Traditions & Encounters

Volume 2
From 1500
to the Present

SEVENTH EDITION

Traditions & Encounters

Volume 2
From 1500
to the Present

Jerry H. Bentley
UNIVERSITY OF HAWAI'I

Herbert F. Ziegler
UNIVERSITY OF HAWAI'I

Heather E. Streets-Salter
NORTHEASTERN UNIVERSITY

Craig Benjamin
GRAND VALLEY STATE UNIVERSITY

Mc
Graw
Hill

TRADITIONS & ENCOUNTERS: VOLUME 2 FROM 1500 TO THE PRESENT, SEVENTH EDITION

ISBN 978-1-264-08815-7 (bound edition)
MHID 1-264-08815-9 (bound edition)
ISBN 978-1-264-08810-2 (loose-leaf edition)
MHID 1-264-08810-8 (loose-leaf edition)

Senior Portfolio Manager: *Jason Seitz*
Marketing Manager: *Rasheité Calhoun*
Content Project Managers: *Sandy Wille; Vanessa McClune*
Product Development Manager: *Dawn Groundwater*
Senior Buyer: *Laura Fuller*
Lead Designer: *David W. Hash*
Senior Content Licensing Specialists: *Brianna Kirschbaum*
Compositor: *Aptara®, Inc.*
Cover Image: *Arp 273: Egyptian Studio/Shutterstock; finger: chaoss/Shutterstock; fern fiddlehead: Zoonar GmbH/ Alamy Stock Photo; Cave of Hands painting: Eduardo Rivero/Shutterstock; shell pattern: andreahast/123RF; Egyptian Rosetta Stone: Photos.com/Getty Images; marble inlay: Glow Images; textile fragment: The Metropolitan Museum of Art, New York, Gift of Henry G. Marquand, 1882; fish mosaics: Lissa Harrison; tunic: The Walters Art Museum, Baltimore, Gift of Georgia and Michael de Havenon, 2016; Greek vase: Digital image courtesy of the Getty's Open Content Program; mosaic of triangles: Alfredo Venturi/Alamy; Roman mosaic: neil harrison/iStock/Getty Images; Ardabil carpet: LACMA -Los Angeles County Museum of Art; Pont du Gard: Bertl123/Shutterstock; Jameh Mosque: Andrea Ricordi, Italy/Moment/Getty Images; Moroccan tile: AlxeyPnferov/iStock/Getty Images; Celtic knot tombstone: Robin Bath/Alamy; Buddhist mani stone: Egmont Strigl/Imagebroker RF/age footstock; bowl: The Metropolitan Museum of Art; New York, The Michael C. Rockefeller Memorial Collection, Purchase, Nelson A. Rockefeller Gift; Vitruvian Man: Janaka Dharmasena/Shutterstock; Romanian carpet; Europeana Collections / INP - National Heritage Institute, Bucharest; dot painting: Paul Pegler/E+/Getty Images; distemper on cloth: The Metropolitan Museum of Art, New York, Purchase, Lita Annenberg Hazen Charitable Trust Gift, 1987; barkcloth: LACMA - Los Angeles County Museum; Moroccan tiles: AlxeyPnferov/iStock/Getty Images; mosaic floor: Digital image courtesy of the Getty's Open Content Program; Pair of Parfleches: The Metropolitan Museum of Art, New York, Ralph T. Coe Collection, Gift of Ralph T. Coe Foundation for the Arts, 2011; Moroccan tile: AlxeyPnferov/iStock/Getty Images; fabric pattern: ADELART/Shutterstock; El Castillo: Kitti Boonnitrod/Getty Images; Buddhist temple: Melba Photo Agency/Alamy; tile: LACMA - Los Angeles County Museum of Art; fan patterns: Jenny Dettrick/Moment/Getty Images; molecules: McGraw Hill; spiral staircase: Rob Tilley/Spaces Images/Blend Images LLC; ceremonial skirt: The Metropolitan Museum of Art, Rogers Fund, 2004; Fleur-de-lis: Exactostock/ SuperStock; Saint Basil's Cathedral: Dave and Les Jacobs/Blend Images LLC; Japanese maple leaf pattern: Photosindia.Com, Llc/Glow Images; DNA: Jezper/Shutterstock; farming village: KingWu/iStockphoto; silk sari: jayk7/Getty Images; bark cloth: Yale University Art Gallery, Photo Credit: Christopher Gardner; silk brocade: Kevin McNeill/iStock/360/Getty Images; Lozenge composition: The Art Institute of Chicago, Gift of Edgar Kaufmann, Jr.; blue technology background: SkillUp/Shutterstock*

All credits appearing on page or at the end of the book are considered to be an extension of the copyright page.

The Internet addresses listed in the text were accurate at the time of publication. The inclusion of a website does not indicate an endorsement by the authors or McGraw Hill Education, and McGraw Hill Education does not guarantee the accuracy of the information presented at these sites.

mheducation.com/highered

Brief Contents

Contents

Maps

Sources from the Past

Power of Process for
Primary Sources

Connecting the Sources

Preface

How do the themes of traditions and encounters continue to help make sense of the entire human past in the twenty-first century?

As Jerry Bentley and Herb Zeigler noted in their original Preface to this book, world history is about both diversity and connections. They began this text with a simple goal: to help our students understand the unique histories of the world's rich variety of peoples, while at the same time allowing them to see the long histories of connections and interactions that have shaped all human communities for millennia. To do this, the authors wrote a story around the dual themes of traditions and encounters to highlight the many different religions and customs embraced by the world's peoples while also exploring the encounters with other cultures that brought about inevitable change.

It is the interaction of these traditions and encounters that continues to provide the key to making sense of our past. Human communities furthered themselves not by remaining isolated, but by interacting with others and exploring the benefits and risks of reaching out. The vitality of history—and its interpretation—lies in understanding the nature of individual cultural traditions and the scope of encounters that punctuated every significant event in human history.

This Seventh Edition of *Traditions & Encounters: A Global Perspective on the Past* provides a genuinely global vision of history that is increasingly meaningful in the shrinking world of the twenty-first century. The theme of *traditions* draws attention to the formation, maintenance, and sometimes collapse of so many distinctive, individual societies. Because the world's peoples have also interacted regularly with one another since the earliest days of human history, the theme of *encounters* directs attention to communications, interactions, networks, and exchanges that have linked individual societies to their neighbors and others in the larger world. Despite many changes in the way world historians have tried to conceptualize the past and present since the appearance of the first edition of *Traditions and Encounters* decades ago, the twin themes of traditions and encounters remain at the heart of every chapter in the text, no matter how extensive revisions might have been. They provide a lens through which to interpret the affairs of humankind and the pressures that continue to shape history. All aspects of the text support these themes—from the organization of chapters, engaging stories of the world's peoples, to the robust map program, updated primary sources, and critical-thinking features that permeate the text.

Some of the changes authors Heather Streets-Salter and Craig Benjamin have introduced to the Seventh Edition of *Traditions and Encounters* include the following:

We have worked hard to eliminate any gendered or out-of-date language throughout the book, in line with most historical writing being done today.

We decided to eliminate the Part Openers and Part Closers to help provide a more seamless narrative and to downplay the somewhat compartmentalized and episodic structure that was more common when earlier editions were prepared.

We have changed the old Eyewitness feature to *Zooming in on Traditions* or *Zooming in on Encounters* to further emphasize the key organizational lens of the book. And we have streamlined the opening stories featured in these *Zooming* features to give greater voice to the many individuals from the past they include. We have also separated these stories from a new *Chapter Overview* that helps better prepare readers for the contents of the chapter that follows.

We have changed the titles of a number of chapters to reflect recent thinking within the field and, in some cases, to be more geographically and politically inclusive. We have also made numerous changes to headers and subheaders throughout, both to reflect new interpretations of how we should "label" various peoples and historical processes and also to make the structure of each chapter clearer.

We have replaced and updated a number of sources in the *Sources from the Past* and *Connecting the Sources* features and have also selected many new images to better illustrate the text. We have added in-line comprehension questions to the sources and also updated reflection questions on most sources, maps, and images to help students practice both their comprehension and analytical thinking skills.

We have changed the old *Reverberations* feature to *How the Past Shapes the Future*, both to further enhance the flow of historical processes and also to more clearly emphasize the continuing relevance of each of the themes explored to the global world of today.

We have changed the old *Summary* feature to a *Conclusion* and modified the language in each to more succinctly sum up the developments described in the chapter. We have also moved the *Chronology* section earlier in the chapter and updated it to incorporate recent date revisions by historians and added new and more relevant secondary courses to the *For Further Reading* section at the end of each chapter.

New to this edition, we have added a feature called *What's Left Out?* to call attention to issues most texts do not usually have space to discuss. Its purpose is to remind students that history is far more complicated and nuanced than any brief narrative can provide. For example, in chapter 9 the authors explore the little-known role of the Kushan King Kanishka the Great in promoting Mahayana Buddhism and helping facilitate its spread into China, enriching the standard account of its transmission by missionaries. In chapter 27 the authors give greater context on non-elite women in Southwest Asia because most textbooks focus on elite women associated with the imperial harem, while in chapter 37 they help students understand that the rivalries of the Cold War in fact originated much earlier in the interwar period.

CHAPTER-BY-CHAPTER CHANGES

The following is a chapter-by-chapter list of topics that are new to this edition or elements that have been substantially revised or updated.

Chapter 22: Transoceanic Encounters and Global Connections

- Reversed subsections in the first section so that Technology of Exploration precedes Motives of Exploration.
- Reversed the sections on Trade and Conflict in Early Modern Asia and Ecological Exchanges so that Ecological Exchanges comes first.
- Added a "What's Left Out?" on the reasons spices were so coveted in European societies.
- Deepened the context for the "Sources from the Past" about Christopher Columbus.
- Added a new "Sources from the Past" by James Cook.
- Updated section on Ecological Exchanges to reflect current scholarship.

Chapter 23: The Transformation of Europe

- Changed title of section on Western Christendom to Western European Christendom to be more specific.
- Clarified relationship between gender and witch-hunting in early modern Europe.
- Added a "What's Left Out?" on the desperate conditions for ordinary Europeans caused by the Thirty Years' War.

Chapter 24: The Integration of the Americas and Oceania with the Wider World

- Changed title to emphasize the relations of these regions with the rest of the world.
- Changed the subsection on the Conquest of Mexico and Peru to simply Mexico and Peru to de-emphasize the idea that conquest was inevitable.
- Changed introductory vignette on Doña Marina to complicate her story.
- Emphasized the critical role of epidemic disease in the devastation of the populations of the Americas.
- Added more detail on the Taíno people so they don't appear passive at the moment of Spanish contact.
- Emphasized previous Spanish practices with slavery and sugar production in the Azores and Canary Islands for informing practices in the Americas.

- Emphasized the brutal treatment of native American peoples by European conquerors and settlers, as well as resistance to such treatment.
- Added a "What's Left Out?" on the widespread practice of British settlers enslaving native American peoples in the eastern colonies.
- Added a new "Sources from the Past" by Miantanamo.
- Streamlined and clarified section on Colonial Society in the Americas to reflect current scholarship.
- Updated the section on slavery in Brazil to reflect current scholarship.
- Added clarity regarding competition among native American groups in North America.

Chapter 25: Africa and the Atlantic World

- Removed several instances of Eurocentric text.
- Brought the sections on the trans-Saharan slave trade and Atlantic slave trade up to date.
- Updated section on consequences of the Atlantic slave trade in Africa to reflect current scholarship.
- Updated section on the African diaspora to reflect current scholarship.
- Added a "What's Left Out?" on the ways women experienced slavery differently than men.
- Updated the section on African diaspora cultures to reflect current scholarship.

Chapter 26: Tradition and Change in East Asia

- Clarified and updated section on foot-binding.
- Added a "What's Left Out?" on the parallels between Chinese foot-binding and the use of corsets in western Europe.
- Streamlined material on Zheng He.
- Rewrote the section on Government and Technology to minimize Eurocentrism.
- Eliminated comparisons of Chinese and European merchants to eliminate Eurocentrism.

Chapter 27: Empires in South and Southwest Asia

- Changed title to de-emphasize Islam for a focus on the region.
- Reversed the two subheads in the section on Empires in Transition to tell the story more clearly.
- Clarified the section on the Battle of Chaldiran.
- Significantly updated the section on the Dynastic State to reflect current thinking on succession.
- Reversed subheads on Steppe Traditions and Women in Politics in the section on the Dynastic State.
- Added a new "Sources from the Past" by Emperor Akbar of the Moghul dynasty.

- Added a "What's Left Out?" on the lives of ordinary Muslim women in the Ottoman Empire.
- Added detail to section on Food Crops.
- Significantly updated section on Economic Difficulties and Military Decline to reflect current scholarship.
- Deleted section on Cultural Conservatism because of Eurocentrism and bias.

Chapter 28: Revolutions and National States in the Atlantic World

- Changed title of first section to Revolutionary Ideas.
- Added a new section on Revolutions to cover the American, French, Haitian, and Latin American revolutions.
- Added a new heading called Consequences and Implications of the Revolutions.
- Changed first subhead under the Consequences section to The Emergence of New Ideologies.
- Changed final section to New Nations and Nationalism in Europe.
- Rewrote chapter overview to reflect extensive changes in the chapter.
- De-emphasized the revolutionary potential of ideas and emphasized the importance of war as a factor in instigating the revolutions of this period.
- Rewrote the subhead on Tightened British Control of the Colonies to reflect the importance of the experience of war.
- Clarified the reasons behind the start of the American Revolution.
- Rewrote the section on why the British lost the American Revolution, with an emphasis on the role of the French.
- Clarified that the French philosophes were deeply inspired by the American Revolution.
- Updated section on the Haitian Revolution.
- Wrote introduction to new section on the consequences of the revolutions.
- Added a "What's Left Out?" on women's participation in the revolutions.

Chapter 29: The Making of Industrial Society

- Added more on the environmental impact of the Industrial Revolution.
- Updated section on the origins of the Industrial Revolution, especially subheads on Ecological Relief and Mechanization, to reflect current scholarship.
- Added a new "Sources from the Past" on Ned Ludd.
- Added a "What's Left Out?" on the introduction of clock time.
- Revised subheads on Big Business and Corporations for greater clarity.

- Deleted claim about the strong link between industrialization and the abolition of slavery.
- Updated and clarified subheads on New Social Classes and Work and Play.
- Updated subheads on women and gender to reflect current scholarship.
- Updated and rewrote subhead on the Global Division of Labor and Economic Interdependence to reflect current scholarship.

Chapter 30: The Americas in the Age of Independence

- Added more in-depth indigenous perspectives to chapter content.
- Clarified and streamlined lead-up to the U.S. Civil War.
- Clarified the process of Canada gaining dominion status.
- Updated and streamlined subhead on Mexico.
- Rewrote the introduction to American Economic Development.
- Significantly rewrote the Section on Latin American Investments.
- Added a "What's Left Out?" on child removal in Australia, Canada, and the United States.
- Updated the section on Societies in the United States to reflect recent scholarship.

Chapter 31: Societies at Crossroads

- Changed section title from The Ottoman Empire in Decline to The Weakening of the Ottoman Empire.
- Changed subhead in this section from The Nature of Decline to Sources of Ottoman Weakness.
- Significantly rewrote opening story on Taiping Rebellion and the Chapter Overview.
- Updated subhead on Ottoman military problems to reflect current scholarship.
- Added a "What's Left Out?" on the global importance of the Russo-Japanese War.
- Updated section on Opium War in China.

Chapter 32: The Apex of Global Empire Building

- Changed title to reflect content changes in chapter.
- Changed subhead under Legacies of Imperialism from Nationalism and Anticolonial Movements to Anticolonial and Nationalist Movements.
- Wrote a new introductory story on Menelik II of Ethiopia.
- Rewrote the Chapter Overview to reflect content changes in the chapter.
- Changed subhead on Political Motives for Imperialism to Geopolitical Motives for Imperialism.
- Substantially rewrote subheads on Geopolitical Motives for Imperialism, Economic Motives for Imperialism, and Cultural Justifications for Imperialism.

- Moved subheads within the section on Foundations of Empire for better flow.
- Rewrote most of the section on the Indian Mutiny.
- Added two new "Sources from the Past," by Raden Kartini and Queen Lili'uokulani.
- Deleted some material on European explorers in Africa and added material on King Leopold's Congo.
- Added material on the British conquest of Egypt and the South African War.
- Updated section on The Emergence of New Imperial Powers to reflect current scholarship.
- Added material on the Can Vuong anti-French movement in Vietnam.
- Updated subhead on Scientific Racism to reflect current scholarship.
- Added a "What's Left Out?" on the unintended consequences of colonialism on gender relations.

Chapter 33: The Great War: The World in Upheaval

- Under the section Global War; added sections on Battles in Southwest Asia and Africa and Africans in the War.
- Streamlined and clarified introductory story.
- Clarified introduction to the section on Understandings and Alliances.
- Clarified the establishment of the Western Front.
- Updated the subhead on Women at War to reflect current scholarship.
- Added a "What's Left Out?" on the German Committee for Indian Independence.
- Added material on battles in Southwest Asia.
- Added material on Africa in the war (originally in chapter 35).
- Clarified section on the mandate system.

Chapter 34: Anxieties and Experiments in Postwar Europe and the United States

- Changed title to reflect content within chapter.
- Changed section on Probing Cultural Frontiers to New Intellectual Frontiers.
- Shortened introductory story on Hitler.
- Significantly rewrote the section on Communism in Russia.
- Added a "What's Left Out?" on the popularity of eugenics in the United States.

Chapter 35: Revolutionaries and Nationalists in the Colonial and Neocolonial World

- Changed title to reflect new content in the chapter.

- Changed section on Asian Paths to Autonomy to Paths to Autonomy in East and Southeast Asia.
- Changed subhead on China's Search for Order to China's Campaigns to End Foreign Domination.
- Added a new "Sources from the Past" by M.N. Roy.
- Changed section on Africa under Colonial Domination to Sub-Saharan Africa under Colonial Domination.
- Deleted section on Africa and Africans in the Great War.
- Significantly rewrote the material on China and India to reflect current scholarly understandings.
- Updated section on sub-Saharan Africa to reflect current scholarship.
- Added a "What's Left Out?" on the League Against Imperialism.
- Updated and clarified subhead on Neighborly Cultural Exchanges.
- Added a new ending to chapter.

Chapter 36: New Conflagrations: World War II and the Cold War

- Updated subhead on Chinese resistance to Japanese invasion to reflect current scholarship.
- Updated subhead on Italian and German Aggression by adding material on Ethiopian invasion.
- Updated and clarified subhead on Peace for Our Time by nuancing the philosophy of appeasement.
- Clarified and rewrote chain of events on the German conquest of western Europe.
- Added to subhead on Women's Roles by adding information about Soviet women.
- Added a "What's Left Out?" on the long history of anti-communism.
- Added material in the section on Cold War that clarifies Soviet perspective.
- Updated section on Cracks in the Soviet-Chinese Alliance to reflect current scholarship.

Chapter 37: The End of Empire in an Era of Cold War

- Changed title to reflect importance of Cold War in decolonization.
- In section on After Independence, added Pan-Arab to the subhead on Islamic Resurgence in Southwest Asia and North Africa.
- Streamlined introductory story on Gandhi and significantly rewrote the chapter overview to reflect new content in the chapter.
- Rewrote introduction to Independence in Asia.
- Rewrote material on Partition in India.
- Rewrote section on nationalism in Vietnam.

- Updated section on Palestine to reflect recent scholarship.
- Rewrote section on the Suez Crisis.
- Substantially rewrote the section on French decolonization in North Africa.
- Added material on the Mau Mau Rebellion in Kenya.
- Added material on apartheid in South Africa.
- Streamlined and updated the material on Mao's China.
- Updated material on postcolonial India to reflect current scholarship.
- Updated material on Islamism and the Iranian Revolution.
- Deleted text on African disunity.
- Added "Sources from the Past" on China's Marriage law (originally in chapter 38).
- Added a "What's Left Out?" on the combination of decolonization and the Cold War in Angola.

Chapter 38: Into the Twenty-First Century

- Changed title to make it sound more current.
- Updated all dates and material to bring it current with second decade of twenty-first century.
- Changed title of section on The End of the Cold War to The End of the Cold War and the Emergence of a Unipolar World.
- Added subhead under this section called The Unipolar Moment.
- Moved the subhead on International Organizations to the section on Cross-Cultural Exchanges.
- Renamed the section on Global Problems to Urgent Global Issues in the Twenty-First Century.

- Added subheads in this section on The Continuing Inequality of Women, Migration, and Global Diseases.
- Deleted final section on Crossing Boundaries.
- Rewrote Chapter Overview to reflect content changes in the chapter.
- Added a new introduction to the section on the End of the Cold War.
- Added new text on the end of the Cold War through 2020.
- Clarified information on GATT and WTO.
- Updated section on the Rise of China.
- Added new material on the EU to Brexit.
- Updated material on OPEC.
- Deleted subhead on Pan-American culture and added material on cultural globalization.
- Deleted subhead on the Age of Access and added material on the Networked World.
- Deleted subheads on the Prominence of the English Language and Adaptations of Technology.
- Updated information on population pressure.
- Added material on climate change.
- Added new material on global diseases, specifically the COVID-19 pandemic, to bring content up to the present.
- Updated material on global terrorism.
- Added new material on women's inequality globally.
- Added a new "Sources from the Past" by Malala.
- Added a "What's Left Out?" on the difficulties about writing the history of the very recent past.
- Added new material on migrants in a global context.

PRIMARY SOURCES HELP STUDENTS THINK CRITICALLY ABOUT HISTORY

Primary sources help students think critically about history and expose them to contrasting perspectives of key events. The Seventh Edition of *Traditions & Encounters* provides four different ways to use primary source documents:

Power of Process for Primary Sources Power of Process is a critical thinking tool for reading and writing about primary sources. As part of Connect History, McGraw Hill's learning platform, Power of Process contains a database of more than 400 searchable primary sources in addition to the capability for instructors to upload their own sources. Instructors can then select a series of strategies for students to use to analyze and comment on a source. The Power of Process framework helps students develop essential academic skills such as understanding, analyzing, and synthesizing readings and visuals such as maps, leading students toward higher-order thinking and writing.

The Power of Process landing page makes it easy for instructors to find pre-populated documents or to add their own.

Sources from the Past These features showcase a significant primary source document of the period, such as a poem, journal account, religious writing, or letter. Thought-provoking questions prompt readers to analyze key issues raised in the document.

Connecting the Sources This feature helps students recognize that historiography is based on scholars' interpretation of historical information. It focuses on two documents or images, asking students to think critically about the different ways information can be interpreted.

McGraw Hill Create Because no two history courses are the same, you can select primary sources that meet the unique needs of your course. Using McGraw Hill's Create allows you to quickly and easily create custom course materials with cross-disciplinary content. Here's what you can do:

- Choose your own content: Create a book that contains only the chapters you want, in the order you want. Create will even renumber the pages for you!

- Add readings: Add readings from our collection or add your own original content such as syllabus or history major requirements.

- Choose your format: Print or ebook? Softcover, spiral, or loose-leaf? Black-and-white or color?

- Customize your cover: Pick your own cover image and include your name and course information right on the cover. Students will know they're purchasing the right book—and using everything they purchase!

- Review your creation: When you are all done, you'll receive a free PDF to review in just minutes. To get started, go to create.mheducation.com and register today.

SMARTBOOK 2.0 TAILORS CONTENT TO THE INDIVIDUAL STUDENT

SMARTBOOK Available within Connect History, SmartBook has been updated with improved learning objectives to ensure that students gain foundational knowledge, while also learning to make connections to help them formulate a broader understanding of historical events. SmartBook 2.0 personalizes learning to individual student needs, continually adapting to pinpoint knowledge gaps and focus learning on topics that need the most attention. Study time is more productive, and as a result, students are better prepared for class and coursework. For instructors, SmartBook 2.0 tracks student progress and provides insights that can help guide teaching strategies.

WRITING ASSIGNMENT

McGraw Hill's new Writing Assignment Plus tool delivers a learning experience that improves students' written communication skills and conceptual understanding with every assignment. Assign, monitor, and provide feedback on writing more efficiently and grade assignments within McGraw Hill Connect® and McGraw Hill Connect Master® 2.0. Writing Assignment Plus gives you time-saving tools with a just-in-time basic writing and originality checker.

Features include:

- Grammar/writing checking with McGraw Hill learning resources.

- Originality checker with McGraw Hill learning resources.

- Writing stats.

- Rubric building and scoring.

- Ability to assign draft and final deadline milestones.

- Tablet ready and tools for all learners.

CONTEXTUALIZE HISTORY

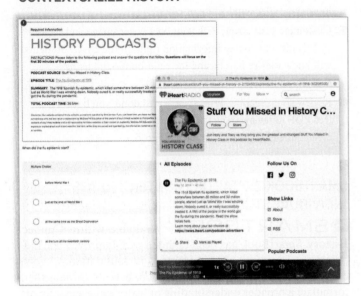

Help students experience history in a whole new way with our new Podcast Assignments. We've gathered some of the most interesting and popular history podcasts currently available and built assignable questions around them. These assignments allow instructors to bring greater context and nuance to their courses while engaging students through the storytelling power of podcasts.

APPLICATION-BASED ACTIVITIES

New to this edition, McGraw Hill's Application-Based Activities are highly interactive, automatically graded, online learn-by-doing exercises that provide students a safe space to apply their knowledge and problem-solving skills in class and in everyday life. Skill-based activities focus on topics such as "How to Read Primary Sources" and "Analyzing Audience" and map activities such as "Roman Imperial Expansion."

INSTRUCTOR RESOURCES

Traditions & Encounters offers an array of instructor resources for the world history course:

Instructor's Manual The Instructor's Manual provides a wide variety of tools and resources for presenting the course, including learning objectives and ideas for lectures and discussions.

Test Bank By increasing the rigor of the test bank development process, McGraw Hill has raised the bar for student assessment. Each question has been tagged for level of difficulty, Bloom's taxonomy, and topic coverage. Organized by chapter, the questions are designed to test factual, conceptual, and higher order thinking.

Test Builder New to this edition and available within Connect, Test Builder is a cloud-based tool that enables instructors to format tests that can be printed and administered within a Learning Management System. Test Builder offers a modern, streamlined interface for easy content configuration that matches course needs, without requiring a download.

Test Builder enables instructors to:

- Access all test bank content from a particular title.
- Easily pinpoint the most relevant content through robust filtering options.
- Manipulate the order of questions or scramble questions and/or answers.
- Pin questions to a specific location within a test.
- Determine your preferred treatment of algorithmic questions.
- Choose the layout and spacing.
- Add instructions and configure default settings.

PowerPoint The PowerPoint presentations highlight the key points of the chapter and include supporting visuals. New to this edition, all slides are WCAG compliant.

About the Authors

Jerry H. Bentley was professor of history at the University of Hawai'i and editor of the *Journal of World History*. His research on the religious, moral, and political writings of the Renaissance led to the publication of *Humanists and Holy Writ: New Testament Scholarship in the Renaissance* (Princeton, 1983) and *Politics and Culture in Renaissance Naples* (Princeton, 1987). More recently, his research concentrated on global history and particularly on processes of cross-cultural interaction. His book *Old World Encounters: Cross-Cultural Contacts and Exchanges in Pre-Modern Times* (New York, 1993) examines processes of cultural exchange and religious conversion before the modern era, and his pamphlet *Shapes of World History in Twentieth-Century Scholarship* (1996) discusses the historiography of world history. His most recent publication is *The Oxford Handbook of World History* (Oxford, 2011), and he served as a member of the editorial team preparing the forthcoming *Cambridge History of the World*. Jerry Bentley passed away in July 2012, although his legacy lives on through his significant contributions to the study of world history. The World History Association recently named an annual prize in his honor for outstanding publications in the field.

Herbert F. Ziegler is an associate professor of history at the University of Hawai'i. He has taught world history since 1980; he previously served as director of the world history program at the University of Hawai'i as well as book review editor of the *Journal of World History*. His interest in twentieth-century European social and political history led to the publication of *Nazi Germany's New Aristocracy: The SS Leadership, 1925-1939* (Princeton, 1990) and to his participation in new educational endeavors in the history of the Holocaust, including the development of an upper-division course for undergraduates. He is at present working on a study that explores from a global point of view the demographic trends of the past ten thousand years, along with their concomitant technological, economic, and social developments. His other current research project focuses on the application of complexity theory to a comparative study of societies and their internal dynamics.

Heather Streets-Salter is Professor and Director of World History Programs at Northeastern University in Boston, Massachusetts. She is the author of *World War One in Southeast Asia: Colonialism and Anticolonialism in an Era of Global Conflict* (Cambridge University Press, 2017); *Martial Races: The Military, Martial Races, and Masculinity in British Imperial Culture, 1857-1914* (Manchester University Press, 2004); and *Empires and Colonies in the Modern World* (Oxford University Press, 2015) with Trevor Getz. Her next book is called *The Chill Before the Cold War: Communism and Anti-Communism in Colonial Southeast Asia in the Interwar Period.*

Craig Benjamin is a Professor of History in the Frederik J. Meijer Honors College at Grand Valley State University in Michigan. He is the author of *The Yuezhi: Origin, Migration and the Conquest of Northern Bactria* (Brepols, 2007); *Empires of Ancient Eurasia. The First Silk Roads Era 100 BCE-250 CE* (Cambridge University Press, 2018); and *Big History: Between Nothing and Everything* (McGraw-Hill, 2014) with David Christian and Cynthia Stokes Brown. He is the editor of Volume 4 of the *Cambridge History of the World* (Cambridge University Press, 2015) and *The Routledge Companion to Big History* (Routledge, 2019) with Esther Quaedackers and David Baker. His next book is called *Eurasia Reconnected. The Second Silk Roads Era 600-1000 CE.*

Acknowledgments

Many individuals have contributed to this book, and the authors take pleasure in recording deep thanks for all the comments, criticism, advice, and suggestions that helped to improve the work. The editorial, marketing, and production teams at McGraw Hill did an outstanding job of seeing the project through to publication. Special thanks go to Jason Seitz, Stephanie Ventura, and Sandy Wille, who provided crucial support by helping the authors work through difficult issues and solve the innumerable problems of content, style, and organization that arise in any project to produce a history of the world. Many colleagues at the University of Hawai'i at Mānoa, most notably Professor Margot A. Henriksen, and elsewhere aided and advised the authors on matters of organization and composition. Finally, we would like to express our appreciation for the advice of the following individuals, who read and commented on the Seventh Edition, as well as previous editions of *Traditions & Encounters*.

Brian C. Black, *Pennsylvania State University*
Beau Bowers, *Central Piedmont Community College*
Erika Briesacher, *Worcester State University*
Stanley Burstein, *California State University, Los Angeles*
David Eaton, *Grand Valley State University*
David Fahey, *Miami University of Ohio*
Amy Forss, *Metropolitan Community College, Omaha*
Melissa Gayan, *Georgia Southern University*
Aimee Harris-Johnson, *El Paso Community College*
Matthew Herbst, *University of California San Diego*
Mark Lee, *University of Nebraska*
Emily G. Miller, *University of Indianapolis*
William Plants, *University of Rio Grande*
Annie Tracy Samuel, *University of Tennessee at Chattanooga*
Pamela Sayre, *Henry Ford Community College*
William Schell Jr., *Murray State University*
Scott Seagle, *University of Tennessee at Chattanooga*
David Simonelli, *Youngstown State University*
Adam Stanley, *University of Wisconsin at Platteville*
Ryan Thompson, *Cleveland State Community College*

Special thanks and gratitude to the McGraw Hill Academic Integrity Board of Advisors who were instrumental in providing guidance on chapter content, illustration program, and language and conventions. Our advisors include:

Susan Bragg, *Georgia Southwestern State University*
Jennifer Epley Sanders, *Texas A & M*
Eileen Ford, *California State University, Los Angeles*
Nicholas Fox, *Houston College*
Rudy Jean-Bart, *Broward Community College*
Darnell Morehand-Olufade, *University of Bridgeport*
Sharon Navarro, *University of Texas at San Antonio*
Jeffrey Ogbar, *University of Connecticut*
Andrea Oliver, *Tallahassee Community College*
Birte Pfleger, *California State University, Los Angeles*
Linda Reed, *University of Houston*

Traditions & Encounters

Volume 2
From 1500
to the Present

22 Transoceanic Encounters and Global Connections

ZOOMING IN ON ENCOUNTERS

Vasco da Gama's Search for Spices

On 8 July 1497 the Portuguese mariner **Vasco da Gama** led a small fleet of four armed merchant vessels with 170 crewmen out of the harbor at Lisbon. His destination was India, which he planned to reach by sailing around the continent of Africa and through the Indian Ocean, and his goal was to enter the highly lucrative trade in spices dominated in Europe by the merchants of Venice. He carried letters of introduction from the king of Portugal as well as cargoes of gold, pearls, wool textiles, bronzeware, iron tools, and other goods that he hoped to exchange for spices in India.

Before there would be an opportunity to trade, however, da Gama and his crew had a prolonged voyage through two oceans. They sailed south from Portugal to the Cape Verde Islands off the west coast of Africa, where they took on water and fresh provisions. On 3 August they headed south into the Atlantic Ocean to take advantage of the prevailing winds. For the next ninety-five days, the fleet saw no land as it sailed through some six thousand nautical miles of open ocean. By October, da Gama came across westerly winds in the southern Atlantic, which helped propel him around the Cape of Good Hope and into the Indian Ocean. The fleet slowly worked its

Vasco da Gama's flagship on the journey to India in 1497, the *San Rafael*.
Photo Researchers/Science History Images/Alamy Stock Photo

Vasco da Gama (VAHS-koh duh GAHM-uh)

way up the east coast of Africa, engaging in hostilities with local authorities at Mozambique and Mombasa, as far as Malindi, where da Gama secured the services of an Indian Muslim pilot to guide his ships across the Arabian Sea. On 20 May 1498—more than ten months after its departure from Lisbon—the fleet anchored at Calicut in southern India.

In India the Portuguese fleet encountered a wealthy, cosmopolitan society. Upon their arrival local authorities in Calicut dispatched a pair of Tunisian merchants who spoke Spanish and Italian to serve as translators for the newly arrived party. The markets of Calicut offered not only pepper, ginger, cinnamon, and other spices sought so eagerly by da Gama, but also rubies, emeralds, gold jewelry, and fine cotton textiles. But apart from gold and some striped cloth, the merchants at Calicut thought the goods that da Gama had brought to trade were worthless and showed no interest in them. Nevertheless, da Gama managed to exchange gold for a cargo of pepper and cinnamon that turned a handsome profit when the fleet returned to Portugal in August 1499. Da Gama's expedition opened the door to direct maritime trade between European and Asian peoples and helped to establish permanent links between the world's various regions.

CHAPTER OVERVIEW

Cross-cultural interactions and encounters have been a persistent feature of historical development. Even in ancient times mass migration, campaigns of imperial expansion, and long-distance trade deeply influenced societies throughout the world. But after 1500 C.E., cross-cultural interactions took place on a much larger geographic scale, and encounters thus affected greater numbers of people than in earlier centuries. Equipped with a variety of technologies and a powerful military arsenal, western European peoples began to cross the world's oceans in large numbers during the early modern era (ca. 1500–ca. 1800). At the same time, Russian adventurers built an enormous Eurasian empire and ventured into the Pacific Ocean.

Europeans were not the only peoples who actively explored the larger world during the early modern era. In the early fifteenth century the Ming emperors of China sponsored a series of seven massive maritime expeditions that visited all parts of the Indian Ocean basin. Although state-sponsored expeditions came to an end after 1435, Chinese merchants and mariners were prominent figures in east Asian and southeast Asian lands throughout the early modern era. In the sixteenth century Ottoman mariners also ventured into the Indian Ocean. Following the Ottoman conquest of Egypt in 1517, both merchant and military vessels established an Ottoman presence throughout the Indian Ocean basin. Ottoman explorers traveled as far as China, but they were most active in Muslim lands from east Africa and Arabia to India and southeast Asia, where they enjoyed especially warm receptions.

Although other peoples also made their way into the larger world, it was Europeans who, initially by chance, linked the lands and peoples of the Eastern Hemisphere, the Western Hemisphere and Oceania. Because they began to travel regularly between the world's major geographic regions, in this period European peoples benefited from unparalleled opportunities to increase their power, wealth, and influence. By 1800, the projection of European influence brought about a decisive shift in the global balance of power. During the millennium 500 to 1500 C.E., the world's most powerful societies had been those organized by imperial states such as the Tang dynasty of China, the Abbasid dynasty in southwest Asia, the Byzantine Empire in the eastern Mediterranean region, and the Mongol Empires that embraced much of Eurasia. After 1500, however, European peoples became more prominent than before in the larger world, and they began to establish vast empires that by the nineteenth century dominated much of the world.

The expansion of European influence also resulted in the establishment of truly global networks of transportation, communication, and exchange. A worldwide diffusion of plants,

CHRONOLOGY	
1394–1460	Life of Prince Henry the Navigator of Portugal
1488	Bartolomeu Dias's voyage around the Cape of Good Hope into the Indian Ocean
1492	Christopher Columbus's first voyage to the Western Hemisphere
1497–1499	Vasco da Gama's first voyage to India
1500	Establishment of Portuguese trading post in Calicut, India
1519–1522	Ferdinand Magellan's circumnavigation of the world
1565–1575	Spanish conquest of the Philippines
1619	Establishment of Batavia by the Dutch on the island of Java
1756–1763	Seven Years' War
1768–1780	Captain James Cook's voyages in the Pacific Ocean

animals, diseases, and human communities followed European ventures across the oceans, and intricate trade networks eventually gave birth to a global economy. The consequences to the peoples of the Americas and Oceania were disastrous, as epidemic diseases killed millions of people. Over much of the rest of the world, however, the spread of food crops and domesticated animals contributed to a dramatic surge in global population. The establishment of global trade networks established in this period ensured that interactions between the world's peoples would continue and intensify.

THE EXPLORATION OF THE WORLD'S OCEANS

Between 1400 and 1800, European mariners launched a remarkable series of exploratory voyages that took them to all the earth's waters, with the exception of those in extreme polar regions. These voyages were very expensive and required the latest technologies for their success. Yet private investors and government authorities had strong motives to underwrite the expeditions and outfit them with advanced nautical technology. The voyages of exploration paid large dividends: they enabled European mariners to chart the world's ocean basins and develop an accurate understanding of world geography. On the basis of that knowledge, European merchants and mariners established global networks of communication, transportation, and exchange that had dramatic consequences for the whole world.

The Technology of Exploration

Without advanced nautical technology and navigational skills, European mariners would not have been able to explore the world's oceans. Embarking on voyages that would keep them out of the sight of land for weeks at a time, mariners needed sturdy ships, navigational equipment, and sailing techniques that would permit them to make their way across the seas and back again. They inherited much of their nautical technology from Mediterranean and northern European maritime traditions and combined it imaginatively with elements of Chinese and Arabic origin.

Ships and Sails From their experiences in the coastal waters of the Atlantic, European sailors learned to construct ships strong enough to survive most adverse conditions. Beginning about the twelfth century, they increased the maneuverability of their craft by building a rudder onto the stern. (The sternpost rudder was a Chinese invention that had diffused across the Indian Ocean and probably became known to Europeans through Arab ships in the Mediterranean.) They outfitted their vessels with two main types of sail, both of which Mediterranean mariners had used since classical times. Square sails enabled them to take full advantage of a following wind (a wind blowing from behind), although these sails did not work well in crosswinds. Triangular lateen sails, on the other hand, were very maneuverable and could catch winds from the side as well as from behind. With a combination of square and lateen sails, European ships were able to use whatever winds arose. Their ability to tack—to advance against the wind by sailing across it—was crucial for the exploration of regions with uncooperative winds.

Navigational Instruments The most important navigational equipment on board these vessels were **magnetic compasses** and **astrolabes** (soon replaced by **cross staffs** and **back staffs**). The compass was a Chinese invention of the Tang or Song dynasty that had diffused throughout the Indian Ocean basin in the eleventh century. By the mid-twelfth century, European mariners used compasses to determine their heading in Mediterranean and Atlantic waters. The astrolabe was a simplified version of an instrument used by Greek and Persian astronomers to determine latitude by measuring the angle of the sun or the pole star (or North Star) above the horizon. Portuguese mariners visiting the Indian Ocean in the late fifteenth century encountered Arab sailors using simpler and more serviceable instruments for determining latitude, which the Portuguese then used as models for the construction of cross staffs and back staffs.

European mariners' ability to determine direction and latitude based on these many borrowed technologies enabled them to assemble a vast body of data about the earth's geography and to find their way around the world's oceans with reasonable accuracy and efficiency. (The measurement of longitude requires the ability to measure time precisely and so had to wait until the late eighteenth century, when dependable, spring-driven clocks became available.)

By using cross staffs to measure the angle of the sun or the pole star above the horizon, mariners could determine latitude.

Knowledge of Winds and Currents   Equipped with the latest technological hardware, European mariners ventured into the oceans and gradually compiled a body of practical knowledge about the winds and currents that determined navigational possibilities in the age of sail. In both the Atlantic and the Pacific Oceans, strong winds blow regularly to create giant "wind wheels" both north and south of the equator, and ocean currents follow a similar pattern. Between about five and twenty-five degrees of latitude north and south of the equator, winds (called "trade winds" by Europeans) blow from the east. Between about thirty and sixty degrees north and south, westerly winds prevail. Winds and currents in the Indian Ocean follow a different, but still regular and reliable, pattern. During the summer months, generally between April and October, monsoon winds blow from the southwest throughout the Indian Ocean basin, whereas during the winter they blow from the northeast. Once mariners understood these patterns, they were able to take advantage of prevailing winds and currents to sail to almost any part of the earth.

The *volta do mar*   Prevailing winds and currents often forced mariners to take indirect routes to their destinations. European vessels sailed easily from the Mediterranean to the Canary Islands, for example, because regular trade winds blew from the northeast. But those same trade winds complicated the return trip. By the mid-fifteenth century, Portuguese mariners had developed a strategy called the ***volta do mar*** ("return through the sea") that enabled them to sail from the Canaries to Portugal. Instead of trying to force their way against the trade winds—a slow and perilous business—they sailed northwest into the open ocean until they found westerly winds and then turned east for the last leg of the homeward journey.

Although the *volta do mar* took mariners well out of their way, experience soon taught that sailing around contrary winds was much faster, safer, and more reliable than butting up against them. Portuguese and other European mariners began to rely on the principle of the *volta do mar* in sailing to destinations other than the Canary Islands. When Vasco da Gama departed for India, for example, he sailed south to the Cape Verde Islands and then allowed the trade winds to carry him southwest into the Atlantic Ocean until he approached the coast of Brazil. There da Gama caught the prevailing westerlies that enabled him to sail east, round the Cape of Good Hope, and enter the Indian Ocean. As they became familiar with the wind systems of the world's oceans, European mariners developed variations on the *volta do mar* that enabled them to travel reliably to coastlines around the world.

Motives for Exploration

A complex combination of motives prompted Europeans to explore the world's oceans. Most important of these motives

MAP 22.1   Wind and current patterns in the world's oceans.

Note how the winds of the Atlantic and Pacific resemble wind wheels, revolving clockwise north of the equator and counterclockwise south of the equator.

How crucial was an understanding of the world's wind patterns to the success of European overseas expansion?

were the search for basic resources and lands suitable for the cultivation of cash crops, the desire to establish new trade routes to Asian markets, and the aspiration to expand the influence of Christianity.

Portuguese Exploration

Mariners from the relatively poor kingdom of Portugal were initially the most prominent in the search for fresh resources to exploit and lands to cultivate. Beginning in the thirteenth century, Portuguese seamen ventured away from the coasts and into the open Atlantic Ocean. They originally sought fish, seals, whales, timber, and lands where they could grow wheat to supplement the meager resources of Portugal. By the early fourteenth century, they had discovered the uninhabited Azores and Madeiras Islands. They also traveled frequently to the Canary Islands, inhabited by the indigenous Guanche people, which Italian and Iberian mariners had visited since the early fourteenth century. Because European demand for sugar was strong and increasing, the prospect of establishing sugar plantations on the Atlantic islands was very tempting. Italian entrepreneurs had organized sugar plantations in Palestine and the Mediterranean islands since the twelfth century, and in the fifteenth century Italian investors worked with Portuguese mariners to establish plantations in the Atlantic islands using slave labor (discussed more fully in chapter 25). Continuing Portuguese voyages also led to the establishment of plantations on more southerly Atlantic islands, including the Cape Verde Islands, São Tomé, Principe, and Fernando Po.

Trade

Even more important than the exploitation of fresh lands and resources was the goal of establishing maritime trade routes to the markets of Asia. During the era of the Mongol Empires, European merchants often traveled overland as far as China to trade in silk, spices, porcelain, and other Asian goods. In the fourteenth century, however, with the collapse of the Mongol Empires and the spread of bubonic plague, travel on what we now call the Silk Roads became much less safe than before. Arab mariners continued to bring Asian goods through the Indian Ocean and the Red Sea to Cairo, where Italian merchants purchased them for distribution in western Europe. But prices at Cairo were high, and Europeans sought ever-larger quantities of Asian goods, particularly spices.

The earliest surviving world globe, produced in 1492 by the German cartographer Martin Behaim, depicts the Eastern Hemisphere quite accurately but shows almost no land west of Iberia except for east Asia.
DEA Picture Library/Getty Images

By the fourteenth century the wealthy classes of Europe regarded Indian pepper and Chinese ginger as expensive necessities, and they especially prized cloves and nutmeg from the spice islands of Maluku. Merchants and monarchs alike realized that by offering direct access to Asian markets and eliminating Muslim intermediaries, new maritime trade routes would increase the quantities of spices and other Asian goods available in Europe—and would also yield enormous profits. This was, indeed, the motive behind Vasco da Gama's voyage to India in 1497 that we read about in the introduction to this chapter.

Europeans were also interested in African trade. Since the twelfth century, camel caravans had delivered west African gold, ivory, and enslaved people to north African ports, where Europeans—along with many others—took part in their trade (for more on the trans-Saharan trade, see chapter 25). Gold was an especially important commodity because the precious metal from west Africa was Europeans' principal form of payment for Asian luxury goods. As in the case of Asian trade, European merchants were interested in maritime routes that eliminated Muslim intermediaries and offered more direct access to African markets.

Missionary Efforts

Alongside material incentives, the goal of expanding the boundaries of Christianity also drove Europeans into the larger world. Like Buddhism and Islam, Christianity is a missionary religion. The New Testament specifically urged Christians to spread their faith throughout the world. Efforts to spread the faith often took peaceful forms. During the era of the Mongol Empires, Franciscan and Dominican missionaries had traveled as far as India, central Asia, and China in search of converts. Yet the expansion of Christianity was by no means always a peaceful affair. Beginning in the eleventh century, western Europeans had launched a series of crusades and holy wars against Muslims in Palestine, the Mediterranean islands, and Iberia. Crusading zeal remained especially strong in Iberia, where the *reconquista* (the "reconquering" of Spain and Iberia from Muslim rulers who had been there for 800 years) came to an end in 1492: the Muslim kingdom of Granada fell to Spanish Christian forces just weeks before Christopher Columbus set sail on his famous first voyage to the Western Hemisphere. Whether through

CALECHVT CELEBERRI MVM INDIÆ EMPORIVM.

A depiction of the Indian port of Calicut in 1572, when Portugal dominated the pepper trade.
FLHC A20/Alamy Stock Photo

persuasion or violence, overseas voyages offered fresh opportunities for western Europeans to spread their faith.

In practice, the various motives for exploration combined and reinforced each other. Prince Henrique of Portugal, often called **Prince Henry the Navigator,** promoted voyages of exploration in west Africa specifically to enter the gold trade, discover profitable new trade routes, gain intelligence about the extent of Muslim power, win converts to Christianity, and make alliances against the Muslims with any Christian rulers he might find. When the Portuguese mariner Vasco da Gama reached the Indian port of Calicut in 1498, local authorities asked him what he wanted there. His reply: "Christians and spices." The goal of spreading Christianity thus became a powerful justification and reinforcement for the more material motives for the voyages of exploration.

European Voyages of Exploration: From the Mediterranean to the Atlantic

In 1291 the Vivaldi brothers departed from Genoa in two ships with the intention of sailing around Africa to India. They did

What's Left Out? ▬▬ ▬ ▬ ▬ ▬

In Europe during the late Middle Ages, spices like pepper, cloves, nutmeg, cinnamon, and ginger were extremely expensive, costing approximately one to three English shillings per pound. Compare this to a whole cow, which cost between six and ten shillings, or a pig, which cost two. An ordinary soldier's wages, by comparison, were about a shilling a day, while a kitchen servant's wages were between 2 and 4 shillings for a whole year. What was it about the spices we now take for granted that made people want to pay such high prices for them and for others to risk their lives and all their material possessions to trade them? Spices were used to enhance the taste and smell of many foods and drinks, to mask bad odors, and as medicines. Pepper, ginger, and cinnamon, for example, were used to treat a myriad of ailments, including headache, insomnia, and digestive problems. But scholars now believe it was the very rarity of spices, and the mythology associated with their mysterious and distant origins, that was the real source of their value. Precisely because they came from so far away and were thus so expensive, spices were viewed as the ultimate status symbols. In addition, many Europeans believed fantastic stories about the way spices were procured. Pepper, for example, was thought to come from trees guarded by serpents who would poison anyone attempting to harvest the peppercorns that grew on them. Stories such as these added to the allure of spices, which in turn helped to explain the very high prices Europeans were willing to pay for them.

Source: John Keay, *The Spice Route: A History* (Berkeley: University of California Press, 2006).

MAP 22.2   European exploration in the Atlantic Ocean, 1486–1498.

Observe the difference between Bartolomeu Dias's journey and Vasco da Gama's journey around the Cape of Good Hope.

Why did da Gama go so far out into the Atlantic before rounding the Cape?

not succeed, but the idea of exploring the Atlantic and establishing a maritime trade route from the Mediterranean to India persisted. During the fourteenth century Genoese, Portuguese, and Spanish mariners sailed frequently into the Atlantic Ocean and rediscovered the Canary Islands. The Guanche people had settled the Canaries from their original home in Morocco, in around the fifth century B.C.E. but there had been no contact between the Guanches and other peoples since the time of the Roman Empire. Iberian mariners began to visit the Canaries regularly, and in the fifteenth century—after a long and brutal war in which the Guanche put up fierce resistance—Castilian forces conquered the islands and made them an outpost for further exploration.

Prince Henry of Portugal   The pace of European exploration quickened after 1415 when Prince Henry of Portugal (1394–1460) conquered the Moroccan port of **Ceuta** and sponsored a series of voyages down the west African coast. Portuguese merchants soon established fortified trading posts at **São Jorge da Mina** (in modern Ghana) and other strategic locations. There they exchanged European horses, leather, textiles, and metalwares for gold and, increasingly, enslaved people (for an in-depth discussion of the emerging Atlantic slave trade, see chapter 25). Portuguese explorations continued after Henry's death, and in 1488 **Bartolomeu Dias** rounded the Cape of Good Hope and entered the Indian Ocean. He did not proceed farther because of storms and a restless crew, but the route to India, China, and the spice-bearing islands of southeast Asia lay open. The sea route to the Indian Ocean offered European merchants the opportunity to buy silk, spices, and pepper at the source, rather than through Muslim intermediaries, and to take part in the flourishing trade of Asia described by Marco Polo.

Vasco da Gama   Portuguese mariners did not immediately follow up Dias's voyage because domestic and foreign problems distracted royal attention from voyages to Asia. In 1497, however, Vasco da Gama departed Lisbon with a fleet of four armed merchant ships bound for India. As we saw in the introduction, his experience—and the experiences of his crew—was not pleasant. His fleet went more than three months without seeing land, and his cargoes excited little interest in Indian markets. His return voyage was especially

Ceuta (SYOO-tuh)

São Jorge da Mina (sou hor-hay dah meena)

Bartolomeu Dias (bahr-tol-uh-MEY-oh dee-as)

SOURCES FROM THE PAST

Christopher Columbus's First Impressions of American Peoples

Christopher Columbus kept journals of his experiences during his voyages to the Western Hemisphere. These journals were not meant to be private, but instead were to be shared with his benefactors, Ferdinand and Isabella of Spain, and also to record his accomplishments for posterity. The journal of his first voyage survives mostly in summary, but it clearly communicates Columbus's first impressions of the people he met in the Caribbean islands. The following excerpts show that Columbus, like other European mariners, had both Christianity and commerce in mind when exploring distant lands. Keep in mind that Columbus treated the indigenous Taíno with brutality even from the first day of his arrival, when he had six people seized as servants. Look for places in the text in which Columbus uses dehumanizing language, or suggests how the Taíno could be useful to Europeans.

Thursday, 11 October [1492]. . . .

I . . . in order that they would be friendly to us—because I recognized that they were people who would be better freed [from error] and converted to our Holy Faith by love than by force—to some of them I gave red caps, and glass beads which they put on their chests, and many other things of small value, in which they took so much pleasure and became so much our friends that it was a marvel. Later they came swimming to the ships' launches where we were and brought us parrots and cotton thread in balls and javelins and many other things, and they traded them to us for other things which we gave them, such as small glass beads and bells. In sum, they took everything and gave of what they had willingly.

But it seemed to me that they were a people very poor in everything. All of them go as naked as their mothers bore them; and the women also, although I did not see more than one quite young girl. And all those that I saw were young people, for none did I see of more than 30 years of age. They are very well formed, with handsome bodies and good faces. Their hair [is] coarse—almost like the tail of a horse—and short. They wear their hair down over their eyebrows except for a little in the back which they wear long and never cut. . . .

They do not carry arms nor are they acquainted with them, because I showed them swords and they took them by the edge and through ignorance cut themselves. They have no iron. Their javelins are shafts without iron and some of them have at the end a fish tooth and others of other things. All of them alike are of good-sized stature and carry themselves well. I saw some who had marks of wounds on their bodies and I made signs to them asking what they were; and they showed me how people from other islands nearby came there and tried to take them, and how they defended themselves and I believed and believe that they come here from *tierra firme* [the continent] to take them captive. They should be good and intelligent servants, for I see that they say very quickly everything that is said to them; and I believe that they would become Christians very easily, for it seemed to me that they had no religion. . . .

> On what basis might Christopher Columbus have been making such an observation about religious faith? What might he have been missing?

Monday, 12 November. . . .

They are very gentle and do not know what evil is; nor do they kill others, nor steal; and they are without weapons and so timid that a hundred of them flee from one of our men even if our men are teasing them. And they are credulous and aware that there is a God in heaven and convinced that we come from the heavens; and they say very quickly any prayer that we tell them to say, and they make the sign of the cross. So that Your Highnesses ought to resolve to make them Christians: for I believe that if you begin, in a short time you will end up having converted to our Holy Faith a multitude of peoples and acquir-

> Does this statement contradict Columbus' earlier assertion that the people he encountered "had no religion"?

ing large dominions and great riches and all of their peoples for Spain. Because without doubt there is in these lands a very great quantity of gold; for not without cause do these Indians that I bring with me say that there are in these islands places where they dig gold and wear it on their chests, on their ears, and on their arms, and on their legs; and they are very thick bracelets. And also there are stones, and there are precious pearls and infinite spicery. . . . And also here there is probably a great quantity of cotton; and I think that it would sell very well here without taking it to Spain but to the big cities belonging to the Grand [Mongol] Khan.

For Further Reflection

■ On the basis of Columbus's account, what inferences can you draw about his plans for American lands and peoples? Based on this small excerpt, is it possible to surmise how contemporary Taíno people might have described Columbus and his men?

Source: Christopher Columbus. *The Diario of Christopher Columbus's First Voyage to America.* Trans. by Oliver Dunn and James E. Kelley Jr. Norman: University of Oklahoma Press, 1989, pp. 65–69, 143–45.

difficult, and more than half of his crew died slow and painful deaths from scurvy (vitamin C deficiency) before making it back to Portugal. Yet his cargo of pepper and cinnamon was hugely profitable, and Portuguese merchants began immediately to organize further expeditions. By 1500 they had built a trading post at Calicut, the site of da Gama's original landing, and Portuguese mariners soon called at ports throughout India and the Indian Ocean basin. By the late sixteenth century, English and Dutch mariners had followed the Portuguese into the Indian Ocean basin.

Christopher Columbus While Portuguese navigators plied the sea route to India, the Genoese mariner Cristoforo Colombo, known in English as **Christopher Columbus** (1451–1506), proposed sailing to the markets of Asia by a western route. On the basis of wide reading of literature on geography, Columbus believed that the Eurasian landmass covered 270 degrees of longitude and that the earth was a relatively small sphere with a circumference of about 17,000 nautical miles. (In fact, the Eurasian landmass from Portugal to Korea covers only 140 degrees of longitude, and the earth's circumference is almost 25,000 nautical miles.) By Columbus's calculations, Japan should be less than 2,500 nautical miles west of the Canary Islands. (The actual distance between the Canaries and Japan is more than 10,000 nautical miles.) This geography suggested that sailing west from Europe to Asian markets would be profitable, and Columbus sought royal sponsorship for a voyage to prove his ideas. The Portuguese court declined his proposal, partly out of skepticism about his geography and partly because Dias's voyage of 1488 already pointed the way toward India.

Fernando and Isabel of Spain eventually agreed to sponsor Columbus's expedition, but it was Italian bankers who actually financed the voyage. In August 1492 his fleet of three ships departed Palos in southern Spain. He sailed south to the Canaries, picked up supplies, and then turned west with the trade winds. On the morning of 12 October 1492, he made landfall at an island in the Bahamas that the native **Taíno** inhabitants called **Guanahaní** and that Columbus rechristened San Salvador (also known as Watling Island). Thinking that he had arrived in the spice islands known familiarly as the Indies, Columbus called the Taíno "Indians." He sailed around the Caribbean for almost three months searching for gold, and at the large island of Cuba he sent a delegation to seek the court of the emperor of China. When Columbus returned to Spain, he reported to his royal sponsors that he had reached islands just off the coast of Asia.

Hemispheric Links In spite of what he believed, Columbus never reached the riches of Asia. Moreover, although he made three additional voyages across the Atlantic Ocean, he obtained very little gold in the Caribbean. Yet news of his voyage spread rapidly throughout Europe, and hundreds of Spanish, English, French, and Dutch mariners soon followed in his wake. Particularly in the early sixteenth century, many of them continued to seek the passage to Asian waters that Columbus himself had pursued. Over the longer term, however, it became clear that the American continents and the Caribbean islands themselves held abundant opportunities for entrepreneurs. Thus Columbus's voyages to the Western Hemisphere had unintended but profound consequences because they established links between the eastern and Western Hemisphere and paved the way for the conquest, settlement, and exploitation of the Americas by European peoples.

European Voyages of Exploration: From the Atlantic to the Pacific

While some Europeans sought opportunities in the Americas, others continued to seek a western route to Asian markets. The Spanish military commander Vasco Nuñez de Balboa sighted the Pacific Ocean in 1513 while searching for gold in Panama, but in the early sixteenth century no one knew how much ocean lay between the Americas and Asia. Indeed, no one even suspected the vast size of the Pacific Ocean, which covers one-third of the earth's surface.

Ferdinand Magellan The initial exploration of the Pacific Ocean basin began with the Portuguese navigator Fernão de Magalhães (1480–1521), better known as **Ferdinand Magellan.** While sailing in the service of Portugal, Magellan had visited ports throughout the Indian Ocean basin and had traveled east as far as the spice islands of Maluku. He believed that the spice islands and Asian markets lay fairly close to the western coast of the Americas, and he decided to pursue Christopher Columbus's goal of establishing a western route to Asian waters. Because Portuguese mariners had already reached Asian markets through the Indian Ocean, they had little interest in Magellan's proposed western route. Thus, on his Pacific expedition Magellan sailed in the service of Spain.

The Circumnavigation Magellan's voyage was an exercise in endurance. He left Spain in September 1519, and then began probing the eastern coast of South America in search of a strait leading to the Pacific. Eventually, he found and sailed through the tricky and treacherous strait, later to bear his name, near the southern tip of South America. After exiting the strait, his fleet sailed almost four months before taking on fresh provisions at Guam. During that period crewmen survived on worm-ridden biscuits only and water gone foul. Ship's rats that were unfortunate enough to fall into the hands of famished sailors quickly became the centerpiece of a meal. A

This 1561 map shows Ferdinand Magellan's name for the Pacific (Mare Pacificum) and the Strait of Magellan (Frenum Magaliani).
The History Collection/Alamy Stock Photo

survivor reported in his account of the voyage that crewmen even ate ox hides, which they softened by dragging them through the sea for four or five days and then grilled on coals. Lacking fresh fruits and vegetables in their diet, many of the crew fell victim to the dreaded disease of scurvy, which caused painful rotting of the gums, loss of teeth, abscesses, hemorrhaging, weakness, loss of spirit, and in most cases death. Scurvy killed twenty-nine members of Magellan's crew during the Pacific crossing.

Conditions improved after the fleet arrived in Guam in March 1521, but its ordeal had not come to an end. From Guam, Magellan proceeded to the Philippine Islands, where he became involved in a local political dispute that took the lives of Magellan himself and 40 of his crew A local chief had asked for Magellan's help in a dispute with a rival tribe, and in the fighting that ensued, Magellan was hit by a poisoned arrow and left to die by his crewmen. The survivors continued on to the spice islands of Maluku, where they took on a cargo of cloves. Rather than brave the Pacific Ocean once again, they sailed home through the familiar waters of the Indian Ocean—and thus completed the first circumnavigation of the world—returning to Spain after a voyage of almost exactly three years. Of Magellan's five ships and 280 men, only a single spice-laden ship with 18 of the original crew returned.

Exploration of the Pacific The Pacific Ocean is so vast that it took European explorers almost three centuries to

SOURCES FROM THE PAST

Captain Cook's Journal from Tahiti

James Cook (1728–1779) was an English explorer from a small village in Yorkshire. He joined the Royal Navy in 1755 and served in North America, where he learned to chart and survey coastal territories. In 1768, the Royal Society and the British Admiralty chose Cook to captain an expedition to find the as-yet-undiscovered "southern continent." Between 1768 and 1771, Cook and his crew sailed the Pacific, landing in Tahiti in 1769 and then making contact with (and claiming) what is now New Zealand. He made two more Pacific voyages before he was killed in hostilities with Hawaiians in a visit there in 1779. Below, he describes in his journal one of the first interactions of his crew with the people of Tahiti in 1769.

Tahiti, Saturday [April] 15th, 1769 . . . This morning several of the Chiefs we had seen Yesterday came on board, and brought with them Hogs, Bread fruit, etc., and for these we gave them Hatchets, Linnen, and such things as they valued. Having not met with yesterday a more Convenient situation for every purpose we wanted than the place we now are, I therefore, without delay, resolved to pitch upon some spot upon the North-East point of the Bay . . . and there to throw up a small fort for our defence. Accordingly I went ashore with a party of men, accompanied by Mr. Banks, Dr. Solander, and Mr. Green. We took along with us one of Mr. Banks's Tents, and after we had fix'd upon a place fit for our purpose we set up the Tent and marked out the ground we intended to Occupy. By this time a number of the Natives had got collected together about us, seemingly only to look on, as not one of them had any weapon, either Offensive or defensive. I would suffer none to come within the lines I had marked out, excepting one who appeared to be a chief . . . we endeavour'd to explain, as well as we could, that we wanted that ground to Sleep upon such a number of nights and then we should go away. Whether they understood us or no is uncertain, but no one appeared the least displeased at what we was about; indeed the Ground we had fixed upon was of no use to them, being part of the sandy Beach upon the shore of the Bay, and not near to any of their Habitations. It being too late in the day to do anything more, a party with a petty officer was left to guard the Tent, while we with another party took a Walk into the woods, and with us most of the natives. We had but just crossed the River when Mr. Banks shott three Ducks at one shott, which surprised them so much that most of them fell down as though they had been shott likewise. I was in hopes this would have had some good effect, but the event did not prove it, for we had not been long from the Tent before the natives again began to gather about, and one of them more daring than the rest pushed one of the Centinels [sic] down, snatched the Musket out of his hand and made a push at him, and then made off, and with him all the rest. Immediately upon this the Officer ordered the party to fire, and the Man who took the musket was shot Dead before he had got far from the Tent, but the musquet was carried quite off when this hapned [sic]. I and Mr. Banks with the other party was about half a Mile off, returning out of the woods, upon hearing the firing of Muskets, and the Natives leaving us at the same time, we Suspected that something was the matter and hastened our march, but before we arrived the whole was over, and every one of the Natives fled except old Owhaa, who stuck by us the whole time . . . [Soon after, Owhaa helped convince some of the Tahitians] to come to the Tent and there sit down with us, and Endeavour'd by every means in our power to Convince them that the Man was kill'd for taking away the Musket, and that we still would be friends with them. At sunset they left us seemingly satisfied, and we struck our Tent and went on board.

> What does Captain Cook's resolve to set up a defensive fort imply about his feelings of entitlement to the land in Tahiti?

> Why might the Tahitians present at the time have been so surprised by Mr. Banks's musket shot? What kind of "good effect" was Captain Cook hoping for here?

For Further Reflection

■ What does this event tell us about the attitudes of Captain Cook and his men toward the indigenous people of Tahiti? Does Cook's language suggest that he and his men saw Tahitians as equals or inferiors, threatening or nonthreatening? Which specific turns of phrase suggest these attitudes?

Source: Captain James Cook, Captain Cook's Journal During His First Voyage Round the World, Made in H.M. Bark "Endeavor," 1768–1771 (London, 1893). https://www.gutenberg.org/files/8106/8106-h/8106-h.htm#ch5

MAP 22.3   Pacific voyages of Magellan and Cook, 1519–1780.

What made exploration of the Pacific Ocean so daunting? What fate befell both Magellan and Cook?

chart its features. Spanish merchants built on information gleaned from Magellan's expedition and established a trade route between the Philippines and Mexico, but they did not continue to explore the ocean basin itself. English navigators, however, ventured into the Pacific in search of an elusive northwest passage from Europe to Asia. In fact, a northwest passage exists, but most of its route lies within the Arctic Circle. It is so far north that ice clogs its waters for much of the year, and it was only in the twentieth century that the Norwegian explorer Roald Amundsen traveled from the Atlantic to the Pacific by way of the northwest passage. Nevertheless, while searching for a passage, English mariners established many of the details of Pacific geography. In the sixteenth century, for example, Sir Francis Drake scouted the west coast of North America as far north as Vancouver Island. By the mid-eighteenth century, French mariners had joined English seafarers in exploring the Pacific Ocean in search of a northwest passage.

Russian expansion was mostly a land-based affair in early modern times, but by the eighteenth century Russians also explored the Pacific Ocean. Russian officials commissioned the Danish navigator **Vitus Bering** to undertake two maritime expeditions (1725–1730 and 1733–1742) in search of a northeast passage to Asian ports. Bering sailed through the icy Arctic Ocean and the Bering Strait, which separates Siberia from Alaska, and reconnoitered northern Asia as far as the Kamchatka peninsula. Other Russian explorers made their way from Alaska down the western Canadian coast to northern California. By 1800, Russian mariners were scouting the Pacific Ocean as far south as the Hawaiian Islands. Indeed, they built a small fort on the island of Kaua`i and engaged in trade there for a few years in the early nineteenth century.

Captain James Cook Along with the Russian explorers and Magellan, one of the most important of the Pacific explorers was **Captain James Cook** (1728–1779), who led three expeditions to the Pacific and died in a scuffle with the indigenous people of Hawai`i. Cook charted eastern Australia and New Zealand, and he added New Caledonia, Vanuatu, and

A portrait of Captain James Cook painted by William Hodges about 1775 depicts a serious and determined man.

Ian Dagnall/Alamy Stock Photo

This European drawing from Captain James Cook's first voyage focuses on the facial tattoos of a Maori chief's son, which would have seemed unusual to Europeans.

BL/Robana/age fotostock

Hawai`i to European maps of the Pacific. He probed the frigid waters of the Arctic Ocean and spent months at a time in the tropical islands of Tahiti, Tonga, and Hawai`i, where he showed deep interest in the manners, customs, and languages of Polynesian peoples. By the time Cook's voyages had come to an end, European geographers had compiled a reasonably accurate understanding of the world's ocean basins, their lands, and their peoples.

ECOLOGICAL EXCHANGES

European explorers and those who followed them established links between all the lands and peoples of the world. Interaction between peoples in turn resulted in an unprecedented volume of exchange across the boundary lines of societies and cultural regions. Some of that exchange involved biological species: plants, food crops, animals, human populations, and disease pathogens all spread to new regions. These biological exchanges had differing and dramatic effects on human populations, destroying some of them through epidemic diseases while enlarging others through

increased food supplies and richer diets. Commercial exchange also flourished in the wake of the voyages of exploration as European merchants traveled to ports throughout the world in search of trade. By the late sixteenth century, they had built fortified trading posts at strategic sites in the Indian, Atlantic, and Pacific Ocean basins. By the mid-eighteenth century, they had established global networks of trade and communication.

The Columbian Exchange

Processes of biological exchange were prominent features of world history well before modern times. The early expansion of Islam, for example, had facilitated the diffusion of plants and food crops throughout much of the Eastern Hemisphere during the period from about 700 to 1100 C.E., and transplanted species helped spark demographic and economic growth in all the lands where they took root. And during the

How the Past Shapes the Future ▷ ▷ ▷ ▷ ▷ ▷ ▷

Short-Term and Long-Term Effects of the Columbian Exchange

Some events or processes in the global past are so momentous that they produce social, political, economic, or environmental changes for centuries—even in places thousands of miles from their points of origin. In other words, we can see the effects of these events or processes in multiple places and in multiple timelines long after they occur, even up to the present. Understanding the spectrum of consequences spurred by such momentous events and processes can help us trace the historical connections between the world's people and places, even when such connections may not have been obvious to people living at the time.

Although the European mariners who first came into contact with the people, plants, and animals of the Americas could not have understood it at the time, their encounters set in motion a process that permanently transformed not just the Americas but the entire world in ways that are still relevant today. Two facets of the exchange demonstrate how this was so: disease and the transfer of flora and fauna.

Disease

In this chapter we have already seen the devastating effect of disease on populations indigenous to the Americas, with scholars estimating between 50 and 90 percent mortality across the entire region. Such high mortality was a key factor in allowing European invaders to conquer, settle, and expand throughout the Americas—a process discussed in chapter 24. In other words, if disease had not ravaged indigenous populations, it seems likely that Europeans would not have been able to use American lands for their own purposes on such a large scale, and also that the population of the present-day Americas would be composed of many more peoples whose ancestors were native to the area. A longer-term consequence of disease during the Columbian exchange was that there were simply not enough laborers in large parts of the Americas to carry out the work required by large-scale agricultural enterprises developed by Europeans after conquest. As a result, first the Portuguese and then many other Europeans began to import enslaved African laborers to the Americas, a process discussed in chapter 25. The Atlantic slave trade, in turn, had profound effects on enslaved individuals, the African states involved, and the eventual composition of populations in the Americas.

Flora and Fauna

In this chapter we have seen that the Columbian exchange involved extensive movement of plants and animals between Eurasia and the Americas. Over the long term, these exchanges transformed landscapes around the world by introducing plant and animal species that became invasive in their new environments (such as dandelions in the Americas or pigs on the island of Barbados). Some introductions to the Americas, like the horse, brought about fundamental cultural changes. For example, Plains Indians adopted horses in order to hunt wild game more effectively, resulting in dramatic changes in gender ideologies and lifestyle. Products that originated in the Americas also had a profound impact on other parts of the world. For example, nutritional foods native to the Americas—including potatoes, corn, and sweet potatoes—helped spur population growth in places like China that were not involved in the initial process of exchange at all. Nonfood crops were important to the Columbian exchange as well: tobacco, introduced from the Americas, was widely and quickly integrated into the cultures of both Europe and the Islamic empires. In fact, in just a little more than one hundred years after being introduced to tobacco for the first time, Europeans had introduced tobacco to Europe, Asia, west Africa, and the Near East. In the present, approximately 1.1 billion of the world's people are smokers, and about 25 percent of smokers die from smoke-related causes.

These are only a small sampling of the historical consequences of the Columbian exchange, both through time and across space. When reading subsequent chapters, try to identify additional developments that may have their origins in this truly momentous process.

Tabacum latifolium.

Tobacco was long used for religious and spiritual purposes in the Americas. After their arrival in the Americas, Europeans quickly popularized tobacco as a trade item and as a recreational drug to be smoked, snuffed, or chewed.
Historical Picture Archive/Corbis Historical/Getty Images

fourteenth century the spread of bubonic plague caused drastic demographic losses when epidemic disease struck Eurasian and north African lands.

Biological Exchanges Yet the **Columbian exchange**—the global diffusion of plants, food crops, animals, human populations, and disease pathogens that took place after voyages of exploration by Christopher Columbus and other European mariners—had consequences much more profound than any of the earlier rounds of biological exchange. Unlike the earlier processes, the Columbian exchange involved lands with radically different flora, fauna, and diseases. For thousands of years the various species of the Eastern Hemisphere, the Western Hemisphere, and Oceania had evolved along separate lines. By creating links between these biological zones, the European voyages of exploration set off a round of biological exchange that permanently altered the world's human geography and natural environment.

Beginning in the early sixteenth century, infectious and contagious diseases brought devastating demographic losses to indigenous peoples of the Americas and the Pacific islands. The most virulent disease was smallpox, but measles, diphtheria, whooping cough, and influenza also took heavy tolls. Before the voyages of exploration, none of these maladies had reached the Western Hemisphere or Oceania, and the peoples of those regions consequently had no inherited or acquired immunities to those pathogens. In the Eastern Hemisphere, these diseases had mostly become endemic: they claimed a certain number of victims from the ranks of infants and small children, but survivors gained immunity to the diseases through exposure at an early age. In some

Smallpox victims in the Aztec Empire. The disease killed most of those it infected and left disfiguring scars on survivors.
Peabody Museum, Harvard University (2004.24.29636).

areas of Europe, for example, smallpox was responsible for 10 to 15 percent of deaths, but most victims were younger than age ten. Although its effects were tragic for individual families and communities, smallpox did not pose a threat to European society as a whole because it did not carry away adults, who were mostly responsible for economic production and social organization.

Epidemic Diseases and Population Decline When infectious and contagious diseases traveled to previously unexposed populations, however, they touched off ferocious epidemics that sometimes destroyed entire societies. Beginning in 1519, epidemic smallpox ravaged the Aztec Empire, often in combination with other diseases, and within a century the indigenous population of Mexico had declined by as much as 90 percent, from about 17 million to 1.3 million. By that time Spanish conquerors had imposed their rule on Mexico, and the political, social, and cultural traditions of the indigenous peoples had either disappeared or fallen under Spanish domination.

Imported diseases took their worst tolls in densely populated areas such as the Aztec and Inca empires, but they did not spare other regions. Smallpox and other diseases were so easily transmissible that they raced to remote areas of North and South America and sparked epidemics even before the first European explorers arrived in those regions. By the 1530s smallpox may have spread as far from Mexico as the Great Lakes in the north and the pampas of Argentina in the south.

When introduced to the Pacific islands, infectious and contagious diseases struck vulnerable populations with the same horrifying effects as in the Americas, albeit on a smaller scale. All told, disease epidemics sparked by the Columbian exchange probably caused the worst demographic calamity in all of world history. Between 1500 and 1800, upwards of 100 million people may have died of diseases imported by Europeans into the Americas and the Pacific islands.

Food Crops and Animals Over the long term, however, the Columbian exchange increased rather than diminished human population because of the global spread of food crops and animals that it sponsored. In the long term, a better-nourished world was an important contributing factor in the growth of the world's population, which began in the eighteenth century and continues in the present. Out of Eurasia to the Western Hemisphere traveled wheat, rice, sugar, bananas, apples, cherries, peaches, peas, and citrus fruits. Wheat in particular grew well on the plains of North America and on the pampas of Argentina, regions either too dry or too cold for the cultivation of maize (corn). Africa contributed yams, okra, collard greens, and coffee. Dairy and meat-yielding animals—horses, cattle, pigs, sheep, goats, and chickens—went from Europe to the Americas, where they sharply increased supplies of food and animal energy.

American Crops Food crops native to the Americas also played prominent roles in the Columbian exchange. American crops that took root in Africa, Asia, and Europe include maize, potatoes, beans, tomatoes, peppers, peanuts, manioc, papayas, guavas, avocados, pineapples, and cacao, to name some of the most important. (A less nutritious transplant was tobacco.) Residents of the Eastern Hemisphere only gradually developed a taste for American crops, but by the eighteenth century maize and potatoes in particular had contributed to a sharply increased number of calories in Eurasian diets. Maize became especially important in China because it grew in eco-niches unsuitable for rice and millet production. With the exception of Bengal (India), Asian lands proved less welcoming to the potato. But in northern Europe, the potato eventually became a staple crop, from Ireland to Russia, because of its impressive nutritional qualities. American bean varieties added protein to diets around the world, and tomatoes and peppers provided vitamins and zesty flavors in lands from western Europe to China. Peanuts and manioc flourished in tropical southeast Asian and west African soils that otherwise would not produce large yields or support large populations. The Americas also supplied medicinal plants. Derived from the bark of the Peruvian cinchona tree, bitter-tasting quinine was the first effective treatment for malaria and proved vital to Europeans trying to survive in tropical areas inhabited by the mosquitoes that spread the disease.

Population Growth The Columbian exchange of plants and animals fueled a surge in world population. In 1500, as Eurasian peoples were recovering from epidemic bubonic plague, world population stood at about 425 million. By 1600 it had increased more than 25 percent to 545 million. Human numbers increased less rapidly during the next century, reaching 610 million in 1700. But thereafter they increased at a faster rate than ever before in world history. By 1750 human population stood at 720 million, and by 1800 it had surged to 900 million, having grown by almost 50 percent during the previous century. Much of the rise was due to the increased nutritional value of diets enriched by the global exchange of food crops and animals.

Migration Alongside disease pathogens and plant and animal species, the Columbian exchange also involved the spread of human populations through transoceanic migration, both voluntary and forced. During the period from 1500 to 1800, the largest contingent of migrants consisted of enslaved Africans transported against their will to South American, North American, and Caribbean destinations. A smaller but still sizable migration involved Europeans who traveled to the Americas as settlers. In some cases, they settled on lands that had previously been depopulated by infectious and contagious diseases, while in others they forced out existing populations through violence and forced relocation. During the nineteenth century, European peoples traveled in massive numbers mostly to the Western Hemisphere but also to south Africa, Australia, and Pacific islands where diseases had diminished indigenous populations, while equal numbers of Asian peoples migrated to tropical and subtropical destinations throughout much of the world. In combination, those migrations have profoundly influenced modern world history.

The Origins of Global Trade

Besides stimulating commerce in the Eastern Hemisphere, the voyages of European merchant mariners encouraged the emergence of a genuinely global trading system. European manufactured goods traveled west across the Atlantic in exchange for silver from Mexican and Peruvian mines and agricultural products such as sugar and tobacco, both of which were in high demand among European consumers. Trade in human beings also figured in Atlantic commerce. European textiles, guns, and other manufactured goods went south to west Africa, where merchants exchanged them for African slaves, who then were forcibly transported to the tropical and subtropical regions of the Western Hemisphere to work on plantations.

The Manila Galleons The experience of the **Manila galleons** illustrates the early workings of the global economy in the Pacific Ocean basin. For 250 years, from 1565 to 1815, Spanish galleons—sleek, fast, heavily armed ships capable of carrying large cargoes—regularly plied the waters of the Pacific Ocean between Manila in the Philippines and Acapulco on the west coast of Mexico. From Manila they took Asian luxury goods to Mexico and exchanged them for silver. Most of the precious metal made its way to China, where a thriving domestic economy demanded increasing quantities of silver, the basis of Chinese currency. In fact, the demand for silver was so high in China that European merchants exchanged it for Chinese gold, which they later traded profitably for more silver as well as luxury goods in Japan. Meanwhile, some of the Asian luxury goods from Manila remained in Mexico or went to Peru, where they contributed to a comfortable way of life for Spanish ruling elites. Most, however, went overland across Mexico and then traveled by ship across the Atlantic to Spain and European markets.

Environmental Effects of Global Trade As the demand for silver fueled growing volumes of global trade, pressures fell on several animal species that had the misfortune to become prominent commodities on the world market. Fur-bearing animals came under particularly intense pressure, as hunters sought their pelts for sale to consumers in China, Europe, and North America. During the seventeenth century, an estimated two hundred to three hundred thousand sable pelts flowed annually from Siberia to the global market, and during the eighteenth century, more than sixteen million North American beaver pelts fed consumers' demands for

This is an artist's rendering of a Spanish galleon. Galleons were large, multidecked, highly stable and maneuverable sailing ships used by Europeans for war or commerce. The Spanish and the Portuguese built the largest types for their profitable overseas trade.

Bettmann/Getty Images

fur hats and cloaks. Wanton hunting of fur-bearing animals soon drove many species into extinction or near-extinction, permanently altering the environments they had formerly inhabited. In addition to fur-bearing animals, early modern hunters harvested enormous numbers of deer, codfish, whales, walruses, seals, and other species as merchants sought to supply skins, food, oil, ivory, and other animal products to global consumers.

By the late sixteenth century, conditions favored the relentless human exploitation of the world's natural and agricultural resources, as European mariners had permanently linked the world's port cities and created global trading networks. During the next two centuries, the volume of global trade expanded, as English, Dutch, French, and other merchants contributed to the development of global markets. During the seventeenth century, for example, Dutch merchants imported, among other commodities, wheat from south Africa, cowry shells from India, and sugar from Brazil. The wheat fed domestic consumers, who increasingly worked as merchants, bankers, or manufacturers rather than as cultivators. English, Dutch, and other merchants eagerly purchased the cowry shells—which served as currency in much of sub-Saharan Africa—and exchanged them for slaves destined for plantations in the Western Hemisphere. The sugar went on the market at Amsterdam and found its way to consumers throughout Europe. During the eighteenth century, world trade became even more intricate as mass markets emerged for commodities

such as coffee, tea, sugar, and tobacco. By 1750 all parts of the world except Australia participated in global networks of commercial relations in which European merchant mariners played prominent roles.

TRADE AND CONFLICT IN EARLY MODERN ASIA

The voyages of exploration taught European mariners how to sail to almost any coastline in the world and return safely. Once they arrived at their destinations, they sought commercial opportunities. In the Eastern Hemisphere they built a series of fortified trading posts that offered footholds in regions where established commercial networks had held sway for centuries. They even attempted to control the spice trade in the Indian Ocean but with limited success. They mostly did not have the human numbers or military power to impose their rule in the Eastern Hemisphere, although Spanish and Dutch forces established small island empires in the Philippines and Indonesia, respectively. In a parallel effort involving expansion across land rather than the sea, Russian explorers and adventurers established a presence in central Asian regions formerly ruled by the Mongols and in the tundra and forests of Siberia, thus laying the foundations for a vast Eurasian empire. Commercial and political competition in both the Eastern and Western Hemispheres led to conflict between European peoples, and by the end of the Seven Years' War in 1763, English military and merchant forces had gained an initiative over their rivals that enabled them to dominate world trade and build the vast British empire of the nineteenth century.

Trading-Post Empires

Portuguese Trading Posts Portuguese mariners built the earliest trading-post empire. Their goal was not to conquer territories but, rather, to control trade routes by forcing merchant vessels to call at fortified trading sites and pay duties there. Vasco da Gama obtained permission from local authorities to establish a trading post at Calicut when he arrived there in 1498. By the mid-sixteenth century, Portuguese merchants had built more than fifty trading posts between west Africa and east Asia. At São Jorge da Mina, they traded in west African slaves, and at Mozambique they attempted to control the south African gold trade. From Hormuz they controlled access to the Persian Gulf, and from Goa they organized trade in Indian pepper. At Melaka they oversaw shipping between the South China Sea and the Indian Ocean, and they channeled trade in cloves and nutmeg through Ternate in the spice islands of Maluku. Posts at Macau and Nagasaki offered access to the markets of China and Japan.

Afonso d'Alboquerque Equipped with heavy artillery, Portuguese vessels were able to overpower most other craft that they encountered, and they sometimes effectively bombarded coastal communities with their cannons. The architect of their aggressive policy was **Afonso d'Alboquerque,** commander of Portuguese forces in the Indian Ocean during the early sixteenth century. Alboquerque's fleets seized Hormuz in 1508, Goa in 1510, and Melaka in 1511. From these strategic sites, Alboquerque sought to control Indian Ocean trade by forcing merchant ships to purchase safe-conduct passes and present them at Portuguese trading posts. Ships without passes were subject to confiscation, along with their cargoes. Alboquerque's forces punished violators of his policy by executing them or cutting off their hands. Alboquerque was confident of Portuguese naval superiority and its ability to control trade in the Indian Ocean. After taking Melaka, he boasted that the arrival of Portuguese ships sent other vessels scurrying and that even the birds left the skies and sought cover.

Alboquerque's boast was an exaggeration. Although heavily armed, Portuguese forces did not have enough vessels to enforce the commander's orders. Arab, Indian, and Malay merchants continued to play prominent roles in Indian Ocean commerce, usually without taking the precaution of securing a safe-conduct pass. Portuguese ships transported perhaps half the pepper and spices that Europeans consumed during the early and middle decades of the sixteenth century, but Arab vessels delivered shipments through the Red Sea, which

Portuguese forces never managed to control, to Cairo and Mediterranean trade routes.

By the late sixteenth century, Portuguese influence in the Indian Ocean weakened. Portugal was a small country with a small population—about one million in 1500—and was unable to sustain a large seaborne trading empire for long. The crews of Portuguese ships often included Spanish, English, and Dutch sailors, who became familiar with Asian waters while in Portuguese service. By the late sixteenth century, investors in other lands began to organize their own expeditions to Asian markets. Most prominent of those who followed the Portuguese into the Indian Ocean were English and Dutch mariners.

English and Dutch Trading Posts Like their predecessors, English and Dutch merchants built trading posts on Asian coasts and sought to channel trade through them, but they did not attempt to control shipping on the high seas. They occasionally seized Portuguese sites, most notably when a Dutch fleet conquered Melaka in 1641. Yet Portuguese authorities held many of their trading posts into the twentieth century: Goa remained the official capital of Portuguese colonies in Asia until independent India reclaimed it in 1961. Meanwhile, English and Dutch entrepreneurs established parallel networks. English merchants concentrated on India and built trading posts at Bombay, Madras, and Calcutta, while the Dutch operated more broadly from Cape Town, Colombo, and Batavia (modern Jakarta on the island of Java).

English and Dutch merchants enjoyed two main advantages over their Portuguese predecessors. They sailed faster, cheaper, and more powerful ships, which offered both an economic and a military edge over their competitors. Furthermore, they conducted trade through an efficient form of commercial organization—the **joint-stock company**—which enabled investors to realize handsome profits while limiting the risk to their investments.

The Trading Companies English and Dutch merchants formed two especially powerful joint-stock companies: the English **East India Company,** founded in 1600, and its Dutch counterpart, the United East India Company, known from its initials as the **VOC** (Vereenigde Oost-Indische Compagnie), established in 1602. Private merchants advanced funds to launch these companies, outfit them with ships and crews, and provide them with commodities and money to trade. Although they enjoyed government support, the companies were privately owned enterprises. Unhampered by political oversight, company agents concentrated strictly on profitable trade. Their charters granted them the right to buy, sell, and build trading posts, and even make war in the companies' interests.

The English and Dutch companies experienced immediate financial success. In 1601, for example, five English ships

Afonso d'Alboquerque (al-FAWN-soo d'AL-buh-kur-kee)

set sail from London with cargoes mostly of gold and silver coins valued at thirty thousand pounds sterling. When they returned in 1603, the spices that they carried were worth more than one million pounds sterling. The first Dutch expedition did not realize such fantastic profits, but it more than doubled the investments of its underwriters. Because of their advanced nautical technology, powerful military arsenal, efficient organization, and relentless pursuit of profit, the English East India Company and the VOC contributed to the early formation of a global network of trade.

European Conquests in Southeast Asia

Following voyages of exploration to the Western Hemisphere, the massive demographic catastrophe caused by the introduction of contagious diseases to indigenous peoples meant that Europeans were able to build territorial empires and establish colonies settled by European migrants. In the Eastern Hemisphere, however, they were mostly unable to force their will on large Asian populations and powerful centralized states. With the decline of the Portuguese effort to

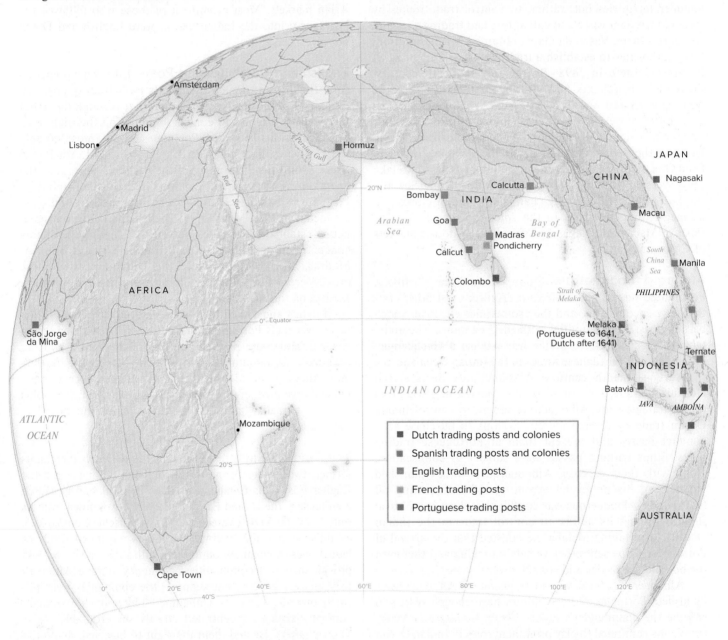

MAP 22.4   European trading posts in Africa and Asia, about 1700.

Note how many more trading posts there were in Asia than in Africa.

What accounts for the difference?

The Tijgersgracht Canal in the Dutch VOC settlement at Batavia (modern Jakarta, Indonesia) during the seventeenth century.
ART Collection/Alamy Stock Photo

control shipping in the Indian Ocean, Europeans mostly traded peacefully in Asian waters alongside Arab, Indian, Malay, and Chinese merchants.

Yet in two island regions of southeast Asia—the Philippines and Indonesia—Europeans were able to make limited conquests during the early modern period. Though densely populated, neither the Philippines nor Indonesia were ruled by a single powerful state when Europeans arrived there in the sixteenth century. Nor did imperial authorities in China or India lay claim to the island regions. Heavily armed ships enabled Europeans to use violence to establish imperial regimes that favored the interests of European merchants.

Conquest of the Philippines Spanish forces approached the Philippines in 1565 under the command of

Miguel López de Legazpi, who named the islands after King Philip II of Spain. Legazpi overcame local authorities in Cebu and Manila in almost bloodless contests. Because the Philippines had no central government, there was no organized resistance to the intrusion. The resistance the Spanish forces faced were from a series of small, disunited chiefdoms, who were not able to fend off Spanish ships and guns. By 1575 Spanish forces controlled the coastal regions of the central and northern islands, and during the seventeenth century they extended their authority to most parts of the archipelago. The main region outside their control was the southern island of Mindanao, where a large Muslim community stoutly resisted Spanish expansion.

Miguel López de Lagazpi (mee-GEHL LOH-pess day la-GAHS-pee)

Manila Spanish policy in the Philippines revolved around trade and Christianity. **Manila** soon emerged as a bustling, multicultural entrepôt—a port city for trade, particularly in silk—and it quickly became the hub of Spanish commercial activity in Asia. Chinese merchants were especially prominent in Manila. They occupied a specially designated commercial district of the city, and they accounted for about one-quarter of Manila's forty-two thousand residents in the mid-seventeenth century. They supplied the silk goods that Spanish traders shipped to Mexico in the so-called Manila galleons. Their commercial success brought suspicion on their community, and resentful Spanish and Filipino residents massacred Chinese merchants by the thousands in at least six major eruptions of violence in 1603, 1639, 1662, 1686, 1762, and 1819. Nevertheless, Spanish authorities continued to rely heavily on the wealth that Chinese merchants brought to Manila.

Apart from promoting trade, Spanish authorities in the Philippines also sought to spread Roman Catholicism throughout the archipelago. Spanish rulers and missionaries pressured prominent Filipinos to convert to Christianity in hopes of persuading others to follow their example. They opened schools to teach the fundamentals of Christian doctrine, along with basic literacy, in densely populated regions throughout the islands. The missionaries encountered stiff resistance in highland regions, where Spanish authority was not as strong as on the coasts, and resistance drew support from opponents of Spanish domination as well as from resentment of the newly arrived faith. Over the long term, however, Filipinos turned increasingly to Christianity, and by the nineteenth century the Philippines had become one of the most fervent Roman Catholic lands in the world.

Conquest of Java Dutch mariners, who imposed their rule on the islands of Indonesia, did not worry about seeking converts to Christianity but concentrated instead on the trade in spices, particularly cloves, nutmeg, and mace. The architect of Dutch policy was **Jan Pieterszoon Coen,** who in 1619 founded Batavia on the island of **Java** to serve as an entrepôt for the VOC. Batavia occupied a strategic site near the Sunda Strait, and its market attracted both Chinese and Malay vessels. Coen's plan was to establish a VOC monopoly over spice production and trade, thus enabling Dutch merchants to reap enormous profits in European markets. Coen brought his naval power to bear on the small Indonesian spice-growing islands and forced them to deliver spices only to VOC merchants. On larger islands such as Java, he took advantage of tensions between local princes and authorities and extracted concessions from many in return for providing them with aid against the others. By the late seventeenth century, the VOC controlled all the ports of Java as well as

most of the important spice-bearing islands throughout the Indonesian archipelago.

Dutch numbers were too few for them to rule directly over their whole southeast Asian empire. They made alliances with local authorities to maintain order in most regions, reserving for direct Dutch rule only Batavia and the most important spice-bearing islands such as clove-producing Amboina and the Banda Islands. They sought less to rule than to control the production of spices. The Dutch did not embark on campaigns of conquest for purposes of adding to their holdings, but they uprooted spice-bearing plants on islands they did not control and mercilessly attacked peoples who sold their spices to merchants not associated with the VOC. In some cases, such as on the island of Banda in 1621, Dutch traders murdered most of the population and burned their villages when they resisted Dutch attempts to monopolize the spice trade on the island. Eventually, monopoly profits from the spice trade not only enriched the VOC but also made the Netherlands the most prosperous land in Europe throughout most of the seventeenth century.

Foundations of the Russian Empire in Asia

While western European peoples were building maritime empires, Russians were laying the foundations for a vast land empire that embraced most of northern Eurasia. This round of expansion began in the mid-sixteenth century, as Russian forces took over several Mongol khanates in central Asia. These acquisitions resulted in Russian control over the Volga River and offered opportunities for trade with the Ottoman empire, Iran, and even India through the Caspian Sea. Because of its strategic location on the Volga delta where the river flows

Modern image of Fort Tolukko, a trading fortification originally built by the Portuguese on the spice island of Ternate. The Dutch occupied it in the early seventeenth century.
Ali Trisno Pranoto/Getty Images

Jan Pieterszoon Coen (yahn PEE-tuhr-sohn KOH-uhn)

into the Caspian Sea, the city of Astrakhan became a bustling commercial center, home to a community of several hundred foreign merchants from as far away as northern India. During the seventeenth and eighteenth centuries, some of the Indian merchants regularly made their way up the Volga River to trade in Moscow and the Russian interior, while others devised plans (which they never realized) to extend their activities to the Baltic Sea and take their business to western Europe. In the eighteenth century, Russian forces extended their presence in the Caspian Sea region by absorbing much of the Caucasus, a multiethnic region embracing the modern-day states of Georgia, Armenia, and Azerbaijan.

Encounters in Siberia Far more extensive were Russian acquisitions in northeastern Eurasia. The frozen tundras and dense forests of **Siberia** posed formidable challenges, but explorers and merchants made their way into the region in a quest for fur. Throughout the early modern era, fur was a lucrative commodity that encouraged Russians to look eastward, just as North American fur attracted the interest of English, French, and Dutch merchants. Russian expansion in northeastern Eurasia began in 1581 when the wealthy Stroganov family hired an adventurer named Yermak to capture the khanate of Sibir in the Ural Mountains. In the following decades, Russian explorers pushed into the interior regions of Siberia by way of the region's great rivers. By 1639 they had made their way across the Eurasian landmass and reached the Pacific Ocean.

Indigenous Peoples of Siberia Siberia was home to about twenty-six major ethnic groups that lived by hunting, trapping, fishing, or herding reindeer. These indigenous peoples varied widely in language and religion, and they responded in different ways to the arrival of Russian adventurers who sought to exact tribute from them by coercing them to supply pelts on a regular basis. Some groups readily accepted iron tools, woven cloth, flour, tea, and liquor for the skins of fur-bearing animals such as otter, lynx, marten, arctic fox, and especially the sleek sable. Others resented the ever-increasing demands for tribute and resisted Russian encroachment on their lands. Russian forces then resorted to punishing raids and hostage taking to induce Siberian peoples to deliver furs. The Yakut people of the Lena and Aldan River valleys in central Siberia mounted a revolt against Russian oppression in 1642 and experienced a brutal retribution that continued for forty years, forcing many Yakut out of their settlements and reducing their population by an estimated 70 percent. Quite apart from military violence, like people in the Americas and Oceania, the peoples of Siberia also reeled from epidemic diseases that reduced many populations by more than half.

As violence and disease sharply diminished the delivery of furs, the Russian government recognized that its interests lay in protection of the "small peoples," as state officials called the indigenous inhabitants of Siberia. Government-sponsored missionaries sought to convert Siberian peoples to Orthodox Christianity and bring them into Russian society, but they had little success. Few Siberians expressed an interest in Christianity, and those few came mostly from the ranks of criminals, abandoned hostages,

This is an engraving of an indigenous Siberian hunter, wearing the fur he helped to collect. He grasps his weapons in one hand while the other holds two fur-pelted animal carcasses.
Science & Society Picture Library/ Getty Images

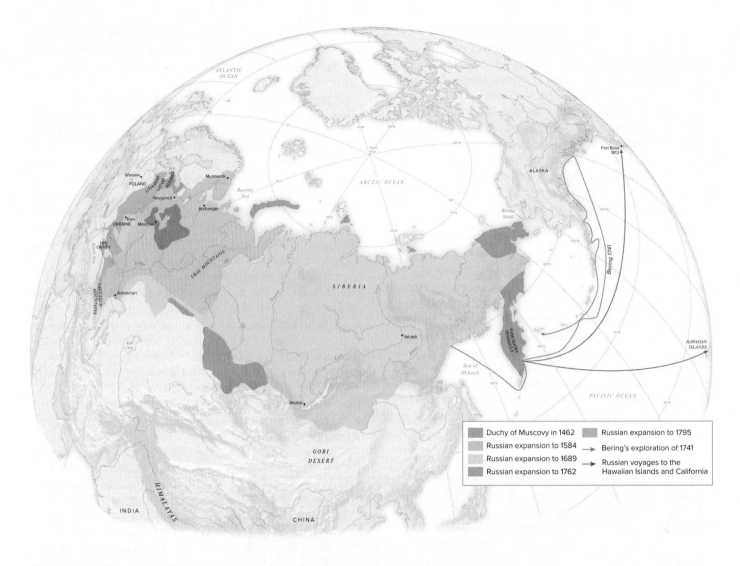

MAP 22.5   Russian expansion, 1462–1795.

Observe how vast the empire became after it added the territory of Siberia.

How did Russians exert their control over such a huge and unforgiving territory?

slaves, and others who had little status in their own societies. Furthermore, once indigenous peoples converted to Christianity, they were exempt from obligations to provide fur tributes, so the Russian government demonstrated less zeal in its religious mission than did the Spanish monarchs, who made the spread of Roman Catholic Christianity a prime goal of imperial expansion. Although they managed to attract a few Siberian converts, Orthodox missionaries mostly served the needs of Russian merchants, adventurers, and explorers in Siberia. For their part, the indigenous peoples of Siberia continued to practice their inherited religions guided by shamans.

The Russian Occupation of Siberia The settlers who established a Russian presence in Siberia included adventurers, convicted criminals, and even prisoners of war. Despite the region's harsh terrain, Russian migrants gradually filtered into Siberia and thoroughly altered its demographic complexion. Small agricultural settlements grew up near many trading posts, particularly in the fertile Amur River valley. Siberian landowners offered working conditions that were much lighter than those of Russia proper, so disgruntled peasants sometimes fled to settlements east of the Ural Mountains. Over time, Siberian trading posts with their garrisons developed into Russian towns with Russian-speaking populations attending Russian Orthodox churches. By 1763 some 420,000 Russians lived in Siberia, nearly double the number of indigenous inhabitants. In the nineteenth century, large numbers of additional migrants moved east to mine Siberian gold, silver, copper, and iron. By this time, the Russian state was well on the way toward consolidating its control over the region.

Commercial Rivalries and the Seven Years' War

Exploration and imperial expansion led to conflicts not only between Europeans and Asians but also among Europeans themselves. Mariners competed vigorously for trade in Asia and the Americas, and their efforts to establish markets—and sometimes monopolies as well—led frequently to clashes with their counterparts from different lands.

Competition and Conflict Indeed, throughout the seventeenth and early eighteenth centuries, commercial and political rivalries led to running wars between ships representing different states. Dutch vessels were most numerous in the Indian Ocean, and they enabled the VOC to dominate the spice trade. Dutch forces expelled most Portuguese merchants from southeast Asia and prevented English mariners from establishing secure footholds there. By the early eighteenth century, trade in Indian cotton and tea from Ceylon had begun to overshadow the spice trade, and English and French merchants working from trading posts in India became the dominant carriers in the Indian Ocean. Fierce competition again generated violence: in 1746 French forces seized the English trading post at Madras, one of the three principal centers of British operations in India.

Commercial competition led to conflict also in the Caribbean and the Americas. English pirates and privateers preyed on Spanish shipping from Mexico, often seizing vessels carrying cargoes of silver. English and French forces constantly skirmished and fought over sugar islands in the Caribbean while also contesting territorial claims in North America. Almost all conflicts between European states in the eighteenth century spilled over into the Caribbean and the Americas.

The Seven Years' War Commercial rivalries combined with political differences and came to a head in the **Seven Years' War** (1756-1763). The Seven Years' War was a global conflict in that it took place in several distinct geographic theaters—Europe, India, the Caribbean, and North America—and involved Asian and indigenous American peoples as well as Europeans. Sometimes called "the great war for empire," the Seven Years' War had deep implications for global affairs because it laid the foundation for 150 years of British imperial hegemony in the world.

In Europe the war pitted Britain and Prussia against France, Austria, and Russia. In India, British and French forces each allied with local rulers and engaged in a contest for dominance in the Indian Ocean. In the Caribbean, Spanish forces joined with the French in an effort to limit British expansion in the Western Hemisphere. In North America—where the Seven Years' War merged with a conflict already under way known as the French and Indian War (1754-1763)—British and French armies made separate alliances with indigenous peoples in an effort to outmaneuver each other.

British Dominance British forces fought little in Europe, where their Prussian allies held off massive armies seeking to surround and crush the expansive Prussian state. Elsewhere, however, British armies and navies fought often and handily overcame their enemies. They ousted French merchants from India and took control of French colonies in Canada, although they allowed French authorities to retain most of their Caribbean possessions. They allowed Spanish forces to retain Cuba but took Florida from the Spanish empire. Despite these victories, Britain couldn't rest easy; powerful states continuously challenged British ambitions. Yet victory in the Seven Years' War placed Britain in a position to dominate world trade for the foreseeable future, and "the great war for empire" paved the way for the establishment of the British empire in the nineteenth century. The war also suggested how close together earlier global exchanges had brought the peoples of the world.

CONCLUSION

Global commercial and biological exchanges and encounters arose from the efforts of European mariners to explore the world's waters and establish sea lanes that would support long-distance trade. Their search for sea routes to Asia accidentally led them to the Western Hemisphere and the vast expanse of the Pacific Ocean. The geographic knowledge that they accumulated enabled them to link the world's regions into an ever more finely articulated network of trade. But commercial exchange was not the only result of this global network. Food crops, animal stocks, disease pathogens, and human migrants also traveled the sea lanes and dramatically influenced societies throughout the world. In the Americas, the Pacific Islands, and (to a lesser extent) Siberia, epidemics sparked by unfamiliar disease pathogens ravaged indigenous populations, while massive migrations of human communities transformed the social and cultural landscape of the Americas. At the same time, in most of the Eastern Hemisphere, transplanted crops and animal species led to improved nutrition and marked population growth. Europeans did not achieve global dominance in early modern times. However, their voyages of exploration and consequent development of transoceanic trading networks meant that European peoples now played a more prominent role in world affairs than any of their ancestors. In addition, their efforts helped foster the development of an increasingly interdependent world.

STUDY TERMS

Afonso d'Alboquerque (465)

astrolabe (450)

back staffs (450)

Bartolomeu Dias (454)

Captain James Cook (459)

Ceuta (454)

Christopher Columbus (456)

Columbian Exchange (462)

cross staffs (450)

East India Company (465)

Ferdinand Magellan (456)

Guanahaní (456)

Jan Pieterszoon Coen (468)

Java (468)

joint-stock company (465)

magnetic compass (450)

Manila (468)

Manila galleons (463)

Miguel López de Legazpi (467)

Prince Henry the Navigator (453)

São Jorge da Mina (454)

Seven Years' War (471)

Siberia (469)

Taíno (456)

Vasco da Gama (448)

Vitus Bering (459)

VOC (465)

volta do mar (451)

FOR FURTHER READING

Rene J. Barendse. *The Arabian Seas.* Eastgate, N.Y., 2002. A pathbreaking and complex work that emphasizes the long predominance of Asia in the world economy.

Jerry Brotton. *A History of the World in 12 Maps.* New York, 2013. A cross-cultural sampling of maps, both ancient and current, and the ideas and beliefs that shaped them.

Christopher Columbus. *The* Diario *of Christopher Columbus's First Voyage to America.* Trans. by Oliver Dunn and James E. Kelley Jr. Norman, Okla., 1989. A careful translation.

Dorothy Crawford. *Deadly Companions: How Microbes Shaped Our History.* Oxford, 2007. Explores how microbes and humans evolved together from earliest humanity to the present.

Alfred W. Crosby. *The Columbian Exchange: Biological and Cultural Consequences of 1492.* Westport, Conn., 1972. Focuses on early exchanges of plants, animals, and diseases between Europe and America.

Charles C. Mann. *1493: Uncovering the New World Christopher Columbus Created.* New York, 2011. A thorough account of the ways the ecological and economic exchanges fundamentally transformed societies in the Americas, Europe, East Asia, and Africa.

Lincoln Paine. *The Sea and Civilization: A Maritime History of the World.* New York, 2013. An accessible, enjoyable, and refreshing maritime history of the world.

John F. Richards. *The Unending Frontier: An Environmental History of the Early Modern World.* Berkeley, 2003. Thoroughly explores the environmental effects of the global historical processes that shaped the early modern world.

Yuri Slezkine. *Arctic Mirrors: Russia and the Small Peoples of the North.* Ithaca, N.Y., 1994. Thoughtful analysis of Russian relations with the hunting, fishing, and herding peoples of Siberia.

Heather Streets-Salter and Trevor Getz. *Empires and Colonies in the Modern World.* New York, 2015. A globally focused exploration of imperialism and colonialism from the fourteenth century to the present.

23 The Transformation of Europe

ZOOMING IN ON TRADITIONS

Martin Luther Challenges the Church

In 1517 an obscure German monk posed a challenge to the Roman Catholic church. Martin Luther of Wittenberg denounced the church's sale of indulgences, a type of pardon that excused individuals from doing penance for their sins, making it easier for their souls to go to heaven when they died. Indulgences had been available since the eleventh century, but to raise funds for the reconstruction of St. Peter's basilica in Rome, church authorities began to sell indulgences aggressively in the early sixteenth century. From their point of view, indulgences were splendid devices: they encouraged individuals to reflect piously on their behavior while also bringing large sums of money into the church's treasury.

To Martin Luther, however, indulgences were signs of greed, hypocrisy, and moral rot in the Roman Catholic church. Luther despised what he saw as the pretentiousness of church authorities who claimed powers that belonged only to God: Luther believed that no human being had the power to absolve individuals of their sins and grant them admission to heaven, so for him the sale of indulgences was a huge moral and religious fraud. In October 1517, following academic custom of the

This detail from a sixteenth-century painting by François Dubois depicts the brutal murder of French Protestants in Paris during the St. Bartholomew's Day Massacre on August 23, 1572.

Alfredo Dagli Orti/Shutterstock

day, he offered to debate publicly with anyone who wished to dispute his views, and he denounced the sale of indulgences in a document called the **Ninety-Five Theses.**

Contrary to popular legend, Luther did not nail his work to the church door in Wittenberg. Nevertheless, news of the *Ninety-Five Theses* spread rapidly: within a few weeks, printed copies were available throughout Europe. Luther's challenge galvanized opinion among many who resented the power of the Roman church. It also drew severe criticism from religious and political authorities seeking to maintain the established order. Church officials subjected Luther's views to examination and judged them erroneous, and in 1520 Pope Leo X excommunicated the unrepentant monk. In 1521 the Holy Roman emperor Charles V, a devout Roman Catholic, summoned Luther to an assembly of imperial authorities and demanded that he publicly renounce his views. Luther's response: "I cannot and will not recant anything, for it is neither safe nor right to act against one's conscience. Here I stand. I can do no other. God help me. Amen."

Martin Luther's challenge held enormous religious and political implications. Though expelled from the church, Luther still considered himself Christian—indeed, he considered his own faith true Christianity—and he held religious services for a community of devoted followers. Wittenberg became a center of religious dissent, which by the late 1520s had spread through much of Germany and Switzerland. During the 1530s these dissenters—who became known as Protestants because of their protest against the established church—organized movements in France, England, the Low Countries, and even Italy and Spain. By midcentury Luther's act of individual rebellion had mushroomed into the Protestant Reformation, which shattered the religious unity of western European Christendom.

CHAPTER OVERVIEW

For all its unsettling effects, the Protestant Reformation was only one of several powerful movements that transformed European society during the early modern era. Another was the consolidation of strong centralized states, which took shape partly because of the Reformation. Between the sixteenth and the eighteenth centuries, monarchs in western Europe took advantage of religious quarrels to tighten control over their societies. By the mid-eighteenth century, some rulers had concentrated so much power in their own hands that historians refer to them as absolute monarchs.

Alongside religious conflict and the building of powerful states, capitalism and early modern science also profoundly influenced western European society in early modern times. Early capitalism—an economic system based on free market conditions and private ownership of goods and services—pushed European merchants and manufacturers into competition with one another and encouraged them to reorganize their businesses in search of maximum efficiency. Early modern science challenged traditional ways of understanding the world and the universe and prompted European intellectuals to seek an entirely rational understanding of the natural world.

As a result of these phenomena, between 1500 and 1800 western Europe underwent a thorough transformation. Although the combination of religious, political, social, economic, intellectual, and cultural change was unsettling and disruptive, it ultimately strengthened European society. The states of early modern Europe competed vigorously and mobilized their human and natural resources in order to do so effectively. By 1800 several of them had become especially powerful, wealthy, and dynamic. They stood poised to play major roles in world affairs during the nineteenth and twentieth centuries.

CHRONOLOGY	
1473–1543	Life of Nicolaus Copernicus
1478	Foundation of the Spanish Inquisition
1483–1546	Life of Martin Luther
1491–1556	Life of Ignatius Loyola
1509–1547	Reign of King Henry VIII
1509–1564	Life of John Calvin
1517	Publication of the *Ninety-Five Theses*
1519–1556	Reign of Emperor Charles V
1540	Foundation of the Society of Jesus
1545–1563	Council of Trent
1556–1598	Reign of King Philip II
1564–1642	Life of Galileo Galilei
1571–1630	Life of Johannes Kepler
1588	Spanish Armada
1618–1648	Thirty Years' War
1642–1727	Life of Isaac Newton
1643–1715	Reign of King Louis XIV
1648	Peace of Westphalia
1706–1749	Life of Émilie du Châtelet

THE FRAGMENTATION OF WESTERN EUROPEAN CHRISTENDOM

Although the peoples of western Europe spoke different languages, ate different foods, and observed different customs, the church of Rome provided them with a common religious and cultural heritage. During the sixteenth and seventeenth centuries, however, revolts against the Roman Catholic church shattered the religious unity of western Europe. Followers of **Martin Luther** and other Protestant reformers established a series of churches independent of Rome, and Roman Catholic leaders strengthened their own church against the challengers. Throughout early modern times, religious controversies fueled social tensions.

The Protestant Reformation

Roots of Reform The **Protestant Reformation** dates from the early sixteenth century, but many of the underlying conditions that prompted reformers to challenge the authority of the Roman Catholic church had existed for hundreds of years. Over the course of centuries, the church and its top officials had become deeply involved in the political affairs of western Europe. But political intrigues, combined with the church's growing wealth and power, also fostered greed and corruption, which undermined the church's spiritual authority and made it vulnerable to criticism. The blatant pursuit of pleasure and crass materialism of church officials—including, in some cases, living in luxury and taking mistresses—only further emphasized the perceived betrayal of Christian ideals. Although the church continued to enjoy the loyalty of most Christians, it faced a disapproval of its abuses that became increasingly strident in the decades before 1517. Alongside such criticism came a growing demand for a more personal involvement with God. Efforts by church authorities to eliminate pre-Christian traditions and alternative kinds of spirituality only intensified the desire among laypeople for forms of devotion that would connect them more directly with God than the church allowed.

Martin Luther Martin Luther coalesced these expressions of religious discontent into a powerful revolt against the church. Martin Luther (1483-1546) attacked the sale of indulgences as an individual, but he soon attracted enthusiastic support from others who resented the policies of the Roman church. Luther was a prolific and talented writer, and he published numerous works condemning the Roman church. His cause benefited enormously from the printing press, which had first appeared in Europe in the mid-fifteenth century.

Johannes Gutenberg (ca. 1395-1468) introduced printing to Europe and his invention of mechanical movable type printing, around 1439, started a printing revolution. From Gutenberg's hometown of Mainz, Germany, printing soon spread to more than two hundred European cities. Luther's translation of the Bible into German stimulated the production and distribution of religious books and pamphlets and proved to be a decisive factor in the spread of literacy. A growing literate public eagerly consumed printed works on both religious and nonreligious themes, as both supporters and critics of Martin Luther took their own works to the printers. Religious controversies kept the presses busy churning out millions of pamphlets and treatises for a century and more.

In his publications, writings, and speeches, Luther attacked the Roman church for a wide range of abuses and called for thorough reform of Christendom. He advocated the closure of monasteries; translation of the Bible from Latin into regional languages; and an end to priestly authority, including the authority of the pope himself. Most important, Luther believed that salvation and the entry to heaven could never be earned through good works or through the prayers of others. Instead, he argued, humans could be saved only through faith in the promises of God as revealed in the Bible. This idea of "justification by faith alone" became the core of Protestant beliefs. When opponents pointed out that his reform program ran counter to church policy, Luther rejected the authority of the church hierarchy and proclaimed that the Bible was the only source of Christian religious authority.

Luther's works drew an enthusiastic popular response, and in Germany they fueled a movement to reform the church along the lines of Luther's teachings. Ordinary Christians flocked to hear Luther preach in Wittenberg, and several princes of the Holy Roman Empire warmed to Luther's views—partly because of personal conviction but partly because religious controversy offered opportunities for them to build their own power bases. During the 1520s and 1530s, many of the most important German cities—Strasbourg, Nuremberg, and Augsburg, among others—passed laws prohibiting Roman Catholic observances and requiring all religious services to follow Lutheran doctrine and procedures.

By the mid-sixteenth century, about half the German population had adopted Lutheran Christianity, and reformers had launched Protestant movements and established alternative churches in other lands as well. By the late 1520s, the prosperous cities of Switzerland—Zurich, Basel, and Geneva—had fledgling Protestant churches. The heavily urbanized Low Countries also responded enthusiastically to Protestant appeals. Protestants appeared even in Italy and Spain, although authorities in those lands handily suppressed their challenge to the Roman church.

John Calvin Meanwhile, an even more influential Reformation was taking shape in France and the French-speaking parts of Switzerland. The initiator was a French lawyer, John Calvin (1509-1564), who in the 1530s converted to Protestant Christianity. Because the French monarchy sought to suppress Protestants, Calvin slipped across the border to French-speaking Geneva in Switzerland. There he organized a Protestant community and worked with local officials to impose a strict code of morality and discipline on the city. Calvin also composed an influential treatise, *Institutes of the Christian Religion* (1536), that codified Protestant teachings and presented them as a coherent and organized package.

Although Calvin believed in the basic elements of Luther's Protestant teachings, his ideas differed from those of Luther in important ways. Most fundamentally, Calvin emphasized the awesome power of God more than Luther did. Indeed, he believed not only that humans could never earn salvation through prayers and good works but also that God had in fact already determined which individuals would be saved from damnation even before they were born. These individuals, known as "the elect," were predestined for salvation regardless of their deeds on earth. This doctrine of "predestination" grew increasingly important to the Calvinist church in the generations after Calvin's death.

Calvin's Geneva was bound by a strict code of morality and discipline. **Calvinists** were expected to dress simply, to study the Bible regularly, and to refrain from activities such as dancing or playing cards. It was, in effect, a Protestant model community. Geneva also became an important missionary center from which Calvinist doctrine spread to other parts of Europe. Calvinist missionaries were most active in France, where they attracted strong interest in the cities, but they ventured also to Germany, the Low Countries, England, Scotland, and even distant Hungary. They established churches in all these lands and worked for reform along Protestant lines. They were most successful in the Netherlands and Scotland.

The English Reformation

In England a Reformation took place for political as well as religious reasons. Lutherans and other Protestants worked to build a following in England from the 1520s, but they faced significant government resistance until King Henry VIII (reigned 1509–1547) came into conflict with the pope. Henry wanted to divorce his wife, who had not given birth to a male heir, but the pope refused to allow him to do so. Henry's response was to cut off relations with the

Inspired by the Catholic Reformation, many devout individuals sought mystic union with God. One of the most famous of the mystics was St. Teresa of Avila (in Spain), who founded a strict order of nuns and often experienced religious visions. A famous sculpture by the Italian artist Gianlorenzo Bernini depicts St. Teresa in an ecstatic trance accompanied by an angel.
Stefano Valeri/Shutterstock

Roman church and make himself Supreme Head of the Anglican church—in essence, an English pope. While Henry reigned, the theology of the English church changed little, but under pressure of reformers, his successors replaced Roman Catholic with Protestant doctrines and rituals. By 1560 England had permanently left the Roman Catholic community. Indeed, by the late sixteenth century, Lutherans, **Anglicans,** and Calvinists together had built communities large enough that a return to religious unity in western Europe was inconceivable.

The Catholic Reformation

Partly in response to the Protestant Reformation, Roman Catholic authorities undertook an enormous reform effort within their own church in the sixteenth century. To some extent their efforts represented a reaction to Protestant success. Yet Roman Catholic authorities also sought to define points of doctrine and thus clarify differences between Roman and Protestant churches, to persuade Protestants to return to the Roman church, and to deepen the sense of spirituality and religious commitment in their own community. Taken together, their efforts constituted the **Catholic Reformation.**

The Council of Trent Two institutions were especially important for defining the Catholic Reformation and advancing its goals—the Council of Trent and the Society of Jesus. The **Council of Trent** was an assembly of bishops, cardinals, and other high church officials who met intermittently between 1545 and 1563 to address matters of doctrine and reform. Drawing heavily on the works of the thirteenth-century scholastic theologian St. Thomas Aquinas (discussed in chapter 19), the council defined the elements of Roman Catholic theology in detail. The council acknowledged that abuses had alienated many people from the Roman church, and it took steps to reform the church. The council demanded that church authorities observe strict standards of morality, and it required them to establish schools and seminaries in their districts to prepare priests properly for their roles.

St. Ignatius Loyola

While the Council of Trent dealt with doctrine and reform, the **Society of Jesus** went on the offensive and sought to extend the boundaries of the reformed Roman church. The society's founder was **St. Ignatius Loyola** (1491-1556), a Basque nobleman and soldier who in 1521 suffered a devastating leg wound that ended his military career. While recuperating he read spiritual works and popular accounts of saints' lives, and he resolved to put his energy into religious work. In 1540, together with a small band of disciples, he founded the Society of Jesus.

The Society of Jesus

Ignatius required that members of the society, known as Jesuits, complete a rigorous and advanced education. They received instruction not only in theology and philosophy but also in classical languages, literature, history, and science. As a result of that preparation—and their unswerving dedication to the Roman Catholic church—the Jesuits made extraordinarily effective missionaries. They were able to outargue most of their opponents and acquired a reputation for discipline and determination. They often served as counselors to kings and rulers and used their influence to promote policies that benefited the Roman church. They also were the most prominent of the early Christian missionaries outside Europe: in the wake of the European reconnaissance of the world's oceans, Jesuits attracted converts in India, China, Japan, the Philippines, and the Americas, thus making Christianity a genuinely global religion.

Witch-Hunts and Religious Wars

Religion was central to the lives of most Europeans in the sixteenth century, and religious divisions helped to fuel social and political conflict. Apart from wars, the most destructive violence that afflicted early modern Europe was the hunt for witches, which was especially prominent in regions such as the Rhineland (in modern Germany) where tensions between Protestants and Roman Catholics ran high.

Like many other peoples, Europeans had long believed that certain individuals possessed unusual powers to influence human affairs or discover secret information such as the identity of a thief. During the late fifteenth century, theologians developed a theory that witches derived their powers from the devil. According to that theory, witches made agreements to worship the devil in exchange for supernatural powers, including the ability to fly through the night on brooms, pitchforks, or animals. Theorists believed that the witches regularly flew off to distant places to attend the "witches' sabbath," a gathering that featured devil worship, lewd behavior, and the concoction of secret potions, culminating in sexual relations with the devil himself.

Witch-Hunting

Although the witches' sabbath was sheer fantasy, fears that individuals were making alliances with the devil sparked an intensive hunt for witches beginning in the sixteenth century. Witchcraft became a convenient explanation for any unpleasant turn of events, including failure of a crop, outbreak of a fire, an unexpected death, or inability to conceive a child. About 110,000 individuals underwent trial as suspected witches during the sixteenth and seventeenth

The Burning of Three Witches (1585), by Johann Jakob Wick. This illustration depicts the execution by burning of three accused "witches" in Baden, Switzerland on November 4, 1585. The History Collection/Alamy Stock Photo

centuries, and about 45,000 of them were executed, either by hanging or by burning at the stake. As a rule, church courts tried large numbers of witches, but they usually imposed non-lethal penalties such as excommunication or imprisonment. It was secular courts that condemned and executed the vast majority of witches.

Witches and Gender Gender played an important role in the **witch-hunts.** Although men were among the victims, most convicted witches were women. Indeed, women may have accounted for 85 percent or more of the condemned. Many of the women were poor, old, single, or widowed—individuals who lived on the margins of their societies and were easy targets for accusers because they had few protectors.

By 1700 the fear of witches had largely diminished. Accusations, trials, and executions occurred only sporadically thereafter. The last legal execution for witchcraft in Europe took place in Switzerland in 1782. For the better part of two centuries, however, the intermittent pursuit of witches clearly revealed the stresses and strains that afflicted European society during early modern times and also the ways women were made to serve as scapegoats for them.

Religious Wars Religious tensions even led to outright war between Protestant and Roman Catholic communities. Religious wars racked France for thirty-six years (1562-1598), for example, and they also complicated relations between Protestant and Roman Catholic states. In 1588 King Philip II of Spain (reigned 1556-1598) attempted to force England to

return to the Roman Catholic church by sending the Spanish Armada—a huge flotilla consisting of 130 ships and 30,000 men—to dethrone the Protestant Queen Elizabeth. The effort collapsed, however, when English forces disrupted the Spanish fleet by sending blazing, unmanned ships into its midst. Then a ferocious gale scattered Spanish vessels throughout the North Sea.

Religious convictions also aggravated relations between the Netherlands and Spain by fueling the revolt of the Dutch provinces from their overlord, the king of Spain. In 1567 Philip sent an army to tighten his control over the provinces and to suppress the Calvinist movement there. Resistance escalated into a full-scale rebellion. By 1610 the seven northern provinces (the modern Netherlands) had won their independence and formed a republic known as the United Provinces, leaving ten southern provinces (modern Belgium) under Spanish and later Austrian rule until the late eighteenth century.

The Thirty Years' War The religious wars culminated in a massive continental conflict known as the **Thirty Years' War** (1618-1648). The war opened after the Holy Roman emperor attempted to force his Bohemian (in modern Czechoslovakia) subjects to return to the Roman Catholic church, though the main battleground was the emperor's territory in Germany. Other parties soon entered the fray, however, and by the time the war ended, Spanish, French, Dutch, German, Swedish, Danish, Polish, Bohemian, and Russian forces had taken part in the conflict.

The Thirty Years' War offered abundant opportunity for undisciplined mercenary soldiers to prey on civilian populations. Only rarely, as in the mass hanging depicted in this engraving of 1633, did soldiers receive punishment for their criminal acts.
Anne S.K. Brown Military Collection, Brown University Library.

What's Left Out? ◼◼ ◼◼◼ ◼◼ ◼◼ ◼◼ ◼◼◼

Chroniclers and historians of the Thirty Years' War have pointed out the brutalities and suffering it caused since the end of the conflict itself. Most textbooks, including this one, rightly point out that the Thirty Years' War was the most destructive European conflict until the even more brutal World Wars of the twentieth century. But the need to be brief and to cover many topics often means that textbooks cannot delve into the details of what such a claim might have meant for the ordinary people who lived through the war. In German territories alone, nearly a quarter of the population died as a result of the war, and in some places the toll was closer to 50 percent. The incredible destruction of the war was due to a number of reasons that had little to do with religion or loyalties. Among the most important was the lack of separation between battle fronts and home fronts, which meant that civilians often found themselves directly in the path of invading or defending armies. In addition, both invading and defending armies required food, clothing, and shelter, and these frequently were taken from civilians by both friendly and enemy troops. Moreover, when civilians had to endure the destruction of their lands, their crops, their homes, their food stores, and the infrastructure of their towns and cities, famines and food shortages became a grim reality. Weakened individuals then died from sickness and disease on a vast scale. People like Hans Heberle—a cobbler from what is now southern Germany—endured staggering losses during the war. He and his wife and children were driven from their home and lost all their possessions. They were then forced to take refuge in forests, in neighboring towns, and in a fortress to protect themselves from invading armies. Heberle watched as those around him were reduced to famine conditions, eating grass and weeds as well as dogs, cats, mice, and horses. In 1635, just one year in the war, fifteen thousand people died from famine and disease in his hometown of Ulm. Over the course of the war, approximately eight million soldiers and civilians died, each of whom could have told an equally horrific story of fear, loss, and brutality.

Source: Hans Medick and Benjamin Marschke, *Experiencing the Thirty Years War: A Brief History with Documents* (Bedford St. Martin's, 2013).

The motives that prompted these states to enter the war were sometimes political or economic, but religious differences complicated the other issues and made them more difficult to resolve. Regardless of the motives, the Thirty Years' War was the most destructive European conflict before the twentieth century. Quite apart from violence and brutalities committed by undisciplined soldiers, the war damaged economies and societies throughout Europe and led to the deaths of about one-third of the German population. The destructiveness of the Thirty Years' War raised questions about the viability of Europe as a region of strong, independent, well-armed, and intensely competitive states.

THE CONSOLIDATION OF SOVEREIGN STATES

Although fundamentally a religious movement, the Reformation had strong political implications, and centralizing monarchs readily made use of religious issues in their efforts to strengthen their states and enhance their authority. Ruling elites had their own religious preferences, and they often promoted a Protestant or Roman Catholic cause out of personal conviction. Religious controversies also offered splendid opportunities for ambitious subordinates who built power bases by appealing to particular religious communities. Over the long run, centralizing monarchs profited most from religious

controversy generated by the Reformation. While the Holy Roman Empire fell into disarray because of political and religious quarrels, monarchs in other lands augmented their revenues, enhanced their authority, and created powerful sovereign states. After the devastation of the Thirty Years' War, rulers of these states devised a diplomatic system that sought to maintain order among the many independent and competitive European states.

The Attempted Revival of Empire

After the dissolution of the **Carolingian** empire in the ninth century C.E., (discussed in chapter 16) there was no effective imperial government in western Europe. The so-called Holy Roman Empire emerged in the tenth century, but its authority extended only to Germany and northern Italy, and even there the emperors encountered stiff opposition from powerful princes and thriving cities. During the early sixteenth century, it seemed that Emperor Charles V (reigned 1519-1556) might establish the Holy Roman Empire as the preeminent political authority in Europe, but by midcentury it was clear that there would be no revival of empire. Thus, unlike China, India, and Ottoman lands in southwest Asia and north Africa, early modern Europe developed as a region of independent states.

Charles V After 1438 the Habsburg family, with extensive dynastic holdings in Austria, dominated the Holy Roman Empire. Through marriage alliances with princely and royal families, the **Habsburgs** accumulated rights and titles to lands

---

Carolingian (kar-uh-LIHN-jee-uhn)

MAP 23.1   Sixteenth-century Europe.

Note the extent of Habsburg territories and the wide boundaries of the Holy Roman Empire.

With such powerful territories, what prevented the Habsburgs from imposing imperial rule on most of Europe?

throughout Europe and beyond. **Charles V** inherited authority over the Habsburgs' Austrian domains as well as the duchy of Burgundy (including the wealthy provinces of the Low Countries) and the kingdom of Spain (including its possessions in Italy and the Americas). When he became emperor in 1519, he acquired authority over Germany, Bohemia, Switzerland, and parts of northern Italy. His empire stretched from Vienna in Austria to Cuzco in Peru.

Imperial Fragmentation In spite of his far-flung holdings, Charles did not extend his authority throughout Europe or even establish a lasting imperial legacy. Throughout his reign Charles had to devote much of his attention and energy to the Lutheran movement and to imperial princes who took advantage of religious controversy to assert their independence. Moreover, Charles did not build an administrative structure for his empire but, instead, ruled each of his lands according to its own laws and customs. He was able to draw on the financial resources of wealthy lands such as the Low Countries and Spain to maintain a powerful army. Yet Charles did not have the ambition to extend his authority by military force. Instead, he used his army mostly to put down rebellions.

Foreign Challenges Foreign difficulties also prevented Charles from establishing his empire as the arbiter of Europe. The prospect of a powerful Holy Roman Empire struck fear in the kings of France, and it caused concern among the sultans of the Ottoman Empire as well. Charles's holdings surrounded France, and the French kings suspected that the emperor wanted to absorb their realm and extend his authority throughout Europe. To forestall that possibility, the French kings created every obstacle they could for Charles. Even though they were staunch Roman Catholics, they aided German Lutherans and encouraged them to rebel. The French kings even allied with the Muslim Ottoman Turks against the emperor.

For their part, the Ottoman sultans did not want to see a powerful Christian empire threaten their holdings in eastern Europe and their position in the Mediterranean basin. With the encouragement of the French king, Turkish forces conquered Hungary in 1526, and three years later they even laid siege briefly to Vienna. Moreover, during the early sixteenth century Ottoman forces imposed their rule beyond Egypt and embraced almost all of north Africa. By midcentury, Turkish holdings posed a serious threat to Italian and Spanish shipping in the Mediterranean.

All of these domestic and foreign problems prevented Charles V from establishing his vast empire as the supreme political authority in Europe. His inability to suppress the Lutherans was especially disappointing to Charles, and in 1556, after agreeing that imperial princes and cities could determine the religious faith observed in their jurisdictions, the emperor abdicated his throne and retired to a monastery in Spain. His empire did not survive. Charles bestowed his holdings in Spain, Italy, the Low Countries, and the Americas on his son, King Philip II of Spain, while his brother Ferdinand inherited the Habsburg family lands in Austria and the imperial throne.

The New Monarchs

In the absence of effective imperial power, guidance of public affairs fell to the various regional states that had emerged during the middle ages. The city-states of Italy were prominent because of their economic power: since the eleventh century they had been Europe's most important centers of trade, manufacturing, and finance. The most powerful European states, however, were the kingdoms of England, France, and Spain. During the late fifteenth and sixteenth centuries, rulers of these lands, known as the "new monarchs," marshaled their resources, curbed the nobility, and built strong centralized regimes.

Finance The new monarchs included Henry VIII of England, Louis XI and Francis I of France, and Fernando and Isabel of Spain. All the new monarchs sought to increase their wealth by developing new sources of revenue. The French kings levied direct taxes on sales, households, and the salt trade. A new sales tax dramatically boosted Spanish royal income in the sixteenth century. For fear of provoking rebellion, the English kings did not introduce new taxes, but they increased revenues by raising fines and fees for royal services. Moreover, after Henry VIII severed ties between the English and Roman churches, he shut down all of the monasteries and took possession of all their land and wealth. This financial windfall enabled Henry to enhance royal power by increasing the size of the state and adding to its responsibilities. After the English Reformation, for example, the state provided relief for the poor and support for orphans, which previously had been left to churches and monasteries.

State Power With their increased income the new monarchs enlarged their administrative staffs, which enabled them to collect taxes and implement royal policies more reliably than before. The French and Spanish monarchs also maintained standing armies that vastly increased their power with respect to the nobility. Their armies with thousands of infantrymen were too large for individual nobles to match, and they equipped their forces with cannons that were too expensive for nobles to purchase. The English kings did not need a standing army to put down the occasional rebellion that flared in their island realm and so did not go to the expense of supporting one. Yet they too increased their power with respect to the nobles by subjecting them to royal justice and forcing them to comply with royal policy.

The debates and disputes launched by the Protestant Reformation helped monarchs increase their authority. In lands that adopted Protestant faiths—including England, much of Germany, Denmark, and Sweden—rulers expropriated the monasteries and used church wealth to expand their powers. That option was not open to Roman Catholic kings, but Protestant movements provided them with a justification to mobilize resources, which they used against political as well as religious adversaries.

The Spanish Inquisition The **Spanish Inquisition** was the most distinctive institution that relied on religious justifications to advance state ends. Fernando and Isabel founded the Spanish Inquisition in 1478, and they obtained the approval of the pope to operate the institution as a royal agency. Its original task was to ferret out those who secretly practiced Judaism or Islam, but Charles also charged it with detecting Protestant heresy (beliefs contrary to the doctrines of the Roman church) in Spain. Throughout the late fifteenth and sixteenth centuries, the Spanish Inquisition served political as well as religious purposes. Moreover, its reach extended well beyond the Iberian peninsula. Just as the fear of witchcraft crossed the Atlantic Ocean and inspired witch-hunts in England's North

American colonies, concerns about heresy also made their way to the Western Hemisphere, where inquisitors worked to protect Spanish colonies from heretical teachings.

Inquisitors had broad powers to investigate suspected cases of heresy. Popular legends have created an erroneous impression of the Spanish Inquisition as an institution running amok, framing innocent victims and routinely subjecting them to torture. In fact, inquisitors usually observed rules of evidence, and they released many suspects after investigations turned up no sign of heresy. Yet, when they detected the scent of heresy, inquisitors could be ruthless. They sentenced hundreds of victims to hang from the gallows or burn at the

This engraving, *Judgment Scene at Spanish Inquisition,* depicts an *auto-da-fé,* or "act of faith," involving the execution of Jews by burning at the stake. An *auto-da-fé* more specifically was the ritual of public penance and punishment of condemned heretics. In 1492, the Catholic monarchy of Spain ordered the expulsion of Jews from Spain.
Bettmann/Getty Images

stake and imprisoned many others in dank cells for extended periods of time. Fear of the inquisition intimidated many into silence, and a strict Roman Catholic orthodoxy prevailed in Spain. The inquisition deterred nobles from adopting Protestant views out of political ambition, and it used its influence on behalf of the Spanish monarchy. From 1559 to 1576, for example, inquisitors imprisoned the archbishop of Toledo—the highest Roman Catholic church official in all of Spain—because of his political independence.

Constitutional States

During the seventeenth and eighteenth centuries, as they sought to restore order after the Thirty Years' War, European states developed along two lines. Rulers in England and the Netherlands shared authority with representative institutions and created constitutional states, whereas monarchs in France, Spain, Austria, Prussia, and Russia concentrated power in their own hands and created a form of state known as absolute monarchy.

Constitutional States The island kingdom of England and the maritime Dutch republic did not have written constitutions specifying the powers of the state, but during the seventeenth century they evolved governments that claimed limited powers and recognized rights pertaining to individuals and representative institutions. Their **constitutional states** took different forms: in England a constitutional monarchy emerged, whereas the Netherlands produced a republic based on representative government. In neither land did constitutional government come easily into being: in England it followed a civil war, and in the Netherlands it emerged after a long struggle for independence. In both lands, however, constitutional government strengthened the state and provided a political framework that enabled merchants to flourish as never before in European experience.

The English Civil War Constitutional government came to England after political and religious disputes led to the **English Civil War** (1642-1649). From the early seventeenth century, the English kings had tried to institute new taxes without approval of the parliament, which for more than three centuries had traditionally approved new levies. While royal financial policies generated political tensions, religious disagreements aggravated matters further. As Anglicans, the kings supported a church with relatively ornate ceremonies and a hierarchy of bishops working under authority of the monarchs themselves. Meanwhile, however, many of the boldest and most insistent voices within parliament belonged to zealous Calvinists known as Puritans because they sought to purify the English church of any lingering elements, such as ornate ceremonies and a hierarchy of bishops, suggestive of Roman Catholic Christianity. By 1641, King Charles I and parliament were in dispute, unable to cooperate or even communicate effectively with each other. Both sides raised armies. In the conflicts that followed, parliamentary forces under the leadership of Oliver

In this contemporary painting, the executioner holds up the just-severed head of King Charles I of England. The spectacle of a royal execution overcomes one woman, who faints (at bottom). How does the image of a beheaded king reflect the ongoing political changes in Europe?

Art Collection 2/Alamy Stock Photo

Cromwell (1599–1658) captured Charles, tried him for tyranny, and in an act that shocked all of Europe, marched him up on a platform and beheaded him in 1649.

The Glorious Revolution In the absence of a king, Cromwell's Puritan regime took power but soon degenerated into a disagreeable dictatorship, prompting parliament to restore the monarchy in 1660 by installing Charles II (the son of the last king). The monarchy and parliament, however, soon resumed their conflicts. The issue came to a head a few decades later in a bloodless change of power known to some as the **Glorious Revolution** (1688–1689), when parliament deposed King James II and invited his daughter Mary and her Dutch husband, William of Orange, to assume the throne. The resulting arrangement provided that kings would rule in cooperation with parliament, thus guaranteeing that nobles, merchants, and other constituencies would enjoy representation in government affairs.

The Dutch Republic As in England, a potent combination of political and religious tensions led to conflict from which constitutional government emerged in the Netherlands. In the mid-sixteenth century, authority over the Low Countries, including modern-day Belgium as well as the Netherlands, rested with King Philip II of Spain. In 1567 Philip, a devout Roman Catholic, moved to suppress an increasingly popular Calvinist movement in the Netherlands—a measure that provoked large-scale rebellion against Spanish rule. In 1579 a group of Dutch provinces formed an anti-Spanish alliance, and in 1581 they proclaimed themselves the independent United Provinces. Representative assemblies organized local affairs in each of the provinces, and on this foundation political leaders built a Dutch republic. Spain did not officially recognize the independence of the United Provinces until the end of the Thirty Years' War in 1648, but the Dutch republic was effectively organizing affairs in the northern Low Countries by the early seventeenth century.

In many ways, the constitutional governments of England and the Dutch republic represented historical experiments. Apart from the Roman republic in classical times and a few Italian city-states of the medieval and Renaissance eras, European peoples had little experience with representative government. In their responses to political crises, popular leaders in both England and the Netherlands found it possible to mobilize support by appealing to the political and religious interests of broad constituencies and making a place for them in the government. The result was a pair of states that effectively harnessed popular support and used it to magnify state power.

Although best known as Louis XIII's "first minister," Cardinal Richelieu also gained fame for his patronage of the arts. Most notably, he founded the Académie Française, the learned society responsible for matters pertaining to the French language.

Alfredo Dagli Orti/Shutterstock

In both England and the Dutch republic, merchants were especially prominent in political affairs, and state policy in both lands favored maritime trade and the building of commercial empires overseas. The constitutional states allowed entrepreneurs to pursue their economic interests with minimal interference from public authorities, and during the late seventeenth and eighteenth centuries, both states experienced extraordinary prosperity as a result of those policies. Indeed, in many ways the English and Dutch states represented an alliance between merchants and rulers that worked to the benefit of both. Merchants supported the state with the wealth that they generated through trade—especially overseas trade—while rulers followed policies that looked after the interests of their merchants.

Absolute Monarchies

Whereas constitutional states devised ways to share power and authority, absolute monarchies found other ways to increase state power. **Absolutism** stood on a theoretical foundation known as the divine right of kings. This theory held that kings derived their authority from God and served as "God's lieutenants upon earth." There was no role in divine-right theory for common subjects or even nobles in public affairs: the monarch made law and determined policy. Noncompliance or disobedience merited punishment, and rebellion was a despicable act tantamount to blasphemy. In practice, absolute monarchs always relied on support from nobles and other social groups, but the claims of divine-right theory clearly reflected efforts at royal centralization.

The most conspicuous absolutist state was the French monarchy. The architect of French absolutism was a prominent church official, Cardinal **Richelieu,** who served as chief minister to King Louis XIII from 1624 to 1642. Richelieu worked systematically to undermine the power of the nobility and enhance the authority of the king. He destroyed nobles' castles and ruthlessly crushed aristocratic conspiracies. As a counterweight to the nobility, Richelieu built a large bureaucracy staffed by commoners loyal to the king. He also appointed officials to supervise the implementation of royal policy in the provinces. Finally, Richelieu attacked French Calvinists, who often allied with independent nobles, and destroyed their political and military power, although he allowed them to continue observing their faith. By midcentury France was under control of a tightly centralized absolute monarchy.

The Sun King The ruler who best epitomized royal absolutism was King **Louis XIV** (reigned 1643–1715), who once reportedly declared that he was himself the state: *"l'état, c'est moi."* Known as *le roi soleil* ("the sun king"), Louis surrounded himself with splendor befitting one who ruled by divine right. During the 1670s he built a magnificent residence at **Versailles,** a royal hunting lodge near Paris, and in the 1680s he moved his court there. Louis's palace at Versailles was the largest building in Europe, with 230 acres of formal gardens and 1,400 fountains. Because Louis did not want to wait years for saplings to grow, he ordered laborers to dig up 25,000 fully grown trees and haul them to Versailles for transplanting.

The sun king was the center of attention at Versailles. Court officials hovered around him and tended to his every need. All prominent nobles established residences at Versailles for their families and entourages. Louis strongly encouraged them to live at court, where he and his staff could keep an eye on them, and ambitious nobles gravitated there anyway in hopes of winning influence with the king. Louis himself was the arbiter of taste and style at Versailles, where he lavishly patronized painters, sculptors, architects, and writers whose creations met with his approval.

While nobles living at Versailles mastered the intricacies of court ritual and attended banquets, concerts, operas, balls, and theatrical performances, Louis and his ministers ran the state.

Richelieu (RISH-uh-loo)
Versailles (vehr-SEYE)

The French painter Hyacinthe Rigaud, renowned for his portrait paintings of the royalty and nobility of Europe, created this vision of Louis XIV. Louis' reign, from 1643 to his death in 1715, lasted seventy-two years, three months, and eighteen days, and is the longest documented reign of any European monarch.

SuperStock/Getty Images

In effect, Louis provided the nobility with luxurious accommodations and endless entertainment in exchange for absolute rule. From Versailles, Louis and his advisers promulgated laws and controlled a large standing army that kept order throughout the land. They also promoted economic development by supporting the establishment of new industries, building roads and canals, abolishing internal tariffs, and encouraging exports. Finally, they waged a series of wars designed to enlarge French boundaries and establish France as the preeminent power in Europe.

Absolutism in Russia

Louis XIV was not the only absolute monarch of early modern Europe: Spanish, Austrian, and Prussian rulers embraced similar policies. The potential of absolutism to increase state power was particularly conspicuous in the case of Russia, where tsars of the Romanov dynasty (1613-1917) tightly centralized government functions. (*Tsar,* sometimes spelled *czar,* is a Russianized form of the term *caesar,* which Russian rulers borrowed from Byzantine emperors, who in turn had borrowed it from the classical Roman Empire to signify their imperial status.) The **Romanovs** inherited a state that had rapidly expanded its boundaries since the mid-fourteenth century. Building on the foundation of a small principality around the trading city of Moscow, by 1600 Russia had become a vast empire extending from the Arctic seas in the north to the Caspian Sea in the south, with an increasing presence in the tundra and forests of Siberia as well.

Peter I Most important of the Romanov tsars was Peter I (reigned 1682-1725), widely known as **Peter the Great,** who inaugurated a thoroughgoing process of state transformation. Peter had a burning desire to make Russia, a huge but underpopulated land, into a great military power like those that had recently emerged in western Europe. In pursuit of that goal, he worked to transform Russia on the model of western European lands. In 1697-1698 he led a large party of Russian observers on a tour of Germany, the Netherlands, and England to learn about western European administrative methods and military technology. His traveling companions often behaved crudely by western European standards: they consumed beer, wine, and brandy in quantities that astonished their hosts, and King William III sent Peter a bill for damages done by his entourage at the country house where they lodged in England. (Among other things, Peter had ruined the gardens by having his men march through them in military formation.)

Upon returning to Moscow, Peter set Russia spinning. He reformed the army by offering better pay and drafting peasants who served for life as professional soldiers. He provided his forces with extensive training and equipped them with modern weapons. He ordered aristocrats to study mathematics and geometry so that they could calculate how to aim cannons accurately, and he began the construction of a navy with an eye toward domination of the Baltic and other northern seas. He also overhauled the government bureaucracy to facilitate tax collection and improve administrative efficiency. His transformation of Russia even involved a cosmetic makeover, as he commanded his aristocratic subjects to wear western European fashions and ordered men to shave their traditional beards. These measures, which were extremely unpopular among conservative Russians, provoked spirited protest among those who resented the influence of western European ways. Yet Peter insisted on observance of his policies—to the point that he reportedly went into the streets and personally hacked the beards off recalcitrants' faces. Perhaps the best symbol of his policies was St. Petersburg, a newly built seaport that Peter opened in 1703 to serve as a magnificent capital city and haven for Russia's fledgling navy.

Catherine II and the Limits of Reform

The most able of Peter's successors was Catherine II (reigned 1762-1796), also known as **Catherine the Great.** Like Peter, Catherine sought to make Russia a great power. She worked to improve governmental efficiency by dividing her vast empire into fifty administrative provinces, and she promoted economic development in Russia's towns. For a while, she even worked to improve the conditions of Russia's oppressed peasantry by restricting the punishments that noble landowners could inflict on the serfs who worked their lands. She sought to eliminate common penalties such as torture, beating, and the mutilation of individuals by cutting off their noses, ears, or tongues.

Yet her interest in social reform cooled rapidly when it seemed to inspire challenges to her rule. She faced a particularly unsettling rebellion in 1773 and 1774, when a disgruntled former soldier named **Yemelian Pugachev** mounted an uprising in the steppe lands north of the Caspian Sea. Pugachev raised a motley army of adventurers, exiles, peasants, and serfs who killed thousands of noble landowners and government officials before imperial forces crushed the uprising. Government authorities took the captured Pugachev to Moscow in chains, beheaded him, quartered his body, and displayed its parts throughout the city as a warning against rebellion. Thereafter, Catherine's first concern was the preservation of autocratic rule rather than the transformation of Russia according to western European models.

Thus, in Russia as in other European lands, absolutist policies resulted in tight centralization and considerable

Russian portrait of the German-born empress of Russia, Catherine II. Although admired by many Russians as a source of national pride, she is also remembered as a ruthless ruler who affirmed absolutism and extended serfdom on a large scale.

DEA/A. Dagli Orti/De Agostini/Getty Images

Tsar Peter the Great, with a pair of shears, readies himself to remove the beard of a conservative noble. Peter had traveled widely in Europe, and he wanted to impose newer European customs on his subjects. That included being more cleanly shaved. Nobles wishing to keep their beloved beards had to pay a yearly tax to do so.

akg-images/Newscom

strengthening of the state. The enhanced power that flowed from absolutism became dramatically clear in the period 1772 to 1797, when Austria, Prussia, and Catherine II's Russia picked the weak kingdom of Poland apart. In a series of three "partitions," the predatory absolutist states seized Polish territory and absorbed it into their own realms, ultimately wiping Poland entirely off the map. The lesson of the partitions was clear: any European state that hoped to survive needed to construct an effective government that could respond promptly to challenges and opportunities.

The European States System

Whether they relied on absolutist or constitutional principles, European governments of early modern times built states much more powerful than those of their medieval predecessors. This round of state development led to difficulties within Europe because conflicting interests fueled interstate competition and

Yemelian Pugachev (yehm-eel-ian puh-gah-chehf)

war. In the absence of an imperial authority capable of imposing and maintaining order in Europe, sovereign states had to find other ways to resolve conflicts.

The Peace of Westphalia The Thirty Years' War demonstrated the chaos and devastation that conflict could bring. In an effort to avoid tearing their society apart, European states ended the Thirty Years' War with the **Peace of Westphalia** (1648), which laid the foundations for a system of independent, competing states. Almost all the European states participated in drafting the Peace of Westphalia, and by the treaty's terms they regarded one another as sovereign and equal. They

also mutually recognized their rights to organize their own domestic affairs, including religious affairs. Rather than envisioning imperial or papal or some other sort of supreme authority, the Peace of Westphalia entrusted political and diplomatic affairs to states acting in their own interests. European religious unity had disappeared, and the era of the sovereign state had arrived.

The Peace of Westphalia did not bring an end to war. Indeed, war was almost constant in early modern Europe. Most conflicts were minor affairs inaugurated by monarchs seeking to extend their authority to new lands or to reclaim territories seized by others, but they nevertheless disrupted

MAP 23.2   Europe after the Peace of Westphalia, 1648.

Compare this map with Map 23.1.

How have the boundaries of the Holy Roman Empire changed, and why?

local economies and drained resources. A few wars, however, grew to sizable proportions. Most notable among them were the wars of Louis XIV and the Seven Years' War. Between 1668 and 1713, the sun king sought to expand his borders east into Germany and to absorb Spain and the Spanish Netherlands into his kingdom. That prospect prompted England, the United Provinces, and Austria to mount a coalition against Louis. Later, the Seven Years' War (1756–1763) pitted France, Austria, and Russia against Britain and Prussia, and it merged with conflicts between France and Britain in India and North America to become a global war for imperial supremacy.

The Balance of Power These shifting alliances illustrate the principal foundation of European diplomacy in early modern times—the balance of power. No ruler wanted to see another state dominate all the others. Thus, when any particular state began to grow too strong, others formed coalitions against it. Balance-of-power diplomacy was risky business: it was always possible that a coalition might repress one strong state only to open the door for another. Yet, in playing balance-of-power politics, statesmen prevented the building of empires and ensured that Europe would be a land of independent, sovereign, competing states.

Military Development Frequent wars and balance-of-power diplomacy drained the resources of individual states but strengthened European society as a whole. European states competed vigorously and sought to develop the most expert military leadership and the most effective weapons for their arsenals. States organized military academies where officers received advanced education in strategy and tactics and learned how to maintain disciplined forces. Demand for powerful weapons stimulated the development of a sophisticated armaments industry that turned out ever more lethal products. Gun foundries manufactured cannons of increasing size, range, power, and accuracy as well as small arms that allowed infantry to unleash withering volleys against their enemies.

In China, India, and Islamic lands, imperial states had little or no incentive to encourage similar technological innovation in the armaments industry. These states possessed the forces and weapons they needed to maintain order within their boundaries, and they rarely encountered foreign threats backed up with superior armaments. In Europe, however, failure to keep up with the latest improvements in arms technology could lead to defeat on the battlefield and decline in state power. Thus Europeans continuously sought to improve their military arsenals, and as a result, by the eighteenth century European armaments outperformed all others.

EARLY CAPITALIST SOCIETY

While the Protestant Reformation and the emergence of sovereign states brought religious and political change, a rapidly expanding population and economy encouraged the development of capitalism, which in turn led to a restructuring of European economy and society. Technologies of communication and transportation enabled businessmen to profit from distant markets, and merchants and manufacturers increasingly organized their affairs with the market rather than local communities in mind.

Capitalism generated considerable wealth, but its effects were uneven and sometimes unsettling. Economic development and increasing prosperity were noticeable in western Europe, particularly England, France, Germany, and the Netherlands. Yet eastern Europe experienced much less economic growth, as Poland and Russia increasingly became suppliers of grain and raw materials rather than centers of trade or production. Even in western Europe, early capitalism encouraged social change that sometimes required painful adjustments to new conditions.

Population Growth and Urbanization

American Food Crops The foundation of European economic expansion in early modern times was a rapidly growing population, which reflected improved nutrition and decreasing mortality. The Columbian exchange enriched European diets by introducing new food crops to European fields and tables. Most notable of the introductions was the potato, which during the sixteenth and seventeenth centuries enjoyed the reputation of being an aphrodisiac. Although potatoes probably did not inspire much romantic ardor, they provided a welcome source of carbohydrates for peasants and laborers who were having trouble keeping up with the rising price of bread. From Ireland to Russia and from Scandinavia to the Mediterranean, cultivators planted potatoes and harvested crops that added calories to European diets. American maize also made its way to Europe. Maize, however, served mostly as feed for livestock rather than as food for human consumption, although peasants sometimes used cornmeal to make bread or porridges like polenta. Other American crops, such as tomatoes and peppers, added vitamins and tangy flavor to European diets.

How the Past Shapes the Future ▶ ▶ ▶ ▶

The Columbian Exchange

As discussed in chapter 22, the Columbian exchange introduced new food crops that provided vital nutrition to ordinary people in Europe, which in turn helped fuel an impressive round of population growth across the region at precisely the same time indigenous American societies were devastated by European diseases. Yet European reliance on certain American food crops—especially the potato—would, over time, result in a dangerous dependency that led to famine when the crop failed, as it did in Ireland in 1845. Consider the ways that the exchange of items as seemingly mundane as new food crops can help shape historical developments over the long term, in both positive and negative ways.

While recently introduced American crops improved European diets, old diseases lost some of their ferocity. Smallpox continued to carry off about 10 percent of Europe's infants, and dysentery, influenza, tuberculosis, and typhus claimed victims among young and old, rich and poor alike. Yet better-nourished populations were better able to resist those maladies. Bubonic plague, a virulent epidemic killer during the fourteenth and fifteenth centuries, receded from European society. After its initial onslaught in the mid-fourteenth century, plague made periodic appearances throughout the early modern era. After the mid-seventeenth century, however, epidemics were rare and isolated events. The last major outbreaks of plague in Europe occurred in London in 1660 and Marseilles in 1720. By the mid-seventeenth century, epidemic disease was almost negligible as an influence on European population.

Population Growth Although European birthrates did not rise dramatically in early modern times, decreasing mortality resulted in rapid population growth. In 1500 the population of Europe, including Russia, was about 81 million. During the sixteenth century, as Europe recovered from epidemic plague, the population rose to 100 million. The Thirty Years' War—along with the famine and disease that the war touched off—led to population decline from about 1620 to 1650, but by 1700 European population had rallied and risen to 120 million. During the next century it grew by an additional 50 percent to 180 million.

Urbanization Rapid population growth drove a process of equally rapid urbanization. Some cities grew because rulers chose them as sites of government. Madrid, for example, was a minor town with a few thousand inhabitants until 1561 when King Philip II decided to locate his capital there. By 1600 the population of Madrid had risen to 65,000, and by 1630 it had reached 170,000. Other cities were commercial and industrial as well as government centers, and their numbers expanded along with the European economy. In the mid-sixteenth century, for example, the population of Paris was about 130,000, and London had about 60,000 inhabitants. A century later the population of both cities had risen to 500,000. Other European cities also experienced growth, even if it was not so dramatic as in Madrid, Paris, and London: Amsterdam, Berlin, Copenhagen, Dublin, Stockholm, Vienna, and others became prominent European cities during the early modern era.

Early Capitalism and Protoindustrialization

The Nature of Capitalism Population growth and rapid urbanization helped spur a round of remarkable economic development. This economic growth coincided with the emergence of **capitalism**—an economic system in which private parties make their goods and services available on a free market and seek to take advantage of market conditions to profit from their activities. Whether they are single individuals or large companies,

private parties own the land, machinery, tools, equipment, buildings, workshops, and raw materials needed for production. Private parties pursuing their own economic interests hire workers and decide for themselves what to produce: economic decisions are the prerogative of capitalist businessmen, not governments or social superiors. The center of a capitalist system is the market in which business owners compete with one another, and the forces of supply and demand determine the prices received for goods and services. If business owners organize their affairs efficiently, they realize handsome profits when they place their goods and services on the market. Otherwise, they incur losses and perhaps even lose their businesses.

The desire to accumulate wealth and realize profits was by no means new. Ever since the introduction of agriculture and the production of surplus crops, some individuals and groups had accumulated great wealth. Indeed, for several thousand years before the early modern era, merchants in China, southeast Asia, India, southwest Asia, the Mediterranean basin, and sub-Saharan Africa had pursued commercial ventures in hopes of realizing profits. Banks, investors, and insurance underwriters had supported privately organized commercial ventures throughout much of the Eastern Hemisphere since the postclassical era (500–1500 C.E.).

Supply and Demand During early modern times, however, European merchants and entrepreneurs transformed their society in a way that none of their predecessors had done. The capitalist economic order developed as individuals learned to take advantage of market conditions by building efficient networks of transportation and communication. Dutch merchants might purchase cheap grain from Baltic lands such as Poland or Russia, for example; store it in Amsterdam until they learned about a famine in the Mediterranean; and then transport it and sell it in southern France or Spain. Their enormous profits fueled suspicions that they took advantage of those in difficulty, but their activities also supplied hungry communities with the necessities of life, even if the price was high.

Private parties organized an array of institutions and services to support early capitalism. Banks, for example, appeared in all the major commercial cities of Europe: they held funds on account for safekeeping and granted loans to merchants or entrepreneurs launching new business ventures. Banks also published business newsletters—forerunners of the *Wall Street Journal* and *Fortune* magazine—that provided readers with reports on prices, information about demand for commodities in distant markets, and political news that could have an impact on business. Insurance companies mitigated financial losses from risky undertakings such as transoceanic voyages. Stock exchanges arose in the major European cities and provided markets where investors could buy and sell shares in joint-stock companies and trade in other commodities as well.

Joint-Stock Companies **Joint-stock companies** were especially important institutions in early capitalist society. Large

The Old Stock Exchange of Amsterdam, depicted here in a painting of the mid-seventeenth century, attracted merchants, investors, entrepreneurs, and businessmen from all over Europe. There they bought and sold shares in joint-stock companies such as the VOC and dealt in all manner of commodities traded in Amsterdam.
Amsterdam Historisch Museum (INV.NR.SA3025)

trading companies such as the English East India Company and its Dutch counterpart, the Vereenigde Oost-Indische Compagnie (VOC), spread the risks attached to expensive business enterprises and also took advantage of extensive communications and transportation networks. The trading companies organized commercial ventures on a larger scale than ever before. They were the principal foundations of the global economy that emerged in early modern times, and they were the direct ancestors of contemporary multinational corporations.

Politics and Empire Capitalism did not develop in a political vacuum. To the contrary, it emerged with the active support of government authorities who saw a capitalist order as the one best suited to their individual and collective interests. Merchants were especially influential in the affairs of the English and Dutch states, so it is not surprising that these lands adopted policies that were most favorable to capitalist enterprises throughout the early modern era. The English and Dutch states recognized individuals' rights to possess private property, enforced their contracts, protected their financial interests, and settled disputes between parties to business transactions. They also chartered joint-stock companies and authorized some of them to explore, conquer, and colonize distant lands in search of commercial opportunities. Thus early capitalism developed in the context of imperialism, as European peoples established fortified trading posts in Asia

An anonymous engraver depicts activity in a Dutch shipyard where workers build a massive, oceangoing sailing ship. In the seventeenth century, Dutch ships were inexpensive to operate, yet they accommodated abundant cargoes. What kinds of cargoes were Dutch ships likely to carry in this period?
North Wind Picture Archives/Alamy Stock Photo

and colonial regimes in both southeast Asia and the Americas. Indeed, imperial expansion and colonial rule were crucial for the development of capitalism because they enabled European merchants to gain access to the natural resources and commodities that they distributed so effectively through their transportation networks.

Quite apart from its influence on trade and the distribution of goods, capitalism encouraged European entrepreneurs to organize new ways to manufacture goods. For centuries, craft guilds had monopolized the production of goods such as textiles and metalwares in European towns and cities. Guilds fixed prices and wages, and they regulated standards of quality. They did not seek to realize profits so much as to protect markets and preserve their members' places in society. As a result, they actively discouraged competition and sometimes resisted technological innovation.

Putting-out System Capitalist entrepreneurs seeking profits found the guilds cumbersome and inflexible, so they sidestepped them and moved production into the countryside. Instead of relying on urban artisans to produce cloth, for example, they organized a "putting-out system" by which they delivered unfinished materials such as raw wool to rural households. Men and women in the countryside would then spin the wool into yarn, weave the yarn into cloth, cut the cloth according to patterns, and assemble the pieces into garments. The entrepreneur paid workers for their services, picked up the finished goods, and sold them on the market. During the seventeenth and eighteenth centuries, entrepreneurs moved the production of cloth, nails, pins, pots, and many other goods into the countryside through the putting-out system.

Because rural labor was usually plentiful, entrepreneurs spent relatively little on wages and realized handsome profits on their ventures. The putting-out system represented an early effort to organize efficient industrial production. Indeed, some historians refer to the seventeenth and eighteenth centuries as an age of **protoindustrialization.** The putting-out system remained a prominent feature of European society until the rise of industrial factories in the nineteenth century.

Social Change in Early Modern Europe

Capitalist economic development brought significant change to European lands. The putting-out system, for example, introduced considerable sums of money into the countryside. Increased wealth brought material benefits, but it also undermined long-established patterns of rural life. The material standards of rural life rose dramatically: peasant households acquired more cabinets, furnishings, and tableware, and rural residents wore better clothes, ate better food, and drank better wine. Individuals suddenly acquired incomes that enabled them to pursue their own economic interests and to become financially independent of their families and neighbors. When young adults and women began to earn their own incomes, however, many feared that they might slip out of the control of their families and abandon their kin who continued to work at agricultural tasks.

The putting-out system did not become a prominent feature of production in eastern Europe, but early capitalism prompted deep social change there as well as in lands to the west. Eastern Europe had few cities in early modern times, so in expansive agrarian states such as Poland, Bohemia, and

Russia, most people had no alternative to working in the countryside. Landlords took advantage of this situation by forcing peasants to work under extremely harsh conditions.

Serfdom in Russia Russia in particular was a vast but sparsely populated empire with little trade or manufacturing. Out of a concern to retain the allegiance of the powerful nobles who owned most of Russia's land, the Romanov tsars restricted the freedoms of most Russian peasants and tied them to the land as serfs. The institution of **serfdom** had emerged in the early middle ages as a labor system that required peasants to provide labor services for landowners and prevented them from marrying or moving away without their landlords' permission. After the fifteenth century, serfdom gradually came to an end in western Europe. In eastern Europe, however, landowners and rulers tightened restrictions on peasants during the sixteenth century, and in Russia the institution of serfdom survived until the nineteenth century. In effect, the Romanovs won the support of the Russian nobles by ensuring that laborers would be available to work their estates, which otherwise would have been worthless. In 1649 the government enacted a law code that provided for tight state control over the Russian labor force by establishing a rigid, castelike social order that sharply restricted both occupational and geographic mobility. The law of 1649 did not legally turn serfs into chattel slaves, but in fact the line between the two was extremely blurred: for example, during the late seventeenth and eighteenth centuries landlords commonly sold serfs to one another as if they were indeed private property. Under those conditions, landlords operated estates with inexpensive labor and derived enormous incomes from the sale of agricultural products on the market.

These arrangements played crucial roles in the emergence of capitalism. In the larger economy of early modern Europe, eastern European lands relied on serfs to cultivate grains and provide raw materials such as timber for export to western Europe, where merchants and manufacturers were able to employ free wage labor in building a capitalist economy. Already by the early sixteenth century, consumers in the Netherlands depended for their survival on grains imported from Poland and Russia through the Baltic Sea. Thus it was possible for capitalism to flourish in western Europe only because the peasants and semifree serfs of eastern Europe provided inexpensive foods and raw materials that fueled economic development. From its earliest days, capitalist economic organization had implications for peoples and lands far removed from the centers of capitalism itself.

Profits and Ethics Capitalism also posed moral challenges. Medieval theologians had regarded profit-making activity as morally dangerous because profiteers looked to their own advantage rather than the welfare of the larger community. Church officials even attempted to forbid the collection of interest on loans because they considered interest an unearned and immoral profit. But profit was the lifeblood of capitalism, and bankers were not willing to risk large sums of money on business ventures without realizing returns on their investments in the form of interest. Even as it transformed the European economy, capitalism found advocates who sought to explain its principles and portray it as a socially beneficial form of economic organization. Most important of the early apostles of capitalism was the Scottish philosopher Adam Smith (1723–1790), who argued that society would prosper when individuals pursued their own economic interests.

Nevertheless, the transition to capitalist society was long and painful. When individuals abandoned the practices of their ancestors and declined to help those who had fallen on hard times, their neighbors readily interpreted their actions as expressions of selfishness rather than economic prudence. Thus capitalist economic practices generated deep social strains, which often manifested themselves in violence. Bandits plagued the countryside of early modern Europe, and muggers turned whole sections of large cities into danger zones. Some historians believe that witch-hunting activities reflected social tensions generated by early capitalism and that accusations of witchcraft represented hostility toward women who were becoming economically independent of their husbands and families.

The Nuclear Family In some ways, capitalism favored the nuclear family as the principal unit of society. For centuries European couples had mostly married late—in their mid-twenties—and set up independent households. Early capitalism offered opportunities for these independent families to increase their wealth by cultivating agricultural crops or producing goods for sale on the market. As nuclear families became more important economically, they also became more socially and emotionally independent. Love between a man and a woman became a more important consideration in the making of marriages than the interests of the larger extended families, and affection between parents and their children became a more important ingredient of family life. Capitalism did not necessarily cause these changes in family life, but it may have encouraged developments that helped to define the nature and role of the family in modern European society.

TRANSFORMATIONS IN SCIENTIFIC THINKING

While experiencing religious, political, economic, and social change, western Europe also underwent intellectual and cultural transformation. Astronomers and physicists rejected classical Greek and Roman authorities, whose theories had dominated scientific thought during the middle ages, and based their understanding of the natural world on direct observation and mathematical reasoning. During the seventeenth and eighteenth centuries, they elaborated a new vision of the earth and the larger universe. Scholars relied on observation and mathematics to transform the natural sciences in a process known as the scientific revolution. The results of early modern science were so powerful that some European

SOURCES FROM THE PAST

Adam Smith on the Capitalist Market

Adam Smith (1723–1790) was a Scottish economist, philosopher, and author who devoted special thought to the nature of early capitalist society and the principles that made it work. In 1776 he published a lengthy book titled An Inquiry into the Nature and Causes of the Wealth of Nations, *a vastly influential work that championed free, unregulated markets and capitalist enterprise as the principal ingredients of prosperity. Smith's optimism about capitalism sprang from his conviction that society as a whole benefits when individuals pursue their own economic interests and trade on a free market.*

Every individual is continually exerting himself to find out the most advantageous employment for whatever capital he can command. It is his own advantage, indeed, and not that of the society, which he has in view. . . .

As every individual, therefore, endeavours as much as he can both to employ his capital in the support of domestic industry, and so to direct that industry that its produce may be of the greatest value, every individual necessarily labours to render the annual revenue of the society as great as he can. He generally, indeed, neither intends to promote the public interest, nor knows how much he is promoting it. By preferring the support of domestic to that of foreign industry, he intends only his own security; and by directing that industry in such a manner as its produce may be of the greatest value, he intends only his own gain, and he is in this, as in many other cases, led by an invisible hand to promote an end which was no part of his intention. Nor is it always the worse for the society that it was no part of it. By pursuing his own interest he frequently promotes that of the society more effectually than when he really intends to promote it. I have never known much good done by those who affected to trade for the public good. It is an affectation, indeed, not very common among merchants, and very few words need be employed in dissuading them from it.

> Smith's notion of an "invisible hand" operating on the economy is famous. What do you think Smith meant by this?

What is the species of domestic industry which his capital can employ, and of which the produce is likely to be of the greatest value, every individual, it is evident, can, in his local situation, judge much better than any statesman or lawgiver can do for him. The statesman, who should attempt to direct private people in what manner they ought to employ their capitals, would not only load himself with a most unnecessary attention, but assume an authority which could safely be trusted, not only to no single person, but to no council or senate whatever, and which would nowhere be so dangerous as in the hands of a man who had folly and presumption enough to fancy himself fit to exercise it.

> Why, according to Smith, are individuals better able to judge how to spend their money than representatives of the state?

To give the monopoly of the home market to the produce of domestic industry, in any particular art or manufacture, is in some measure to direct private people in what manner they ought to employ their capitals, and must, in almost all cases, be either a useless or a hurtful regulation. If the produce of domestic industry can be brought there as cheap as that of foreign industry, the regulation is evidently useless. If it cannot, it must generally be hurtful. It is the maxim of every prudent master of a family, never to attempt to make at home what it will cost him more to make than to buy. The tailor does not attempt to make his own shoes, but buys them of the shoemaker. The shoemaker does not attempt to make his own clothes, but employs a tailor. The farmer attempts to make neither the one nor the other, but employs those different artificers. All of them find it for their interest to employ their whole industry in a way in which they have some advantage over their neighbours, and to purchase with a part of its produce, or, what is the same thing, with the price of a part of it, whatever else they have occasion for.

For Further Reflection

■ To what extent do you think Adam Smith's analysis reflected the experiences of his own times, and to what extent did they represent universally valid observations?

Source: Adam Smith. *An Inquiry into the Nature and Causes of the Wealth of Nations.* Edinburgh: 1863, pp. 198–200.

intellectuals sought to overhaul moral, social, and political thought by adapting scientific methods and relying on reason rather than traditional cultural authorities. Over time, their efforts weakened the influence of churches in western Europe and encouraged the development of secular values.

The Reconception of the Universe

The Ptolemaic Universe   Until the seventeenth century, European astronomers based their understanding of the universe on the work of the Greek scholar Claudius Ptolemy of Alexandria. About the middle of the second century C.E., Ptolemy composed a work known as the *Almagest* that synthesized theories about the universe. Ptolemy envisioned a motionless earth surrounded by a series of nine hollow, concentric spheres that revolved around it. Each of the first seven spheres had one of the observable heavenly bodies—the sun, the moon, Mercury, Venus, Mars, Jupiter, and Saturn—embedded in its shell. The eighth sphere held the stars, and an empty ninth sphere surrounded the whole cosmos and provided the spin that kept all the others moving. Beyond the spheres Christian astronomers located heaven, the realm of God.

Following Ptolemy, astronomers believed that the heavens consisted of matter unlike any found on earth. Glowing like perfect jewels in the night skies, heavenly bodies were composed of a pure substance that did not experience change or corruption, and they were not subject to the physical laws that governed the world below the moon. They followed perfect circular paths in making their revolutions around the earth.

Planetary Movement Although theoretically attractive, this earth-centered, or geocentric, cosmology did not mesh readily with the erratic movements of the planets—a term that comes from the Greek word *planetes,* meaning "wanderer." From the vantage point of the earth, the planets often followed regular courses through the skies, but they sometimes slowed down, stopped, or even turned back on their courses—motions that would be difficult to explain if the planetary spheres revolved regularly around the earth. Astronomers went to great lengths to explain planetary behavior as the result of perfect circular movements. The result was an awkward series of adjustments known as epicycles—small circular revolutions that planets made around a point in their spheres, even while the spheres themselves revolved around the earth.

The Copernican Universe As astronomers accumulated data on planetary movements, most of them sought to reconcile their observations with Ptolemaic theory by adding increasing numbers of epicycles to their cosmic maps. In 1543, however, the Polish astronomer **Nicolaus Copernicus** published a treatise, *On the Revolutions of the Heavenly Spheres,* that broke with Ptolemaic theory and pointed European science in a new direction. Copernicus argued that the sun rather than the earth stood at the center of the universe and that the planets, including the earth, revolved around the sun.

Compared with Ptolemy's earth-centered universe, this new sun-centered, or heliocentric, theory harmonized much better with observational data, but it did not receive a warm welcome. Copernicus's ideas not only challenged prevailing scientific theories but also threatened cherished religious beliefs. His theory implied that the earth was just another planet and that humans did not occupy the central position in the universe. To some it also suggested the unsettling possibility that there might be other populated worlds in the universe—a notion that would be difficult to reconcile with Christian teachings, which held that the earth and humanity were unique creations of God.

The Scientific Revolution

Although it was unpopular in many quarters, Copernicus's theory inspired some astronomers to examine the heavens in fresh ways. As evidence accumulated, it became clear that the **Ptolemaic universe** simply did not correspond with reality. Astronomers based their theories on increasingly precise observational data, and they relied on mathematical reasoning to organize the data. Gradually, they abandoned the Ptolemaic in favor of the Copernican model of the universe. Moreover, some of them began to apply their analytical methods to mechanics—the branch of science that deals with moving bodies—and by the mid-seventeenth century accurate observation and mathematical reasoning dominated both mechanics and astronomy. Indeed, reliance on observation and mathematics transformed the study of the natural world and brought about the process we now call the **scientific revolution.**

Galileo Galilei The works of two scientists—**Johannes Kepler** of Germany and **Galileo Galilei** of Italy—rang the death knell for the Ptolemaic universe. Kepler (1571-1630) demonstrated that planetary orbits are elliptical, not circular as in Ptolemaic theory. Galileo (1564-1642) showed that the heavens were not the perfect, unblemished realm that Ptolemaic astronomers assumed but, rather, a world of constant change. Galileo took a recently invented instrument—the telescope—turned it skyward, and reported observations that astonished his contemporaries. With his telescope he could see spots on the sun and mountains on the moon—observations that discredited the notion that heavenly bodies were smooth, immaculate, unchanging, and perfectly spherical. He also noticed four of the moons that orbit the planet Jupiter—bodies that no human being had ever before observed—and he caught sight of previously unknown distant stars, which implied that the universe was much larger than anyone had previously suspected.

In addition to his astronomical discoveries, Galileo contributed to the understanding of terrestrial motion. He designed ingenious experiments to show that the velocity of falling bodies depends not on their weight but, rather, on the height from which they fall. This claim brought him scorn from scientists who subscribed to scientific beliefs deriving from Aristotle. But it offered a better explanation of how moving bodies behave under the influence of the earth's gravitational pull. Galileo also anticipated the modern law of

Ptolemaic (TAWL-oh-may-ihk)

In this seventeenth-century engraving, Galileo Galilei faces the Inquisition, a Roman Catholic institution that prosecuted individuals accused of a wide variety of crimes related to heresy. At a trial in 1633, the Inquisition found Galileo "vehemently suspect of heresy," forced him to recant Copernicanism, and placed him under house arrest for the remainder of his life.

Stefano Bianchetti/Corbis Historical/Getty Images

inertia, which holds that a moving body will continue to move in a straight line until some force intervenes to check or alter its motion.

Isaac Newton The new approach to science culminated in the work of the English mathematician **Isaac Newton** (1642–1727), who depended on accurate observation and mathematical reasoning to construct a powerful synthesis of astronomy and mechanics. Newton outlined his views on the natural world in an epoch-making volume of 1687 titled *Mathematical Principles of Natural Philosophy.* Newton's work united the heavens and the earth in a vast, cosmic system. He argued that a law of universal gravitation regulates the motions of bodies throughout the universe, and he offered precise mathematical explanations of the laws that govern movements of bodies on the earth. Newton's laws of universal gravitation and motion enabled him to synthesize the sciences of astronomy and

mechanics. They also allowed him to explain a vast range of seemingly unrelated phenomena, such as the ebb and flow of the tides, which move according to the gravitational pull of the moon, and the eccentric orbits of planets and comets, which reflect the gravitational influence of the sun, the earth, and other heavenly bodies. Until the twentieth century, Newton's universe served as the unquestioned framework for the physical sciences.

Newton's work symbolized the scientific revolution, but it by no means marked the end of the process by which observation and mathematical reasoning transformed European science. Inspired by the dramatic discoveries of astronomers and physicists, other scientists began to turn away from classical authorities and to construct fresh approaches to the understanding of the natural world. During the seventeenth and eighteenth centuries, anatomy, physiology, microbiology, chemistry, and botany underwent a thorough overhaul, as

SOURCES FROM THE PAST

Galileo Galilei, Letter to the Grand Duchess Christina

The Italian physicist and astronomer Galileo Galilei (1564–1642) was one of the most important European scientists in the early 1600s. His staunch defense of Nicolaus Copernicus's theory of a sun-centered universe threatened Catholic clergy, who were worried that such a theory threatened the authority of both the Bible and the Church. In 1615 Galileo, himself a devout Catholic, defended his scientific beliefs and argued why they should not be condemned by the church in a published letter to Christina, the grand duchess of Tuscany. Although the Church forced Galileo to publicly renounce his scientific beliefs in 1632, over the long term his writings contributed greatly to the reconception of the universe using the new scientific methodology.

I am inclined to believe, that the intention of the sacred Scriptures is to give to mankind the information necessary for their salvation, and which, surpassing all human knowledge can by no other means be accredited than by the mouth of the Holy Spirit. But I do not hold it necessary to believe, that the same God who has endowed us with senses, with speech, and intellect, intended that we should neglect the use of these, and seek by other means for knowledge which they are sufficient to procure us; especially in a science like astronomy, of which so little notice is taken in the Scriptures, that none of the planets, except the sun and moon, and, once or twice only, Venus under the name of Lucifer, are so much as named there. This therefore being granted, methinks that in the discussion of natural problems we ought not to begin at the authority of texts of Scripture, but at sensible experiments, and necessary demonstrations: for, from the divine word, the sacred Scripture and nature did both alike proceed, and I conceive that, concerning natural effects, that which either sensible experience sets before our eyes, or necessary demonstrations do prove unto us, ought not upon any account to be called into question, much less condemned, upon the testimony of Scriptural texts. . . Again, to command the very professors of astronomy that they of themselves see to the confuting of their own observations and demonstrations, is to enjoin a thing beyond all possibility of doing; for it is not only to command them not to see that which they do see, and not to understand that which they do understand, but it is to order them to seek for and to find the contrary of that which they happen to meet with. I would entreat these wise and prudent fathers, that they would with all diligence consider the difference that is between opinionative and demonstrative doctrines; . . . that it is not in the power of the professors of demonstrative sciences to change their opinions at pleasure, and adopt first one side and then another; and that there is a great difference between commanding a mathematician or a philosopher, and the disposing of a lawyer or a merchant; and that the demonstrated conclusions touching the things of nature and of the heavens cannot be changed with the same facility as the opinions are touching what is lawful or not in a contract, bargain, or bill of exchange. Therefore, first let these men apply themselves to examine the arguments of Copernicus and others, and leave the condemning of them as erroneous and heretical to whom it belongeth. . .

> By what process does Galileo argue that people should explain natural phenomena?

> What argument is Galileo using to demonstrate that the Bible, and religious figures, should not be used as an authority on matters of astronomy?

For Further Reflection

■ Why might religious authorities have found Galileo's astronomical observations threatening?

Source: Life of Galileo: With Illustrations of the Advancement of Experimental Philosophy (Boston, William Hyde and Company, 1832), 143–145.

A portrait of Sir Isaac Newton (1642–1727) by Sir Godfrey Kneller (1646–1723), the leading portrait painter in England during the late seventeenth and early eighteenth centuries. Although commonly hailed as one of the most influential scientists of all time, Newton was more humble when judging his own achievements, writing to a fellow scientist: "If I have seen further it is by standing on the shoulders of giants."
Imagno/Hulton Fine Art Collection/Getty Images

scientists tested their theories against direct observation of natural phenomena and explained them in rigorous mathematical terms.

Women and Science

In the sixteenth and seventeenth centuries, Europe's learned men challenged some of the most hallowed traditions concerning the nature of the physical universe and supplanted them with new scientific principles. Yet, when male scientists studied female anatomy, female physiology, and women's reproductive organs, they were commonly guided not by scientific observation but by tradition, prejudice, and fanciful imagination. William Harvey (1578–1657), the English physician who discovered the principles of the circulation of human blood, also applied his considerable talents to the

study of human reproduction. After careful dissection and observation of female deer, chickens, and roosters, he hypothesized that women, like hens, served as mere receptacles for the "vivifying" male fluid. According to him, it was the male semen—endowed with generative powers so potent that it did not even have to reach the uterus to work its magic—from which the unfertilized egg received life and form. Anatomy, physiology, and limited reproductive function seemed to confirm the innate inferiority of women, adding a "scientific" veneer to the traditionally limited images, roles, and functions of women. With the arrival of printing, men were able to disseminate more widely those negative conclusions about women.

Émilie du Châtelet Despite prevailing critical attitudes, some women found themselves drawn to the new intellectual currents of the time. **Émilie du Châtelet** (1706–1749) established her reputation as a scientist with her three-volume work on the German mathematician Gottfried Leibniz (1646–1716)

Émilie du Châtelet was perhaps the most exceptional female scientist of the eighteenth century. Although she had to contend with the conventional demands on women, she remained committed to her study of Newton and science.
DEA/G. Dagli Orti/De Agostini/Getty Images

in 1740. Her crowning achievement, however, was her translation of Isaac Newton's monumental work *Principia Mathematica*, which has remained the standard French translation of the work. She did not simply render Newton's words into another language, however; rather, she explained his complex mathematics in graceful prose, transformed his geometry into calculus, and assessed the current state of Newtonian physics. She finished her work in the year of her death, at age forty-three, six days after giving birth to a child. Underscoring the difficulty of reconciling a woman's reproductive duties with her intellectual aspirations was her lover Voltaire's commentary. He declared in a letter to his friend Frederick II, King of Prussia (reigned 1740–1786), that du Châtelet was "a great man whose only fault was being a woman."

CONCLUSION

During the early modern era, European society experienced a series of profound and sometimes painful changes. The Protestant Reformation ended the religious unity of western Europe, and intermittent religious conflict disrupted European society for a century and more. Centralizing monarchs strengthened their realms and built a society of sovereign, autonomous, and intensely competitive states with distinctive traditions. Capitalist entrepreneurs reorganized the production and distribution of manufactured goods, and although their methods led to increased wealth, their quest for efficiency and profits clashed with traditional values. Modern science based on direct observation and mathematical explanations emerged as a powerful tool for the investigation of, and encounters with, the natural world. At just the time that European merchants, colonists, and adventurers were seeking new opportunities and encounters in the larger world, European society was becoming more powerful, more experimental, and more competitive than ever before. Given that Europeans now possessed the latest armaments and were willing to use them to achieve political and economic goals, this combination would have profound effects for many regions of the world in the future.

STUDY TERMS

absolutism (485)
Anglicans (477)
Calvinists (477)
capitalism (490)
Carolingian (480)
Catherine the Great (486)
Catholic Reformation (477)
Charles V (481)
constitutional states (483)
Council of Trent (477)
Émilie du Châtelet (498)
English Civil War (483)
Galileo Galilei (495)
Glorious Revolution (484)
Habsburgs (480)
Isaac Newton (496)

Johannes Gutenberg (476)
Johannes Kepler (495)
joint-stock companies (490)
Louis XIV (485)
Martin Luther (476)
Nicolaus Copernicus (495)
Ninety-Five Theses (475)
Peace of Westphalia (488)
Peter the Great (486)
Protestant Reformation (476)
protoindustrialization (492)
Ptolemaic universe (495)
Richelieu (485)
Romanov (486)
scientific revolution (495)
serfdom (493)

Society of Jesus (478)
Spanish Inquisition (482)
St. Ignatius Loyola (478)
Thirty Years' War (479)

Versailles (485)
witch-hunts (479)
Yemelian Pugachev (487)

FOR FURTHER READING

Paul Dukes. *The Making of Russian Absolutism, 1613–1801.* 2nd ed. London, 2015. A succinct study of two disparate centuries, the seventeenth and eighteenth, and two influential tsars, Peter and Catherine.

Patricia Fara. *Pandora's Breeches: Women, Science, and Power in the Enlightenment.* London, 2004. An engaging account of the contributions women made to science in the seventeenth and eighteenth centuries.

Philip S. Gorski. *The Disciplinary Revolution: Calvinism and the Rise of the Early Modern State.* Chicago, 2003. Argues that the formation of strong European states was a result of religious and social control policies initiated by the Protestant Reformation.

Thomas S. Kuhn. *The Structure of Scientific Revolutions.* 3rd ed. Chicago, 1997. An influential theoretical work that views scientific thought in larger social and cultural contexts.

Brian P. Levack. *The Witch-Hunt in Early Modern Europe.* New York, 2006. A compact but comprehensive survey of European witchcraft beliefs and pursuit of witches in the sixteenth and seventeenth centuries.

Jerry Z. Muller. *The Mind and the Market: Capitalism in Modern European Thought.* New York, 2002. Broad history of the development of capitalism through the eyes of major European thinkers, including Adam Smith, Joseph Schumpeter, and Karl Marx.

Andrew Pettegree. *Reformation and the Culture of Persuasion.* Cambridge, 2005. Investigates why people chose to support the Reformation in an era before mass literacy.

Paolo Rossi. *The Birth of Modern Science.* Malden, Mass., 2001. Explores specific seventeenth-century value systems and traditions that were central to the rise of modern science.

Merry Wiesner-Hanks. *Women and Gender in Early Modern Europe,* 4th ed. Cambridge, 2019. Comprehensive overview of women's lives and of ideas about gender in the early modern period, with attention to race, migration, and global issues.

Peter Wilson. *The Thirty Years' War: Europe's Tragedy.* Cambridge, Mass., 2011. Comprehensive study of the destructiveness of the war and its social, political, and economic causes as well as its religious causes.

The Integration of the Americas and Oceania with the Wider World

ZOOMING IN ON ENCOUNTERS

The Complicated Choices of Doña Marina

A remarkable young woman played a pivotal role in the Spanish conquest of Mexico. Sometimes called **Malintzin,** over the years she has come to be better known as **Doña Marina,** the name bestowed on her by Spanish forces. Doña Marina was born about 1500 in central Mexico. Her mother tongue was **Nahuatl,** the principal language of the Aztec Empire. When she was a girl, Doña Marina's family sent her to the Mexican coast as a slave, and later, her slaveholders sent her to their neighbors in the Yucatan peninsula. On her journey, she became fluent in Maya as well as her native Nahuatl language.

When **Hernán Cortés** arrived on the Mexican coast in 1519, his small army included a Spanish soldier who had learned the Maya language during a period of captivity in the Yucatan. But he had no way to communicate with the Nahuatl-speaking peoples of central Mexico until a Maya chieftain presented him with twelve young women, including Doña Marina, when he entered into an alliance with Cortes against the Aztecs. Doña Marina's linguistic abilities enabled Cortés to communicate

Malintzin (mal-een-tzeen)
Nahuatl (na-watl)
Hernán Cortés (er-NAHN kor-TEZ)

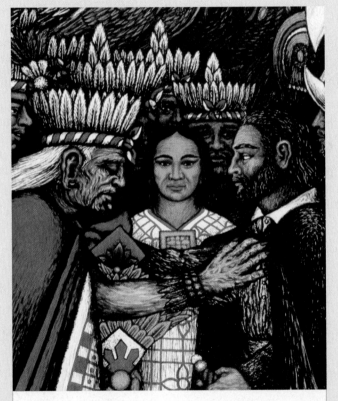

A contemporary mural by Tlaxala artist Desiderio Hernández Xochitiotzin—which is based on a sixteenth-century indigenous painting—suggests the central place of Doña Marina in facilitating encounters between Hernán Cortés (on the right) and the indigenous peoples of Mexico.
Benson Latin American Collection, General Libraries, University of Texas at Austin.

through an improbable chain of languages—from Spanish to Maya to Nahuatl and then back again—while making his way to the Aztec capital of **Tenochtitlan.** Before long, Doña Marina learned Spanish and thus eliminated the Maya link in the linguistic chain.

Doña Marina provided Cortés with information and diplomatic services as well. On several occasions she learned of plans by indigenous peoples to destroy the tiny Spanish army, and she alerted Cortés in time for him to prevent an attack. Once, she was able to report the precise details of a planned ambush because she played along with an effort by Cortes' enemies to bring her into the scheme. She also helped Cortés negotiate with emissaries from Tenochtitlan and other major cities of central Mexico. In fact, without Doña Marina's help, it is difficult to see how Cortés's small band could have survived to see the Aztec capital.

Precisely because of her pivotal role in aiding Cortés in his invasion of the Aztec Empire, Doña Marina earned another name commonly bestowed on her in Mexican history: La Malinche, or the traitor. The belief that she betrayed her people by collaborating with the Spanish underscores the complicated choices Doña Marina was faced with in their encounters with Europeans. Mesoamerican societies were not monolithic, and many people chose to ally themselves with the Spanish because of their disaffection from Aztec imperial rule. In Doña Marina's specific case, it is also important to remember her lack of power as a slave woman. After being given to Cortes, she may have felt the need to protect her new membership in his group by making herself valuable. Using her linguistic and diplomatic talents to aid Cortes may well have been a means of survival. Whatever her motives, it is clear that Doña Marina's aid was crucial to the success of Cortes' small group.

In addition to facilitating the Spanish conquest of the Aztec Empire, Doña Marina played a role in the formation of a new society in Mexico. In 1522, one year after the fall of Tenochtitlan, she gave birth to a son fathered by Cortés, and in 1526 she bore a daughter to a Spanish captain whom she had married. Given her status as a slave, historians have no way of knowing whether Doña Marina conceived her children willingly or not. Nevertheless, although her offspring were not the first children born in the Western Hemisphere of indigenous and Spanish parentage, they symbolize the early emergence of a mestizo population in Mexico. Doña Marina died soon after the birth of her daughter, probably in 1527, but during her short life she contributed to the thorough transformation of Mexican society.

Tenochtitlan (teh-noch-tee-TLAHN)

CHAPTER OVERVIEW

Until 1492 the peoples of the Eastern and Western Hemispheres had few dealings with one another. After 1492, however, the voyages of European mariners led to permanent and sustained contact between the peoples of the Eastern Hemisphere, the Western Hemisphere, and Oceania. The resulting encounters brought profound and violent change to both American and Pacific lands. European peoples possessed powerful military weapons, horses, and sailing ships that provided them with technological advantages over the peoples they encountered in the Americas and the Pacific Islands. Moreover, most Europeans also enjoyed complete or partial immunity to diseases that caused demographic disasters when introduced to the Western Hemisphere and Oceania. Because of their technological advantages and the wholesale depopulation that followed from epidemic diseases, European peoples were able to establish a strong presence throughout the Americas and much of the Pacific Ocean basin.

In Australia and the Pacific Islands, the European presence laid a foundation for dramatic and often traumatic change in the nineteenth and twentieth centuries. In the Western Hemisphere, however, large numbers of European migrants helped to bring about a profound transformation of American societies in early modern times. In Mexico and Peru, Spanish conquerors established territorial empires that were ruled from Spain. In Brazil, Portuguese entrepreneurs founded sugar plantations and imported African slaves to perform the heavy labor required for their operation. In North America, French, English, and Dutch fur traders allied with indigenous peoples who provided them with animal skins, and their more sedentary compatriots founded settler societies concentrating on the production of cash crops for export. Throughout the Western Hemisphere, peoples of European, African, and American ancestry interacted to fashion altogether new societies.

COLLIDING WORLDS

When European peoples first sought to establish their presence in the Americas, they brought a range of technology unavailable to the peoples they encountered in the Western

CHRONOLOGY

1492	First voyage of Christopher Columbus to the Western Hemisphere
1494	Treaty of Tordesillas
1500	Brazil claimed for Portugal by Pedro Alvares de Cabral
1500–1527	Life of Doña Marina
1502–1520	Reign of Motecuzoma
1518	Smallpox epidemic in the Caribbean
1519–1521	Spanish conquest of Mexico
1525	Execution of Cuauhtémoc
1531	Juan Diego's vision of the Virgin of Guadalupe
1532–1540	Spanish conquest of Peru
1545	Spanish discovery of silver near Potosí
1604	Foundation of Port Royal (Nova Scotia)
1607	Foundation of Jamestown
1608	Foundation of Quebec
1619	First enslaved Africans brought to Virginia
1623	Foundation of New Amsterdam
ca. 1642–1698	French and Iroquois Wars
1630	Foundation of the Massachusetts Bay Colony
1688	Smallpox epidemic on Guam
1754–1763	French and Indian war in North America
1763	Transfer of French Canadian possessions to British rule
1768–1779	Captain James Cook's exploration of the Pacific Ocean
1788	Establishment of first European colony in Australia

Hemisphere. Even more important than technology, however, was the combination of devastating epidemic disease Europeans brought with them and European willingness to exploit existing divisions between indigenous peoples. With the help of technology, disease, and ruthless political maneuvering, Spanish conquerors toppled the Aztec and Inca empires and imposed their own rule in Mexico and Peru. In later decades Portuguese planters built sugar plantations on the Brazilian coastline. French, English, and Dutch migrants displaced indigenous peoples in North America and established settler colonies under the rule of European peoples.

The Spanish Caribbean

The Taíno When Spanish mariners arrived in the Caribbean, the **Taíno** (also known as Arawaks) were the most prominent people in the region. During the late centuries B.C.E., the

Taíno (tah-EE-noh)
encomienda (ehn-KOH-mee-ehn-dah)

ancestors of the Taíno sailed in canoes from the Orinoco River valley in South America to the Caribbean islands, and by about 900 C.E. they had settled throughout the region. The Taíno cultivated manioc and other crops, and they lived in small villages under the authority of chiefs who allocated land to families and supervised community affairs. They showed interest in the glass, beads, and metal tools that Spanish mariners brought as trade goods because these were new to them. Meanwhile, the Spanish showed great interest in trading for the gold jewelry worn by the Taíno. Although at first the Taíno received the Spanish warmly, within a few months relations between the Taíno and the Spanish turned sour when it became clear that the Spanish were not satisfied with the amount of gold they were getting through trade alone.

Spanish Arrival Christopher Columbus and his immediate followers made the island of Hispaniola (which embraces modern Haiti and the Dominican Republic) the base of Spanish operations in the Caribbean. There, Spanish settlers established the fort of Santo Domingo, and the city, officially founded in 1498, became the capital of the Spanish Caribbean. Columbus's original plan was to build forts and trading posts where merchants could trade with local peoples for products desired by European consumers. Within a few years of Spanish arrival, however, it became clear that the Caribbean region offered no silks or spices for the European market. If Spanish settlers wanted to maintain their presence in the Caribbean, they would need to find some way to make a living.

The settlers first attempted to support their society by mining gold. Spanish settlers were too few in number to mine gold—and in any case they were not inclined to perform heavy physical labor—so the miners came largely from the ranks of the Taíno. Recruitment of labor came through an institution known as the ***encomienda,*** which involved Spanish *encomenderos* ("settlers") forcing the Taíno to work in their mines or fields. In return for labor, *encomenderos* were supposed to look after their workers' health and welfare and to encourage their conversion to Christianity.

Conscription of Taíno labor was a brutal business that, in practice, functioned like a system of slavery. *Encomenderos* worked their charges hard and punished them severely when they did not deliver the expected quantities of gold or work sufficiently hard in the fields. The Taíno occasionally organized rebellions, but their bows, arrows, and slings had little effect against horse-mounted Spanish forces wielding steel swords and firearms. By about 1515, enslavement

One of the earliest European depictions of Native Americans was this engraving of 1505. The caption informed readers that American peoples lived in communal society, where men took several wives but none had private possessions, and that they routinely smoked and consumed the bodies of slain enemies. How might such representations have shaped European ideas about Native Americans?

North Wind Picture Archives/Alamy Stock Photo

and physical abuse had brought dramatic decline to Taíno populations on the large Caribbean islands of Hispaniola, Jamaica, Puerto Rico, and Cuba. On the island of Hispaniola alone, by 1514 the Taíno population had declined to about 32,000 from a pre-contact population of several hundred thousand.

Smallpox Another serious demographic decline then set in after 1518, when **smallpox** reached the Caribbean region and touched off devastating epidemics among the peoples of the Western Hemisphere. To replace laborers lost to disease, *encomenderos* launched raiding parties to kidnap and enslave Taíno and other peoples. This tactic exposed additional victims to introduced diseases and hastened the decline of indigenous populations.

Under pressure of **epidemic disease,** the indigenous population of the Caribbean plummeted from about four million in 1492 to a few thousand in the 1540s. As a result, some indigenous societies passed almost completely out of existence. Only a few Taíno cultural elements survived: *canoe, hammock, hurricane, barbecue, maize,* and *tobacco* all derive from Taíno words, but the society that generated them had largely disappeared by the middle of the sixteenth century.

From Mining to Plantation Agriculture Deposits of gold were not plentiful in the Caribbean, but optimistic Spanish adventurers continued to seek treasure there for a century and more. After the mid-sixteenth century, however, when Spanish explorers located exceptionally rich sources of silver in Mexico and Peru, the Caribbean became a much

How the Past Shapes the Future

The Columbian Exchange

Recall that the spread of epidemic diseases like smallpox, measles, and influenza from Eurasia to the Americas was one of the key features of the Columbian exchange—a process that began almost immediately after contact between Europeans and indigenous Americans in the late fifteenth century. Since indigenous Americans had no immunity to Eurasian diseases, they took a staggering toll: in some cases, as in colonial Mexico, the mortality rate may have been as high as 90 percent. If epidemic disease had not caused such high mortality among indigenous Americans, in what ways might the history of the Americas in the sixteenth and seventeenth centuries have been different?

less important part of the Spanish Empire. English pirates lurked in Caribbean waters hoping to intercept imperial fleets carrying American silver to Spain, but the region was not a center of production. Then, in about the 1640s, French, English, and Dutch settlers began to flock to the Caribbean with the intention of establishing plantations. It became clear that even if the Caribbean islands lacked precious metals, they offered ideal conditions for the cultivation of cash crops, particularly sugar, which would fetch high prices in European markets. Later, tobacco also became a prime cash crop of the region. Meanwhile, because indigenous populations had been decimated, planters lacked the labor they needed to operate their estates. Based on earlier Spanish practices in the Azores and Canary Islands, Europeans solved the labor shortage by forcibly importing several million slaves from Africa. By 1700 Caribbean society consisted of a small class of European landowners and large numbers of enslaved Africans.

Mexico and Peru at the Time of Contact

Spanish interest soon shifted from the Caribbean to the American mainland, where settlers hoped to find more resources to exploit. During the early sixteenth century, Spanish *conquistadores* ("conquerors") pressed beyond the Caribbean islands, moving west into Mexico and south into Panama and Peru. Aided especially by the spread of epidemic disease, between 1519 and 1521 Hernán Cortés and a small band of men brought down the Aztec Empire in Mexico, and between 1532 and 1533 **Francisco Pizarro** and his followers toppled the Inca Empire in Peru. Those conquests laid the foundations for colonial regimes that would transform the Americas.

In Mexico and Peru, Spanish explorers found societies quite different from those of the Caribbean islands. Both

Mexico and Peru had been sites of agricultural societies, cities, and large states for more than a millennium. In the early fifteenth century, both lands fell under the sway of powerful imperial states: the Mexica people and their allies founded the Aztec Empire that expanded to embrace most of Mesoamerica, while the Incas imposed their rule on a vast realm extending from modern Ecuador in the north to modern Chile in the south—the largest state South America had ever seen. But neither the Inca nor the Aztec Empire could count on all its subjects to rally to its defense. In fact, the very success of Spanish military campaigns often rested on the support of indigenous allies, who were eager to shake off Aztec or Inca rule. As allies they played a crucial role in the conquest, supplying auxiliary troops, logistical support, and secure bases in friendly territory.

Hernán Cortés The conquest of Mexico began with an expedition to search for gold on the American mainland. In 1519 Cortés led about 450 soldiers to Mexico and made his way from Veracruz on the Gulf coast to the island city of Tenochtitlan, the large and vibrant Aztec capital situated in Lake Texcoco. They seized the emperor **Motecuzoma** II, who died in 1520 during a skirmish between Spanish forces and residents of Tenochtitlan. Fierce Aztec resistance soon drove the conquistadores from the capital, and Cuauhtémoc (ca. 1502–1525)—the nephew and son-in-law of Motecuzoma—emerged as the last Aztec emperor. Cortés built a small fleet of ships, placed Tenochtitlan under siege, and in 1521 starved the city into surrender. Cuauhtémoc withstood the torture Cortés inflicted upon him in an attempt to uncover the whereabouts of Aztec gold and treasures. However, he ultimately could not escape the execution ordered by Cortés in 1525.

Steel swords, muskets, cannons, and horses offered Cortés and his soldiers some advantage over the forces they met and help to account for the Spanish conquest of the Aztec Empire. Yet weaponry alone clearly would not enable Cortés's tiny force to overcome a large, densely populated society. Quite apart from military technology, Cortés's expedition forged alliances with peoples who resented domination by the Mexica, the leaders of the Aztec Empire, and who reinforced the small Spanish army with thousands of veteran warriors. Indigenous allies also provided Spanish forces with logistical support and secure bases in friendly territory.

Epidemic Disease On the mainland, as in the Caribbean, epidemic disease aided Spanish efforts. During the siege of Tenochtitlan, smallpox raged through the city, killing inhabitants by the tens of thousands and fatally sapping the strength of defensive forces. Smallpox rapidly spread beyond the capital, raced through Mexico, and killed so many people that Aztec society was unable to function. Only in the context of

conquistadores (kon-kees-tah-DOH-rayz)
Motecuzoma (mo-tek-oo-ZO-mah)

SOURCES FROM THE PAST

First Impressions of Spanish Forces

As the Spanish army made its way to Tenochtitlan, Motecuzoma dispatched a series of emissaries to communicate with Cortés and learn his intentions. The following document, based on indigenous accounts but filtered through the Spanish sensibilities of Bernardino de Sahagun, suggested that Motecuzoma reacted with fright when presented with reports that were less than reassuring because they focused on fearsome weapons and animals of the Spanish. Given the vigorous resistance by the Aztecs to the Spanish invaders, it seems highly likely that the source exaggerated Motecuzoma's terror. At the same time, at the very least it suggests that Motecuzoma took the threat posed by the Spanish very seriously.

And when [Motecuzoma] had heard what the messengers reported, he was terrified, he was astounded. . . .

Especially did it cause him to faint away when he heard how the gun, at [the Spaniards'] command, discharged [the shot]; how it resounded as if it thundered when it went off. It indeed bereft one of strength; it shut off one's ears. And when it discharged, something like a round pebble came forth from within. Fire went showering forth; sparks went blazing forth. And its smoke smelled very foul; it had a fetid odor which verily wounded the head. And when [the shot] struck a mountain, it was as if it were destroyed, dissolved. And a tree was pulverized; it was as if it vanished; it was as if someone blew it away.

> For someone who had never seen a firearm in action before, does this description seem to do an adequate job of relaying its effects?

All iron was their war array. In iron they clothed themselves. With iron they covered their heads. Iron were their swords. Iron were their crossbows. Iron were their shields. Iron were their lances.

And those which bore them upon their backs, their deer [that is, horses], were as tall as roof terraces.

And their bodies were everywhere covered; only their faces appeared. They were very white; they had chalky faces; they had yellow hair, though the hair of some was black. Long were their beards; they also were yellow. They were yellow-headed. [The black men's hair] was kinky, it was curly.

> Why might the Aztecs have paid particular attention to the Europeans with blond hair?

And their food was like fasting food—very large, white, not heavy like [tortillas]; like maize stalks, good-tasting as if of maize stalk flour; a little sweet, a little honeyed. It was honeyed to eat; it was sweet to eat.

And their dogs were very large. They had ears folded over; great dragging jowls. They had fiery eyes—blazing eyes; they had yellow eyes—fiery yellow eyes. They had thin flanks—flanks with ribs showing. They had gaunt stomachs. They were very tall. They were nervous; they went about panting, with tongues hanging out. They were spotted like ocelots; they were varicolored.

And when Motecuzoma heard all this, he was much terrified. It was as if he fainted away. His heart saddened; his heart failed him.

For Further Reflection

■ What did the Spanish and their indigenous allies hope to gain by presenting this image of Motecuzoma?

Source: Bernardino de Sahagún. *Florentine Codex: General History of the Things of New Spain,* 13 vols. Trans. by Arthur J. O. Anderson and Charles E. Dibble. Salt Lake City: University of Utah Press, 1950–82, 13:19–20. (Translation slightly modified.)

this drastic depopulation is it possible to understand the Spanish conquest of Mexico.

Francisco Pizarro Francisco Pizarro experienced similar results when he led a Spanish expedition from Central America to Peru. Pizarro set out in 1530 with 180 soldiers, later joined by reinforcements to make a force of about 600. The conquistadores arrived in Peru just after a bitter dispute between Huascar (1503–1532) and **Atahualpa** (ca. 1502–1533), two brothers within the Inca ruling house, and Pizarro's

forces exploited the differences between those factions. Already by 1533 they had taken the Inca capital at Cuzco. Under pretext of holding a conference, they called the Inca ruling elites together, seized them, and killed most of them. They spared the Inca ruler Atahualpa until he had delivered a large quantity of gold to Pizarro. Then they strangled him and decapitated his body. The search for treasure continued after the end of Inca rule. Pizarro and his conquistadores

Atahualpa (ah-tah-WAHL-pah)

Tlaxcalan allies of the Spanish on their way to the Aztec capital of Tenochtitlan. A Spanish warrior is at the front right of the drawing on his horse. Taken from the sixteenth-century *Lienzo de Tlaxcala* manuscript.

looted gold and silver plaques from Cuzco's temples and public buildings, melted down statuettes fashioned from precious metals, and even stole jewelry and ornaments from the embalmed bodies of deceased Inca rulers.

Several considerations help to explain how Pizarro's tiny force was able to topple the Inca Empire. Many subjects of the empire despised the Incas as overlords and tax collectors. Indeed, many allied with the Spanish invaders. Epidemic disease also discouraged resistance: smallpox had spread from Mexico and Central America to Peru in the 1520s, long before Pizarro's arrival, and had already significantly weakened Andean populations. Hence, by 1540 Spanish forces had established themselves securely in Peru.

Spanish and Portuguese Empires in the Americas

During the early days after the conquests, Cortés and Pizarro allocated lands and labor rights to their troops on their own authority. Gradually, however, the Spanish monarchy extended its control over the growing American empire, and by about 1570 the semiprivate regime of the conquistadores had given way to formal rule under the Spanish crown. Bureaucrats charged with the implementation of royal policy and the administration of royal justice replaced the soldiers of fortune who had conquered Mexico and Peru. The conquistadores did not welcome the arrival of the bureaucrats, but with the aid of Spanish lawyers, tax collectors, and military forces, royal officials had their way.

Spanish Colonial Administration

Spanish administrators established two main centers of authority in the Americas—Mexico (which they called **New Spain**) and Peru (known as New Castile)—each governed by a viceroy who was responsible to the king of Spain. In Mexico they built a new capital, Mexico City, on top of Tenochtitlan. In Peru they originally hoped to rule from the Inca capital of Cuzco, but they considered the high altitude unpleasant and also found the Andean city too inaccessible for their purposes. In 1535 they founded Lima and transferred the government to the coast where it was accessible to Spanish shipping.

The viceroys were the king's representatives in the Americas, and they wielded considerable power. The kings of Spain, attempting to ensure that their viceroys would not build personal power bases and become independent, subjected them to the review of courts known as *audiencias* staffed by university-educated lawyers. The *audiencias* heard appeals against the viceroys' decisions and policies and had the right to address their concerns directly to the Spanish king. Furthermore, the *audiencias* conducted reviews of viceroys' performance at the end of their terms, and negative reviews could lead to severe punishment.

In spite of this structure, in many ways Spanish administration in the Americas was a ragged affair. Transportation and communication difficulties limited the ability of viceroys to supervise their territories. In many regions, local administration fell to *audiencias* or town councils. Meanwhile, the Spanish monarchy exercised even less influence on American affairs than the viceroys. It often took two years for the central government in Spain to respond to a query from Mexico or Peru, and many replies simply asked for further information rather than providing firm directives. When viceroys received clear orders that they did not like, they found ways to procrastinate: they often responded to the king that "I obey, but I do not enforce," implying that with additional information the king would alter his decision.

New Cities

Spanish rule in the Americas led to the rapid establishment of cities throughout the viceroyalties. Like their compatriots in Spain, colonists preferred to live in cities even when they derived their income from the agricultural

In this illustration from Peru native Felipe Guaman Poma de Ayala's letter of complaint to the Spanish king—a record of grievances against Spanish overlords—conquistadores decapitate Atahualpa after executing him by strangulation in 1533.
DEA/G. DAGLI ORTI /De Agostini/Getty Images

production of their landed estates. As the numbers of migrants increased, they expanded the territory under Spanish imperial authority and built a dense network of bureaucratic control based in recently founded cities. The jurisdiction of the viceroyalty of New Spain reached from Mexico City as far as St. Augustine in Florida (founded in 1565). Administrators in Lima oversaw affairs from Panama (founded in 1519) to Concepción (founded in 1550) and Buenos Aires (founded in 1536).

The Portuguese in Brazil

While Spanish conquistadores and administrators built a territorial empire in Mexico and Peru, Portuguese forces established an imperial presence in **Brazil.** The Portuguese presence came about by an odd twist of diplomatic convention. In 1494 Spain and Portugal signed the Treaty of Tordesillas, which divided the world along an imaginary north-south line 370 leagues west of the Azores and Cape Verde Islands. According to this agreement, Spain could claim any land west of that line, so long as it was not already under Christian rule, and Portugal gained the same rights for lands east of the line. Thus Portugal gained territory along the northeastern part of the South American continent, a region known as Brazil from the many brazilwood trees that grew along the coast, while the remainder of the Western Hemisphere fell under Spanish control. Of course, this treaty completely disregarded preexisting indigenous claims to any of these lands—an indication of the conceit of both the Spanish and the Portuguese.

The Portuguese mariner Pedro Alvares de Cabral stopped in Brazil briefly in 1500 while making a tack through the Atlantic Ocean en route to India. His compatriots did not display much immediate interest in the land. When French and Dutch mariners began to visit Brazilian shores, however, the Portuguese king decided to consolidate his claim to the land. He made vast land grants to Portuguese nobles in the expectation that they would develop and colonize their holdings, and later he dispatched a governor to oversee affairs and implement royal policy. Portuguese interest in Brazil rose dramatically after mid-century when entrepreneurs established profitable sugar plantations—based on slave labor—on the coast.

audiencias (AW-dee-ehns-see-ahs)

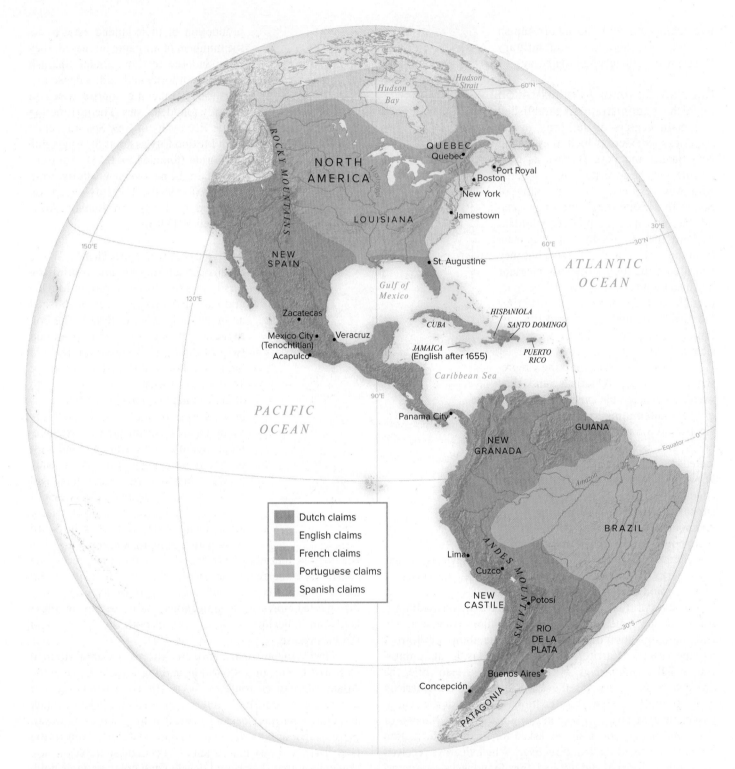

MAP 24.1   European empires and colonies in the Americas about 1700.

Locate the major cities and settlements of each imperial power.

What factors decided where settlements would be placed? Why are so few settlements in the interior of either North or South America?

Colonial American Society The cities of the Spanish and Portuguese empires became centers of European-style society in the Americas: the spires of churches and cathedrals defined their skylines, and Spanish and Portuguese were the languages of government, business, and society. Beyond the urban districts, however, indigenous ways of life persisted. In the Amazon basin and Paraguay, for example, indigenous peoples produced little agricultural surplus, and there were no mineral deposits to attract European migrants. The few Spanish and Portuguese colonists who ventured to those regions learned to adapt to indigenous societies and customs: they ate bread made of manioc flour, made use of native hammocks and canoes, and communicated in the Guaraní and Tupí languages. Indeed, indigenous languages flourish even today throughout much of Latin America: among the more prominent are Nahuatl in Mexico; K'iché in Guatemala; Guaraní in Paraguay; and Quechua in the Andean highlands of Peru, Ecuador, and Bolivia.

Spanish and Portuguese peoples saw the Western Hemisphere more as a land to exploit and administer than as a place to settle and colonize. Nevertheless, sizable contingents of migrants settled permanently in the Americas. Between 1500 and 1800, upwards of five hundred thousand Spanish migrants crossed the Atlantic, alongside one hundred thousand Portuguese. Their presence contributed to the making of a much more globalized world—a world characterized by meaningful encounters between the peoples of Europe, Africa, and the Americas—in the Western Hemisphere.

Settler Colonies in North America

Throughout the sixteenth century, Spanish explorers sought opportunities north of Mexico and the Caribbean. They established towns, forts, and missions from modern Florida as far north as Virginia on the east coast of North America, and they scouted shorelines off Maine and Newfoundland. On the west coast they ventured into modern Canada and established a fort on Vancouver Island. By mid-century, French, English, and Dutch mariners sailed the North Atlantic in search of fish and a northwest passage to Asia, and by the early seventeenth century they were dislodging Spanish colonists north of Florida. Their search for a northwest passage proved fruitless, but they harvested immense quantities of fish from the cod-filled banks off Labrador, Newfoundland, Nova Scotia, and New England.

Foundation of Colonies In the early seventeenth century explorers began to establish permanent colonies on the North American mainland. French settlers established colonies at Port Royal (Nova Scotia) in 1604 and Quebec in 1608. During the seventeenth and eighteenth centuries, French migrants settled in eastern Canada, and French explorers and traders scouted the St. Lawrence, Ohio, and Mississippi Rivers, building forts all the way to the Gulf of Mexico. Meanwhile, English migrants founded Jamestown in 1607 and the Massachusetts Bay Colony in 1630, and proceeded to establish colonies along the east coast of the present-day United States of America. Dutch entrepreneurs built a settlement at New Amsterdam in 1623, but the colony did not remain long in Dutch hands: an English fleet seized it in 1664, rechristened it New York, and absorbed it into English colonial holdings.

Life in those early settlements was extremely difficult. Most of the settlers did not expect to cultivate food crops but, rather, hoped to sustain their communities by producing valuable commodities such as fur, pitch, tar, or lumber, if not silver and gold. They relied heavily on provisions sent from Europe, and when supply ships did not arrive as expected, they sometimes avoided starvation only because indigenous peoples provided them with food. In Jamestown (located in present-day Virginia in the United States), food shortages and disease became so severe that only sixty of the colony's five hundred inhabitants survived the winter of 1609–1610.

Colonial Government The French and English colonies in North America differed in several ways from Spanish and Portuguese territories to the south. Whereas Iberian explorations had royal backing, private investors played larger roles in French and English colonial efforts. Individuals put up the money to finance expeditions to America, and they retained much more control over their colonies' affairs than did their Iberian counterparts. Although English colonies were always subject to royal authority, for example, they also maintained their own assemblies and influenced the choice of royal governors: there were no viceroys or *audiencias* in the North American colonies. At the conclusion of the Seven Years' War in 1763, the French colony in Canada fell under British control, and it, too, soon acquired institutions of self-government.

Relations with Indigenous Peoples French and English colonies differed from Iberian territories also in their relationships with indigenous peoples. French and English migrants did not find large, centralized states like the Aztec and Inca empires. Nor did they encounter agricultural peoples living in densely settled societies. Rather, the peoples of eastern North America had formed dozens of distinct societies, even though most spoke Algonquian, Iroquois, or Lakota languages. Many practiced agriculture, but most also relied on hunting and consequently moved their villages frequently in pursuit of game. They did not claim ownership of precisely bounded territories, but they regularly migrated between well-defined regions and utilized the resources of the land as they did so.

But when European settlers saw forested lands not bearing crops or supporting villages, they viewed them as "empty" and unclaimed. Even when lands had been in use by multiple Native American groups over many hundreds of years, Europeans believed they had the right to claim such lands. Thus, they staked out farms and excluded the indigenous peoples who had, over many centuries, used the lands during the

This painting of the English settlement at Jamestown in the early seventeenth century illustrates the precarious position of European settlers trying to live in the midst of indigenous people. Note the heavy palisades surrounding the settlement.
MPI/Archive Photos/Getty Images

course of their migrations. The availability of fertile farmland soon attracted large numbers of European migrants. Upwards of 150,000 English migrants moved to North America during the seventeenth century alone, and sizable French, German, Dutch, and Irish contingents joined them in the search for land.

European migrants took pains to justify their claims to American lands. English settlers in particular brought with them English legal structures such as treaties and property deeds that suggested land could be permanently transferred to individuals or groups. They fundamentally did not understand that the Native American way of life in the region depended on a very different way of using, and laying claim to, land. For Native American groups, using the land productively entailed keeping hunting grounds healthy, while for Europeans land could only be considered productive if under cultivation.

Conflict French and English settlers frequently clashed with indigenous peoples who resented intrusions on their hunting grounds and thus their means of survival, but the conflicts differed from the campaigns of conquest carried out by the conquistadores in Mexico and Peru. Although English settlers negotiated rights to American lands by treaty, native peoples did not accept that land should be used exclusively for one owner. When Europeans tried to insist on their exclusive use of land, Native Americans resisted by mounting raids on farms and villages. During an assault of 1622, for example, they killed almost one-third of the English settlers in the Chesapeake region. Attacks on European communities brought equally severe reprisals on Native American communities,

including the ruthless destruction of entire towns and villages. Edward Waterhouse, who survived the raid of 1622, went so far as to advocate annihilation of the indigenous population: "Victorie may bee gained many waies: by force, by surprize, by [causing] famine [through] burning their Corne, by destroying and burning their Boats, Canoes, and Houses, by breaking their fishing Weares [nets], by assailing them in their huntings, whereby they get the greatest part of their sustenance in Winter, by pursuing and chasing them with our horses, and blood-Hounds to draw after them, and Mastives [mastiffs] to teare them."

Indeed, a combination of epidemic disease and violent conflict dramatically reduced the indigenous population of North America between the sixteenth and nineteenth centuries. In 1492 the native population of the territory now embraced by the United States was greater than five million, perhaps as high as ten million. By the mid-sixteenth century, however, smallpox and other diseases had begun to spread north from Mexico and ravage native societies in the plains and eastern woodlands of North America. Between 1600 and 1800 about one million English, French, German, Dutch, Irish, and Scottish migrants crossed the Atlantic and sought to displace indigenous peoples as they pursued economic opportunities in North America. By 1800, indigenous peoples in the territory of the present-day United States numbered only six hundred thousand, as against almost five million settlers of European ancestry and about one million enslaved people of African ancestry. As with the Iberian incursions in the South, the European settlement of North America fundamentally transformed the Western Hemisphere.

SOURCES FROM THE PAST

Miantanamo's Call for Unity

Miantanamo (ca. 1600–1643) was a chief of the Narragansett tribe, which claimed territories in what is now Rhode Island, Connecticut, and eastern Massachusetts. In 1637 Miantanamo and the Narragansetts (along with other tribes) allied with the English against the Pequot tribe in what became known as the Pequot War. English settlers in Massachusetts nevertheless suspected him of trying to plot against them, and in 1640 he was brought to Boston where he successfully defended himself against these charges. In 1643 he assembled a force to attack his enemy of the Mohegan tribe, Uncas, but was caught. Uncas turned Miantanamo over to the English authorities in Connecticut. There they recommended the death penalty but asked Uncas to carry it out on Mohegan land. Miantanamo was executed at the command of Uncas in 1643. The speech below was given sometime in 1642 or 1643.

Brothers, we must be as one as the English are, or we shall all be destroyed. You know our fathers had plenty of deer and skins and our plains were full of game and turkeys, and our coves and rivers were full of fish.

But, brothers, since these Englishmen have seized our country, they have cut down the grass with scythes, and the trees with axes. Their cows and horses eat up the grass, and their hogs spoil our bed of clams; and finally we shall all starve to death; therefore, stand not in your own light, I ask you, but resolve to act like men. All the sachems both to the east and the west have joined with us, and we are resolved to fall upon them at a day appointed, and therefore I come secretly to you, cause you can persuade your Indians to do what you will.

> What are Miantanamo's main complaints about the presence of the English?

For Further Reflection

■ Given Miantanamo's complicated history of alliances with the English and against some other Native American tribes, is it possible to read Miantanamo's plea here at face value? How realistic was such a call to unity given this history of shifting alliances?

Source: http://www.digitalhistory.uh.edu/disp_textbook.cfm?smtid=3&psid=656 Original source: Herbert Milton Sylvester, *Indian Wars of New England* (Cleveland, 1910), vol. I, p. 386.

COLONIAL SOCIETY IN THE AMERICAS

The European migrants who flooded into the Western Hemisphere interacted both with the indigenous inhabitants and with African peoples whom they forcibly imported as enslaved laborers. Throughout the Americas, relations between individuals of American, European, and African ancestry soon led to the emergence of what were known at the time as **mestizo** populations. Notwithstanding such intercultural mixing, European peoples and their Euro-American offspring increasingly dominated political and economic affairs in the Americas. Using enslaved labor and Native American knowledge, they mined precious metals, cultivated cash crops such as sugar and tobacco, and trapped fur-bearing animals to supply capitalist markets that met the voracious demands of European and Asian consumers. Over time they also established their Christian religion as the dominant faith of the Western Hemisphere.

The Formation of Multicultural Societies

European migrants radically transformed the social order in the regions where they established imperial states or settler colonies, although it is important to remember that their influence only reached the American interior gradually. All European territories became multicultural societies where peoples of varied ancestry lived together under European or Euro-American dominance. Spanish and Portuguese territories soon became not only multicultural but ethnically mixed as well, largely because of migration patterns. Migrants to the Iberian colonies were overwhelmingly men: about 85 percent of the Spanish migrants were men, and the Portuguese migration was even more male-dominated than the Spanish. Because of the small numbers of European women, Spanish and Portuguese migrants tended to enter into relationships with indigenous women, which soon gave rise to an increasingly mixed ("mestizo") society.

Mestizo Society

Most Spanish migrants went to Mexico, where there was soon a growing population of mestizos—those of Spanish and native parentage, like the children of Doña Marina. Women were more prominent among the migrants to Peru

Indigenous Zapotec painter Miguel Mateo Maldonado y Cabrera (1695–1768) created this domestic portrait of a multicultural family in the viceroyalty of New Spain, today's Mexico. A Spanish man gazes at his Mexican Indian wife and their mestizo daughter.

Album/Alamy Stock Photo

than to Mexico, and Spanish colonists there lived mostly in cities, where they maintained a more distinct community than did their counterparts in Mexico. In the colonial cities, Spanish migrants married among themselves and re-created a European-style society. In less settled regions, however, Spanish men associated with indigenous women and gave rise to mestizo society.

With few European women available in Brazil, Portuguese men readily entered into relations—some consensual and some forced—both with indigenous women and with enslaved African women. Brazil soon had large populations not only of mestizos but also of people known as mulattoes, who were born of Portuguese and African parents; those known

as *zambos,* who were born of indigenous and African parents; and other combinations arising from these groups. Indeed, marriages between members of different racial and ethnic communities became common in colonial Brazil and generated a society even more thoroughly mixed than that of Mexico.

The Social Hierarchy In both Spanish and Portuguese colonies, migrants born in the Iberian peninsula in Europe (known as *peninsulares*) stood at the top of the social hierarchy. They were followed by *criollos,* or *creoles,* those born in the Americas of Iberian parents. In the early days of the colonies, mestizos lived on the fringes of society. As time went on, however, the numbers of mestizos grew, and they became essential contributors to their societies, especially in Mexico and Brazil. Meanwhile, mulattoes, *zambos,* and others of mixed parentage became prominent groups in Brazilian society, although they were usually subordinate to European migrants, Euro-American creoles, and even mestizos. In all the Iberian colonies, enslaved and conquered peoples stood at the bottom of the social hierarchy.

Sexual Hierarchies Race and ethnicity were crucial in shaping a person's position and role in colonial society. But the defining factor in both Spanish and Portuguese America was the existence of a clear sexual hierarchy that privileged men. Women lived in a patriarchal world, where men occupied positions of power and delineated the boundaries of acceptable female behavior. Although there were exceptions to the rule, women's power tended to be expressed informally through their influence on relationships and in domestic duties. Only when it came to punishing disobedient slaves did society ignore gender—both male and female slaves could count on the same harsh punishment, which usually took the form of flogging.

Gender alone, however, did not explain the diverse experiences of women in colonial society. Commonly, the ratio of men to women in a given community either enhanced or limited women's choices. Women's experiences also varied with the degree of prosperity and the nature of the local economy. As women moved from childhood through marriage and motherhood, to being widows or "spinsters," their experiences and roles in society likewise underwent change. Race and class usually figured as powerful forces shaping women's lives. Women of European descent, though under strict patriarchal control and under pressure to conform to the stereotype of female dependence and passivity, sometimes used their elite position to their advantage. By necessity, women of color and those from the low class became part of the colonial labor force, performing tasks closely tied to the commercialization of traditional female work such as food preparation, laundering, and weaving. Although poor, these women were freer to move about in public and to interact with others than were their elite counterparts. The most disadvantaged women were black, mulatta, and zamba slaves,

peninsulares (pehn-IHN-soo-LAH-rayz)
criollos (kree-OH-lohs)

who were required to perform hard physical tasks such as planting and cutting cane or working as laundresses. Since they had few powerful protectors, such women were also frequently the targets of forced sexual relationships with European men.

North American Societies The social structure of the French and English colonies in North America differed markedly from that of the Iberian colonies. Women were more numerous among the French and especially the English migrants than in Spanish and Portuguese communities, and settlers tended to marry within their own groups. Although French fur traders often associated with native women and generated *métis* (French for "mixed") in regions around forts and trading posts, in French colonial cities such as Port Royal and Quebec, liaisons between French and native peoples were less common.

Mingling between peoples of different ancestry was least common in the English colonies of North America. Colonists disdained the indigenous peoples they encountered and regarded them as heathens who did not recognize private property and did not exert themselves to cultivate the land. Later, they also scorned imported enslaved Africans as inferior beings. Those attitudes fueled a virulent racism, as English settlers attempted to maintain sharp boundaries between themselves and peoples of Native American and African ancestry.

Yet English settlers nevertheless interacted with American and African peoples, and they readily borrowed useful cultural elements from other communities. They learned about American plants and animals, for example, and they used indigenous terms to refer to unfamiliar animals such as raccoons and opossums or trees such as hickory and pecan. They adapted moccasins and deerskin clothes, and they gave up European military customs of marching in massed ranks and announcing their presence with drums and flying colors. From enslaved peoples they borrowed African food crops and techniques for the cultivation of rice. Yet, unlike their Iberian neighbors to the south, the English settlers discouraged relationships between individuals of different ancestry and sometimes refused to accept or even acknowledge offspring of mixed parentage.

Mining and Agriculture in the Spanish Empire

From the Spanish perspective the greatest attractions of the Americas were precious metals, which drew thousands of migrants from all levels of Spanish society. The conquistadores thoroughly looted the easily accessible treasures of the Aztec and Inca empires. Ignoring the artistic or cultural value of artifacts, the conquerors simply melted down silver and gold treasures and fashioned them into ingots. Their followers opened mines to extract the mineral wealth of the Americas in more systematic fashion.

Silver Mining Gold was not the most abundant American treasure. Silver far outweighed gold in quantity and value, and much of Spain's American enterprise focused on its extraction. Silver production concentrated on two areas: the thinly populated Mexican north, particularly the region around **Zacatecas,** and the high, cold central Andes, particularly the stunningly rich mines of **Potosí** (present-day Bolivia). Both sites employed large numbers of indigenous laborers. Many laborers went to Zacatecas voluntarily as their home villages experienced the pressures of conquest and disease. Over time they became professional miners, spoke Spanish, and lost touch with the communities of their birth.

Meanwhile, Spanish prospectors discovered a large vein of silver near Potosí in 1545 and began large-scale mining there in the 1580s. By 1600 Potosí was a boomtown with a population of 150,000. Rapid growth created an explosive demand for labor. As in the Mexican mines, Spanish administrators relied mostly on voluntary labor, but they also adapted the Inca practice of requisitioning draft labor, known as the ***mita system,*** to recruit workers for particularly difficult and dangerous chores that free laborers would not accept. Under the *mita* system, Spanish authorities annually required each village to send one-seventh of its male population to work for four months in the mines at Potosí. Draft laborers received payment for their work, but wages were very low, and the conditions of work were extremely harsh. Some *mita* laborers hauled heavy baskets of silver ore up steep mine shafts, while others worked with toxic mercury, which miners used to separate the silver from its ore. Death rates of draft laborers were high, and many indigenous men sought to evade *mita* obligations by fleeing to cities or hiding in distant villages. Thus, even though at any given moment draft laborers represented only about 10 percent of the workforce at Potosí, the *mita* system touched a large portion of the indigenous population and influenced settlement patterns throughout the Andean region.

The Global Significance of Silver The mining industries of Mexico and Peru powered the Spanish economy in the Americas and even stimulated the world economy of early modern times. Silver produced profits for private investors and revenues for the crown. The Spanish government reserved a fifth of the silver production for itself. This share, known as the ***quinto***, represented the principal revenue that the crown derived from its American possessions. American silver helped Spanish kings finance a powerful army and bureaucracy, but much of it also went well beyond Spain to lubricate the European and the larger world economies.

---

métis (may-TEE)

Zacatecas (sah-kah-TEH-kahs)

Potosí (paw-taw-SEE)

quinto (KEEN-toh)

Mining operations at Potosí in South America gave rise to a large settlement that housed miners and others who supplied food, made charcoal, fashioned tools, and supported the enterprise. In this illustration from the mid-1580s, llamas laden with silver ore descend the mountain (background) while laborers work in the foreground to crush the ore and extract pure silver from it.
Courtesy of the Hispanic Society of America, New York.

Most American silver made its way across the Atlantic to Spain and markets throughout Europe, and from there European merchants traded it for silk, spices, and porcelain in the markets of Asia. Some silver went from Acapulco on the west coast of Mexico across the Pacific to the Philippines in the **Manila galleons,** and from Manila it also made its way to Asian markets, especially China. No matter which direction it went or which oceans it crossed, American silver quickly traveled throughout the world and powerfully stimulated global trade.

The Hacienda Apart from mining, the principal occupations in Spanish America were farming, stock raising, and craft production. The organization of mining industries created opportunities for cultivators, herders, and artisans to provision mining towns with food, wine, textiles, tools, furniture, and craft items. By the seventeenth century the most prominent site of agricultural and craft production in Spanish America was the estate, or **hacienda,** which produced foodstuffs for its own use as well as for sale to local markets in nearby mining districts, towns, and cities. The products of the hacienda were mostly of European origin: wheat, grapes, and meat from pigs and cattle were the most prominent agricultural products. Bordering the large estates were smaller properties owned by Spanish migrants or creoles as well as sizable

tracts of land held by indigenous peoples who lived in native villages and practiced subsistence agriculture.

Labor Systems The major source of labor for the haciendas was the indigenous population. Spanish conquerors first organized native workforces under the *encomienda* system. As originally developed in Spain during the era of the *reconquista* (see chapter 19), the *encomienda* system rewarded Spanish conquerors by allowing them to exact both labor and tribute from defeated Moorish populations, while in theory requiring the *encomenderos* to look after the physical and spiritual welfare of their workers. Later, Spanish conquerors transferred the system to the Caribbean, Mexico, Central America, and Andean South America. From the 1520s to the 1540s, the *encomienda* system led to rampant abuse of indigenous peoples, as Spanish landowners overworked their laborers and skimped on their maintenance. After mid-century, *encomenderos* in agriculturally productive regions increasingly required their subject populations to provide tribute but not labor. Populations living under indigenous leadership owned much of the land that they cultivated in villages. In some ways, their payments to Spanish colonists resembled the tributes their ancestors had provided to Aztec rulers.

As the *encomienda* system gradually went out of use, Spanish landowners resorted to a system of debt peonage to recruit labor for their haciendas. Under this system, landowners advanced loans to native peoples so that they could buy

hacienda (ah-SYEN-dah)

seeds, tools, and supplies. The debtors then repaid the loans with labor, but wages were so low that they were never able to pay off their debts. Because legal restrictions often prevented debtors from leaving their lands and escaping their obligations, landowners had in effect a captive labor force to work their estates. In effect, then, the line between debt peonage and slavery was not always clear, and indeed the system is sometimes referred to as "debt slavery."

Resistance to Spanish Rule The Spanish regimes in the Americas met considerable resistance from indigenous peoples. Resistance took various forms: rebellion, work slowdowns, and retreat into the mountains and forests where Spanish power did not reach. In 1680, for example, after experiencing nearly a century of forced labor on Spanish estates, several indigenous groups in northern Mexico (the modern-day American state of New Mexico) mounted a large uprising known as the Pueblo revolt. Led by an indigenous shaman named Popé, the rebels attacked missions, killed priests and colonists, and drove Spanish settlers out of the region for twelve years. Spanish forces in Peru faced an even larger rebellion in 1780, when a force of about sixty thousand native peoples revolted in the name of Túpac Amaru, the last of the Inca rulers, whom Spanish conquistadores had beheaded in 1572. This rebellion raged for almost two years before Spanish forces suppressed it and executed thousands of its participants.

On some occasions, indigenous peoples turned also to Spanish law and administrators in search of aid against oppressive colonists. In 1615, for example, Felipe Guaman Poma de Ayala, a native of Peru, fired off a 1,200-page letter—accompanied by some four hundred hand-drawn illustrations—to King Philip III of Spain asking for protection for indigenous

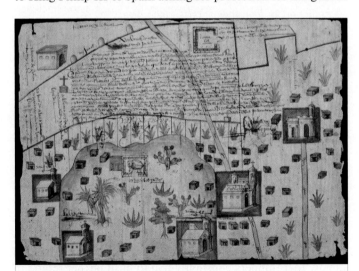

Map drawn in 1569 of Spanish settlement around the Hacienda de Santa Ines in New Spain. The map was intended to be a legal document between Spanish settlers and indigenous inhabitants of the area. Newberry Library.

peoples against greedy colonists. Although Guaman Poma's letter never made it to the king, it somehow made its way to Denmark, where it remained undiscovered in a library until 1908.

Nevertheless, Guaman Poma's complaint serves as a record of grievances against the Spanish. The author wrote passionately of men ruined by overtaxation and women driven to prostitution, of Spanish colonists who grabbed the lands of indigenous peoples and Spanish priests who preyed sexually upon the wives of indigenous men. Guaman Poma warned the king that the peoples of Peru were dying fast because of disease and abuse and that if Philip wanted anything to remain of his Andean empire, he should intervene and protect the indigenous peoples of the land.

Sugar and Slavery in Brazil

Whereas the Spanish American empire concentrated on the extraction of silver, the Portuguese Empire in Brazil depended on the production and export of sugar. The different economic and social foundations of the Spanish and Portuguese empires led to different patterns of labor recruitment. Spanish conquistadores subjugated sedentary peoples with effective administrative systems and compelled them to provide labor in the mines and estates of Mexico and Peru. Portuguese nobles and entrepreneurs established sugar plantations in regions without the administrative machinery to recruit workers and relied instead on imported enslaved Africans as laborers. Indeed, Africans and their descendants became the majority of the population in Brazil, not simply an auxiliary labor force as in Spanish America.

The Engenho Colonial Brazilian life revolved around the sugar mill, or *engenho.* Strictly speaking, the term *engenho* (related to the English word *engine*) referred only to the mill itself, but it came to represent a complex of land, labor, buildings, animals, capital, and technical skills related to the production of sugar. Unlike other crops, sugarcane required extensive processing to yield molasses or refined sugar as a profitable export. Thus *engenhos* always combined agricultural and industrial enterprises. They depended both on heavy labor for the planting and harvesting of cane and on the specialized skills of individuals who understood the intricacies of the sugar-making process. As a result, *engenhos* were among the most complex business enterprises in the Americas.

In a colonial economy where sugar figured as the most important export, the Portuguese planters and owners of sugar mills were a privileged class, exercising political, social, and economic power. As long as they contributed to the government's revenues, they could usually count on strong royal support. The planters acted like landed nobility, but the nature of their enterprises required them to pay attention to affairs like businessmen. They operated on very small profit margins. Their exalted social position often disguised difficult financial predicaments, and turnover in the business was always high.

engenho (en-GEHN-ho)

The Search for Labor Like their Spanish counterparts, Portuguese colonists first tried to enlist local populations as laborers. Unlike the inhabitants of Mexico and Peru, however, the peoples of Brazil were not sedentary cultivators. They resisted efforts to commandeer their labor, evaded Portuguese forces by retreating to interior lands, and took every opportunity to escape captors who managed to force them into servitude. In addition, as elsewhere in the Americas, epidemic diseases devastated indigenous populations in Brazil. During the 1560s, smallpox and measles ravaged the whole Brazilian coast, making it difficult for Portuguese settlers even to find potential laborers, let alone force them to work.

Slavery Faced with those difficulties, the colonists turned to another labor source: enslaved Africans. As we saw in chapter 22, Iberians had been using the labor of enslaved Africans on the Canary and Madeira islands since the late fifteenth century. Using this experience as their guide, Portuguese plantation managers in Brazil imported enslaved people as early as the 1530s, but they began to rely on African labor on a large scale only in the 1580s. The labor demands of cane cultivation and sugar production exacted a heavy toll from enslaved communities, who faced arduous working conditions, physical and sexual abuse, tropical heat, poor nutrition, and inadequate housing. These conditions resulted in high rates of disease and mortality for enslaved Africans in Brazil. In any given year, 5 to 10 percent of slaves on engenhos died from such conditions. In Brazil, as in most other plantation societies, the number of deaths in the slave population usually exceeded the number of births, so there was a constant demand for more slaves.

Although a few Portuguese criticized this brutal system, government officials mostly left matters of labor management to slaveholders. To them the balance sheet of sugar production dictated practices that paid scant heed to the preservation of the lives of enslaved people, as long as the owners realized profits. Indeed, if an enslaved person lived five to six years, the investment of the average slaveholder doubled and permitted him to purchase a new and healthy enslaved person without taking a monetary loss. As a result, slaveholders had little economic incentive to improve conditions for enslaved people or to increase their birthrates. Children required financial outlays for at least twelve years, which from the perspective of the slaveholder represented a financial loss. All told, the business of producing Brazilian sugar was so brutal that every ton of the sweet substance cost one human life.

Fur Traders and Settlers in North America

The Fur Trade European mariners first frequented North American shores in search of fish. Although fishing was a profitable enterprise, trade in furs became far more lucrative. The North American **fur trade** began when fishermen bartered for fur with local peoples. After explorers found a convenient entrance to rich fur-producing regions through the Hudson Strait and Hudson Bay, they began the systematic exploitation

An illustration from a nineteenth-century painting showing Native Americans trading pelts onboard Henry Hudson's ship, in Nova Scotia in 1609. Hudson (born ca. 1560s/1570s) was an English explorer and navigator, who repeatedly searched for a northwest passage to Asia.
Bettmann/Getty Images

of the northern lands. Royal agents, adventurers, businessmen, and settlers began to connect large parts of the North American interior by a chain of forts and trading posts. Indigenous peoples trapped animals for Europeans and exchanged the pelts for manufactured goods such as wool blankets, iron pots, firearms, and distilled spirits. The hides went mostly to Europe, where capitalist markets experienced burgeoning demand for beaver skin hats and fur clothing.

Effects of the Fur Trade The fur trade generated tremendous conflict in North America. American beaver populations, which were the chief targets of the trade, declined so rapidly that trappers constantly had to push farther inland in search of untapped beaver grounds. When hunting grounds became depleted, indigenous peoples poached or invaded others' territories, which sometimes led to war. Among the most brutal of those conflicts were the French and Iroquois Wars (also called the Beaver Wars) of the seventeenth century, which pitted Iroquois against Hurons and their French allies.

The Iroquois sought to expand their diminished hunting grounds into the territory of the Hurons (and others) to the north and thus maintain their livelihoods in the fur trade.

Competition between Native American groups over the fur trade was complicated by rivalries between European groups. During the French and Iroquois Wars, the Iroquois were allied with the Dutch, while the Huron were allied with the French. The Iroquois used firearms supplied by the Dutch in their campaign to control the fur trade in Huron territory, and in the process tried to eliminate their enemies. Hurons survived the war, although in greatly diminished numbers, but the Iroquois vastly increased their strength and destroyed Huron power.

Settler Society European settler-cultivators posed an even more serious challenge to native ways of life than did the fur traders because they displaced indigenous peoples from the land and turned hunting grounds into plantations. The earliest colonists experienced difficult times because European crops such as wheat did not grow well in their settlements. Indeed, many of the early colonies would have perished except for maize, game, and fish supplied by indigenous peoples. Over time, however, French and especially English migrants stabilized their societies and distinguished them sharply from those of indigenous peoples.

Tobacco and Other Cash Crops As colonists' numbers increased, they sought to integrate their American holdings into the larger capitalist economy of the Atlantic Ocean basin by producing cash crops that they could market in Europe. In the English colonies of Virginia and Carolina, settlers concentrated on the cultivation of **tobacco,** a plant they learned about from Native American societies. Christopher Columbus had observed Taíno people smoking the leaves of a local plant through a pipe called a *tobago*—the origin of the word *tobacco*. Later, European visitors frequently observed

This painting features the "first smoke" of Sir Walter Raleigh (1552–1618). He was an English aristocrat, writer, poet, soldier, courtier, spy, and explorer. He is also well known for popularizing tobacco in England.
The Picture Art Collection/Alamy Stock Photo

tobacco consumption among indigenous peoples, who had been using the plant for two thousand years for ritual, medicinal, and social purposes. Maya worshipers blew tobacco smoke from their mouths as offerings to the gods. Priests of the Aztec Empire both smoked tobacco and took it in the form of snuff as an accompaniment to religious sacrifices.

The widespread popularity of this plant was due to the addictive nature of nicotine, an oily, toxic substance present in tobacco leaves. The word "nicotine" comes from the French diplomat, Jean Nicot, who introduced tobacco use to Paris in

What's Left Out? ▬▬ ▬▬ ▬▬ ▬▬ ▬▬

The history of slavery in North America has, until recently, focused mainly on enslaved Africans in what became the American South. Although many textbooks acknowledge that the northern colonies also permitted slavery for a time, these colonies have nevertheless usually been depicted as less dependent on slave labor. Moreover, a large body of historical work once argued that Native Americans were unwilling or unable to tolerate slavery and thus were not commonly enslaved by Europeans. Recent scholarship, however, is revising these longstanding perceptions. Indeed, during the seventeenth and eighteenth centuries, New England colonists enslaved many thousands of Native Americans and depended on their labor to build new lives for themselves. During both the Pequot War (1630s) and King Philip's War (1670s), thousands of Native Americans were captured and sold into slavery. King Philip's War, in fact, had erupted in part because a Wampanoag-led coalition protested the use of forced Indian labor. But the war ended in defeat for the Wampanoags and did not end the practice of enslaving indigenous peoples. Instead, one study shows that after the war nearly 40 percent of Indians remaining in the southern portion of New England were serving as slaves or indentured servants in English households. In addition, European colonists in Virginia, North Carolina, and South Carolina similarly enslaved and traded indigenous peoples. These practices continued until the late eighteenth century, when large numbers of enslaved Africans began to displace indigenous slaves. In what ways can new information such as this add, nuance or even alter our perceptions about the early history of the United States?

Source: Margaret Ellen Newell, *Brethren by Nature: New England Indians, Colonists, and the Origins of American Slavery* (Ithaca: Cornell University Press, 2015).

1560. Spanish and English promoters first touted the health benefits of tobacco to European consumers. Many physicians ascribed miraculous healing powers to tobacco, which they referred to as "the herb panacea," "divine tobacco," or the "holy herb nicotine." Merchants and mariners soon spread the use of tobacco throughout Europe and beyond to all parts of the world that European ships visited.

In 1612, English settlers cultivated the first commercial crop of tobacco in Virginia. By 1616, Virginia colonists exported 2,300 pounds of tobacco. European demand for the addictive weed resulted in skyrocketing exports amounting to 200,000 pounds in 1624 and three million pounds in 1638. By the late seventeenth century, most consumers used tobacco socially and for pleasure because tobacco's alleged health benefits never lived up to expectations. By the eighteenth century settlers in the southern colonies had established plantation complexes that produced rice and indigo as well as tobacco, and by the nineteenth century cotton also had become a prominent plantation crop.

Indentured Labor The plantations created high demand for inexpensive labor. Colonists in North America enslaved indigenous peoples in large numbers, but still the demand for labor grew. By the seventeenth century, colonists began to recruit indentured servants from Europe to increase the supply of labor. People who had little future in Europe—the chronically unemployed, orphans, political prisoners, and criminals—were often willing to sell a portion of their working lives in exchange for passage across the Atlantic and a new start in life. Throughout the seventeenth and eighteenth centuries, indentured servants came to the American colonies in hopes that after they had satisfied their obligation to provide four to seven years of labor they might become independent artisans or planters themselves. (The **indentured labor** trade in the Americas continued on a smaller scale even into the early twentieth century.) Some indentured servants went on to become prominent figures in colonial society, but many died of disease or overwork before completing their terms of labor, and others found only marginal employment.

Slavery in North America Most indentured servants eventually gained their freedom, but other laborers remained in bondage all their lives. Like Iberian colonists, English settlers also used the labor of enslaved Africans in their colonial territories. In 1619 a group of about twenty Africans was brought to Virginia. While it took some time to determine the legal status of Africans, in 1661 Virginia law recognized all Africans as slaves. After 1680, planters increasingly replaced indigenous slaves and indentured servants with enslaved Africans. By 1750 about 120,000 enslaved Africans tilled Chesapeake tobacco, and 180,000 more cultivated Carolina rice.

Plantation labor was not prominent in the agricultural production of the northern colonies, principally because the land and the climate were not suitable for the cultivation of labor-intensive cash crops. But European settlers in the northern colonies also exploited both indigenous and African slave labor until slavery was outlawed in the late eighteenth and early nineteenth centuries. In addition, the economies of these colonies also profited handsomely from slavery. Many New England merchants traded in enslaved people destined for the West Indies: by the mid-eighteenth century, half the merchant fleet of Newport carried human cargo. The economies of New York and Philadelphia benefited from the building and outfitting of slave vessels, and the seaports of New England became profitable centers for the distillation of rum. The chief ingredient of this rum was slave-produced sugar from the West Indies, and merchants traded much of the distilled spirits for enslaved people on the African coast. Thus, although the southern plantation societies became most directly identified with a system that exploited African labor, all the North American colonies participated in and profited from the slave trade.

Christianity and Indigenous Religions in the Americas

Like Buddhists and Muslims in earlier centuries, Christian explorers, conquerors, merchants, and settlers took their religious traditions with them when they traveled overseas. Centuries of warfare against Muslims had convinced the Spanish monarchs that non-Christians should be converted to Christianity. In the aftermath of Christopher Columbus's voyages, Queen Isabella of Spain asserted that the indigenous peoples of the Western Hemisphere were her subjects, and as such had to be converted to Christianity. Thus, when Spanish conquistadores, colonists, and priests came to the Americas, they came both as conquerors as well as evangelists. In the long term, their conversion efforts succeeded, but in the process Catholicism evolved into a religion that integrated Christian concepts with aspects of indigenous beliefs and traditions.

Spanish Missionaries From the beginning of Spanish colonization in Mexico and Peru, Roman Catholic priests served as representatives of the crown and reinforced civil administrators. Franciscan, Dominican, Jesuit, and other missionaries campaigned to Christianize indigenous peoples. In Mexico, for example, a group of twelve Franciscan missionaries arrived in 1524. They founded a school in Tlatelolco, the bustling market district of the Aztec capital of Tenochtitlan, where they educated the sons of prominent noble families in Latin, Spanish, and Christian doctrine. The missionaries themselves learned native languages and sought to explain Christianity in terms their audiences could understand. They also compiled a vast amount of information about indigenous societies in hopes of learning how best to communicate their message. The work of the Franciscan Bernardino de Sahagún was especially important. Sahagún preserved volumes of information about the language, customs, beliefs, literature, and history of Mexico before the arrival of Spanish forces there (a tiny portion of which can be seen in the first "Sources of the Past"

An eighteenth-century engraving depicts work on a tobacco plantation: several enslaved Africans prepare flour and bread from manioc (left), while others hang tobacco leaves to dry in a shed (right). The illustration helps capture the labor intensity of plantation life for enslaved peoples.
Everett Collection/age fotostock

selection in this chapter). His work remained largely unstudied until the twentieth century, but in recent times it has shed enormous light both on Aztec society and on the methods of early missionaries in Mexico.

Survival of Indigenous Religions Christian missionaries encountered considerable resistance in the Americas. In both Mexico and Peru, indigenous peoples continued to observe their inherited faiths into the seventeenth century and beyond, even though Spanish authorities sponsored the Roman Catholic faith and tried to eliminate the worship of indigenous gods. In the face of Spanish persecution, indigenous peoples often continued their religious practices in locations inaccessible to Catholic priests.

Yet Christianity also won adherents in Spanish America. In the wake of conquest and epidemic disease, many indigenous leaders in Mexico concluded that their gods had abandoned them and looked to the missionaries for spiritual guidance. When indigenous peoples adopted Christianity, however, they blended their own interests and traditions with the faith taught by Spanish missionaries. When they learned about Roman Catholic saints, for example, they revered saints with qualities like those of their inherited gods or those whose feast days coincided with traditional celebrations.

The Virgin of Guadalupe In Mexico, Roman Catholicism became especially popular after the mid-seventeenth century. One reason for this was the **Virgin of Guadalupe,** who came to be worshipped almost as a national symbol. According to legends, the Virgin Mary appeared before the devout peasant Juan Diego on a hill near Mexico City in 1531. The site of the apparition soon became a popular local shrine visited mostly by Spanish settlers. By the 1640s the shrine attracted pilgrims from all parts of Mexico, and the Virgin of Guadalupe gained a reputation for working miracles on behalf of individuals who visited her shrine. The Virgin of Guadalupe, with her darker, indigenous complexion, came to symbolize a distinctly Mexican faith, and in later years she became transformed as a result into a powerful symbol of Mexican nationalism. The popularity of the Virgin of Guadalupe helped to ensure not only that Roman Catholic Christianity would dominate cultural and religious matters in Mexico but also that Mexican religious faith would retain strong indigenous influences.

French and English Missions French and English missionaries did not attract nearly as many converts to Christianity in North America as their Spanish counterparts did in Mexico and Peru. In part this was because French and English colonists did not rule over conquered populations of sedentary cultivators: it was much more difficult to conduct missions among peoples who frequently moved about the countryside than among those who lived permanently in villages, towns, or cities. English colonists, moreover, displayed little interest in converting indigenous peoples to Protestantism. The colonists did not discourage converts, but they made little effort to seek them, nor did they welcome converted indigenous people into their agricultural and commercial society. In contrast, Catholic French missionaries worked actively among native communities in the St. Lawrence, Mississippi, and Ohio River valleys Their efforts, however, were only modestly successful. Yet even though native peoples did not embrace Christianity, the burgeoning settlements of French and especially English colonists guaranteed that European religious traditions would figure prominently in North American society.

Virgin of Guadalupe (gwah-dah-LOO-pay)

Famed Mexican painter Miguel Cabrera crafted this eighteenth-century depiction of the Virgin of Guadalupe. Recognized as the greatest painter in New Spain, he featured in this work one of Mexico's most powerful religious icons.
Album/Alamy Stock Photo

EUROPEANS IN THE PACIFIC

Though geographically distant from the Americas, Australia and the Pacific Islands underwent experiences similar to those that transformed the Western Hemisphere in early modern times. Like their American counterparts, the peoples of Oceania had no inherited or acquired immunities to diseases that were common to peoples throughout the Eastern Hemisphere, and their numbers plunged when epidemic disease struck their populations. For the most part, however, the peoples of Australia and the Pacific Islands experienced epidemic disease and the arrival of European migrants later than did the peoples of the Americas. European mariners thoroughly explored the Pacific basin between the sixteenth and eighteenth centuries, but only in Guam and the Mariana Islands did they establish permanent settlements before the late eighteenth century. Nevertheless, their scouting of the region laid a foundation for much more intense interactions between European, Euro-American, Asian, and Oceanic peoples during the nineteenth and twentieth centuries.

Australia and the Larger World

At least from the second century C.E., European geographers had speculated about *terra australis incognita* ("unknown southern land") that they thought must exist in the world's southern hemisphere to balance the huge landmasses north of the equator. As European mariners explored the Atlantic and Pacific Oceans during early modern times, they searched expectantly for a southern continent. Yet their principal interest was trade, and they rarely abandoned the pursuit of profit to sail out of their way in search of an unknown land.

Dutch Exploration   Europeans first approached the Australian continent from the west in Southeast Asia. Portuguese mariners likely charted much of the western and northern coast of Australia as early as the 1520s, but Dutch sailors made the first recorded European sighting of the southern continent in 1606. The Dutch VOC (see chapter 22) authorized exploratory voyages, but mariners found little to encourage further efforts. In 1623, after surveying the dry landscapes of western Australia, the Dutch mariner Jan Carstenzs reported that his party had not seen "one fruit-bearing tree, nor anything that man could make use of: there are no mountains or even hills, so that it may be safely concluded that the land contains no metals, nor yields any precious woods." He went on to describe the land as "the most arid and barren region that could be found anywhere on earth."

Nevertheless, Dutch mariners continued to visit Australia. By the mid-seventeenth century, they had scouted the continent's northern, western, and southern coasts, and they had ascertained that New Guinea and Tasmania were islands separate from Australia itself. Dutch explorers were so active in the reconnaissance of Australia that Europeans referred to the southern continent as "New Holland" throughout the seventeenth century. Yet neither Dutch nor any other European seamen visited the eastern coast until **James Cook** approached Australia from the southeast and charted the region in 1770, barely escaping destruction on the Great Barrier Reef.

Although European mariners explored Australian coastlines in the seventeenth and eighteenth centuries, they made only brief landfalls and had only fleeting encounters with

MAP 24.2   Manila galleon route and the lands of Oceania, 1500–1800.

Note the route taken by the Manila galleons in relation to the majority of the Pacific Islands.

Why did Spanish mariners not explore the Hawaiian Islands and the more southerly Pacific Islands as they made their way to the Philippines?

indigenous peoples. The aboriginal peoples of Australia had formed many distinct foraging and fishing societies, but European visitors did not linger long enough to become familiar with either the peoples or their societies. Because they were nomadic foragers rather than sedentary cultivators, Europeans did not hold them in high regard. In the absence of tempting opportunities to trade, European mariners made no effort to establish permanent settlements in Australia.

British Colonists   Only after Cook's charting of the eastern coast in 1770 did European peoples become seriously interested in Australia. Cook dropped anchor for a week at Botany Bay (near modern Sydney) and reported that the region was suitable for settlement. In 1788 a British fleet arrived at Sydney carrying about one thousand passengers, eight hundred of them convicts, who established the first European settlement in Australia as a penal colony. For half a century Europeans in Australia numbered only a few thousand, most of them convicts who herded sheep. Free settlers did not outnumber convicted criminals until the 1830s. Thus exploratory voyages of the seventeenth and eighteenth centuries led to fleeting encounters between European and aboriginal Australian peoples, but only in the nineteenth and twentieth centuries did a continuing stream of European settlers link Australia more directly to the larger world.

The Pacific Islands and the Larger World

The entry of European mariners into the Pacific Ocean basin did not bring immediate change to most of the Pacific Islands. In these islands, as in Australia, European merchants and settlers did not arrive in large numbers until the late eighteenth century. Guam and the Mariana Islands underwent dramatic change already in the sixteenth century, however, and the ventures of European merchants and explorers in the Pacific basin set the stage for profound upheavals in other island societies during the nineteenth and twentieth centuries.

Spanish Voyages in the Pacific   In 1521 Ferdinand Magellan and his crew became the first Europeans to cross the Pacific Ocean. Before reaching the Philippines, they encountered only one inhabited island group—the Marianas, dominated by Guam. In 1565 Spanish mariners inaugurated the Manila galleon trade between Manila and Acapulco. Because their primary goal was to link New Spain to Asian markets, they rarely went out of their way to explore the Pacific Ocean or to search for other islands. Spanish vessels visited the Marquesas, Tuamotu, Cook, Solomon, and New Hebrides islands in the sixteenth century, and it is likely that one or more stray ships accidentally ended up in Hawai'i. Yet Spanish mariners found little to interest them in most of the Pacific islands and did not establish regular communications with island peoples. They usually sailed before the trade winds from Acapulco to Manila on a route that took them south of Hawai'i and north of other Polynesian islands. On the return trip they sailed before the westerlies on a route that took them well north of all the Pacific Islands.

Guam The only Pacific Islands that attracted substantial Spanish interest in the sixteenth century were Guam and the northern Mariana Islands. Manila galleons called regularly at Guam, which lay directly on the route from Acapulco to Manila. For more than a century, they took on fresh provisions and engaged in mostly peaceful trade with the indigenous Chamorro people. During the 1670s and 1680s, Spanish authorities decided to consolidate their position in Guam and bring the Mariana Islands under the control of the viceroy of New Spain in Mexico. They dispatched military forces to the islands to impose Spanish rule and subject the Chamorro to the spiritual authority of the Roman Catholic church. The Chamorro strongly opposed those efforts, but a smallpox epidemic in 1688 severely reduced their numbers and crippled their resistance. By 1695 the Chamorro population had declined from about fifty thousand at mid-century to five thousand, partly because of Spanish campaigns but mostly because of smallpox. By the end of the seventeenth century, Spanish forces had established garrisons throughout the Mariana Islands and relocated surviving Chamorro into communities supervised by Spanish authorities.

Visitors and Trade Like the aboriginal peoples of Australia, the indigenous peoples of the Pacific Islands had mostly fleeting encounters with European visitors during early modern times. By the late eighteenth century, however,

growing European and Euro-American interest in the Pacific Ocean basin led to sharply increased interactions between islanders and mariners. English and French mariners explored the Pacific basin in search of commercial opportunities and the elusive northwest passage from Europe to Asia. They frequently visited Tahiti after 1767, and they soon began to trade with the islanders, whose societies were complex and highly stratified by social class and by occupation (discussed in greater depth in chapter 20). European mariners received provisions and engaged in sexual relations with Tahitian women in exchange for nails, knives, iron tools, and textiles. Although trade was mostly peaceful, misunderstandings based on European ignorance about social practices often led to skirmishes and acts of violence, and European captains occasionally trained their cannons on fleets of war canoes or villages in the Pacific Islands.

Captain Cook and Hawai'i The experiences of Captain James Cook in Hawai'i illustrate a common pattern. In 1778, while sailing north from Tahiti in search of the northwest passage, Cook happened across the Hawaiian Islands. He immediately recognized Hawaiians as a people related to Tahitians and other Polynesians whose lands he had visited during his explorations of the Pacific Ocean since 1768, and he was able to communicate with Hawaiians on the basis of familiarity with Polynesian languages. Cook and his crew mostly got along well with Hawaiians, who readily traded pigs and provisions for ironwares. Sailors and island women avidly consorted with one another, resulting in the transmission of venereal diseases to Hawai'i, even though Cook had ordered infected crewmen to remain aboard ship. After a few weeks' stay in the islands, Cook resumed his northern course to seek the northwest passage. When he revisited Hawai'i late in 1779, he faced a very different climate, one in which islanders were

As depicted in 1816 by artist Ludwig Choris, the port of Honolulu in the Hawaiian Islands was home to European ships, horses, cattle, and warehouses as well as Hawaiians inhabiting traditional dwellings.
Honolulu Museum of Art, Gift of the Honolulu Art Society, 1944 (12,161).

less accommodating than before. Indeed, he lost his life when disputes over petty thefts escalated into a bitter conflict between his crew and islanders of Hawai'i.

Nevertheless, in the wake of Cook, whose reports soon became known throughout Europe, whalers began to venture into Pacific waters in large numbers, followed by missionaries, merchants, and planters. By the early nineteenth century, European and Euro-American peoples had become prominent figures in all the major Pacific Islands groups. During the nineteenth and twentieth centuries, interactions among islanders, visitors, and migrants brought rapid and often unsettling change to Pacific Islands societies.

CONCLUSION

The Americas underwent thorough transformation in early modern times. Smallpox and other diseases sparked ferocious epidemics that devastated indigenous populations and undermined their societies. In the wake of severe depopulation, European peoples toppled imperial states, established mining and agricultural enterprises, imported enslaved African laborers, and founded colonies throughout much of the Western Hemisphere. Some indigenous peoples disappeared entirely as distinct groups. Others maintained their communities, identities, and cultural traditions but fell increasingly under the influence of European migrants and their Euro-American offspring. In Oceania only Guam and the Mariana Islands felt the full effects of epidemic disease and migration in the early modern era. By the late eighteenth century, however, European and Euro-American peoples with advanced technologies had thoroughly explored the Pacific Ocean basin, and epidemic diseases featured largely in their encounters with the peoples of Australia and the Pacific Islands. As a result, during the nineteenth and twentieth centuries, Oceania underwent a social transformation similar to the one experienced earlier by the Americas. These encounters in both regions profoundly shaped the course of their history into the modern era.

STUDY TERMS

Atahualpa (505)	mestizo (511)
audiencias (507)	*métis* (513)
Brazil (507)	*mita system* (513)
conquistadores (504)	Motecuzoma II (504)
criollos (512)	Nahuatl (500)
Doña Marina (500)	New Spain (507)
encomienda (502)	*peninsulares* (512)
engenho (515)	Potosí (513)
epidemic disease (503)	*quinto* (513)
Francisco Pizarro (504)	smallpox (503)
fur trade (516)	Taíno (502)
hacienda (514)	Tenochtitlan (501)
Hernán Cortés (500)	*terra australis incognita* (520)
indentured labor (518)	tobacco (517)
James Cook (520)	Virgin of Guadalupe (519)
Malintzin (500)	Zacatecas (513)
Manila galleons (514)	*zambos* (512)

FOR FURTHER READING

Rolena Adorno. *Guaman Poma: Writing and Resistance in Colonial Peru.* Austin, 2000. A native Andean, who came of age after the fall of the Inca Empire, tells Philip III of Spain of the evils of colonialism and the need for reform.

Colin G. Callaway. *New Worlds for All: Indians, Europeans, and the Remaking of Early America.*, 2nd ed. Baltimore, 2013. Scholarly synthesis examining interactions and cultural exchanges between European and indigenous American peoples.

William Cronon. *Changes in the Land: Indians, Colonists, and the Ecology of New England,* rev. ed. New York, 2003. New York, 1983. Brilliant study concentrating on the different ways English colonists and native peoples in colonial New England used the environment.

John H. Elliot. *Empires of the Atlantic World: Britain and Spain in America 1492–1830.* New Haven, 2006. Excellent comparative study of Spanish and English colonies in the Americas.

K. R. Howe. *Where the Waves Fall: A New South Sea Island History from First Settlement to Colonial Rule.* Honolulu, 1984. A thoughtful survey of Pacific Islands history emphasizing interactions between islanders and visitors.

John E. Kicza. *Resilient Cultures: America's Native Peoples Confront European Colonization, 1500–1800.* Upper Saddle River, N.J., 2002. A comprehensive comparative study assessing the impact of colonization on indigenous American peoples as well as native influences on American colonial history.

Karen Ordahl Kupperman. *Indians and English: Facing Off in Early America.* Ithaca, N.Y., 2000. Fascinating reconstruction of the early encounters between English and indigenous American peoples, drawing on sources from all parties to the encounters.

Kathleen Ann Meyers. *Neither Saints nor Sinners: Writing the Lives of Women in Spanish America.* New York, 2003. Examines female self-representation through the life writings of six seventeenth-century women in Latin America.

Matthew Restall, Lisa Sousa, and Kevin Terraciano, eds. *Mesoamerican Voices: Native Language Writings from Colonial Mexico, Yucatan, and Guatemala.* Cambridge, 2005. Composed between the sixteenth and eighteenth centuries, this collection of texts offers access to an important historical source.

Daniel Richter. *Facing East from Indian Country: A Native History of North America.* Cambridge, 2003. Explores the active ways Native American communities engaged with European colonization efforts into the interior of North America.

David J. Weber. *Bárbaros: Spaniards and Their Savages in the Age of Enlightenment.* New Haven, 2005. Pathbreaking and nuanced study of how Spanish administrators tried to forge a more enlightened policy toward native peoples.

Richard White. *The Middle Ground: Indians, Empires, and Republics in the Great Lakes Region, 1650–1815.* Cambridge, 1991. Insightful study of relations between French, English, and indigenous peoples in the Great Lakes region.

Africa and the Atlantic World

ZOOMING IN ON TRADITIONS AND ENCOUNTERS

An Enslaved Man's Long Trip Back to Africa

SLAVES PACKED BELOW AND ON DECK.

Young people held on board an illegal slave ship captured by the British in 1857.
Historia/Shutterstock

Between 1760 and 1792, a west African man named Thomas Peters crossed the Atlantic Ocean four times. In 1760, slave raiders captured Peters, whose original African name is unknown, marched him to the coast, and sold him to French slave merchants. He traveled in a slave ship to the French colony of Louisiana, where he probably worked on a sugar plantation. But Peters was not a docile servant. He attempted to escape at least three times, and his slaveholder punished him by beating him, branding him with a hot iron, and forcing him to wear shackles around his legs. During the 1760s his French slaveholder sold Peters to an English planter, and about 1770 a Scottish landowner in North Carolina bought him.

During the 1770s, as English colonists in North America prepared to rebel against the British government in the interests of "life, liberty, and the pursuit of happiness," enslaved people of African ancestry considered their own prospects and looked for ways to obtain freedom. Peters was among them. When war broke out in 1776, he made his way with his wife and daughter to British lines and joined the Black Pioneers, a company of people who had escaped slavery and who fought to maintain British rule in the colonies. When the colonists won the war, Peters escaped to Nova Scotia with his family and many other formerly enslaved people.

Slavery was illegal in Nova Scotia, but the white ruling elites forced people of African ancestry to till marginal lands and live in segregated villages. In hopes of improving their lot, some two hundred black families designated Peters as their spokesman and sent him to London to petition the government for better treatment or resettlement in a more favorable land. In 1790 Peters sailed to England, where he promoted the establishment of a colony for formerly enslaved people in Sierra Leone. His efforts succeeded, and the next year he returned to Nova Scotia to seek recruits for the colony. In 1792 he led 1,196 formerly enslaved people aboard a convoy of fifteen ships and began his fourth crossing of the Atlantic Ocean. The colonists arrived safely at Freetown, where Peters served as a leader of the new community. His time in Freetown was tense and short—the conditions Peters and his fellow colonists encountered fell far short of what they had been promised, and then only four months after arriving, Peters fell ill and died of malarial fever. Nevertheless, through his own life and experiences, Thomas Peters personified the links connecting the lands and peoples of the Atlantic Ocean basin and is remembered for his fight for black justice and self-determination in North America and West Africa.

CHAPTER OVERVIEW

The establishment of global trade networks in the early modern period brought deep change to sub-Saharan Africa. Commercial opportunities drew European vessels to the coast of west Africa, and maritime trade soon turned the attention of west African leaders to the Atlantic. Maritime commerce did not put an end to the trans-Saharan caravan trade that linked west Africa to the Mediterranean, but it helped promote the emergence of prosperous port cities and the establishment of powerful coastal kingdoms that traded through the ocean rather than the desert. In central and south Africa, European merchants brought the first substantial opportunities for long-distance trade because Muslim merchants had not ventured previously to those regions in large numbers.

Trade through the Atlantic profoundly affected African society because it included trade in human beings. Africans had made a place for slavery within their societies for centuries, and they had also supplied enslaved people to Muslim merchants who transported them to markets in the Mediterranean and the Indian Ocean basin. The Atlantic slave trade, however, operated on a vastly larger scale than the trans-Saharan slave trade, and it had more serious consequences for African society. Between the fifteenth and the nineteenth centuries, it not only siphoned millions of people from their societies but also provoked turmoil in large portions of sub-Saharan Africa because some peoples raided others' communities in search of captives for sale to slave traders.

The vast majority of Africans sold into the Atlantic slave trade went to destinations in the Caribbean or the Americas. Most worked on plantations cultivating cash crops for export, although some worked as domestic servants, miners, or laborers. Together they made up the largest forced migration in history before the nineteenth century and gave rise to an African diaspora in the Western Hemisphere. Under the restrictive conditions of slavery, they could not reconstitute African societies, but neither did people of European ancestry permit them to join Euro-American society. Instead, people of African ancestry preserved some African traditions and blended them with European and American traditions to create hybrid societies.

CHRONOLOGY	
1441	Beginning of the Portuguese slave trade
1464–1493	Reign of Sunni Ali
1464–1591	Songhay Empire
1506–1542	Reign of King Afonso I of Kongo
1623–1663	Reign of Queen Nzinga of Ndongo
1706	Execution of Dona Beatriz
1745–1797	Life of Olaudah Equiano
1793–1804	Haitian revolution
1807	End of the British slave trade
1865	Abolition of slavery in the United States

AFRICAN POLITICS AND SOCIETY IN EARLY MODERN TIMES

For perhaps three millennia (2000 B.C.E. to 1000 C.E.), Bantu-speaking peoples migrated throughout sub-Saharan Africa. Many organized themselves into villages governed by kinship groups rather than formal states. As their numbers grew, they devised political structures and built a series of chiefdoms and regional kingdoms. After the eighth century increased transregional trade encouraged the formation of large kingdoms and empires in west Africa and thriving city-states in east Africa.

In the early modern era, the influence of maritime trade across the Atlantic and Indian Oceans changed patterns of state development. Regional kingdoms replaced the imperial states of west Africa as peoples organized their societies to

Timbuktu, the commercial and cultural center of the Mali and Songhay empires, as sketched by a French traveler in 1828. Though in decline by that time, the city's mosques, mud-brick dwellings, and crowds of people suggest the prosperous city of an earlier era.
Everett Historical/Shutterstock

take advantage of Atlantic as well as trans-Saharan commerce. The city-states of east Africa fell under the domination of Portuguese merchant-mariners seeking commercial opportunities in the Indian Ocean basin. The extension of trade networks also led to the formation of regional kingdoms in central Africa and south Africa. As the volume of long-distance trade grew, both Islam and Christianity became more prominent in sub-Saharan African societies.

The States of West Africa and East Africa

Between the eighth and the sixteenth centuries, powerful kingdoms and imperial states ruled the savannas of west Africa. The earliest was the kingdom of **Ghana,** which originated perhaps as early as the fourth or fifth century and established its dominance in the region in the eighth century. By controlling and taxing the trans-Saharan trade in gold, the kings of Ghana gained the financial resources they needed to field a large army and influence affairs in much of west Africa. In the thirteenth century the **Mali Empire**

replaced Ghana as the preeminent power in west Africa, but the Mali rulers continued the Ghana policy of controlling trans-Saharan trade.

The Songhay Empire By the fifteenth century the Mali Empire had begun to weaken, and the expansive state of Songhay emerged to take its place as the dominant power of the western grasslands. Based in the trading city of Gao, Songhay rulers built a flourishing city-state perhaps as early as the eighth century. In the early fifteenth century, they rejected Mali authority and mounted raids deep into Mali territory. In 1464 the Songhay ruler **Sunni Ali** (reigned 1464–1493) embarked on a campaign to conquer his neighbors and consolidated the **Songhay Empire** (1464–1591). He brought the important trading cities of **Timbuktu** and **Jenne** under his control and used their wealth to dominate the central Niger valley.

Songhay Administration Sunni Ali built an elaborate administrative and military apparatus to oversee affairs in his realm. He appointed governors to provinces and instituted a hierarchy of command that turned his army into an effective military force. He also created an imperial navy to patrol the Niger River, which was an important commercial highway in the Songhay Empire. Songhay military might enabled Sunni Ali's successors to extend their authority north into the Sahara, east toward Lake Chad, and west toward the upper reaches of the Niger River.

Ghana (GAH-nuh)

Songhay (song-AHY)

Sunni Ali (soon-ee ah-lee)

Jenne (jehn-neh)

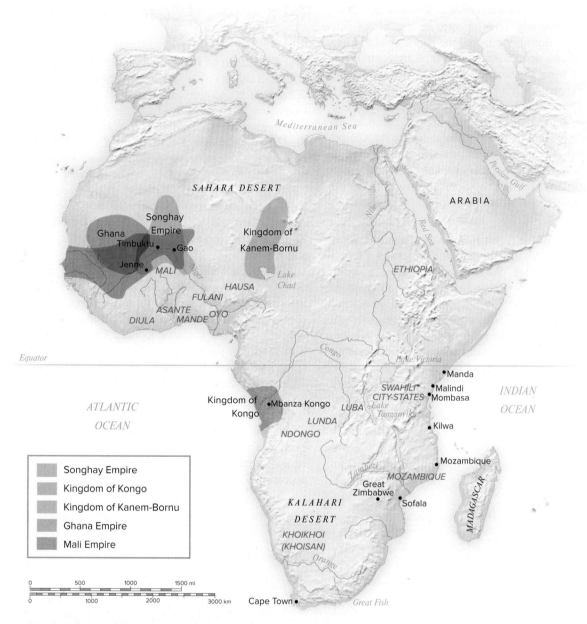

MAP 25.1 African states, 1500–1650.

Locate the three largest states of Songhay, Kongo, and Kanem-Bornu.

What was it about their respective locations that favored the development of such large polities?

The Songhay emperors presided over a prosperous land. The capital city of Gao had about seventy-five thousand residents, many of whom participated in the lucrative trans-Saharan trade that brought salt, textiles, and metal goods south in exchange for gold and enslaved people. The emperors were Muslim: they supported mosques, built schools to teach the Quran, and maintained an Islamic university at Timbuktu. Like the rulers of Ghana and Mali, the Songhay emperors valued Islam as a cultural foundation for cooperation with Muslim merchants and Islamic states in north Africa. Nevertheless, the Songhay emperors

did not abandon traditional religious practices: Sunni Ali himself often consulted non-Muslim African diviners and magicians.

Fall of Songhay The Songhay Empire dominated west Africa for most of the sixteenth century, but it was the last of the great imperial states of the grasslands. In 1591 a musket-bearing Moroccan army trekked across the Sahara and attacked the previously invincible Songhay military machine. Songhay forces withered under the assault, and subject peoples took the opportunity to revolt against Songhay domination.

As the Songhay Empire crumbled, a series of small, regional kingdoms and city-states emerged in west Africa. The kingdom of Kanem-Bornu dominated the region around Lake Chad, and the Hausa people established thriving commercial city-states to the west. In the forests south of the grasslands, Oyo and **Asante** peoples built powerful regional kingdoms. On the coasts Diula, Mande, and other trading peoples established a series of states that entered into commercial relations with European merchant-mariners who called at west African ports after the fifteenth century. The increasing prominence of Atlantic trade in west African society worked against the interests of imperial states like Mali and Songhay, which had relied on control of trans-Saharan trade to finance their empires.

Swahili Decline While regional states displaced the Songhay Empire in west Africa, the **Swahili** city-states of east Africa fell on hard times. When the Portuguese mariner Vasco da Gama made his way up the east African coast en route to India in 1497 and 1498, he skirmished with local forces at Mozambique and Mombasa. On his second voyage to India in 1502, he forced the ruler of Kilwa to pay tribute, and his followers trained their cannons on Swahili ports all along the east African coast. In 1505 a massive Portuguese naval expedition subdued all the Swahili cities from Sofala to Mombasa. Portuguese forces built administrative centers at Mozambique and Malindi and constructed forts throughout the region in hopes of controlling trade in east Africa. They did not succeed in that effort, but they disrupted trade patterns enough to send the Swahili cities into a decline from which they never fully recovered.

The Kingdoms of Central Africa and South Africa

The Kingdom of Kongo

As trade networks multiplied and linked all regions of sub-Saharan Africa, an increasing volume of commerce encouraged state building in central Africa and south Africa. In central Africa the principal states were the kingdoms of Kongo, Ndongo, Luba, and Lunda in the basin of the Congo River (also known as the Zaire River). Best known of them was the kingdom of **Kongo** because abundant written records throw light on its experience in early modern times. The kingdom emerged in the fourteenth century. Its rulers built a centralized state with officials overseeing military, judicial, and financial affairs, and by the late fifteenth century Kongo embraced much of the modern-day Republic of Congo and Angola.

In 1483 a small Portuguese fleet mapped out the estuary of the Congo River and initiated commercial relations with the kingdom of Kongo. Within a few years, Portuguese merchants had established a close political and diplomatic relationship with the kings of Kongo. They supplied the kings with advisers; provided a military garrison to support the kings and protect Portuguese interests; and brought tailors, shoemakers, masons, miners, and priests to Kongo.

The kings of Kongo converted to Christianity and thus established closer commercial relations with Portuguese merchants and diplomatic relations with the Portuguese monarchy. The kings appreciated the fact that Christianity offered a strong endorsement of their monarchical rule. The new faith was appealing also because the saints of the Roman Catholic church

An engraving depicts São Salvador in Angola in the late seventeenth century. A flag flies over the royal palace while the Portuguese citadel (to the right of the palace) guards the city. Churches appear at the center and on the far right side of the engraving.
Rare Book Division/New York Public Library

Engraving from 1626 showing Queen Nzinga of Matamba, who is sitting on a prostrate man while having an audience with a group of Portuguese men.
Fotosearch/Stringer/Getty Images

were similar to spirits long recognized in Kongolese religion. **King Nzinga Mbemba** of Kongo, also known as King Afonso I (reigned 1506–1542), became a devout Roman Catholic and sought to convert all his subjects to Christianity. Portuguese priests in Kongo reported that he attended religious services daily and studied the Bible so zealously that he sometimes neglected to eat. The Kongo capital of Mbanza—known to Europeans as São Salvador—had so many churches during the sixteenth century that contemporaries referred to it as "Kongo of the Bell."

Slave Raiding in Kongo Relations with Portugal brought wealth and foreign recognition to Kongo but led eventually to the destruction of the kingdom and the establishment of a Portuguese colony in Angola. In exchange for the textiles, weapons, advisers, and artisans that they brought to Kongo, Portuguese merchants sought high-value merchandise such as copper; ivory; and, most of all, enslaved people. They sometimes embarked on slaving expeditions themselves, but more often they made alliances with local authorities in interior regions and provided them with weapons in exchange for captured people. Some of their local allies were enemies of the kings of Kongo, while others were royal subordinates. In either case, Portuguese tactics undermined the authority of the kings, who appealed repeatedly but unsuccessfully for the Portuguese to cease or at least to limit their trade in slaves.

In spite of these problems, Kongo remained strong until the mid-seventeenth century. Portuguese forces aided Kongo in expelling invaders, but at the same time they continued to trade in slaves. Some Portuguese merchants settled in Kongo, took local wives, and henceforth looked more after the interests of their adoptive home than their native land. Over time, though, relations between Kongo and Portugal deteriorated, particularly after Portuguese agents began to pursue opportunities south of Kongo. By 1665 Portuguese colonists to the south even went to war with Kongo. Portuguese forces quickly defeated the Kongolese army and decapitated King Antonio I (also called Nvita a Nkanga) that same year. Soon thereafter, Portuguese merchants began to withdraw from Kongo in search of more profitable business in the kingdom of Ndongo to the south. By the eighteenth century the kingdom of Kongo had largely disintegrated.

The Kingdom of Ndongo Meanwhile, Portuguese explorers were developing a brisk slave trade to the south in the kingdom of **Ndongo,** which the Portuguese referred to as **Angola** from the title of the king, *ngola*. During the sixteenth century, Ndongo had grown from a small chiefdom subject to the kings of Kongo to a powerful regional kingdom in its own right, largely on the basis of the wealth it was able to attract by trading directly with Portuguese merchants rather than through Kongolese intermediaries. Portuguese merchants founded a small coastal colony in Ndongo as early as 1575. After 1611 they steadily increased their influence inland by allying with neighboring peoples who delivered increasing

---

Nzinga Mbemba (N-zinga MEHM-bah)
Ndongo (n'DAWN-goh)

numbers of war captives to feed the growing slave trade. Over the next several decades, Portuguese forces campaigned in Ndongo in an effort to establish a colony that would support large-scale trading in slaves.

Queen Nzinga The conquest of Ndongo did not come easily. For forty years **Queen Nzinga** (reigned 1623–1663) led spirited resistance against Portuguese forces. Nzinga came from a long line of warrior kings. She dressed as a male warrior when leading troops in battle and insisted that her subjects refer to her as king rather than queen. She sometimes went so far in playing male roles as to travel with a group of "concubines"—young men dressed as women companions of the "king." She mobilized central African peoples against her Portuguese adversaries, and she also allied with Dutch mariners, who traded frequently on the African coast during the mid-seventeenth century. Her aim was to drive the Portuguese from her land, expel the Dutch, and then to create a vast central African empire embracing the entire lower Congo basin.

The Portuguese Colony of Angola Although she was a cunning strategist and an effective military leader, Nzinga was unable to oust Portuguese forces from Ndongo. She stymied Portuguese efforts to extend their influence, but with their powerful arms and considerable wealth, Portuguese forces were able to exploit the political divisions that perennially plagued central Africa. When Nzinga died in 1663, Portuguese forces faced less capable resistance, and they both extended and tightened their control over the region they now called Angola, the first European colony in sub-Saharan Africa.

Regional Kingdoms in South Africa Historical records do not shed as much light on the political structures of south Africa as they do on Kongo and Angola, but it is clear that in the south, as in central Africa, regional kingdoms dominated political affairs. Kingdoms had begun to emerge as early as the eleventh century, largely as a result of increasing trade. Merchants from the Swahili city-states of coastal east Africa sought gold, ivory, and people to enslave from the interior regions of south Africa. By controlling commerce, chieftains increased their wealth, enhanced their power, and extended their authority. By 1300 rulers of one such kingdom had built

A bronze plaque from Benin offers an early African view of Europeans: it depicts a Portuguese soldier armed with a musket and accompanied by a dog.
Werner Forman/Universal Images Group/Getty Images

a massive, stone-fortified city known as **Great Zimbabwe,** near the city of Nyanda in modern Zimbabwe, and they dominated the gold-bearing plain between the Zambesi and Limpopo rivers until the late fifteenth century.

European Arrival in South Africa After the fifteenth century a series of smaller kingdoms displaced the rulers of Great Zimbabwe, and Portuguese and Dutch mariners began to play a role in south African affairs. In search of commercial opportunities, Europeans struck alliances with local peoples and intervened in disputes with the aim of supporting their allies and advancing their own interests. They became especially active after Dutch mariners built a trading post at Cape Town in 1652. There they encountered the hunting and gathering **Khoikhoi** people, whom they referred to pejoratively as Hottentots. With the aid of firearms, they claimed lands for themselves and commandeered Khoikhoi labor with relative ease. By 1700 large numbers of Dutch colonists had begun to arrive in south Africa, and by mid-century they had established settlements throughout the region bounded by the Orange and the Great Fish rivers. Their conquests laid the foundation for a series of Dutch and British colonies, which eventually became the most prosperous European possessions in sub-Saharan Africa.

Islam and Christianity in Early Modern Africa

Indigenous religions remained influential throughout sub-Saharan Africa in early modern times. Although many Africans recognized a supreme, remote creator god, they also devoted attention to powerful spirits who were thought to intervene directly in human affairs. Many of these spirits were associated with prominent geographic features such as mountains, waters, or forests. Others were thought of as the "living dead"—spirits of ancestors who roamed the world, not only distributing rewards to descendants who led worthy lives and who honored the memories of departed kin but also meting out punishments to those who did not.

Islam in Sub-Saharan Africa Although most Africans continued to observe indigenous religions, both Islam and Christianity attracted increasing interest in sub-Saharan Africa. Islam was most widely adopted in the commercial centers of west Africa and the Swahili city-states of east Africa. In the

An illustration from the Dutch work called the *Description of Africa*, published in 1688, shows King Alvaro I of Kongo receiving Dutch ambassadors.
DEA/A. Dagli Orti/Getty Images

sixteenth century the trading city of Timbuktu had a prominent Islamic university and 180 schools that taught the Quran. Students flocked to Timbuktu by the thousands from all parts of west Africa.

African Muslims often blended Islam with indigenous beliefs and customs. The result was a syncretic style of Islam that not only made a place for African beliefs in spirits and magic but also permitted men and women to associate with each other on much more familiar terms than was common in north Africa, Arabia, and southwest Asia. Although it appealed to Africans, this syncretic Islam struck many devout Muslims as impure. Muslim merchants and travelers from north Africa and Arabia often commented on their shock at seeing women in tropical Africa who went out in public with bare breasts and socialized freely with men outside their own families.

The Fulani and Islam Some Muslims in sub-Saharan Africa also shared these concerns about the purity of Islam. Most important of them were the **Fulani,** originally a pastoral people who for centuries kept herds of cattle in the savannas of west Africa. By the late seventeenth century, many Fulani had settled in cities, where they observed a strict form of Islam like that practiced in north Africa and Arabia. Beginning about 1680 and continuing through the nineteenth century, the Fulani led a series of military campaigns to establish Islamic states and impose their own style of Islam in west Africa.

The Fulani did not by any means stamp out African religions, nor did they eliminate indigenous elements from the syncretic Islam practiced in west Africa. But they founded powerful states in what is now Guinea, Senegal, Mali, and northern Nigeria, and they promoted the spread of Islam beyond the cities to the countryside. They even established schools in remote towns and villages to teach the Quran and Islamic doctrine. Their campaigns strengthened Islam in sub-Saharan Africa and laid a foundation for new rounds of Islamic state building and conversion efforts in the nineteenth and twentieth centuries.

Christianity in Sub-Saharan Africa Like Islam, Christianity in sub-Saharan Africa was a syncretic blend of Christian doctrine and indigenous traditions and beliefs. The Portuguese community in Kongo and Angola supported priests and missionaries who introduced Roman Catholic Christianity to central Africa. They found strong interest among rulers such as King Afonso I of Kongo and his descendants, who eagerly adopted European-style Christianity. Beyond the ruling courts, however, Christian teachings frequently blended with African traditions. Some Africans wore crosses and other Christian symbols as amulets to ward off danger from angry spirits.

The Antonian Movement A particularly influential form of Christianity was the **Antonian movement** in Kongo, which flourished in the early eighteenth century, when the Kongolese monarchy faced challenges throughout the realm. The Antonian movement began in 1704 when an aristocratic woman named **Dona Beatriz** proclaimed that St. Anthony of Padua had possessed her and chosen her to communicate his messages.

St. Anthony was a thirteenth-century Franciscan missionary and popular preacher. Born in Lisbon, St. Anthony died near Padua in Italy, where his followers built a large church in his honor. He was extremely popular among Portuguese Christians, who introduced his cult to Kongo. Dona Beatriz gained a reputation for working miracles and curing diseases, and she used her prominence to promote an African form of Christianity. She taught that Jesus Christ had been a black African man, that Kongo was the true holy land of Christianity, and that heaven was for Africans. She urged Kongolese to ignore European missionaries and heed her disciples instead, and she sought to harness the widespread popular interest in her teachings and use it to end the wars plaguing Kongo.

Dona Beatriz's movement was a serious challenge to Christian missionaries in Kongo. In 1706 they persuaded King Pedro IV of Kongo to arrest the charismatic prophetess on suspicion of heresy. Upon examining her, the missionaries satisfied themselves that Dona Beatriz was a false prophet and that she knowingly taught false doctrine. On their recommendation the royal government sentenced her to death and burned her at the stake. Yet the Antonian movement did not disappear: Dona Beatriz's disciples continued working to strengthen the monarchy and reconstruct Kongolese society. In 1708 an army of almost twenty thousand Antonians challenged King Pedro, whom they considered an unworthy ruler. Their efforts illustrate clearly the tendency of Kongolese Christians to fashion a faith that reflected their own needs and concerns.

Social Change in Early Modern Africa

Despite increased state-building activity and political turmoil, African societies followed long-established patterns during the early modern era. Kinship groups, for example, continued to serve as the basis of social organization and sometimes political organization as well. Within agricultural villages throughout sub-Saharan Africa, clans under the leadership of prominent individuals organized the affairs of their kinship groups and disciplined those who violated community standards. In

MAP 25.2   The Atlantic slave trade, 1500–1800.

Note the "triangular" pattern of the Atlantic trade routes between Europe, Africa, and the Americas.

Why were most enslaved people in the Atlantic system taken from west and central Africa, and where were they taken?

regions where kingdoms and empires had not emerged, clan leaders consulted with one another and governed large regions. Indeed, even in lands ruled by formal states, clan leaders usually implemented state policy at the village level.

American Food Crops in Sub-Saharan Africa In the mid-sixteenth century, American crops such as manioc, maize, and peanuts arrived in Africa aboard Portuguese ships. These crops supplemented bananas, yams, rice, and millet, the principal staple foods of sub-Saharan Africa. The most important American crop was **manioc** because of its high yield and because it thrived in tropical soils not well suited to cultivation of the other crops.

Population Growth By the eighteenth century, bread made from manioc flour had become a staple food in much of west Africa and central Africa, where it helped provide a foundation for steady population growth. In 1500 C.E. the population of sub-Saharan Africa was about thirty-four million. By 1600 it had increased by almost one-third to forty-four million, and it continued climbing to fifty-two million in 1700 and sixty million in 1800. This strong demographic expansion is all the more remarkable because it took place precisely when millions of Africans underwent involuntary, forced migration to destinations in the Caribbean and the Americas. Even in spite of the loss of millions of people to the slave trade and the violence surrounding it, American food crops supported expanding populations in all regions of sub-Saharan Africa during early modern times.

THE ATLANTIC SLAVE TRADE

Of all the processes that linked Africa to the larger Atlantic world in early modern times, the most momentous was the **Atlantic slave trade.** From the fifteenth to the nineteenth centuries millions of Africans were brutally enslaved and sent to the Americas to work on European-owned agricultural plantations. In exchange for providing enslaved people, African slave traders sought European manufactured products—most notably firearms, which they sometimes used to strengthen military forces that then sought to capture more people for the slave trade. Only in the early nineteenth century did the Atlantic slave trade come to an end. During the course of that century, most states abolished the institution of slavery itself.

Foundations of the Slave Trade

Slavery in Africa The institution of slavery was already in existence in remote antiquity, and until the nineteenth century most settled agricultural societies in the world utilized slave labor in some form. Slavery was common throughout Africa after the Bantu-speaking people spread agriculture to all parts of the continent. As in other societies, most enslaved people in Africa came from the ranks of war captives, although criminals and individuals expelled from their clans also frequently fell into slavery. Once enslaved, an individual had no personal or civil rights. Owners could order enslaved people to perform

Below decks on an illegal slave ship seized by a British antislavery patrol in 1846. Note the extremely cramped quarters in which captives were forced to spend most of their time. They were both deeply uncomfortable and contributed to dangerously unsanitary conditions.
The Art Archive/Shutterstock

any kind of work, punish them at will, and sell them as chattel (property). Enslaved Africans usually worked as cultivators in societies far from their homes, although some worked as administrators, soldiers, or even highly placed advisers. The Songhay emperors, for example, often employed enslaved people as administrators and soldiers because the rulers distrusted free nobles, whom they considered excessively ambitious. Agricultural plantations in the Songhay Empire often had hundreds of enslaved laborers, many of them working under the management of slave administrators.

Yet despite similarities with slavery in other places like Europe and Asia, African slavery was also distinct in some ways. African law did not recognize private property but, rather, vested ownership of land in communities. Thus wealth and power in Africa came not from the possession of land but from control over the human labor that made the land productive. Enslaved people were a form of private investment, a type of heritable property, and a means of measuring wealth. Those who controlled large numbers of enslaved people were able to harvest more crops and accumulate more wealth than others. Africans routinely purchased enslaved people to enlarge their families and enhance their power. Often, they assimilated them into their kinship groups, so that within a generation an enslaved person might obtain both freedom and an honorable position in a new family or clan.

The Trans-Saharan Slave Trade After the eighth century, Muslim merchants from north Africa, Arabia, and Persia sought slaves in sub-Saharan Africa for sale and distribution to destinations in the Mediterranean basin, southwest Asia, India, and even southeast Asia and China. When demand for enslaved people outstripped supply, merchants resorted to raiding villages, capturing innocent individuals, and forcing them into slavery. State officials sometimes allied with the merchants by providing cavalry forces to mount lightning raids on undefended communities. Merchants then transported the victims of these raids across the Sahara desert by camel caravan for distribution in the Mediterranean basin. Alternatively, they forced them to board ships at the Swahili port cities of east Africa for delivery to destinations across the Indian Ocean. During a millennium and more of the trans-Saharan slave trade, which lasted into the twentieth century, as many as ten million Africans may have been enslaved.

By the time Europeans ventured to sub-Saharan Africa in the fifteenth and sixteenth centuries, traffic in enslaved people was a well-established feature of African society, and a system for capturing, selling, and distributing enslaved people had functioned effectively for more than five hundred years. But when Europeans began to pursue commercial interests in Africa and the Americas, the slave trade expanded dramatically. After 1450, European peoples initially tapped existing networks and then greatly expanded commerce in enslaved Africans from the Mediterranean and the Indian Ocean to the Atlantic Ocean basin. This Atlantic slave trade brought about an enormous forced migration that influenced the development of societies throughout the Atlantic Ocean basin.

Human Cargoes

The Atlantic slave trade began small, but it grew steadily and eventually reached enormous proportions. The earliest European slave traders were Portuguese explorers who navigated and mapped the west African coast in the mid-fifteenth century. In 1441 a raiding party seized twelve African men and took them to Portugal as slaves. Portuguese mariners encountered stiff resistance when they attempted to capture people into slavery as African warriors fired thousands of poison-tipped arrows at gangs of would-be slave raiders. Soon, however, the mariners learned that they could purchase enslaved people rather than capturing them, and by 1460 they were delivering five hundred enslaved people per year to Portugal and Spain. In Europe, enslaved Africans usually worked as miners, porters, or domestic servants because free peasants and serfs cultivated the land.

The Early Slave Trade Slave traders also delivered their human cargoes to Portuguese island colonies in the Atlantic. There was no supply of labor to work plantations in the Azores, Madeiras, Cape Verde Islands, and São Tomé, all of which were uninhabited when explorers discovered them in the fifteenth century. The Portuguese population was too small to provide large numbers of colonists, let alone laborers. Sugar planters on the island of São Tomé in particular

How the Past Shapes the Future

The Columbian Exchange

Think back to the effects of Eurasian diseases on the original inhabitants of the Americas after 1492. In what ways was the massive death toll among indigenous Americans related to the origins of the Atlantic slave trade?

called for slave labor to solve this labor shortage. By the 1520s some two thousand enslaved people per year went to São Tomé, which allowed sugar production on the island to soar. Soon thereafter Portuguese entrepreneurs extended the use of slave labor to South America. During the 1530s Portuguese planters imported enslaved people directly from Kongo and Angola to Brazil, which eventually became the wealthiest of the sugar-producing lands of the Western Hemisphere.

Meanwhile, Spanish explorers and conquerors also sought laborers to work lands in the Caribbean and the Americas. As imported diseases ravaged indigenous populations in the Western Hemisphere, the conquerors found themselves in possession of vast stretches of land but few laborers to work them. The Spanish attempted to harness the labor of those who survived the diseases, but their desire for labor exceeded the number of available indigenous people. Gradually, Spanish settlers began to rely on enslaved people from Africa as well. In 1518 the first shipment of enslaved Africans went directly from west Africa to the Caribbean, where they worked on recently established sugar plantations. During the 1520s Spanish authorities introduced enslaved Africans to Mexico, where they worked as cultivators and miners. By the early seventeenth century, English colonists had introduced enslaved Africans also to the North American mainland.

Triangular Trade The demand for labor in the Western Hemisphere stimulated a profitable commerce known as the **triangular trade** because European ships often undertook voyages of three legs. On the first leg they carried horses and European manufactured goods—mostly cloth and metalwares, especially firearms—that they exchanged in sub-Saharan Africa for enslaved people. The second leg took enslaved Africans to Caribbean and American destinations. Upon arrival merchants sold their human cargoes to plantation owners for two to three times what they had cost on the African coast. Sometimes they exchanged enslaved people for cash, but in sugar-producing regions they often bartered them for sugar or molasses. Then they filled their vessels' hulls with American products before embarking on their voyage back to Europe.

At every stage of the process, the slave trade was a brutal and inhumane business. The original capture of Africans into slavery was almost always a violent affair. As European demand for enslaved people grew, some African chieftains

SOURCES FROM THE PAST

Olaudah Equiano on the Middle Passage

Olaudah Equiano (1745–1797) was a native of Benin in west Africa. When he was ten years old, slave raiders seized him and his sister at their home while their parents were tending the fields. He spent the next twenty-one years in slavery. Eventually, Equiano purchased his freedom and worked against the slave trade for the rest of his life. In his autobiography published in 1789, Equiano described the horrors of the middle passage.

The first object which saluted my eyes when I arrived on the coast was the sea, and a slave ship which was then riding at anchor and waiting for its cargo. These filled me with astonishment, which was soon converted into terror when I was carried on board. I was immediately handled and tossed up to see if I were sound by some of the crew, and I was now persuaded that I had gotten into a world of bad spirits and that they were going to kill me. . . .

I was not long suffered to indulge my grief; I was soon put down under the decks, and there I received such a salutation in my nostrils as I had never experienced in my life: so that with the loathsomeness of the stench and crying together, I became so sick and low that I was not able to eat, nor had I the least desire to taste anything. I now wished for the last friend, death, to relieve me; but soon, to my grief, two of the white men offered me eatables, and on my refusing to eat, one of them held me fast by the hands and laid me across I think the windlass and tied my feet while the other flogged me severely. I had never experienced anything of this kind before, and although not being used to the water I naturally feared that element the first time I saw it, yet nevertheless if I could have gotten over the nettings I would have jumped over the side, but I could not; and besides, the crew used to watch very closely over those of us who were not chained down to the decks, lest we should leap into the water: and I have seen some of these poor African prisoners most severely cut for attempting to do so, and hourly whipped for not eating. This indeed was often the case with myself. . . .

> Why was it so important to the ship's crew that the Africans on board eat?

One day when we had a smooth sea and moderate wind, two of my wearied countrymen who were chained together (I was near them at the time), preferring death to such a life of misery, somehow made through the nettings and jumped into the sea: immediately another quite dejected fellow, who on account of his illness was suffered to be out of irons, also followed their example; and I believe many more would very soon have done the same if they had not been prevented by the ship's crew, who were instantly alarmed. Those of us that were the most active were in a moment put down under the deck, and there was such a noise and confusion amongst the people of the ship as I never heard before, to stop her and get the boat to go after the slaves. However, two of the wretches were drowned, but they got the other and afterwards flogged him unmercifully for thus attempting to prefer death to slavery. In this manner we continued to undergo more hardships than I can now relate, hardships which are inseparable from this accursed trade.

> Consider how terrible the conditions on board the ship must have been to encourage some of the Africans on board to choose death over survival.

For Further Reflection

■ On the basis of Equiano's account, what measures did the crews of slave ships take to ensure maximum profits from their business of transporting human cargoes?

Source: Olaudah Equiano. *The Interesting Narrative of the Life of Olaudah Equiano, or Gustavus Vassa, the African, Written by Himself.* 2 vols. London, 1789. (Translation slightly modified.)

organized raiding parties to seize individuals from neighboring societies. Others launched wars for the purpose of capturing victims for the slave trade. They often snatched individuals right out of their homes, fields, or villages: millions of lives changed instantly, as slave raiders grabbed their victims and then immediately spirited them away in captivity.

The Middle Passage Following capture, enslaved individuals underwent a forced march to the coast, where they lived in holding pens until a ship arrived to transport them to the Western Hemisphere. Then they embarked on the dreadful **middle passage,** the trans-Atlantic journey aboard filthy and crowded slave ships. Enslaved passengers traveled below decks in

Connecting the Sources

Using indirect sources to reconstruct the lives of slaves

In order to write about the past, historians must find and interpret primary sources. Primary sources can include material objects, archaeological evidence, oral traditions, texts (including official documents, letters, accounts, newspapers), or images. They provide the evidence on which historical narratives rest. This exercise highlights some of the challenges of interpreting original primary sources by asking you to consider the kinds of contextual information you might need to interpret such documents accurately and by asking you to consider what individual documents can and cannot tell you.

The problem   Sometimes historians want to find out about the experiences of groups that may not have had much power in the past, such as women, peasants, or enslaved people. This can be difficult, however, because such groups frequently did not leave many textual records behind. In the case of Africans who became part of the Atlantic slave trade, it is difficult to find primary sources created by individual enslaved people themselves, particularly in the seventeenth and eighteenth centuries. Many enslaved people were not literate in European languages, and even when they were the documents they created may not have been saved for later inclusion in historical archives. Some voices—like Olaudah Equiano's—have survived from that period, as we see in this chapter. But to understand the varieties of experiences enslaved people might have had, historians must use many primary sources written by others, including those written by slave traders, slave owners, courts, and governments. Let us consider two such sources as a way of thinking about what indirect sources can and cannot tell us about the experience of slavery in the eighteenth century.

The documents   Read the documents below, and consider carefully the questions that follow.

FL Historical 28/Alamy Stock Photo

Document 1:

This advertisement comes from the New London Summary (Connecticut) on March 30, 1764.

The text reads:

Ran away from me the subscriber, the 14th instant, a Molatto named Bilhah, a tall, thick-built well-proportioned Wench; had on a brown short stuff Gown, batt'd with Yellow, a blue camblet Quilt, and check'd linnen Apron, black silk Bonnet, a large pair flower'd silver Shoe-Buckles; may possibly pretend to be a Free Woman, or may Change her Apparel for Men's Cloathing. All Masters of Vessels are cautioned from carrying off said Molatto—Any Person who shall secure said Molatto Wench in any of His Majesty's Goals, shall have FOUR DOLLARS Reward, and necessary Charges paid by Jared Eliot. Killingworth, Mar. 21, 1764.

hideously cramped quarters. Most ships provided enslaved people with enough room to sit upright, although not to stand, but some forced them to lie in chains on shelves with barely half a meter (twenty inches) of space between them. Conditions were so bad that many prisoners attempted to starve themselves to death or mounted revolts. Ship crews attempted to preserve the lives of enslaved people, intending to sell them for a profit at the end of the voyage, but they nevertheless treated the unwilling passengers with cruelty and contempt. Crew members used tools to pry open the mouths of those who

Document 2:

This broadside advertisement was posted in Charlestown, South Carolina, in 1769.

The text reads:

CHARLESTOWN, April 27, 1769
TO BE SOLD,
On Wednesday the Tenth Day of
May next,
A CHOICE CARGO OF
Two Hundred & Fifty
NEGROES:

ARRIVED in the Ship
Countess of Sussex, Thomas Davies,
Master, directly from Gambia, by
JOHN CHAPMAN, & Co.

THIS is the Vessel that had the Small-Pox on Board at the Time of her Arrival the 31st of March last:
Every necessary Precaution hath since been taken to cleanse both Ship and Cargo thoroughly, so that
those who may be inclined to purchase need not be under the least Apprehension of Danger from Infliction.

The NEGROES are allowed to be the likeliest Parcel that have been imported this Season.

Questions

1. What can these advertisements definitively tell you about their respective situations? What facts can be gleaned from these brief sources?
2. In Document 1, what might this advertisement imply about the experience of slavery from Bilhah's point of view? For example, does it imply that Bilhah was unhappy with her status as a slave, or is it simply impossible to know?
3. Also in Document 1, what might this advertisement imply about Bilhah's treatment prior to her departure? Are there any clues that indicate how she lived under Jared Eliot's care?
4. In Document 2, what kinds of information can you glean about the possible experience of the enslaved people held aboard the *Countess of Sussex*? For example, what might it have been like to cross the Atlantic with smallpox aboard?
5. Taking both documents together, what kinds of contextual information would you need in order to understand these advertisements more fully? For example, would your conclusions about the meaning of Document 1 change if you knew that hundreds of slaves ran away every year or, alternatively, if Bilhah was a rare exception? Would your conclusions regarding Document 2 be different if you knew that the *Countess of Sussex* was one of many slave ships to arrive in port at Charlestown in 1769, or if you knew such a landing was a rare occurrence? What further information would you need in order to use these documents to interpret the experience of enslaved people in North America in the eighteenth century?
6. Sources such as these make up the building blocks on which historians base their interpretations of the past. In most cases, however, historians discover that they must use a variety of primary and secondary sources in order to make accurate interpretations.

Source Websites: **Document 1:** http://www.yale.edu/glc/citizens/stories/module1/documents/runaway_slave.html **Document 2:** http://www.pbs.org/wgbh/aia/part1/1h304.html

refused to eat and pitched sick individuals into the ocean rather than have them infect others or waste limited supplies of food.

In good sailing conditions, the journey to Caribbean and American destinations took four to six weeks, during which heat, cold, and disease levied a heavy toll on the enslaved people aboard the ships. During the early days of the slave trade on particularly cramped ships, mortality sometimes exceeded 50 percent. As the volume of the trade grew, slavers built larger ships, carried more water, and provided better nourishment and facilities for their cargoes, and mortality eventually declined to

Numbers and Destinations of Enslaved People in the Transatlantic Slave Trade by Year.

	Europe	Mainland North America	British Caribbean	French Caribbean	Dutch Americas	Danish West Indies	Spanish Americas	Brazil	Africa	Totals
1501–1600	903	0	0	0	0	0	241,917	34,686	0	277,506
1601–1700	3,639	19,956	405,117	50,356	145,980	22,610	313,301	910,361	4,312	1,875,631
1701–1800	6,256	358,845	2,139,819	1,178,518	339,559	81,801	175,438	2,210,931	3,451	6,494,619
1801–1866	0	93,581	218,475	99,549	28,654	25,455	860,589	2,376,141	171,137	3,873,580
Totals	10,798	472,381	2,763,411	1,328,422	514,192	129,867	1,591,245	5,532,118	178,901	12,521,336

Source: *The Trans-Atlantic Slave Trade Database. Emory University.*

about 5 percent per voyage. Over the course of the Atlantic slave trade, however, approximately 25 percent of individuals enslaved in Africa died during the middle passage.

The Impact of the Slave Trade in Africa

Volume of the Slave Trade Before 1600 the Atlantic slave trade operated on a modest scale. Figures varied considerably from one year to the next, but on average about two thousand enslaved people left Africa annually during the late fifteenth and sixteenth centuries. During the seventeenth century, the trade in humans from Africa rose dramatically to twenty thousand per year, as European peoples settled in the Western Hemisphere and sought African labor to cultivate their lands. The high point of the slave trade came in the eighteenth century, when the number of enslaved people brought to the Americas averaged fifty-five thousand per year. During the 1780s slave arrivals averaged eighty-eight thousand per year, and in some individual years they exceeded one hundred thousand. From beginning to end, the Atlantic slave trade brought about the forced migration of about twelve million Africans to the Western Hemisphere. An additional four million or more died resisting seizure or during captivity before arriving at their intended destination.

The impact of the slave trade varied over time and from one African society to another. The kingdoms of Rwanda and Bugunda on the great lakes and the herding societies of the Masai and Turkana of east Africa largely escaped the worst effects of the slave trade, partly because they resisted it and partly because their lands were distant from the major slave ports on the west African coast. Other societies flourished during early modern times and benefited economically from the slave trade. Those Africans who raided, took captives, and sold enslaved people to Europeans profited handsomely from the trade, as did the port cities and the states that coordinated trade with European merchants. Asante, Dahomey, and Oyo peoples, for example, took advantage of the slave trade to obtain firearms from European merchants and build powerful states in west

Africa. In the nineteenth century, after the abolition of slavery, some African merchants complained bitterly about losing their livelihood and tried to undermine the efforts of the British navy to patrol Atlantic waters and put an end to slave trading.

Social Effects of the Slave Trade On the whole, however, sub-Saharan Africa suffered serious losses from the slave trade. The Atlantic slave trade alone deprived African societies of about sixteen million individuals, in addition to several million others forced into the continuing trans-Saharan slave trade during the early modern era. Although total African population rose during the early modern era, partly because American food crops enriched diets, several individual societies experienced severe losses because of the slave trade. West African societies between Senegal and Angola were especially vulnerable to slave raiding because of their proximity to the most active slave ports.

Gender and Slavery While diverting labor from sub-Saharan Africa to other lands, the slave trade also distorted sex ratios both in the Americas and in Africa. Approximately two-thirds of all Africans enslaved were young men between fourteen and thirty-five years of age. This reflected European preferences because men in their physical prime had the best potential to repay their buyers' investments by providing heavy labor over an extended period of time. It also coincided with the desire of African slavers to retain enslaved women for use in households. The resulting gender imbalance meant, at least initially, that enslaved African communities could not reproduce quickly enough through childbirth. When combined with the high mortality rate among enslaved Africans due to brutal conditions and hard physical work, the result was a continuous demand for new shipments of enslaved people from Africa. The need to replenish populations of enslaved men was especially acute on Caribbean sugar plantations, where death rates were especially high. The preference for men to enslave also had implications for sub-Saharan societies. By the late eighteenth

Armed escorts march a group of captured Africans to the coast for sale on slave markets. Chained together are African men, women, and children. What motivated states and individuals in Africa to take part in capturing people to sell in the Atlantic slave trade?

North Wind Picture Archives

century, for example, women made up more than two-thirds of the adult population of Angola, encouraging Angolans to embrace polygyny, the practice of having more than one wife at a time. In addition, women by necessity took on duties that earlier had been the responsibility of men.

Political Effects of the Slave Trade Apart from its demographic and social effects, the slave trade brought turmoil to African societies. While African groups fought a variety of wars that had little or nothing to do with the slave trade during the early modern period, the existence of the trade also encouraged people to participate in conflicts that might never have occurred in its absence.

Violence escalated especially after the late seventeenth century, when African states and kingdoms increasingly exchanged enslaved people for European firearms. When the kingdom of Dahomey obtained effective firearms, for example, its armies were able to capture people from unarmed neighboring societies and exchange them for more weapons. During the eighteenth century, Dahomey expanded rapidly and absorbed neighboring societies by increasing its arsenal of

firearms and maintaining a constant flow of enslaved people to the coast. Indeed, the Dahomey army, which included a regiment of women soldiers, became largely a slave-raiding force. By no means did all African states take such advantage of the slave trade, but Dahomey's experience illustrates the potential of the slave trade to alter the patterns of African politics and society.

THE AFRICAN DIASPORA

Some enslaved Africans worked as urban laborers or domestic servants, and in Mexico and Peru many worked also as miners. The vast majority, however, worked as agricultural laborers on plantations in the Caribbean or the Americas. There they cultivated cash crops that made their way into commercial arteries linking lands throughout the Atlantic Ocean basin. Although deprived of their freedom and frequently treated with brutality, enslaved people often resisted their bondage, and they built hybrid cultural traditions compounded of African, European, and American elements. Most European and American states ended the slave trade

Enslaved men and women cutting sugar cane on the island of Antigua, 1823.

Chronicle of World History/Alamy Stock Photo

and abolished slavery during the nineteenth century. By that time the **African diaspora**—the dispersal of African peoples and their descendants—had left a permanent mark throughout the Western Hemisphere.

Plantation Societies

Most enslaved Africans went to plantations in the tropical and subtropical regions of the Western Hemisphere. When European peoples arrived in the Caribbean and the Americas, they envisioned taking the vast stretches of fertile land they found for themselves. Their goal was to establish profitable **plantations** that would produce agricultural commodities like tobacco and sugar for European and global markets. Spanish colonists established the first of these plantations in 1516 on the island of Hispaniola (which is now modern

Haiti and the Dominican Republic) and soon extended them to Mexico as well. Beginning in the 1530s Portuguese entrepreneurs established plantations in Brazil, and by the early seventeenth century English, Dutch, and French settlers had also established plantations in the Caribbean and the Americas.

Cash Crops Many of these plantations produced sugar, which was one of the most lucrative cash crops of early modern times. But plantations produced other crops as well. During the seventeenth century, tobacco rivaled sugar as a profitable product. Rice also became a major plantation product, as did indigo (which was used as a dye). By the eighteenth century many plantations concentrated on the cultivation of cotton, and coffee had begun to emerge as a plantation cash crop.

Regardless of the crops they produced, Caribbean and American plantations had certain elements in common. All of them specialized in the production of some agricultural

diaspora (die-AS-per-uh)

crop in high demand. Plantations often maintained gardens that produced food for the local community, but their purpose was to profit from the production and export of commercial crops. These plantations relied almost exclusively on slave labor. Plantation communities often included a hundred or more enslaved individuals whose unpaid labor helped keep their agricultural products competitive. Plantations also featured a sharp racial division of labor. Small numbers of European or Euro-American supervisors governed plantation affairs, while large numbers of enslaved Africans or people of African-descent performed most of the community's physical labor.

Regional Differences In spite of their structural similarities, plantation societies differed considerably from one region to another. In the Caribbean and South America, slave populations usually were unable to sustain their numbers. Many enslaved people fell victim to tropical diseases such as malaria and yellow fever. On the plantations, they faced brutal working conditions and low standards of sanitation and nutrition. Moreover, enslaved people had low rates of reproduction because plantation owners mostly imported men and allowed only a few to establish families. Thus, in the Caribbean and South America, plantation owners imported continuing streams of enslaved Africans to maintain their workforces. Of all the people forced from Africa to the Western Hemisphere, about half went to the Caribbean, and about one-third went to Brazil. Smaller numbers went to other destinations in South America and Central America.

Only about 5 percent of enslaved Africans went to North American destinations. Diseases there were less threatening than in the Caribbean and Brazil, and in some ways conditions were less harsh than in the more southerly regions. North American planters imported larger numbers of enslaved women, and encouraged them to form families and bear children. Their support for natural reproduction was especially strong in the eighteenth century, when the prices of individual slaves from Africa rose dramatically.

Resistance to Slavery No matter where they lived, enslaved people did not meekly accept their servile status. Instead, like Thomas Peters—who we met in the introduction—they resisted it in numerous ways. Some forms of resistance were mild but costly to slave owners: individuals might purposefully work slowly for their masters but diligently in their own gardens, for example. Some enslaved people might also sabotage plantation equipment or work routines. A more serious form of resistance involved running away from the plantation community. Runaways known as *maroons* gathered in mountainous, forested, or swampy regions and built their own self-governing communities. Maroons often raided nearby plantations for arms, tools, provisions, and even other enslaved people to increase their own numbers or to provide labor for their communities. Many maroons had gained military experience in Africa, and they organized runaways into effective military forces. Maroon communities flourished throughout slave-holding regions of the Western Hemisphere, and some of them survived for centuries. In

Enslaved people were vulnerable to cruel treatment that often provoked them to run away from their plantations or even mount revolts. A French visitor to Brazil in the early nineteenth century depicted a Portuguese overseer administering a brutal whipping to a bound man on a plantation near Rio de Janeiro.

Pictorial Press Ltd/Alamy Stock Photo

What's Left Out?   ▆▆▆ ▆▆ ▆▆ ▆▆ ▆▆▆

While we know that both African men and women were forced into the Atlantic slave trade, we also know that there were differences in the ways enslaved women and enslaved men experienced slavery. In the case of enslaved women, European slave traders and settlers often wrongly believed that African women were hypersexual and that they were uninhibited about sexual encounters. These beliefs, combined with the power of ownership over enslaved women's bodies, contributed to a strong sense of entitlement over their reproductive capacities. Indeed, slave owners viewed enslaved women not only as laborers but as profitable vessels for producing additional slaves. Sexual violence by Europeans was a routine part of enslaved women's lives and resulted in many unwanted pregnancies. Even when enslaved women gave birth to children by partners of their own choosing, their children were subject to sale, and thus they could not control basic aspects of their futures. Enslaved women often resisted these practices, but the structure of slave societies meant that they could not turn to the law or to the larger society for assistance. It is important to remember that the practice of slavery in the Americas and the Caribbean involved control over labor as well as the most intimate aspects of daily life. For women, this involved significant loss of control over their bodies and their reproductive capacities.

Source: Jennifer Morgan, *Laboring Women: Reproduction and Gender in New World Slavery* (Philadelphia: University of Pennsylvania Press, 2004).

present-day Suriname, for example, the Saramaka people maintain an elaborate oral tradition that traces their descent from eighteenth-century maroons.

Slave Revolts The most dramatic form of resistance to slavery was organized revolt. Enslaved people far outnumbered others in most plantation societies, and they had the potential to organize and overwhelm slaveholders. Slave revolts brought stark fear to plantation owners and supervisors, and they often resulted in widespread death and destruction. Yet these revolts almost never brought slavery itself to an end because the European and Euro-American ruling elites had access to arms, horses, and military forces that extinguished most rebellions. Only in the French sugar colony of **Saint-Domingue** did a revolt abolish slavery as an institution (1793). Indeed, the enslaved Africans of Saint-Domingue declared independence from France, renamed the land **Haiti,** and established a self-governing republic (1804). The Haitian revolution terrified slaveholders and inspired enslaved people throughout the Western Hemisphere, but no other rebellion matched its accomplishments.

Slavery and Economic Development The physical labor of enslaved people made crucial contributions to the building of new societies in the Americas and also to the making of the early modern world as a whole. Enslaved people cultivated many of the crops and extracted many of the minerals that made their way around the world in the global trade networks of the early modern era. They themselves did not enjoy the fruits of their labors, which flowed disproportionately to European peoples and their Euro-American descendants. Had it not been for the labor of enslaved African peoples and

their African descendants, however, it would have been impossible for prosperous new societies to emerge in the Americas during the early modern era.

The Making of Hybrid Cultural Traditions

When Africans were forced into the Atlantic slave trade, they were not allowed to bring any of their material culture with them—including clothing, artwork, furniture, and tools. Once in the Americas and Caribbean, individuals found themselves enslaved with other Africans from many regions who spoke a wide variety of languages. As a result, it was difficult for enslaved Africans to maintain their cultural traditions in the Western Hemisphere. Instead, enslaved people adapted by constructing hybrid languages and religions based on many African traditions combined with new European and American elements. In adapting to new circumstances, enslaved people constructed distinctive hybrid cultural traditions.

African and Creole Languages European languages were dominant in the plantation societies of the Western Hemisphere, but African languages also influenced communication. Occasionally, enslaved Africans from a particular region were numerous enough to speak among themselves in their native tongues. More often, they spoke a **creole language** that drew on several African and European languages. In the low country of South Carolina and Georgia, for example, enslaved people made up about three-quarters of the population in the eighteenth century and regularly communicated in the creole languages **Gullah** and **Geechee,** respectively.

African-Influenced Religions Like their languages, religions of enslaved Africans also combined elements from

Gullah (GUHL-uh)

different societies. Some enslaved people brought from Africa were Muslims, some were Christians, and many others converted to Christianity after their arrival in the Western Hemisphere. Most Africans and African descendants did not practice European Christianity, however, but rather a syncretic faith that made considerable room for African interests and traditions. Because they developed mostly in plantation societies under conditions of slavery, these syncretic religions usually did not create an institutional structure or establish a hierarchy of priests and other church officials. Yet in several cases—most notably **Voudou** in Haiti, **Santeria** in Cuba, and **Candomblé** in Brazil—they became exceedingly popular among enslaved people.

All the syncretic religions with African elements drew inspiration from Christianity: they met in parish churches; sought personal salvation; and made use of European Christian paraphernalia such as holy water, candles, and statues. Yet they also preserved African traditions. They associated African deities with Christian saints and relied heavily on African rituals such as drumming, dancing, and sacrificing animals. Indeed, the core of these syncretic faiths was often participation in rituals like those observed in Africa. They also preserved beliefs in spirits and supernatural powers: magic, sorcery, witchcraft, and spirit possession all played prominent roles in the new hybrid religions.

Hybrid African Music

As in language and religion, enslaved people relied on African traditions in creating new, hybrid musical forms because they were not allowed to bring material items from their homelands. Music was one of the means by which enslaved Africans reminded themselves of their homes and communities. Once in the Americas, enslaved Africans adapted African musical traditions, including both rhythmic and lyrical elements, to their new environments. Under the brutal circumstances of slavery, music may have been one of the means by which enslaved people resisted their new lives and survived its brutal conditions. In the process, they created new musical forms that influenced not only enslaved communities but also the multicultural societies of the Caribbean and the Americas over the long term.

Enslaved people fashioned new identities in part by blending west African instruments and musical traditions with European languages, Christian religion, and the work routines of American plantations. Musicians played drums and stringed instruments such as banjos that closely resembled traditional African instruments. They adapted west African call-and-response patterns of singing to the rhythms of field work on plantations. The call-and-response format also found its way into the music of spirituals that blended Christian, European, and African influences.

Some slave owners sought to ban music out of fear that it harbored subversive potential. Slave owners in South Carolina recalled, for example, that enslaved people had used drums to signal one another to rise up during the Stono

An 1823 engraving of enslaved men practicing the martial art of Capoeira. Enslaved people often practiced this extremely physically demanding martial art to music, but its purpose was to teach enslaved people a method of self-defense. Capoeira originated in Angola, and was brought by enslaved people to Brazil. It is still practiced today.

The Picture Art Collection/Alamy Stock Photo

rebellion of 1739. Despite efforts to suppress African influences, the music of enslaved people and later of their free descendants survived and testified to the continuing relevance of music as a means of shaping community identity and resistance to oppression. From work songs and spirituals to the blues, jazz, and soul, African-inspired music evolved to mirror the difficult and often brutal circumstances of life in the Americas.

African-Inspired Cultural Traditions

African traditions also made their effects felt throughout much of the Western Hemisphere. Enslaved people introduced African foods to Caribbean and American societies and helped give rise to distinctive hybrid cuisines. They combined African okra, for example, with European-style sautéed vegetables and American shellfish to produce magnificent gumbos, which found their way to Euro-American tables and the tables of Africans and their descendants. (*Okra* and *gumbo* are both African words.) Enslaved people introduced rice cultivation to tropical and subtropical regions, including South Carolina, Georgia, and Louisiana, and added variety to American diets. They also built houses, fashioned clay pots, and wove grass baskets in west African styles. In many ways, the African diaspora influenced the ways all people lived in plantation societies.

Voudou (voo-doo)

Santeria (sahn-tuh-REE-uh)

Candomblé (kan-duhm-BLEH)

The End of the Slave Trade and the Abolition of Slavery

Almost as old as the Atlantic slave trade itself were voices calling for its abolition. The American and French revolutions stimulated the abolitionist cause. The American call for "life, liberty, and the pursuit of happiness" and the French appeal for "liberty, equality, and fraternity" suggested that there was a universal human right to freedom and equality.

Olaudah Equiano Africans also took up the struggle to abolish commerce in human beings. Frequent revolts in the eighteenth and nineteenth centuries made the institution of slavery an expensive and dangerous business. Some formerly enslaved people contributed to the abolitionist cause by writing books that exposed the brutality of institutional slavery. Most notable of them was the west African **Olaudah Equiano** (1745–1797), who in 1789 published an autobiography detailing his experiences as an enslaved and as a free man. Captured at age ten in his native Benin (in modern Nigeria), Equiano was enslaved in the West Indies, Virginia, and Pennsylvania. He accompanied one of his slaveholders on several campaigns of the Seven Years' War before purchasing his freedom in 1766. Equiano's book became a best-seller, and the author traveled throughout the British isles giving speeches and denouncing slavery as an evil institution. He lobbied government officials and members of Parliament, and his efforts strengthened the antislavery movement in England.

The Economic Costs of Slavery Quite apart from moral and political arguments, economic forces contributed to the end of slavery and the slave trade. Plantations, slavery, and the slave trade continued to flourish as long as they were profitable, notwithstanding the efforts of abolitionists. Yet it gradually became clear that slave labor did not come cheap. The possibility of rebellion forced plantation societies to maintain expensive military forces. Even in peaceful times enslaved people often worked unenthusiastically, but owners had to provide basic food and shelter for them throughout

Olaudah Equiano as depicted in the first edition of his autobiography (1789).
The British Library/Robana/Getty Images

their lives no matter how hard they worked. Furthermore, in the late eighteenth century a rapid expansion of Caribbean sugar production led to declining prices. About the same time, African slave traders and European merchants sharply increased the prices they charged for individual enslaved people.

As the profitability of slavery declined, Europeans began to shift their investments from sugarcane and other agricultural products to newly emerging manufacturing industries. Investors soon found that wage labor in factories was less expensive than slave labor on plantations. As an additional benefit, free workers spent much of their income on manufactured goods. Meanwhile, European investors realized that leaving Africans in Africa where they could secure raw materials and buy manufactured goods in exchange was profitable. Thus European entrepreneurs began to look upon Africa less as a source of slave labor and more as a source of raw materials and as a market for manufactured goods.

End of the Slave Trade In 1803 Denmark abolished the slave trade, and other lands followed the Danish example: Great Britain in 1807, the United States in 1808, France in 1814, the Netherlands in 1817, and Spain in 1820. The end of the legal commerce in enslaved people did not abolish the institution of slavery itself, however, and as long as plantation slavery continued, a clandestine trade shipped enslaved people across the Atlantic. British naval squadrons sought to prevent this trade by patrolling the west coast of Africa and conducting search and seizure operations, so gradually the illegal slave trade ground to a halt. The last documented ship that carried enslaved people across the Atlantic arrived in Cuba in 1867.

The Abolition of Slavery The abolition of the institution of slavery itself was a long and drawn-out process: emancipation of all enslaved people came in 1833 in British colonies, 1848 in French colonies, 1865 in the United States, 1886 in Cuba, and 1888 in Brazil. Saudi Arabia and Angola abolished slavery in the 1960s. Officially, slavery no longer exists, but millions of people live in various forms of slavery even today.

Olaudah Equiano (oh-LAU-duh eh-kwee-AHN-oh)

SOURCES FROM THE PAST

A Cargo of Black Ivory, 1829

In 1807, the British Parliament passed a bill prohibiting the slave trade in the British Empire. To enforce the law, a naval force, the West African Squadron, patrolled the west coast of Africa seizing slave ships, fining their captains, and freeing the enslaved people on board. In the following excerpt, from a piece entitled "A Cargo of Black Ivory," the outspoken abolitionist Reverend Robert Walsh in 1829 recounted the horrifying conditions found aboard a slaving ship bound for Brazil from Africa. His British vessel had stopped the ship on suspicion of piracy or illegal trafficking.

. . . **Our boat was now hoisted out,** and I went on board with the officers. When we mounted her decks, we found her full of slaves. She was called the Veloz, commanded by Captain Jose Fiarbosa, bound to Bahia. She was a very broad-decked ship, with a mainmast, schooner-rigged, and behind her foremast was that large formidable gun, which turned on a broad circle of iron, on deck, and which enabled her to act as a pirate, if her slaving speculation had failed. She had taken in, on the coast of Africa, 336 males, and 226 females, making in all 562, and had been out seventeen days, during which she had thrown overboard fifty-five. The slaves were all enclosed under grated hatchways, between decks. The space was so low, that they sat between each other's legs, and stowed so close together, that there was no possibility of their lying down, or at all changing their position, by night or day. As they belonged to, and were shipped on account of different individuals, they were all branded, like sheep, with the owners' marks of different forms. . . These were impressed under their breasts, or on their arms, and as the mate informed me, with, perfect indifference. . . "burnt with the red-hot iron."

Over the hatchway stood a ferocious looking fellow, with a scourge of many twisted thongs in his hand, who was the slave-driver of the ship, and whenever he heard the slightest noise below, he shook it over them, and seemed eager to exercise it. . . .

> Why were the enslaved individuals on board the ship branded with hot irons?

The heat of these horrid places was so great, and the odour so offensive, that it was quite impossible to enter them, even had there been room. They were measured as above when the slaves had left them. The officers insisted that the poor suffering creatures should he admitted on deck to get air and water. This was opposed by the mate of the slaver, who, from a feeling that they deserved it, declared they would murder them all. The officers, however, persisted, and the poor beings were all turned up together. It is impossible to conceive the effect of this eruption—517 fellow-creatures of all ages and sexes, some children, some adults, some old men and women, all in a state of total nudity, scrambling out together to taste the luxury of a little fresh air and water. They came swarming up, like bees from the aperture of a hive, till the whole deck was crowded to suffocation, from stem to stern; so that it was impossible to imagine where they could all have come from, or how they could have been stowed away. On looking into the places where they had been crammed, there were found some children next to the sides of the ship, in the places most remote from light and air; they were lying nearly in a torpid state, after the rest had turned out. The little creatures seemed indifferent as to life or death, and when they were carried on deck, many of them could not stand. . .

It was not surprising that they should have endured much sickness and loss of life, in their short passage. They had sailed from the coast of Africa on the 7th of May, and had been out but seventeen days, and they had thrown overboard no less than fifty-five, who had died of dysentery and other complaints, in that space of time, though they had left the coast in good health. Indeed, many of the survivors were seen lying about the decks in the last stage of emaciation, and in a state of filth and misery not to be looked at. Even-handed justice had visited

> Why did the author think it was justice that so many of the ship's crew had become sick with fever?

the effects of this unholy traffic, on the crew who were engaged in it. Eight or nine had died, and at that moment six were in hammocks on board, in different stages of fever. This mortality did not arise from want of medicine. There was a large stock ostentatiously displayed in the cabin, with a manuscript book, containing directions as to the quantities; but the only medical man on board to prescribe it was a black, who was as ignorant as his patients.

While expressing my horror at what I saw, and exclaiming against the state of this vessel for conveying human beings, I was informed by my friends, who had passed so long a time on the coast of Africa, and visited so many ships, that this was one of the best they had seen. The height, sometimes, between decks, was only eighteen inches; so that the unfortunate beings could not turn round, or even on their sides, the elevation being less than the breadth of their shoulders; and here they are usually chained to the decks, by the neck and legs. . . .

For Further Reflection

■ The Reverend Walsh clearly expressed his horror and moral outrage at the conditions suffered by the slaves. What did this presumably precious "cargo" have to endure? What treatment did the reverend find especially offensive?

Source: Walsh, Reverend Robert. "A Cargo of Black Ivory." As found in American History told by Contemporaries. Edited by Albert Bushnell Hart. 5 volumes. New York: Macmillan Company, 1898–1953.

Enslaved people in chains on the island of Zanzibar (off the east coast of modern Tanzania) where slavery was abolished on 5 March 1873. Zanzibar had served as east Africa's principal port for the slave trade between Africa and Asia.
Bojan Brecelj/Corbis Historical/Getty Images

According to the Anti-Slavery Society for the Protection of Human Rights, debt bondage, contract labor, sham adoptions, servile marriages, and other forms of forced servitude still oppress more than two hundred million people, mostly in Africa, south Asia, and Latin America. Meanwhile, the legacy of the Atlantic slave trade remains visible throughout much of the Western Hemisphere, where the African diaspora has given rise to distinctive communities as well as cultural traditions that have shaped societies as a whole throughout the Americas and Caribbean.

CONCLUSION

During the early modern era, many sub-Saharan Africans continued the tradition of living in small kinship groups as they had for centuries. Others built states and traded with Muslim societies as they had since the eighth century C.E. Yet Africans also experienced dramatic changes as they participated in the formation of an integrated Atlantic Ocean basin. Among the agents of change were European merchant-mariners who sought commercial opportunities in sub-Saharan Africa. They brought European manufactured goods and introduced American food crops that fueled population growth throughout Africa. But they also encouraged a vast expansion of existing slave-trading networks as they sought unfree laborers for plantations in the Western Hemisphere. The Atlantic slave trade violently removed sixteen million or more individuals from their home societies and traditions, which led to political turmoil and social disruption throughout much of sub-Saharan Africa. Enslaved Africans and their descendants were mostly prohibited from building independent states in the Western Hemisphere. But they formed an African diaspora from multiple encounters between peoples from all over sub-Saharan

Africa and, as a result, were able to maintain some African traditions and to build new ones inspired by African knowledge. The individuals who made up the African diaspora profoundly influenced the development of societies in all slave-holding regions of the Caribbean and the Americas as well as in Africa itself, like Thomas Peters from the introduction to this chapter, who brought former enslaved people back to Africa. Ultimately, Africans and African-descended people took action and collaborated with others to bring about an end to the slave trade and the abolition of slavery itself.

STUDY TERMS

African diaspora (540)	Dona Beatriz (531)
Angola (529)	Fulani (531)
Antonian movement (531)	Geechee (542)
Asante (528)	Ghana (526)
Atlantic slave trade (533)	Great Zimbabwe (530)
Candomblé (543)	Gullah (542)
creole language (542)	Haiti (542)

Jenne (526)

Khoikhoi (530)

King Nzinga
    Mbemba (529)

Kongo (528)

Mali Empire (526)

manioc (533)

middle passage (535)

Ndongo (529)

Olaudah Equiano (544)

plantations (540)

Queen Nzinga (530)

Saint-Domingue (542)

Santeria (543)

Songhay Empire (526)

Sunni Ali (526)

Swahili (528)

Timbuktu (526)

triangular trade (534)

Voudou (543)

FOR FURTHER READING

Vince Brown. *The Reaper's Garden: Death and Power in the World of Atlantic Slavery*. Cambridge, Mass., 2008. A fascinating exploration about the ways death shaped multiple aspects of life in Jamaica in the time of slavery.

Michael L. Conniff and Thomas J. Davis. *Africans in the Americas: A History of the Black Diaspora*. New York, 2002. A comprehensive survey of African-European relations, the slave trade, and the African diaspora.

Christopher Ehret. *The Civilizations of Africa: A History to 1800*. Charlottesville, Va., 2002. An important contribution that views Africa in the context of world history.

Olaudah Equiano and Vincent Carretta. *The Interesting Life of Olaudah Equiano*. Rev. ed. New York, 2003. Autobiography of an enslaved man who turned into an abolitionist, with an informative introduction and editorial comments.

Philip Gould. *Barbaric Traffic: Commerce and Antislavery in the Eighteenth-Century Atlantic World*. Cambridge, 2003. Compelling study of Anglo-American antislavery literature that suggests the discourse was less a debate over the morality of slavery than a concern with the commercial aspects of the slave trade.

Patrick Manning. *The African Diaspora: A History through Culture*. New York, 2010. A truly global exploration of the connections wrought between Africans as they interacted across the continents after 1400.

Stephanie Smallwood. *Saltwater Slavery: A Middle Passage from Africa to American Diaspora*. Cambridge, Mass., 2008. A harrowing look at the process of becoming enslaved from the perspective of enslaved people themselves.

James H. Sweet. *Recreating Africa: Culture, Kinship, and Religion in the African-Portuguese World, 1441–1770*. Chapel Hill, N.C., 2006. Engaging study of African slave culture in Portuguese Brazil and the process of creolization.

Dale W. Tomich. *Through the Prism of Slavery: Labor, Capital, and World Economy*. Lanham, Md., 2004. Brief overview of slavery's role in the development of global capitalism.

Jan Vansina. *Paths in the Rainforest: Toward a History of Political Tradition in Equatorial Africa*. Madison, 1990. A thoughtful analysis that considers both indigenous traditions and external influences on African history.

ZOOMING IN ON ENCOUNTERS
Matteo Ricci and Chiming Clocks in China

In January 1601 a mechanical clock chimed the hours for the first time in the city of Beijing. In the early 1580s, devices that Chinese people called "self-ringing bells" had arrived at the port of Macau, where Portuguese merchants impressed local authorities with their chiming clocks. Reports of them soon spread throughout southern China and beyond to Beijing. The Roman Catholic missionary **Matteo Ricci** conceived the idea of capturing the emperor's attention with mechanical clocks and then persuading him and his subjects to convert to Christianity. From his post at Macau, Ricci let imperial authorities know that he could supply the emperor with a chiming clock. When the emperor **Wanli** (r. 1572–1620) granted him permission to travel to Beijing and establish a mission, Ricci took with him both a large mechanical clock intended for public display and a smaller, self-ringing bell for the emperor's personal use.

Emperor Wanli was enchanted by the chiming clocks, and they soon became the rage in elite society throughout China.

Matteo Ricci (maht-TAY-oh REE-chee)
Wanli (wahn-LEE)

European-style buildings on the waterfront in eighteenth-century Guangzhou, where foreign merchants conducted their business.
The Picture Art Collection/Alamy Stock Photo

Wealthy Chinese merchants paid handsome sums for the devices, and Europeans often found that their business in China went better if they presented gifts of self-ringing bells to the government officials they dealt with. By the eighteenth century the imperial court maintained a workshop to manufacture and repair mechanical clocks and watches. While most Chinese people could not afford to purchase mechanical clocks, commoners also had opportunities to encounter self-ringing bells. Outside their residence in Beijing, Matteo Ricci and his missionary colleagues installed a large mechanical clock that regularly attracted crowds of curious neighbors when it struck the hours.

But chiming clocks did not have the effect that Ricci desired. The emperor showed no interest in Christianity, and the missionaries attracted only small numbers of Chinese converts. Yet, by opening the doors of the imperial court to the missionaries, the self-ringing bells symbolized the increasing frequency of encounters between East Asian and European peoples.

CHAPTER OVERVIEW

By linking all the world's regions and peoples, the European voyages of exploration inaugurated a new era in world history. Yet transoceanic connections influenced different societies in very different ways. In contrast to sub-Saharan Africa, where the Atlantic slave trade bred instability and provoked turmoil, for the most part east Asian lands benefited from long-distance trade because it brought silver that stimulated their economies. East Asian societies benefited also from American plant crops that made their way across the seas as part of the Columbian exchange.

Unlike the Americas, where Europeans profoundly influenced historical development from the time of their arrival, east Asian societies controlled their own affairs until the nineteenth century. Europeans were active on the coastlines, but they had little influence on internal affairs in the region. Because of its political and cultural preeminence, China remained the dominant power in east Asia. Established during the Qin (221–206 B.C.E.) and Han (206 B.C.E.–220 C.E.) dynasties, long-standing political, social, and cultural traditions endowed Chinese society with a sense of stability and permanence. China was also a remarkably prosperous land. Indeed, with its huge population, enormous productive capacity, and strong demand for silver, China was a lead-ing economic powerhouse driving world trade in early modern times. By the late eighteenth century, however, China experienced social and economic change that eventually caused problems both for state authorities and for Chinese society as a whole.

During the seventeenth and eighteenth centuries, Japan also underwent major transformations. The Tokugawa shoguns unified the Japanese islands for the first time and laid a foundation for long-term economic growth. While tightly restricting contacts and relations with the larger world, Tokugawa Japan generated a distinctive set of social and cultural traditions. Those developments helped fashion a Japan that would play a decisive role in global affairs by the twentieth century.

CHRONOLOGY

1368–1644	Ming dynasty (China)
1368–1398	Reign of Hongwu
1403–1424	Reign of Yongle
1552–1610	Life of Matteo Ricci
1572–1620	Reign of Emperor Wanli
1600–1867	Tokugawa shogunate (Japan)
1616–1626	Reign of Nurhaci
1642–1693	Life of Ihara Saikaku
1644–1911	Qing dynasty (China)
1661–1722	Reign of Kangxi
1736–1795	Reign of Qianlong

THE QUEST FOR POLITICAL STABILITY

During the thirteenth and fourteenth centuries, China experienced the trauma of rule by the Yuan dynasty (1279–1368) of nomadic Mongol warriors (discussed in chapter 17). Mongol overlords ignored Chinese political and cultural traditions, and they displaced Chinese bureaucrats in favor of Turkish, Persian, and other foreign administrators. When the Yuan dynasty came to an end, the Ming emperors who succeeded it sought to erase all signs of Mongol influence and restore traditional ways to China. Looking to the Tang and Song dynasties for inspiration, they built a powerful imperial state, revived the civil service staffed by Confucian scholars, and promoted Confucian thought. Rulers of the succeeding **Qing dynasty** were themselves Manchus of nomadic origin, but they too worked zealously to promote Chinese ways. Ming and Qing emperors alike were deeply conservative: their principal

Qing (ching)

MAP 26.1   Ming China, 1368–1644.

Locate the old Ming capital at Nanjing and the new Ming capital at Beijing.

Why would the Ming emperors have wanted to move so far north?

concern was to maintain stability in a large agrarian society, so they adopted policies that favored Chinese political and cultural traditions. The state they fashioned governed China for more than half a millennium.

The Ming Dynasty

Ming Government When the Yuan dynasty collapsed, the **Ming dynasty** (1368–1644) restored Han Chinese rule to China. **Hongwu** (reigned 1368–1398), founder of the Ming ("brilliant") dynasty, drove the Mongols out of China and built a tightly centralized state. As emperor, Hongwu made extensive use of mandarins, imperial officials who traveled throughout the land and oversaw implementation of government policies. He also placed great trust in **eunuchs** based on

the thinking that they could not generate families and hence would not build power bases that would challenge imperial authority. The emperor **Yongle** (reigned 1403–1424) launched a series of naval expeditions that sailed throughout the Indian Ocean basin and showed Chinese colors as far away as Malindi in east Africa (discussed in chapter 21). Yongle's successors discontinued the expensive maritime expeditions but maintained the tightly centralized state that Hongwu had established.

The Ming emperors were determined to prevent new invasions. In 1421 Yongle moved the capital from Nanjing in the south to Beijing to keep closer watch on the Mongols and other nomadic peoples in the north. The early Ming emperors commanded powerful armies that controlled the Mongols militarily, but by the mid-fifteenth century they had lost their effectiveness. Mongol forces massacred several Chinese armies in the 1440s, and in 1449 they captured the Ming emperor himself.

eunuchs (YOO-nihks)

Yongle (YAWNG-leh)

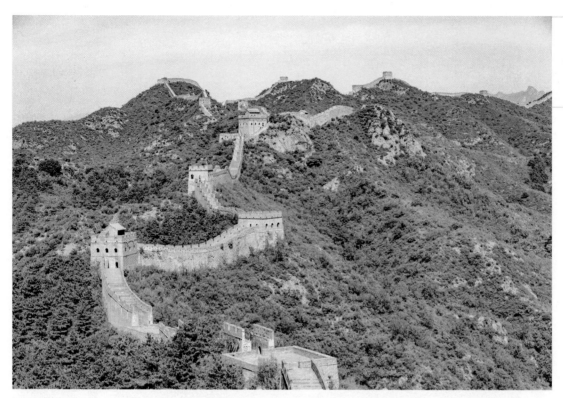

A portion of the Great
Wall in Jinshanlang,
Hebei province.
Benjamin B/Shutterstock

The Great Wall The later Ming emperors sought to protect their realm by building new fortifications, including the **Great Wall** of China, along the northern border. The Great Wall had precedents dating back to the fourth century B.C.E., and the first emperor of the Qin dynasty had ordered construction of a long defensive wall during the third century B.C.E. Those early walls had all fallen into ruin, however, and thus the Great Wall was a Ming dynasty project. Workers by the hundreds of thousands labored throughout the late fifteenth and sixteenth centuries to build a massive stone and brick barrier that ran some 2,500 kilometers (1,550 miles). The Great Wall was 10 to 15 meters (33 to 49 feet) high, and it featured watchtowers, signal towers, and accommodations for troops stationed at the border.

The Ming emperors also set out to eradicate Mongol and other foreign influences and to create a stable society in the image of the Chinese past. With Ming encouragement, for example, individuals abandoned the Mongol names and dress that many had adopted during the Yuan dynasty. Respect for Chinese traditions facilitated the restoration of institutions that the Mongols had ignored or suppressed. The government sponsored study of Chinese cultural traditions, especially Confucianism (discussed in chapter 8), and provided financial support for imperial academies and regional colleges. Most important, the Ming state restored the system of civil service examinations that Mongol rulers had neglected.

Ming Decline The vigor of early Ming rule did not survive beyond the mid-sixteenth century, when a series of problems weakened the dynasty. From the 1520s to the 1560s, pirates and smugglers operated almost at will along the east coast of China. (Although Ming officials referred to the pirates as Japanese, in fact most of them were Chinese.) Both the Ming navy and coastal defenses proved ineffective, and conflicts with pirates often led to the disruption of coastal communities and sometimes even interior regions. In 1555, for example, a band of sixty-seven pirates went on a three-month rampage during which they looted a dozen cities in three provinces and killed more than four thousand people.

Suppression of pirates took more than forty years, partly because of serious problems in the imperial government. The later Ming emperors lived extravagantly in the Forbidden City, a vast complex in Beijing that was isolated from the outside world and only received news about what was happening in the rest of China from eunuch servants and administrators. The emperors sometimes ignored government affairs for decades while satisfying their various appetites. Throughout his long reign, for example, the emperor Wanli (1572–1620) refused to meet with government officials. Instead, while indulging his taste for wine, he conducted business through eunuch intermediaries. Powerful eunuchs won the favor of the later Ming emperors by procuring concubines for them and providing for their amusement. The eunuchs then used their power and position to enrich themselves and lead lives of luxury. Over time, corruption and inefficiency spread throughout the government and weakened the Ming state.

Ming Collapse When a series of famines struck China during the early seventeenth century, the government was unable to organize effective relief efforts. Peasants in stricken

Bird's-eye view of the Forbidden City, which was built by the Emperor Yongle (r. 1402–1424) as a vast, walled imperial retreat at the center of Beijing. Note the extent of the grounds.
Sovfoto/Getty Images

regions resorted to eating grass roots and tree bark. By the 1630s peasants organized revolts throughout China, and they gathered momentum as one city after another withdrew its loyalty from the Ming dynasty. To complicate matters further, **Manchu** forces invaded from the north in search of opportunities for expansion in China. In 1644, Chinese rebel forces captured the Ming capital at Beijing. Manchu invaders allied with an army loyal to the Ming, crushed the rebels, and recovered Beijing. The Manchus portrayed themselves as avengers who saved the capital from dangerous rebels, but instead of restoring Ming rule, they moved their own capital to Beijing and displaced the Ming dynasty.

The Qing Dynasty

The Manchus When the Ming dynasty fell, Manchus poured into China from their homeland of Manchuria north of the Great Wall. The victors proclaimed a new dynasty, the Qing ("pure"), which ruled China until the early twentieth century (1644–1911).

The Manchus were primarily pastoral nomads, although many had turned to agriculture and settled in the rich farmlands of southern Manchuria. Their remote ancestors had traded with China since the Qin dynasty, and they had frequently clashed with their neighbors over land and resources in northern China and southern Manchuria. During the late

sixteenth and early seventeenth centuries, an ambitious chieftain named **Nurhaci** (reigned 1616–1626) unified Manchu tribes into a centralized state, established a code of laws, and organized a powerful military force. During the 1620s and 1630s, the Manchu army expelled Ming garrisons in Manchuria, captured Korea and Mongolia, and launched small-scale invasions into China. After their seizure of Beijing in 1644, the Manchus moved to extend their authority throughout China. For almost forty years they waged campaigns against Ming loyalists and other rebels in southern China until by the early 1680s the Manchus had consolidated the Qing dynasty's hold throughout the land.

The establishment of the Qing dynasty was due partly to Manchu military might and partly to Chinese support for the Manchus. During the 1630s and 1640s, many Chinese generals deserted the Ming dynasty because of its corruption and inefficiency. Confucian scholar-bureaucrats also worked against the Ming because they despised the eunuchs who dominated the imperial court. The Manchu ruling elites were schooled in Chinese language and Confucian thought, and they were often more respected by Chinese scholar-bureaucrats than the emperor and high administrators of the Ming dynasty itself.

Yet the Manchus were also careful to preserve their own ethnic and cultural identity. They not only outlawed intermarriage between Manchus and Chinese but also forbade Chinese from traveling to Manchuria and from learning the Manchurian language. Qing authorities also forced Chinese

Nurhaci (NOOR-hacheh)

MAP 26.2　The Qing empire, 1644–1911.

Compare this map with Map 26.1.

Why would the Qing emperors have wanted to incorporate such extensive territories in Mongolia and Tibet into their empire?

men to shave the front of their heads and grow a Manchu-style queue (somewhat like a pony-tail) as a sign of submission to the dynasty.

Kangxi and His Reign Until the nineteenth century, strong imperial leadership muted tensions between Manchu rulers and Chinese subjects. The long reigns of two particularly effective emperors, **Kangxi** (1661–1722) and **Qianlong** (1736–1795), helped the Manchus consolidate their hold on China. Kangxi was a Confucian scholar as well as an enlightened ruler. He was a voracious reader and occasionally composed poems. He studied the Confucian classics and sought to apply their teachings through his policies. For example, he organized flood-control and irrigation projects in observance of the Confucian precept that rulers should look after the welfare of their subjects and promote agriculture. He also generously patronized Confucian schools and academies.

Kangxi was also a conqueror, and he oversaw the construction of a vast empire. He conquered the island of Taiwan, where Ming loyalists had retreated after being expelled from southern China, and absorbed it into his empire. Like

his predecessors of the Han and Tang dynasties, Kangxi sought to forestall problems with nomadic peoples by projecting Chinese influence into central Asia. His conquests in Mongolia and central Asia extended almost to the Caspian Sea, and he imposed a Chinese protectorate over Tibet. Kangxi's grandson Qianlong continued this expansion of Chinese influence. Qianlong sought to consolidate Kangxi's conquests in central Asia by maintaining military garrisons in eastern Turkestan (the territory now known as Xinjiang province in western China) and encouraging merchants to settle there in hopes they would stabilize the region. Under Qianlong's reign, Vietnam, Burma, and Nepal became tributary states to China.

Qianlong and His Reign Qianlong's reign marked the height of the Qing dynasty. Like Kangxi, Qianlong was a sophisticated and learned man. He reportedly composed more than one hundred thousand poems, and he was a discriminating connoisseur of painting and calligraphy. During his long,

---

Kangxi (kahng-shee)

Qianlong (chyahn-lawng)

stable, and prosperous reign, the imperial treasury collected so much wealth that on four occasions Qianlong cancelled tax collections. Toward the end of his reign, Qianlong paid less attention to imperial affairs and delegated many responsibilities to his favorite eunuchs. His successors continued that practice, devoting themselves to hunting and court life, and by the nineteenth century the Qing dynasty faced serious difficulties. Throughout the reign of Qianlong, however, China remained a wealthy and well-organized land.

The Son of Heaven and the Scholar-Bureaucrats

Although Qing rulers usually appointed Manchus to the highest political posts, they relied on the same governmental apparatus that the Ming emperors had established. Both the Ming and the Qing dynasties presided over a tightly centralized state, which they administered through a bureaucracy staffed by Confucian scholars. For more than five hundred years, the autocratic state created by the Ming emperor Hongwu governed China's fortunes.

The Son of Heaven Although the emperor of China during the Ming and Qing dynasties was not quite a god, he was more than a mere mortal. Chinese tradition held that he was the **"Son of Heaven,"** the human being designated by heavenly powers to maintain order on the earth. He led a privileged life within the walls of the Forbidden City. Hundreds of concubines resided in his harem, and thousands of eunuchs looked after his every need. His daily activities were carefully choreographed performances and included inspections, audiences, banquets, and other official duties. Everything about his person and the institution he represented conveyed a sense of awesome authority. The imperial wardrobe and personal effects bore designs no one else was allowed to wear, for instance, and it was forbidden throughout the realm to write the characters of the emperor's name. Individuals who had the rare privilege of a personal audience with the emperor had to perform the kowtow—three kneelings and nine head knockings. Those who gave even minor offense faced severe punishment. Even the highest official could have his bare buttocks flogged with bamboo canes, a punishment that sometimes brought victims to the point of death.

Though painted in the nineteenth century, this portrait depicts Kangxi in his imperial regalia as he looked at about age fifty. Kangxi reigned for sixty-one years, making him the longest-ruling emperor in Chinese history.

Universal History Archive/Getty Images

The Scholar-Bureaucrats Day-to-day governance of the empire fell to scholar-bureaucrats appointed by the emperor. With few exceptions these officials came from the class of well-educated and highly literate men known as the scholar-gentry. These men had earned academic degrees by passing rigorous civil service examinations, and they dominated China's political and social life.

Preparations for the examinations began at an early age. Sometimes they took place in local schools, which like the civil service examinations were open only to males. Wealthy families often engaged the services of tutors, who made formal education available also to girls. By the time students were eleven or twelve years old, they had memorized several thousand characters that were necessary to deal with the Confucian curriculum, including the ***Analects* of Confucius** and other standard works. They followed those studies with instruction in calligraphy, poetry, and essay composition. Diligent students also acquainted themselves with a large corpus of commentaries, histories, and literary works in preparing for **civil service examinations.**

Civil Service Examinations The examinations consisted of a battery of tests administered at the district, provincial, and metropolitan levels. Stiff official quotas restricted the number of successful candidates in each examination—only three hundred students could pass metropolitan examinations—and students frequently took the examinations several times before earning a degree.

Writing the examinations was a grueling ordeal. At the appointed hour, candidates presented themselves at the examination compound. Each candidate brought a water pitcher, a chamber pot, bedding, food, an inkstone, ink, and brushes. After guards had verified their identities and searched them for hidden printed materials, the new arrivals proceeded along narrow lanes to a honeycomb of small, cell-like rooms barely large enough to accommodate one man and his possessions. Aside from a bench, a makeshift bed, and boards that served as a desk, the rooms were empty. For three days and two nights, the cramped rooms were home to the candidates, who spent all their time writing "eight-legged essays"—literary compositions with eight distinct sections—on questions posed by the examiners. There were no interruptions, nor was there any communication between candidates. If someone died

Imperial civil-service examination hall in Suzhou, 1759. Note the tiny cells in which students took the exams.
The Picture Art Collection/ Alamy Stock Photo

during the examination period, officials wrapped his body in a straw mat and tossed it over the high walls that ringed the compound.

The Examination System and Chinese Society

The possibility of bureaucratic service—with prospects for rich social and financial rewards—ensured that competition for degrees was ferocious at all levels. Yet a degree did not ensure government service. During the Qing dynasty the empire's one million degree holders competed for twenty thousand official civil service positions. Those who passed only the district exams had few opportunities for bureaucratic employment and usually spent their careers "plowing with the writing brush" by teaching in local schools or serving as family tutors. Those who passed the metropolitan examinations, however, could look forward to powerful positions in the imperial bureaucracy.

The examination system was a pivotal institution. By opening the door to honor, power, and rewards, the examinations encouraged serious pursuit of a formal education. Furthermore, since the system did not erect social barriers before its recruits, it provided an avenue for upward social mobility. Years of education and travel to examination sites were expensive, so candidates from wealthy families certainly enjoyed advantages over others, but the exams themselves were open to all males regardless of age or social class. Finally, in addition to selecting officials for government service, the education and examination system molded the personal values of those who managed day-to-day affairs in imperial China. By concentrating on Confucian classics and neo-Confucian commentaries, the examinations guaranteed that Confucianism would be at the heart of Chinese education and that Confucians would govern the state.

ECONOMIC AND SOCIAL CHANGES

By modeling their governmental structure on the centralized imperial states of earlier Chinese dynasties, the Ming and Qing emperors succeeded in their goal of restoring and maintaining traditional ways in China. They also sought to preserve the traditional hierarchical and patriarchal social order. Yet, while the emperors promoted conservative political and social policies, China experienced economic and social changes, partly as a result of influences and encounters from abroad. Agricultural production increased dramatically—especially after the introduction of new food crops from the Americas—and fueled rapid population growth. Meanwhile, global trade brought China enormous wealth, which stimulated the domestic economy by encouraging increased trade, manufacturing, and urban growth. These developments deeply influenced Chinese society and partly undermined the stability that the Ming and Qing emperors sought to preserve.

The Patriarchal Family

Filial Piety Moralists portrayed the Chinese people as one large family, and they extended family values to the larger society. **Filial piety,** for example, implied not only duties of children toward their parents but also loyalty of subjects toward the emperor. Like the imperial government, the Chinese family ideal was hierarchical, patriarchal, and authoritarian. The father was head of the household, and he passed leadership of the family to his eldest son. The veneration of ancestors, which the state promoted, strengthened the authority of the patriarchs by honoring the male line of descent in formal family rituals. Filial piety was the cornerstone of family values. Children had the duty to look after their parents' happiness and well-being, and a crucial obligation was to support parents in their old age. Young children heard stories of sons who went so far as to cut off parts of their bodies to ensure that their parents had enough to eat!

The Chinese family ideal extended into patrilineal (tracing descent through the male line) descent groups such as the clan. Sometimes numbering into the thousands, clan members came from all social classes, though members of the gentry usually dominated a given clan. Clans assumed responsibilities that exceeded the capacities of the nuclear family, such as the maintenance of local order, organization of local economies, and provision for welfare. Clan-supported education gave poor but promising relatives the opportunity to succeed in the civil service examinations. The principal motives behind such charity were self-interest as well as altruism. A government position brought prestige and prosperity to the entire clan, so educational support was a good investment. As a result of educating their members for a chance to take the civil service examinations, clans served as a means for the transmission of Confucian values from the gentry leaders to all social classes within the clan.

Gender Relations

Within the family, Confucian principles subjected women to the authority of men. The subordination of females began at an early age. Chinese parents preferred boys over girls. Whereas a boy might have the opportunity to take the official examinations, become a government official, and thereby bring honor and financial reward to the entire clan, parents regarded a girl as a social and financial liability. After years of expensive upbringing, most girls would marry and become members of other households. Under those circumstances some people even resorted to female infanticide when a girl was born to them.

During the Ming and Qing dynasties, patriarchal authority over females probably became tighter than ever before in China. Since ancient times, relatives had discouraged widows from remarriage, but social pressures increased during the Ming dynasty. Friends and relatives not only encouraged widows to honor the memory of their departed husbands but also heaped honors on those who committed suicide and followed their spouses to the grave.

Foot Binding

Foot binding, a custom that probably originated in the Song dynasty, became exceptionally popular during the late Ming and Qing dynasties. Because small and dainty feet were considered attractive and even erotic, some families bound the feet of girls with strips of linen to make their feet even smaller. Bound feet could not grow naturally and so would not support the weight of an adult woman. For this reason, the practice of foot binding became most widespread among the wealthy classes because it demonstrated an ability to support women who could not perform physical labor. Sometimes, however, commoners bound the feet of girls who they hoped could attract marriage prospects that would enhance the family's social standing.

Marriage itself was a contractual affair whose principal purpose was to continue the male line of descent. A bride became a member of the husband's family, and there was no ambiguity about her position in the household. On her wedding day, as soon as she arrived at her husband's home, the bride performed ritual acts demonstrating subservience to her husband and her new family. Women could not divorce their husbands, but men could divorce their wives in cases where there was no offspring or where the wife was guilty of adultery, theft, disobedience to her husband's family, or even being too talkative.

Thus custom and law combined to strengthen patriarchal authority in Chinese families during the Ming and Qing

What's Left Out?

The practice of foot-binding in China was certainly painful for the (mostly elite) women who underwent the process. There is also no doubt that it permanently limited women's mobility, increasing their dependency on others around them. Westerners certainly saw the practice as a grotesque symbol of the oppression of women in Qing culture. But it is important to remember that foot-binding was only one example of many around the world in which women altered or deformed their bodies in the name of beauty. In fact, in the eighteenth and nineteenth centuries—the very same period westerners were pointing out the cruelties and pain associated with foot-binding—middle-class and elite western European women were wearing whale-bone corsets around their torsos to alter their shapes significantly. Like foot-binding, corseting was painful and could permanently deform women's bodies so that they assumed an ideal shape. Corseting also had significant adverse health effects for women, including breathing and lung disorders, prolapsed uteruses, digestive problems, an inability to move quickly or vigorously, and back pain. The point here is that it is important to remember that while ideals of female beauty differed from place to place, Chinese society during the Qing period was not distinctive for encouraging some women to alter their bodies to achieve a physical ideal. Moreover, many of the methods for attaining these ideals of female beauty, including foot-binding and corseting, also had secondary effects of limiting the mobility of women.

Sources: John Robert Shepherd, *Foot-Binding as Fashion: Ethnicity, Labor, and Status in Traditional China* (Seattle: University of Washington Press, 2019); Leigh Summers, *Bound to Please: A History of the Victorian Corset* (Oxford: Berg Publishers, 2001).

To encourage widows to remain unmarried, the Ming and Qing governments constructed arches in honor of those who did not marry again after the death of their husbands. These arches erected during the Qing dynasty still stand in Anhui province in the Yangzi River valley.

Imagemore/age fotostock

dynasties. Yet, while family life continued to develop along traditional lines, the larger Chinese society underwent considerable change between the sixteenth and the eighteenth centuries.

Population Growth and Economic Development

China was a predominantly agricultural society, a fact that meshed agreeably with the Confucian view that land was the source of everything praiseworthy. The emperor himself acknowledged the central importance of agriculture by plowing

the first furrow of the season. Yet only a small fraction of China's land is suitable for planting: even today only about 11 percent is in cultivation. To feed the country's large population, China's farmers relied on intensive, garden-style agriculture that was highly productive. On its strong agrarian foundation, China supported a large population and built the most highly commercialized economy of the preindustrial world.

American Food Crops By intensively cultivating every available parcel of land, Chinese peasants increased their yields of traditional food crops—especially rice, wheat, and millet—until the seventeenth century. Beginning about the mid-seventeenth century, as peasants approached the upper limits of agricultural productivity, Spanish merchants coming by way of the Philippines introduced American food crops to China. American maize (corn), sweet potatoes, and peanuts permitted Chinese farmers to take advantage of soils that previously had gone uncultivated. The introduction of new crops increased the food supply and supported further population growth.

Population Growth In spite of recurring epidemic diseases such as plague, which claimed the lives of millions, China's population rose rapidly from 100 million in 1500 to 160 million in 1600. Partly because of rebellion and war during the transition between the Ming and Qing empires, it fell to 140 million in the mid-seventeenth century, but

How the Past Shapes the Future ▷ ▷ ▷ ▷

The Columbian Exchange

Prior to the sixteenth century, crops such as corn, sweet potatoes, and peanuts had only been known in the Americas. As a result of the Columbian exchange, however, food crops native to the Americas were brought not only to Europe but also to Asia and Africa. The introduction of such crops to China during the sixteenth century both changed Chinese cuisine and also allowed more land to be cultivated. The result was dramatic population growth, which had both positive and negative effects for Chinese people over the long term. In this case, consider the ways that events and processes that occurred in the Americas played an important but unforeseen role in shaping historical developments in east Asia.

A Ming-era vase painting depicts a woman weaving silk as an attendant pours tea. Silk and tea were among the exports China produced for global trade.
DeAgostini/Getty Images

Foreign Trade Global trade brought prosperity to China, especially during the early Qing dynasty. Chinese workers produced vast quantities of silk, porcelain, lacquerware, and tea for consumers in the Indian Ocean basin, central Asia, and Europe. The silk industry was especially well organized: weavers worked in workshops for regular wages producing fine satins and brocades for export. Chinese imports were relatively few: they included spices from Maluku, exotic products such as birds and animal skins from tropical regions, and small quantities of woolen textiles from Europe. Payment for exports came most importantly in the form of silver bullion, which supported the silver-based Chinese economy and fueled manufacturing.

Economic growth and commercial expansion took place mostly in an atmosphere of tight government regulation. Although the emperor Yongle had sought to establish a Chinese presence in the Indian Ocean during the early fifteenth century through the expeditions of admiral **Zheng He,** after his reign the Ming government withdrew its support for expensive maritime expeditions and even tried to prevent Chinese subjects from dealing with foreign peoples. In its effort to pacify southern China during the later seventeenth century, the Qing government tried to end maritime activity altogether. An imperial edict of 1656 forbade "even a plank from drifting to the sea," and in 1661 the emperor Kangxi ordered evacuation of the southern coastal regions. Those policies had only a limited effect—small Chinese vessels continued to trade actively in Japan and southeast Asian ports—and when Qing forces pacified southern China in the 1680s, government authorities rescinded the strictest measures. Thereafter, however, Qing authorities closely supervised the activities of foreign merchants in China. They permitted Portuguese merchants to operate only at the port of Macau, and British agents had to deal exclusively with the official merchant guild in Guangzhou.

While limiting the activities of foreign merchants, government policies also discouraged the organization of large-scale commercial ventures by Chinese merchants. In the absence of government approval, it was impossible, for example, to maintain shipyards that could construct large sailing ships like the mammoth, nine-masted treasure ships that Zheng He had led throughout the Indian Ocean. Similarly, it was impossible to organize large trading firms like the English East India Company or the Dutch VOC.

Trade and Migration to Southeast Asia Nevertheless, thousands of Chinese merchants worked either individually or in partnerships, plying the waters of the China seas to link China with global trade networks. Chinese merchants were especially prominent in Manila (in the Philippines), where they exchanged silk and porcelain for American silver that came across the Pacific Ocean with the Manila galleons. They were also frequent visitors at the Dutch colonial capital of Batavia, where they supplied the VOC with silk and porcelain in exchange for silver and Indonesian spices. Entrepreneurial

returned to 160 million by 1700 and then surged to 225 million by 1750—an increase of more than 40 percent in just half a century. This rapid demographic growth set the stage for economic and social problems because agricultural production could not keep pace with population over the long term. Acute problems did not occur until the nineteenth century, but per capita income in China began to decline as early as the reign of Qianlong.

While an increasing population placed pressure on Chinese resources, the growing commercial market offered opportunities for entrepreneurs. Because of demographic expansion, entrepreneurs had access to a large, mobile labor force, and they were able to recruit workers readily at low cost. After the mid-sixteenth century, the Chinese economy benefited also from the influx of Japanese and American silver, which stimulated trade and financed further commercial expansion.

Zheng He (jehng huh)

SOURCES FROM THE PAST

Qianlong on Chinese Trade with England

Qing administrators tightly restricted foreign trade. Foreign merchants had to deal with government-approved agents outside the city walls of Guangzhou and had to depart as soon as they had completed their business. In 1793 a British diplomat representing King George III of England bestowed gifts on the emperor Qianlong (r. 1735–1796) and petitioned for the right to trade at ports other than Guangzhou. In a letter to King George, Qianlong outlined his views on Chinese trade with England. His letter also clearly demonstrates the active role of the imperial government in the formation of commercial and economic policies.

You, O king, from afar have yearned after the blessings of our civilization, and in your eagerness to come into touch with our influence have sent an embassy across the sea bearing a memorandum. I have already taken note of your respectful spirit of submission, have treated your mission with extreme favor and loaded it with gifts, besides issuing a mandate to you, O king, and honoring you with the bestowal of valuable presents. . . .

Yesterday your ambassador petitioned my ministers to memorialize me regarding your trade with China, but his proposal is not consistent with our dynastic usage and cannot be entertained. Hitherto, all European nations, including your own country's barbarian merchants, have carried on their trade with our Celestial Empire at Guangzhou. Such has been the procedure for many years, although our Celestial Empire possesses all things in prolific abundance and lacks no product within its own borders. There was therefore no need to import the manufactures of outside barbarians in exchange for our own produce. But as the tea, silk, and porcelain which the Celestial Empire produces are absolute necessities to European nations and to yourselves, we have permitted, as a signal mark of favor, that trading agents should be established at Guangzhou, so that your wants might be supplied and your country thus participate in our beneficence. But your ambassador has now put forward new requests which completely fail to recognize our throne's principle to "treat strangers from afar with indulgence," and to exercise a pacifying control over barbarian tribes the world over. . . . Your England is not the only nation trading at Guangzhou. If other nations, following your bad example, wrongfully importune my ear with further impossible requests, how will it be possible for me to treat them with easy indulgence? Nevertheless, I do not forget the lonely remoteness of your island, cut off from the world by intervening wastes of sea, nor do I overlook your excusable ignorance of the usages of our Celestial Empire. I have consequently commanded my ministers to enlighten your ambassador on the subject, and have ordered the departure of the mission. . . .

> Does the language of emperor Qianlong here signal an attitude of deference or an attitude of superiority to the English?

If, after the receipt of this explicit decree, you lightly give ear to the representations of your subordinates and allow your barbarian merchants to proceed to Zhejiang and Tianjin, with the object of landing and trading there, the ordinances of my Celestial Empire are strict in the extreme, and the local officials, both civil and military, are bound reverently to obey the law of the land. Should your vessels touch the shore, your merchants will assuredly never be permitted to land or to reside there, but will be subject to instant expulsion. In that event your barbarian merchants will have had a long journey for nothing. Do not say that you were not warned in due time! Tremblingly obey and show no negligence! A special mandate!

> What will the consequences be for English traders who try to trade outside Guangzhou in spite of the emperor's ban?

For Further Reflection

■ What considerations might have prompted the Chinese government to take such a restrictive approach to foreign trade?

Source: J. O. P. Bland. *Annals and Memoirs of the Court of Peking.* Boston: Houghton Mifflin, 1914, pp. 325–31. (Translation slightly modified.)

Chinese merchants ventured also to lands throughout southeast Asia—including Borneo, Sumatra, Malaya, Thailand, and elsewhere—in search of tropical products for Chinese consumers. Indeed, the early modern era was an age when merchants established a prominent Chinese presence throughout southeast Asia.

Government and Technology During the Tang and Song dynasties, Chinese engineers had produced a veritable flood of inventions, and China was the world's leader in technology. Yet by early Ming times, technological innovation had slowed. Imperial armed forces adopted European cannons and advanced firearms for their own uses—thus borrowing

Chinese peasants plowing, ca. 1770.

Chronicle/Alamy Stock Photo

forms of gunpowder technology that had originated in China and that Europeans had refined and improved—but little innovation in agricultural and industrial technologies occurred during the Ming and Qing dynasties.

Part of the explanation for the slowdown had to do with the role of the government in the formation of economic and social policies. During the Tang and Song dynasties, the imperial government had encouraged technological innovation as a foundation of military and economic strength. In contrast, the Ming and Qing regimes favored political and social stability over technological innovation, which they thought would lead to unsettling change. Alongside government policy, the abundance and availability of skilled workers also discouraged technological innovation. When employers wanted to increase production, they found that hiring additional workers was cost-effective, and thus there was little need for new technologies. In the short term this tactic maintained relative prosperity in China while keeping most of the population gainfully employed. Over the longer term, however, the fact that Europeans were investing in a variety of technological innovations by the late eighteenth century meant that there would be an imbalance in technological knowledge that would favor Europeans by the nineteenth century.

Gentry, Commoners, Soldiers, and "Mean" People

Privileged Classes Aside from the emperor and his family, scholar-bureaucrats and people from the highest social classes occupied the most exalted positions in Chinese society. Because of their official positions, the scholar-bureaucrats ranked slightly above gentry. Nevertheless, scholar-bureaucrats had much in common with the gentry: they came largely from gentry ranks, and after leaving government service they usually rejoined gentry society. The scholar-bureaucrats and gentry functioned as intermediaries between the imperial government and local society. By organizing water control projects and public security measures, they played a crucial role in the management of local society.

Scholar-bureaucrats and gentry wore distinctive clothing—black gowns with blue borders adorned with various rank insignia—and commoners addressed them with honorific terms. They received favorable legal treatment that reflected their privileged status. As a rule, commoners could not call members of privileged classes to appear as witnesses in legal proceedings. They also enjoyed immunity from corporal punishment and exemption from labor service and taxes.

Most of the gentry owned land, which was their major source of income. As long as they did not have to perform physical labor, some gentry also supplemented their income by operating pawn and rice shops. Many of them were also silent business partners of merchants and entrepreneurs. Their principal source of income, however, came from the government service to which only they had access by virtue of their academic degrees. In contrast to landed elites elsewhere, who often lived on rural estates, China's gentry resided largely in cities and towns, where they tended to political, social, and financial affairs.

Working Classes Confucian tradition ranked three broad classes of commoners below the gentry: peasants, artisans or workers, and merchants. By far the biggest class consisted of peasants, a designation that covered everyone from day laborers to tenant farmers, to small landlords. Confucian principles regarded peasants as the most honorable of the three classes because they provided the food that supported the entire population.

The category of artisans and workers encompassed a wide spectrum of occupations. Despite their lower status, crafts workers, tailors, barbers, physicians, and workers in manufacturing plants generally enjoyed higher income than peasants. Artisans and workers were usually employees of the state or of gentry and merchant families, but they also pursued their occupations as self-employed persons.

Merchants Merchants, from street peddlers to individuals of enormous wealth and influence, ranked at the bottom level of the Confucian social hierarchy. Because moralists looked upon them as unscrupulous social parasites, merchants enjoyed little legal protection, and government policy was always critically important to their pursuits. Yet Chinese merchants often garnered official support for their enterprises, either through bribery of government bureaucrats or through profit-sharing arrangements with gentry families. Indeed, the participation of gentry families in commercial ventures such as warehousing, money lending, and pawnbroking blurred the distinction between gentry and merchants. Merchants blurred the distinction further by providing their sons with an educa-

Portrait of Howqua (Wu Bingjian—1769–1843) in the early nineteenth century. His elegant clothing and surroundings suggest the great wealth of merchants in late Imperial China.
IanDagnall Computing/Alamy Stock Photo

tion that prepared them for government examinations, which in turn could result in promotion to gentry status and appointment to civil service positions.

Although Qing China was still a basically agricultural land, the increasing wealth of the merchant classes signaled that manufacturing and commerce had become much more economically important than in ancient times.

Lower Classes Beyond the Confucian social hierarchy were members of the military forces and the "mean" people. Confucian moralists regarded armed forces as a wretched but necessary evil and attempted to avoid military dominance of society by placing civilian bureaucrats in the highest command positions, even at the expense of military effectiveness. The "mean" people included enslaved people, indentured servants, entertainers, prostitutes, and other marginal groups such as the "beggars of Jiangsu" and the "boat people of Guangdong."

THE CONFUCIAN TRADITION AND NEW CULTURAL INFLUENCES

The Ming and Qing emperors looked to Chinese traditions for guidance in framing their cultural as well as their political and social policies. They provided generous support for Confucianism, particularly in the form of neo-Confucianism articulated by the twelfth-century scholar **Zhu Xi,** and they ensured that formal education in China revolved around Confucian thought and values. Yet the Confucian tradition was not the only cultural alternative in Ming and Qing China. Demographic and urban growth encouraged the emergence of a vibrant popular culture in Chinese cities, and European missionaries reintroduced Roman Catholic Christianity to China and introduced Chinese intellectuals to European science and technology as well.

Neo-Confucianism and Pulp Fiction

Imperial sponsorship of Chinese cultural traditions meant primarily support for the Confucian tradition, especially as systematized by the Song dynasty scholar Zhu Xi, the most prominent architect of neo-Confucianism. Zhu Xi combined the moral, ethical, and political values of Confucius with the logical rigor and speculative power of Buddhist philosophy. He emphasized the values of self-discipline, filial piety, and obedience to established rulers, all of which appealed to Ming and Qing emperors seeking to maintain stability in their vast realm. Cultural policies of the Ming and Qing dynasties made the neo-Confucian tradition the reigning imperial ideology from the fourteenth to the early twentieth century.

Confucian Education To promote Confucian values, the Ming and Qing emperors supported educational programs at several levels. They funded the Hanlin Academy, a research institute for Confucian scholars in Beijing, and maintained provincial schools throughout China where promising students could study for the civil service examinations. The exams themselves encouraged the cultivation of Confucian values because they focused largely on Confucian texts and neo-Confucian commentaries.

Ming and Qing courts also provided generous funding for other projects emphasizing Chinese cultural traditions. The Ming emperor Yongle sponsored the compilation of the *Yongle Encyclopedia,* a vast collection of Chinese philosophical, literary, and historical texts that filled almost twenty-three thousand scrolls. During the Qing dynasty both Kangxi and Qianlong organized similar projects. Kangxi's *Collection of Books* was smaller than the *Yongle Encyclopedia,* but it was more influential because the emperor had it printed and distributed, whereas Yongle's compilation was available only in

Zhu Xi (JHOO SHEE)

three manuscript copies. Qianlong's *Complete Library of the Four Treasures* was too large to publish—it ran to 93,556 pamphlet-size volumes—but the emperor deposited manuscript copies in seven libraries throughout China.

Popular Culture

While the imperial courts promoted Confucianism, a lively popular culture took shape in the cities of China. Most urban residents did not have an advanced education and knew little about Confucius, Zhu Xi, or other intellectual luminaries. Many of them were literate merchants, however, and they preferred intellectually engaging entertainment and diversion over the type typically found in local teahouses and wine shops. Popular novels met their needs.

Popular Novels

Confucian scholars looked down on popular novels as crude fiction that had little to do with the realities of the world. Printing made it possible to produce books cheaply and in mass quantities, however, and urban residents eagerly consumed the fast-paced novels that flooded Chinese cities during the Ming and Qing eras. Many of the novels had little literary merit, but their tales of conflict, horror, wonder, excitement, and sometimes unconcealed pornography appealed to readers.

Yet many popular novels also offered thoughtful reflections on the world and human affairs. The historical novel *The Romance of the Three Kingdoms,* for example, explored the political intrigue that followed the collapse of the Han dynasty. *The Dream of the Red Chamber* told the story of cousins deeply in love who could not marry because of their families' wishes. Through the prism of a sentimental love story, the novel explored the complicated dynamics of wealthy scholar-gentry families. In a different vein, *Journey to the West* dealt with the seventh-century journey to India of the famous Buddhist monk Xuanzang. In the popular novel, Xuanzang's traveling companion was a monkey with magical powers who, among other things, could jump 10,000 kilometers (6,215 miles) in a single bound. While promoting Buddhist values, *Journey to the West* also made the trickster monkey a wildly popular and celebrated character in Chinese literature. As recently as 1987, Chinese-American novelist Maxine Hong Kingston adapted this character to modern times in her novel *Tripmaster Monkey.*

Italian Jesuit Matteo Ricci (left) with Xu Quangqi, his most famous Chinese disciple. Both men wear the distinctive Chinese gowns of educated, refined scholar-gentry. A distinguished scholar who held an appointment at the Hanlin Academy, Xu helped Ricci translate Euclid's geometrical works into Chinese.
Private Collection/AF Fotografie/Alamy Stock Photo

The Return of Christianity to China

Nestorian Christians had established churches and monasteries in China as early as the seventh century C.E., and Roman Catholic communities were prominent in Chinese commercial centers during the Yuan dynasty. After the outbreak of epidemic plague and the collapse of the Yuan dynasty in the fourteenth century, however, Christianity disappeared from China. When Roman Catholic missionaries returned in the sixteenth century, they had to start from scratch in their efforts to win converts and establish a Christian community.

Matteo Ricci

The most prominent of the missionaries were the **Jesuits,** who worked to strengthen Roman Catholic Christianity in Europe and also to spread their faith abroad. Founder of the mission to China was the Italian Jesuit Matteo Ricci (1552–1610), who had the ambitious goal of converting China to Christianity, beginning with the Ming emperor Wanli. Ricci was a brilliant and learned man as well as a polished diplomat, and he became a popular figure at the Ming court. Upon arrival at Macau in 1582, Ricci immersed himself in the study of the Chinese language and the Confucian classics. He had a talent for languages, and his phenomenal memory enabled him to master the thousands of characters used in literary Chinese writing. By the time he first traveled to Beijing and visited the imperial court in 1601, Ricci was able to write learned Chinese and converse fluently with Confucian scholars.

Ricci's mastery of Chinese language and literature opened doors for the Jesuits, who then impressed their hosts with European science and gadgetry. Ricci and his colleagues had an advanced education in mathematics and astronomy, and they were able to correct Chinese calendars that consistently miscalculated solar eclipses. The Jesuits also prepared maps of the world—with China placed diplomatically at the center—on the basis of geographic knowledge that Europeans had gained during their voyages through the world's seas. The Jesuits even supervised the casting of high-quality bronze cannons for Ming and early Qing armies.

Confucianism and Christianity

The Jesuits piqued Chinese curiosity with mechanical devices. Finely ground glass prisms became popular because of their refraction of sunlight into its various colors. Harpsichords also drew attention, and Jesuits with musical talents often composed songs for their hosts. Most popular of all, as we saw in the introduction, were the devices that Chinese called "self-ringing bells"—spring-driven mechanical clocks that kept tolerably accurate time, chimed the hours, and sometimes even struck the quarter hours as well.

The Jesuits sought to capture Chinese interest with European science and technology, but their ultimate goal was always to win converts. They portrayed Christianity as a faith very similar to Chinese cultural traditions. Ricci, for example, wrote a treatise titled *The True Meaning of the Lord of Heaven* in which he argued that the doctrines of Confucius and Jesus were very similar, if not identical. Over the years, according to Ricci, neo-Confucian scholars had altered Confucius's own teachings, so adoption of Christianity by Chinese would represent a return to a more pure and original Confucianism. The Jesuits also held religious services in the Chinese language and allowed converts to continue the time-honored practice of venerating their ancestors.

In spite of their tolerance, flexibility, and genuine respect for their hosts, the Jesuits attracted few converts in China. By the mid-eighteenth century, Chinese Christians numbered about 200,000—a tiny proportion of the Chinese population of 225 million. Chinese people hesitated to adopt Christianity partly because of its exclusivity: for centuries, Chinese had honored Confucianism, Daoism, and Buddhism at the same time. Like Islam, though, Christianity claimed to be the only true religion, so conversion implied that Confucianism, Daoism, and Buddhism were inferior or even fallacious creeds—a proposition most Chinese people were unwilling to accept.

End of the Jesuit Mission Ultimately, the Roman Catholic mission in China came to an end because of squabbles between the Jesuits and members of the Franciscan and Dominican orders, who also sought converts in China. Jealous of the Jesuits' presence at the imperial court, the Franciscans and Dominicans complained to the pope about their rivals' tolerance of ancestor veneration and willingness to conduct Chinese-language services. The pope sided with the critics and in the early eighteenth century issued several proclamations ordering missionaries in China to suppress ancestor veneration and conduct services according to European standards. In response to that demand, the emperor Kangxi ordered an end to the preaching of Christianity in China. Although he did not strictly enforce the ban, the mission weakened, and by the mid-eighteenth century it had effectively come to an end.

The Roman Catholic mission to China did not attract large numbers of Chinese converts, but it nonetheless had important cultural effects. Besides making European science and technology known in China, the Jesuits made China known in Europe. In letters, reports, and other writings distributed widely throughout Europe, the Jesuits described China as an orderly and rational society. The Confucian civil service system attracted the attention of European rulers, who began to design their own civil service bureaucracies in the eighteenth century. The rational morality of Confucianism also appealed to European thinkers, who sought alternatives to Christianity as the foundation for ethics and morality. For the first time since Marco Polo, the Jesuits made firsthand observations of China available to Europeans and stimulated strong European interest in east Asian societies.

THE UNIFICATION OF JAPAN

During the late sixteenth and early seventeenth centuries, the political unification of Japan ended an extended period of civil disorder. Like the Ming and Qing emperors in China, the **Tokugawa** shoguns sought to lay a foundation for long-term political and social stability, and they provided generous support for neo-Confucian studies in an effort to promote traditional values. Indeed, the shoguns went even further than their Chinese counterparts in promoting conservative values and tightly restricting foreign influence in Japan. As in China, however, demographic expansion and economic growth fostered social and cultural change in Japan, and merchants introduced Chinese and European influences into Japan.

The Tokugawa Shogunate

From the twelfth through the sixteenth century, a *shogun* ("military governor") ruled Japan through retainers who received political rights and large estates in exchange for military services. Theoretically, the shogun ruled as a temporary stand-in for the Japanese emperor, the ultimate source of political authority. In fact, however, the emperor was nothing more than a figurehead, and the shogun sought to monopolize power. After the fourteenth century the conflicting ambitions of shoguns and retainers led to constant turmoil, and by the sixteenth century Japan was in a state of civil war. Japanese historians often refer to the sixteenth century as the era of *sengoku*—"the country at war."

Tokugawa Ieyasu Toward the end of the sixteenth century, powerful states emerged in several regions of Japan, and a series of military leaders brought about the unification of the land. In 1600 the last of these chieftains, **Tokugawa Ieyasu** (reigned 1600–1616), established a military government known as the Tokugawa *bakufu* ("tent government" because it theoretically was only a temporary replacement for the emperor's rule). Ieyasu and his descendants ruled the *bakufu* as shoguns from 1600 until the end of the Tokugawa dynasty in 1867.

The principal aim of the Tokugawa shoguns was to stabilize their realm and prevent the return of civil war. Consequently, the shoguns needed to control the *daimyo* ("great names"), powerful territorial lords who ruled most of Japan from their vast, hereditary landholdings. The 260 or so daimyo functioned as near-absolute rulers within their domains.

Tokugawa (TOH-koo-GAH-wah)

daimyo (DEYEM-yoh)

MAP 26.3 Tokugawa Japan, 1600–1867.

Consider Japan's position with regard to China, Korea, and Russia.

Would it have been easy or difficult to enforce the ban on foreign trade during most of the period?

Each maintained a government staffed by military subordinates, supported an independent judiciary, established schools, and circulated paper money. Moreover, after the mid-sixteenth century, many daimyo established relationships with European mariners, from whom they learned how to manufacture and use gunpowder weapons. During the last decades of the *sengoku* era, cannons and personal firearms played prominent roles in Japanese conflicts.

Control of the Daimyo From the castle town of Edo (modern Tokyo), the shogun governed his personal domain and sought to extend his control to the daimyo. The shoguns instituted the policy of "alternate attendance," which required daimyo to maintain their families at Edo and spend every other year at the Tokugawa court. This policy enabled the shoguns to keep an eye on the daimyo, and as a side benefit it encouraged daimyo to spend their money on lavish residences and comfortable lives in Edo rather than investing

it in military forces that could challenge the *bakufu*. The shoguns also subjected marriage alliances between daimyo families to *bakufu* approval, discouraged the daimyo from visiting one another, and required daimyo to obtain permits for construction work on their castles. Even meetings between the daimyo and the emperor required the shogun's permission.

In an effort to prevent European influences from destabilizing the land, the Tokugawa shoguns closely controlled relations between Japan and the outside world. They knew that Spanish forces had conquered the Philippine Islands in the sixteenth century, and they feared that Europeans might jeopardize the security of the *bakufu* itself. Even if Europeans did not conquer Japan, they could cause serious problems by making alliances with daimyo and supplying them with weapons.

Control of Foreign Relations Thus during the 1630s the shoguns issued a series of edicts sharply restricting Japanese relations with other lands: these remained in effect for more than two centuries. The policies forbade Japanese from going abroad on pain of death and prohibited the construction of large ships. It expelled Europeans from Japan, prohibited foreign merchants from trading in Japanese ports, and even forbade the import of foreign books. The policies did allow carefully controlled trade with Asian lands, and it also permitted small numbers of Chinese and Dutch merchants to trade under tight restrictions at the southern port city of Nagasaki.

During the seventeenth century, Japanese authorities strictly enforced these policies. In 1640 a Portuguese merchant ship arrived at Nagasaki in hopes of engaging in trade in spite of the ban. Officials beheaded sixty-one of the party and spared thirteen others so that they could relate the experience to their compatriots. Yet authorities gradually loosened the restrictions, and the policy never led to the complete isolation of Japan from the outside world. Throughout the Tokugawa period, Japan carried on a flourishing trade with China, Korea, Taiwan, and the Ryukyu Islands, and Dutch merchants regularly brought news of European and larger world affairs.

Economic and Social Change

By ending civil conflict and maintaining political stability, the Tokugawa shoguns set the stage for economic growth in Japan. Ironically, peace and a booming economy encouraged social change that undermined the order that the *bakufu* sought to preserve.

Economic growth had its roots in increased agricultural production. New crop strains, new methods of water control and irrigation, and the use of fertilizer brought increased yields of rice. Production of cotton, silk, indigo, and sake (rice wine) also increased dramatically. In many parts of Japan, villages moved away from subsistence farming in favor of production for the market. Between 1600 and 1700, agricultural production doubled.

Population Growth Increased agricultural production brought about rapid demographic growth: during the seventeenth century the Japanese population rose by almost one-third, from twenty-two million to twenty-nine million. Thereafter, however, Japan underwent a demographic transition, as many families practiced population control to maintain or raise their standard of living. Between 1700 and 1850 the Japanese population grew moderately, from twenty-nine million to thirty-two million. Contraception, late marriage, and abortion all played roles in limiting population growth, as did infanticide, euphemistically referred to as "thinning out the rice shoots." Japanese families resorted to those measures primarily because Japan was land poor. During the seventeenth century, populations in some areas strained resources, causing financial difficulties for local governments and distress for rural communities.

The Tokugawa era was an age of social as well as demographic change in Japan. Because of Chinese cultural influence, the Japanese social hierarchy followed Confucian precepts in ranking the ruling elites—including the shogun, daimyo, and

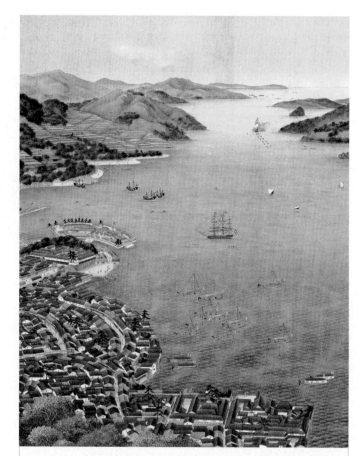

Dutch sailing ships and smaller Japanese vessels mingle in Nagasaki harbor, the only place the Japanese government allowed the Dutch to trade. Dutch merchants conducted their business on the artificial island of Deshima, at left.
CPA Media Pte Ltd/Alamy Stock Photo

samurai warriors—as the most prominent and privileged class of society. Beneath them were peasants and artisans. Merchants ranked at the bottom, as they did in China.

Social Change The extended period of peace ushered in by Tokugawa rule undermined the social position of the ruling elites. Since the twelfth century the administration of local affairs had fallen mostly to daimyo and samurai warriors. Once Japan was stable, however, the interest of Tokugawa authorities was to reduce the numbers of armed professional warriors, so they pushed daimyo and samurai to become bureaucrats and government functionaries. They even encouraged daimyo and samurai to turn their talents to scholarship, a pursuit that their martial ancestors would have utterly despised. As they lost their accustomed place in society, many of the ruling elite also fell into financial difficulty. Their principal income came in the form of rice collected from peasant cultivators of their lands. They readily converted rice into money through brokers, but the price of rice did not keep pace with other costs. Moreover, daimyo and samurai lived in expensive

This hanging scroll depicts the pleasure quarters or courtesan district of Kyoto in the late seventeenth century. Courtesans awaited clients behind the wooden grill.

Ashmolean Museum/Heritage Images/Getty Images

and sometimes ostentatious style—particularly daimyo who sought to impress others with their wealth while residing at Edo in alternate years. Many of them became indebted to rice brokers and gradually declined into genteel poverty.

Meanwhile, as in China, merchants in Japan became increasingly wealthy and prominent. Japanese cities flourished throughout the Tokugawa era—the population of Edo approached one million by 1700—and merchants prospered handsomely in the vibrant urban environment. Rice dealers, pawnbrokers, and sake merchants soon controlled more wealth than ruling elites. Those who became especially wealthy sometimes purchased elite ranks or contracted marriages with elite families in efforts to improve their social standing.

Neo-Confucianism and Floating Worlds

Japan had been deeply influenced by Chinese culture in the past, and the influence of China continued throughout the Tokugawa era. Formal education began with study of Chinese language and literature. As late as the nineteenth century,

many Japanese scholars wrote their philosophical, legal, and religious works in Chinese. The common people embraced Buddhism, which had come to Japan from China, and Confucianism was the most influential philosophical system.

Neo-Confucianism in Japan Like the Ming and Qing emperors in China, the Tokugawa shoguns promoted the **neo-Confucianism** of Zhu Xi. With its emphasis on filial piety and loyalty to superiors, neo-Confucianism provided a respectable ideological underpinning for the *bakufu*. The shoguns patronized scholars who advocated neo-Confucian views, which figured prominently in the educational curriculum. All those who had a formal education—including the sons of merchants as well as offspring of government officials—received constant exposure to neo-Confucian values. By the early eighteenth century, neo-Confucianism had become the official ideology of the Tokugawa *bakufu*.

Native Learning Yet even with Tokugawa sponsorship, neo-Confucianism did not dominate intellectual life in Japan.

A colored woodcut by Okumura Masanobu depicts the audience at a seventeenth-century kabuki theater. Enthusiastic actors often ran down wooden ramps and played their roles among the audience.

Universal History Archive/Getty Images

Although most scholars recognized Japan's debt to Chinese intellectual traditions, some sought to establish a sense of Japanese identity that did not depend on cultural kinship with China. Particularly during the eighteenth century, scholars of "native learning" scorned neo-Confucianism and even Buddhism as alien cultural imports and emphasized instead the importance of folk traditions and the indigenous Shinto religion for Japanese identity. Many scholars of native learning viewed Japanese people as superior to all others and regarded foreign influence as dangerous. They urged the study of Japanese classics and glorified the supposed purity of Japanese society before its corruption by Chinese and other foreign influences.

While scholars of neo-Confucianism and native learning debated issues of philosophy and Japanese identity, the emergence of a prosperous merchant class encouraged the development of a vibrant popular culture. During the seventeenth and eighteenth centuries, an exuberant middle-class culture flourished in cities such as Kyoto, the imperial capital; Edo, Japan's largest city and home to bureaucrats and daimyo; and Osaka, the commercial hub of the islands. In those and other cities, Japan's finest creative talents catered to middle-class appetites.

Floating Worlds The centers of Tokugawa urban culture were the *ukiyo* (**"floating worlds"**), entertainment and pleasure quarters where teahouses, theaters, brothels, and public baths offered escape from social responsibilities and the rigid rules of conduct that governed public behavior in Tokugawa society. In contrast to the solemn, serious proceedings of the imperial court and the *bakufu,* the popular culture of urban residents was secular and satirical. The main expressions of this lively culture were prose fiction and new forms of theater.

Ihara Saikaku (1642–1693), one of Japan's most prolific poets, helped create a new genre of prose literature, the "books of the floating world." Much of his fiction revolved around the themes of sex and love. In ***The Life of a Man Who Lived for Love,*** for example, Ihara chronicled the experiences of a townsman who devoted his life, beginning at the tender age of eight,

This fresco, entitled the "Twenty-six Martyrs of Japan," famously illustrates the crucifixion of Christians, mainly Japanese converts, ordered by Hideyoshi Toyotomi during the shogunate's repression of the religion.
Pontino/Alamy Stock Photo

to a quest for sexual pleasure. Ihara's treatment of love stressed the erotic, and the brief, episodic stories that made up his work appealed to literate urban residents who were not inclined to pore over dense neo-Confucian treatises.

Beginning in the early seventeenth century, two new forms of drama became popular in Japanese cities. One was *kabuki* theater, which usually featured several acts consisting of lively and sometimes bawdy skits where stylized acting combined with lyric singing, dancing, and spectacular staging. A crucial component of kabuki was the actor's ability to improvise and embellish the dialogue, for the text of plays served only as guides for the dramatic performance. The other new dramatic form was *bunraku,* the puppet theater. In bunraku, chanters accompanied by music told a story acted out by puppets. Manipulated by a team of three, each puppet could execute the subtlest and most intricate movements, such as brushing a tear from the eye with the sleeve of a kimono. Both kabuki and bunraku attracted enthusiastic audiences in search of entertainment and diversion.

Christianity and Dutch Learning

Christian Missions Alongside neo-Confucianism, native learning, and middle-class popular culture, Christian missionaries and European merchants contributed their own distinctive threads to the cultural fabric of Tokugawa Japan. The Jesuit **Francis Xavier** traveled to Japan in 1549 and opened a mission to seek converts to Christianity. In the early decades of their mission, Jesuits experienced remarkable success in Japan. Several powerful daimyo adopted Christianity and ordered

Francis Xavier (fran-sis ZEY-vee-er)
Christovão Ferreira (kris-TOH-vo feh-RAY-rah)

their subjects to do likewise. The principal interest of the daimyo was to establish trade and military alliances with Europeans, but many Japanese converts became enthusiastic Christians and worked to convert their compatriots to the new faith. By the 1580s about 150,000 Japanese had converted to Christianity, and by 1615 Japanese Christians numbered about 300,000.

Although Christians were only a tiny minority of the Japanese population, the popularity of Christianity generated a backlash among government officials and moralists seeking to preserve Japanese religious and cultural traditions. The Tokugawa shoguns restricted European access to Japan largely because of concerns that Christianity might serve as a cultural bridge for alliances between daimyo and European adventurers, which in turn could lead to destabilization of Japanese society and even threats to the *bakufu.* Meanwhile, Buddhist and Confucian scholars resented the Christian conviction that their faith was the only true doctrine. Some Japanese converts to Christianity themselves eventually rejected their adopted faith out of frustration because European missionaries refused to allow them to become priests or play leadership roles in the mission.

Anti-Christian Campaign Between 1587 and 1639, shoguns promulgated several decrees ordering a halt to Christian missions and commanding Japanese Christians to renounce their faith. In 1612 the shoguns began rigorous enforcement of those decrees. They tortured and executed European missionaries who refused to leave the islands as well as Japanese Christians who refused to abandon their faith. They often executed victims by crucifixion or burning at the stake, which Tokugawa authorities regarded as especially appropriate punishments for Christians. The campaign was so effective that even some European missionaries abandoned Christianity. Most notable of them was the Portuguese Jesuit **Christovão Ferreira,** head of

SOURCES FROM THE PAST

Fabian Fucan Rejects Christianity

Fabian Fucan (ca. 1565–1621) was a Japanese Buddhist who converted to Christianity and entered the Jesuit order as a novice in 1586. In the early seventeenth century, however, his relations with the Jesuits soured, and he eventually left the order. In 1620 he composed a treatise titled Deus Destroyed *that leveled a spirited attack at Christianity and its God ("Deus" in Latin). His work reveals deep concerns about European imperial expansion as well as Christian doctrine.*

I joined this creed at an early age; diligently, I studied its teachings and pursued its practices. Due to my stupidity, however, I was long unable to realize that this was a perverse and cursed faith. Thus fruitlessly I spent twenty years and more! Then one day I clearly perceived that the words of the adherents of Deus were very clever and appeared very near reason—but in their teaching there was little truth. So I left their company. Some fifteen years have passed since: every morning I have lamented my desertion of the Great Holy True Law [of Buddhism]; every evening I have grieved over my adherence to the crooked path of the barbarians. All that effort to no effect! But I had a friend who remonstrated with me, saying: "'If you have made a mistake, do not be afraid of admitting the fact and amending your ways' [a Confucian precept]. Here, this is the Confucians' golden rule of life—act on it! Before, you learned all about the cursed faith of Deus; take pen in hand now, commit your knowledge to writing, and counter their teachings. Not only will you thereby gain the merit of destroying wickedness and demonstrating truth; you will also supply a guide toward new knowledge."

> Does Fucan indicate what it was that caused him to turn away from Christianity?

All right. Though I am not a clever man, I shall by all means try to act on this advice. I shall gather the important points about the teachings of the Deus sect and shall skip what is not essential; my aim is to write concisely. Thus shall I mount my attack; and I shall call my volume DEUS DESTROYED. . . .

Japan is the Land of the Gods. The generations of our rulers have received the Imperial Dignity from [the gods] Amaterasu Omikami, through U-gaya-fuki-awsezu no Mikoto and his August Child Jimmu Tenno, who became the progenitor of our Hundred Kings. The Three Divine Regalia [symbols of rule received from the gods] became the protectors of the Empire, so that among all the customs of our land there is not one which depends not on the Way of the Gods. . . .

And this, the adherents of Deus plan to subvert! They bide their time with the intent to make all of Japan into their own sectarians, to destroy the Law of Buddha and the Way of the Gods. Because the Law of Buddha and the Way of the Gods are planted here, the Royal Sway also flourishes; and since the Royal Sway is established here the glory of the Buddhas and the gods does grow. And therefore the adherents of Deus have no recourse but to subvert the Royal Sway, overthrow the Buddhas and the gods, eliminate the customs of Japan, and then to import the customs of their own countries; thus only will advance the plot they have concocted to usurp the country themselves.

They have dispatched troops and usurped such countries as Luzon [the Philippines] and Nova Hispania [Mexico], lands of barbarians with nature close to animal. But our land by far surpasses others in fierce bravery; and therefore the ambition to diffuse their faith in every quarter and thus to usurp the country, even if it take a thousand years, has penetrated down to the very marrow of their bones. Ah!—but what a gloomy prospect awaits them! For the sake of their faith they value their lives less than trash, than garbage. *Martyr,* they call this. When a wise sovereign rules the Empire good is promoted and evil is chastised. Rewards promote good and punishments chastise evil. There is no greater punishment than to take away life; but the adherents of Deus, without even fearing that their lives be cut, will not change their religion. How horrible, how awful it is!

> According to Fucan, what makes Japan different than the Phillipines or Mexico in terms of conversion to Christianity?

For Further Reflection

■ Discuss the various religious, cultural, historical, political, and social aspects of Fabian Fucan's attack on Christianity.

Source: George Elison. *Deus Destroyed: The Image of Christianity in Early Modern Japan.* Cambridge, Mass.: Harvard University Press, 1973, pp. 259–60, 283–84.

the Jesuit mission in Japan, who gave up Christianity under torture, adopted Buddhism, and interrogated many Europeans who fell into Japanese hands in the mid-seventeenth century. By the late seventeenth century, the anti-Christian campaign had claimed tens of thousands of lives, and Christianity survived as a secret, underground religion observed only in rural regions of southern Japan.

Dutch Learning Tokugawa policies ensured that Christianity would not soon reappear in Japan, but they did not entirely prevent contacts between Europeans and Japanese. After 1639, Dutch merchants trading at Nagasaki became Japan's principal source of information about Europe and the world beyond east Asia. A small number of Japanese scholars learned Dutch in order to communicate with the foreigners. Their studies, which they called **Dutch learning,** brought considerable knowledge of the outside world to Japan. After 1720, Tokugawa authorities lifted the ban on foreign books, and Dutch learning began to play a significant role in Japanese intellectual life.

European art influenced Japanese scholars interested in anatomy and botany because of its accurate representations of objects. Scholars translated Dutch medical and scientific treatises into Japanese and learned to draw according to the principles of linear perspective, which enabled them to prepare textbooks that were more accurate than the Chinese works they had previously used. European astronomy was also popular in Japan because it enabled scholars to improve calendars and issue accurate predictions of eclipses and other celestial events. By the mid-eighteenth century, the Tokugawa shoguns themselves had become enthusiastic proponents of Dutch learning, and schools of European medicine and Dutch studies flourished in several Japanese cities.

CONCLUSION

Both China and Japan controlled their own affairs throughout the early modern era and avoided the turmoil that afflicted societies in the Americas and much of sub-Saharan Africa. After driving the Mongols to the steppe lands of central Asia, rulers of the Ming dynasty built a powerful centralized state in China. They worked diligently to eradicate all vestiges of Mongol rule and restore traditional ways by reviving Chinese political institutions and providing state sponsorship for neo-Confucianism. In the interest of stability, authorities also restricted encounters with foreigners by limiting foreign merchants' access to China and the activities of Christian missionaries. The succeeding Qing dynasty pursued similar policies. The Ming and Qing dynasties both brought political stability, but China experienced considerable social and economic change in early modern times. American food crops helped increase agricultural production, which fueled rapid population growth, and global trade stimulated the Chinese economy, which improved the position of merchants and artisans in society. The experience of the Tokugawa era in Japan was much like that of the Ming and Qing eras in China. The Tokugawa *bakufu* brought political order to the Japanese islands and closely controlled encounters with foreigners, but a vibrant economy promoted social change that enhanced the status of merchants and artisans.

STUDY TERMS

Analects of Confucius (554)	*Complete Library of the*
bakufu (563)	*Four Treasuries* (562)
bunraku (568)	*daimyo* (563)
Christovão Ferreira (568)	*The Dream of the Red*
civil service examinations (554)	*Chamber* (562)
Collection of Books (561)	Dutch learning (570)

eunuch (550)	Qianlong (553)
filial piety (555)	Qing dynasty (549)
floating worlds (567)	*The Romance of the Three*
foot binding (556)	*Kingdoms* (562)
Francis Xavier (568)	*sengoku* (563)
Great Wall (551)	*shogun* (563)
Hongwu (550)	Son of Heaven (554)
Jesuits (562)	Tokugawa (563)
Journey to the West (562)	Tokugawa Ieyasu (563)
kabuki (568)	*The True Meaning of the Lord*
Kangxi (553)	*of Heaven* (563)
The Life of a Man Who Lived	*ukiyo* (567)
for Love (567)	Wanli (548)
Manchu (552)	Yongle (550)
Matteo Ricci (548)	*Yongle Encyclopedia* (561)
Ming dynasty (550)	Zheng He (558)
neo-Confucianism (566)	Zhu Xi (561)
Nurhaci (552)	

FOR FURTHER READING

Timothy Brook. *The Confusions of Pleasure: Commerce and Culture in Ming China.* Berkeley, 1998. Fascinating social and cultural analysis of Ming China focusing on the role of commerce as an agent of social change.

———. *The Troubled Empire: China in the Yuan and Ming Dynasties.* Cambridge, Mass., 2010. A readable and intriguing account of the Yuan and Ming dynasties.

Adam Clulow. *The Company and the Shogun: The Dutch Encounter with Tokugawa Japan.* New York, 2013. Explores the Dutch East India Company's clashes with Tokugawa Japan over trade and diplomacy.

Mark C. Elliott. *The Manchu Way: The Eight Banners and Ethnic Identity in Late Imperial China.* Stanford, 2001. Important scholarly study focusing on relations between Manchus and Chinese during the Qing dynasty.

Benjamin A. Elman. *A Cultural History of Civil Examinations in Late Imperial China.* Berkeley, 2000. A meticulous study of one of the most important institutions in Chinese history.

Susan Mann and Yu-Ying Cheng, eds. *Under Confucian Eyes: Writings on Gender in Chinese History.* Berkeley, 2001. A rich anthology of primary texts documenting the lives of women in imperial China.

Kenneth Pomeranz. *The Great Divergence: China, Europe, and the Making of the Modern World Economy.* Princeton, 2000. Pathbreaking scholarly study that illuminates the economic history of the early modern world through comparison of economic development in Asian and European lands.

William T. Rowe. *China's Last Empire: The Great Qing.* Cambridge, Mass., 2009. Revisionist history that challenges ideas of the Qing Empire as inward-looking.

Ronald P. Toby. *State and Diplomacy in Early Modern Japan: Asia in the Development of the Tokugawa Bakufu.* Princeton, 1984. An important study dealing with Japanese trade and relations with other lands under Tokugawa rule.

H. Paul Varley. *Japanese Culture.* 4th ed. Honolulu, 2000. Places the cultural history of the Tokugawa era in its larger historical context.

27 Empires in South and Southwest Asia

ZOOMING IN ON TRADITIONS

Shah Jahan's Monument to Love and Allah

In 1635 **Shah Jahan,** the emperor of Mughal India, took his seat on the Peacock Throne. Seven years in the making, the Peacock Throne is probably the most spectacular seat on which any human being has rested. Shah Jahan ordered the throne encrusted with ten million rupees' worth of diamonds, rubies, emeralds, and pearls. Atop the throne itself stood a magnificent, golden-bodied peacock with a huge ruby and a fifty-carat, pear-shaped pearl on its breast and a brilliant elevated tail fashioned of blue sapphires and other colored gems.

Yet, for all its splendor, the Peacock Throne ranks a distant second among the artistic projects Shah Jahan sponsored: pride of place goes to the Taj Mahal. Built over a period of eighteen years as a tomb for Shah Jahan's beloved wife, **Mumtaz Mahal,** who died during childbirth in 1631, the Taj Mahal is a graceful and elegant monument both to the departed empress and to Shah Jahan's Islamic faith.

The Taj Mahal was a sumptuous mosque and tomb built between 1632 and 1649 by Shah Jahan in memory of his wife, Mumtaz Mahal.
Andrea Pistolesi/The Image Bank/Getty Images

Shah Jahan (shah jah-han)
Mumtaz Mahal (moom-tahz muh-HAHL)

The emperor and his architects conceived the Taj Mahal as a vast allegory in stone symbolizing the day when Allah would cause the dead to rise and undergo judgment before his heavenly throne. Its gardens represented the gardens of paradise, and the four water channels running through them symbolized the four rivers of the heavenly kingdom. The domed marble tomb of Mumtaz Mahal represented the throne of Allah, and the four minarets surrounding the structure served as legs supporting the divine throne. Craftsmen carved verses from the Quran throughout the Taj Mahal. The main gateway to the structure features the entire text of the chapter promising that on the day of judgment, Allah will punish the wicked and gather the faithful into his celestial paradise.

CHAPTER OVERVIEW

The Peacock Throne and the Taj Mahal testify to the wealth of the Mughal empire, while the tomb of Mumtaz Mahal highlights the Islamic character of the ruling dynasty. But the Mughal empire, which ruled most of the Indian subcontinent for more than three hundred years, was not the only well-organized empire in south and southwest Asia during early modern times. The Ottoman Empire was a dynastic Muslim state centered in what is today Turkey. At the height of its power, it controlled a vast area from southeastern Europe to western Asia and North Africa. It was also the longest-lived of the empires in these two regions, as it remained intact until the early twentieth century. On the eastern borders of the Ottoman Empire lay the ancient lands of Persia, where yet another powerful empire emerged during the early sixteenth century. Ruled by the Safavid dynasty, this state never expanded far beyond its heartland of present-day Iran, but its Shiite rulers challenged the Sunni Ottomans for dominance in southwest Asia. The Safavid realm prospered from its place in trade networks linking China, India, Russia, southwest Asia, and the Mediterranean basin.

All three empires in this broad region had Turkish ruling dynasties. The Ottomans, Safavids, and Mughals came from nomadic, Turkish-speaking peoples of central Asia who conquered the settled agricultural lands of Anatolia, Persia, and India, respectively. All three dynasties retained political and cultural traditions that their ancestors had adopted while leading nomadic lives on the steppes, but they also adapted readily to the city-based agricultural societies that they conquered. The Ottoman dynasty made especially effective use of the gunpowder weapons that transformed early modern warfare, and the Safavids and the Mughals also incorporated gunpowder weapons into their arsenals. All three dynasties officially embraced Islam and drew cultural guidance from Islamic values.

During the sixteenth and early seventeenth centuries, the three empires presided over expansive and prosperous societies. About the mid-seventeenth century, however, they all began to weaken. Their waning fortunes reflected the fact that they had ceased to expand territorially and gain access to new sources of wealth. Instead, each empire waged long, costly wars that drained resources without bringing compensating benefits. The empires also faced domestic difficulties. Each of them was an ethnically and religiously diverse realm, and each experienced tensions when conservative Muslim leaders lobbied for strict observance of Islam while members of other communities sought greater freedom for themselves. All three empires—especially the Mughal and Ottoman—relied increasingly on trade with Europeans, who came to their lands with textiles, food items, and armaments. Although it could not have been predicted initially, such reliance eventually put the empires at both an economic and technological disadvantage to Europeans, who increasingly sought to dominate the world around them. By the mid-eighteenth century, the Safavid empire had collapsed, and the Ottoman and Mughal realms were rapidly falling under European influence.

CHRONOLOGY	
1289–1923	Ottoman dynasty
1451–1481	Reign of Mehmed the Conqueror
1453	Ottoman conquest of Constantinople
1501–1524	Reign of Shah Ismail
1501–1722	Safavid dynasty
1502–1558	Life of Hurrem Sultana
1514	Battle of Chaldiran
1520–1566	Reign of Süleyman the Magnificent
1526–1858	Mughal dynasty
1556	Construction of Süleymaniye Mosque
1556–1605	Reign of Akbar
1588–1629	Reign of Shah Abbas the Great
ca. 1600	Introduction of tobacco to the Ottoman Empire
1632–1649	Construction of the Taj Mahal
1659–1707	Reign of Aurangzeb

FORMATION OF THE EMPIRES OF SOUTH AND SOUTHWEST ASIA

By the sixteenth century, Turkish warriors had transformed much of south and southwest Asia into vast regional empires. These empires divided up the greater part of the Islamic world at the time: the **Ottoman Empire,** which was distinguished by its multiethnic character; the **Safavid empire** of Persia, which served as the center of Shiite Islam; and the **Mughal empire,** which had been imposed over a predominantly Hindu Indian subcontinent. The creation of these durable and powerful political entities attempted centralization throughout south and southwest Asia.

All three empires began as small warrior principalities in frontier areas. They expanded at varying rates and with varying degrees of success at the expense of neighboring states. As they grew, they devised elaborate administrative and military institutions. Under the guidance of talented and energetic rulers, each empire organized an effective governmental apparatus and presided over a prosperous society.

Mughal (MOO-guhl)

ghazi (GAH-zee)

The Ottoman Empire

Osman The Ottoman Empire was an unusually successful frontier state. The term *Ottoman* derived from **Osman Bey,** founder of the dynasty that continued in unbroken succession from 1289 until the dissolution of the empire in 1923. Osman was *bey* (chief) of a band of seminomadic Turks who migrated to northwestern Anatolia in the thirteenth century. Osman and his followers sought above all to become *ghazi,* Muslim religious warriors, who fought in the name of Islam against non-Muslims.

Ottoman Expansion The Ottomans' location on the borders of the Byzantine Empire afforded them ample opportunity to wage war against non-Muslims. Their first great success came in 1326 with the capture of the Anatolian city of Bursa, which became the capital of the Ottoman principality. Around 1352 they established a foothold in Europe when they seized the fortress of Gallipoli while aiding a claimant to the Byzantine throne. Numerous *ghazi,* many of them recent converts to Islam, soon flocked to join the Ottomans. The city of Edirne (Adrianople) became a second Ottoman capital and served as a base for further expansion into the Balkans. As warriors settled in frontier districts and pushed their boundaries

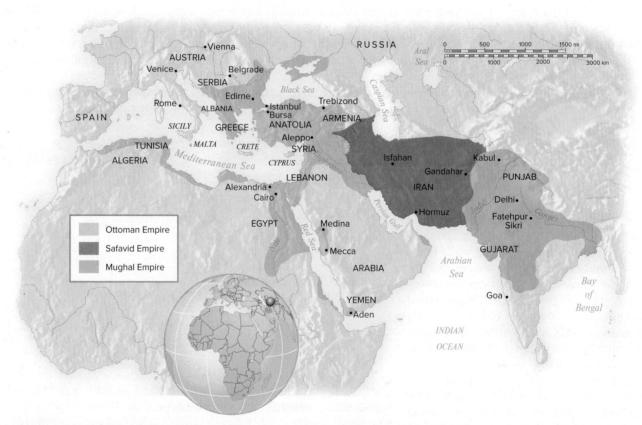

MAP 27.1   The Empires of South and Southwest Asia.

Locate the Ottoman capital of Istanbul, the Safavid capital of Isfahan, and the Mughal capital of Delhi.

What strategic or commercial purposes did each of these capitals fulfill, and how would their locations have aided or hindered imperial administration?

forward, they took spoils and gathered revenues that enriched both the *ghazi* and the central government. Bursa, for example, developed into a major commercial and intellectual center with inns, shops, schools, libraries, and mosques.

A formidable military machine drove Ottoman expansion. Ottoman military leaders initially organized *ghazi* recruits into two forces: a light cavalry and a volunteer infantry. As the Ottoman state became more firmly established, it added a professional cavalry force equipped with heavy armor and financed by land grants. After expanding into the Balkans, the Ottomans created a powerful force composed of slave troops. Through an institution known as the **devshirme,** the Ottomans required the Christian population of the Balkans to contribute young boys to become slaves of the sultan. The boys received special training, learned Turkish, and converted to Islam. According to individual ability, they entered either the Ottoman civilian administration or the military. Those who became soldiers were known as **Janissaries,** from the Turkish *yeni cheri* ("new troops"). Despite the fact that they did not choose these roles for themselves, the Janissaries quickly gained a reputation for intense group pride, loyalty to the sultan, and readiness to employ new military technology. Besides building powerful military forces, the Ottomans outfitted their forces with gunpowder weapons and used them effectively in battles and sieges.

Mehmed the Conqueror The capture of Constantinople in 1453 by Mehmed II (reigned 1451–1481)—known as **Mehmed the Conqueror**—opened a new chapter in Ottoman expansion. With its superb location and illustrious heritage, Constantinople became the new Ottoman capital, subsequently known as Istanbul, and Mehmed worked energetically to stimulate its role as a commercial center. With the capture of the great city behind him, Mehmed presented himself not just as a warrior-sultan but also as a true emperor, ruler of the "two lands" (Europe and Asia) and the "two seas" (the Black Sea and the Mediterranean). He laid the foundations for a tightly centralized, absolute monarchy, and his army faced no serious rival. He completed the conquest of Serbia; moved into southern Greece and Albania; eliminated the last Byzantine outpost at Trebizond on the Black Sea; captured Genoese ports in the Crimea; initiated a naval war with Venice in the Mediterranean; and reportedly hoped to cross the Strait of Otranto, march on Rome, and capture the pope himself. Toward the end of his life, he launched an invasion of Italy and briefly occupied Otranto, but his successors abandoned Mehmed's plans for expansion in western Europe.

Süleyman the Magnificent The Ottomans continued their expansion in the early sixteenth century when sultan Selim the Grim (reigned 1512–1520) occupied Syria and Egypt. Ottoman expansion climaxed in the reign of **Süleyman the Magnificent** (reigned 1520–1566). Süleyman vigorously promoted Ottoman conquests both in southwest Asia and in

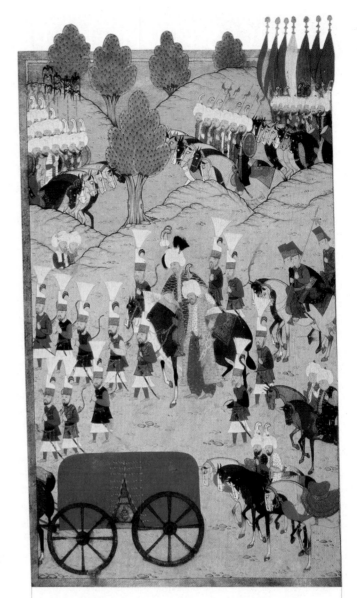

Sultan Süleyman (center, on horse) leads Ottoman forces as they march on Europe. How does this illustration promote the power and prominence of Süleyman and his Ottoman forces?
Leemage/Universal Images Group/Newscom

Europe. In 1534 he conquered Baghdad and added the Tigris and Euphrates valleys to the Ottoman domain. In Europe he kept the rival Hapsburg Empire on the defensive throughout his reign. He captured Belgrade in 1521, defeated and killed the king of Hungary at the battle of Mohács in 1526, consolidated Ottoman power north of the Danube, and in 1529 subjected the Hapsburgs' prized city of Vienna to a brief siege.

Süleyman (SOO-lee-mahn)

SOURCES FROM THE PAST

Ghiselin de Busbecq's Concerns about the Ottoman Empire

Ogier Ghiselin de Busbecq (1522–1592) was a diplomat who traveled to Istanbul in 1555 as a representative of Hapsburg King Ferdinand of Hungary and Bohemia to negotiate a border dispute between Ferdinand and Sultan Süleyman the Magnificent. In a series of four letters to a friend, Ghiselin commented on the Ottoman state, society, customs, and military forces. His observations left him deeply concerned about the prospects of Christian Europe in the event of conflict with the Ottoman realm.

The Sultan [Süleyman "the Lawgiver"] was seated on a very low ottoman, not more than a foot from the ground, which was covered with a quantity of costly rugs and cushions of exquisite workmanship; near him lay his bow and arrows . . .; The Sultan then listened to what I had to say; but the language I used was not at all to his taste, for the demands of his Majesty breathed a spirit of independence and dignity, which was by no means acceptable to one who deemed that his wish was law; and so he made no answer beyond saying in an impatient way, "Giusel, giusel," that is, "well, well." After this we were dismissed to our quarters.

The Sultan's hall was crowded with people, among whom were several officers of high rank. Besides these, there were all the troopers of the Imperial guard, and a large force of Janissaries [the elite infantry corps], but there was not in all that great assembly a single man who owed his position to anything save his valor and his merit. No distinction is attached to birth among the Turks; the respect to be paid to a man is measured by the position he holds in the public service. There is no fighting for precedence; a man's place is marked out by the duties he discharges . . ., It is by merit that men rise in the service, a system which ensures that posts should only be assigned to the competent. Each man in Turkey carries in his own hand his ancestry and his position in life, which he may make or mar as he will. Those who receive the highest offices from the Sultan are for the most part the sons of shepherds or herdsmen, and so far from being ashamed of their parentage, they actually glory in it, and consider it a matter of boasting that they owe nothing to the accident of birth; for they do not believe that high qualities are either natural or hereditary, nor do they think, that they can be handed down from father to son, but that they are partly the gift of God, and partly the result of good training, great industry, and unwearied zeal; arguing that high qualities do not descend from a father to his son or heir, any more than a talent for music, mathematics or the like . . .; Among the Turks, therefore, honors, high posts, and judgeships are the rewards of great ability and good service. If a man is dishonest, or lazy, or careless, he remains at the bottom of the ladder, an object of contempt; for such qualities there are no honors in Turkey!

This is the reason that they are successful in their undertakings, that they lord it over others, and are daily extending the bounds of their empire. These are not our ideals, with us there is no opening left for merit; birth is the standard for everything; the prestige of birth is the sole key to advancement in public service.

It makes me shudder to think of what the result of a struggle between such different systems must be; one of us must prevail and the other be destroyed, at any rate we cannot both exist in safety. On their side is the vast wealth of their empire, unimpaired resources, experience and practice in arms, a veteran soldiery, an uninterrupted series of victories, readiness to endure hardships, union, order, discipline, thrift, and watchfulness. On ours are found an empty exchequer, luxurious habits, exhausted resources, broken spirits, a raw and insubordinate soldiery, and greedy generals; there is no regard for discipline, license runs riot, the men indulge in drunkenness and debauchery, and worst of all, the enemy are accustomed to victory, we, to defeat. Can we doubt what the result must be?

> Does de Busbecq seem surprised by the fact that merit is valued more highly than birth by the Ottomans? Why?

> What advantages, according to de Busbecq, does a system of rewarding merit have over a system of rewarding birth?

For Further Reflection

■ What was de Busbecq's purpose in writing this letter? Was he trying to prompt a reaction and, if so, from whom?

Source: Foster, C. T., and F. H. Blackburne Daniell. "Süleyman 'the Lawgiver.'" in *The Life and Letters of Ogier Ghiselin de Busbecq.* vol. 1. London: Hakluyt Society, 1881. pp. 152–156.

Under Süleyman the Ottomans also became a major naval power. In addition to their own Aegean and Black Sea fleets, the Ottomans inherited the navy of the Mamluk rulers of Egypt. A Turkish corsair, Khayr al-Din Barbarossa Pasha, who had challenged Spanish forces in Tunisia and Algeria, placed his pirate fleet under the Ottoman flag and became Süleyman's leading admiral. Thus Süleyman was able to challenge Christian vessels throughout the Mediterranean as well as Portuguese fleets in the Red Sea and the Indian Ocean. The Ottomans seized the island of Rhodes from the Knights of St. John, besieged Malta, secured Yemen and Aden, and even dispatched a squadron to attack the Portuguese fleet at Diu in India.

The Safavid Empire

In 1499 a twelve-year-old boy named **Ismail** left the swamps of Gilan near the Caspian Sea, where he had hidden from the enemies of his family for five years, to seek his revenge. Two years later he entered Tabriz (in modern Iran) at the head of an army and laid claim to the ancient Persian imperial title of shah. The young Shah Ismail (reigned 1501–1524) also proclaimed that the official religion of his realm would be **Twelver Shiism,** and he proceeded to impose it, by force when necessary, on the formerly **Sunni** population. Over the next decade he seized control of the Iranian plateau and launched expeditions into the Caucasus, Anatolia, Mesopotamia, and central Asia.

The Safavids For propaganda purposes, Shah Ismail and his successors carefully controlled accounts of their rise to power—and expediently changed the story when circumstances warranted. They traced their ancestry back to Safi al-Din (1252–1334), leader of a Sufi religious order in northwestern Persia. Sufism, a mystical belief and practice, formed an important Islamic tradition (discussed in chapter 14). The goal of a Sufi mystic, such as Safi al-Din, was to recover the lost intimacy between God and the human soul and to find the truth of divine knowledge and love through a direct personal experience of God. The famous tomb and shrine of Safi al-Din at Ardabil became the home of Shah Ismail's family (named "Safavids" after the holy man himself); the headquarters of his religious movement; and the center of a determined, deliberate campaign to win political power for his descendants. The Safavids changed their religious preferences several times in the hope of gaining popular support before settling on a form of **Shiism** that appealed to the nomadic Turkish tribes moving into the area in the post-Mongol era.

Twelver Shiism Twelver Shiism held that there had been twelve infallible imams (or religious leaders) after Muhammad, beginning with the prophet's cousin and son-in-law Ali. The twelfth, "hidden" imam had gone into hiding around 874 to escape persecution, but the Twelver Shiites believed he was still alive and would one day return to take power and spread his true religion. Ismail's father had instructed his Turkish followers to wear a distinctive red hat with twelve pleats in memory of the twelve Shiite imams, and they subsequently became known as the *qizilbash* ("red heads"). Safavid propaganda also suggested that Ismail was himself the hidden imam or even an incarnation of Allah. Although most Muslims, including most Shiites, would have regarded those claims as utterly blasphemous, the *qizilbash* enthusiastically accepted them because they resembled traditional Turkish conceptions of leadership that associated military leaders with divinity. The *qizilbash* believed that Ismail would make them invincible in battle, and they became extremely loyal to the Safavid cause.

Battle of Chaldiran Shah Ismail's curious blend of Shiism and Turkish traditions gave his regime a distinctive identity, particularly since he made conversion to Shiite Islam mandatory for the largely Sunni population. At the same time,

it also created some powerful enemies. Foremost among them were the staunchly Sunni Ottomans, who believed that the first legitimate successor to Mohammed was Mohammed's father-in-law Abu Bakr, not Ali as the Safavids believed. The Ottoman Sunni detested the Shiite Safavids and feared not only Safavid territorial expansion but also the spread of Safavid propaganda among the nomadic Turks in their territory. As soon as Selim the Grim became sultan, he launched a persecution of Shiites in the Ottoman Empire and prepared for a full-scale invasion of Safavid territory.

At the critical battle of **(battle of) Chaldiran** (1514), the Ottomans deployed heavy artillery and thousands of Janissaries equipped with firearms behind a barrier of carts. Although the Safavids knew about gunpowder technology and had access to firearms, the Ottomans maintained a clear technological advantage. Trusting in the protective charisma of Shah Ismail, the *qizilbash* cavalry strenuously attacked the Ottoman line and suffered devastating casualties. Ismail had to slip away, and the Ottomans temporarily occupied his capital at Tabriz. The Ottomans badly damaged the Safavid state but lacked the resources to destroy it, and the two empires remained locked in intermittent conflict for the next two centuries.

Later Safavid rulers recovered from the disaster at Chaldiran. They relied more heavily than Ismail had on the Persian bureaucracy and its administrative talents. Ismail's successors abandoned the extreme Safavid ideology that associated the emperor with Allah in favor of more conventional Twelver Shiism, from which they still derived legitimacy as descendants and representatives of the imams. They also assigned land grants to the *qizilbash* officers to retain their loyalty and give them a stake in the survival of the regime.

Shah Abbas the Great Shah **Abbas the Great** (reigned 1588–1629) fully revitalized the Safavid empire. He moved the capital to the more central location of Isfahan, encouraged trade with other lands, and reformed the administrative and military institutions of the empire. He incorporated male slaves of the royal household into the army, increased the use of gunpowder weapons, and sought European assistance against the Ottomans and the Portuguese in the Persian Gulf. With newly strengthened military forces, Shah Abbas led the Safavids to numerous victories. He attacked and defeated the nomadic Uzbeks in central Asia, expelled the Portuguese from Hormuz, and engaged the Ottomans in a series of wars from 1603 to the end of his reign. His campaigns brought most of northwestern Iran, the Caucasus, and Mesopotamia under Safavid rule.

The Mughal Empire

Babur In 1523 Zahir al-Din Muhammad, known as **Babur** ("the Tiger"), a Chaghatai Turk who claimed descent from both Chinggis Khan and Tamerlane (see chapter 17), suddenly appeared in northern India. Unlike the Ottomans, who sought to be

---

qizilbash (gih-ZIHL-bahsh)
Babur (BAH-ber)

Shah Ismail and the *qizilbash*. This miniature painting from a Safavid manuscript depicts the shah and his *qizilbash* warriors wearing the distinctive red pleated cap that was their emblem of identity.

Album/Alamy Stock Photo

This colorful scene at a spring in Kabul highlights Babur (1483–1530), founder of the Mughal dynasty, who stands in a central position near the life-giving water.

Angelo Hornak/Corbis Historical/Getty Images

renowned *ghazis,* or the Safavids, who acted as champions of Shi-ism, Babur made little pretense to be anything more than an adventurer and soldier of fortune in the manner of his illustrious ancestors. His father had been the prince of Farghana (in modern Uzbekistan), and Babur's great ambition was to transform his inheritance into a glorious central Asian empire. Yet envious relatives and Uzbek enemies frustrated his ambitions.

Never able to extend his authority much beyond Kabul and Qandahar (both in modern Afghanistan) and reduced at times to hardship and a handful of followers, Babur turned his attention to India. With the aid of gunpowder weapons, including both artillery and firearms, Babur mounted invasions in 1523 and 1525, and successfully conquered Delhi in 1526. Ironically, Babur cared little for the land he had conquered. Many in his entourage wanted to take their spoils of war and leave the hot

and humid Indian climate, which among other things ruined their finely crafted compound bows, but Babur elected to stay. He probably hoped to use the enormous wealth of India to build a vast central Asian empire like that of Tamerlane—an elusive dream that his successors would nonetheless continue to cherish. By the time of his death in 1530, Babur had built a loosely knit empire that stretched from Kabul through the Punjab to the borders of Bengal. He founded a dynasty called the *Mughal* (a Persian term for "Mongol"), which eventually embraced almost all the Indian subcontinent.

Akbar The real architect of the Mughal empire was Babur's grandson **Akbar** (reigned 1556–1605), a brilliant and charismatic

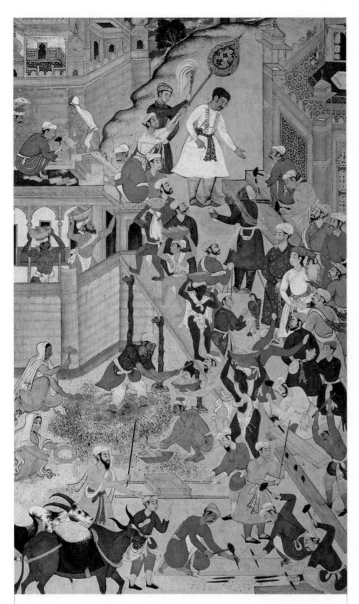

This manuscript illustration from about 1590 depicts Akbar (at top, shaded by attendants) inspecting construction of a new imperial capital at Fatehpur Sikri.

Picturenow/Universal Images Group/Getty Images

ruler. Akbar gathered the reins of power in his own hands in 1561 following a violent argument with Adham Khan, a powerful figure at the imperial court and commander of the Mughal army. Akbar murdered Adham Khan during the argument and thereafter took personal control of the Mughal government and did not tolerate challenges to his rule. He created a centralized administrative structure with ministries regulating the various provinces of the empire. His military campaigns consolidated Mughal power in Gujarat to the west and Bengal to the east. He also began to absorb the recently defeated Hindu kingdom of Vijayanagar, thus laying the foundation for later Mughal expansion in southern India.

Akbar was a thoughtful, reflective man deeply interested in religion and philosophy. He pursued a policy of religious toleration that he hoped would reduce tensions between Hindu and Muslim communities in India. Although illiterate (probably due to dyslexia), he was extremely intelligent and had books read to him daily. Instead of imposing Islam on his subjects, he encouraged the elaboration of a syncretic religion called the "divine faith" that focused attention on the emperor as a ruler common to all the religious, ethnic, and social groups of India.

Aurangzeb The Mughal empire reached its greatest extent under **Aurangzeb** (reigned 1659–1707). During his long reign, Aurangzeb waged a relentless campaign to push Mughal authority deep into southern India. By the early eighteenth century, Mughals ruled the entire subcontinent except for a small region at the southern tip.

Although he greatly expanded Mughal boundaries, Aurangzeb presided over a troubled empire. He faced rebellions throughout his reign, and religious tensions generated conflicts between Hindus and Muslims. Aurangzeb was a devout Muslim, and he broke with Akbar's policy of religious toleration. He demolished several famous Hindu temples and replaced them with mosques. He also imposed a tax on Hindus in an effort to encourage conversion to Islam. His promotion of Islam appealed strongly to the Mughals themselves and other Indian Muslims, but it provoked deep hostility among Hindus and enabled local leaders to organize movements to resist or even rebel against Mughal authority.

IMPERIAL SOCIETY

Despite their ethnically and religiously diverse populations, there were striking similarities in the development of Ottoman, Safavid, and Mughal societies. All relied on bureaucracies that drew inspiration from the steppe traditions of Turkish and Mongol peoples as well as from the heritage of Islam. They adopted similar economic policies and sought ways to maintain harmony in societies that embraced many different religious and ethnic groups. Rulers of all the empires also sought to enhance the legitimacy of their regimes by providing for public welfare and associating themselves with literary and artistic talent.

The Dynastic State

The Ottoman, Safavid, and Mughal empires were all military creations, regarded by their rulers as their personal possessions by right of conquest. The rulers exercised personal command of the armies, appointed and dismissed officials at will, and adopted policies of their own making. In theory, the emperors owned all land and granted use of it to peasant families on a hereditary basis in return for the payment of fixed taxes. The emperors and their families derived revenues from crown lands, and revenues from other lands supported military and administrative officials.

The Emperors and Islam In the Ottoman, Safavid, and Mughal empires, the prestige and authority of the dynasty

SOURCES FROM THE PAST

The *Ain I Akbari* on Akbar's Imperial Harem

From 1590 until his death in 1602, Abu'l-Fazl—Akbar's court historian—wrote a history of Akbar's reign, which became known as the Akbar Nama (Chronicle of Akbar). *Book three of this expansive, three-volume work is called the* Ain I Akbari (Institutes of Akbar) *and presents a detailed look at both Mughal institutions and Mughal India more generally. Abu'l-Fazl used vast quantities of imperial records in his work and set the standard for royal chronicles in the region for centuries. Throughout the* Akbar Nama, *Abu'l-Fazl presented Akbar as a semi-divine ruler who presided over a multiethnic and multireligious empire. Below, he describes Akbar's harem.*

His majesty forms matrimonial alliances with princes of Hindustan, and of other countries; and secures by these ties of harmony the peace of the world.

As the sovereign, by the light of his wisdom, has raised fit persons from the dust of obscurity, and appointed them to various offices, so does he also elevate faithful persons to the several ranks in the service of the seraglio [women's apartments] . . . "The saying of the wise is true that the eye of the exalted is the elixir for producing goodness." Such also are the results flowing from the love of order of his majesty [Akbar], from his wisdom, insight, regard to rank, his respect for others, his activity, his patience. . . .

His majesty has made a large enclosure with fine buildings inside, where he reposes. Though there are more than five thousand women, he has given to each a separate apartment. He has also divided them into sections, and keeps them attentive to their duties. Several chaste women have been appointed as *daroghas* [officials], and superintendents over each section, and one has been appointed as a writer [record-keeper] . . .

The inside of the Harem is guarded by sober and active women; the most trustworthy of them are placed about the apartments of his Majesty. Outside of the enclosure the eunuchs are placed; and at a proper distance, there is a guard of faithful *Rajputs* [soldiers from a Hindu military caste], beyond whom are the porters of the gates . . . Notwithstanding the great number of faithful guards, his Majesty does not dispense with his own vigilance, but keeps the whole in proper order.

> Why would marriage with women from princely Hindu families have secured "peace" in Akbar's realm?

> What is the author trying to say here about Akbar's ideas about merit versus birth?

For Further Reflection

■ Why was it so important to keep Akbar's harem under such heavy guard? Was he more concerned with keeping people out of the harem or keeping people in? Was there reason to be concerned about maintaining armed order inside the harem, given the many conflicts over succession in the Mughal empire?

Source: This translation taken from Abul Fazl'Allami (trans by H. Blockman), *Ain I Akbari,* Volume I (Calcutta, 1873), pp. 44–45. Available on the Hathi Trust website: https://babel.hathitrust.org/cgi/pt?id=mdp.39015005602431&view=image&seq=7

derived from the personal piety and the military prowess of the ruler and his ancestors. The Safavids were prominent leaders of a Sufi religious order, and the Ottomans and Mughals associated closely with famous **Sufis.** Devotion to Islam encouraged rulers to extend their faith to new lands. The *ghazi* ideal of spreading Islam by fighting non-believers or heretics meshed well with the traditions of Turkish and Mongolian peoples, which emphasized the glory of battle.

Women and Politics Even though Muslim theorists agreed that women should have no role in public affairs and decried the involvement of women in politics as a sure sign of decadence, in practice women played important roles in managing all three empires. Many Ottoman, Safavid, and Mughal emperors followed the example of Chinggis Khan, who bestowed special privileges and authority on his mother and his first, and favorite, wife. Ottoman courtiers often complained loudly about the "rule of women," thus offering eloquent testimony to the power that women could wield. Süleyman the Magnificent, for example, fell in love with Hürrem Sultana (also known as Roxelana), a concubine of Ukrainian origin who had been brought to the sultan's harem as a slave. Eventually, Süleyman elevated her to the status of a legal wife, consulted her on state policies, and deferred to her judgment on a variety of matters. It was rumored that Hürrem counseled Süleyman to have his son and heir by another wife executed. While it is not clear if this was the case, Süleyman did have his oldest son executed, and his son with Hürrem, Selim II, eventually became sultan. After Hürrem's unexpected death in 1558, a devastated Süleyman constructed a mausoleum for her next to his own in the courtyard of the great mosque in Istanbul.

This romantic portrait of Shah Jahan (reigned 1628–1658) and his most beloved wife, Mumtaz Mahal (died 1631), suggested the strong bond between them that drove him to build a white marble mausoleum, the Taj Mahal.

Dinodia Photos/Alamy Stock Photo

A sixteenth century portrait of Hürrem Sultan (1510-1588), born Aleksandra Lisowska and also known as Roxelana.

ART Collection/Alamy Stock Photo

Women also played prominent political roles in the Safavid and Mughal empires. In Safavid Persia, Khayr al-Nesa, better known as Mahd-e Olya and mother of the future Shah Abbas I, gained enormous influence over her husband. Her efforts to limit the power of the *qizilbash* so enraged them that in 1579 they murdered her. The aunt of another shah scolded the ruler for neglecting his duties and used her own money to raise an army to put down a revolt. The Mughal emperor **Jahangir** was content to let his wife Nur Jahan run the government, while Aurangzeb often followed his daughter's political advice.

Steppe Traditions The autocratic authority wielded by the rulers of all three empires reflected the steppe traditions of their origins. The early emperors largely did as they pleased, regardless of religious and social norms in the areas they conquered. The Ottoman sultans, for example, unilaterally issued numerous legal edicts. The greatest of these were the many *kanun* ("laws") issued by Süleyman—Europeans called him Süleyman the Magnificent, but the Ottomans referred to him as Süleyman Kanuni, "the Lawgiver." Safavid and Mughal rulers went even further than the Ottomans in asserting their spiritual authority. Shah Ismail did not hesitate to force his Shiite

religion on his subjects. Akbar issued a decree in 1579 claiming broad authority in religious matters, and he promoted his own eclectic religion, which glorified the emperor as much as Islam.

Steppe practices also brought succession problems. In the steppe empires the ruler's relatives often managed components of the states, and succession to the throne became a hot contest between competing members of the family. Problems of succession were compounded by the fact that rulers of all three empires maintained large harems that could include many wives and concubines as well as their children, and thus rivalry for succession was deeply intertwined with the desire of different wives to maintain their position at court. The Mughal empire in particular became tied up in family controversies: conflicts among Mughal princes and rebellions of sons against fathers were recurrent features throughout the history of the empire. The Safavids also engaged in murderous struggles for the throne. Shah Abbas himself lived in fear that another member of the family would challenge him. He kept his sons confined to the palace and killed or blinded relatives he suspected, almost wiping out his family in the process.

The early Ottomans assigned provinces for the sultan's sons to administer but kept the empire as a whole tightly unified. After the fifteenth century, however, the sultans moved to protect their position by eliminating family rivals. Mehmed the Conqueror decreed that a ruler could legally kill off his brothers—many of whom would have been half-siblings by different mothers—after taking the throne. His successors observed that tradition until 1595, when the new sultan executed nineteen brothers, many of them infants, as well as fifteen expectant mothers. After that episode, sultans confined their sons in special quarters of the imperial harem and forbade them to go outside except to take the throne.

Agriculture and Trade

Food Crops Productive agricultural economies were the foundations of all three empires. Each extracted surplus agricultural production and used it to finance armies and bureaucracies. For the most part, all three empires relied on crops of wheat and rice that had flourished for centuries in the lands they ruled. In addition, European merchants introduced maize, potatoes, tomatoes, and other crops from the Americas to each of the empires, and the new arrivals soon found a place in regional cuisines. Potatoes appeared in the curries of southern India, and tomatoes enlivened dishes in the Ottoman Empire as well as other Mediterranean lands. Maize did not win a place in the cuisine of the empires of south and southwest Asia, but it became popular as feed for animal stocks, especially in the Ottoman Empire.

Global trade networks also strongly encouraged consumption of coffee and tobacco, especially in the Ottoman and Safavid empires. Although native to Ethiopia and cultivated in southern Arabia by the fifteenth century, coffee did not become popular in Islamic lands until the sixteenth century. Like sugar, coffee became a cash crop in the Americas, which then was sold for profit in markets around the world. By the eighteenth century, American producers and European merchants supplied Muslim markets with both coffee and sugar.

Tobacco According to the Ottoman historian Ibrahim Pechevi, English merchants introduced tobacco around 1600, claiming it was useful for medicinal purposes. Within a few

Ottoman coffeehouse. This nineteenth-century depiction of a coffeehouse in Istanbul demonstrates the centrality of tobacco smoking to the experience. Beginning in the seventeenth century, men in the Ottoman Empire socialized in coffeehouses while smoking from elaborate water pipes called hookahs.

Historical Picture Archive//Corbis/Getty Images

decades it had spread throughout the Ottoman Empire. The increasing popularity of coffee drinking and pipe smoking encouraged entrepreneurs to establish coffeehouses where customers could indulge their appetites for caffeine and nicotine at the same time. The popularity of coffeehouses provoked protest from moralists who worried that these popular attractions were dens of iniquity that distracted patrons from their religious duties and encouraged idleness. Pechevi complained

What's Left Out? ■■■ ▬▬ ▬ ▬ ▬

In textbook overviews such as this, women in the empires of south and southwest Asia tend to appear only briefly, usually in the context of imperial harems. There is a reason for this: Extensive records were kept about (and sometimes by) the elite women who inhabited these harems. But it would be a mistake to imagine that the lives of most women in the Ottoman, Mughal, and Safavid empires were similar to the lives of women in imperial harems. If we take the Ottoman Empire during the seventeenth century as an example, we would see that only a tiny proportion of Ottoman women lived in the secluded and isolated conditions of harems. Instead, Ottoman women were visible in multiple contexts, though their visibility depended upon their social class and geographical location. Elite women, as was the case in many parts of the world, were more constrained in their mobility than those from laboring classes but nevertheless could be seen moving through towns and cities with their bodies covered. Women of the farming and agricultural classes, in contrast, were integral to family labor and were visible in the fields driving horses and threshing grain. In cities and large towns, laboring women could be seen selling crafts on the streets. And in both rural and urban areas, slave women were constantly visible in public while they performed a wide variety of tasks for their owners. In the realm of law, Ottoman women were highly visible in the courts, where they frequently brought suits against others. Additionally, Ottoman law allowed women to own property in their own names and to dispose of it as they pleased. Thus, while it is important to remember that Ottoman women were not considered equal to men (such a status did not exist anywhere in the world at this time), they also were not the invisible, secluded, highly controlled creatures that images of the harem tend to suggest.

Source: Ebru Boyar and Kate Fleet, eds. *Ottoman Women in Public Space* (Leiden: Brill, 2016).

about the odor of tobacco, the messy ashes, and the danger that smoking could cause fires. Religious leaders claimed that coffee was an illegal beverage and that it was worse to frequent a coffeehouse than a tavern that served alcoholic beverages. Sultan Murad IV (r. 1623–1640) went so far as to outlaw coffee and tobacco and to execute those who continued to partake. That effort, however, was a losing battle. Both pastimes eventually won widespread acceptance, and the coffeehouse became a prominent social institution in all three empires.

Population Growth
The population of India surged during early modern times, growing from 105 million in 1500 to 135 million in 1600, 165 million in 1700, and 190 million in 1800. This population growth resulted more from intensive agriculture along traditional lines than from any other factor. The Safavid population grew less rapidly, from 5 million in 1500 to 6 million in 1600, and to 8 million in 1800. Ottoman numbers grew from 9 million in 1500 to 28 million in 1600, as the empire enlarged its boundaries to include populous regions in the Balkans, Egypt, and southwest Asia. After 1600, however, the Ottoman population declined to about 24 million, where it remained until the late 1800s. The decline reflected loss of territory more than a shrinking population, but even in the heartland of Anatolia, Ottoman numbers did not expand nearly as dramatically as those of other lands in early modern times. From 6 million in 1500, the population of Anatolia rose to 7.5 million in 1600, 8 million in 1700, and 9 million in 1800.

Trade
The Islamic empires ruled lands that had figured prominently in long-distance trade for centuries and participated actively in global trade networks in early modern times. In the Ottoman Empire, for example, the early capital at Bursa was also the terminus of a caravan route that brought raw silk from Persia to supply the Italian market. The Ottomans also granted special trading concessions to merchants from England and France to cement alliances against common enemies in Spain and central Europe. Aleppo became an emporium for foreign merchants engaged primarily in the spice trade and served as local headquarters for the operations of the English Levant Company.

Shah Abbas promoted Isfahan as a commercial center, extending trading privileges to foreign merchants and even allowing Christian monastic orders to set up missions there to help create a favorable environment for trade. European merchants sought Safavid raw silk, carpets, ceramics, and high-quality craft items. The English East India Company, the French East India Company, and the Dutch VOC all traded actively with the Safavids. To curry favor with them, the English company sent military advisers to introduce gunpowder weapons to Safavid armed forces and provided a navy to help them retake Hormuz in the Persian Gulf from the Portuguese.

The Mughals did not pay as much attention to foreign trade as the Ottomans and the Safavids did, partly because of the enormous size and productivity of the domestic Indian economy and partly because the Mughal rulers concentrated on their land empire and had little interest in maritime affairs. Nevertheless, the Mughal treasury derived significant income from foreign trade. The Mughals allowed the creation of trading stations and merchant colonies by Portuguese, English, French, and Dutch merchants. Meanwhile, Indian merchants formed trading companies

In this anonymous painting produced about 1670, Dutch and English ships lie at anchor in the harbor of the busy port of Surat in northwestern India. Surat was the major port on the west coast of India, and it served as one of the chief commercial cities of the Mughal empire.
Rijksmuseum, Amsterdam

of their own, ventured overland as far as Russia, and sailed the waters of the Indian Ocean to port cities from Persia to Indonesia.

Religious Affairs

Religious Diversity Each of the empires had populations that were religiously and ethnically diverse, and imperial rulers had the daunting challenge of maintaining harmony between different religious communities. The Ottoman Empire included large numbers of Christians and Jews in the Balkans, Armenia, Lebanon, and Egypt. The Safavid empire embraced sizable Zoroastrian and Jewish communities as well as many Christian subjects in the Caucasus. The Mughal empire was especially diverse. Most Mughal subjects were Hindus, but large numbers of Muslims lived alongside smaller communities of Jains, Zoroastrians, Christians, and Sikhs.

Christian Mission in India Portuguese Goa became the center of a Christian mission in India. Priests at Goa sought to attract converts to Christianity and established schools that provided religious instruction for Indian children. In 1580 several Portuguese Jesuits traveled to the Mughal court at Akbar's invitation. They had visions of converting the emperor to Christianity and then spreading their faith throughout India, but their hopes went unfulfilled.

In a seventeenth-century painting, the emperor Akbar presides over discussions between representatives of various religious groups. Two Jesuits dressed in black robes kneel at the left.
DeAgostini/Getty Images

who combined elements of Hinduism and Islam in a new syncretic faith. He also attempted to elaborate his own "divine faith" that emphasized loyalty to the emperor while borrowing eclectically from different religious traditions. Akbar never explained his ideas systematically, but it is clear that they drew most heavily on Islam. The divine faith was strictly monotheistic, and it reflected the influence of Shiite and Sufi teachings. But it also glorified the emperor: Akbar even referred to himself as the "lord of wisdom," who would guide his subjects to understanding of the world's creator god. The divine faith was tolerant of Hinduism, and it even drew inspiration from Zoroastrianism in its effort to bridge the gaps between Mughal India's many cultural and religious communities.

Status of Religious Minorities Each of the empires relied on a long-established model to deal with subjects who were not Muslims. They did not require conquered peoples to convert to Islam but extended to them the status of *dhimmi* ("protected people"). In return for their loyalty and payment of a special tax known as *jizya, dhimmi* communities retained their personal freedom, kept their property, practiced their religion, and handled their legal affairs. In the Ottoman Empire, for example, autonomous religious communities known as *millet* retained their civil laws, traditions, and languages. *Millet* communities usually also assumed social and administrative functions in matters concerning birth, marriage, death, health, and education.

Akbar received the Jesuits cordially and welcomed their participation in religious and philosophical discussions at his court, but he was not interested in conversion.

Akbar's Divine Faith Indeed, Akbar was not fervent even about his own Islamic faith. In his efforts to find a religious synthesis that would serve as a cultural foundation for unity in his diverse empire, he supported the efforts of the early Sikhs,

The situation in the Mughal empire was different because its large number of religious communities made a *millet* system impractical. Mughal rulers reserved the most powerful military and administrative positions for Muslims, but in the day-to-day management of affairs, Muslims and Hindus cooperated closely. Some Mughal emperors sought to forge links between religious communities. Akbar in particular worked to integrate

dhimmi (DIHM-mee)
jizya (JIHZ-yuh)

Muslim and Hindu elites. In an effort to foster communication and understanding among the different religious communities of his realm, he abolished the *jizya;* tolerated all faiths; and sponsored discussions and debates between Muslims, Hindus, Jains, Zoroastrians, and Christians.

Promotion of Islam Some Indian Muslims worried that policies of religious toleration would lead to the loss of their religious identity or that they might be absorbed into Hindu society as another caste. Some therefore insisted that Mughal rulers create and maintain an Islamic state based on Islamic law. When Aurangzeb reached the Mughal throne in 1659, these ideas gained strength. Aurangzeb reinstated the *jizya* and promoted Islam as the official faith of Mughal India. His policy satisfied zealous Muslims but at the cost of deep bitterness among his Hindu subjects. Tension between Hindu and Muslim communities in India persisted throughout the Mughal dynasty and beyond.

Cultural Patronage

As the empires matured, the rulers of all three empires sought to enhance their prestige through public works projects and patronage of scholars. They competed to attract outstanding religious scholars, poets, artists, and architects to their courts. They lavished resources on mosques, palaces, government buildings, bridges, fountains, schools, hospitals, and soup kitchens for the poor.

Istanbul Capital cities and royal palaces were the most visible expressions of imperial majesty. The Ottomans beautified both Bursa and Edirne, but they took particular pride in **Istanbul.** Dilapidated and deserted after the conquest, it quickly revived and became a bustling, prosperous city of more than a million people. At its heart was the great **Topkapi palace,** which housed government offices, such as the mint, and meeting places for imperial councils. At its core was the sultan's residence with its harem, gardens, pleasure pavilions, and a repository for the most sacred possessions of the empire, including the mantle of the prophet Muhammad. Sultan Süleyman the Magnificent was fortunate to be able to draw on the talents of the architectural genius **Sinan Pasha** (1489–1588) to create the most celebrated of all the monuments of Istanbul. Sinan built a vast religious complex called the **Süleymaniye,** which blended Islamic and Byzantine architectural elements. It combined tall, slender minarets with large domed buildings supported by half domes in the style of the Byzantine church Hagia Sofia (which the Ottomans converted into the mosque of Aya Sofya).

Isfahan Shah Abbas made his capital, **Isfahan,** into one of the leading Persian cities and the prime center of urban

Topkapi (TOHP-kah-pih)
Sinan Pasha (sih-NAHN pah-cha)

The massive Süleymaniye mosque built for Sultan Süleyman the Magnificent by the Ottoman architect Sinan Pasha in 1556.
Anadolu Agency/Getty Images

Isfahan Royal Mosque. The Royal Mosque of Isfahan, centerpiece of the city as rebuilt by Shah Abbas at the end of the sixteenth century. With its combination of an open space flanked by markets, the palace, and religious structures, Isfahan stands as a unique example of urban planning in Islamic lands.
DrRave/E+/Getty Images

architectural development anywhere in the world: its inhabitants still boast that "Isfahan is half the world." Abbas concentrated markets, the palace, and the royal mosque around a vast polo field and public square. Broad, shaded avenues and magnificent bridges linked the central city to its suburbs. Safavid architects made use of monumental entryways; vast arcades; spacious courtyards; and intricate, colorful decoration. Unlike the sprawling Ottoman and Mughal palaces, the Safavid palaces in Isfahan were relatively small and emphasized natural settings with gardens and pools. They were also much more open than Topkapi, with its series of inner courts and gates. Ali Qapu, the palace on the square in Isfahan, had a striking balcony, and most of the palaces had large, open verandas. The point was not only to enable the shah to observe outside activities but also to emphasize his visibility and accessibility, qualities long esteemed in the Persian tradition of kingship.

Fatehpur Sikri   To some extent, in accordance with steppe traditions, the early Mughals regarded the capital as wherever the ruler happened to camp. Yet they too came to sponsor urban development. Their work skillfully blended central Asian traditions with elements of Hindu architecture, and they built on a scale that left no doubt about their wealth and resources. They constructed scores of mosques, fortresses, and palaces and sometimes created entire cities. The best example was **Fatehpur Sikri,** a city planned and constructed by Akbar that served as his capital from 1569 to 1585. It commemorated his conquest of the prosperous commercial province of Gujarat in a campaign that enabled Akbar to head off both Portuguese attacks and Ottoman intervention there. With its mint, records office, trea-

sury, and audience hall, the new city demonstrated Akbar's strength and imperial ambitions. Fatehpur Sikri was also a private residence and retreat for the ruler, reproducing in stone a royal encampment with exquisite pleasure palaces where Akbar indulged his passions for music and conversation with scholars and poets. At yet another level, it was a dramatic display of Mughal piety and devotion, centered on the cathedral mosque and the mausoleum of Akbar's Sufi guru, **Shaykh Salim Chishti.** Despite their intensely Islamic character, many of the buildings consciously incorporated Indian elements such as verandas supported by columns and decorations of stone elephants. Even the tomb of Shaykh Chishti bore some resemblance to a Hindu shrine. Unfortunately, Akbar selected a poor site for the city and soon abandoned it because of its bad water supply.

The Taj Mahal   The most famous of the Mughal monuments was the **Taj Mahal**, which we read about in the introduction to this chapter. Shah Jahan had twenty thousand workers toil for eighteen years to erect the exquisite white marble mosque and tomb. He originally planned to build a similar mausoleum out of black marble for himself, but his son Aurangzeb deposed him before he could carry out the project. Shah Jahan spent his last years confined to a small cell with a tiny window, and only with the aid of a mirror was he able to catch the sight of his beloved wife's final resting place.

THE EMPIRES IN TRANSITION

The empires of south and southwest Asia underwent dramatic change between the sixteenth and the eighteenth centuries. The Safavid empire disappeared entirely. In 1722 a band of Afghan tribesmen marched all the way to Isfahan, blockaded the city until its starving inhabitants resorted to cannibalism, forced the shah to abdicate, and executed thousands of Safavid

Fatehpur Sikri (fah-teh-poor SIH-kree)
Shaykh Salim Chishti (sheyk sah-LEEM CHEESH-tee)

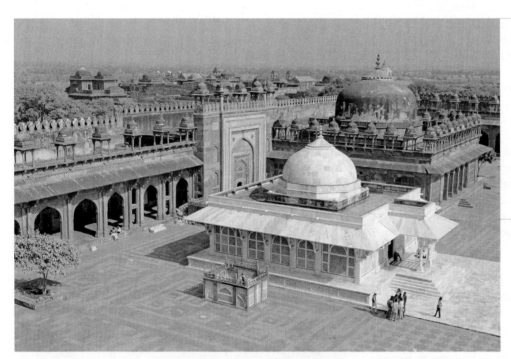

Fatehpur Sikri, built by Akbar in the 1570s, commemorated the emperor's military conquests and housed the tomb of his religious guide. It included a palace, an audience hall where Akbar attended religious and philosophical debates, and a great mosque.
Gavin Hellier/robertharding/Alamy Stock Photo

officials as well as many members of the royal family. After the death of Aurangzeb in 1707, Mughal India experienced provincial rebellions and foreign invasions. By mid-century the subcontinent was falling under British imperial rule. By 1700 the Ottomans, too, were on the defensive: the sultans lost control over remote provinces such as Lebanon and Egypt, and throughout the eighteenth and nineteenth centuries European and Russian states placed political, military, and economic pressure on the shrinking Ottoman realm.

Economic and Military Decline

In the sixteenth century, each of the empires had strong domestic economies and played prominent roles in global trade networks. By the eighteenth century, however, domestic economies were under great stress, and foreign trade had declined dramatically or had fallen under the control of European powers. The empires were well on their way to becoming dependent on goods produced elsewhere.

Economic Difficulties The high cost of maintaining an expensive military and administrative apparatus helped to bring about economic decline in each of the empires. As long as the empires were expanding, they were able to finance their armies and bureaucracies with fresh resources extracted from newly conquered lands. When expansion slowed, ceased, or reversed, however, they faced the problem of supporting their institutions with limited resources. The long, costly, and unproductive wars fought by the Ottomans with the Hapsburgs in central Europe, by the Safavids and the Ottomans in Mesopotamia, and by Aurangzeb in southern India exhausted the treasuries of the empires without making fresh resources available to them. As early as 1589 the Ottomans tried to pay the Janissaries in debased coinage and immediately provoked

a mutiny. The next 150 years witnessed at least six additional military revolts.

As expansion slowed and the empires lost control over remote provinces, officials reacted to the loss of revenue by raising taxes, selling public offices, accepting bribes, or resorting to simple extortion. All those measures were counterproductive. Although they might provide immediate cash, they did long-term economic damage. Foreign trade initially seemed to provide a partial solution, as the goods they brought provided extra revenue for the state and helped satisfy consumer demands for things like textiles and tobacco. The Ottomans therefore expanded the privileges enjoyed by foreign merchants, while the Mughals encouraged the establishment of Dutch and English trading outposts and welcomed the expansion of their business in India. Imperial authorities were content to have foreign traders come to them. Only later did it become clear that welcoming European traders to their lands gave Europeans the leverage to become economically dominant and, in the case of India, conquerors.

Military Decline As they lost initiative to western European peoples in economic and commercial affairs, the empires of south and southwest Asia also experienced military decline. As early as the fifteenth century, the Ottomans had relied heavily on European technology in gunnery; indeed, the cannon that Mehmed the Conqueror used in 1453 to breach the defensive wall of Constantinople was the product of a Hungarian gun-founder. During the sixteenth and early seventeenth centuries, the Islamic empires were able to purchase European weapons in large numbers and attract European expertise that kept their armies supplied with powerful gunpowder weapons. In 1605, for example, the cargo of an English ship bound for Anatolia included seven hundred barrels of gunpowder, one thousand musket barrels, five hundred fully assembled muskets, and two thousand sword blades, alongside wool textiles and bullion.

Although each of the empires of south and southwest Asia continued to be able to purchase European weapons and expertise, this ready availability was one of the reasons none of them developed large armament industries of their own. When combined with financial difficulties within each of the empires, the result was an inability to buy the latest technologies. Over time, their equipment and arsenals became increasingly dated. By the late eighteenth century, the Ottoman navy, which had long influenced maritime affairs in the Mediterranean, Red Sea, Persian Gulf, and Arabian Sea, closed its own ship-building operations. From then on, the Ottomans ordered all new military ships from European shipyards.

The Deterioration of Imperial Leadership

Strong and effective central authority had long been essential to the empires of south and southwest Asia, and Muslim political theorists never tired of emphasizing the importance of rulers who were diligent, virtuous, and just. Weak, negligent, and corrupt rulers would allow institutions to become dysfunctional and social order to break down. The Ottomans were fortunate in having a series of talented sultans for three centuries, and the Safavids and Mughals produced their share of effective rulers as well.

Dynastic Decline Eventually, however, all three dynasties had rulers who were incompetent or more interested in spending vast sums of money on personal pleasures than in tending to affairs of state. Moreover, all three dynasties faced difficulties because of suspicion and fighting among competing members of their ruling houses. The Ottomans sought to limit problems by confining princes in the palace, but that measure had several negative consequences. The princes had no opportunity to gain experience in government, but they were frequently exposed to plots and intrigues of the various factions maneuvering to bring a favorable candidate to the throne. Notorious examples of problem rulers included Süleyman's successor Selim the Sot (reigned 1566–1574) and Ibrahim the Crazy (reigned 1640–1648), who taxed and spent to such excess that government officials deposed and murdered him. Several energetic rulers and talented ministers attempted to keep the government on track. Nonetheless, after the late seventeenth century, weak rule increasingly provoked mutinies in the army, provincial revolts, political corruption, economic oppression, and insecurity throughout the Ottoman realm.

Religious Tensions Political troubles often arose from religious tensions. Conservative Muslim clerics strongly objected to policies and practices that they considered affronts to Islam. Muslim leaders had considerable influence in each of the empires because of their monopoly of education and their deep involvement in the everyday lives and legal affairs of ordinary subjects. The clerics mistrusted the emperors' interests

in unconventional forms of Islam such as Sufism, objected when women or subjects who were not Muslims played influential political roles, and protested any exercise of royal authority that contradicted Islamic law.

In the Ottoman Empire, disaffected religious students often joined the Janissaries in revolt. A particularly serious threat came from the **Wahhabi movement** in Arabia, which denounced the Ottomans as dangerous religious innovators who were unfit to rule. Conservative Muslims fiercely protested the construction of an astronomical observatory in Istanbul and forced the sultan to demolish it in 1580. In 1742

Each of the empires in south and southwest Asia fought numerous wars, many of which exhausted resources without adding to the productive capacities of the empires. This illustration depicts Ottoman forces (right) clashing with heavily armored Austrian cavalry near Budapest in 1540.
Images & Stories/Alamy Stock Photo

they also forced the closure of the Ottoman printing press, which they regarded as an impious technology.

The Safavids, who began their reign by crushing Sunni religious authorities, fell under the domination of the very Shiites they had supported. Shiite leaders pressured the shahs to persecute Sunnis, non-Muslims, and even the Sufis who had helped establish the dynasty. Religious tensions also afflicted Mughal India. Already in the seventeenth century, the conservative Shaykh Ahmad Sirhindi (1564–1624)

fearlessly rebuked Akbar for his policy of religious tolerance and his interest in other faiths. In the mid-eighteenth century, as he struggled to claim the Mughal throne, Aurangzeb drew on Sirhindi's ideas when he required non-Muslims to pay the poll tax and ordered the destruction of Hindu temples. Those measures inflamed tensions between the various Sunni, Shiite, and Sufi branches of Islam and also fueled animosity among Hindus and other Mughal subjects who were not Muslims.

CONCLUSION

Like China and Japan, the empires of south and southwest Asia remained strong and powerful throughout the early modern era. Ruling elites of the Ottoman, Safavid, and Mughal empires came from nomadic Turkish stock, and they all drew on steppe traditions in organizing their governments. But the rulers also adapted steppe traditions to the needs of settled agricultural societies they encountered and devised institutions that maintained order over the long term. During the sixteenth and seventeenth centuries, each of the empires enjoyed productive economies and participated actively in the global trade networks of early modern times. Their leaders sponsored magnificent architectural and artistic projects as well as campaigns for expansion, and their populations boomed. Each of the empires was religiously and ethnically diverse, and their leaders devised policies to accommodate non-Muslims. By the early eighteenth century, however, these same empires were experiencing difficulties that led to political and military decline. Extensive military campaigns eventually drained the imperial treasuries, while slowed territorial expansion decreased imperial revenues. The diversity that characterized each of the realms also led to religious tensions, and a series of weak rulers encouraged resistance and rebellion. By the late eighteenth century, the Safavid empire had collapsed, and economic difficulties and cultural insularity had severely weakened the Ottoman and Mughal empires and made them vulnerable to outside influences.

STUDY TERMS

Akbar (578)	Janissaries (574)
Aurangzeb (579)	*jizya* (584)
Babur (577)	*kanun* (581)
(battle of) Chaldiran (577)	Mehmed the
devshirme (574)	Conqueror (574)
dhimmi (584)	*millet* (584)
Fatehpur Sikri (586)	Mughal Empire (574)
ghazi (574)	Mumtaz Mahal (572)
Isfahan (585)	Osman Bey (574)
Ismail (575)	Ottoman Empire (574)
Istanbul (585)	*qizilbash* (577)
Jahangir (581)	Safavid empire (574)

Shah Abbas the Great (577)	Süleymaniye (585)
Shah Jahan (572)	Sunni (575)
Shaykh Salim Chishti (586)	Taj Mahal (586)
Shiism (575)	Topkapi palace (585)
Sinan Pasha (585)	Twelver Shiism (575)
Sufis (580)	Wahhabi movement (588)
Süleyman the Magnificent (575)	

FOR FURTHER READING

Giancarlo Casale. *The Ottoman Age of Exploration.* New York, 2010. This work argues convincingly that the Ottoman Turks were important players in the maritime explorations of the sixteenth century.

Stephen F. Dale. *The Muslim Empires of the Ottomans, Safavids, and Mughals.* Cambridge, 2010. This is a learned but approachable comparative study of three Islamic empires from 1300 to 1923.

Andrew de la Garza. *The Mughal Empire at War: Babur, Akbar and the Indian Military Revolution, 1500–1605.* London, 2016. Argues that the military innovations introduced in the early Mughal empire constituted a fundamental military revolution.

Carter Vaughn Findley. *The Turks in World History.* New York, 2005. A highly readable account that connects the two-thousand-year history of the Turkic peoples with larger global processes.

Douglas Howard. *A History of the Ottoman Empire.* Cambridge, 2017. Covers the entire social and political history of the Ottoman Empire from its origins to the twentieth century.

Kemal H. Karpat. *The Politicization of Islam: Reconstructing Identity, State, Faith, and Community in the Late Ottoman State.* New York, 2001. Scholarly study of the Ottoman state's role in constructing Muslim identity.

Moazzen Maryam. *Formation of a Religious Landscape: Shii Higher Learning in Safavid Iran.* Leiden, 2017. Explores the ways religious information was produced and transmitted during the second half of Safavid rule via institutions of higher learning.

Andrew J. Newman. *Safavid Iran: Rebirth of a Persian Empire.* London and New York, 2008. Based on meticulous scholarship, this is the definitive single volume work on the subject.

Leslie Pierce. *The Imperial Harem: Women and Sovereignty in the Ottoman Empire.* Oxford, 1993. Challenges many stereotypes about the role of women in the imperial Ottoman elite.

John F. Richards. *The Mughal Empire.* Cambridge, 1993. A concise and reliable overview of Mughal history, concentrating on political affairs.

Revolutions and National States in the Atlantic World

ZOOMING IN ON TRADITIONS

Olympe de Gouges Declares the Rights of Women

Marie Gouze was a French butcher's daughter who educated herself by reading books before moving to Paris and marrying a junior army officer. Under the name **Olympe de Gouges,** she won fame as a journalist, actress, and playwright. Gouges was as flamboyant as she was talented, and news of her well-publicized love affairs scandalized Parisian society.

Gouges was also a revolutionary and a strong advocate of women's rights. She responded enthusiastically when the French revolution broke out in July 1789, and she applauded in August when revolutionary leaders proclaimed freedom and equality for all citizens in the Declaration of the Rights of Man and the Citizen. It soon became clear, however, that in the view of revolutionary leaders, freedom and equality pertained only to male citizens. They welcomed women's contributions to the revolution but withheld the right to vote and left women under the patriarchal authority of their fathers and husbands.

Gouges campaigned fervently to raise the standing of women in French society. She called for more education and demanded that women share equal rights in family property. She challenged

François Toussaint L'Ouverture (1743–1803) proclaims the constitution of the Republic of Haiti in the midst of the Haitian Revolution on July 1, 1801.
World History Archive/Alamy Stock Photo

Olympe de Gouges (oh-LAHMP de gouj)

traditions associated with patriarchal authority and appealed to Queen Marie Antoinette to use her influence to advance women's rights. In 1791 Gouges published a Declaration of the Rights of Woman and the Female Citizen, which claimed the same rights for women that revolutionary leaders had granted to men in August 1789. She asserted that freedom and equality were inalienable rights of women as well as men, and she insisted on the rights of women to vote, speak their minds freely, participate in the making of law, and hold public office.

Gouges's declaration attracted a great deal of attention but little support. Revolutionary leaders dismissed her appeal as a publicity stunt and refused to put women's rights on their political agenda. In 1793 they executed her because of her affection for Marie Antoinette and her persistent crusade for women's rights. Yet Gouges's campaign illustrated the power of the Enlightenment ideals of freedom and equality, which played an important role in inspiring all of the Atlantic revolutions. Indeed, once revolutionaries in France and elsewhere had proclaimed freedom and equality as universal human rights, they were unable to suppress demands to extend them to other groups—such as women, enslaved people, and people of color—who the revolutionaries often originally intended to exclude.

CHAPTER OVERVIEW

Violence rocked lands throughout much of the Atlantic Ocean basin in the late eighteenth and early nineteenth centuries as a series of revolutions and wars of independence brought dramatic political and social change. People attempted to restructure their societies—if necessary by violent means—by abolishing traditional social and political institutions and replacing them with new ones. Politically active people now sought not only to participate in government but also actually viewed it as their inherent right to do so, and they rejected the idea that god had created a division between rulers and ruled. And while each revolution was different, they all shared several features. First, all were at least partially inspired by Enlightenment ideals. Second, wars fought between the major imperial powers created the conditions for each of the revolutions to erupt. Finally, the revolutions were deeply interlinked: in fact, beginning with the American revolution, each successive revolution helped to create the conditions for the next.

Revolution broke out first in the British colonies of North America, where colonists asserted their independence and founded a new republic. Partly as a result of the lavish spending of the French on helping the American revolutionaries, revolution broke out in France just a few years later. There, revolutionaries abolished the French monarchy and thoroughly reorganized French society. During the French revolution, enslaved people in the French sugar island of St. Domingue seized the opportunity to revolt against French rule and establish their independence. The Napoleonic wars (1799–1815) then created the conditions for the peoples of Latin America to seek independence from Spain and Portugal. By the 1830s, peoples had reorganized political and social structures throughout western Europe and the Americas.

The revolutions of the late eighteenth and early nineteenth centuries had two results of

CHRONOLOGY	
1694–1778	Life of Voltaire
1712–1778	Life of Jean-Jacques Rousseau
1744–1803	Life of Toussaint Louverture
1748–1793	Life of Olympe de Gouges
1753–1811	Life of Miguel Hidalgo y Costilla
1756–1763	Seven Years' War
1769–1821	Life of Napoleon Bonaparte
1773–1859	Life of Klemens von Metternich
1774–1793	Reign of King Louis XVI
1775–1781	American revolution
1783–1830	Life of Simón Bolívar
1789–1799	French revolution
1791–1803	Haitian revolution
1799–1814	Reign of Napoleon
1805–1872	Life of Giuseppe Mazzini
1810–1825	Wars of independence in Latin America
1814–1815	Congress of Vienna
1815–1898	Life of Otto von Bismarck
1821–1827	War of Greek independence
1859–1870	Unification of Italy
1864–1871	Unification of Germany

deep global significance. First, they helped to spread a cluster of Enlightenment ideas concerning freedom, equality, and popular sovereignty. Revolutionary leaders argued that political authority arose from the people and worked to establish states in the interests of the people rather than the rulers. In fact, early revolutionaries extended political rights to a privileged group of white men, but they justified their actions in general terms that invited excluded groups to seek the same rights. By the mid-twentieth century, nearly every state in the world formally recognized the freedom and equality of all its citizens—even if they did not always honor their official positions—and claimed authority to rule on the basis of popular sovereignty.

Second, while promoting Enlightenment values, the revolutions of this period also encouraged the consolidation of national states as the principal form of political organization. As peoples defended their states from enemies and sometimes mounted attacks on foreign lands, they developed a powerful sense of identity with their compatriots, and nationalist convictions inspired them to work toward the foundation of states that would advance the interests of the national community. During the nineteenth century, strong national identities and movements to build national states profoundly influenced the political experiences of European states. During the late nineteenth and twentieth centuries, efforts to harness nationalist sentiments and form states based on national identity became one of the most powerful and dynamic movements in world history.

REVOLUTIONARY IDEAS

Revolutionaries of the eighteenth and nineteenth centuries sought to fashion an equitable society by instituting governments that were responsive to the needs and interests of the peoples they governed. In justifying their policies, revolutionaries attacked monarchical and aristocratic regimes and argued for popular sovereignty—the idea that legitimate political authority resides not in kings but, rather, in the people who make up a society. In North America, colonists declared independence from British rule and instituted a new government founded on the principle of popular sovereignty. Soon thereafter, French revolutionaries abolished the monarchy and restructured the social order. French revolutionaries resented royal, noble, and clerical privileges and sought freedom of religion, liberty, and republicanism. Their goals resonated with many others in the Atlantic basin, including people in the Caribbean and Latin America, who fought their own revolutions in the name of liberty and freedom. Meanwhile, Napoleon Bonaparte's invasions of states in western Europe helped spread revolutionary ideas to much of the region.

The Enlightenment

Isaac Newton's vision of the universe (discussed in chapter 23) was so powerful and persuasive that its influence extended well beyond science. His work suggested that rational analysis could lead to fresh insights about the human as well as the natural world. From Scotland to Sicily, and from Philadelphia to Moscow, European and Euro-American thinkers launched an ambitious project to transform human thought and to use reason to transform the world. Like the early modern scientists, they abandoned Aristotelian philosophy, Christian theology, and other traditionally recognized authorities, and they sought to subject the human world to purely rational

analysis. The result of their work was a movement known as the **Enlightenment.**

Science and Society Enlightenment thinkers sought to discover natural laws that governed human society in the same way that Newton's laws of universal gravitation and motion regulated the universe. Their search took different forms. The English philosopher **John Locke** (1632–1704) worked to discover natural laws of politics. He attacked theories that promoted the idea that monarchs had a divine right to rule and, instead, advocated constitutional government on the grounds that sovereignty resides in the people rather than the state or its rulers. Indeed, he provided much of the theoretical justification for the Glorious Revolution of 1688 and the establishment of constitutional monarchy in England (discussed in chapter 23). The Scottish philosopher **Adam Smith** turned his attention to economic affairs and held that laws of supply and demand determine what happens in the marketplace. The French nobleman Charles Louis de Secondat, better known as the **Baron de Montesquieu** (1689–1755), sought to establish a science of politics and discover principles that would foster political liberty in a prosperous and stable state.

The center of Enlightenment thought was France, where prominent intellectuals known collectively as *philosophes* ("philosophers") advanced the cause of reason. The philosophes were not philosophers in the traditional sense of the term so much as public intellectuals. They addressed their works more to the educated public than to scholars: instead of formal philosophical treatises, they mostly composed histories, novels, dramas, satires, and pamphlets on religious, moral, and political issues.

Voltaire More than any other philosophe, François-Marie Arouet (1694–1778) epitomized the spirit of the Enlightenment. Writing under the pen name **Voltaire,** he published his first book at age seventeen. By the time of his death at age eighty-four, his published writings included some ten thousand letters and filled seventy volumes. With stinging wit and sometimes bitter irony, Voltaire championed individual freedom and

---

Montesquieu (MON-teh-skew)

philosophes (fil-uh-sofs)

Voltaire (vohl-TAIR)

attacked any institution sponsoring intolerant or oppressive policies. Targets of his caustic wit included the French monarchy and the Roman Catholic church. When the king of France sought to save money by reducing the number of horses kept in royal stables, for example, Voltaire suggested that it would be more effective to get rid of the asses who rode the horses. Voltaire also waged a long literary campaign against the Roman Catholic church, which he held responsible for fanaticism, intolerance, and incalculable human suffering. Voltaire's battle cry was *écrasez l'infame* ("crush the damned thing"), meaning the church that he considered an agent of oppression.

Deism Some philosophes were conventional Christians, while a few turned to atheism. Like Voltaire, however, most of them were **deists** who believed in the existence of a god but denied the supernatural teachings of Christianity, such as Jesus' virgin birth and his resurrection. To the deists the universe was an orderly realm. Deists held that a powerful god set the universe in motion and established natural laws that govern it, but did not take a personal interest in its development or intervene in its affairs. In a favorite simile of the deists, this god was like a watchmaker who did not need to interfere constantly in the workings of his creation because it operated by itself according to rational and natural laws.

The Theory of Progress Most philosophes were optimistic about the future of the world and humanity. They expected knowledge of human affairs to advance as fast as modern science, and they believed that rational understanding of human and natural affairs would bring about a new era of constant progress. In fact, progress became almost an ideology of the philosophes, who believed that natural science would lead to greater human control over the world while rational sciences of human affairs would lead to individual freedom and the construction of a prosperous, just, and equitable society.

The philosophes' fond wishes for progress, prosperity, and social harmony did not come to pass. Yet the Enlightenment helped to bring about a thorough cultural transformation of European society. It weakened the influence of organized religion, although it by no means destroyed institutional churches. Enlightenment thought encouraged the replacement of Christian values, which had guided European thought on religious and moral affairs for more than a millennium, with a new set of secular values. Furthermore, the Enlightenment encouraged political and cultural leaders to subject society to rational analysis and intervene actively in its affairs in the interests of promoting progress and prosperity.

Popular Sovereignty

Since ancient times, kings or emperors ruled almost all settled agricultural societies. Small societies occasionally instituted democratic governments, in which all citizens participated in political affairs, or republican governments, in which delegates represented the interests of various constituencies. Some societies, especially those with weak central leadership, also relied on aristocratic governments, in which privileged elites supervised public affairs. But hierarchical rule flowing from a king or an emperor was by far the most common form of government in settled agricultural societies.

In justifying their rule, kings and emperors throughout the world often identified themselves with gods or claimed divine sanction for their authority. Some rulers were priests, although most cooperated closely with religious authorities. On the basis of their association with divine powers, kings and emperors claimed sovereignty—the authority to rule. In imperial China, for example, dynastic houses claimed to rule in accordance with the "mandate of heaven," and in early modern Europe monarchs often asserted a "divine right of kings" as the foundation of their authority.

During the seventeenth and eighteenth centuries, philosophes and other advocates of Enlightenment ideas began to question these long-standing notions of sovereignty. The philosophes rarely challenged monarchical rule but sought instead to make kings responsible to the people they governed. They commonly regarded government as the result of a contract between rulers and ruled. The English philosopher John Locke (1632–1704) formulated one of the most influential theories of contractual government. In his *Second Treatise of Civil Government,* published in 1690, Locke held that government arose in the remote past when people decided to work together, form civil society, and appoint rulers to protect and promote their common interests. Individuals granted political rights to their rulers but retained personal rights to life, liberty, and property. Any ruler who violated those rights was subject to being overthrown. Furthermore, according to Locke, because individuals voluntarily formed society and established government, rulers derived their authority from the consent of those whom they governed. If subjects withdrew their consent, they had the right to replace their rulers. In effect, Locke's political thought relocated sovereignty, removing it from rulers as divine agents and vesting it in the people of a society.

Individual Freedom Enlightenment thinkers addressed issues of freedom and equality as well as sovereignty. Philosophes such as Voltaire resented the persecution of religious minorities and censorship by royal officials, who had the power to prevent printers from publishing works that did not meet the approval of political and religious authorities. Philosophes called for religious toleration and freedom to express their views openly. When censors prohibited the publication of their writings in France, they often worked with French-speaking printers in Switzerland or the Netherlands who published their books and smuggled them across the border into France.

Political and Legal Equality Many Enlightenment thinkers also called for equality. They condemned the legal and social privileges enjoyed by aristocrats, who in the philosophes' view made no more contribution to the larger society than a peasant, an artisan, or a crafts worker. They recommended the

Socially prominent women deeply influenced the development of Enlightenment thought by organizing and maintaining salons—gatherings where philosophes, scientists, and intellectuals discussed the leading ideas of the day. Although produced in 1814, this painting depicts the Parisian salon of Mme. Geoffrin (center left), a leading patron of the French philosophes, about 1775. In the background is a bust of Voltaire, who lived in Switzerland at the time.

The Picture Art Collection/Alamy Stock Photo

creation of a society in which all individuals would be equal before the law. The most prominent advocate of political equality was the French-Swiss thinker **Jean-Jacques Rousseau** (1712–1778), who identified with simple working people and deeply resented the privileges enjoyed by elite classes. In his influential book *The Social Contract* (1762), Rousseau argued that members of a society were collectively the sovereign. In an ideal society all individuals would participate directly in the formulation of policy and the creation of laws. In the absence of royalty, aristocrats, or other privileged elites, the general will of the people would carry the day.

Enlightenment thought on freedom, equality, and popular sovereignty reflected the interests of educated and talented individuals who sought to increase their influence and enhance their status in society. Most Enlightenment thinkers

were of common birth but comfortable means. Although seeking to limit the prerogatives of ruling and aristocratic classes, most did not envision a society in which they would share political rights with women, children, peasants, laborers, enslaved people, or people of color.

Global Influence of Enlightenment Values Enlightenment thought constituted a serious challenge to long-established notions of political and social order. Revolutionary leaders in Europe and the Americas readily adopted Enlightenment ideas when justifying their efforts to overhaul the political and social structures they inherited. Over time, Enlightenment political thought influenced the organization of states and societies throughout the world. In part, this was because reformers and revolutionaries around the Atlantic basin had access to a vibrant print culture that allowed people in distant places to read about—and be inspired by—ideologies and events happening elsewhere.

Jean-Jacques Rousseau (zhahn-zhahk roo-soh)

REVOLUTIONS

The American Revolution

In the mid-eighteenth century there were few signs that North America might become a center of revolution. Residents of the thirteen British colonies there regarded themselves as British subjects: they recognized British law, read English-language books, and often braved the stormy waters of the North Atlantic Ocean to visit friends and family in England. Trade brought prosperity to the colonies, and British military forces protected colonists' interests. From 1754 to 1763, for example, British forces waged an extremely expensive conflict in North America known as the French and Indian War. This conflict merged with a larger contest for imperial supremacy, the Seven Years' War (1756–1763), in which British and French forces battled each other in Europe and India as well as North America. Victory in the Seven Years' War ensured that Britain would dominate global trade and that British possessions, including the North American colonies, would prosper.

Tightened British Control of the Colonies But the Seven Years' War also provided the circumstances in which American colonists became increasingly discontented with British rule. The war had been enormously expensive for the British government and had increased the tax burden of ordinary people living in Britain, so when it was over, the British government wanted the American colonists to help pay their fair share for the continuing maintenance and protection of the colonies. To achieve this, the British Parliament passed legislation to levy new taxes on goods and services in the colonies. But the American colonists had become accustomed to a degree of autonomy from the British government. Nearly every colony had an elective legislative assembly that controlled legislation affecting taxation and defense and that ultimately controlled the salaries paid to royal officials. They had also grown used to very lax enforcement of taxes and duties on imported goods. Thus, when the British attempted to increase its control in the colonies, the colonists resisted. Colonists especially resented the imposition of taxes on molasses by the Sugar Act (1764), on publications and legal documents by the Stamp Act (1765), on a wide variety of imported items by the Townshend Act (1767), and on tea by the Tea Act (1773). They objected to strict enforcement of navigation laws—some of them a century old, but widely disregarded—that required cargoes to travel in British ships and clear British customs. Colonists also took offense at the Quartering Act (1765), which required them to provide housing and accommodations for British troops.

In responding to British policies, the colonists argued that Parliament could not make policy for the colonies without the consent of the colonists themselves because they were protected by all the common-law rights of British citizens. The colonists in effect embraced legal traditions that were first demonstrated during the English civil war (1641–1651),

Engraved likeness of Deborah Sampson (1760–1827). During the American revolution, Sampson disguised herself as a man in order to serve as a soldier in the Continental army. She served as Robert Shirtliff for seventeen months, until she was discovered after being wounded in combat. She was honorably discharged in 1783.
FLHC 12/Alamy Stock Photo

establishing the constitutional precedent that an English monarch cannot govern without Parliament's consent. This concept was legally enshrined in the Bill of Rights (1689), which established, among other rights, that the consent of Parliament is required for the implementation of new taxes. Thus, the colonists responded to the imposition of new taxes by Parliament with the slogan "no taxation without representation." They boycotted British products; physically attacked British officials; and mounted protests such as the Boston Tea Party (1773), in which colonists dumped a cargo of tea into Boston harbor rather than pay duties under the Tea Act. They also organized the **Continental Congress** (1774), which coordinated the resistance to British policies across the thirteen colonies. By 1775 tensions were so high that British troops and a colonial militia skirmished at the village of Lexington, near Boston. The **American revolution** had begun.

The Declaration of Independence On 4 July 1776 the Continental Congress adopted a document titled "The unanimous Declaration of the thirteen united States of America." This **Declaration of Independence** drew deep inspiration from Enlightenment political thought in justifying the colonies' quest for independence. The document asserted "that all men are created equal, that they are endowed by their Creator with certain unalienable Rights, that among these are Life, Liberty, and the pursuit of Happiness." It echoed John Locke's contractual theory of government in arguing that individuals established governments to secure those rights and that governments derive their power and authority from "the consent of the governed." When any government infringes upon individuals' rights, the document continued, "it is the Right of the People to alter or abolish it, and to institute new Government." The Declaration of Independence presented a long list of specific abuses charged to the British crown and concluded by proclaiming the colonies "Free and Independent States" with "full Power to levy War, conclude Peace, contract Alliances, establish Commerce, and to do all other Acts and Things which Independent States may of right do."

Divided Loyalties It was one thing to declare independence, but a different matter altogether to make independence a reality. At the beginning of the war for independence, Britain enjoyed many advantages over the rebels: a strong government with clear lines of authority, the most powerful navy in the world, a competent army, a sizable population of loyalists in the colonies, and an overall colonial population with mixed sentiments about revolution and independence from Britain. In their political views and attitudes, the colonial population was far from homogeneous. Political loyalties varied between and within regions and communities and frequently shifted during the course of the revolution. Although "patriots," those who supported the revolution, were in the majority, not every colonist favored a violent confrontation with the British Empire. An estimated 20 percent of the white population of the colonies were "loyalists" or "Tories" who remained loyal to the British monarchy. A minority of people tried to stay neutral in the conflict, most notably the Religious Society of Friends of Pennsylvania, a religious movement better known as the Quakers. Native Americans were also divided in their loyalties. Tribes that depended on colonial trade usually threw their

Washington Crossing the Delaware is an 1851 oil-on-canvas painting by German American artist Emanuel Leutze. It commemorates Washington's crossing of the Delaware on 25 December 1776, during the American revolutionary war. A copy of this painting hangs in the West Wing reception area of the White House The painting emphasizes the mythological qualities of Washington as hero.
The Metropolitan Museum of Art, New York, Gift of John Stewart Kennedy, 1897

weight behind the patriots, but most Native Americans east of the Mississippi distrusted the colonists based on plentiful past experience and thus supported the British cause.

Colonial Advantages In spite of Britain's many advantages, it nevertheless lost the war. This can be explained in part by the distance between Britain and the colonies because the British had to ship supplies and troops across the Atlantic in order to engage in combat. **George Washington** (1732-1799) also provided strong and imaginative military leadership for the colonial army while local militias employed guerrilla tactics effectively against British forces. Most important, however, was the eventual support rival European powers—especially France—gave to the American colonists. The French had reason to help the colonists because they wanted revenge against the British for their recent losses in the Seven Years' War. Once the Americans proved they could fight effectively by defeating a British army at Saratoga in 1777, the French entered into a formal alliance with them. By 1780, the French were providing the Americans with not only substantial sums of money but also naval support and a large force of trained soldiers and officers.

In fact, the French were critical in forcing the British to surrender at Yorktown in October 1781. An army of French and American soldiers had surrounded the British forces of Charles Cornwallis at Yorktown, Virginia, and laid siege to his encampment. Cornwallis had planned to escape via the sea but found his way blocked by a French naval force in the Chesapeake Bay and was forced to surrender. Although the war continued into 1782, Cornwallis' surrender ensured an eventual American victory. In September 1783 diplomats concluded the Peace of Paris, by which the British government formally recognized American independence, thanks in very large measure to French aid.

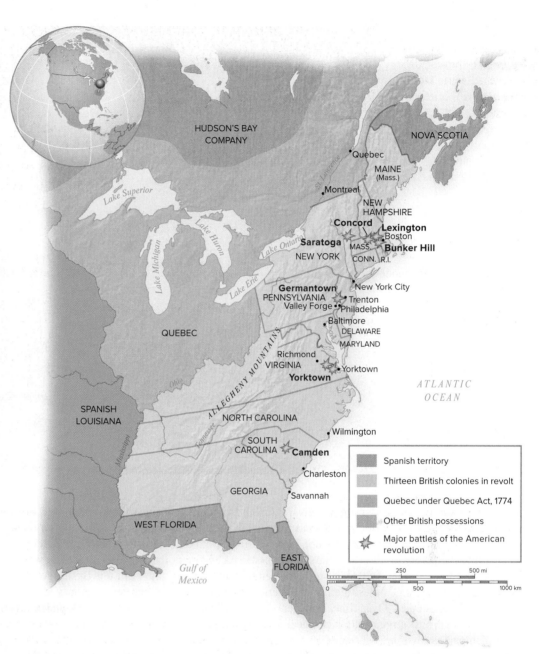

MAP 28.1   The American revolution, 1781.

Note both the location of the major towns and cities in the colonies and the location of the major battles that occurred during the revolution.

Why were both situated so close to the eastern coast?

Building an Independent State The leaders of the fledgling republic organized a state that reflected Enlightenment principles. In 1787 a constitutional convention drafted the blueprint for a new system of government—the Constitution of the United States—which emphasized the rights of individuals. American leaders based the federal government on popular

A contemporary print depicts the storming of the Bastille in 1789. The deeds of common people working in crowds became a favorite theme of artists after the outbreak of the French revolution.
PRISMA ARCHIVO/Alamy Stock Photo

sovereignty, and they agreed to follow this written constitution that guaranteed individual liberties such as freedom of speech, of the press, and of religion. They did not, however, grant political and legal equality to all inhabitants of the newly independent land. They accorded full rights only to men of property, withholding them from landless men, women, enslaved people, and indigenous peoples. Over time, however, disenfranchised groups claimed and struggled for political and legal rights. Their campaigns involved considerable personal sacrifice and sometimes led to violence because those in possession of rights did not share them readily with others. Yet in spite of its imperfections, the early American republic served as an inspiration to others around the Atlantic basin, who similarly sought to create governments based on popular sovereignty.

The French Revolution

Among those most inspired by the success of the American revolution were the French philosophes and their followers, who for decades had been arguing in favor of popular sovereignty and greater social and political equality. Although French Enlightenment thinkers drew inspiration from the

American example, the **French revolution** that began in 1789 was a more radical affair than its American counterpart. American revolutionary leaders sought independence from British imperial rule, but they were content to retain British law and much of their British social and cultural heritage. In contrast, French revolutionary leaders repudiated existing society; often referred to as the *ancien régime* ("old order"); and sought to replace it with new political, social, and cultural structures.

The Estates General Serious fiscal problems within the French government provided the opportunity for French revolutionaries to put their ideas into practice. In the 1780s approximately half of the French royal government's revenue went to pay off war debts—nearly a quarter of which were amassed as a result of French support for colonists in the war of American independence. Combined with the need to maintain the French armed forces and the lavish spending of the French court, by 1789 the French government faced complete bankruptcy. King **Louis XVI** (reigned 1774-1793) was unable to raise more revenue from the overburdened peasantry, so he sought to increase taxes on the French nobility. The nobility, which had traditionally been exempt from taxation, protested. This then forced Louis to summon the **Estates General,** which was an assembly that represented the entire French population through groups known as estates, to get the money he needed.

ancien régime (ahn-syen REY-zheem)
Louis (LOO-ee)

In the ancien régime there were three estates, or political classes. The first estate consisted of about one hundred thousand Roman Catholic clergy, and the second included some four hundred thousand nobles. The third estate embraced the rest of the population—about twenty-four million serfs; free peasants; and urban residents ranging from laborers, artisans, and shopkeepers to physicians, bankers, and attorneys. Though founded in 1303, the Estates General had not met since 1614. The third estate had as many delegates as the other two estates combined, but that numerical superiority offered no advantage when the assembly voted on issues because voting took place by estate—one vote for each—rather than by individuals.

In May 1789 King Louis called the Estates General into session at the royal palace of Versailles in hopes that it would authorize new taxes and save the kingdom from financial ruin. Louis never controlled the assembly. Representatives of the third estate arrived at Versailles demanding political and social reform based on Enlightenment thinking regarding popular sovereignty. Although some members of the lower clergy and a few prominent nobles supported such reforms, in general the first and second estates were far more socially and politically conservative than the third estate and actively thwarted efforts to push reforms through the Estates General.

The National Assembly On 17 June 1789, after several weeks of fruitless debate, representatives of the third estate took the dramatic step of seceding from the Estates General and proclaiming themselves to be the **National Assembly.** Three days later, meeting in an indoor tennis court, members of the new Assembly swore not to disband until they had provided France with a new constitution. On 14 July 1789 a Parisian crowd, fearing that the king sought to undo events of the previous weeks, stormed the Bastille, a royal jail and arsenal, in search of weapons. The military garrison protecting the Bastille surrendered to the crowd but only after killing many

of the attackers. To vent their rage, members of the crowd hacked the defenders to death. One assailant used his pocketknife to sever the garrison commander's head, which the victorious crowd mounted on a pike and paraded around the streets of Paris. News of the event soon spread, sparking insurrections in cities throughout France.

Emboldened by popular support, the National Assembly undertook a broad program of political and social reform. The **Declaration of the Rights of Man and the Citizen,** which the National Assembly promulgated in August 1789, articulated its guiding principles. Reflecting the influence of American revolutionary ideas, the Declaration of the Rights of Man and the Citizen proclaimed the equality of all men; declared that sovereignty resided in the people; and asserted individual rights to liberty, property, and security.

Liberty, Equality, and Fraternity Between 1789 and 1791 the National Assembly reconfigured French society. Taking "liberty, equality, and fraternity" as its goals, the Assembly abolished the old social order along with the many fees and labor services that peasants owed to their landlords. It dramatically altered the role of the church in French society by seizing church lands, abolishing the first estate, defining clergy as civilians, and requiring clergy to take an oath of loyalty to the state. It also issued a constitution that made the king the chief executive official but deprived him of legislative authority. France became a constitutional monarchy in which men of property—about half the adult male population—had the right to vote in elections to choose legislators. In these ways, the French revolution represented an effort to put Enlightenment political thought into practice.

The Convention The revolution soon took a radical turn. The French nobility, who were not happy with their diminished status, sought to mobilize foreign powers in support of

The guillotine was an efficient killing machine during the French revolution. In this contemporary print the executioner displays the just-severed head of King Louis XVI to the crowd assembled to witness his execution.
adoc-photos/Corbis Historical/Getty Images

SOURCES FROM THE PAST

Declaration of the Rights of Man and the Citizen

This declaration, which became part of the official revolutionary platform in France in August 1789, was written in close collaboration with Thomas Jefferson, the principal author of the American Declaration of Independence and the U.S. ambassador to France that year. Thus it is not surprising that the Declaration of the Rights of Man and the Citizen reflects the strong influence of American revolutionary ideas.

First Article. Men are born and remain free and equal in rights. Social distinctions may be based only on common utility.

Article 2. The goal of every political association is the preservation of the natural and inalienable rights of man. These rights are liberty, property, security, and resistance to oppression.

Article 3. The principle of all sovereignty resides essentially in the nation. No body and no individual can exercise authority that does not flow directly from the nation. ——— *According to this statement, was it possible for kings to be sovereign?*

Article 4. Liberty consists in the freedom to do anything that does not harm another. The exercise of natural rights of each man thus has no limits except those that assure other members of society their enjoyment of the same rights. These limits may be determined only by law . . .

Article 6. Law is the expression of the general will. All citizens have the right to participate either personally or through their representatives in the making of law. The law must be the same for all, whether it protects or punishes. Being equal in the eyes of the law, all citizens are equally eligible for all public honors, offices, and occupations, according to their abilities, without any distinction other than that of their virtues and talents.

Article 7. No person shall be accused, arrested, or imprisoned except in the cases and according to the forms prescribed by law. Any one soliciting, transmitting, executing, or causing to be executed, any arbitrary order, shall be punished. But any citizen summoned or arrested in virtue of the law shall submit without delay, as resistance constitutes an offense . . .

Article 9. As all persons are held innocent until they shall have been declared guilty, if arrest shall be deemed indispensable, all harshness not essential to the securing of the prisoner's person shall be severely repressed by law . . .

Article 11. The free communication of thoughts and opinions is one of the most precious rights of man: every citizen may thus speak, write, and publish freely, but will be responsible for abuse of this freedom in cases decided by the law . . . ——— *Is it possible to learn something of French society under the ancien régime by reading these articles?*

Article 13. For the maintenance of public military force and for the expenses of administration, common taxation is necessary: it must be equally divided among all citizens according to their means . . .

Article 15. Society has the right to require from every public official an accounting of his administration.

Article 16. Any society in which guarantees of rights are not assured and separation of powers is not defined has no constitution at all.

Article 17. Property is an inviolable and sacred right. No one may be deprived of property except when public necessity, legally determined, clearly requires it, and on condition of just and prearranged compensation.

For Further Reflection

■ In what ways do the principles established in the Declaration reflect the political transformations taking place throughout the age of Atlantic revolutions?

Source: *Déclaration des droits de l'homme et du citoyen.* Translated by Jerry H. Bentley.

the king and to restore the ancien régime. This gave the Assembly the pretext to declare war against Austria and Prussia in April 1792. Adding to the military burden of France, revolutionary leaders declared war in the following year on Spain, Britain, and the Netherlands. Fearing military defeat and counterrevolution, revolutionary leaders created the Convention, a new legislative body elected by universal manhood suffrage, which abolished the monarchy and proclaimed France a republic. The Convention rallied the French population by instituting the *levée en masse* ("mass levy"), or universal conscription that drafted people and resources for use in the war against invading forces. The Convention also rooted

levée en masse (le-VAY ahn mahs)

out enemies at home. It made frequent use of the guillotine, a recently invented machine that brought about supposedly humane executions by quickly severing a victim's head. In 1793 King Louis XVI and his wife, Queen Marie Antoinette, themselves were killed by guillotine when the Convention found them guilty of treason.

Revolutionary chaos reached its peak in 1793 and 1794 when Maximilien Robespierre (1758–1794) and the radical Jacobin party dominated the Convention. A lawyer by training, Robespierre had emerged during the revolution as a ruthless but popular radical known as "the Incorruptible," and he dominated the Committee of Public Safety, the executive authority of the Republic. The Jacobins believed passionately that France needed complete restructuring, and they unleashed a campaign of terror to promote their revolutionary agenda. They sought to eliminate the influence of Christianity in French society by closing churches and forcing priests to take wives. They promoted a new "cult of reason" as a secular alternative to Christianity. They reorganized the calendar, keeping months of thirty days but replacing seven-day weeks with ten-day units that recognized no day of religious observance. The Jacobins also proclaimed the inauguration of a new historical era with the Year I, which began with the declaration of the First Republic on 22 September 1792. They encouraged citizens to display their revolutionary zeal by wearing working-class clothes. They granted increased rights to women by permitting them to inherit property and divorce their husbands, although they did not allow women to vote or participate in political affairs. The Jacobins also made frequent use of the guillotine: between the summer of 1793 and the summer of 1794, they executed about forty thousand people and imprisoned three hundred thousand suspected enemies of the revolution. Even the feminist Olympe de Gouges (1748–1793)—to whom we were introduced in the introduction to this chapter—was a victim of the Jacobins, who did not appreciate her efforts to extend the rights of freedom and equality to women.

The Directory Many victims of this **reign of terror** were fellow radicals who fell out of favor with Robespierre and the Jacobins. The instability of revolutionary leadership eventually undermined confidence in the regime itself. In July 1794 the Convention arrested Robespierre and his allies, convicted them of tyranny, and sent them to the guillotine. A group of conservative men of property then seized power and ruled France under a new institution known as the Directory (1795–1799). Though more pragmatic than previous revolutionary leaders, members of the Directory were unable to resolve the economic and military problems that plagued revolutionary France. In seeking a middle way between the ancien régime and radical revolution, they lurched from one policy to another and faced constant challenges to their authority. The Directory came to an end in November 1799 when a young general named Napoleon Bonaparte staged a coup d'état and seized power.

Jacques-Louis David's *Napoleon on Horseback at the St. Bernard Pass* (1800) presents a famously heroic image of Napoleon's attack on Italy in 1800. David's art clearly served the interests of Napoleon's political regime. The powerful and dynamic image was intended to convey Napoleon's greatness and his place in the history of conquering heroes.
Leemage/Corbis/Getty Images

The Reign of Napoleon

Born to a minor noble family of Corsica, a Mediterranean island annexed by France in 1768, **Napoleon Bonaparte** (1769–1821) studied at French military schools and became an officer in the army of King Louis XVI. A brilliant military leader, he became a general at age twenty-four. He was a fervent supporter of the revolution and defended the Directory against a popular uprising in 1795. In a campaign of 1796–1797, he drove the Austrian army from northern Italy and established French rule there. In 1798 he mounted an invasion of Egypt to gain access to the Red Sea and threaten British control of the sea route to India, but the campaign ended in a complete British victory. Politically ambitious, Napoleon returned to France in 1799; overthrew the Directory; and set up a new government, the Consulate. Although he ostensibly shared power with two other consuls, it was Napoleon who

Napoleon Bonaparte (nuh-POH-lee-uhn BOH-nuh-pahrt)

was henceforth the real master of France. Having established a dictatorship, he crowned himself emperor in 1804.

Napoleonic France Napoleon brought political stability to a land torn by revolution and war. He made peace with the Roman Catholic church and in 1801 concluded an agreement with the pope. The pact, known as the Concordat, provided that the French state would retain church lands seized during the revolution, but the state agreed to pay clerics' salaries, recognize Roman Catholic Christianity as the preferred faith of France, and extend freedom of religion to Protestant Christians and Jews. This measure won Napoleon a great deal of support from people who supported the political and social goals of the revolution but balked at radicals' efforts to replace Christianity with a cult of reason.

In 1804 Napoleon issued the **Civil Code,** a revised body of civil law, which also helped stabilize French society. The Civil Code affirmed the political and legal equality of all adult men and established a merit-based society in which individuals qualified for education and employment because of talent rather than birth or social standing. The code protected private property, and Napoleon allowed aristocratic opponents of the revolution to return to France and reclaim some of the property that had been taken from them. The Civil Code confirmed many of the moderate revolutionary policies of the National Assembly but retracted measures passed by the more radical Convention. For example, the code restored patriarchal authority in the family by making women and children subservient to male heads of households. And although he approved the Enlightenment ideal of equality, Napoleon was no champion of intellectual freedom or representative government. He limited free speech and routinely censored newspapers and other publications. He established a secret police force that relied heavily on spies and detained suspected political opponents by the thousands. He made systematic use of propaganda to manipulate public opinion. He ignored elective bodies and surrounded himself with loyal military officers who ensured that representative assemblies did not restrict his authority. When he crowned himself emperor, he founded a dynasty that set his family above and apart from the people in whose name they ruled.

Napoleon's Empire While working to stabilize France, Napoleon also sought to extend his authority throughout Europe. Napoleon's armies conquered Spain, Portugal, and Italy; occupied the Netherlands; and inflicted humiliating defeats on Austrian and Prussian forces. Napoleon sent his brothers and other relatives to rule the conquered and occupied lands, and he forced Austria, Prussia, and Russia to ally with him and respect French hegemony in Europe. But Napoleon's empire began to unravel in 1812, when he decided to invade Russia. Convinced that the tsar was conspiring with his British enemies, Napoleon led a Grand Army of six hun-

dred thousand soldiers to Moscow. He captured the city, but the tsar withdrew and refused to surrender. Russians set Moscow ablaze, leaving Napoleon's massive army without adequate shelter or supplies. By the end of the campaign, more than 400,000 French soldiers had died.

The Fall of Napoleon Napoleon's disastrous Russian campaign emboldened his enemies. A coalition of British, Austrian, Prussian, and Russian armies converged on France and forced Napoleon to abdicate his throne in April 1814. The victors restored the French monarchy and exiled Napoleon to the tiny Mediterranean island of Elba, near Corsica. But Napoleon's adventure had not yet come to an end. In March 1815 he escaped from Elba, returned to France, and reconstituted his army. For a hundred days he ruled France again before a British army defeated him at **Waterloo** in Belgium. Unwilling to take further chances with the wily general, European powers banished Napoleon to the remote and isolated island of St. Helena in the South Atlantic Ocean, where he died of natural causes in 1821.

The Haitian Revolution

The success of the American revolution appealed not only to French social reformers but also to enslaved people and free people of color in the Caribbean. But on the French portion of the island of Hispaniola it was the French revolution that provided the immediate inspiration and the opportunity for the revolution that broke out there in 1791.

Indeed, the only successful slave revolt in history took place on Hispaniola in the midst of the French revolution. By the eighteenth century, Hispaniola was a major center of sugar production with hundreds of prosperous plantations. The Spanish colony of Santo Domingo occupied the eastern part of the island (modern Dominican Republic), and the French colony of Saint-Domingue occupied the western part (modern Haiti). Saint-Domingue was one of the richest of all European colonies in the Caribbean: sugar, coffee, and cotton produced there accounted for almost one-third of France's foreign trade.

Saint-Domingue Society On the eve of the **Haitian revolution,** the population of Saint-Domingue was comprised of three major groups. There were about forty thousand white colonials, subdivided into several classes: European-born Frenchmen who monopolized colonial administrative posts; a class of plantation owners, chiefly minor aristocrats who hoped to return to France as soon as possible; and lower-class whites, who included artisans, shopkeepers, slave dealers, and day laborers. A second group comprised about twenty-eight thousand *gens de couleur* (French for "people of color"), most of whom were mixed race. Many of them were artisans, domestic servants, or overseers, but a small and influential proportion owned small plots of land and held enslaved people. The remainder of the population made up the third group, consisting of some five hundred thousand enslaved people,

---

gens de couleur (zhen de coo-LEHR)

MAP 28.2   Napoleon's empire in 1812.

Observe the number of states dependent on or allied with Napoleon in contrast to those who were at war with him.

Were there geographic conditions that allowed some states to resist Napoleon's efforts at conquest better than others?

some of whom were mixed-race and born in St. Domingue but most of whom were African-born.

Most of the colony's enslaved people toiled in fields under brutal conditions. Planters worked enslaved people so hard and provided them with so little care that mortality was very high. Not surprisingly, white planters and enslaved people frequently had violent conflicts. Aware that they were outnumbered by enslaved people by a factor of more than ten, plantation owners lived in constant fear of rebellion. Many enslaved people ran away into the mountains. By the late eighteenth century, Saint-Domingue had many large communities of maroons (enslaved people who had run away), who maintained their own societies and sometimes attacked plantations in search of food, weapons, tools, and additional recruits. As planters lost laborers as a result of death and escape, they imported new enslaved people from Africa and other Caribbean islands. This pattern continued throughout the eighteenth century, until prices of new slaves from Africa rose dramatically.

The American and French revolutions both inspired and helped to ignite violent political and social revolution in Saint-Domingue. Because the French government supported North American colonists against British rule, colonial governors in Saint-Domingue sent about five hundred *gens de couleur* to fight in the American war of independence. Having seen revolutionary ideals in practice, they returned to Saint-Domingue with the intention of reforming society there. Then, when the French revolution broke out a few years later in 1789, white settlers in Saint-Domingue sought the right to govern themselves, but they opposed proposals to grant political and legal equality to the *gens de couleur*. By May 1791 civil war had broken out between white settlers and *gens de couleur*.

Slave Revolt The conflict expanded dramatically when a charismatic Voudou priest named Boukman organized a slave revolt. In August 1791 some twelve thousand enslaved people began a campaign of killing white settlers, burning their homes, and destroying their plantations. Within a few weeks the rebels attracted almost one hundred thousand enslaved people into their ranks. Many enslaved people were battle-tested veterans of wars in Africa, and they drew on their military experience to organize large armies. Slave leaders also found recruits and reinforcements in Saint-Domingue's maroon communities. Foreign armies soon complicated the situation: French troops arrived in 1792 to restore order, and British and Spanish forces intervened in 1793 in hopes of benefiting from France's difficulties.

Toussaint Louverture Boukman died while fighting shortly after launching the revolt, but slave forces eventually overcame white settlers, *gens de couleur,* and foreign armies. Their successes were due largely to the leadership of François-Dominique **Toussaint** (1744–1803), who after 1791 called himself **Louverture**—from the French *l'ouverture,* meaning "the

Nineteenth-century mural of Jean-Jacques Dessalines (1758–1806), a leader of the Haitian Revolution and the first ruler of independent Haiti under the constitution of 1805.
Historic Images/Alamy Stock Photo

opening," to indicate the one who created an opening in enemy ranks. The son of enslaved parents, Toussaint learned to read and write from a Roman Catholic priest. Because of his education and intelligence, he rose to the position of livestock overseer on the plantation where he was enslaved. Later, he leased land for planting coffee, where he used "rented" slaves for labor. He was able to buy his freedom in 1776. When the slave revolt broke out in 1791, Toussaint helped his masters escape to a safe place, then left the plantation and joined the rebels.

Toussaint was a skilled organizer, and by 1793 he had taken a leadership role in the revolt and built a strong, disciplined army. He shrewdly played French, British, and Spanish forces against one another while also jockeying for power with

Toussaint Louverture (too-SAHNT loo-vehr-TOOR)

A French depiction of the Battle of Crête à Pierrot (March 4–12, 1802) during the Haitian Revolution.
Niday Picture Library/Alamy Stock Photo

other African and mixed-race generals. By 1797 he led an army of twenty thousand and controlled most of Saint-Domingue. In 1801 he issued a constitution that granted equality and citizenship to all residents of Saint-Domingue. He stopped short of declaring independence from France, however, because he did not want to provoke Napoleon—who had by that time seized power in France—into attacking the island.

The Republic of Haiti Toussaint's worries about Napoleon were well founded. In 1802 Napoleon dispatched forty thousand troops to restore French authority in Saint-Domingue. Toussaint attempted to negotiate a peaceful settlement, but the French commander arrested him and sent him to France, where he died in jail of maltreatment in 1803. By the time he died, however, yellow fever had ravaged the French army in Saint-Domingue, and the generals who took Toussaint's place had defeated the remaining troops and driven them out of the colony. Late in 1803 they declared independence, and on 1 January 1804 they proclaimed the establishment of Haiti, meaning "land of mountains," which became the second independent republic in the Western Hemisphere after the United States.

Wars of Independence in Latin America

Latin American Society Revolutionary ideals also traveled to the Spanish and Portuguese colonies in the Americas. Though governed by *peninsulares* (colonial officials from Spain or Portugal), the Iberian colonies all had a large, wealthy, and powerful class of *criollos* (creoles), or people of European descent who had been born in the Americas. In 1800 the *peninsulares* numbered about 30,000, while the creole population was 3.5 million. The Iberian colonies also had a large population—about 10 million in all—of less privileged classes. Enslaved people formed a majority in Brazil, but elsewhere indigenous peoples and individuals of mixed European and African or European and indigenous ancestry were most numerous.

Creoles benefited greatly during the eighteenth century as they established plantations and ranches in the colonies and participated in rapidly expanding trade with Spain and Portugal. Yet the creoles also had grievances. Like British colonists in North America, the creoles resented administrative control and economic regulations imposed by the Iberian powers. They drew inspiration from Enlightenment political thought and occasionally took part in tax revolts and popular uprisings. The creoles desired neither social reform like that promoted by Robespierre nor the establishment of an egalitarian society like Haiti. Rather, they sought to displace the *peninsulares* but retain their privileged position in society: political independence on the model of the United States in North America struck them as an attractive alternative to colonial status. Their opportunity came as a result of the Napoleonic Wars in Europe because Napoleon invaded and conquered Portugal in 1807 and Spain in 1808. In the Spanish case, this effectively left Spanish settlers in the Americas to rule themselves until Napoleon was defeated and the Spanish king was restored in 1814. As a result of their experiences with self-rule, between 1810 and 1825 creoles led movements that brought independence to all Spanish colonies

peninsulares (peh-neen-soo-LAH-rehs)
criollos (kree-OH-yohs)

MAP 28.3   Latin America in 1830.

Note the dates each state won its independence.

Since most states became independent in very close succession, what conditions prevented Latin American states from joining together in a federation like that in the United States?

in the Americas—except Cuba and Puerto Rico—and established creole-dominated republics.

Mexican Independence By 1810, weakened royal authority in the Americas spurred revolts against Spanish rule in Argentina, Venezuela, and Mexico. The most serious was a peasant rebellion in Mexico led by a parish priest, **Miguel Hidalgo y Costilla** (1753–1811), who rallied indigenous peoples and mestizos—people of mixed European and indigenous descent—against colonial rule. Many contemporaries viewed Hidalgo's movement for independence from Spanish rule as social and economic warfare by the masses against the elites of Mexican society, particularly since he called for the death of Spaniards. Conservative creoles soon captured Hidalgo and executed him, but his rebellion continued to flare for three years after his death. Hidalgo became the symbol of Mexican independence, and the day on which he proclaimed his revolt—16 September 1810—is Mexico's principal national holiday.

Colonial rule in Mexico actually came to an end in 1821, when the creole general Augustín de Iturbide (1783–1824) declared independence from Spain. In the following year, he declared himself emperor of Mexico. Neither Iturbide nor his empire survived for long. Though an able general, Iturbide was an incompetent administrator, and in 1823 creole elites deposed him and established a republic. Two years later the southern regions of the Mexican empire declared their own independence. They formed a Central American Federation until 1838, when they split into the independent states of Guatemala, El Salvador, Honduras, Nicaragua, and Costa Rica.

Simón Bolívar In South America, creole elites such as **Simón Bolívar** (1783–1830) led the movement for independence. Born in Caracas (in modern Venezuela), Bolívar was a fervent republican steeped in Enlightenment ideas about popular sovereignty. Inspired by the example of George Washington, he took up arms against Spanish rule in 1811, during the period of weakened royal authority when the Spanish king had been deposed. In the early days of his struggle, Bolívar experienced many reversals and twice went into exile. In 1819, however, he assembled an army that surprised and crushed the Spanish army—sent by the Spanish King Ferdinand VII almost immediately after his restoration to power in 1814—in Colombia. Later, he campaigned in Venezuela, Ecuador, and Peru, coordinating his efforts with other creole leaders, such as

Simón Bolívar, creole leader of the independence movement in Latin America, was a favorite subject of painters in the nineteenth century.
Photo Researchers/Science Source

José de San Martín (1778–1850) in Argentina and Bernardo O'Higgins (1778–1842) in Chile. By 1825 creole forces had overcome Spanish armies and deposed Spanish rulers throughout South America.

Bolívar's goal was to weld the former Spanish colonies of South America into a great confederation like the United States in North America. During the 1820s independent Venezuela, Colombia, and Ecuador formed a republic called **Gran Colombia,** and Bolívar attempted to bring Peru and Bolivia (named for Bolívar himself) into the confederation as well. By 1830, however, strong political and regional differences had undermined Gran Colombia. As the confederation disintegrated, a bitterly disappointed Bolívar pronounced South America "ungovernable" and lamented that "those who have served the revolution have plowed the sea." Shortly after the breakup of Gran Colombia, Bolívar died of tuberculosis while en route to self-imposed exile in Europe.

Brazilian Independence Independence came to Portuguese Brazil at the same time as to Spanish colonies, but by a different process. When Napoleon invaded Portugal in 1807, the royal court fled Lisbon and established a government in exile in Rio de Janeiro. In 1821 the king returned to Portugal, leaving his son Pedro in Brazil as regent. The next year Brazilian creoles called for independence from Portugal, and Pedro agreed to their demands. When the Portuguese *Cortes* (parliament) tried to curtail his power, Pedro declared Brazil's independence and accepted appointment as Emperor Pedro I (reigned 1822–1834).

Creole Dominance Although Brazil achieved independence as a monarchy rather than a republic, creole elites dominated Brazilian society just as they did in former Spanish colonies. Indeed, independence brought little social change in Latin America. The *peninsulares* returned to Europe, but Latin American society remained as rigidly stratified as it had been in 1800. The newly independent states granted military authority to local charismatic strongmen, known as *caudillos,* who allied with creole elites. The new states also permitted the continuation of

---

Miguel Hidalgo y Costilla (mee-GEL hee-DAHL-goh ee koh-STEE-ya)
Simón Bolívar (see-MOHN boh-LEE-vahr)
caudillos (KAW-dee-ohs)

slavery, confirmed the wealth and authority of the Roman Catholic church, and repressed the poor. The principal beneficiaries of independence in Latin America were the creole elites.

CONSEQUENCES AND IMPLICATIONS OF THE REVOLUTIONS

The ideals of the Atlantic revolutions resulted in the birth of new ideologies, including especially the ideologies of conservatism and liberalism. An ideology is a coherent vision of human nature, human society, and the larger world that proposes some particular form of political and social organization as ideal. Whereas conservatism sought to justify the current state of affairs, liberalism sharply criticized the status quo and argued for the need to improve society. The revolutions also encouraged social reformers to organize broader programs of liberation. Whereas the American, French, and Latin American revolutions guaranteed political and legal rights to white men, social reformers sought to extend those rights to women and slaves of African ancestry. During the nineteenth century all European and American states abolished slavery, but former slaves and their descendants remained an underprivileged and oppressed class in most of the Atlantic world. The quest for women's rights also proceeded slowly during the nineteenth century.

The Emergence of New Ideologies

Conservatism The modern ideology of **conservatism** arose as political and social theorists responded to the challenges of the American and especially the French revolutions. Conservatives viewed society as an organism that changed slowly over the generations. The English political philosopher Edmund Burke (1729–1797) held, for example, that society was a compact between a people's ancestors, the present generation, and their descendants as yet unborn. While admitting the need for gradual change that came about by general consensus, Burke condemned radical or revolutionary change, which in his view could only lead to anarchy. Thus Burke approved of the American revolution, which he took as an example of natural change in keeping with the historical development of North American society, but he denounced the French revolution as a chaotic and irresponsible assault on society.

Liberalism In contrast to conservatives, liberals took change as normal and welcomed it as the agent of progress. They viewed conservatism as an effort to justify the status quo, maintain the privileges enjoyed by favored classes, and avoid dealing with injustice and inequality in society. For liberals the task of political and social theory was not to stifle change but, rather, to manage it in the best interests of society. Liberals championed the Enlightenment values of freedom and equality, which they believed would lead to higher standards of morality and increased prosperity for the whole society. They usually favored republican forms of government in which citizens elected representatives to legislative bodies, and they

called for written constitutions that guaranteed freedom and equality for all citizens and that precisely defined the political structure and institutions of their societies.

The **liberalism** that emerged from the Atlantic revolutions was concerned with civil rights but was not as concerned with political and social rights. Most liberals, for example, held the view that voting was more of a privilege than a right and therefore was legitimately subject to certain qualifications. Limitations on voting were in fact characteristic of postrevolutionary societies, and citizens were routinely denied the vote on the basis of class, age, gender, and race, among other factors. But as the nineteenth century progressed liberalism changed its character. As general populations became more assertive, liberalism could not concern itself mainly with interests of the more privileged strata of society. Consequently, there was a shift from early classical liberalism to a more democratic variety. Equality before the law was supplemented by equality before the ballot box. Liberalism's traditional emphasis on minimizing the role and power of government was reversed, and by the end of the nineteenth century, liberals started to look to government to minimize or correct the problems that accompanied industrialization.

The most prominent exponent of early liberalism was John Stuart Mill (1806–1873), an English philosopher, economist, and social reformer. Mill tirelessly promoted the freedom of individuals to pursue economic and intellectual interests. He tried to ensure that powerful minorities, such as wealthy businessmen, would not curb the freedoms of the poorly organized majority, but he also argued that it was improper for the majority to impose its will on minorities with different interests and values. He advocated universal suffrage as the most effective way to advance individual freedom, and he called for taxation of business profits and high personal incomes to limit the power of the wealthiest classes. Mill went further than most liberals of his time in seeking to extend the rights of freedom and equality to women and working people as well as men of property.

Voting Rights and Restrictions As Mill recognized, the age of revolutions in the Atlantic world illustrated the centrality of suffrage in establishing a people's and a nation's sense of democratic legitimacy and political sovereignty. **Suffrage** refers to the right or the privilege to vote in order to elect public officials or to adopt laws. The concept of suffrage derived its revolutionary significance from Enlightenment notions about self-government and about governments deriving authority from the consent of the people. Voting rights and restrictions evolved into powerful political concerns both during and after the age of revolutions.

Testing the Limits of Revolutionary Ideals: Slavery

The Enlightenment ideals of freedom and equality were watchwords of revolution in the Atlantic Ocean basin. Yet different revolutionaries understood the implications of freedom and equality in very different ways. In North America revolution led to political independence, a broad array of individual freedoms, and the legal equality of adult white men. In France it destroyed the hierarchical social order of the ancien régime and temporarily extended political and legal rights to all citizens, although Napoleon and later rulers effectively curbed some of those rights. In Haiti revolution brought independence from French rule and the end of slavery. In South America it led to independence from Iberian rule and societies dominated by creole elites. In the wake of the Atlantic revolutions, social activists in Europe and the Americas considered the possibility that the ideals of freedom and equality might have further implications as yet unexplored. They turned their attention especially to the issues of slavery and women's rights.

Movements to End the Slave Trade

The campaign to end the slave trade and abolish slavery began in the eighteenth century. Formerly enslaved people such as Olaudah Equiano (1745-1797) were among the earliest critics of slavery. Beginning in the 1780s European Christian moralists also voiced opposition to slavery.

Only after the American, French, and Haitian revolutions, however, did the antislavery movement gain momentum. The leading spokesman of the movement was **William Wilberforce** (1759-1833), a prominent English philanthropist elected in 1780 to a seat in Parliament. There he tirelessly attacked slavery on moral and religious grounds. After the Haitian revolution he attracted supporters who feared that continued reliance on enslaved labor would result in more and larger slave revolts, and in 1807 Parliament passed Wilberforce's bill to end the slave trade. Under British pressure, other states also banned commerce in enslaved people: the United States in 1808, France in 1814, the Netherlands in 1817, and Spain in 1845. The British navy, which dominated the North Atlantic Ocean, patrolled the west coast of Africa to ensure compliance with the law. But the slave trade died slowly because illegal trade continued on a small scale: the last documented ship to carry slaves across the Atlantic Ocean arrived in Cuba in 1867.

Movements to Abolish Slavery

The abolition of slavery itself was a much bigger challenge than ending the slave trade because owners had property rights in the people they enslaved. Planters and merchant elites strongly resisted efforts to alter the system that provided them with abundant supplies of inexpensive labor. Nevertheless, the end of the slave trade doomed the institution of slavery in the Americas. In Haiti the end of slavery came with the revolution. In much of South America, slavery ended with independence from Spanish rule, as Simón Bolívar freed enslaved people who joined his forces and provided constitutional guarantees of free status for all residents of Gran Colombia. In Mexico slavery was abolished in 1829, though not solely for humanitarian reasons. Rather, abolition in Mexico served as a mechanism to stop the influx of residents from the southern United States coming in with enslaved people to grow cotton.

Meanwhile, as they worked to ban traffic in human labor, Wilberforce and other moralists also launched a campaign to free enslaved people and abolish the institution of slavery itself. In 1833, one month after Wilberforce's death, Parliament provided twenty million pounds sterling as compensation to slave holders and abolished slavery throughout the British Empire. Other states followed the British example: France abolished slavery in 1848, the United States in 1865, Cuba in 1886, and Brazil in 1888.

Freedom without Equality

Abolition brought legal freedom for African and African American people, but it did not bring political equality. In most lands other than Haiti, African American peoples had little influence in society. Property requirements, literacy tests, poll taxes, and campaigns of intimidation effectively prevented them from voting. Nor did emancipation bring social and economic improvements for former enslaved people and their descendants. White elites owned most of the property in the Americas, and they kept people of color subordinated by forcing them to accept low-paying work. A few African Americans owned small plots of land, but they could not challenge the economic and political power of creole elites.

Testing the Limits of Revolutionary Ideals: Women's Rights

Women participated alongside men in the movement to abolish slavery, and their experience inspired some social reformers to seek equality with men. They argued that women suffered many of the same legal disabilities as enslaved people: they had little access to education, they could not enter professional occupations that required advanced education, and they were legally deprived of the right to vote. They drew on Enlightenment thought in making a case for women's rights, but in spite of support from prominent liberals such as John Stuart Mill, they had little success before the twentieth century.

Enlightenment Ideals and Women

Enlightenment thought called for the restructuring of government and society, but the philosophes mostly held conservative views on women and their roles in family and society. Rousseau, for example, advised that girls' education should prepare them to become devoted wives and mothers. Yet social reformers found Enlightenment thought extremely useful in advocating for women's rights. Drawing on the political thought of John Locke, for example, the English writer Mary Astell (1666-1731) argued that absolute sovereignty was no more appropriate in a family than in a state. Astell also reflected Enlightenment influence in asking why, if all men were born free, all women were born slaves.

During the eighteenth century, advocates of women's rights were particularly active in Britain, France, and North

Portrait of Mary Wollestonecraft (1759–1797) in 1790–1791, painted by John Opie.

Niday Picture Library/Alamy Stock Photo

America. Among the most prominent was the British writer **Mary Wollstonecraft** (1759–1797). Although she had little schooling, Wollstonecraft avidly read books at home and gained an informal self-education. In 1792 she published an influential essay titled *A Vindication of the Rights of Woman.* Like Astell, Wollstonecraft argued that women possessed all the rights that Locke had granted to men. She insisted on the right of women to education: it would make them better mothers and wives, she said, and would enable them to contribute to society by preparing them for professional occupations and participation in political life.

Women and Revolution Women played crucial roles in the revolutions of the late eighteenth and early nineteenth centuries. Some women supported the efforts of men by sewing uniforms; rolling bandages; or managing farms, shops, and businesses. Others actively participated in revolutionary activities. In October 1789, for example, about six thousand Parisian women marched to Versailles to protest the high price of bread. Some of them forced their way into the royal apartments and demanded that the king and queen return with them to Paris—along with the palace's supply of flour. In the early 1790s, pistol-wielding members of the Republican Revolutionary Women patrolled the streets of Paris. The fate of Olympe de Gouges made it clear, however, that revolutionary women had little prospect of holding official positions or playing a formal role in public affairs.

Under the National Assembly and the Convention, the French revolution brought increased rights for women. The republican government provided free public education for girls as well as boys, granted wives a share of family property, and legalized divorce. Yet the French Revolution did not bring

What's Left Out?

In the eighteenth century, women were barred from serving in the military almost everywhere in the world. While some women defied this restriction in by disguising themselves as men and fighting alongside them, many more played active roles in military conflicts as spies. Female secret agents were particularly active during the American revolution and provided critical intelligence for both the American and British sides. Spying was dangerous work because the punishment for being caught was death. But women took advantage of the fact that they were seldom suspected of espionage: men on both sides of the conflict thought women were too busy with mundane household tasks or else were too delicate to pose a serious threat to either side. As a result, women were often able to carry out their work in plain sight, by hiding messages in their clothing, by posing as peddlers in army camps, and by serving food and drink to officers planning their next moves. One example of hiding in plain sight was Anna Smith Strong, whose main job was to let other agents know where to pick up secret messages and anti-British intelligence. Her system was simple: when information was ready to be picked up, she hung a black petticoat outside on her laundry line. The location of the pickup was signaled by the number of handkerchiefs she hung out to dry, which corresponded to different locations. Sometimes the information provided by female spies changed the course of the war. An example of this was when a woman (still known only as "Agent 355") provided information to the Continental Army that the British planned to attack French forces in Newport, Rhode Island. American forces then used this information to prevent the surprise attack from occurring. Anna Strong and Agent 355 are only two examples of many, which should help us remember that even before women were permitted to join national military forces in the twentieth century, they were still able to play active roles in military conflicts.

Source: Jeanne Munn Bracken, ed. *Women in the American Revolution* (Auburndale, MA: History Compass, 2009).

SOURCES FROM THE PAST

Declaration of the Rights of Woman and the Female Citizen

In 1791 Olympe de Gouges, a butcher's daughter and playwright of some note, wrote and published the **Declaration of the Rights of Woman and the Female Citizen.** *She directly challenged the 1789 Declaration of the Rights of Man and the Citizen, which limited citizenship to males. By publicly asserting the equality of women, Gouges questioned barriers that most revolutionary leaders wanted to leave in place. Charged with treason during the rule of the National Convention, Gouges was executed by guillotine on 3 November 1793.*

Article 1. Woman is born free and remains the equal of man in rights. Social distinctions can only be founded on a common utility.

Article 2. The purpose of all political organisations must be the protection of the natural and imprescriptible rights of Woman and Man: these rights are liberty, property, security and above all the right to resist oppression.

Article 3. The principle of sovereignty is vested primarily in the Nation, which is but the union of Woman and Man: no body, no individual, can exercise authority that does not explicitly emanate from it.

Article 4. Liberty and justice exist to render unto others what is theirs; therefore the only limit to the exercise of the natural rights of woman is the perpetual tyranny that man opposes to it: these limits must be reformed by the laws of nature and reason . . .

Article 6. The law must embody the will of the majority; all Female and Male citizens must contribute personally, or through their representatives, to its development; it must be the same for one and all: all Female and all Male citizens, being equal in law, must be equally entitled to all public honours, positions and employment according to their capacities and with no other distinctions than those based solely on talent and virtue.

> How might Article 6 in de Gouges' Declaration have changed French society?

Article 7. No woman may be exempt; she must be accused, arrested and imprisoned according to the law. Women, like men, will obey this rigorous law . . .

Article 11. The free expression of thoughts and opinions is one of the most precious rights of woman given that this liberty ensures the legitimacy of fathers and their children. Any Female citizen can therefore freely declare 'I am the mother of your child' without a barbrous prejudice forcing them to hide the truth, unless in response to the abuse of this freedom in cases determined by the law . . .

> Why might de Gouges have included this article about acknowledging parenthood?

Article 13. Women and men are to contribute equally to the upkeep of the forces of law and order and to the costs of administration: woman shares all the labour, all the hard tasks; she should therefore have an equal share of positions, employment, responsibilities, honours and professions.

Article 14. Female and male citizens have a right to decide for themselves, or through their representatives, the necessity of public contribution. Female citizens can only subscribe to it if they are allowed an equal share not only of wealth but also of public administration and in determining the amount, assessment, collection and duration of the tax . . .

Article 17. Property belongs to both sexes, united or separated; for each it is an inviolable and sacred right; no one can be deprived of a true natural heritage unless a general necessity, legally verified, obviously requires it and on condition of a fair indemnity agreed in advance.

For Further Reflection

■ How does Olympe de Gouges's restatement of the Declaration of the Rights of Man and the Citizen intensify its radical precepts?

Source: Gouges, Olympe de. The Declaration of the Rights of Woman. Translation by Clarissa Palmer. 1791. www.olympedegouges.eu. Translation reprinted with permission.

women the right to vote or to play major roles in public affairs. Under the Directory and Napoleon's rule, women lost even the rights that they had won in the early days of the revolution. In other places, women never gained as much as they did in revolutionary France. In the United States and the independent states of Latin America, revolution brought legal equality and political rights only for adult white men, who retained patriarchal authority over their wives and families.

Women's Rights Movements Nevertheless, throughout the nineteenth century social reformers pressed for women's rights as well as the abolition of slavery. The American **Elizabeth Cady Stanton** (1815–1902) was an especially prominent figure in this movement. In 1840 Stanton went to London to attend an antislavery conference but found that the organizers barred women from participation. Infuriated, Stanton returned to the United States and began to build a movement for women's rights. She organized a conference of women who met at Seneca Falls, New York, in 1848. The conference passed twelve resolutions demanding that lawmakers grant women rights equivalent to those enjoyed by men. The resolutions called specifically for women's rights to vote, attend public schools, enter professional occupations, and participate in public affairs.

The women's rights movement experienced limited success in the nineteenth century. More women received formal education than before the American and French revolutions, and women in Europe and North America participated in academic, literary, and civic organizations. Rarely did they enter the professions, however, and nowhere did they enjoy the right to vote. Yet by seeking to extend the promises of Enlightenment political thought to people of color and women as well as white men, social reformers of the nineteenth century laid a foundation that would lead to large-scale social change in the twentieth century.

THE NEW NATIONS AND NATIONALISM IN EUROPE

The Enlightenment ideals of freedom, equality, and popular sovereignty inspired political revolutions in much of the Atlantic Ocean basin, and the revolutions in turn helped spread Enlightenment values. The wars of the French revolution and the Napoleonic era also inspired the development of a particular type of community identity that had little to do with Enlightenment values—**nationalism.** Revolutionary wars involved millions of French citizens in the defense of their country against foreign armies and the extension of French influence to neighboring states. Wartime experiences encouraged peoples throughout Europe to think of themselves as members of distinctive national communities. Throughout the nineteenth century, European nationalist leaders worked to fashion states based on national identities and mobilized citizens to work in the interests of their own national communities, sometimes by fostering jealousy and suspicion of other national groups. By the late nineteenth century, national identities were so strong that peoples throughout Europe responded enthusiastically to ideologies of nationalism, which promised glory and prosperity to those who worked in the interests of their national communities.

Johann Gottfried von Herder
(YOH-hahn GAWT-freet fuhn HER-duhr)

A portrait of the Italian nationalist leader Giuseppe Mazzini (1805–1872). By the mid-nineteenth century, Mazzini's views had inspired nationalist movements not only in Italy but in other European states as well.

bauhaus1000/Getty Images

Nations and Nationalism

One of the most influential concepts of modern political thought is the idea of the nation. The word *nation* refers to a type of community that became especially prominent in the nineteenth century. At various times and places in history, individuals have associated themselves primarily with families, clans, cities, regions, and religious faiths. During the nineteenth century, European peoples came to identify strongly with communities they called nations. Members of a nation considered themselves a distinctive people born into a unique community that spoke a common language, observed common customs, inherited common cultural traditions, held common values, and shared common historical experiences. Often, they also honored common religious beliefs, although they sometimes overlooked differences of faith and construed the nation as a political, social, and cultural, rather than religious, unit.

Intense feelings of national identity fueled ideologies of nationalism. Advocates of nationalism insisted that the nation must be the focus of political loyalty. Zealous nationalist leaders maintained that members of their national communities had a common destiny that they could best advance by organizing independent national states and resolutely pursuing their national interests. Ideally, in their view, the boundaries of the national state embraced the territory occupied by the national community, and its government promoted the interests of the national group, sometimes through conflict with other peoples.

Cultural Nationalism Early nationalist thought often sought to deepen appreciation for the historical experiences of the national community and foster pride in its cultural accomplishments. During the late eighteenth century, for example, **Johann Gottfried von Herder** (1744–1803) sang the praises of the German *Volk* ("people") and their powerful and expressive language. In reaction to Enlightenment thinkers and their quest for a scientific, universally valid understanding of the world, early cultural nationalists such as Herder focused their attention on individual communities and relished their uniqueness. They emphasized historical scholarship, which they believed would illuminate the distinctive characteristics of their societies. They also valued the study of literature, which they considered the best guide to the *Volksgeist,* the popular soul or essence of their community. For that reason the German brothers Jakob and Wilhelm Grimm collected popular poetry, stories, songs, and tales (known in the present day as fairy tales) as expressions of the German *Volk.*

Political Nationalism

During the nineteenth century, nationalist thought became much more strident than the cultural nationalism of Herder or the brothers Grimm. Advocates of nationalism demanded loyalty and solidarity from members of the national group. In lands where they were minorities or where they lived under foreign rule, they sought to establish independent states to protect and advance the interests of the national community.

In Italy, for example, the nationalist **Giuseppe Mazzini** (1805–1872) formed a group called **Young Italy** that promoted independence from Austrian and Spanish rule and the establishment of an Italian national state. Mazzini likened the nation to a family and the nation's territory to the family home. Austrian and Spanish authorities forced Mazzini to lead much of his life in exile, but he used the opportunity to encourage the organization of nationalist movements in other states. By the mid-nineteenth century, Young Italy had inspired the development of nationalist movements in Ireland, Switzerland, and Hungary.

While it encouraged political leaders to work toward the establishment of national states for their communities, nationalism also had strong potential to stir up conflict between different groups of people. The more nationalists identified with their own national communities, the more they distinguished themselves both from peoples in other places and from minority groups within their societies.

A determined Theodor Herzl (1860–1904) founded the Zionist movement, which sought to confront anti-Semitism in Europe by establishing a home for the Jews in Palestine.
The History Collection/Alamy Stock Photo

Nationalism and Anti-Semitism

The divisive potential of nationalism helps to explain the emergence of **Zionism,** a political movement that holds that the Jewish people constitute a nation and have the right to their own national homeland. Unlike Mazzini's Italian compatriots, Jews did not inhabit a well-defined territory but, rather, lived in states throughout Europe and beyond. As national communities tightened their bonds, nationalist leaders often became distrustful of minority populations. Suspicion of Jews fueled **anti-Semitism** in many parts of Europe including Austria-Hungary, Germany, and eastern Europe. In Russia and in the Russian-controlled areas of Poland, anti-Semitism often turned violent, climaxing in a series of pogroms, or organized massacres. Beginning in 1881 and lasting into the early twentieth century, these massacres claimed the lives and property of thousands of Jews.

During the late nineteenth and twentieth centuries, millions of Jews migrated to other European states or to North America to escape persecution and violence. Anti-Semitism was not as violent in France as in central and eastern Europe, but it reached a fever pitch there after a military court convicted Alfred Dreyfus, a Jewish army officer, of spying for Germany in 1894. Although he was innocent of the charges and eventually had the verdict reversed on appeal, Dreyfus was the focus of bitter debates about the trustworthiness of Jews in French society.

Zionism

Among the reporters at the Dreyfus trial was a Jewish journalist from Vienna, **Theodor Herzl** (1860–1904). As Herzl witnessed mobs shouting "Death to the Jews" in what was supposed to be the land of enlightenment and liberty, he concluded that anti-Semitism could not be solved by assimilation into the larger society. In 1896 Herzl published the pamphlet *Judenstaat,* which argued that the only defense against anti-Semitism lay in the mass migration of Jews from all over the world to a land that they could call their own. In the following year, Herzl organized the first Zionist Congress in Basel, Switzerland, which founded the World Zionist Organization. The delegates at Basel formulated the basic platform of the Zionist movement, declaring that "Zionism seeks to establish a home for the Jewish people in Palestine," the location of the ancient Kingdom of Israel.

Giuseppe Mazzini (joo-ZEP-peh maht-TSEE-nee)
Theodor Herzl (TEY-aw-dohr HER-tsuhl)
Judenstaat (yoo-dehn-STAHT)

The charming and polished courtier Prince Klemens von Metternich (standing at left center) dominated the Congress of Vienna. Here, delegates to the Congress are gathered at the Hapsburg palace in Vienna.
DeAgostini/Getty Images

The Emergence of National Communities

The French revolution and the wars that followed it heightened feelings of national identity throughout Europe. In France the establishment of a republic based on liberty, equality, and fraternity inspired patriotism and encouraged citizens to rally to the defense of the revolution when foreign armies threatened it. Revolutionary leaders took the tricolored flag as a symbol of the French nation, and they adopted a rousing marching tune, the "Marseillaise," as an anthem that inspired pride in and identity with the national community. In Spain, the Netherlands, Austria, Prussia, and Russia, national consciousness surged in reaction to the invasions and occupations of revolutionary and Napoleonic armies. Opposition to Napoleon, and especially fears over French invasion, also inspired national feeling in Britain.

The Congress of Vienna After the fall of Napoleon, conservative political leaders feared that heightened national consciousness and ideas of popular sovereignty would encourage further experimentation with revolution and undermine European stability. In response, representatives of the "great powers" that defeated Napoleon—Britain, Austria, Prussia,

and Russia—attempted to restore the prerevolutionary order at a meeting known as the **Congress of Vienna** (1814–1815). Under the guidance of the influential foreign minister of Austria, Prince **Klemens von Metternich** (1773–1859), the Congress dismantled Napoleon's empire, returned sovereignty to Europe's royal families, restored them to the thrones they had lost during the Napoleonic era, and created a diplomatic order based on a balance of power that prevented any one state from dominating the others. One of Metternich's central goals was to suppress national consciousness, which he viewed as a serious threat to the multicultural Austrian Empire that included Germans, Italians, Magyars, Czechs, Slovaks, Poles, Serbs, and Croats among its subjects.

The efforts of Metternich and the Congress of Vienna to restore the ancien régime had limited success. The European balance of power established at Vienna survived for almost a century, until the outbreak of World War I in 1914. Metternich and the conservative rulers installed by the Congress of Vienna took measures to forestall further revolution: they censored publications to prevent communication of seditious ideas and relied on spies to identify nationalist and republican activists. By 1815, however, it was impossible to suppress national consciousness and ideas of popular sovereignty.

Nationalist Rebellions From the 1820s through the 1840s, a wave of rebellions inspired by nationalist sentiments swept through Europe. The first uprising occurred in 1821 in the

Klemens von Metternich (kleh-men fuhn MET-er-nik)

MAP 28.4 The unification of Italy.

The unification of Italy and Germany (see Map 28.5) as national states in the nineteenth century fundamentally altered the balance of power in Europe.

Why did unification result from diplomacy and war conducted by conservative statesmen rather than popular nationalist action?

Balkan peninsula, where the Greek people sought independence from the Ottoman Turks, who had ruled the region since the fifteenth century. Many western Europeans sympathized with the Greek cause. The English poet Lord Byron even joined the rebel army and in 1824 died (of a fever) while serving. With the aid of Britain, France, and Russia, the rebels overcame the Ottoman forces in the Balkans by 1827 and won formal recognition of Greek independence in 1830.

In 1830 rebellions occurred throughout Europe. In France, Spain, Portugal, and some of the German principalities, revolutionaries inspired by liberalism called for constitutional government based on popular sovereignty. In Belgium, Italy, and Poland, they demanded independence and the formation of national states as well as popular sovereignty. Revolution in Paris drove Charles X from the throne, while uprisings in Belgium

resulted in independence from the Netherlands. By the mid-1830s authorities had put down the uprisings elsewhere, but in 1848 a new round of rebellions shook European states. The uprisings of 1848 brought down the French monarchy and seriously threatened the Austrian Empire, where subject peoples clamored for constitutions and independence. Prince Metternich resigned his office as Austrian foreign minister and unceremoniously fled Vienna as rebels took control of the city. Uprisings also rocked cities in Italy, Prussia, and German states in the Rhineland.

By the summer of 1849, the veteran armies of conservative rulers had put down the last of the rebellions. Advocates of national independence and popular sovereignty remained active, however, and the potential of their ideals to mobilize popular support soon became dramatically apparent.

How the Past Shapes the Future ▷▷▷▷▷▷▷▷

The Birth of Nationalism

The consequences of the birth of nationalism for world history have been enormous, beginning in the period 1750–1914 and continuing right down to the present. From its beginnings, nationalism was intimately linked with powerful emotive phenomena such as folk traditions, songs, and literature that symbolized common heritage and common values. As a result, nationalism had the power to awaken deep feelings of love and unity, and also of hatred and ferocity, among its adherents. Such feelings often spurred individuals to work on behalf of the nation even at the expense of their own interests. They also encouraged individuals to exclude—sometimes brutally—those they defined as "outside the nation," and to see the interests of their own nation in competition with the interests of others. As a result, people around the world have done extraordinary things—both altruistic and cruel—in the name of nationalism.

In this chapter, we have already seen some of the first instances (in Italy and Germany) of individuals using the power of nationalism to create unified state governments where there were none before—a process that has been attempted multiple times (e.g., Greater Serbia, Palestine) since then. We have also seen that nationalism was used from its beginnings as a tool to exclude unwelcome groups, in this case European Jews. In fact, nationalism has often served as the double-edged sword of unity. On the one side, its symbols and myths have been used by diverse populations as the glue uniting them into one people, as in many of the newly formed North, South, and Central American nations during the nineteenth century (chapter 30). On the other side, by emphasizing particular languages and heritages, nationalism often inspires some groups to seek the exclusion of others, as people of European ancestry tried to do to Native Americans through-

A French sans-culottes holding the French tricolor flag. Behind him is the countryside of France, and his clothes indicate his common status. Images like these were used to evoke emotions in viewers about their national identity.
Heritage Images/Hulton Fine Art Collection/Getty Images

out the Americas (chapter 30). Nationalism has also spurred deep feelings of animosity or competition between people of different nations, which has increased the incidence of serious conflict between states (chapters 32 and 33).

One of the hallmarks of nationalism is that its emotive power has often been exploited by state governments for self-interested purposes. In late-nineteenth-century Japan, for example, reformers tried to inculcate a strong sense of national pride in Japanese citizens in order to garner support for a rapid program of industrialization that would allow Japan to be competitive on the world stage (chapter 31). While the process did foster national identification among ordinary Japanese people as well as rapid industrialization, the result was a far stronger state buttressed by a handful of extremely powerful corporations. In Europe, meanwhile, states played upon nationalist sentiments among their citizens—especially the specter of being bested by other nations—to garner support for imperial expansion in Asia and Africa (chapter 32). Indeed, by framing expansionist programs in terms of national aggrandizement, states were able to win the support for imperial conquests. Somewhat ironically, European imperial expansion ensured that people all over the world would be introduced to the concept of nationalism during the nineteenth and twentieth centuries—with consequences that would ultimately bring all of the European empires down (chapters 31 and 32).

The birth of nationalism profoundly shaped identities, loyalties, and both individual and state actions around the world from the late eighteenth century onward, with effects that continue to be felt in the present. In subsequent chapters, think about the many and varied ways that the force of nationalism—born in the context of the Atlantic revolutions—has shaped the world we live in today.

The Unifications of Italy and Germany

The most striking demonstration of the power that national sentiments could unleash involved the unification of Italy and of Germany. A variety of regional kingdoms, city-states, and ecclesiastical states ruled the Italian peninsula for more than a thousand years, and princes divided Germany into more than three hundred semiautonomous jurisdictions. The Holy Roman Empire claimed authority over Germany and much of Italy, but the emperors were rarely strong enough to enforce their claims.

When delegates at the Congress of Vienna dismantled Napoleon's empire and sought to restore the ancien régime, they placed much of northern Italy under Austrian rule. Southern Italy was already under close Spanish supervision because of dynastic ties between the Kingdom of the Two Sicilies and the Spanish Bourbon monarchy. As national sentiment surged throughout nineteenth-century Europe, Italian political leaders worked to win independence from foreign rule and establish an Italian national state. Mazzini's Young Italy movement attracted discontented idealists throughout the peninsula. In 1820, 1830, and 1848, they mounted major uprisings that threatened but did not dislodge foreign rule in Italy.

Cavour and Garibaldi

The **unification of Italy** came about when practical political leaders such as Count **Camillo di Cavour** (1810-1861), prime minister to King Vittorio Emanuele II of Piedmont and Sardinia, combined forces with nationalist advocates of independence. Cavour was a cunning diplomat, and the kingdom of Piedmont and Sardinia was the most powerful of the Italian states. In alliance with France, Cavour expelled Austrian authorities from most of northern Italy in 1859. Then he turned his attention to southern Italy, where **Giuseppe Garibaldi** (1807-1882), a charismatic soldier for hire and a passionate nationalist, led the unification movement. With an army of about one thousand men outfitted in distinctive red shirts, Garibaldi swept through Sicily and southern Italy, outmaneuvering government forces and attracting enthusiastic recruits. In 1860 Garibaldi met King Vittorio Emanuele near Naples. Not ambitious to rule, Garibaldi delivered southern Italy into Vittorio Emanuele's hands, and the kingdom of Piedmont and Sardinia became the kingdom of Italy. During the next decade the new monarchy absorbed several additional territories, including Venice, Rome, and their surrounding regions.

Otto von Bismarck

In Germany as in Italy, unification came about when political leaders harnessed nationalist aspirations. The Congress of Vienna created a German Confederation composed of thirty-nine states dominated by Austria. Metternich and other conservative German rulers stifled nationalist movements, and the suppression of the rebellions of 1848 left German nationalists frustrated at their inability to found a national state. In 1862 King Wilhelm I of Prussia appointed a wealthy landowner, **Otto von Bismarck** (1815-1898), as his prime minister. Bismarck was a master of *Realpolitik* ("the politics of reality"). He succinctly expressed his realistic approach in his first speech as prime minister: "The great questions of the day will not be settled by speeches or majority votes—that was the great mistake of 1848 and 1849—but by blood and iron."

It was indeed blood and iron that brought about the **unification of Germany.** As prime minister, Bismarck reformed and expanded the Prussian army. Between 1864 and 1870 he intentionally provoked three wars—with Denmark, Austria, and France—and whipped up German sentiment against the enemies. In all three conflicts Prussian forces quickly shattered their opponents, swelling German pride. In 1871 the Prussian

The German realist painter Franz von Lenbach (1836–1904) painted many leaders of his time, including the German chancellor Otto von Bismarck depicted here. Bismarck is commonly credited with the unification of Germany and the creation of the German empire in 1871. Bismarck is shown here wearing a *Pickelhaube,* a spiked helmet worn by German military, firefighters, and police in the nineteenth and twentieth centuries.
ART Collection/Alamy Stock Photo

king proclaimed himself emperor of the Second Reich—meaning the Second German Empire, following the Holy Roman Empire—which embraced almost all German-speaking peoples outside Austria and Switzerland in a powerful and dynamic national state.

The unification of Italy and Germany made it clear that, when coupled with strong political, diplomatic, and military leadership, nationalism had enormous potential to mobilize

Camillo di Cavour (kah-MEE-loh dee kah-VOHR)
Giuseppe Garibaldi (juh-SEP-eh gar-uh-BAHL-dee)
Otto von Bismarck (oht-toh fuhn BIZ-mahrk)

MAP 28.5   The unification of Germany.

Note the vast size of the territory in central Europe that united to become Germany in just five years.

Does the map give a sense about why the state of Prussia dominated the newly unified nation?

people who felt a sense of national kinship. Italy, Germany, and other national states went to great lengths to foster a sense of national community. They adopted national flags to serve as symbols of unity, national anthems to inspire patriotism, and national holidays to focus public attention on individuals and events of special importance for the national community. They established bureaucracies that took censuses of national populations and tracked vital national statistics involving birth, marriage, and death. They built schools that instilled patriotic values in students, and they recruited young men into armies that defended national interests and sometimes went on the offensive to enhance national prestige. By the end of the nineteenth century, the national state had proven to be a powerful model of political organization in Europe. By the mid-twentieth century, it had become nearly universal as political leaders adopted the national state as the principal form of political organization throughout the world.

CONCLUSION

The Enlightenment ideals of freedom, equality, and popular sovereignty inspired revolutionary movements throughout much of the Atlantic Ocean basin in the late eighteenth and early nineteenth centuries. While Enlightenment ideals may have served as inspiration, war provided the opportunity and dictated the timing of the revolutions. Just as important, each successive revolution drew inspiration from the ones that went before. In North America, tensions caused by the Seven Years' War provided the context in which colonists threw off British rule and founded an independent federal republic. In France, where aid to the American revolutionaries helped to cause a massive financial crisis, revolutionaries abolished the monarchy, established a republic, and abandoned traditions to refashion the social order. In Saint-Domingue rebellious slaves who were inspired by revolutionary ideas took advantage of the chaos caused by the French Revolution to throw off French rule, establish an independent Haitian republic, and grant freedom and equality to all citizens. In Latin America creole elites led movements to expel Spanish and Portuguese colonial authorities during the power vacuum created by the invasion of Spain and Portugal by Napoleon's armies, and eventually founded independent republics. And although most of these revolutionary movements sought to extend the ideals of freedom and equality to adult white men, during the nineteenth century social reformers launched campaigns to extend them to enslaved people and women.

Meanwhile, as wars rocked the Atlantic basin in the late eighteenth and early nineteenth centuries, people around the region developed strong feelings of national identity and worked to establish states that advanced the interests of national communities. Nationalist thought was often divisive: it pitted national groups against one another and fueled tensions, especially in large multicultural states. But nationalism also had strong potential to contribute to state-building movements, and nationalist appeals played prominent roles in the unification of Italy and Germany and in the aspiration to establish a Jewish state. During the nineteenth and twentieth centuries, peoples throughout the world drew inspiration from egalitarian revolutionary ideals and nationalism when seeking to build or restructure their societies.

STUDY TERMS

Adam Smith (592)
American revolution (595)
ancien régime (598)
anti-Semitism (613)
Baron de Montesquieu (592)
Camillo di Cavour (617)
caudillos (607)
Civil Code (602)
Congress of Vienna (614)
conservatism (608)
Continental Congress (595)
criollos (605)
Declaration of Independence (596)
Declaration of the Rights of Man and the Citizen (599)
Declaration of the Rights of Woman and the Female Citizen (611)
deists (593)
Elizabeth Cady Stanton (611)
Enlightenment (592)
Estates General (598)
French revolution (598)
gens de couleur (602)
George Washington (597)
Giuseppe Garibaldi (617)
Giuseppe Mazzini (613)
Gran Colombia (607)
Haitian revolution (602)
Jean-Jacques Rousseau (594)
Johann Gottfried von Herder (612)
John Locke (592)
Judenstaat (613)
Klemens von Metternich (614)
levée en masse (600)
liberalism (608)
Louis XVI (598)
Mary Wollstonecraft (610)
Miguel Hidalgo y Costilla (607)
Napoleon Bonaparte (601)
National Assembly (599)
nationalism (612)
Olympe de Gouges (590)
Otto von Bismarck (617)
peninsulares (605)
philosophes (592)
Realpolitik (617)
reign of terror (601)
Simón Bolívar (607)
The Social Contract (594)
suffrage (608)
Theodor Herzl (613)
Toussaint Louverture (604)
unification of Germany (617)
unification of Italy (617)
Volksgeist (612)
Voltaire (592)
Waterloo (602)
William Wilberforce (609)
Young Italy (613)
Zionism (613)

FOR FURTHER READING

Benedict Anderson. *Imagined Communities: Reflections on the Origin and Spread of Nationalism.* Rev. ed. London, 1991. A pioneering work that analyzes the means and the processes by which peoples came to view themselves as members of national communities.

David A. Bell. *The First Total War: Napoleon's Europe and the Birth of Warfare as We Know It.* Boston, 2007. A fine work that argues that nearly every "modern" aspect of war was born in the Revolutionary and Napoleonic wars.

Suzanne Desan, Lynn Hunt, and William Max Nelson, eds. *The French Revolution in Global Perspective.* Ithaca, N.Y., 2013. A collection of essays that offers a new approach to the understanding of the international origins and worldwide effects of this seminal revolution.

Laurent Dubois. *Avengers of the New World: The Story of the Haitian Revolution.* Cambridge, Mass., 2005. Comprehensive study of how the French slave colony of Saint-Domingue became a unique example of a successful black revolution that challenged the boundaries of freedom, citizenship, and empire.

François Furet. *Revolutionary France 1770–1880.* Oxford, 1995. In a brilliant work of synthesis, a leading historian places the revolutions of 1789, 1830, 1848, and 1871 within the grand scheme of democratic traditions.

David Geggus, ed. *The Impact of the Haitian Revolution in the Atlantic World.* Columbia, S.C., 2001. Focuses on the wider impact of the revolution for the region in terms of ideology, economics, and precedent.

Jay Kinsbruner. *Independence in Spanish America: Civil Wars, Revolutions, and Underdevelopment.* 2nd ed. Albuquerque, 2000. A compelling reinterpretation of the independence movements of sixteen nations, their similarities, and their regional differences.

Robert Middlekauff. *The Glorious Cause: The American Revolution, 1763–1789.* 2nd ed. Oxford, 2005. Masterful exploration of the causes, events, and consequences of the revolution.

Anthony Pagden. *The Enlightenment: And Why It Still Matters.* New York, 2013. This sweeping and fascinating work is an enlightening look at the Enlightenment that argues for the continuing relevance of this intellectual movement.

The Making of Industrial Society

ZOOMING IN ON TRADITIONS AND ENCOUNTERS

Betty Harris, a Woman Chained in the Coal Pits

In 1827, shortly after marrying at the age of twenty-three, Betty Harris took a job as a drawer in a coal pit near Manchester, England. A drawer's job involved crawling down narrow mine shafts and hauling loads of coal from the bottom of the pit (where miners chipped it from the earth) to the surface. From there the coal went to fuel the steam engines that powered the factories and the mills of early industrial society. Drawers performed unskilled labor for low wages, but their work was essential for the emergence of industrial production.

While working, Harris wore a heavy belt around her waist. Hitched to the belt was a chain that passed between her legs and attached to the coal cart that she pulled through the mine shafts, often while creeping along on her hands and knees. The belt strained against her body, and the mine shafts were steep and slippery. Yet every workday, even when she was pregnant, Harris strapped on her belt and chain at 6:00 A.M., removing her bindings only at the end of the shift twelve hours later.

Work conditions for Betty Harris were exhausting and dangerous. She labored in the coal pit with six other women and six boys and girls. All members of the crew experienced hardships and exploitation. Harris reported that drawing coal was "very hard work for a woman," and she did not exaggerate. She

An 1831 painting by D. O. Hill depicting the St. Rollox Chemical Works in Glasgow, Scotland, on the occasion of the opening of the Garnkirk and Glasgow railway. Note the juxtaposition between the picnicking spectators and the black smoke emanating from the St. Rollox factory chimney stacks.
FLHC 15/Alamy Stock Photo

and her companions often had to crawl through water that collected in the mine shafts during rainstorms, and the men who mined coal in the pits showed little respect for the ill-paid drawers. The belts and chains worn by drawers often chafed their skin raw, and miners contributed to their physical discomfort by beating them for slow or clumsy work. The miners, many of whom shed their clothes and worked naked in the hot, oppressive coal pits, also sometimes sexually abused the women and girl drawers: Harris personally knew several women who became pregnant after being raped in the coal pits.

Harris's work schedule made comfortable family life impossible. A cousin cared for her two children during the day, and Harris tended to them and her husband at night after a twelve-hour workday with only a single one-hour break to eat bread and butter. After fourteen years in the mines, at age thirty-seven, Harris put it mildly when she said, "I am not so strong as I was, and cannot stand my work so well as I used to."

CHAPTER OVERVIEW

Not all industrial workers suffered as much as coal drawers, but Betty Harris's experience nonetheless illustrates some of the deep changes that industrialization wrought in patterns of work and family life. Beginning in the late eighteenth century, workers and their families had little choice but to adjust to the sometimes harsh demands of the machine age. First in Britain, then in parts of western Europe, North America, Russia, and Japan, machines and factories transformed agricultural societies into industrial societies. At the heart of this transformation were technological changes based on newly developed, inanimate sources of power—especially fossil fuels—that led to the extensive use of machinery in manufacturing. Machine production raised worker productivity, encouraged economic specialization, and promoted the growth of large-scale enterprise. Industrial machinery transformed economic production by turning out high-quality products quickly, cheaply, and efficiently. The process of industrialization encouraged rapid technological innovation and over the long term raised material standards of living in much of the world.

But the impact of industrialization went beyond economics, generating widespread environmental and social change as well. Perhaps most important, the use of fossil fuels and the transition to industrial production had enormous environmental consequences. Coal-fired furnaces pumped thick pollution into the air, while factories dumped poisonous by-products into nearby rivers, lakes, and oceans. By the turn of the twentieth century, many of the world's soils and waters were deeply polluted, and the air near industrial areas posed a serious health risk. Social change was also far-reaching. Early industrialists created a new work environment, the factory, which concentrated large numbers of workers under one roof to operate complicated machinery. Factories also enabled managers to impose work discipline and closely supervise the quality of production at their plants. By moving work outside the home, however, factories drew fathers, mothers, and children in different directions, altered traditional patterns of domestic life, and strained family relations.

Industrialization also encouraged rapid urbanization and migration. New cities mushroomed to house workers who left the countryside for jobs in factories. Millions of migrants traveled even farther, crossing the seas in search of opportunities in new lands. Often, however, early industrial workers found themselves living in squalor and toxic pollution while laboring under dangerous conditions.

Social critics and reformers worked to alleviate the social problems caused by early industrial society. Most scathing and influential of the critics were the German theorists Karl Marx and Friedrich Engels, who called for the destruction of capitalism and the establishment of a more just and equitable socialist society. Despite their appeals, capitalism and industrialization flourished and spread rapidly from Britain to continental Europe, North America, and Asia. Although industrialization spread unevenly around the globe, during the nineteenth century it became clear that it affected the entire world. This was because the industrial revolution upset the balance of power between industrialized and nonindustrialized countries, allowing industrialized countries to dominate temporarily—both economically and militarily—those that had not yet industrialized. In addition, in hindsight, it is clear that earth, air, and water in much of the world were negatively affected as a result of the demands of the industrial revolution for raw materials.

CHRONOLOGY	
1733	John Kay develops the flying shuttle
1765	James Watt patents an improved steam engine
1779	Samuel Crompton develops the spinning mule
1785	Edmund Cartwright develops the power loom
1797	Eli Whitney introduces interchangeable parts to the manufacturing process
1829	George Stephenson's locomotive, the Rocket, attains a speed of 45 kilometers (28 miles) per hour
1832	Reform Bill expands electorate to House of Commons
1833	Factory Act restricts employment of women and children in textile factories
1842	Mines Act restricts employment of women and children in mines
1848	Karl Marx and Friedrich Engels publish *Manifesto of the Communist Party*
1851	Crystal Palace exhibition in London
1856	Bessemer converter developed
1913	Henry Ford introduces the assembly line to the manufacture of automobiles

PATTERNS OF INDUSTRIALIZATION

Industrialization refers to a process that transformed economics previously centered around agriculture and handicrafts to those distinguished by industry and machine manufacture. Critical to industrialization were productivity-increasing technological developments that made it possible to produce goods by machines rather than by hand and that harnessed inanimate sources of energy such as coal and petroleum.

Organizational changes accompanied technological developments. By the end of the nineteenth century, the factory had become the predominant site of industrial production in Europe, the United States, and Japan. Factory production strongly encouraged the emergence of new divisions of labor as interchangeable parts and belt-driven assembly lines made the mass production of goods a hallmark of industrialized societies. The need to invest in increasingly expensive equipment encouraged the formation of large businesses: by the mid-nineteenth century, many giant corporations had joined together to control trade through trusts and cartels.

Foundations of Industrialization

By the mid-eighteenth century, several areas of the world—Great Britain in western Europe, the Yangzi Delta in China, Japan—exhibited growing and dynamic economies that shared many common features. High agricultural productivity in those regions resulted in significant population growth. High population densities in turn encouraged occupational specialization and permitted many individuals to work at tasks other than cultivation. Navigable rivers and networks of canals facilitated trade and transport, and cities and towns were home to sophisticated banking and financial institutions. At the same time, these dynamic economies ran up against difficult ecological obstacles—especially soil depletion and deforestation—that threatened continued population growth and consumption levels. First Great Britain and then the other regions of western Europe overcame those ecological constraints by exploiting coal deposits found near large centers of population and by utilizing natural resources found abroad.

Coal and Colonies   Coal played a crucial role in the industrialization of Great Britain. Until the eighteenth century, wood had served as the primary source of fuel for iron production, home heating, and cooking. Prodigious uses of wood, however, resulted in and caused deforestation and serious wood shortages. Geographic luck had placed some of western Europe's largest coal deposits in Great Britain, within easy reach of water transport, centers of commerce, and pools of skilled labor. Humans in many parts of the world had known for at least a millennium that coal can burn. In Britain, however, it did not seem necessary to seek it out in large quantities until wood became scarce. Once it became clear that wood was in increasingly short supply, the fortunate combination of coal deposits and the skills necessary to extract it encouraged the substitution of coal for wood, thus creating a promising framework for industrialization. If coal had not been easily accessible in Britain, it is unlikely that the economy could have supported an expanding iron production and the application of steam engines to mining and industry—both crucial to the industrial process in Great Britain. In that respect, Britain's experience differed from that of China, where industrialization occurred later. In China, the largest coal deposits were hundreds of miles from the area in the Yangzi Delta where large populations of skilled laborers lived. As a result, it did not make sense to shift to a reliance on coal in China in this period.

A woman working as a drawer in a British coal mine drags her coal cart with the aid of a belt and chain, much as Betty Harris—who we met in the introduction to this chapter—would have done. Manually produced coal fueled the machines of early industrial society, though its extraction was often dangerous and difficult for workers involved in the industry.

Hulton Deutsch/Corbis Historical/Getty Images

An 1835 engraving depicts female workers at a textile factory. The shift to machine-based manufacturing commonly started with the mechanization of the textile industries not only in Great Britain but also in other industrializing lands, such as the United States and Japan. What cannot be communicated by images like this was the deafening clatter made by the machines while they were being operated throughout the day.

Bettmann/Getty Images

Ecological Relief The unique economic relationship between Europe and the Americas gave Great Britain in particular an additional resource to overcome ecological obstacles. After decimating the indigenous populations of the Americas and then settling the land, European colonizers overcame European land constraints by supplying European societies with a growing volume of raw materials—like sugar and cotton—that could never have been grown in the cool climate of western Europe. During the eighteenth century the slave-based plantations of northeastern Brazil, the Caribbean islands, and later the southern United States supplied Europe with huge amounts of sugar and cotton; each of which helped to fuel the industrial revolution in its own way. Sugar was high in calories and quickly converted to energy when eaten. By the mid-nineteenth century, sugar provided workers with low-cost meals that helped them work long hours. Cotton, for its part, was a vital raw material in the emerging textile industries. The plantation economies of the Caribbean islands in particular also created significant markets for manufactured imports from Europe, especially in the form of inexpensive cotton textiles to clothe enslaved people. Indeed, almost one-half of the proceeds from sugar exports paid for the importation of manufactured goods from Europe. The significance of valuable American resources grew after 1830, when large amounts of grain, timber, and beef were sent across the Atlantic to European destinations. All these products grew on colonial acreage, which expanded Europe's land base. Later in the century, American lands also served as outlets for Europe's surplus population.

Mechanization of the Cotton Industry Among the first industries to mechanize was British textile manufacturing. During the seventeenth century, English consumers had become fond of **calicoes**—inexpensive, brightly printed textiles imported from India, which carried on a vibrant international trade in finished cotton textiles. Cotton cloth came into demand because it was lighter, easier to wash, and quicker to dry than wool, which was the principal fabric of European clothes before the nineteenth century. Threatened by the popularity of Indian cotton products, British wool producers persuaded Parliament to pass a series of laws to protect the domestic wool industry. The Calico Acts of 1720 and 1721 prohibited imports of printed cotton cloth and restricted the sale of calicoes at home. Parliament even passed a law requiring corpses to be buried in woolen shrouds, but legislation did not dampen consumers' enthusiasm for cotton. By the 1730s, some British entrepreneurs turned their attention not to banning the use of cotton but to manufacturing their own. After the 1750s, British cotton textile producers convinced Parliament to set high tariffs on Indian textiles so their own finished goods would be less expensive. Given the demand for cotton, producers sought methods of speeding up the processes of spinning and weaving to supply growing domestic and foreign markets. To increase production, they turned to inventions that rapidly mechanized the cotton textile industry. In the early 1730s, artisans began to develop labor-saving devices for spinning and weaving cotton, thereby moving away from hand-based techniques derived from the wool and linen industries. The first important technological breakthrough came in 1733 when Manchester mechanic

John Kay invented the **flying shuttle.** This device speeded up the weaving process and stimulated demand for cotton thread. Within a few years, competitions among inventors resulted in the creation of several mechanical devices to spin thread. The most important was Samuel Crompton's **"mule,"** built in 1779. Adapted for steam power by 1790, the mule became the device of choice for spinning cotton thread. A worker using a steam-driven mule could produce a hundred times more thread than a worker using a manual spinning wheel.

The new spinning machines created an imbalance in manufacturing because weavers could not keep up with the production of thread, so innovators turned their attention next to weaving. In 1785 Edmund Cartwright, a clergyman without training or experience in either mechanics or textiles, patented a water-driven **power loom** that mechanized the weaving process. Within two decades steam moved the power loom, and by the 1820s it had largely taken the place of hand weavers in the cotton industry. Collectively, these technological developments permitted the production of textile goods in great volume and variety and at low cost. By 1830 half a million people worked in the cotton business, Britain's leading industry, which accounted for 40 percent of exports.

Steam Power Among the most crucial technological breakthroughs of the early industrial era was the development of a general-purpose steam engine in 1765 by **James Watt,** an instrument maker at the University of Glasgow in Scotland. Steam engines burned coal to boil water and create steam, which drove mechanical devices that performed work. Even before Watt's time, primitive steam engines had powered pumps that drew water out of coal mines, but those devices consumed too much fuel to be useful for other purposes. Watt's version relied on steam to force a piston to turn a wheel, whose rotary motion converted a simple pump into an engine that had multiple uses. Watt's contemporaries used the term *horsepower* to measure the energy generated by his steam engine, which did the work of numerous animals. By 1800 more than a thousand of Watt's steam engines were in use in the British isles. They were especially prominent in the textile industry, where their application resulted in greater productivity for manufacturers and cheaper prices for consumers.

Iron and Steel The iron and steel industries also benefited from technological refinement in this period, and the availability of inexpensive, high-quality iron and steel reinforced the move toward mechanization. After 1709, British smelters began to use coke (a purified form of coal) rather than more expensive charcoal as a fuel to produce iron. As we know, deforestation in England had made wood—the principal source of charcoal—scarce. Besides being cheaper than charcoal, coke was a more efficient fuel and made it possible for producers to build bigger blast furnaces and turn out larger lots of iron. As a result, British iron production skyrocketed during the eighteenth century, and prices to consumers fell. Inexpensive iron fittings and parts made industrial machinery stronger, and iron soon became common in bridges, buildings, and ships.

The nineteenth century was an age of steel rather than iron. Steel is much harder, stronger, and more resilient than iron, but until the nineteenth century it was very expensive to produce. Between 1740 and 1850 a series of improvements simplified the process. In 1856 Henry Bessemer—an English inventor—built a refined blast furnace known as the Bessemer converter that made it possible to produce steel cheaply and in large quantities. Steel production rose sharply, and steel quickly began to replace iron in tools, machines, and structures that required high strength.

Transportation Steam engineering and metallurgical innovations both contributed to improvements in transportation technology. James Watt's steam engine did not adapt well to transportation uses because it consumed too much coal. After his patent expired, however, inventors devised high-pressure engines that required less fuel. In 1815 **George Stephenson,** a self-educated Englishman, built the first steam-powered locomotive. In 1829 his Rocket won a contest by reaching a speed of 45 kilometers (28 miles) per hour. Although they were more efficient than Watt's invention, Stephenson's engines still burned too much coal for use at sea. Sailing ships remained the most effective means of transport over the seas until the middle of the nineteenth century, when refined engines of high efficiency began to drive steamships.

Because they had the capacity to carry huge cargoes, steam trains and steamships dramatically lowered transportation costs. They also contributed to the creation of dense transportation networks that linked remote interior regions and distant shores more closely than ever before. Between 1830 and 1870, British entrepreneurs laid about 20,000 kilometers (13,000 miles) of railroads, which linked industrial centers, coalfields, iron deposits, and port cities. Railroads also carried some 322 million passengers as well as cargoes of raw materials and manufactured goods. Meanwhile, steamships proved their versatility by advancing up rivers to points that sailboats could not reach because of inconvenient twists, turns, or winds. Railroads and steamships benefited from the innovations that drove the industrialization process and in turn encouraged continuing industrialization by providing rapid and inexpensive transport.

The Factory System

In the emerging capitalist society of early modern Europe (discussed in chapter 23), most manufacturing took place under what was known as the putting-out system. Under this system, entrepreneurs in early modern Europe paid individuals to work on materials in their households. During the seventeenth and early eighteenth centuries, new and larger units of production supplemented the putting-out system. Rising demand for certain products such as textiles and the growing use of water and wind power led to the formation of nonmechanized factories, where workers performed specialized tasks under one roof.

The Factory The **factory system** replaced both the putting-out system and nonmechanized factories and became the characteristic method of production in industrial economies. It began to emerge in the late eighteenth century, when technological advances transformed the British textile industry. By the mid-nineteenth century, most cotton production took place in factories. Many of the newly developed machines were too large and expensive for home use, and it became necessary to move work to locations where entrepreneurs and engineers built complicated machinery for large-scale production. This centralization of production brought together more workers doing specialized tasks than ever before. Most industrial workers came from the countryside. A combination of factors provided a plentiful supply of cheap labor for the new factories, including rural overpopulation and the land pressure and declining job opportunities that went with it.

The newly mechanized factory system became associated with a new division of labor, one that called for a production process in which each worker performed a single task rather than one in which a single worker completed the entire job, as was typical of handicraft traditions. In the first chapter of the

George Stephenson's North Star engine of 1837. Although Stephenson did not invent the locomotive, his refinements of locomotive technology, his application of civil engineering to the development of efficient railroad lines, and his vision of the future impact of railway systems on commerce earned him the nickname "Father of the Railways."
Science & Society Picture Library/SSPL/Getty Images

Wealth of Nations (1776), Adam Smith used a pin factory to describe the new system of manufacture: "One man draws out the wire, another straights it, a third cuts it, a fourth points it, a fifth grinds it at the top for receiving the head; . . . and the important business of making a pin is, in this manner, divided into about eighteen distinct operations." Factories also enabled managers to impose strict work discipline and closely supervise employees. Thus Josiah Wedgwood (1730–1795), an Englishman who owned a pottery plant, held his employees to high standards in an effort to produce the highest quality pottery. When he spotted inferior work, he frequently dumped it on the factory floor and crushed it, saying, "This will not do for Josiah Wedgwood!"

Working Conditions With its new divisions of labor, the factory system allowed managers to improve worker productivity and realize spectacular increases in the output of manufactured goods. But the new environment also changed the nature of work in unsettling ways. The factory system led to the emergence of an owner class whose capital financed equipment and machinery that were too expensive for workers to acquire. Industrial workers themselves became mere wage

What's Left Out? ▰ ▰ ▰ ▰ ▰

How might you experience time if you had no clocks and no watches and you had no way to know the exact time to wake up, take a break, eat lunch, or go home from work? It is difficult to imagine now, but that is how most people experienced time before the industrial revolution. For almost everyone, time was dictated by the rhythm of the seasons, tasks that needed to be completed, and the progression of the day. Even if someone were wealthy enough to own their own timepiece (most were not), almost every town kept its own local time without reference to the world around it. The industrial revolution changed all that. With the advent of railroads, it became important to know exactly when a train would arrive and when a train would depart. To solve the problem of widely varying local times, in 1847 the railroads in Britain uniformly adopted Greenwich Mean Time. Over the next few decades, most towns abandoned local time for this single, standardized time. The factory system also revolutionized the way people experienced time. Unlike earlier forms of work, the scale of the workforce in factories and the expense of running complicated machines prompted factory owners to insist that workers arrive to work, take breaks, and leave from work at exact times. Suddenly, people needed to know precisely when to get up, go to work, eat, and sleep. Towns erected large clocks that loudly chimed the hour so all could hear, and those who could afford it purchased pocket watches or clocks for their homes. As a result, people began to experience time not in terms of natural rhythms but almost exclusively as something dictated by the discipline of clocks—a discipline that has become a permanent part of modern life right into the present.

Source: Trish Ferguson, *Victorian Time: Technologies, Standardizations, Catastrophes*, 3rd ed. (London: Palgrave Macmillan, 2013).

earners who had only their labor services to offer and who depended on their employers for their livelihood. In addition, any broad-range skills that workers may have previously acquired as artisans often became obsolete in a work environment that rewarded narrowly defined skills. The repetitive and boring nature of many industrial jobs, moreover, left many workers alienated or estranged from their work and the products of their labor.

Equally disturbing was the new work discipline and the pace of work. Those accustomed to rural labor soon learned that the seasons, the rising and setting of the sun, and fluctuations in the weather no longer dictated work routines. Instead, clocks, machines, and shop rules established new rhythms of work. Industrial workers commonly labored six days a week for twelve to fourteen hours daily. The factory whistle sounded the beginning and the end of the working day, and throughout the day workers had to keep pace with the monotonous movements of machines. At the same time, they faced strict and immediate supervision, which made little allowance for a quick nap or socializing with friends. Floor managers pressured men, women, and children to speed up production and punished them when they did not meet expectations. Because neither the machines nor the methods of work took safety into account, early industrial workers constantly faced exposure to toxic chemicals, harmful levels of noise, and the possibility of accidents—some of which could be fatal.

Industrial Protest In some instances, machine-centered factories sparked violent protest. Between 1811 and 1816, organized bands of English handicraft workers known as **Luddites** went on a rampage and destroyed textile machines that they blamed for their low wages and unemployment. They called their leader King Lud, after a legendary boy named Ludlam who broke a knitting frame to spite his father. The movement broke out in the hosiery and lace industries around Nottingham (central England) and then spread to the wool and cotton mills of Lancashire in the north of the country. The Luddites usually wore masks and operated at night. Because they avoided violence against people (even though they threatened it), they enjoyed considerable popular support. Nevertheless, by hanging fourteen Luddites in 1813, the government served notice that it was unwilling to tolerate violence even against machines, and the movement gradually died out.

The Early Spread of Industrialization

Industrialization and the technological, organizational, and social transformations that accompanied it might have originated in many parts of the world where abundant craft skills, agricultural production, and investment capital could support the industrialization process. For half a century, however, industrialization took place only in Great Britain. Aware of their head start, British entrepreneurs and government officials forbade the export of machinery, manufacturing techniques, and skilled workers.

Yet Britain's monopoly on industrialization did not last forever because enterprising entrepreneurs recognized profitable opportunities in foreign lands and circumvented government regulations to sell machinery and technical know-how abroad. Moreover, European and North American businesspeople often took such knowledge by force. European and North American entrepreneurs did not hesitate to bribe or even kidnap British engineers, and they also smuggled advanced machinery out of the British isles. Sometimes they got poor value for their investments: they found that it was difficult to attract the best British experts to foreign lands and had to make do with drunkards or second-rate specialists who demanded high pay but made little contribution to industrialization.

Industrialization in Western Europe Nevertheless, by the mid-nineteenth century, industrialization had spread to parts of France, Germany, Belgium, and the United States. The French revolution and the Napoleonic wars helped set the stage for industrialization in western Europe by abolishing internal trade barriers and dismantling craft guilds that discouraged technological innovation and restricted the movement of laborers. The earliest center of industrial production in continental Europe was Belgium, where coal, iron, textile, glass, and armaments production flourished in the early nineteenth century. About the same time, France also moved toward industrialization. By 1830, French firms employed about fifteen thousand skilled British workers who helped establish mechanized textile and metallurgical industries in France. By the mid-nineteenth century, French engineers and inventors were devising refinements and innovations that led to greater efficiencies in metallurgical industries. Later in the century a boom in railroad construction stimulated economic development while also leading to decreased transportation costs.

German industrialization proceeded more slowly than in Belgium and France, partly because of political instability resulting from competition between the many German states. After the 1840s, however, German coal and iron production soared, and by the 1850s an extensive railroad network was under construction. After the unification of Germany in 1871 (discussed in chapter 28), Bismarck's government sponsored rapid industrialization. In the interests of strengthening military capacity, Bismarck encouraged the development of heavy industry, and the formation of huge businesses became a hallmark of German industrialization. The giant Krupp firm, for example, dominated mining, metallurgy, armaments production, and shipbuilding.

Industrialization in North America Industrialization transformed North America as well as western Europe in the nineteenth century. In 1800 the United States possessed abundant land and natural resources but few laborers and little money to invest in business enterprises. Both labor and investment capital came largely from Europe: migrants crossed the

SOURCES FROM THE PAST

Ned Ludd's Angry Letter to a Shearing Frame Holder

Many ordinary people in Britain were not happy with the mechanization that accompanied industrialization in the early nineteenth century. Skilled artisans like weavers rightly worried that the new machines would put them out of a job. In fact, it was true that a single person could do the work of several people by operating one of the shearing frames being introduced into the weaving industry. Between 1811 and 1816, groups of men claiming to be led by "Ned Ludd" or "General Ludd" banded together in order to destroy the new machines and to protest cuts in their wages. They sent threatening letters to business owners who utilized the new machines, broke into factories to break the machines, attacked employers, and fought with government soldiers. Although some of these protesters were caught and executed, most Luddites escaped capture because local communities seem to have protected them. The letter below was written around March 9, 1812, to a Mr. Smith, an owner of a factory with shearing frames in Yorkshire.

Information has just been given in that you are a holder of those detestable Shearing Frames, and I was desired by my Men to write to you and give you fair Warning to pull them down, and for that purpose I desire you will now understand I am now writing to you. you will take Notice that if they are not taken down by the end of next Week, I will detach one of my Lieutenants with at least 300 Men to destroy them and furthermore take Notice that if you give us the Trouble of coming so far we will increase your misfortune by burning your Buildings down to Ashes and if you have Impudence to fire upon any of my Men, they have orders to murder you, & burn all your Housing, you will have the Goodness to your Neighbours to inform them that the same fate awaits them if their Frames are not speedily taken down as I understand their are several in your Neighbourhood, Frame holders.

> What will happen to Mr. Smith and his fellow industrialists if they do not voluntarily take down their shearing frames, according to the letter?

And as the Views and Intentions of me and my Men have been much misrepresented I will take this opportunity of stating them, which I desire you will let all your Brethren in Sin know of. I would have the Merchants, Master Dressers, the Government & the public to know that the Grievances of such a Number of Men are not to be made sport of for by the last Returns there were 2782 Sworn Heroes bound in a Bond of Necessity either to redress their Grievances or gloriously perish in the Attempt in the Army of Huddersfield alone, nearly double sworn Men in Leeds . . . we hope for assistance from the French Emperor in shaking off the Yoke of the Rottenest, Wickedest and most Tyranious Government that ever existed; then down come the Hanover Tyrants [the current line of British kings], and all our Tyrants from the greatest to the smallest.

And we will be governed by a just Republic, and may the Almighty hasten those happy Times is the Wish and Prayer of Millions in this Land, but we won't only pray but we will fight, the Redcoats shall know that when the proper time comes We will never lay down our Arms.

> What indication do we have that the author of this letter has only a basic education? Can that tell us anything about who he might have been?

Signed by the General of the Army of Redressers
Ned Ludd Clerk

Redressers for ever Amen,
You may make this Public
[March 9th or 10th]

For Further Reflection

■ What is the ultimate goal of Ned Ludd and his army of redressers, according to the letter above, and how will they achieve it?

■ What can this document tell us about how ordinary people might have viewed the changes associated with the industrial revolution?

Source: Clerk Ludd, Ned. Letter from "Ned Ludd Clerk" addressed "To Mr Smith Shearing Frame Holder at Hill End Yorkshire." 1812. http://ludditebicentenary.blogspot.com/2012/03/9th-march-1812-letter-from-ned-ludd.html

Workers tend to a massive steam hammer, which was used for forging metal. Note the proximity of the workers to the molten metal.
Ann Ronan Pictures/Print Collector/ Getty Images

Atlantic in large numbers throughout the nineteenth century, and European bankers and businesspeople eagerly sought opportunities to invest in businesses that made use of American natural resources. American industrialization began in the 1820s when entrepreneurs lured British crafts workers to New England and built a cotton textile industry. By mid-century well over a thousand mills were producing fabrics from raw cotton grown in the southern states, and New England had emerged as a site for the industrial production also of shoes, tools, and handguns. In the 1870s heavy iron and steel industries emerged in areas such as western Pennsylvania and central Alabama where there were abundant supplies of iron ore and coal. By 1900 the United States had become an economic powerhouse, and industrialization had begun to spill over into southern Canada.

The vast size of the United States was advantageous to industrialists because it made abundant natural resources available to them, but it also hindered travel and communication between the regions. To facilitate transportation and distribution, state governments built canals, and private investors established steamship lines and railroad networks. By 1860 rails linked the industrial northeast with the agricultural south and the midwestern cities of St. Louis and Chicago, where brokers funneled wheat and beef from the plains to the more densely populated eastern states. As in other lands, railroad construction in the United States spurred industrialization by providing cheap transportation and stimulating the coal, iron, and steel industries.

Industrial Capitalism

Mass Production Cotton textiles were the major factory-made products during the early phase of industrialization, but new machinery and techniques soon made it possible to extend the factory system to other industries. Furthermore, with refined manufacturing processes, factories could mass-produce standardized items. An important contribution to the evolving factory system came from the American inventor **Eli Whitney** (1765–1825). Though best remembered as the inventor of the cotton gin (1793), Whitney also developed the technique of using machine tools to produce large quantities of interchangeable parts in the making of firearms. In conventional methods a skilled worker made a complete musket, forming and fitting each unique part; Whitney designed machine tools with which unskilled workers made only a particular part that fit every musket of the same model. Before long, entrepreneurs applied Whitney's method to the manufacture of everything from clocks and sewing machines to uniforms and shoes. By the middle of the nineteenth century, mass production of standardized items was becoming the hallmark of industrial societies.

In 1913 **Henry Ford** improved manufacturing techniques further when he introduced the assembly line to automobile production. Instead of organizing production around a series of stations where teams of workers assembled each individual car using standardized parts, Ford designed a conveyor system that carried components past workers at the proper height and speed. Each worker performed a specialized task

Legend:
- 20% of population in cities of 100,000 or more
- 6–10% of population in cities of 100,000 or more
- 5% or less of population in cities of 100,000 or more
- ┼┼┼┼ Railroads, ca. 1850
- ★ Emerging industrial areas
- Major exposed coal deposits

North Sea

FINLAND

KINGDOM OF NORWAY AND SWEDEN

Baltic Sea

DENMARK

RUSSIAN EMPIRE

SCOTLAND
Glasgow

IRELAND
Dublin

ENGLAND
Manchester
Liverpool
Sheffield
Birmingham
WALES
Bristol ★
London
Plymouth

English Channel

NETH.

Elbe

Berlin
KINGDOM OF PRUSSIA
POLAND
RUHR
Essen
Oder
SILESIA

BELGIUM
Brussels
Lille
Liège
GERMAN
CONFEDERATION
Prague ★

ATLANTIC OCEAN

Seine
Paris

Loire

FRANCE
Le Creusot ★
Lyons
Rhône
Garonne

Mulhouse

SWITZ.

AUSTRIAN EMPIRE
Vienna

HUNGARY

Milan ★

Danube

Marseilles

Adriatic Sea

PORTUGAL
Lisbon

SPAIN
Madrid

CORSICA

ITALIAN STATES

SARDINIA

GREECE

Mediterranean Sea

SICILY

0   250   500 mi
0   500   1000 km

MAP 29.1 Industrial Europe ca. 1850.

Locate the places marked as emerging industrial areas.

Are there any features those areas have in common? If so, what are they?

at a fixed point on the assembly line, which churned out a complete chassis (the base frame for an automobile) every 93 minutes—a task that previously had taken 728 minutes. The subdivision of labor and the coordination of operations resulted in enormous productivity gains. By the early twentieth century, Ford Motor Company produced half the world's automobiles. With gains in productivity, car prices plummeted, allowing millions of people to purchase automobiles. The age of the motor car had arrived.

The Corporation As the factory evolved, so too did the organization of business. Industrial machinery and factories were expensive investments, and they encouraged businesses to organize on a large scale. During the 1850s and 1860s, government authorities in Britain and France laid the legal foundations for the modern corporation, which quickly became the most common form of business organization in industrial societies. Instead of individual or small partnerships owning businesses, corporations were formed as legal entities that were separate and distinct from its owners. This meant that individual people could not be held liable for claims or losses incurred, thus spreading financial risk. It also allowed groups of people to raise money by selling shares, which allowed large

sums of capital to be raised for expensive ventures. By the late nineteenth century, **corporations** controlled most businesses requiring large investments in land, labor, or machinery, including railroads, shipping lines, and industrial concerns that produced iron, steel, and armaments. Meanwhile, an array of investment banks, brokerage firms, and other businesses offering financial services arose to serve the needs of industrial capitalists organized in corporations.

Monopolies, Trusts, and Cartels To protect their investments, some big businesses of the late nineteenth century sought not only to outperform their competitors in the capitalist marketplace but also to eliminate competition. Business firms formed associations to restrict markets or establish monopolies in their industries. Large-scale business organizations formed **trusts** and **cartels.** The difference between the two was largely a technical one, and both shared a common goal: to control the supply of a product and hence its price in the marketplace. Some monopolists sought to control industries through vertical organization, by which they would dominate all facets of a single industry. The industrial empire of the American petroleum producer John D. Rockefeller, for example, which he ruled through Standard Oil Company and

This is a 1911 photograph of Standard Oil's refinery in Richmond, California. Established in 1870 as an Ohio corporation, Standard Oil was the largest oil refiner in the world at the time and operated as a major company trust. It was one of the world's first and largest multinational corporations until it was broken up by the United States Supreme Court in 1911. John D. Rockefeller, the company's founder, became the richest man in history.
Library of Congress/Corbis Historical/Getty Images

Trust, controlled almost all oil drilling, processing, refining, marketing, and distribution in the United States. Control over all aspects of the petroleum industry enabled Standard Oil to operate efficiently, cut costs, and undersell its competitors. Vertical organization of this kind offered large corporations great advantages over smaller companies.

Other monopolists tried to eliminate competition by means of horizontal organization, which involved the consolidation or cooperation of independent companies in the same business. Thus cartels sought to ensure the prosperity of their members by absorbing competitors, fixing prices, regulating production, or dividing up markets. The German firm IG Farben, the world's largest chemical company until the middle of the twentieth century, grew out of a complex merger of chemical and pharmaceutical manufacturers that controlled as much as 90 percent of production in chemical industries. By the end of the nineteenth century, some governments outlawed these combinations and broke them up because such organizations actively worked against market competition that might result in lower prices for consumers and because they tended to keep wages low for workers so profits could be maintained. When governments proved unwilling to confront large businesses or when the public remained ignorant or indifferent, monopolistic practices continued even into the present.

INDUSTRIAL SOCIETY

Over time, industrialization brought material benefits in its train, including inexpensive manufactured products and rising standards of living. Yet industrialization also unleashed dramatic and often unsettling social and evironmental change. Massive internal and external migrations took place as millions of people moved from the countryside to work in new industrial cities, populations grew, and European migrants crossed the Atlantic by the tens of millions to seek opportunities in the less densely populated lands of the Western Hemisphere. Industrialization encouraged the emergence of new social classes—especially the middle class and the working class—and forced men, women, and children to adjust to distinctly new patterns of family and work life. Reformers sought to alleviate the social, economic, and environmental problems that accompanied industrialization. The most influential critics were the socialists, who did not object to industrialization per se but worked toward the building of a more equitable and just society.

Industrial Demographics

Industrialization brought efficiencies in production that flooded markets with affordable manufactured goods. In 1851 the bounty of industry went on display in London at the **Crystal Palace,** a magnificent structure made of iron and glass that enclosed trees, gardens, fountains, and manufactured products from around the world. Viewers flocked to the exhibition to see industrial products such as British textiles, iron goods, and machine tools. Colt revolvers and sewing machines from the United States also attracted attention as representatives of the "American system of manufacture," which used interchangeable parts in producing large quantities of standardized goods at low prices. Observers marveled at the Crystal Palace exhibits and congratulated themselves on the achievements of industrial society.

For many people, industrialization raised material standards of living. Industrial production led to dramatic reductions in the cost of clothing, for example, so individuals were able to add variety to their wardrobes. By the early nineteenth century, all but the desperately poor could afford several changes of clothes, and light, washable underwear came into widespread use with the availability of inexpensive manufactured cotton. Industrial factories turned out tools that facilitated agricultural work, while steam-powered locomotives delivered produce quickly and cheaply to distant markets, so industrialization contributed as well to a decline in the price of food. Consumers in early industrial Europe also filled their homes with more furniture, cabinets, porcelain, and decorative objects than any but the most wealthy of their ancestors.

Population Growth The populations of European and Euro-American peoples rose sharply during the eighteenth and nineteenth centuries, and they reflected the rising prosperity and standards of living that came with industrialization. Between 1700 and 1800 the population of Europe increased from 105 million to 180 million, and during the nineteenth century it more than doubled to 390 million. Demographic growth in the Americas—fueled by migration from Europe—was even more remarkable. Between 1700 and 1800 the population of North America and South America rose from 13 million to 24 million and then surged to 145 million by 1900. Demographic growth was most spectacular in the temperate regions of the Western Hemisphere. In Argentina, for example, population expanded from 300,000 in 1800 to 4.75 million in 1900—a 1,583 percent increase. In temperate North America—what is now the United States—population rose from 6 million to 76 million (1,266 percent) during the 1800s.

The rapid population growth in Europe and the Americas reflected changing patterns of fertility and mortality. In most preindustrial societies fertility was high, but famines and epidemics resulted in high mortality, especially child mortality, which prevented explosive population growth.

Medical advances over time supplied the means to control disease better and reduce mortality. A case in point was smallpox, an ancient, highly contagious, and often fatal viral disease that had killed more people than any other malady in world history. The experiments of the English physician Edward Jenner dealt an effective blow against smallpox. Knowing that milkmaids—women who milked cows—often contracted cowpox, in 1797 Jenner inoculated an eight-year-old boy with cowpox and followed it six weeks later with the smallpox virus. The boy became ill but soon recovered fully, leading Jenner to deduce that cowpox conferred immunity against smallpox. Later called vaccination (from *vacca,* the Latin word for "cow"), Jenner's procedure not only created a powerful weapon in the

Exhibitors from around the world displayed fine handicrafts and manufactured goods at the Crystal Palace exhibition of 1851 in London. Industrial products from Britain and the United States particularly attracted the attention of visitors to the enchanting and futuristic exhibition hall.
Time Life Pictures/Mansell/The LIFE Picture Collection/Getty Images

war against smallpox but also laid the foundation for scientific immunology. Although it took a century and more, physicians eventually developed vaccines that prevented sickness and death from polio, tetanus, typhoid, whooping cough, and many other diseases that once plagued humankind.

Death rates fell markedly during the industrial revolution because better diets and improved disease control reduced child mortality. Since more infants survived to adulthood, the population of early industrializing societies grew rapidly. By the late nineteenth century, better diets and improved sanitation led to declining levels of adult as well as child mortality, so populations of industrial societies expanded even faster. Britain and Germany, the most active sites of early industrialization, experienced especially fast population growth. Between 1800 and 1900 the British population increased from 10.5 million to 37.5 million, while German numbers rose from 18 million to 43 million.

The Demographic Transition Beginning in the nineteenth century, industrializing lands experienced a social change known as the **demographic transition,** which refers to shifting patterns of fertility and mortality. As industrialization transformed societies, fertility—the number of children born—declined. In the short run, mortality fell even faster than fertility, so the populations of industrial societies continued to increase. Over time, however, declining birthrates led to lower population growth and relative demographic stability. The principal reason for declining fertility in industrial lands was voluntary birth control through contraception.

The reasons for this demographic transition are not completely clear. Some couples might have chosen to have fewer offspring because raising them cost more in industrial than in agricultural societies or because declining child mortality meant that any children born were more likely to survive to adulthood. Whatever the reasons, the demographic transition

A French newspaper sponsored free smallpox vaccinations in 1905; in this image, the serum of a cow infected with cowpox is being injected into waiting Parisians.
World History Archive/Alamy Stock Photo

accompanied industrialization in western Europe, the United States, Japan, and other industrializing lands as well.

Birth Control For thousands of years, people tried to find deliberate ways of preventing or reducing the probability of pregnancy resulting from sexual intercourse. Some of the methods, such as withdrawal before insemination, proved not to be particularly reliable, and others, such as sexual abstinence, turned out to be unrealistic. More ingenious methods of birth control such as vaginal suppositories, cervical caps, or drinkable concoctions designed to prevent pregnancies or induce miscarriages often carried serious health risks for women. Because none of those methods proved effective, people throughout the world sometimes resorted to abortion or infanticide.

The first efficient means of contraception without negative side effects was the male condom. Initially made of animal intestines, it came into use in the seventeenth century. The effectiveness and popularity of the condom soared in the mid-nineteenth century with the arrival of the latex condom,

which served both as a contraceptive device and as a barrier against syphilis, a much-feared venereal disease.

Urbanization and Migration

Industrialization and population growth strongly encouraged migration and urbanization. Within industrial societies, migrants flocked from the countryside to urban centers in search of work. Industrial Britain led the world in urbanization. In 1800 about one-fifth of the British population lived in towns and cities of 10,000 or more inhabitants. During the following century a largely rural society became predominantly urban, with three-quarters of the population working and living in cities. That pattern repeated itself in continental Europe, the United States, Japan, and the rest of the industrialized world. By 1900 at least 50 percent of the population in industrialized lands lived in towns with populations of 2,000 or more. The increasing size of cities reflected this internal migration. In 1800 there were barely twenty cities in Europe with populations as high as 100,000, and there were none in the Western Hemisphere. By 1900 there were more than 150 large cities in Europe and North America combined. With a population of 6.5 million, London was the largest city in the world, followed by New York with 4.2 million, Paris with 3.3 million, and Berlin with 2.7 million.

The Urban Environment With urbanization came intensified environmental pollution. Although cities had always been putrid and unsanitary places, the rapid increase in urban populations during the industrial age dramatically increased the magnitude and severity of water and air pollution. The widespread burning of fuels, such as wood and coal, fouled the air with vast quantities of chemicals and particulate matter. This pollution led to typical occupational diseases among some trades. Chimney sweeps, for instance, contracted cancer of the scrotum from hydrocarbon deposits found in chimney soot. Effluents from factories and mills and an increasing amount of untreated sewage dirtied virtually every major river. No part of a city was immune to the constant stench coming from air and water pollution. Worse, tainted water supplies and unsanitary living conditions led to periodic epidemics of cholera and typhus, and dysentery and tuberculosis were also common maladies. Until the latter part of the nineteenth century, urban environments remained dangerous places in which death rates commonly exceeded birthrates, and only the constant stream of new arrivals from the country kept cities growing.

Income determined the degree of comfort and security offered by city life. The wealthy typically tried to insulate themselves the best they could from urban discomforts by retreating to their elegant homes in the newly growing suburbs. The working poor, in contrast, crowded into the centers of cities to live in shoddy housing constructed especially for them. The rapid influx of people to expanding industrial cities such as Liverpool and Manchester encouraged the quick but slipshod construction of dwellings close to the mills and factories. Industrial workers and their families occupied overcrowded tenements lacking in comfort and amenities. The cramped spaces in apartments obliged many to share the same bed, increasing the likelihood of disease transmission. The few open spaces outside the buildings were usually home to herds of pigs living in their own dung or were depositories for pools of stagnant water and human waste. Whenever possible, the inhabitants of such neighborhoods flocked to parks and public gardens.

By the later nineteenth century, though, government authorities were tending to the problems of the early industrial cities. They improved the safety of municipal water supplies, expanded sewage systems, and introduced building codes that outlawed the construction of rickety tenements to accommodate poorly paid workers. Those measures made city life safer and brought improved sanitation that eventually helped to eliminate epidemic disease. City authorities also built parks and recreational facilities to encourage wholesome recreation and to make cities more livable. Nevertheless, the emissions from fossil fuel combustion that accompanied industrialization and rapid economic development were responsible for the

increased amount of greenhouse gases, and hence the rise in the average temperature of earth's cities, atmosphere, and oceans: a process that has continued to the present.

Transcontinental Migration While workers moved from the countryside to urban centers, rapid population growth in Europe encouraged massive migration to the Americas, especially to the United States. During the nineteenth and early twentieth centuries, about fifty million Europeans migrated to the Western Hemisphere, and this flow of humanity accounts for much of the stunning demographic growth of the Americas. Many of the migrants intended to stay for only a few years and fully expected to return to their homelands with a modest fortune made in the Americas. Indeed, some did return to Europe: about one-third of Italian migrants to the Americas made the trip back across the Atlantic. The vast majority, however, remained in the Western Hemisphere.

Most of the migrants came from the British isles in the early nineteenth century; from Germany, Ireland, and Scandinavia in the middle decades; and from eastern and southern Europe in the late nineteenth century. Migration reflected difficult political, social, and economic circumstances in Europe: British migrants often sought to escape dangerous factories and the squalor of early industrial cities, most Irish migrants departed during the potato famines of the 1840s, and millions of Jews left the Russian Empire in the 1890s because of the tsar's anti-Semitic policies. Many of those migrants entered the workforce of the United States, where they settled in new industrial centers such as New York City, Pittsburgh, and Cleveland. Indeed, labor from abroad made it possible for the United States to undergo rapid industrialization in the late nineteenth century.

Industry and Society

As millions of people moved from the countryside to industrial centers, society began a process of dramatic transformation. Before industrialization, the vast majority of the world's peoples worked in rural areas as cultivators or herders. Rulers, aristocrats, priests, and a few others enjoyed privileged status, and small numbers of people worked in cities as artisans, crafts workers, bureaucrats, or professionals. Many societies also made use of enslaved labor, occasionally on a large scale.

New Social Classes Industrialization helped bring new social classes into being, which eventually replaced older social structures. Owners of industry and enterprising businesspeople became fabulously wealthy and powerful enough to overshadow the military aristocracy and other traditionally privileged classes. In addition to this new class of elites, a new **middle class** emerged in this period, consisting of small business owners; factory managers; engineers; accountants; skilled employees of large corporations; and professionals such as teachers, physicians, and attorneys. Industrial production generated great wealth, and a large portion of it flowed to the middle class, which was a principal beneficiary of industrialization. Meanwhile, manufacturing, or commerce, family members worked together and contributed to the welfare of the larger group. Industrialization challenged the family economy and reshaped family life by moving economic production outside the home and introducing a sharp distinction between work and family life. During the early years of industrialization, family economies persisted as fathers, mothers, and children pooled their wages and sometimes even worked together in factories. Over time, however, it became less common for family members to work together in the same factory. Instead, workers left their homes each day to labor an average of fourteen hours in factories, and family members led increasingly separate lives.

laborers who worked in factories and mines constituted a new **working class.** Their work did not require the skill of artisans and craftsmen of earlier times because most of the new industries required either physical strength or the ability to tend to machines while performing a single task. Because individuals could be easily replaced by others seeking work in the growing cities, their wages tended to be quite low. By the mid-nineteenth century, the low wages and poor working conditions of the working class led them to organize for greater political rights.

Industrial Families The most basic unit of social organization—the family—also underwent fundamental change during the industrial age. In preindustrial societies the family was the basic productive unit. Whether engaged in agriculture, domestic

A More Masculine World of Work and Play When production moved outside the home and work increasingly dominated public life, men gained greater stature and responsibility. While western European society was patriarchal prior to the industrial revolution and women enjoyed few legal or political rights, family production had nevertheless been a joint venture to which women and children contributed. But once men began to earn the bulk of their families' income in jobs outside the home, the domestic work traditionally done by women was increasingly devalued as an economic contribution to family life. This was especially true of upper-class and middle-class men, who now set the cultural standard for their societies. These men often insisted on being the sole wage-earners in the family. Indeed, they envisioned ideal family life as one in

The blood sport known as bear baiting had roots back to the early modern period, but was still practiced in the Victorian era. Usually, a bear was chained by the neck or leg, and trained hunting dogs were set upon it to attack. Dogs were replaced as they were wounded, killed, or became too tired to continue.

Topham Partners LLP/ Alamy Stock Photo

which men went to work outside the home while women and children remained at home in comfortable surroundings.

Middle-class men also sought to instill their values about work and family life in members of the industrial workforce. They used their positions of power as factory owners and managers to threaten workers with fines, beatings, and dismissal if they did not obey factory rules against absenteeism, tardiness, and swearing. Through their support for churches and Sunday schools, factory owners also sought to persuade workers to adopt middle-class ideals of family, respectability, and morality.

Given their very low wages and substandard housing, it was impossible for all but the most skilled workers to live like the middle class. Realizing this, workers often resisted the work discipline and moral pressures they encountered at the factory. Some observed "Holy Monday" and stayed home to lengthen their weekly break from work on Sundays. They also made the most of their limited leisure time. Some joined sports teams, while others gambled, socialized at bars and pubs, or engaged in the very old tradition of "blood sports," in which spectators bet on fights between dogs, roosters, or even between dogs and bears. Although all classes had once engaged in blood sports, in the industrial era the middle and upper classes tried to suppress these activities and established urban police forces to control workers' public behavior. But efforts at regulation had limited success, and workers persistently pursued their own interests.

Women at Home and Work Industrialization dramatically changed the terms of work for women. When industry moved production from the home to the factory, married women were unable to work unless they left their homes and

children in someone else's care. At the same time, middle-class men increasingly insisted that women should not leave the household to work but, rather, that they should devote themselves to raising children and managing their homes.

By the mid-nineteenth century, one of the hallmarks of belonging to the industrial middle class was that women did not work outside the home. For these women, industrialization brought increasing confinement to the domestic sphere and pressure to conform to new models of behavior revolving around their roles as mothers and wives. In a book titled *Woman in Her Social and Domestic Character* (1833), Mrs. John Sandford—who referred to herself by her husband's name rather than her own—described the ideal British woman. "Domestic life is the chief source of her influence," Sandford proclaimed, adding that "there is, indeed, something unfeminine in independence." (By *independence* Sandford meant taking a job.) The model woman, according to Sandford, "knows that she is the weaker vessel" and takes pride in her ability to make the home a happy place for her husband and children.

But for working-class women, who formed the largest proportion of women in industrialized societies, remaining at home without working was a nearly impossible ideal. Working-class men generally made low wages and thus could not support a whole family on a single income. Young, unmarried women were expected to support themselves by going into domestic service in middle-class households or by taking low-wage factory jobs. Married women, too, often had to supplement the family income by working outside the home. During the early stages of industrialization, it was in fact easy for working-class women to find factory jobs. This was especially true for the flourishing low-wage textile industry, where

This 1909 photograph shows a young girl being instructed by a male supervisor on how to use a spinning machine. Women, not men, made up the bulk of the early labor force in the textile industry, principally because it was presumed that women were easier to discipline than men and because women's smaller hands allegedly made them better suited for working with machines.
Bettmann/Getty Images

labor-saving devices made their first appearance. Both inventors and manufacturers mistakenly believed that women (and also children) were best suited to operate the new machines because their small hands and fingers gave them superior dexterity. As a result, by the middle of the nineteenth century, women made up the majority of the British industrial workforce. But the preference for women in factory jobs was short-lived, as male workers demanded access to industrial employment. Over the last half of the nineteenth century, women were increasingly replaced by mechanized labor-saving devices, while men were hired for factory jobs.

The largest employment sector available to working-class women was in domestic service. Industrialization increased the demand for domestic servants as the middle class grew in both numbers and wealth. One of every three European women became a domestic servant at some point in her life. Rural women sometimes had to move long distances to take positions in middle-class homes in cities, where they experienced independence from family control but also hard work, exploitation, and sexual abuse. Their employers replaced their parents as guardians, but high demand for servants ensured that women could switch jobs readily in search of more attractive positions. Young women servants often sent some of their earnings home, but many also saved wages for their future lives: amassing a dowry, for example, or building funds to start careers as clerks or secretaries.

Child Labor Industrialization profoundly influenced children's lives as well. Like their elders, children in preindustrial societies had always worked in and around the family home.

Industrial work, which took children away from home and parents for long hours with few breaks, made abuse and exploitation of **child labor** more likely. Early reports from British textile mills described overseers who forced children to work from dawn until dark and beat them to keep them awake. Yet many families needed their children's wages to survive, so they had little choice but to send them to the factories and mines. By the 1840s the British Parliament began to pass laws regulating child labor and ultimately restricted or removed children from the industrial workforce. In the long term, industrial society was responsible for removing children from the labor process altogether, even in the home. Whereas agricultural settings continued to demand that children make a contribution to the family income, urban industrial societies redefined the role of children. Motivated in part by moral concerns and in part by the recognition that modern society demanded a highly skilled and educated labor force, governments established the legal requirement that education, and not work for monetary gain, was the principal task of childhood. In England, for instance, education for children age five to ten became mandatory by 1881.

The Socialist Challenge

Among the most vocal and influential critics of early industrial society were the socialists, who worked to alleviate the social and economic problems generated by capitalism and industrialization. Socialists deplored economic inequalities, as represented by the vast difference in wealth between a captain of industry and a factory laborer, and they condemned the

SOURCES FROM THE PAST

Testimony for the Factory Act of 1833: Working Conditions in England

During the 1830s and 1840s, deplorable conditions in England's factories and mines led the British Parliament to conduct a series of investigations on the subject. Investigators asked doctors, workers, and factory owners many questions about working conditions and their effects on laborers. The results of these investigations led to parliamentary legislation, such as the Factory Act of 1833, designed to protect workers from the worst effects of industrialization.

Testimony of John Wright.

How long have you been employed in a silk-mill?—More than thirty years.

Did you enter it as a child?—Yes betwixt five and six.

How many hours a day did you work then?—The same thirty years ago as now.

What are those hours?—Eleven hours per day and two over-hours: over-hours are working after six in the evening until eight. The regular hours are from six in the morning to six in the evening, and two others are two over-hours. . . .

> If one worked thirteen hours a day, six days a week, how might this have affected family life?

Why, then, are those employed in them said to be in such a wretched condition?—In the first place, the great number of hands congregated together, in some rooms forty, in some fifty, in some sixty, and I have known some as many as 100, which must be injurious to both health and growing. In the second place, the privy [toilet] is in the factory, which frequently emits an unwholesome smell; and it would be worth while to notice in the future erection of mills, that there be betwixt the privy door and the factory wall a kind of a lobby of cage-work. 3dly, The tediousness and the everlasting sameness in the first process preys much on the spirits, and makes the hands spiritless. 4thly, the extravagant number of hours a child is compelled to labour and confinement, which for one week is seventy-six hours. . . . 5thly, About six months in the year we are obliged to use either gas, candles, or lamps, for the longest portion of that time, nearly six hours a day, being obliged to work amid the smoke and soot of the same; and also a large portion of oil and grease is used in the mills.

What are the effects of the present system of labor? —From my earliest recollections, I have found the effects to be awfully detrimental to the well-being of the operative; I have observed frequently children carried to factories, unable to walk, and that entirely owing to excessive labour and confinement. The degradation of the workpeople baffles all description: frequently have two of my sisters been obliged to be assisted to the factory and home again, until by-and-by they could go no longer, being totally crippled in their legs. And in the next place, I remember some ten or twelve years ago working in one of the largest firms in Macclesfield, . . . with about twenty-two men, where they were scarce one half fit for His Majesty's service. Those that are straight in their limbs are stunted in their growth; much inferior to their fathers in point of strength. 3dly, Through excessive labour and confinement there is often a total loss of appetite; a kind of langour steals over the whole frame—enters to the very core—saps the foundation of the best constitution—and lays our strength prostrate in the dust. In the 4th place, by protracted labour there is an alarming increase of cripples in various parts of this town, which has come under my own observation and knowledge. —

> In addition to the extremely difficult physical conditions, what kinds of emotional toll did working in the silk mills take on workers, according to John Wright?

Are all these cripples made in the silk factories?—Yes, they are, I believe. . . .

For Further Reflection

■ In Wright's opinion, what aspect of labor in the silk factories was the most damaging for children?

Source: Commission for Inquiry into the Employment of Children in Factories, Second Report, with Minutes of Evidence and Reports by the Medical Commissioners, vol. V, Session 29 January–20 August, 1833. London: His Majesty's Printing Office, 1833, pp. 5, 26–28.

system that permitted the exploitation of laborers, including women and children. Early socialists sought to expand the Enlightenment understanding of equality: they understood equality to have an economic as well as a political, legal, and social dimension, and they looked to the future establishment of a just and equitable society. Although most socialists shared this general vision, they held very different views on the best way to establish and maintain an ideal socialist society.

Utopian Socialists The term *socialism* first appeared around 1830, when it referred to the ideas of social critics such as Charles Fourier (1772–1837) and Robert Owen (1771–1858). Often called **utopian socialists,** Fourier, Owen, and their followers worked to establish ideal communities that would point the way to an equitable society. Fourier spent most of his life as a salesman, but he loathed the competition of the market system and called for social transformations that would better serve

Robert Koehler's 1886 painting *The Strike* depicts a situation verging toward violence as workers mill about in a confrontation with factory owners and one angry laborer crouches to pick up a stone.

Art Collection 2/Alamy Stock Photo

the needs of humankind. He painstakingly planned model communities that were supposed to be held together by love rather than coercion, in which everyone performed work in accordance with personal temperament and inclination. Owen,

How the Past Shapes the Future ▷ ▷ ▷ ▷

The Birth of Nationalism

One of the attractions of nationalism was a sense of belonging to a defined community based on language, heritage, and culture. But revolutionary socialism as expressed in the *Communist Manifesto* saw the main division between peoples not in terms of nationality but in terms of membership in either the capitalist or proletariat classes. Capitalists and proletarians could be from any nation and theoretically would have more in common with others in their same group—from any nation—than with members of the opposing group, even if they were of the same nationality. Consider how revolutionary socialism could exist side by side with nationalism, and why revolutionary socialism did not replace nationalism in the areas where it developed.

a successful businessman, transformed a squalid Scottish cotton mill town called New Lanark into a model industrial community. At New Lanark, Owen raised wages, reduced the workday from seventeen to ten hours, built spacious housing, and opened a store that sold goods at fair prices. Despite the costs of those reforms, the mills of New Lanark generated profits. Out of the two thousand residents of the community, five hundred were young children from the poorhouses of Glasgow and Edinburgh, and Owen devoted special attention to their education. He kept young children out of the factories and sent them to a school that he opened in 1816. Owen's indictment of competitive capitalism, his stress on cooperative control of industry, and his advocacy of improved educational standards for children left a lasting imprint on the socialist tradition.

The ideas of the utopian socialists resonated widely in the nineteenth century, and their disciples established experimental communities from the United States to Romania. But in spite of the enthusiasm of the founders, most of the communities soon encountered economic difficulties and political problems that forced them to fold. By the mid-nineteenth century, most socialists looked not to utopian communities but to large-scale organization of working people as the best means to bring about a just and equitable society.

Marx and Engels Most prominent of the nineteenth-century socialists were the German theorists **Karl Marx** (1818–1883) and **Friedrich Engels** (1820–1895). They scorned the utopian socialists as unrealistic dabblers whose ideal communities had no hope of resolving the problems of the early industrial era. Marx and Engels believed that the social problems of the nineteenth century were inevitable results of a capitalist economy. They held that capitalism divided people into two main classes, each with its own economic interests and social status: the capitalists, who owned industrial machinery and factories (which Marx and Engels called the means of production), and the proletariat, consisting of wageworkers who had only their labor to sell. Intense competition between capitalists trying to realize a profit resulted in ruthless exploitation of the working class. To make matters worse, according to Marx and Engels, the state and its coercive institutions, such as police forces and courts of law, were agencies of the capitalist ruling class. Their function was to maintain capitalists in power and enable them to continue their exploitation of the proletariat. Even music, art, literature, and religion served the purposes of capitalists, according to Marx and Engels, since they amused the working classes and diverted attention from their misery. Marx once referred to religion as "the opiate of the masses" because it encouraged workers to focus on a hypothetical realm of existence in heaven rather than the difficulties they faced in the world of the living.

The *Communist Manifesto* Marx developed those views fully in a long, theoretical work called *Capital*. Together with Engels, Marx also wrote a short, spirited tract titled *Manifesto of the Communist Party* (1848). This work, which became popularly known as the *Communist Manifesto*, Marx and Engels aligned themselves with the communists, who worked toward the abolition of private property and the institution of a radically egalitarian society. The *Manifesto* asserted that all human history has been the history of struggle between social classes. It argued that the future lay with the working class because the laws of history dictated that capitalism would inexorably grind to a halt. Crises of overproduction, underconsumption, and diminishing profits would shake the foundations of the capitalist order. Meanwhile, members of the constantly growing and thoroughly exploited proletariat would come to view the forcible overthrow of the existing system as the only alternative available to them. Marx and Engels believed that a socialist revolution would result in a "dictatorship of the proletariat," which would abolish private property and destroy the capitalist order. After the revolution was secure, the state would wither away. Coercive institutions would also disappear because there would no longer be an exploiting

Contemporary photograph of Karl Marx (1818–1883), German political philosopher and founder of modern socialism. His most important theoretical work, *Das Kapital* (*Capital,* in the English translation), is an extensive treatise on political economy that offers a highly critical analysis of capitalism.
Bettmann/Getty Images

class. Thus socialism would lead to a fair, just, and egalitarian society infinitely more humane than the capitalist order.

The doctrines of Marx and Engels came to dominate European and international socialism, and socialist parties grew rapidly throughout the nineteenth century. Political parties, trade unions, newspapers, and educational associations all worked to advance the socialist cause. Yet socialists disagreed strongly on the best means to reform society. Revolutionary socialists such as Marx, Engels, and other communists urged workers to seize control of the state, confiscate the means of production, and distribute wealth equitably throughout society. Doubting that a revolution could succeed, evolutionary socialists placed their hopes in representative governments and called for the election of legislators who supported socialist reforms.

Once held almost exclusively by men, clerical jobs increasingly went to women as industrial society matured. This photograph features the typewriting department of a large company in Dayton, Ohio. Note the absence of men in their ranks.
Everett Collection Historical/ Alamy Stock Photo

Social Reform Although socialists did not win control of any government until the Russian revolution of 1917, their critiques—along with those of conservatives and liberals—persuaded government authorities to attack the abuses of early industrialization and provide at least some security for the working classes. The British Parliament prohibited underground employment for women, like the drawer Betty Harris, as well as for boys and girls under age ten. It also stipulated that children under age nine not work more than nine hours a day. The 1830s and 1840s saw the inception of laws that regulated women's working hours, while leaving men without protection and constraints. The intention behind this legislation was to protect women's family roles according to middle-class ideals, but it also reduced women's economic opportunities on the grounds of their perceived frailty. Coming under pressure from the voting public and labor unions, governments increasingly accepted that the state was responsible for the social and economic welfare of its citizens. Beginning in the late nineteenth century, European countries, led by Germany, adopted social reform programs, including retirement pensions; minimum wage laws; sickness, accident, and unemployment insurance; and the regulation of hours and conditions of work. These reforms of liberal capitalist society were a prelude to the modern welfare state that emerged in the twentieth century.

Trade Unions **Trade unions** also sought to advance the quest for a just and equitable society. As governments regu-

lated businesses and enhanced social security, workers struggled to eliminate abuses of early industrial society and improve workers' lives by organizing to seek higher wages and better working conditions for their members. Through most of the nineteenth century, both employers and governments considered trade unions illegal associations whose purpose was to restrain trade. Tensions ran high when union members went on strike, especially when employers sought to keep their businesses going by hiring replacement workers. In those cases, violence frequently broke out, prompting government authorities to send in police or military forces to maintain order. Over the longer run, though, trade unions gradually improved the lives of working people and reduced the likelihood that a disgruntled proletariat would mount a revolution to overthrow industrial capitalist society. Indeed, trade unions became an integral part of industrial society because they did not seek to destroy capitalism but, rather, to make employers more responsive to their employees' needs and interests.

Global Effects of Industrialization

Early industrialization was a British affair, which then spread to western Europe and North America by the early nineteenth century. By the late nineteenth century, Russia and Japan were also beginning to industrialize (see chapter 31). In addition to its spread beyond western Europe, industrialization had deep global implications because industrial powers used their tools, technologies, business organization, financial influence, and transportation networks to obtain raw materials from societies around the world. Many places that possessed natural resources became increasingly oriented to exporting raw materials but maintained little control over them because representatives of industrial countries dominated the commercial and financial institutions associated with the trade. Some societies saw their home markets flooded with inexpensive manufactured products from industrial states, which devastated traditional industries and damaged local economies.

The International Division of Labor Industrialization brought great economic and military strength to societies that now relied on mechanized production. Their power encouraged other societies to work toward industrialization. Before the mid-twentieth century, however, those efforts were hampered either by outright imperial conquests undertaken by industrial states or by deliberate attempts by the same states to discourage industrialization via economic or political pressure. In India, for example, entrepreneurs had established a thriving industry in the production of cotton textiles by the eighteenth century. But since the East India Company had conquered Bengal in 1757, by the early nineteenth century British businessmen were able to crush the industry by forcing imports of inexpensive British textiles and by raising tariffs on Indian textiles.

Indeed, industrialization tilted the global balance of power in favor of industrial states and gave rise to a new international division of labor. Industrial societies needed minerals, agricultural products, and other raw materials to power their industries and to feed their growing populations. The mechanization of the textile industry, for example, produced a demand for large quantities of raw cotton, which came mostly from India,

Egypt, and the southern rim of the United States. Similarly, new industrial technologies increased demand for products such as rubber, the principal ingredient of belts and tires that were essential to industrial machinery, which came from Brazil, Malaya, and the Congo River basin. When state leaders did not wish to trade on the terms offered by representatives of industrial societies, these representatives did not hesitate to use force, the threat of force, or economic intimidation to get what they wanted.

Economic Development In some places, specialization in the production and export of primary goods paved the way for economic development and eventual industrialization. This pattern was especially noticeable in European settler colonies, including Canada, South Africa, Australia, and New Zealand, each of which enjoyed a special relationship with Great Britain. Britons directly controlled the government in each of these colonies, and British investors were directly and heavily invested in their infrastructure and economies. European migrants flocked to the settler colonies, where they set up businesses that exported primary products to feed the economies of the industrial states. European settlers commanded high wages, and the spending power of these incomes created flourishing markets for industrial goods within the settler colonies. Over time, European entrepreneurs in the settler colonies developed mechanized industries themselves based on technologies brought from Europe.

Economic Interdependence Other places did not benefit from the same advantages as European settler colonies. In most of Latin America, sub-Saharan Africa, south Asia, and southeast Asia representatives of industrialized states sought to impose their will either by outright colonial

This is an image of the Clermont Paddlesteamer invented by Robert Fulton and launched in 1807. Steamboats transported passengers and cargo and aided in the exploitation of raw materials around the world.
Chronicle/Alamy Stock Photo

conquest (discussed in chapter 32) or by using economic and political pressure. In most areas, they sought raw materials—especially sugar, cotton, and rubber—and encouraged whole economies to move toward an export-oriented agricultural economy based on cash crops. They actively discouraged industrialization, seeking instead to create reliable supplies of raw materials to feed their own industrial economies. They often set controls on the prices of agricultural goods, thus keeping prices—and thus the profits for producers—artificially low.

This new geographic division of labor, in which some of the world's peoples provided raw materials while others processed and consumed them, increased the volume of world trade and led to increased transportation on both sea and land. Bigger ships, larger docks, and deeper canals facilitated trade and transport around the world. However, the benefits of this new system flowed primarily to Europe, North America, and Japan. Other places realized few benefits from the process of industrialization, even though the process increasingly linked the fortunes of all the world's peoples.

CONCLUSION

The process of industrialization involved the harnessing of inanimate sources of energy, the replacement of handicraft production with machine-based manufacturing, and the generation of new forms of business and labor organization. Along with industrialization came demographic growth, large-scale migration, and rapid urbanization, which increased the demand for manufactured goods by working people, who formed the majority of the population. Societies that underwent industrialization enjoyed sharp increases in economic productivity: they produced large quantities of high-quality goods at low prices, and their increased productivity eventually translated into higher material standards of living. Yet industrialization brought costs, in the form of unsettling social problems. Family life changed dramatically in the industrial age as men, women, and children increasingly left their homes to work in factories and mines, often under appalling conditions. In response, socialist critics sought to bring about a more just and equitable society, and government authorities eventually responded by curtailing the worst abuses of the early industrial era. Governments and labor unions both worked to raise living standards and provide security for working people. Meanwhile, industrialization increasingly touched the lives of peoples around the world. Western European, North American, and Japanese societies followed Britain's lead into industrialization, while many African, Asian, and Latin American places had little choice but to become dependent on the export of raw materials to industrial societies.

STUDY TERMS

calicoes (623)	Friedrich Engels (640)
cartels (630)	George Stephenson (624)
child labor (637)	Henry Ford (628)
Communist Manifesto (639)	James Watt (624)
corporations (630)	Karl Marx (640)
Crystal Palace (631)	Luddites (626)
demographic transition (632)	middle class (634)
Eli Whitney (628)	mule (624)
factory system (625)	power loom (624)
flying shuttle (624)	*socialism* (638)

trade unions (641)	utopian socialists (638)
trusts (630)	working class (635)

FOR FURTHER READING

Daniel R. Headrick. *Power over Peoples: Technology, Environments, and Western Imperialism, 1400 to the Present.* Princeton, 2009. Explores the important relationship between technology and imperialism.

Penelope Lane, Neil Raven, and K. D. M. Snell, eds. *Women, Work and Wages in England, 1600-1850.* Rochester, N.Y., 2004. Study of women's contributions to British industrialization and how it was rewarded.

Karl Marx and Friedrich Engels. *The Communist Manifesto.* Trans. by Samuel Moore. Harmondsworth, 1967. English translation of the most important tract of nineteenth-century socialism, with an excellent introduction by historian A. J. P. Taylor.

David R. Meyer. *The Roots of American Industrialization.* Baltimore, 2003. Interdisciplinary study that ties America's industrialization to increasing agricultural productivity of the antebellum period.

Prasannan Parthasarathi. *Why Europe Grew Rich and Asia Did Not: Global Economic Divergence, 1600-1800.* Cambridge, 2011. Argues that British economic policies were crucial in crushing the thriving cotton textile industry in India.

Kenneth Pomeranz. *The Great Divergence: China, Europe, and the Making of the Modern World Economy.* Princeton, 2000. Argues that the fortuitous location of coal deposits and access to the resources of the Americas created a uniquely advantageous framework for English industrialization.

William Rosen. T*he Most Powerful Idea in the World: A Story of Steam, Industry, and Invention.* New York, 2010. Dismissing traditional explanations for the origins of British industrialization, the author argues that England's patent system proved the decisive factor.

Peter N. Stearns. *The Industrial Revolution in World History.* 4th ed. Boulder, Colo., 2012. This concise account places industrialization and its effects in a global perspective.

E. P. Thompson. *The Making of the English Working Class.* New York, 1966. A classic work that analyzes the formation of working-class consciousness in England from the 1790s to the 1830s.

Louise A. Tilly. *Industrialization and Gender Inequality.* Washington, D.C., 1993. A brief historiographical survey of debates on gender and industrialization in England, France, Germany, the United States, Japan, and China.

The Americas in the Age of Independence

ZOOMING IN ON ENCOUNTERS

Fatt Hing Chin Searches for Gold from China to California

Fatt Hing Chin was a village fish peddler who lived in a coastal town in southern China. One day at the wharves, he heard people talking about a place across the ocean where the mountains were laden with gold. Chin was nineteen years old and full of energy, and he longed for the chance to see if he could find some of this gold for himself. He learned that he could purchase passage on a foreign ship, and in 1849—after reconciling his parents to his plans—he boarded a Spanish ship to sail to California and join the gold rush.

Chin felt some uncertainty once at sea. Surprised at the large number of young Chinese men crammed in with him in the ship's hold, he shared their dismay as they remained confined to the cargo areas of the ship, where the smell of vomit was overpowering. Ninety-five days and nights passed before the hills of San Francisco came into view. Upon arrival the travelers met Chinese veterans of life in the United States who explained the strategy of sticking together in order to survive and prosper.

Chin hired himself out as a gold miner and headed for the mountains of gold. After digging and sifting for two years, he had accumulated his own little pile of gold. He wrote to his

Seven miners stand near a sluice box in California around 1852. Note the four Chinese miners standing to the right.
Fotosearch/Archive Photos/Getty Images

brothers and cousins, urging them to join him, and thus helped fuel a large-scale overseas migration that brought 24,000 Chinese workers to California in the four years between 1849 and 1853. Having made his fortune, though, Chin decided to return to China. Now wealthy, on the way home he traveled much more comfortably in a cabin with a bunk. Although he gambled away half his gold before his ship docked in China at Guangzhou, what remained still amounted to a small fortune.

California gold provided him with the means to take a wife, build a house, and buy some land.

Although settled and prosperous, Chin remained restless and longed to return to California. Leaving his pregnant wife, he sailed for California again after only a year. He returned to mining with his brother (who had taken his advice and made the trip to California), but the gold had become more difficult to find. Inspired by the luck of another migrant, Tong Ling, who managed to get one dollar for each meal he sold, Chin's cousins in San Francisco decided to open a restaurant. As one of them said, "If the foreign devils will eat his food, they will eat ours." Chin found the city much more comfortable than the mountains.

"Let the others go after the gold in the hills," he said. "I'll wait for the gold to come to the city."

Fatt Hing Chin was one of the earliest Chinese migrants to settle in the Americas. His career path—from a miner in search of quick riches to an urban resident committed to a new homeland and hoping to profit from the service industry—was typical of Chinese migrants to the United States. Some went from mining to railroad construction or agricultural labor, but all contributed to the transformation of the Americas. Along with millions of others from Europe and Asia, Chinese migrants increased the ethnic diversity of American populations and stimulated political, social, and economic development in the Western Hemisphere.

CHAPTER OVERVIEW

During the late eighteenth and early nineteenth centuries, almost all the territories in the Western Hemisphere won their independence from European colonial powers. American peoples then struggled throughout the nineteenth century to build states and societies that realized their potential in an age of independence. The United States embarked on a westward push that brought most of the temperate regions of North America under U.S. control. Canada built a federal state under British Canadian leadership. The varied lands of Latin America built smaller states that often fell under the sway of local military leaders. One issue that most American peoples wrestled with, regardless of their region, was the legacy of the Enlightenment. The effort to build societies based on freedom, equality, and constitutional government was a monumental challenge only partially realized in lands characterized by enormous social, economic, and cultural divisions. Both the institution of slavery and its ultimate abolition complicated the process of building societies in the Americas, particularly in regard to defining a new type of workforce for free and increasingly industrial economies. Asian and European migrants joined native-born workers and formerly enslaved people in labor systems—from plantations and factories to debt peonage—that often demonstrated the hollowness of American promises of welcome and freedom.

The age of independence for the United States, Canada, and Latin America was a contentious era characterized by continuous mass migration and explosive economic growth, occasionally followed by deep economic stagnation, and punctuated with civil war, ethnic violence, class conflict, and battles for racial and sexual equality. Independence clearly did not solve the political and social problems of the Western Hemisphere but, rather, created a new context in which American peoples struggled to build effective states, enjoy economic prosperity, and attain cultural cohesion. Those goals were

CHRONOLOGY	
1803	Louisiana Purchase
1804–1806	Lewis and Clark expedition
1812–1814	War of 1812
1829–1852	Rule of Juan Manuel de Rosas in Argentina
1838–1839	Trail of Tears
1846–1848	Mexican-American War
1848	Seneca Falls Convention
1849	California gold rush
1850s	La Reforma in Mexico
1861–1865	U.S. Civil War
1867	Establishment of the Dominion of Canada; French troops withdraw from Mexico
1867–1877	Reconstruction in the United States
1869	Completion of the transcontinental railroad line in the United States
1876	Battle of the Little Bighorn
1876–1911	Rule of Porfirio Díaz in Mexico
1885	Completion of the Canadian Pacific Railroad; Northwest Rebellion
1890	Massacre at Wounded Knee
1910–1920	Mexican revolution

elusive throughout the nineteenth century (and in many ways remain so in the present day). Nevertheless, the histories of these first territories to win independence from colonial powers inspired other peoples who later sought freedom from imperial rule. At the same time, they also served as portents of the difficulties faced by newly free states.

THE BUILDING OF AMERICAN STATES

After winning independence from Britain in 1783, the United States fashioned a government and began to expand rapidly to the west. By mid-century the new republic had forcibly absorbed almost all the temperate lands of North America. Yet the United States was an unstable society composed of varied regions with diverse economic and social structures. Differences over slavery and the rights of individual states as opposed to the federal government sparked a devastating civil war in the 1860s. That conflict resulted in the abolition of slavery and the strengthening of the federal state. The experience of Canada was very different from that of the United States. Canada gained independence from Britain without fighting a war, and, despite also being a land of great diversity, avoided fighting a civil war. Although intermittently nervous about the possibility that the United States might expand to the north, Canada established a relatively weak federal government, which presided over provinces that had considerable power over local affairs. Latin American states were even more diverse than their counterparts to the north, and in spite of the efforts of some individuals they were unable to join together in a confederation. Throughout the nineteenth century Latin America was politically fragmented, and many individual states faced serious problems and divisions within their own societies.

The United States: Westward Expansion and Civil War

After gaining independence the United States faced the need to construct a framework of government. During the 1780s leaders from the rebellious colonies drafted a constitution that entrusted responsibility for general issues to a federal government, reserved authority for local issues for individual states, and provided for the admission of new states and territories to the confederation. Although the Declaration of Independence had declared that "all men are created equal," most individual states limited the vote to men of property. But the Enlightenment ideal of equality encouraged political leaders to extend the franchise: by the late 1820s most property qualifications had disappeared, and by mid-century almost all adult white men were eligible to participate in the political affairs of the republic.

Westward Expansion and Manifest Destiny While working to settle constitutional issues, residents of the United States also began to expand rapidly to the west. After the American revolution, Britain ceded to the new republic all lands between the Appalachian Mountains and the Mississippi

River, and the United States doubled in size. In 1803 Napoleon Bonaparte needed funds immediately to protect revolutionary France from its enemies, and he allowed the United States to purchase France's Louisiana Territory, which extended from the Mississippi River to the Rocky Mountains. Overnight the United States doubled in size again. Between 1804 and 1806 a geographic expedition led by Meriwether Lewis and William

Sitting Bull (ca. 1831–1890) was a Hunkpapa Lakota Sioux holy man who also led his people as a war chief during years of resistance to United States government policies. The battle of the Little Bighorn, also known by the indigenous Americans as the battle of Greasy Grass Creek, was the most famous action of the Great Sioux War against the United States cavalry in 1876–1877. It was an overwhelming victory for the Lakota and Northern Cheyenne, overseen by Sitting Bull.
The Art Archive/Shutterstock

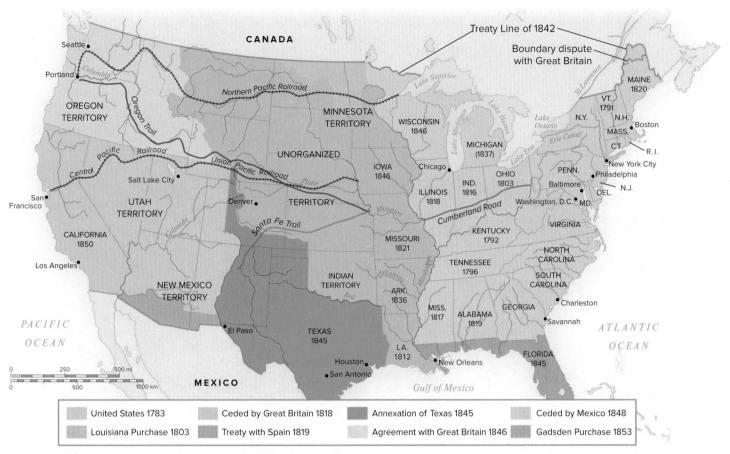

MAP 30.1 Westward expansion of the United States during the nineteenth century.

Note the large land claims ceded by Britain, France, and Mexico.

Why were there no portions of North America purchased from or ceded by Native Americans?

Clark mapped the territory and surveyed its resources. Settlers soon began to flock west in search of cheap land to cultivate. By the 1840s westward expansion was well under way, and many U.S. citizens spoke of a **manifest destiny.** According to this idea, the United States was destined, even divinely ordained, to expand across the North American continent from the Atlantic seaboard to the Pacific and beyond. Manifest destiny was often invoked to justify U.S. expansion.

Conflict with Indigenous Peoples Although gaining territory from Britain and France gave westward expansion legal legitimacy from the American point of view, from the perspective of indigenous people it was nothing less than forcible conquest of lands on which they had lived for thousands of years. Indeed, westward expansion brought settlers and government forces into conflict with the indigenous peoples of North America, who resisted efforts to push them from their ancestral lands and hunting grounds. Native Americans forged alliances among themselves and also sought the backing of British colonial officials in Canada, but U.S. officials and military forces supported Euro-American settlers and violently

forced the continent open to white expansion. Their efforts, however, did not stop at opening the land to white colonists. Instead, with the **Indian Removal Act of 1830,** the United States government determined to move all Native Americans west of the Mississippi River onto marginal lands they called "Indian Territory" (Oklahoma). Among the tribes affected by this forced removal from the east were the Seminoles, some of whom managed to avoid capture and the long march to Oklahoma by resisting and retreating to Florida's swampy lowlands. The Cherokees also suffered a harrowing 800-mile migration from the eastern woodlands to Oklahoma on the **Trail of Tears** (1838–1839), so known because thousands died from disease, starvation, and the difficulties of relocation.

After 1840 the site of conflict between Euro-American and indigenous peoples shifted to the plains region west of the Mississippi River. Settlers and ranchers in the trans-Mississippi west encountered peoples such as the Sioux, Comanche, Pawnee, and Apache, who possessed firearms and outstanding equestrian skills. The indigenous peoples of the plains offered effective resistance to encroachment by white settlers and at times celebrated powerful victories over U.S. forces.

This photograph of an 1890s Plains Indian camp in South Dakota offers a pastoral and peaceful image of the indigenous societies in the United States who were in the process of being violently forced off their lands.

Buyenlarge/Archive Photos/Getty Images

In 1876, for example, thousands of Lakota Sioux and their allies defeated an army under the command of Colonel George Armstrong Custer in the **battle of the Little Bighorn** (in southern Montana). However, despite occasional successes in battle, Native Americans on the plains ultimately lost the war against the forces of U.S. expansionism. The weaponry employed against native peoples included cannons and deadly, rapid-fire Gatling guns. Those weapons—plus ever greater numbers of settlers and military reinforcements—aided U.S. forces in breaking Native American resistance and opened the western plains to U.S. conquest.

One last symbolic conflict took place in 1890 at Wounded Knee Creek in South Dakota. Frightened and threatened by the Sioux adoption of the Ghost Dance, an expression of religious beliefs that included a vision of an afterlife in which all white peoples disappeared, whites wanted these religious ceremonies suppressed. U.S. cavalry forces chased the Sioux who were fleeing to safety in the South Dakota Badlands. At Wounded Knee Creek, a Sioux man accidentally shot off a

gun, and the cavalry overreacted badly, slaughtering more than two hundred men, women, and children with machine guns. Emblematic of harsh U.S. treatment of native peoples, **Wounded Knee** represented the place where "a people's dream died," as one Native American leader put it.

The Mexican-American War Westward expansion also generated tension between the United States and Mexico, whose territories included Texas, California, and New Mexico (the territory that is now the American southwest). Texas declared independence from Mexico in 1836, largely because the many U.S. migrants who had settled there wanted to run their own affairs. In 1845 the United States accepted Texas as a new state—against vigorous Mexican protest—and moved to consolidate its hold on the territory. Those moves led to conflicts that rapidly escalated into the **Mexican-American War** (1846–1848), or, as it is known in Mexico, *la intervención norteamericano* (the North American Intervention) or *la guerra del 47* (the War of 1847). U.S. forces instigated the war by sending troops into a disputed zone along the Rio Grande. When Mexican cavalry attacked U.S. soldiers in this zone, the United States sent in reinforcements and inflicted a punishing defeat on the Mexican army. By the Treaty of Guadalupe Hidalgo (1848), the United States took possession of approximately one-half of Mexico's territory, paying a mere fifteen million dollars in exchange for Texas north of the Rio Grande, California, and New Mexico. Thousands of U.S. and Mexican soldiers died in the conflict, and thousands of Mexican families found themselves stranded in the territories annexed by the United States. Some moved to be within the new borders of Mexico, but most stayed where they were and attained U.S. citizenship. This conflict nonetheless fueled Mexican nationalism, as well as hostility toward the United States.

Westward expansion also created problems within the republic by aggravating tensions between regions. The most serious and divisive issue had to do with slavery, which had been a serious problem in American politics since independence. The Enlightenment ideal of equality clearly suggested that the appropriate policy was to abolish slavery, but the leaders of the American revolution and framers of the Constitution recognized the sanctity of private property, which legally included enslaved people. U.S. independence initially promoted a surge of antislavery sentiment, as states north of Delaware abolished slavery within their jurisdictions. Abolition did not bring full equality for former enslaved people in northern states, but it hardened divisions between what became known as "slave" and "free" states. Westward expansion aggravated tensions further by raising the question of whether settlers could extend slavery to newly acquired territories.

Sectional Conflict Opponents of slavery had hoped that the institution would die a natural death with the decline of tobacco cultivation. Their hopes faded, however, with the invigoration of slavery as a result of the rise of cotton as a cash crop in the early nineteenth century, and then by westward expansion. The number of enslaved people in the United States rose sharply, from five hundred thousand in 1770 to almost two million in 1820. As the numbers of enslaved people grew, antislavery forces fought to limit the spread of slavery to new territories. Beginning with the Missouri Compromise of 1820, a series of political compromises attempted to maintain a balance between slave and free states as the republic admitted new states carved out of western territories. As proslavery and antislavery forces became more strident, however, those compromises could not endure. **Abraham Lincoln** (1809–1865) predicted in 1858 that "a house divided against itself cannot stand," and he made the connection to slavery explicit: "I believe this government cannot endure permanently half *slave* and half *free*. . . . It will become *all* one thing, or *all* the other."

The election of Abraham Lincoln to the presidency in 1860 was the spark that ignited war between the states (1861–1865). Lincoln was an explicitly sectional candidate, was convinced that slavery was immoral, and was committed to the idea of free

The Peacemakers, an 1868 painting by George Healy, depicts Abraham Lincoln in a strategy session with his top army and navy commanders aboard the *River Queen* during the final days of the Civil War. From left to right are General William Tecumseh Sherman, General Ulysses S. Grant, Abraham Lincoln, and Admiral David Dixon Porter.
ARCHIVIO GBB/Alamy Stock Photo

soil—territories without slavery. Although slavery stood at the center of the conflict, President Lincoln had insisted from the beginning of the war that his primary aim was the restoration of the Union, not the abolition of slavery. He was therefore reluctant to adopt an abolitionist policy. There were reasons for his hesitancy. Not only had Lincoln been elected on a platform of noninterference with slavery within the states, but he also doubted the constitutionality of any federal action. He was also concerned about the difficulties of assimilating four million former enslaved people—if abolition were to go into effect—into the nation's social and political fabric. Most important, Lincoln feared that an abolitionist program would prompt Delaware, Maryland, Kentucky, and Missouri—all slave states—into leaving the Union to join the southern states in the Confederacy. The Civil War also revolved around issues central to the United States as a society: the nature of the Union, states' rights as opposed to the federal government's authority, and the imperatives of a budding industrial-capitalist system against those of an export-oriented plantation economy.

The U.S. Civil War Eleven southern states withdrew from the Union in 1860 and 1861, affirming their right to dissolve the Union and their support for states' rights. Slavery and the cultivation of cotton as a cash crop had isolated the southern states from economic developments in the rest of the United States. By the mid-nineteenth century, the southern states were the world's major source of cotton, and the bulk of the crop went to the British isles to feed the textile factories of the industrial revolution. Manufactured goods consumed in the southern states came mostly from Britain, and almost all food came from the region's farms. Many southerners thus considered themselves self-sufficient and believed they did not need the rest of the United States. Northerners saw the situation differently. They viewed secession as illegal insurrection and an act of betrayal. They fought not only against slavery but also against the concept

of a state subject to blackmail by its constituent parts. They also fought for a way of life—their emerging industrial society—and an expansive western agricultural system based on free labor.

The first two years of the war ended in stalemate. The war changed character, however, when Abraham Lincoln signed the Emancipation Proclamation, which made the abolition of slavery an explicit goal of the war. As the war progressed, Lincoln increasingly viewed the destruction of slavery as the only way to preserve the Union. Five days after the Union victory at the battle of Antietam, President Lincoln issued a preliminary **Emancipation Proclamation.** The final version, issued January 1, 1863, freed enslaved people in the states that had rebelled. Ironically, in the states that remained loyal to the Union, slavery remained protected by the U.S. Constitution. The solution to this problem, one that Lincoln urged, was the Thirteenth Amendment to the Constitution, ratified in 1865, which completely abolished slavery throughout the United States.

Ultimately, the northern states prevailed in the Civil War, after the bloody battle at Gettysburg in July 1863 turned the military tide against southern forces. The northern states brought considerable resources to the war effort—some 90 percent of the country's industrial capacity and approximately two-thirds of its railroad lines—but still they fought four bitter years against a formidable enemy. The victory of the northern states had enormous consequences for the United States. Most immediately, it permanently ended slavery throughout the country. Moreover, it ensured that the United States would remain politically united, and it enhanced the authority of the federal government in the republic. Thus, as European lands were building powerful states on the foundations of revolutionary ideals, liberalism, and nationalism, the United States also forged a strong central government to oversee settler colonialism to the west and to deal with the political and social issues that divided the nation. That strength came at a horrible cost for both sides, however, especially in terms of the enormous

This photograph depicts the bodies of northern soldiers who died in the bloody battle of Antietam (Maryland) in 1862. With 620,000 military deaths, the Civil War was the most costly in U.S. history in terms of lives lost.
Library of Congress, Prints & Photographs Division [LC-DIG-cwpb-01097]

human casualties. About 1,556,000 soldiers served in the Union armies and suffered a total of over 634,000 casualties, 360,000 of whom died. Approximately 800,000 men served in the Confederate forces, which sustained approximately 483,000 casualties, including 258,000 dead.

The Canadian Dominion: Independence without War

Autonomy and Division Canada did not fight a war for independence, and in spite of deep regional divisions, it did not experience bloody internal conflict. Instead, Canadian independence came gradually as Canadians and the British

government agreed on general principles of autonomy. The distinctiveness of the two dominant European ethnic groups, the British Canadians and the French Canadians, ensured that the process of building an independent society would not be smooth, but intermittent fears of U.S. expansion and concerns about the possibility of an invasion from the south helped submerge ethnic differences. By the late nineteenth century, Canada was a state in control of its own destiny, despite continuing ties to Britain and the sometimes threatening presence of the United States to the south.

Originally colonized by trappers and settlers from both Britain and France, the colony of New France was incorporated into the British Empire after the British victory in the Seven Years' War (1756-1763). Until the late eighteenth

MAP 30.2 The Dominion of Canada in the nineteenth century.

Note the provinces that make up the modern state of Canada and the dates in which they were incorporated into the Dominion.

At what date were eastern and western Canada geographically united?

century, however, French Canadians outnumbered British Canadians, so to avoid unnecessary conflict imperial officials made a number of concessions to their subjects of French descent. For example, officials recognized the Roman Catholic church and permitted continued observance of French civil law in Quebec and other areas of French Canadian settlement, which they governed through appointed councils staffed by local elites. British Canadians, in contrast, were Protestants who lived mostly in Ontario, followed British law, and governed themselves through elected representatives. Then, as the American revolution was ending in 1781, large numbers of British loyalists fled the newly formed United States to the south and sought refuge in Canada, thus greatly enlarging the size of the English-speaking community.

The War of 1812 Ethnic divisions and political differences could easily have splintered Canada, but the **War of 1812** stimulated a sense of unity against an external threat. The United States declared war on Britain in retaliation for encroachments on U.S. rights during the Napoleonic wars, and the British colony of Canada formed one of the front lines of the conflict. U.S. military leaders assumed they could easily invade and conquer Canada to pressure their foes. Despite the greater resources of the United States, however, Canadian forces repelled U.S. incursions. Their victories promoted a sense of Canadian pride, and anti-U.S. sentiment became a means for covering over differences among French Canadians and British Canadians.

After the War of 1812, Canada experienced an era of rapid growth. Expanded business opportunities drew English-speaking migrants, who swelled the population. However, that influx threatened the identity of French Canadians in Quebec, and discontent in Canada reached a critical point in the 1830s. The British imperial governors of Canada did not want a repeat of the American revolution, so between 1840 and 1867 they defused tensions by expanding home rule in Canada and permitting the provinces to govern their own internal affairs. Inspiring this imperial move toward Canadian autonomy was the **Durham Report,** issued in 1839 by John George Lambton (1782–1840), the first earl of Durham and recent governor-general and lord high commissioner of Canada. He advocated a good deal of self-government for a united Canada, and his report became a model for later British imperial policy toward other white settler colonies, including Australia and New Zealand.

Dominion Over the next few decades, Canadians developed a federal structure for their developing state. The **British North America Act of 1867** joined Quebec, Ontario, Nova Scotia, and New Brunswick and recognized them as the **Dominion of Canada.** (Other provinces joined the Dominion later.) The term *dominion* signaled the continuing connection of Canada to the British government, while Canadians took control of internal affairs. Under this arrangement, each province had its own seat of government, provincial legislature, and lieutenant governor representing the British crown. The act created a federal government headed by a governor-general who acted as the British

representative. An elected House of Commons and appointed Senate rounded out the framework of governance. Provincial legislatures reserved certain political matters for themselves, whereas others fell within the purview of the federal government. Without waging war, the Dominion of Canada had won control over all Canadian internal affairs, while Britain retained jurisdiction over foreign affairs until 1931.

John A. Macdonald (1815–1891) became the first prime minister of Canada, and he moved to incorporate all of British North America into the Dominion. He negotiated the purchase of the huge Northwest Territories from the Hudson's Bay Company in 1869, and he persuaded Manitoba, British Columbia, and Prince Edward Island to join the Dominion. Macdonald believed, however, that Canada's Dominion would remain symbolic—a mere "geographic expression," as he put it—until the government took concrete action to make Canadian unity a reality. To strengthen the union, he oversaw construction of a transcontinental railroad, completed in 1885. The railroad facilitated transportation and communications throughout Canada and eventually helped bring new provinces into the Dominion: Alberta and Saskatchewan in 1905 and Newfoundland in 1949. Internal conflicts never disappeared, but the Dominion provided a foundation for Canadian independence and unity. While maintaining ties to Britain and struggling to forge an identity distinct from that of its powerful neighbor to the south, Canada developed as a culturally diverse yet politically unified society.

Latin America: Fragmentation and Political Experimentation

Political unity was short-lived in Latin America. Simón Bolívar (1783–1830), hailed as South America's liberator, worked for the establishment of a large confederation that would provide Latin America with the political, military, and economic strength to resist encroachment by foreign powers. The wars of independence that he led encouraged a sense of solidarity in Latin America. But Bolívar once admitted that "I fear peace more than war," and after the defeat of the common colonial enemy, solidarity proved impossible to sustain. Bolívar's Gran Colombia broke into its three constituent parts—Venezuela, Colombia, and Ecuador—and the rest of Latin America fragmented into numerous independent states.

Creole Elites and Political Instability Following the example of the United States, creole (people of European descent born in the Americas) elites usually established republics with written constitutions in most newly independent states of Latin America. Yet constitutions were much more difficult to frame in Latin America than in the United States. Before gaining independence, Latin American leaders had less experience with self-government because Spanish and Portuguese colonies were ruled far more directly by representatives of the crown than the British colonies in North America. Creole elites responded enthusiastically to Enlightenment

MAP 30.3   Latin America in the nineteenth century. Date is year of independence.

Note the many states that emerged from the independence movements early in the century.

Why was it difficult for large, federated republics, such as the Republic of Colombia, founded by Simón Bolívar, to survive?

values and republican ideals but found it difficult to put these principles into practice. As a result, several Latin American states lurched from one constitution to another as leaders struggled to create a machinery of government that would lead to political and social stability.

Creole elites themselves were part of the problem because they dominated the newly independent states and effectively prevented mass participation in public affairs. Less than 5 percent of the male population was active in Latin American politics in the nineteenth century, and millions of indigenous peoples lived entirely outside the political system. Without institutionalized means of expressing discontent or opposition, those disillusioned with the system had little choice beyond rebellion. Aggravating political instability were differences among elites. Whether they were urban merchants or rural landowners, Latin American elites divided into different camps as liberals or conservatives, centralists or federalists, secularists or Roman Catholics.

Conflicts with Indigenous Peoples

Like their neighbors in the United States, one thing elites agreed on was the policy of claiming South American land for agriculture and ranching. That meant pushing aside indigenous peoples and establishing hegemony in Latin America. Conflict was most intense in Argentina and Chile, where cultivators and ranch-

caudillos (KAHW-dee-yohs)

Juán Manuel de Rosas (HWAHN mahn-WEL deh roh-sahs)

ers longed to take over the South American plains. During the mid-nineteenth century, as the United States was crushing indigenous resistance to western expansion in North America, Argentine and Chilean forces brought modern weapons to bear in their campaign to conquer the indigenous peoples of those states. By the 1870s, they had forced indigenous peoples on the most productive lands to retreat to marginal lands or to assimilate to Euro-American society.

Caudillos

Although creole elites agreed on the policy of conquering indigenous peoples, division and discord in the newly independent states helped **caudillos,** or regional military leaders, come to power in much of Latin America. The wars of independence had lasted well over a decade, and they provided Latin America with military rather than civilian heroes. After independence, military leaders took to the political stage, appealing to populist sentiments and exploiting the discontent of the masses. One of the most notable caudillos was **Juan Manuel de Rosas,** who from 1829 to 1852 ruled an Argentina divided between the cattle-herding gaucho (cowboy) society of the pampas (the interior grasslands) and the urban elite of Buenos Aires. Rosas himself emerged from the world of cattle ranching, and he used his skills to subdue other caudillos and establish control in Buenos Aires. Rosas called for regional autonomy in an attempt to reconcile competing interests, but at the same time he worked to centralize the government he now controlled. He quelled rebellions, but he did so in bloody fashion. Critics often likened Rosas to well-known political

Edouard Manet's painting (one of a series painted between 1867 and 1869) depicts the execution by firing squad of Emperor Maximilian, whose death in 1867 ended attempted French rule in Mexico.
World History Archive/ Alamy Stock Photo

manipulators or dictators from the past, calling him "the Machiavelli of the pampas" and "the Argentine Nero," and they accused him of launching a reign of terror to stifle opposition. One exiled writer compiled a chart that counted the number of Rosas's victims and the violent ways they met their ends; of the 22,404 total victims killed, most met their end in armed clashes but others died by poisoning, hanging, or assassination.

Rosas did what caudillos did best: he restored order. In doing so, however, he made terror a tool of the government, and he ruled as a despot through his own personal army. Rosas also, however, embodied the charismatic personality traits most exemplified by caudillos. He attained great popularity through his identification with the people and with gauchos, and he demonstrated his physical strength and machismo.

Mexico: War and Reform
Independent Mexico experienced a succession of governments, from monarchy to republic to caudillo rule, but it also generated a liberal reform movement. The Mexican-American War (1846-1848) caused political turmoil in Mexico and helped the caudillo General **Antonio López de Santa Anna** (1797-1876) perpetuate his intermittent rule of the country. After the defeat and disillusion of the war, however, a liberal reform movement attempted to reshape Mexican society. Led by President **Benito Juárez** (1806-1872), a Mexican of indigenous ancestry, La Reforma of the 1850s aimed to limit the power of the military and the Roman Catholic church in Mexican society. Juárez and his followers called for reforms that were designed, in part, to create a rural middle class. The Constitution of 1857 curtailed the prerogatives of priests and military elites, and it guaranteed universal male suffrage and other civil liberties, such as freedom of speech. Land reform efforts centered on breaking up jointly held properties, which had the effect of parceling out communal Indian lands and villages as private property. However, the reforms did not have the desired effect, as much of this land ended up in the hands of large landowners rather than indigenous peoples.

Mexico: Revolution
La Reforma challenged some of the fundamental conservatism of Mexican elites, who led a determined opposition to political, social, and economic reform.

Emiliano Zapata (1879–1919), who hailed from the southern state of Morelos, was the very picture of a revolutionary leader, heavily armed and sporting his trademark moustache.

Cultural Heritage Images/Universal Images Group/Newscom

Liberals and conservatives in Mexico stayed bitterly divided, and in fact conservatives forced the Juárez government out of the capital in Mexico City. In 1861, Juarez sought to reestablish his authority and restore order to the country. To lessen Mexico's financial woes, Juárez chose to suspend loan payments to foreign powers that had invested heavily in Mexico's infrastructure, which in turn led to French, British, and Spanish intervention as Europeans sought to recover and protect their investments in Mexico. France's Napoleon III proved especially intrusive, and in 1862 he even sent an invasion force whose goal was to re-create a monarchy in Mexico, this time controlled by France. But on May 5, 1862, Mexican forces beat back the French invaders at the city of Puebla, a date thereafter celebrated as Cinco de Mayo. Napoleon III then sent tens of thousands of troops to conquer Mexico and proclaimed the creation of a Mexican empire. In 1867, however, Napoleon III had no choice but to accept defeat and withdraw his forces after a Mexican firing squad killed the man he had appointed emperor, the Austrian archduke Maximilian (1832-1867). Juárez managed to restore a semblance of liberal government following the French invasion, but Mexico remained beset by political divisions.

By the early twentieth century, Mexico was a divided land moving toward civil war. The Mexican revolution (1910-1920), a bitter and bloody conflict, broke out when middle-class Mexicans joined with peasants and workers to overthrow the powerful dictator **Porfirio Díaz** (1830-1915). The revolt in Mexico was the first major, violent effort in Latin America to attempt to topple the grossly unequal system of landed estates in which 95 percent of all peasants remained landless. As those denied land and representation armed themselves and engaged in guerrilla warfare against government forces, the revolt turned increasingly radical. The lower classes took up weapons and followed the revolutionary leaders **Emiliano Zapata** (1879-1919) and **Francisco (Pancho) Villa** (1878-1923), charismatic men of agrarian backgrounds who organized massive armies fighting

Benito Juárez (beh-NEE-toh HWAHR-ez)
Porfirio Díaz (pohr-FEER-eeo DEE-ahs)
Emiliano Zapata (eh-mee-LYAH-no zuh-PAH-tuh)
Francisco Villa (frahn-SEES-kow VEE-yuh)

for the goals of *tierra y libertad* (land and liberty). Zapata, the son of a mestizo peasant, and Villa, the son of a field worker, embodied the ideals and aspirations of the indigenous Mexican masses and enjoyed tremendous popular support. They discredited what they viewed as timid governmental efforts at reform and challenged governmental political control. For example, Zapata confiscated hacienda lands and began distributing the lands to the peasants, while Villa attacked and killed U.S. citizens in retaliation for U.S. support of Mexican government officials—and succeeded in eluding capture by either U.S. or Mexican forces.

Despite the power and popularity enjoyed by Zapata and Villa, they were unable to capture Mexico's major cities, and they did not command the resources and wealth to which government forces had access. The Mexican revolution came to an end soon after government forces ambushed and killed Zapata in 1919. Villa was assassinated a few years later in 1923, when his car was ambushed in the town of Hidalgo de Parral. Government forces regained control over Mexico, but the human cost of so many years of war had been appalling: as many as two million Mexicans had died during the conflicts. Although radicals such as Zapata and Villa were ultimately defeated, the Mexican government that came to power in 1917 issued a constitution that did in fact address some of the concerns of the revolutionaries. These included providing for land redistribution, universal suffrage, state-supported education, minimum wages and maximum hours for workers, and restrictions on foreign ownership of Mexican property and mineral resources. Although these constitutional provisions were not all implemented right away, they provided inspiration for the future.

Instability and conflict plagued Latin America throughout the nineteenth century in the form of division, rebellion, caudillo rule, and civil war. Many Latin American peoples continued to lack education, profitable employment, and political representation. Simón Bolívar himself once said that "independence is the only blessing we have gained at the expense of all the rest."

AMERICAN ECONOMIC DEVELOPMENT

During the nineteenth and early twentieth centuries, two principal influences—mass migration and British financial investment—shaped economic development throughout the Americas. But American states reacted in different ways to migration and foreign investment. The United States and Canada absorbed waves of migrants, exploited British capital, built industrial societies, and established economic independence. The results of mass migration and financial investment were much more mixed in Latin America, however. In both South America and the Caribbean, migrants tended to arrive as contract or indentured laborers to take the place of enslaved people after abolition, and thus remained quite poor. In terms of foreign financial investments, in much of Latin America these tended to benefit only the investors themselves and the small elite classes that controlled most countries.

Migration to the Americas

Underpinning the economic development of the Americas was large-scale migration of European and Asian peoples to the United States, Canada, and Latin America. Internal migration within the Americas also contributed to a new economic landscape, particularly as Latin Americans journeyed to the United States in search of work and financial opportunities. As we saw in the introduction, gold discoveries drew prospectors hoping to make a quick fortune: the California gold rush of 1849 drew the largest numbers (about three hundred thousand) but Canadian gold also lured migrants by the tens of thousands. Outnumbering gold prospectors were millions of European and Asian migrants who made their way to the factories, railroad construction sites, and plantations of the Americas. Following them were others who offered the support services that made life for migrant workers more comfortable and at the same time transformed the ethnic and cultural landscape of the Americas. Fatt Hing Chin's restaurant in San Francisco's Chinatown fed Chinese migrants, but it also helped introduce Chinese cuisine to American society. Migrants from other parts of the world found similar comforts as their foods, religious beliefs, and cultural traditions migrated with them to the Americas.

Industrial Migrants After the mid-nineteenth century, European migrants flocked to North America, where they filled the factories of the growing industrial economy of the United States. Their lack of skills made them attractive to industrialists seeking workers to operate machinery or perform heavy labor at low wages. By keeping labor costs down, migrants helped increase the profitability and fuel the expansion of U.S. industry.

In the 1850s 2.3 million Europeans migrated to the United States—almost as many as had crossed the Atlantic during the half century from 1800 to 1850—and the volume of migration continued to surge until the early twentieth century. Increasing rents and indebtedness drove cultivators from Ireland, Scotland, Germany, and Scandinavia to seek opportunities in North America. Some of them moved to the Ohio and Mississippi River valleys in search of cheap and abundant land, but many stayed in the eastern cities and contributed to the early industrialization of the United States. By the late nineteenth century, most European migrants were coming from southern and eastern Europe. Poles, Russian Jews, Slavs, Italians, Greeks, and Portuguese escaping either persecution or poverty were most prominent among the later migrants, and they settled largely in the industrial cities of the eastern states. They dominated the textile industries of the northeast, and without their labor, the remarkable industrial expansion that the United States experienced in the late nineteenth century would not have been possible.

Asian migrants further swelled the U.S. labor force and contributed to the construction of an American transportation infrastructure. Chinese migration grew rapidly after the 1840s, when officials of the Qing government permitted foreigners to

Italian migrants construct a railway in New York. Italians were just one of many migrant groups coming to the Americas in the nineteenth century, including Irish and Chinese.

Michael Maslan/Corbis Historical/Getty Images

seek indentured laborers in China and approved their migration to distant lands. Between 1852 and 1875 some two hundred thousand Chinese migrated to California alone. Some, like Fatt Hing Chin, negotiated their own passage and sought to make their fortune in the gold rush, but most traveled on indentured labor contracts that required them to cultivate crops or work on the Central Pacific Railroad. An additional five thousand Chinese entered Canada to search for gold in British Columbia or work on the Canadian Pacific Railroad.

Plantation Migrants Whereas migrants to the United States contributed to the development of an industrial society, those who went to Latin American lands mostly worked on agricultural plantations. Some Europeans figured among these migrants. About four million Italians sought opportunities in Argentina in the 1880s and 1890s, for example, and the Brazilian government paid Italian migrants to cross the Atlantic and work for coffee growers, who experienced a severe labor shortage after the abolition of slavery in 1888. Many Italian workers settled permanently in Latin America, especially Argentina, but some, popularly known as *golondrinas* ("swallows") because of their regular migrations, traveled back and forth annually between

Europe and South America to take advantage of different growing seasons in the northern and southern hemispheres.

Asian laborers also worked on plantations in the Western Hemisphere. More than fifteen thousand indentured laborers from China worked in the sugarcane fields of Cuba during the nineteenth century, and Indian migrants traveled to Jamaica, Trinidad, Tobago, and Guyana. Laborers from both China and Japan migrated to Peru, where they worked on cotton plantations in coastal regions, mined guano deposits for fertilizer, and built railroad lines. After the middle of the nineteenth century, expanding U.S. influence in the Pacific islands also led to Chinese, Japanese, Filipino, and Korean migrations to Hawai`i, where planters sought indentured laborers to tend sugarcane. About twenty-five thousand Chinese went to Hawai`i during the 1850s and 1860s, and later 180,000 Japanese also made their way to island plantations.

Economic Expansion in the United States

British Capital British investment capital in the United States proved crucial to the early stages of industrial development by helping businesspeople establish a textile industry.

In the late nineteenth century, it also spurred a vast expansion of U.S. industry by funding entrepreneurs, who opened coal and iron ore mines, built iron and steel factories, and constructed railroad lines. The flow of investment monies was a consequence of Britain's own industrialization, which generated enormous wealth and created a need for investors to find profitable outlets for their funds. British investors were especially keen to invest in white settler states and colonies, and this investment in turn often provided the impetus for industrial expansion and economic independence in those regions. In the case of the United States, it helped create a rival industrial power that would eventually outperform Britain's economy.

After the 1860s, U.S. businesses made effective use of foreign investment capital as the country recovered from the Civil War. The war had determined that the United States would depend on wage labor rather than enslaved labor, and entrepreneurs set about tapping American resources and building a continental economy.

Railroads Perhaps the most important economic development of the later nineteenth century was the construction of railroad lines that linked all U.S. regions and helped create an integrated national economy. Because of its enormous size and environmental diversity, the United States offered an abundance of natural resources for industrial exploitation. But vast distances made it difficult to maintain close economic ties between regions until a boom in railroad construction created a dense transportation, communication, and distribution network. Before the U.S. Civil War, the United States had about 50,000 kilometers (31,000 miles) of railroad lines, most of them short routes east of the Mississippi River. By 1900 there were more than 320,000 kilometers (200,000 miles) of track, and the U.S. rail network stretched from coast to coast. Most prominent of the new lines was a transcontinental route, completed in 1869, running from Omaha, Nebraska (where connections provided access to eastern states), to San Francisco.

Railroads decisively influenced U.S. economic development. They provided cheap transportation for agricultural

AMERICAN EXPRESS TRAIN.

In this lithograph of Frances F. Palmer's well-known painting *American Express Train* (ca. 1864), the railroad is depicted as a cheerful and industrious master of the landscape.
Yale University Art Gallery

commodities, manufactured goods, and individual travelers. Railroads hauled grain, beef, and hogs from the plains states; cotton and tobacco from the south; lumber from the northwest; iron and steel from the mills of Pittsburgh; and finished products from the eastern industrial cities. In addition to the transportation services they provided, railroads spurred the development of other industries because they required huge amounts of coal, wood, glass, and rubber. Indeed, by the 1880s some 75 percent of U.S. steel went to the railroad industry. Railroads also required the development of new managerial skills to operate large, complicated businesses. In 1850 few if any U.S. businesses had more than a thousand employees. By the early 1880s, however, the Pennsylvania Railroad alone employed almost fifty thousand people, and the size of the business called for organization and coordination on an unprecedented scale. Railroads were the testing grounds where managers developed the techniques they needed to run big businesses.

Space and Time Railroads led to drastic changes in the ways people organized, controlled, and even thought about space and time. Railroads altered the landscape in often extreme fashion, and the transformations consequent to the building of railroads—in land control and development, the transportation of migrants and settlers to the west, and the exploitation of natural resources—only furthered the environmental impact of the railroad. The westward expansion driven by the railroad led to broadscale land clearing and the extension of farming and mining lands, and brought about both human suffering for indigenous peoples and environmental damage through soil erosion and pollution. Irrigation and the politics of water also sparked trouble, especially as settlers and farmers entered the drier plains and even desert regions. The dark smoke emanating from railroad engines undoubtedly represented progress to industrial promoters, but it also symbolized an ever-widening intrusion into the natural environment.

Railroads even shaped the sense of time in the United States. Until rapid and regular rail transportation became available, communities set their clocks by the sun. As a result, New York time was eleven minutes and forty-five seconds behind Boston time. When the clock showed 12 noon in Chicago, it was 11:50 A.M. in St. Louis and 12:18 P.M. in Detroit. Those differences in local sun times created scheduling nightmares for railroad managers, who by the 1880s had to keep track of more than fifty time standards. Observance of local time also created hazards because a small miscalculation in scheduling could bring two trains hurtling unexpectedly toward each other on the same track. To simplify matters, in 1883 railroad companies divided the North American continent into four zones in which all railroad clocks read precisely the same time. The general public quickly adopted **railroad time** in place of local sun time, and in 1918 the U.S. government legally established the four time zones as the nation's official framework of time.

Economic Growth Led by railroads, the U.S. economy expanded rapidly between 1870 and 1900. Inventors designed new products and brought them to market: electric lights, telephones, typewriters, phonographs, film photography, motion picture cameras, and electric motors all made their appearance during this era. Strong consumer demand for those and other products fueled rapid industrial expansion and suggested to observers that the United States had found the road to continuous progress and prosperity.

Yet the march of U.S. industrialization did not go entirely unopposed: large-scale labor unions emerged alongside big business in the period from 1870 to 1900, and confrontations between business owners seeking profits and workers seeking higher wages or job security sometimes grew ugly. A nationwide, coordinated strike of rail workers in 1877 shut down two-thirds of the nation's railroads. Violence stemming from the strike took the lives of one hundred people and resulted in ten million dollars' worth of property damage. Nevertheless, big business prevailed in its disputes with workers during the nineteenth century, often with support from federal or state governments, and by the early twentieth century the United States had emerged as one of the world's major industrial powers.

Canadian Prosperity

British investment deeply influenced the development of the Canadian as well as the U.S. economy in the nineteenth and early twentieth centuries. Canadian leaders, like U.S. leaders, took advantage of British capital to industrialize without allowing their economy to fall under British control. During the early nineteenth century, Britain paid relatively high prices for Canadian agricultural products and minerals, partly to keep the colony stable and to discourage the formation of separatist movements. As a result, white Canadians enjoyed a high standard of living even before industrialization.

The National Policy After the establishment of the Dominion of Canada in 1867, politicians started a program of economic development known as the **National Policy.** The idea was to attract migrants, protect nascent industries through tariffs, and build national transportation systems. The centerpiece of the transportation network was the transcontinental **Canadian Pacific Railroad,** built largely with British investment capital and completed in 1885. The Canadian Pacific Railroad opened the western prairie lands to commerce, stimulated the development of other industries, and promoted the emergence of a Canadian national economy. The National Policy created some violent conflicts with indigenous peoples who resisted encroachment on their lands and with trappers who resented disruption of their way of life, but at the same time it also promoted economic growth and independence. In Canada as in the United States, the ability to control and direct economic affairs was crucial to limiting the state's dependence on British capital.

As a result of the National Policy, Canada experienced booming agricultural, mineral, and industrial production in the late nineteenth and early twentieth centuries. Canadian population surged as a result of both migration and natural increase. Migrants flocked to Canada's shores from Asia and especially from Europe: between 1903 and 1914 some 2.7 million eastern European migrants settled in Canada. Fueled in part by this population growth, Canadian economic expansion took place on the foundation of rapidly increasing wheat production and the extraction of rich mineral resources, including gold, silver, copper, nickel, and asbestos. Industrialists also tapped Canadian rivers to produce the hydroelectric power necessary for manufacturing.

U.S. Investment Canada remained wary of its powerful neighbor to the south but did not keep U.S. economic influence entirely at bay. British investment dwarfed U.S. investment throughout the nineteenth century: in 1914 British investment in Canada totaled $2.5 billion, compared with $700 million from the United States. Nevertheless, the U.S. presence in the Canadian economy grew. By 1918, Americans owned 30 percent of all Canadian industry, and thereafter the U.S. and Canadian economies became increasingly interdependent. Canada began to undergo rapid industrialization after the early twentieth century, as the province of Ontario benefited from the spillover of U.S. industry in the northeastern states.

Latin American Investments

Latin American states did not undergo industrialization or enjoy economic development like the United States or Canada. When the colonies of Spain and Portugal became independent in the early nineteenth century, European investors from Britain, France, and Germany jumped at the chance to establish trading relationships in a region where they had long been prevented from investing. Both Central and South America offered attractive prospects for extracting raw materials such as wheat, beef, fish, and guano (bat dung—a critical source for

A contemporary photograph of the Metlac railway bridge in Mexico, constructed in 1903 during the rule of Porfirio Diaz.
George Rinhart/Corbis/Getty Images

fertilizer), and European investors were happy to supply the investment for railroads and other types of infrastructure necessary to bring raw materials to ports. Because Latin American elites retained control over local economies, European investors only needed to make sure their economic plans were attractive to them. And indeed, elites profited handsomely from European trade and investment and thus had little incentive to seek different economic policies or work toward industrialization. As a result, foreign investment and trade had more damaging effects in Latin America than in the United States or Canada. In fact, foreign investment in Latin America during this period has come to be known by scholars as "informal imperialism," meaning that foreign entities gain so much control of an economy that they are then able to exert political pressure on the governments in question as well.

British Investment British investors were particularly active in Latin America during the nineteenth century. Although they did not believe Latin American countries could offer attractive markets for British manufactured items, they were quite interested in their potential for producing raw materials. In Argentina, for example, British investors encouraged the development of cattle and sheep ranching. After the 1860s and the invention of refrigerated cargo ships, meat became Argentina's largest export and Britain its principal market. Because British investors controlled the industry at almost every stage; they also reaped the profits, and British business interests gained considerable control over the Argentine economy as a whole. Meanwhile, between 1880 and 1914, European migrants labored in the new export industries and contributed to the explosive growth of urban areas such as Buenos Aires: by 1914 the city's population exceeded 3.5 million. Although migrant laborers rarely shared in the profits controlled by elites, the domination of urban labor by European migrants represented yet another form of foreign influence in Latin American economic affairs.

Attempted Industrialization Latin American elites did make attempts to encourage industrialization in a few places, but these had limited success. The most notable of those efforts was when the dictatorial general Porfirio Díaz ruled Mexico (1876–1911). Díaz represented the interests of large landowners, wealthy merchants, and foreign investors. Under his rule, railroad tracks and telegraph lines connected all parts of Mexico, and the production of mineral resources surged. A small steel industry produced railroad track and construction materials, and entrepreneurs also established glass, chemical, and textile industries. The capital, Mexico City, underwent a transformation during the Díaz years: it acquired paved streets, streetcar lines, and electric streetlights. But the profits from Mexican enterprises did not support continuing industrial development. Instead, they went into the pockets of the Mexican elites and foreign investors who supported Díaz, while a growing and discontented urban working class seethed with resentment at low wages, long hours, and foreign managers. Even as agriculture, railroad construction,

and mining were booming, the standard of living for average Mexicans had begun to decline by the early twentieth century. Frustration with that state of affairs helps explain the sudden outbreak of violent revolution in 1910.

Latin American economies expanded rapidly in the late nineteenth century. Exports geared toward foreign markets drove that growth: copper and silver from Mexico, bananas and coffee from Central America, rubber and coffee from Brazil, beef and wheat from Argentina, copper from Chile, and tobacco and sugar from Cuba. Because foreign investors controlled the markets and their infrastructure, however, they were also able to keep prices for commodities low. Latin American economies were thus subject to decisions made in the interests of foreign investors, and unstable governments could do little in the face of strong foreign intervention. Controlled by the very elites who profited from foreign intervention at the expense of their citizens, Latin American governments helped account for the region's slower economic development, despite growth in industrial and export economies.

AMERICAN CULTURAL AND SOCIAL DIVERSITY

In his "Song of Myself" (1855), a poetic celebration of himself as well as the vast diversity of his nation, the U.S. poet Walt Whitman asked:

> Do I contradict myself?
> Very well then I contradict myself,
> (I am large, I contain multitudes.)

Much of the allure of the Americas derived from their vast spaces and diverse populations. The Americas were indeed large, and they did indeed contain multitudes. While diversity distinguished the Americas, that same diversity also provided abundant fuel for conflicts between ethnic groups, social classes, and those segregated into groups based on race and gender. The social and cultural diversity of American societies challenged their ability to achieve cultural cohesion as well as political unity and democratically inclusive states. The lingering legacies of European conquest, slavery, migration, and patriarchy highlighted contradictions between the Enlightenment ideals of freedom and equality and the realities of life for indigenous and African American peoples as well as recent migrants and women. American societies experienced abundant strife in the age of independence. In efforts to maintain their own position and preserve social stability, the dominant political forces in the Americas often repressed demands for recognition by dispossessed groups.

Societies in the United States

By the late nineteenth century, the United States had become a boisterous multicultural society—the most culturally diverse land of the Western Hemisphere—whose population included

Apache youths at the Carlisle Indian School in Pennsylvania, where Native American children were removed from their families in an attempt to assimilate them into the larger American society.
Historical/Corbis Historical/Getty Images

indigenous peoples, Euro-Americans African Americans, and growing numbers of migrants from Europe and Asia. Walt Whitman described the United States as "not merely a nation but a teeming nation of nations." Yet political and economic power rested almost exclusively with white male elites of European ancestry. The United States experienced tension and occasional conflict as members of various constituencies worked for dignity, prosperity, and a voice in society.

Native Peoples As they expanded to the west, Euro-American settlers and ranchers pushed indigenous peoples off their own lands and onto marginal tracts of land called reservations. Even though the reservations were supposed to be sovereign land for Native Americans, the U.S. government nevertheless permitted settlers and railroads to encroach on the reservations, which forced indigenous people onto ever smaller and less productive territories. In the latter half of the nineteenth century

A lithograph called "The First Vote" from *Harper's Weekly* in 1867. It depicts black Americans of several occupations— including an artisan, a businessman, and a Union Soldier—casting their votes for the first time in their lives.
Historical/Corbis Historical/Getty Images

the United States government embarked on a policy designed to reduce indigenous autonomy even further through laws and reforms aimed at forcibly assimilating tribes to American culture and destroying Native American cultural traditions. Some indigenous tribes on the plains, for example, had developed material cultures largely centered on the hunting of bison, or buffalo, and the skillful exploitation of those animal resources. Beginning in 1850 but accelerating after the Civil War, white migrants, railroad employees, hunters, and "wild west" men such as Buffalo Bill Cody shot and killed hundreds of thousands of bison, which deliberately exterminated the buffalo and the economy of the Plains Indians. Herds numbering at least fifteen million were reduced to a mere thousand by 1875.

Other U.S. actions also attempted to destroy Native Americans' communal traditions and cultural practices. The Dawes Severalty Act of 1887, for example, sought to lessen the influence

What's Left Out?

The practice of separating indigenous children from their parents was not just a United States policy. In fact, all of the white settler colonies—including the United States, Canada, and Australia—used child separation as a tool of colonial rule in the late nineteenth and early twentieth centuries. Although agents of these settler colonies sometimes learned from one another when implementing the practice of child separation, these policies largely originated within each colony as part of the logic of settler colonialism itself. One of the primary goals of settler colonies was to dispossess indigenous populations of their lands and then to repopulate them with settlers of European descent. Yet in spite of trying to accomplish this goal by battling with, murdering, and forcibly removing indigenous people, indigenous populations nevertheless persisted. By the late nineteenth century, this persistence led agents of the settler colonies to attempt to eradicate indigenous culture by the forcible and systematic assimilation of children. In Australia, aboriginal people were removed to isolated areas, where children were separated from their parents in segregated dormitories. In the United States, settlers founded one hundred and fifty-four boarding schools for Native American children by 1902, each located far from their home communities. In Canada, authorities studied the U.S. model and established a network of boarding schools for indigenous children. Once removed from their homes, children were taught to adopt the language and behavior of the settler culture in the hope that this would permanently eliminate their own cultures and customs. But indigenous people seldom gave up their children voluntarily. In fact, so many resisted that most were taken by force or the threat of force. In the United States, for example, authorities often withheld food rations on reservations until communities gave up their children. When thinking about this global practice of child separation, it is worth considering that the 1948 United Nations Convention on Genocide defined one of the methods of genocide as "forcibly transferring children of one group to another group."

Source: Margaret D. Jacobs, *White Mother to a Dark Race: Settler Colonialism, Maternalism, and the Removal of Indigenous Children in the American West and Australia, 1880–1940* (Lincoln: University of Nebraska Press, 2009).

of tribal culture by shifting land policies away from collective tribal reservations and toward individual tracts of land. Even more traumatic for Native Americans, government officials began a policy of removing indigenous children from their families and tribes and enrolling them in white-controlled boarding schools. These schools, such as the Carlisle Indian School and the Toledo Indian School, illustrated the extent to which white society sought to eliminate tribal influences and inculcate what they believed were Christian, U.S. values. Tribal languages as well as tribal dress and hair fashions were banned, further distancing the children from their cultures. Native Americans, however, resisted these policies designed to destroy their culture, often fleeing from boarding schools or refusing to agree to new governmental land policies. Indeed, in spite of these inhumane and concentrated efforts to deny them their heritage, Native American tribes managed not only to survive but to rebuild their communities over the following decades.

Freed African Americans The Civil War ended slavery, but it did not bring about equality for formerly enslaved African Americans and their descendants. In an effort to establish a place for formerly enslaved people in American society, northern forces sent armies of occupation to the southern states and forced them to undergo a program of social and political **Reconstruction** (1867–1877). Reconstruction extended civil rights to formerly enslaved people and legislated that black men would be able to vote. Black and white citizens in southern states elected biracial governments

for the first time in U.S. history, and formerly enslaved people began to participate actively in the political affairs of the republic.

After Reconstruction, however, the armies of occupation went back north, and a violent backlash soon dismantled the program's reforms. Reconstruction had not included land grants or other economic support for formerly enslaved people, so many had to work as sharecroppers for former owners of enslaved people. Under those circumstances it was relatively easy for white southerners to take away the political and civil liberties that former enslaved people had gained under Reconstruction. By the turn of the century, U.S. blacks faced violence and intimidation when they tried to vote. Southern states fashioned a rigidly segregated society that deprived the

How the Past Shapes the Future

The Birth of Nationalism

The most powerful group of people in the United States during the nineteenth century—white males of European ancestry—defined the nation in terms of the legacies of the American revolution and a common western European heritage. This group often resisted incorporating other peoples from different traditions into the nation, including former enslaved people, immigrants from Asia and southern Europe, and Native Americans. Think about the methods that people of western European ancestry used to exclude people from other traditions from full participation in national life, and about the consequences of such exclusionary practices on the development of the United States from the nineteenth century all the way to the present. Why do ideas about who belongs in the nation have the potential to generate so much conflict?

African American population of educational, economic, and political opportunities. Although freedom was better than slavery, it was far different from the hopeful visions of the enslaved people who had won their emancipation.

Women Even before the Civil War, a small but growing women's movement had emerged in the United States. At the **Seneca Falls Convention** in 1848, feminists—people who advocate for women's rights based on equality of the sexes—issued a "declaration of sentiments" modeled on the Declaration of Independence, and they demanded equal political and economic rights for U.S. women:

> Now, in view of this entire disenfranchisement of one-half the people of this country, their social and religious degradation—in view of the unjust laws above mentioned, and because women do feel themselves aggrieved, oppressed, and fraudulently deprived of their most sacred rights, we insist that they have immediate admission to all the rights and privileges which belong to them as citizens of the United States.

Some groups of women fought for equal rights throughout the nineteenth century, and new opportunities for education and employment slowly began to offer alternatives to marriage and domesticity. Women's colleges, reform activism, and professional industrial jobs allowed some women to pursue careers instead of marriage. Yet abundant economic and political opportunities for women awaited the twentieth century, and even these mainly benefited white women rather than women of color.

Migrants Between 1840 and 1914 some twenty-five million European migrants landed on American shores, and by the late nineteenth century most of them hailed from southern and eastern European countries. Migrants introduced new foods, music, dances, holidays, sports, and languages to U.S. society and contributed to the cultural diversity of the Western Hemisphere. Yet white, native-born citizens of the United States whose descendants came from western Europe often did not welcome the newer arrivals. Distaste for foreigners frequently resulted in hostility to the migrants who moved into the expanding industrial cities. Migrants and their families tended to concentrate in certain districts, such as Little Italy and Chinatown. They did this partly out of choice because they preferred neighbors with familiar cultural traditions, but partly also because native-born citizens discouraged migrants from moving into other neighborhoods. Concerns about growing numbers of migrants with different cultural and social traditions eventually led to the exclusion of new arrivals from Asia: the U.S. government ordered a complete halt to migration from China in 1882 and from Japan in 1907.

Canadian Cultural Contrasts

Ethnic Diversity British and French settlers each viewed themselves as Canada's founding people. This cleavage, which

This nineteenth-century engraving provides an idealized representation of European migrants, many of them women and children, arriving in New York under the gaze of the Statue of Liberty.
Stefano Bianchetti/Corbis/Getty Images

profoundly influenced Canadian political development, masked much greater cultural and ethnic diversity in Canada. French and British settlers displaced indigenous peoples, who remain a significant minority of Canada's population today. Slavery likewise left a mark on Canada. Slavery was legal in the British Empire until 1833, and many early settlers brought enslaved people to Canada. After the 1830s, enslaved people who escaped from the United States also reached Canada by way of the Underground Railroad. Black people in Canada were free but not equal, segregated and isolated from the political and cultural mainstream. Chinese migrants also came to Canada; attracted by gold rushes such as the Fraser River rush of 1858 and by opportunities to work on the Canadian Pacific Railway in the 1880s, Chinese migrants lived mostly in segregated Chinatowns in the cities of British Columbia, and like black people they had little voice in public affairs. In the late nineteenth and early twentieth centuries, waves of migrants brought even greater ethnic diversity to Canada. Between 1896 and 1914

SOURCES FROM THE PAST

The Meaning of Freedom

Once an enslaved man in Tennessee on the plantation of Colonel P. H. Anderson, Jourdan Anderson gained his freedom in 1864, before the conclusion of the Civil War. He and his family then relocated to Dayton, Ohio. The letter below is a response to a letter from Colonel Anderson, who asked Jourdan to return to the Tennessee plantation. Jourdan's thoughtful reply, tinged with sarcastic humor, underscores his sense of dignity and self-worth.

Dayton, Ohio, August 7, 1865

To my Old Master, Col. P. H. Anderson, Big Spring, Tennessee

Sir: I got your letter and was glad to find that you had not forgotten Jourdan, and that you wanted me to come back and live with you again, promising to do better for me than anybody else can. I have often felt uneasy about you. I thought the Yankees would have hung you long before this for harboring Rebs they found at your house. I suppose they never heard about your going to Col. Martin's to kill the Union soldier that was left by his company in their stable. Although you shot at me twice before I left you, I did not want to hear of your being hurt and I am glad you are still living. . . . I would have gone back to see you all when I was working in the Nashville Hospital, but one of the neighbors told me Henry intended to shoot me if he ever got the chance.

> What indications does Jourdan Anderson give here about the kind of treatment he received from Colonel Anderson while he was enslaved?

I want to know particularly what the good chance is you propose to give me. I am doing tolerably well here; I get $25 a month, with victuals and clothing; have a comfortable home for Mandy (the folks here call her Mrs. Anderson) and the children, Milly, Jane, and Grundy, go to school and are learning well; the teacher says Grundy has a head for a preacher. They go to Sunday-School, and Mandy and me attend church regularly. We are kindly treated. . . . Now, if you will write and say what wages you will give me, I will be better able to decide whether it would be to my advantage to move back again.

As to my freedom, which you say I can have, there is nothing to be gained on that score, as I got my free-papers in 1864 from the Provost-Marshal-General of the Department at Nashville. Mandy says she would be afraid to go back without some proof that you are sincerely disposed to treat us justly and kindly—and we have concluded to test your sincerity by asking you to send us our wages for the time we served you. This will make us forget and forgive old scores, and rely on your justice and friendship in the future. I served you faithfully for thirty-two years, and Mandy twenty years, at $25 a month for me, and $2 a week for Mandy. Our earnings would amount to $11,680. . . . Please send the money by Adams Express, in care of V. Winters, esq., Dayton, Ohio. If you fail to pay us for faithful labors in the past we can have little faith in your promises in the future. We trust the good Maker has opened your eyes to the wrongs which you and your fathers have done to me and my fathers, in making us toil for you for generations without recompense. . . . Surely there will be a day of reckoning for those who defraud the laborer of his hire.

> Do you think Jourdan Anderson was serious about this request or that he made it to make a point about how much the labor of enslaved people was worth?

In answering this letter please state if there would be any safety for my Milly and Jane, who are now grown up and both good looking girls. . . . I would rather stay here and starve and die if it come to that than have my girls brought to shame by the violence and wickedness of their young masters. You will also please state if there has been any schools opened for the colored children in your neighborhood, the desire of my life now is to give my children an education, and have them form virtuous habits.

From your old servant, Jourdan Anderson.

P. S.—Say howdy to George Carter, and thank him for taking the pistol from you when you were shooting at me.

For Further Reflection

■ What does Colonel Anderson's request for Jourdan Anderson to return tell us about the colonel's understanding of what slavery had been like? What does Jourdan Anderson's response tell us about what it meant to him to be free?

■ In what clever ways does Jourdan Anderson test the seriousness of his former owner's offer of employment, and what does his approach say about the meaning of black freedom?

Source: "Letter from a Freedman to His Old Master," *New York Daily Tribune,* 22 August 1865, p. 7.

three million migrants from Britain, the United States, and eastern Europe arrived in Canada.

Despite the diversity of Canada's population, communities descended from British and French settlers dominated Canadian society, and conflict between the two communities was the most prominent source of ethnic tension throughout the nineteenth and twentieth centuries. After 1867, as British Canadians led the effort to settle the Northwest Territories and incorporate them into the Dominion, frictions between the two groups intensified. Westward expansion brought British Canadian settlers and cultivators into conflict with French Canadian fur traders and lumberjacks. The fur traders in particular often lived on the margins between European and indigenous societies. They frequently married or lived with indigenous women, giving rise to the métis, individuals of mixed European and indigenous ancestry.

The Métis and Louis Riel A major outbreak of civil strife took place in the 1870s and 1880s. Indigenous peoples and métis had moved west throughout the nineteenth century to preserve their land and trading rights, but the drive of British Canadians to the west threatened them. **Louis Riel** (1844–1885) emerged as the leader of the métis and indigenous peoples of western Canada. A métis himself, Riel abandoned his studies for the priesthood in Montreal and returned to his home in the Red River Settlement (in the southern part of modern Manitoba). Sensitive to his community's concern that the Canadian government threatened local land rights, Riel assumed the presidency of a provisional government in 1870. He led his troops in capturing Fort Garry (modern Winnipeg) and negotiated the incorporation of the province of Manitoba into the Canadian Dominion. Canadian government officials and

troops soon outlawed his government and forced Riel into years of exile, during which he wandered through the United States and Quebec, even suffering confinement in asylums.

Work on the Canadian Pacific Railroad in the 1880s renewed the threat of white settlement to indigenous and métis society. The métis asked Riel to lead resistance to the railroad and British Canadian settlement. In 1885 he organized a military force of métis and indigenous peoples in the Saskatchewan river country and led an insurrection known as the **Northwest Rebellion.** Canadian forces quickly subdued the makeshift army, and government authorities executed Riel for treason.

Although the Northwest Rebellion never had a chance of success, the execution of Riel nonetheless reverberated throughout Canadian history. French Canadians took it as an indication of the state's readiness to subdue individuals who were culturally distinct and politically opposed to the drive for a nation dominated by British Canadian elites. In the very year when completion of the transcontinental railroad signified for some the beginnings of Canadian national unity, Riel's execution foreshadowed a long term of cultural conflict between Canadians of British, French, and indigenous ancestry.

Ethnicity, Identity, and Gender in Latin America

The heritage of Spanish and Portuguese colonialism and the legacy of slavery inclined Latin American societies toward the establishment of hierarchical distinctions based on ethnicity and color. At the top of society stood the creoles, individuals of European ancestry born in the Americas, while indigenous peoples, former enslaved people, and their descendants occupied the lowest rungs of the social ladder. In between were various groups of mixed ancestry, which were known by names

A contemporary depiction of the Battle of Cut Knife during the Northwest Rebellion led by Louis Riel. Although the rebellion was defeated, Cut Knife was an early victory for Riel's forces. The History Collection/ Alamy Stock Photo

such as mestizos, mulattoes, zambos, and castizos. Although most Latin American states ended the legal recognition of these groups after independence, the distinctions themselves persisted and limited the opportunities available to peoples of indigenous, African, or mixed ancestry.

Migration and Cultural Diversity Large-scale migration brought added cultural diversity to Latin America in the nineteenth century. Indentured laborers who went from parts of Asia to Peru, Brazil, Cuba, and other Caribbean destinations carried with them many of their native cultural practices. When their numbers were relatively small, as in the case of Chinese migrants to Cuba, they mostly intermarried and assimilated into the working classes without leaving much foreign influence on the societies they joined. When they were relatively more numerous, however, as in the case of Indian migrants to Trinidad and Tobago, they formed distinctive communities in which they spoke their native languages, prepared foods from their homelands, and observed their inherited cultural and social traditions. Migration of European workers to Argentina brought a lively diversity to the capital of Buenos Aires, which was perhaps the most cosmopolitan city of nineteenth-century Latin America. With its broad avenues, smart boutiques, and handsome buildings graced with wrought iron, Buenos Aires enjoyed a reputation as "the Paris of the Americas."

Latin American intellectuals seeking cultural identity usually saw themselves either as heirs of Europe or as products of the American environment. One spokesperson who identified with Europe was the Argentine president **Domingo Faustino Sarmiento** (1811–1888). Sarmiento despised the rule of caudillos that had emerged after independence and worked for the development of a society based on European values. In his widely read book *Facundo: Civilization and Barbarism* (1845), Sarmiento argued that it was necessary for Buenos Aires to bring discipline to the disorderly Argentine countryside. Deeply influenced by the Enlightenment, he characterized books, ideas, law, education, and art as products of cities, and he argued that only when cities dominated the countryside would social stability and genuine liberty be possible.

Gauchos Sarmiento admired the bravery and independence of Argentina's *gauchos* ("cowboys"), but he thought it necessary that urban residents rather than ranchers make society's crucial decisions. Most, but not all, gauchos were of mixed race, but race was not the determining factor in becoming a gaucho. Instead, anyone who adopted gaucho ways became a gaucho, and gaucho society acquired an ethnic egalitarianism rarely found elsewhere in Latin America. Gauchos were most prominent in the Argentine pampas, but their cultural practices linked them to the cowboys, or vaqueros, found throughout the Americas. As pastoralists herding cattle and horses on the pampas, gauchos stood apart from both the indigenous peoples and the growing urban and agricultural elites who

An 1868 photograph of an Argentinian gaucho dressed in typical gear.
Historic Collection/Alamy Stock Photo

gradually displaced them with large landholdings and cattle ranches that spread to the pampas.

The gauchos led independent and self-sufficient lives that appealed broadly to many Latin Americans who lived in hierarchical societies. Legend had it that gauchos lived off their own skills and needed only their horses to survive. They dressed distinctively, with sashed trousers, ponchos, and boots. Countless songs and poems lauded their courage, skills, and romantic allure. Yet independence and caudillo rule disrupted gaucho life as the cowboys increasingly entered armies, either voluntarily or by force, and as settled agriculture and ranches surrounded by barbed wire enclosed the pampas. The gauchos did not leave the pampas without resistance.

Domingo Faustino Sarmiento
(doh-MING-oh fow-STEEN-oh sahr-MYEN-toh)

gauchos (GOW-chohs)

668 Chapter 30 ■ The Americas in the Age of Independence

The poet José Hernandez offered a romanticized vision of the gaucho life and protested its decline in his epic poem *The Gaucho Martín Fierro* (1873). Hernandez conveyed the pride of gauchos, particularly those who resisted assimilation into Euro-American society, by having Martín Fierro proclaim his independence and assert his intention to stay that way:

> I owe nothin' to nobody;
> I don't ask for shelter, or give it;
> and from now on, nobody
> better try to lead me around by a rope.

Nevertheless, by the late nineteenth century, gauchos were mostly echoes of the Latin American past.

Male Domination Even more than in the United States and Canada, male domination was a central characteristic of Latin American society in the nineteenth century. Women could not vote or hold office, nor could they work or manage estates without permission from their male guardians. In rural areas, women were liable to rough treatment by men steeped in the values of *machismo*—a social ethic that honored male strength, courage, aggressiveness, assertiveness, and cunning. A few women voiced their discontent with male domination and machismo. In her poem "To Be Born a Man" (1887), for example, the Bolivian poet Adela Zamudio lamented bitterly that talented women could not vote, but ignorant men could, just by learning how to sign their names. Although Latin American states had not yet generated a strong women's movement, they did begin to expand educational opportunities for girls and young women after the mid-nineteenth century. In large cities most girls received some formal schooling, and women usually filled teaching positions in the public schools that proliferated throughout Latin America in the late nineteenth century.

Female Activism Women did carve spaces for themselves outside or alongside the male world of machismo, and this was especially true in the home and in the marketplace, where Latin American women exerted great influence. In the early twentieth century, women also served in conjunction with men in the Mexican revolution, most famously as Zapatistas, or followers of Emiliano Zapata. Many women supporting Zapata labored within the domestic realm to provide food for the soldiers, but others became soldiers and officers themselves. Although those women who became *soldaderas* (female soldiers or supporters of soldiers) demonstrated the most extreme forms of activism during the Mexican revolution, Mexican women on the whole made major contributions to the success of the revolution and shared in the radical spirit of change that characterized much of early-twentieth-century Latin America.

CONCLUSION

After gaining independence from European colonial powers, the states of the Western Hemisphere worked to build stable and prosperous societies. The independent American states faced difficult challenges—including vast territories, diverse populations, social tensions, and cultural differences—as they sought to construct viable societies based partly on the Enlightenment principles of freedom, equality, and constitutional government. People in the United States and Canada built large federal societies in North America, whereas people in Latin America built a series of smaller states. Encounters, at times violent, between the various groups in the Americas and their varying traditions, proved a significant challenge to the emerging states in the Western Hemisphere. The United States in particular was an expansive, colonial society, absorbing Texas, California, and the northern territories of Mexico while extending its authority from the Atlantic to the Pacific Ocean. Throughout the hemisphere, descendants of European settlers violently conquered indigenous American peoples and built societies dominated by Euro-American peoples. They established agricultural economies, exploited natural resources, and in some places launched processes of industrialization. Millions of people from Europe and Asia migrated to the Americas, contributing not only to American cultural diversity but also to the transformations in labor practices caused by the abolition of slavery and the rise of industry. All American states experienced tensions arising from social, economic, cultural, and ethnic differences, which led occasionally to violent civil conflict and often to smoldering resentments and grievances. While the making of independent American societies was not a smooth process, it nevertheless reflected the increasing interdependence of all the world's peoples.

STUDY TERMS

Abraham Lincoln (649)
Antonio López de
  Santa Anna (655)
battle of the
  Little Bighorn (648)
Benito Juárez (655)
British North America
  Act of 1867 (652)
Canadian Pacific
  Railroad (659)
caudillos (654)
Domingo Faustino
  Sarmiento (667)

Dominion of Canada (652)
Durham Report (652)
Emancipation
  Proclamation (650)
Emiliano Zapata (655)
Francisco (Pancho) Villa (655)
gauchos (667)
Indian Removal Act
  of 1830 (647)
John A. Macdonald (652)
Juan Manuel de Rosas (654)
Louis Riel (666)
machismo (668)

manifest destiny (647)
Mexican-American War (648)
National Policy (659)
Northwest Rebellion (666)
Porfirio Díaz (655)
railroad time (659)
Reconstruction (663)

Seneca Falls Convention (664)
soldaderas (668)
Trail of Tears (647)
U.S. Civil War (650)
War of 1812 (652)
Wounded Knee (648)

FOR FURTHER READING

David Barry Gaspar and Darlene Clark Hine, eds. *Beyond Bondage: Free Women of Color in the Americas*. Chicago, 2004. Collection of essays on free black women and their unique abilities to negotiate social and legal institutions in the era of slavery.

Pekka Hämäläinen. *The Comanche Empire*. New Haven, 2008. An ambitiously revisionist history that challenges the accepted understanding of colonial America and westward expansion.

Tom Holm. *The Great Confusion in Indian Affairs: Native Americans and Whites in the Progressive Era*. Austin, 2005. Study of Native American resistance to the American government's attempts at subjugation.

Patricia Nelson Limerick. *The Legacy of Conquest: The Unbroken Past of the American West*. New York, 1987. A provocative work exploring the influences of race, class, and gender in the conquest of the American west.

Adam McKeown. *Melancholy Order: Asian Migration and the Globalization of Borders*. New York, 2008. Documents the global scale of Asian migration in the nineteenth and twentieth centuries and argues that it triggered exclusionary border policies in the United States and Europe.

J. R. Miller. *Skyscrapers Hide the Heavens: A History of Indian-White Relations in Canada*. 3rd ed. Toronto, 2000. An important study of Canadian policies toward indigenous peoples.

Desmond Morton. *A Short History of Canada*. 6th ed. Toronto, 2006. This is a well-balanced, popular history of Canada.

Paul Ortiz. *An African American and Latinx History of the United States*. Boston, 2018. A radical revisionist exploration of U.S. history from the perspective of marginalized people in a global context.

Robert L. Scheina. *Latin American Wars*. Vol. 1: *The Age of the Caudillos, 1791–1899*. Washington, D.C., 2003. By examining the wars of independence, this work uncovers the reasons behind the failures of Latin American state building.

Allison Sneider. *Suffragists in an Imperial Age: US Expansion and the Woman Question, 1870–1929*. Oxford, 2008. Explores the women's suffrage movement in the United States and U.S. imperialism as intertwined and inseparable phenomena.

ZOOMING IN ON TRADITIONS AND ENCOUNTERS

"Heavenly King" Hong Xiuquan, Empress Dowager Cixi, and Qing Reform

China's Empress Dowager Cixi in 1903. Beginning her political career as a concubine in the harem of the Xianfeng emperor, she developed into a powerful and charismatic figure who became the de facto ruler of the Manchu Qing dynasty in China for over forty years, from 1861 until her death in 1908.

Art Images/Chinese School/Getty Images

Hong **Xiuquan,** the third son of a poor family, grew up in a farming village in southern China about 50 kilometers (31 miles) from Guangzhou. Although he was arrogant and irritable, he showed intellectual promise. His neighbors made him village teacher so that he could study and prepare for the civil service examinations, the principal avenue to government employment, because a position in the Qing bureaucracy would bring honor and wealth to both his family and his village. Between 1828 and 1837, Hong took the exams three times but failed to obtain even the lowest degree. This outcome was not surprising because thousands of candidates competed for degrees while only a few obtained one. But the disappointment was too much for Hong. He suffered an emotional collapse, lapsed into a delirium that lasted about forty days, and experienced visions.

Upon recovering from his breakdown, Hong resumed his position as village teacher and studied to take the civil service examinations again. After failing yet again in 1843, Hong began studying the works of a Chinese missionary who explained the

Xiuquan (shee-OH-chew-ahn)

basic elements of Christianity. As he pondered the religious tracts, Hong came to believe that during his illness he had visited heaven and learned from God that he was the younger brother of Jesus Christ. He believed further that God had revealed to him that his destiny was to reform China and pave the way for the heavenly kingdom. Inspired by these convictions, Hong baptized himself and worked to build a community of disciples.

Hong's personal religious vision soon evolved into a political program: Hong believed that God had charged him with the establishment of a new order, one that necessitated the destruction of the **Qing** dynasty, which had ruled China since 1644. In 1847 he emerged as the leader of the Society of God Worshipers, a religious group recently founded by his own disciples, whose supporters were poor peasants and miners from Guangxi province in southern China. In 1850, Hong led about ten thousand of these followers in rebellion against the Qing dynasty. On his thirty-seventh birthday, 11 January 1851, he assumed the title of "Heavenly King" and proclaimed his own dynasty, the Taiping tianguo ("Heavenly Kingdom of Great Peace"). Hong's followers, known as the Taipings, quickly grew from a ragtag band to a disciplined and zealous army of over one million men and women who nearly toppled the Qing dynasty. The Taiping rebellion lasted until 1864, and at its height included two million followers. Although the Taipings were eventually defeated by Qing dynasty forces under the command of the Dowager Empress **Cixi**, the rebellion—which claimed at least twenty million lives—pointed to massive turmoil within Chinese society and deep dissatisfaction with Qing rule. Given Hong's inspiration from Christianity, the Taiping rebellion also signaled the growing importance of encounters with western ideas, influence, and interference in nineteenth-century China.

Qing (ching)
Taiping (TEYE-pihng)
Cixi (tsuh-shee)

CHAPTER OVERVIEW

China was not the only place that faced serious turmoil in the nineteenth century: the Ottoman Empire, the Russian Empire, and Tokugawa Japan also experienced similar problems in this period. One problem common to the four societies was military weakness that left them vulnerable to foreign interference. The Ottoman, Russian, Qing, and Tokugawa armies all fought wars or engaged in military confrontations with the nations of western Europe and the United States in the nineteenth century, and all discovered suddenly and unexpectedly that industrialization had allowed their rivals to develop far more effective military weaponry than they now commanded. The result was a new power dynamic in which the industrialized states increasingly sought to impose their will on states that had not yet industrialized. Sometimes this meant that industrialized states seized territories and conquered them by force. Often, however, Euro-American states used force or the threat of force to extract favorable economic arrangements with their weaker rivals. These arrangements allowed capitalists from industrialized states to profit enormously at the expense of the weaker societies.

Other problems common to Tokugawa Japan and the Ottoman, Russian, and Qing empires were internal, including population pressure, declining agricultural productivity, famine, falling government revenue, and corruption at all

CHRONOLOGY	
1805–1848	Reign of Muhammad Ali in Egypt
1808–1839	Reign of Sultan Mahmud II
1814–1864	Life of Taiping leader Hong Xiuquan
1839–1842	Opium War
1839–1876	Tanzimat era
1850–1864	Taiping rebellion
1853	Arrival of Commodore Perry in Japan
1853–1856	Crimean War
1855–1881	Reign of Tsar Alexander II
1860–1895	Self-Strengthening Movement
1861	Emancipation of the Russian serfs
1868	Meiji restoration
1876	Promulgation of the Ottoman constitution
1889	Promulgation of the Meiji constitution
1894–1917	Reign of Tsar Nicholas II
1898	Hundred Days reforms
1900	Boxer rebellion
1904–1905	Russo-Japanese War
1905	Revolution of 1905 in Russia
1908–1918	Young Turk era

levels of government. Each experienced serious domestic turmoil, especially during the second half of the nineteenth century, as peasants mounted rebellions, dissidents struggled for reform, and political factions fought among themselves or conspired to organize coups. Moreover, when leaders of the four societies were unable to respond effectively to domestic strife, this sometimes provided western European powers and the United States with an excuse to intervene to protect their business interests.

By the late nineteenth century, leaders of the Ottoman Empire, the Russian Empire, Qing China, and Tokugawa Japan recognized that their societies were at a critical crossroads: they could either institute reforms that would enable them to compete with industrial states, or they could continue to be increasingly dominated by them. Thus, reformers in all four societies promoted plans to introduce written constitutions, limit the authority of rulers, make governments responsive to the needs and desires of the people, guarantee equality before the law, restructure educational systems, and begin processes of industrialization. Many reformers had traveled in Europe and the United States, where they experienced constitutional government and industrial society firsthand, and they sought to remodel their own societies along the lines of the industrial states.

Vigorous reform movements emerged in all four territories, but they had very different results. In the Ottoman Empire, the Russian Empire, and Qing China, ruling elites and wealthy classes opposed changes that might threaten their status. Reform in those three territories was halting and tentative, and by the early twentieth century the Ottoman, Romanov, and Qing dynasties were on the verge of collapse. In Japan, however reform, was much more thorough. By the early twentieth century, Japan was an emerging industrial power poised to expand its influence in the larger world.

THE WEAKENING OF THE OTTOMAN EMPIRE

During the eighteenth century the Ottoman Empire experienced military reverses and challenges to its rule. By the early nineteenth century, the Ottoman state could no longer ward off extensive European economic interference or prevent territorial dismemberment. As Ottoman officials launched reforms to regenerate imperial vigor, Egypt and other north African provinces declared their independence, and European states seized territories in the northern and western parts of the Ottoman Empire. At the same time, pressure from ethnic, religious, and nationalist groups threatened to fragment the empire from within. By the late nineteenth century, the once-powerful realm found that its sovereignty was now severely compromised by the same European powers that exploited its economy.

The Sources of Ottoman Weakness

Military Difficulties By the late seventeenth century, the Ottoman Empire had reached the limits of its expansion. In the late seventeenth and eighteenth centuries, Ottoman armies suffered humiliating defeats on the battlefield, especially at the hands of Austrian and Russian foes. Part of the reason for these defeats was that Ottoman forces had begun to lag behind their rivals in terms of strategy, tactics, weaponry, and training. Equally serious was a breakdown in the discipline of the elite Janissary corps (discussed in chapter 27), which had served as the backbone of the imperial armed forces since the fifteenth century. The **Janissaries** repeatedly masterminded palace coups during the seventeenth and eighteenth centuries and by the nineteenth century had become a powerful political force within the Ottoman state. The Janissaries neglected their military training and turned a blind eye to advances in weapons technology. As its military capacity declined, the Ottoman realm became vulnerable to its more powerful neighbors.

Loss of military power translated into reduced effectiveness of the central government, which was losing power in the provinces to its own officials. By the early nineteenth century, semi-independent governors and local notables had formed private armies of mercenaries and enslaved peoples to support the sultan in Istanbul in return for recognition of autonomy. Increasingly these independent rulers also turned fiscal and administrative institutions to their own interests, collecting taxes for

By the latter part of the nineteenth century, European imperialism directly affected the fortunes of the Ottoman Empire. This undated political cartoon shows England as a lion and Russia as a bear threatening Turkey (shown as a turkey). The illustration is labeled "Be my ally, or I'll give you the worst thrashing you ever had in your life."
Bettmann/Getty Images

themselves and sending only nominal payments to the imperial treasury, thus depriving the central state of revenue.

Territorial Losses The Ottoman government managed to maintain its authority in Anatolia (present-day Turkey), the heart of the empire, as well as in Iraq, but it suffered serious territorial losses elsewhere, especially in the nineteenth century. Russian forces took over poorly defended territories in the Caucasus and in central Asia, and the Austrian Empire nibbled away at the western frontiers. Nationalist uprisings forced Ottoman rulers to recognize the independence of Balkan provinces, notably Greece (1830) and Serbia (1867).

Most significant, however, was the loss of Egypt. In 1798 the ambitious French general Napoleon invaded Egypt in hopes of using it as a springboard for an attack on the British Empire in India. His campaign was a miserable failure: Napoleon had to abandon his army and sneak back to France, where he proceeded to overthrow the Directory. But the invasion sparked turmoil in Egypt, as local elites battled to seize power after

Napoleon's departure. The ultimate victor was the energetic general **Muhammad Ali,** who built a powerful army modeled on European forces and ruled Egypt from 1805 to 1848. He drafted peasants to serve as infantry soldiers, and he hired French and Italian officers to train his troops. He also launched a program of industrialization, concentrating on cotton textiles and armaments. Although he remained technically subordinate to the Ottoman sultan, by 1820 it was clear that he had established himself as the effective ruler of Egypt, which was the most powerful land in the Muslim world. In 1839 he even invaded Syria and Anatolia, threatening to capture Istanbul and topple the Ottoman state. Indeed, the Ottoman dynasty survived only because British forces intervened out of fear that Ottoman collapse would result in a sudden and dangerous expansion of Russian influence. Nevertheless, Muhammad Ali made Egypt an essentially autonomous region within the Ottoman Empire.

Economic Difficulties Economic problems aggravated the military and political problems of the Ottoman state.

MAP 31.1 Territorial losses of the Ottoman Empire, 1800–1923.

Compare the borders of the Ottoman Empire in 1800 with what was left of the empire in 1914.

What might have been the strategic value of the remaining Ottoman territories?

The volume of trade passing through the Ottoman Empire declined throughout the later seventeenth and eighteenth centuries, as European merchants increasingly bypassed Ottoman territories in the Mediterranean to trade directly with their counterparts in India and China. By the eighteenth century the focus of European trade had shifted to the Atlantic Ocean basin, where the Ottomans had no presence at all. Meanwhile, as European producers began to industrialize in the eighteenth and nineteenth centuries, their textiles and manufactured goods began to flow into the Ottoman Empire. Because those items were inexpensive and high-quality products, they were in high demand by Ottoman consumers. At the same time, they placed considerable pressure on Ottoman artisans and crafts workers, who frequently led urban riots to protest foreign imports. Ottoman exports consisted largely of raw materials such as grain, cotton, hemp, indigo, and opium, but they did not offset the value of imported European manufactures. Gradually, the Ottoman Empire moved toward fiscal insolvency and financial dependency. After the middle of the nineteenth century, economic development in the Ottoman Empire depended heavily on foreign loans, as European capital financed the construction of railroads, utilities, and mining enterprises. Interest payments on foreign loans grew to the point that they consumed more than half of the empire's revenues. In 1882 the Ottoman state was unable to pay interest on its loans and had no choice but to accept administration of its debts by Europeans.

The Capitulations Nothing symbolized foreign interference more than the **capitulations,** agreements that exempted European visitors from Ottoman law and provided European powers with extraterritoriality—the right to exercise jurisdiction over their own citizens according to their own laws. The practice dated back to the sixteenth century, when Ottoman sultans signed capitulation treaties to avoid the burden of administering justice for communities of foreign merchants. By the nineteenth century, however, Ottoman officials regarded the capitulations as humiliating intrusions on their sovereignty. Capitulations also served as instruments of economic power by European businesspeople who established tax-exempt banks and commercial enterprises in the Ottoman Empire, and they permitted foreign governments to levy duties on goods sold in Ottoman ports.

By the early twentieth century, the Ottoman state lacked the resources to maintain its costly

Sultan Abdül Hamid II (1842–1918) ruled the Ottoman Empire from 1876 to 1909, when the Young Turks deposed him and sent him into exile.
Universal History Archive/UIG/Shutterstock

bureaucracy. Expenditures exceeded revenues, and the state experienced growing difficulty paying the salaries of its employees in the palace household, the military, and the religious hierarchy. Declining incomes led to reduced morale, recruitment difficulties, and a rise in corruption. Increased taxation designed to offset revenue losses only led to increased exploitation of the peasantry and a decline in agricultural production. The Ottoman Empire was in trouble and it needed a major restructuring to survive.

Reform and Reorganization

In response to recurring and deepening crises, Ottoman leaders launched a series of reforms designed to strengthen and preserve the state. Reform efforts began as early as the seventeenth century, when sultans sought to limit taxation, increase agricultural production, and end official corruption. Reform continued in the eighteenth century, as **Sultan Selim III** (reigned 1789–1807) embarked on a program to remodel his army along the lines of European forces. But the establishment of this new fighting force, trained by European instructors and equipped with modern weapons, threatened the elite Janissary corps, which reacted violently by rising in revolt, killing the new troops, and locking up the sultan. When Selim's successor tried to revive the new military force, rampaging Janissaries killed all male members of the dynasty except one, Selim's cousin **Mahmud II,** who became sultan (reigned 1808–1839).

The Reforms of Mahmud II
The increasing interventions by European powers and the separatist ambitions of local rulers persuaded Mahmud to launch his own reform program. Given what had happened to his predecessors, Mahmud tried to ensure that his reforms were not perceived as dangerous innovations but, rather, as a restoration of the traditional Ottoman military. Nevertheless, his proposal for a new European-style army in 1826 brought him into conflict with the Janissaries. When the Janissaries mutinied in protest, Mahmud had them massacred by troops loyal to the sultan. That incident cleared the way for a series of reforms that unfolded during the last thirteen years of Mahmud's reign.

Mahmud's program remodeled Ottoman institutions along western European lines. Highest priority went to the creation of a more effective army. European drillmasters dressed Ottoman soldiers in European-style uniforms and instructed them in European weapons and tactics. Ottoman recruits studied at military and engineering schools and learned European curricula. Mahmud's reforms also went beyond military affairs. His government created a system of secondary education for boys to facilitate the transition from mosque schools, which provided most primary education, to newly established scientific, technical, and military academies. Mahmud also tried to transfer power from traditional elites to himself and his cabinet by taxing rural landlords, abolishing the system of military land grants, and undermining the ulama, the Islamic leadership. To make his authority more effective, the sultan established European-style ministries, constructed new roads, built telegraph lines, and inaugurated a postal service. By the time of Mahmud's death in 1839, the Ottoman Empire had shrunk in size, but it was also more manageable and stronger than it had been since the early seventeenth century.

Legal and Educational Reform Continuing defeats on the battlefield and the rise of separatist movements among subject peoples prompted the ruling classes to undertake more radical restructuring of the Ottoman state after Mahmud's reign. The tempo of reform increased rapidly during the **Tanzimat** ("reorganization") **era** (1839–1876). Once again, the army was a principal target of reform efforts, but legal and educational reforms also had wide-ranging implications for Ottoman society. In designing their program, Tanzimat reformers drew considerable inspiration from Enlightenment thought and the constitutional foundations of western European states.

Tanzimat reformers attacked Ottoman law with the aim of making it acceptable to Europeans so they could have the capitulations lifted and recover Ottoman sovereignty. Using the French legal system as a guide, reformers issued a commercial code (1850), a penal code (1858), a maritime code (1863), and a new civil code (1870–1876). Tanzimat reformers also issued decrees designed to safeguard the rights of subjects. Key among them were measures that guaranteed public trials, rights of privacy, and equality before the law for all Ottoman subjects, whether Muslim or not. Matters pertaining to marriage and divorce still fell under religious law. But because state courts administered the new laws, legal reform undermined the ulama and enhanced the authority of the Ottoman state. Educational reforms also undermined the ulama, who controlled religious education for Muslims. A comprehensive plan for educational reform, introduced in 1846, provided for a complete system of primary and secondary schools leading to university-level instruction, all under the supervision of the state ministry of education. A still more ambitious plan, inaugurated in 1869, provided for free and compulsory primary education.

Opposition to the Tanzimat Although reform and reorganization strengthened Ottoman society, the Tanzimat provoked spirited opposition from several distinct quarters. Harsh criticism came from religious conservatives, who argued that reformers posed a threat to the empire's Islamic foundation. Many devout Muslims viewed the extension of legal equality to Jews and Christians as an act contrary to the basic principles of Islamic law. Even some minority leaders opposed legal equality, fearing that it would diminish their own position as intermediaries between their communities and the Ottoman state. Criticism arose also from a group known collectively as the Young Ottomans. Although they did not share a common political or religious program—their views ranged from secular revolution to uncompromising Islam—Young Ottomans agitated for individual freedom, local autonomy, and political decentralization. Many Young Ottomans desired the establishment of a constitutional government along the lines of the British system. A fourth and perhaps the most dangerous critique of Tanzimat emerged from within the Ottoman bureaucracy itself. In part because of their exclusion from power, high-level bureaucrats were determined to impose checks on the sultan's power by forcing him to accept a constitution and, if necessary, even to depose him.

The Young Turk Era

Reform and Repression In 1876 a group of radical dissidents from the Ottoman bureaucracy seized power in a coup, formed a cabinet that included advocates of reform, and installed **Abdül Hamid II** as sultan (reigned 1876–1909). Convinced of the need to check the sultan's power, reformers persuaded Abdül Hamid to accept a constitution that limited his authority and established a representative government. Within a year, however, the sultan suspended the constitution, dissolved parliament, exiled many liberals, and executed others. For thirty years he ruled autocratically in an effort to rescue the empire from dismemberment by European powers. He continued, however, to develop the army and administration according to Tanzimat principles, and he oversaw the formation of a police force, educational reforms, economic development, and the construction of railroads.

Abdül Hamid's despotic rule generated many liberal opposition groups. Though intended to strengthen the state, reform and reorganization actually undermined the position of the sultan. As Ottoman bureaucrats and army officers received an education in European curricula, they not only learned modern science and technology but also became acquainted with European political, social, and cultural traditions. Many of them fell out of favor with Abdül Hamid and spent years in exile, where they experienced European society firsthand. Educated subjects came to believe that the biggest problem of the Ottoman Empire was the political structure that vested unchecked power in the sultan. For these dissidents, Ottoman society was in dire need of political reform and especially of a written constitution that defined and limited the sultan's power.

شیخ نظام رکوردای دولت در کاج دوای ۱۳۲۶   تبریز

Young Turks pose for a photograph during the revolution of 1908, which forced the sultan to establish a constitutional government.
Historia/Shutterstock

The Young Turks The most active dissident organization was the Ottoman Society for Union and Progress, better known as the Young Turk Party, although many of its members were neither young nor Turkish. Founded in 1889 by exiled Ottoman subjects living in Paris, the Young Turk Party vigorously promoted reform, and its members made effective use of recently established newspapers to spread their message. **Young Turks** called for universal suffrage, equality before the law, freedom of religion, free public education, secularization of the state, and the emancipation of women. In 1908 the Young Turks inspired an army coup that forced Abdül Hamid to restore parliament and the constitution of 1876. In 1909 they dethroned him and established Mehmed V Rashid (reigned 1909-1918) as a puppet sultan. Throughout the Young Turk era (1908-1918), Ottoman sultans reigned but no longer ruled.

While pursuing reform within Ottoman society, the Young Turks sought to maintain Turkish hegemony in the larger empire. They worked to make Turkish the official language of the empire, even though many subjects spoke Arabic or a Slavic language as their native tongue. As a result, Young Turk policies aggravated tensions between Turkish rulers and subject peoples outside the Anatolian heartland of

the Ottoman Empire. Syria and Iraq were especially active regions of Arab resistance to Ottoman rule. In spite of their efforts to shore up the ailing empire, reformers could not adequately strengthen the empire to ward off either external or internal threats. By the early twentieth century, the Ottoman Empire survived principally because European governments could not agree on how to dismantle the empire without upsetting the European balance of power.

THE RUSSIAN EMPIRE UNDER PRESSURE

Like the Ottoman Empire, the Russian Empire experienced battlefield reverses that exposed the economic and technological disparity between Russia and the industrialized powers of western Europe. Determined to preserve Russia's status as a great land power, the tsarist government embarked on a program of reform. The keystone of those efforts was the emancipation of Russian serfs, who were peasants tied to the land on which they were born. Social reform paved the way for government-sponsored industrialization, which began to transform Russian society during the last decades of the nineteenth century. Political liberalization did not accompany social and economic reform because the tsars refused to yield their autocratic powers. The oppressive political environment sparked opposition movements that turned increasingly radical in the late nineteenth century. In the early twentieth century, domestic discontent reached crisis proportions and exploded in revolution.

Military Defeat and Social Reform

The nineteenth-century tsars ruled a multiethnic, multilingual, multicultural empire that stretched from Poland to the Pacific Ocean. Only about half the population spoke the Russian language or observed the Russian Orthodox faith. The Romanov tsars ruled their diverse and sprawling realm through a dictatorial regime in which all initiative came from the central administration. The tsars enjoyed the support of the Russian Orthodox church and a small but powerful class of nobles who owned most of the land and were exempt from taxes and military duty. Peasants made up the vast majority of the population, and most of them were serfs. Serfdom was in fact almost indistinguishable from slavery, but most landowners, including the state, considered it a guarantee of social stability.

The Crimean War During the nineteenth century the Russian Empire expanded in three directions: east into Manchuria, south into the Caucasus and central Asia, and southwest toward the Mediterranean. This last thrust led to interference in the Balkan provinces of the Ottoman Empire. After defeating Turkish forces in a war from 1828 to 1829, Russia tried to establish a protectorate over the weakening Ottoman Empire. This expansive effort threatened to upset the balance of power in Europe, which led to military conflict between Russia and a coalition including Britain, France, the kingdom of Sardinia, and the Ottoman Empire. The **Crimean War** (1853–1856) clearly revealed the weakness of the Russian Empire, which could hold its own against Ottoman and Qing forces but not against the industrial powers of western Europe. In September 1854, allied forces mounted a campaign against Sevastopol in the Crimean peninsula, headquarters of Russia's Black Sea Fleet. Unable to mobilize, equip, and transport troops to defeat European forces that operated under a mediocre command, Russian armies suffered devastating and humiliating defeats on their own territory. Russia's economy could not support the tsars' expansionist ambitions, and the Crimean War clearly demonstrated the weakness of an agrarian economy based on unfree labor. Military defeat compelled the tsarist autocracy to reevaluate the Russian social order and undertake an extensive restructuring program.

Emancipation of the Serfs The most significant social reform in Russia was emancipation of the serfs. Opposition to serfdom had grown steadily since the eighteenth century, not only among radicals but also among high officials. Although some Russians objected to serfdom on moral grounds, many believed that it had become an obstacle to economic development and a viable state. Besides being economically inefficient, serfdom was a source of rural instability and peasant revolt: hundreds of insurrections broke out during the first four decades of the nineteenth century. As **Tsar Alexander II** (reigned 1855–1881) succinctly suggested to the nobility of Moscow, "It is better to abolish serfdom from above than to wait until the serfs begin to liberate themselves from below." Accordingly, in 1861, the tsar issued the **Emancipation Manifesto,**

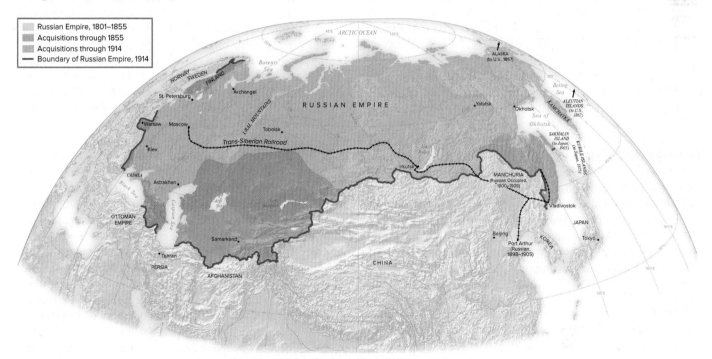

MAP 31.2 The Russian Empire, 1801–1914.

Note the sheer size of Russian territory in this period and that the state included parts of Europe, central Asia, and east Asia.

How would straddling so much space and so many cultures have affected the process of industrialization and nationalism in Russia?

which abolished the institution of serfdom and granted liberty to some twenty-three million serfs. This newfound freedom encompassed the right to full citizenship, the right to marry without consent, and the right to own property.

Although the government sought to balance the interests of nobles and serfs, on balance the terms of emancipation were unfavorable to most peasants. The government compensated landowners for the loss of their land and the serfs who had worked it. Serfs won their freedom, had their labor obligations gradually canceled, and gained opportunities to become landowners. But the peasants won few political rights, and they had to pay tax on most of the lands they received. Many disappointed peasants believed that their rulers forced them to pay for land that was theirs by right. Complicating this situation further was the fact that the majority of peasants held their land in communal ownership within a *mir* (society). Although the mir had the power to distribute land given to recently freed serfs by the government, the concept of communal ownership of the land prohibited individual peasants from selling their land. The years between 1906 and 1914 were marked by the implementation of agrarian reforms designed to break up the communes and create a class of individual peasant landowners. These so-called Stolypin reforms, named after Prime Minister Pyotr Arkadyevich Stolypin (1862–1911), ended with the outbreak of the Great War in 1914. A few peasants prospered and improved their position as the result of emancipation, but most found themselves in debt for the rest of their lives. In addition, emancipation resulted in little if any increase in agricultural production.

Political and Legal Reform Other important reforms came in the wake of the serfs' emancipation. To deal with local issues of health, education, and welfare, the government created elected district assemblies, or *zemstvos,* in 1864. Although all classes, including peasants, elected representatives to these assemblies, the *zemstvos* remained subordinate to the tsarist autocracy, which retained exclusive authority over national issues, and the landowning nobility, which possessed a disproportionately large share of both votes and seats. Legal reform was more fruitful than experimentation with representative government. The revision of the judiciary system in 1864 created a system of law courts based on western European models, complete with independent judges and a system of appellate courts. Legal reforms also instituted trial by jury for criminal offenses and elected justices of the peace who dealt with minor offenses. These reforms encouraged the emergence of attorneys and other legal experts, whose professional standards contributed to a decline in judicial corruption.

Industrialization

Social and political reform coincided with industrialization in nineteenth-century Russia. Tsar Alexander II emancipated the serfs partly with the intention of creating a mobile labor force

Tsar Alexander II of Russia (1818–1881). After signing the Treaty of Paris in 1856, ending the Crimean War, Alexander abolished serfdom in the Russian Empire in 1861.
Universal History Archive/UIG/Shutterstock

for emerging industries, and the tsarist government encouraged industrialization as a way of strengthening the Russian Empire. Thus, although Russian industrialization took place within a framework of capitalism, it differed from western European industrialization in that the motivation for development was political and military and the driving force was government policy rather than entrepreneurial initiative. Industrialization proceeded slowly at first, but it surged during the last two decades of the nineteenth century.

The Witte System The prime mover behind Russian industrialization was Count **Sergei Witte,** minister of finance from 1892 to 1903. His first budget, submitted to the government in 1893, outlined his aims as "removing the unfavorable conditions which hamper the economic development of the country" and "kindling a healthy spirit of enterprise." Availing himself of the full power of the state, Witte implemented policies designed to stimulate economic development. The centerpiece of his industrial policy was an ambitious program of railway construction, which linked the far-flung regions of the Russian Empire and also stimulated the development of other industries. Most important of the new lines was the trans-Siberian railway, which opened Siberia to large-scale settlement, exploitation, and industrialization. To raise domestic capital for industry, Witte remodeled the state bank and encouraged the establishment of savings banks. Witte supported infant

Sergei Witte (SAYR-gay VIHT-te)

Russian merchants in nineteenth-century Novgorod wear both western European and traditional Russian dress while taking tea. What does this mixed fashion suggest about Russian society at this time?
Hulton Archive/Getty Images

industries with high protective tariffs while also securing large foreign loans from western Europe to finance industrialization. His plan worked. French and Belgian capital played a key role in developing the steel and coal industries, and British funds supported the booming petroleum industry in the Caucasus.

Industrial Discontent For a decade the Witte system played a crucial role in the industrialization of Russia, but peasant rebellions and strikes by industrial workers indicated that large segments of the population were unwilling to tolerate the low standard of living that Witte's policies required. Recently freed serfs often did not like factory work, which forced them to follow new routines and adapt to the rhythms of industrial machinery. Industrial growth began to generate an urban working class, which endured dismal conditions similar to those experienced by workers in other societies during the early stages of industrialization. Employers kept wages of overworked and poorly housed workers at the barest minimum. The industrial sections of St. Petersburg and Moscow became notorious for the miserable working and living conditions of factory laborers. In 1897 the government limited the maximum working day to 11.5 hours, but that measure did little to alleviate the plight of workers. The government prohibited the formation of trade unions and outlawed strikes, which continued to occur in spite of the restrictions. Economic exploitation and the lack of political freedom made workers increasingly receptive to revolutionary propaganda, and underground movements soon developed among them.

Not everyone was dissatisfied with the results of intensified industrialization. Besides foreign investors, a growing Russian business class benefited from government policy that protected domestic industries and its profits. Russian entrepreneurs reaped rich rewards for their roles in economic development, and they had little complaint with the political system. In contrast to western European capitalists, who had both material and ideological reasons to challenge the power of absolute monarchs and the nobility, Russian businesspeople generally did not challenge tsarist rule.

Repression and Revolution

Protest During the last three decades of the nineteenth century, antigovernment protest and revolutionary activity increased. Hopes aroused by government reforms inspired reform movements, and social tensions arising from industrialization fueled protest by groups whose aims became increasingly radical. Peasants seethed with discontent because they had little or no land, while newly mobile workers spread rebellious ideas between industrial cities. At the center of opposition were university students and a class of intellectuals collectively known as the intelligentsia. Their goals and methods varied, but they generally sought substantial political reform and comprehensive social change. Most dissidents drew inspiration from western European socialism (discussed in chapter 29), but they despised the individualism and materialism of western Europe and thus worked toward a socialist system more in keeping with Russian cultural traditions. Many revolutionaries were anarchists, who opposed all forms of government and believed that individual freedom cannot be realized until all government is abolished. Some anarchists relied on terror tactics and assassination to achieve their goals. Insofar as they had a positive political program, the anarchists wanted all authority to stem from local governing councils elected by universal suffrage.

Repression Some activists saw the main potential for revolutionary action in the countryside, and between 1873 and 1876 hundreds of anarchists and other radicals traveled to rural areas to rouse the peasantry. However, police soon arrested

Japanese infantry charging during the Russo-Japanese War, 1904–1905.
Chris Hellier/Corbis NX/Getty Images

the idealists. Tsarist authorities sentenced some to prison and banished others to the remote provinces of Siberia. Frightened by the increasing radicalism within their realm, tsarist authorities resorted to a campaign of repression: they censored publications and sent secret police to infiltrate and break up radical organizations. Repression, however, only served to radicalize revolutionaries further and gave them new determination to overthrow the tsarist regime.

In the Baltic provinces, Poland, Ukraine, Georgia, and central Asia, dissidents opposed the tsarist autocracy on ethnic as well as political and social grounds. In those places, subject peoples speaking their own languages often used schools and political groups as foundations for separatist movements as they sought autonomy or independence from the Russian Empire. Tsarist officials responded with a heavy-handed program of Russification to repress the use of languages other than Russian and to restrict educational opportunities only to those loyal to the tsarist state. Throughout the Russian Empire, Jews also were targets of suspicion, and tsarist authorities tolerated frequent **pogroms** (anti-Jewish riots) by subjects jealous of their Jewish neighbors' success in business affairs. To escape this violence, Jews in the Russian Empire migrated by the hundreds of thousands to western Europe and the United States in the late nineteenth century.

Terrorism In 1876 a recently formed group called the Land and Freedom Party began to promote the assassination of prominent officials as a means of forcing the government into political reform. In 1879 a terrorist faction of the party, the People's Will, resolved to assassinate Alexander II, who had emancipated the serfs and had launched a program of political and social reform. After several unsuccessful attempts, an assassin exploded a bomb under Alexander's carriage in 1881. The first blast did little damage, but as Alexander inspected his carriage, a second and more powerful explosion killed the reforming tsar. The attack brought the era of reform to an end and prompted the tsarist autocracy to adopt an uncompromising policy of repression.

In 1894 **Nicholas II** (reigned 1894–1917) ascended the throne. A weak ruler, Nicholas championed oppression and police control. To deflect attention from domestic issues and neutralize revolutionary movements, the tsar's government embarked on expansionist ventures in east Asia. However, Russian designs on Korea and Manchuria clashed with similar Japanese intentions, leading to a rivalry that ended in war. The Russo-Japanese War began with a Japanese surprise attack on the Russian naval squadron at Port Arthur in February 1904 and ended in May 1905 with the destruction of the Russian navy.

The Revolution of 1905 Russian military defeats in the Russo-Japanese War brought to a head simmering political and social discontent and triggered widespread protests. In January 1905 a group of workers marched on the tsar's Winter Palace in St. Petersburg to petition Nicholas for a popularly elected assembly and other political concessions. Government

What's Left Out? ■■ ■■ ■■ ■■ ■■

We know that the Russo-Japanese War of 1904–1905 played an important role in the massive disturbances that erupted in the Russian revolution of 1905. But the effects of the war were much more far-reaching than that. Indeed, while textbooks tend to gloss over the war in favor of World War I, scholars are beginning to understand that the Russo-Japanese War represented a fundamental turning point for people in the non-Western world—especially those living under colonial rule or foreign domination. This was because the Japanese victory was interpreted by millions of people to be the first time members of an Asian "race" decisively beat members of a European "race" in a modern war. This had major consequences for the ways people of color—whether from Asia, Africa, the Middle East, or even the United States—viewed European notions of white superiority. Ordinary people in places as far flung as Egypt, India, the Dutch East Indies, Indochina, and China avidly tracked the progress of the Japanese army during the war through newspaper reports. When the Japanese emerged victorious, these same people joined in celebrations and congratulated one another, elated that an Asian nation had turned the tables on a European foe. Key revolutionaries and future nationalist leaders—including Jawaharlal Nehru of India, Sun Yat-Sen of China, and Phan Boi Chau of Indochina—were deeply inspired by the Japanese victory, and anticolonialists all over the world became more assertive and more hopeful. Some even began to send anticolonial revolutionaries to Japan so they could learn the secret to Japanese success and then use it against their colonial oppressors. So even though most textbooks do not cover the Russo-Japanese war extensively, it is worth remembering that it had profound consequences for the growing anticolonial movements that would soon convulse the world.

Source: Cemil Aydin, *The Politics of Anti-Westernism in Asia: Visions of World Order in Pan-Islamic and Pan-Asian Thought* (New York: Columbia University Press, 2007), chapter 4.

troops met the petitioners with rifle fire, killing 130. The news of this Bloody Sunday massacre caused an angry uproar throughout the empire that culminated in labor unrest, peasant insurrections, student demonstrations, and mutinies in both the army and the navy. Organizing themselves at the village level, peasants discussed seizing the property of their landlords. Urban workers created new councils known as soviets to organize strikes and negotiate with employers and government authorities. Elected delegates from factories and workshops served as members of these soviets.

Revolutionary turmoil paralyzed Russian cities and forced the government to make concessions. Sergei Witte, whom Nicholas had appointed to conduct peace negotiations with Japan, urged the tsar to create an elected legislative assembly. The tsar reluctantly consented and permitted the establishment of the **Duma,** Russia's first parliamentary institution. Although the Duma lacked the power to create or bring down governments, from the Romanov perspective this act was a major concession. Still, the creation of the Duma did not end unrest. Between 1905 and 1907 disorder continued, and violence flared, especially in the Baltic provinces, Poland, Ukraine, Georgia, and central Asia, where ethnic tensions added to revolutionary sentiments. Through bloody reprisals the government eventually restored order, but by this time the Romanov empire had been fundamentally weakened.

THE CHINESE EMPIRE UNDER SIEGE

The Qing dynasty in China experienced even more difficulties than did the Ottoman and Russian empires during the nineteenth century. European powers inflicted military defeats on Qing forces and compelled China's leaders to accept a series of humiliating treaties. The provisions of these treaties undermined Chinese sovereignty, carved China into spheres of influence that allowed profound economic exploitation, and handicapped the Qing dynasty's ability to deal with domestic disorder. As the government tried to cope with foreign challenges, it also faced dangerous internal upheavals, the most important of which was the Taiping rebellion, which we read about in the introduction. Caught between aggressive foreigners and insurgent rebels, China's ruling elites developed reform programs designed to maintain social order, strengthen the state, and preserve the Qing dynasty. The reforms had limited effect, however, and by the early twentieth century, China too was in a seriously weakened condition.

The Opium War and the Unequal Treaties

In 1759 the Qianlong emperor restricted the European commercial presence in China to the waterfront at Guangzhou, where European merchants were allowed to establish warehouses. There, Chinese authorities controlled not only European merchants but also the terms of trade. Foreign merchants could deal only with specially licensed Chinese firms known as *cohongs,* which bought and sold goods at set prices and operated under strict regulations established by the government. At the same time, Chinese consumers created very little demand for European products. As a result, European merchants had to pay for the Chinese products European consumers desperately wanted—including silk, porcelain, lacquerware, and tea—largely with silver.

The Opium Trade Seeking increased profits in the late eighteenth century, officials of the British East India Company sought alternatives to silver to exchange for Chinese goods. They gradually turned to trade in a product that was as

Chinese opium smokers around 1870. The Chinese government's attempt to stop the importation of opium resulted in a major defeat in the Opium War of 1839–1842. Here, opium smokers recline and sleep on the hard beds characteristic of opium dens.
Chronicle/Alamy Stock Photo

profitable as it was criminal—opium. Using Turkish and Persian expertise, the East India Company oversaw the production of opium grown in India and shipped it to China, where company officials exchanged it for Chinese silver coin. The silver then flowed back to British-controlled Calcutta and London, where company merchants used it to buy Chinese products in Guangzhou. Once it was clear that opium was in high demand in China, the trade expanded rapidly: annual imports of opium in the early nineteenth century amounted to about 4,500 chests, each weighing 60 kilograms (133 pounds), but by 1839 some 40,000 chests of opium entered China annually to satisfy the habits of consumers. With the help of this new commodity, the East India Company easily paid for luxury Chinese products.

Trade in opium was illegal, but it continued unabated for decades because of the efforts of European and Chinese smugglers and because some Chinese officials benefited personally by allowing the illegal trade to go on. By the late 1830s, however, government officials had become aware that opium had caused both a trade problem and a drug problem in China. The opium trade not only drained large quantities of silver from China but also created serious social problems, especially in southern China. When Chinese government authorities took steps in 1838 to halt the illicit trade, British merchants started losing money. In 1839 the Chinese government stepped up its campaign by charging a government official named **Lin Zexu** with the task of destroying the opium trade. Commissioner Lin acted quickly, confiscating and destroying some 20,000 chests of opium. His uncompromising policy, however, ignited a war that ended in a major defeat for China.

Lin Zexu (lin zuh-SHOO)

SOURCES FROM THE PAST

Commissioner Lin on Banning Opium in China

In the following passages, Commissioner Lin Zexu (1785–1850), who was appointed by the emperor to end the illegal traffic in opium, enumerated in 1839 four reasons British traders should surrender their smuggled opium. Although opium was illegal in Britain and China, the British East India Company knowingly smuggled huge quantities of opium into China in order to improve the trade deficit produced by its importation of Chinese products. Lin, whose actions touched off the Opium War that began in 1839, was a steadfast opponent of opium and its negative effects on public health and society.

First. You ought to make haste and deliver up the opium, by virtue of that reason which Heaven hath implanted in all of us. . . . [W]hile you have been scheming after private advantage, with minds solely bent on profit, our people have been wasting their substance and losing their lives; and if the reason of Heaven be just, think you that there will be no retribution? If, however, you will now repent and deliver up your opium, by a well-timed repentance you may yet avert judgment and calamities; if not, then your wickedness being greater, the consequences of that wickedness will fall more fearfully upon you! . . .

Now our great emperor, being actuated by the exalted virtue of Heaven itself, wishes to cut off this deluge of opium, which is the plainest proof that such is the intention of high Heaven! . . .

Secondly. You ought to make immediate delivery of this opium, in order to comply with the law of your own countries, which prohibits the smoking of opium, and he who uses it is adjudged to death! . . . If, then, your laws forbid it to be consumed by yourselves, and yet permit it to be sold that it may be consumed by others, this is not in conformity with the principle of doing unto others what you would that they should do unto you. . . .

Our great emperor looks upon the opium trade with the most intense loathing, and burns to have it cut off forever; and I, the high commissioner, looking up to the great emperor, and feeling in my own person his sacred desire to love and cherish the men from afar, do mercifully spare you your lives. I wish nothing more than that you deliver up all the opium you have got, and forthwith write out a duly prepared bond, to the effect that you will henceforth never more bring opium to China, and, should you bring it, agreeing that the cargo be confiscated and the people who bring it, put to death.

> When Commissioner Lin says he will spare the lives of traders here, what kind of power was he assuming over them?

Thirdly. You ought to make immediate delivery of this opium, by reason of your feelings as men. You come to this market of Canton to trade, and you profit thereby full threefold. Every article of commerce that you bring with you, no matter whether it be coarse or fine, in whole pieces or in small, there is not one iota of it that is not sold off and consumed; and of the produce of our country, whether it be for feeding you, for clothing you, for any kind of use, or for mere sale, there is not a description that we do not permit you to take away with you; so that not only do you reap the profit of the inner land by the goods which you bring, but, moreover, by means of the produce of our central land, do you gather gold from every country to which you transport it. Supposing that you cut off and cast away your traffic in the single article of opium, then the other business which you do will be much increased, and you will thereon reap your threefold profit comfortably.

> This is the only place in the passage where Commissioner Lin discusses the economics of the trade. What does he think the economic consequences of cutting off the trade will be?

Fourthly. You ought to make a speedy delivery of your opium by reason of the necessity of the case. You foreigners from afar, in coming hither to trade, have passed over an unbounded ocean; your prospect for doing business depends entirely on your living on terms of harmony with your fellow-men, and keeping your own station in peace and quietness. Thus may you reap solid advantage and avoid misfortune! But if you will persist in selling your opium, and will go on involving the lives of our foolish people in your toils, there is not a good or upright man whose head and heart will not burn with indignation at your conduct; they must look upon the lives of those who have suffered for smoking and selling the drug as sacrificed by you; the simple country folk and the common people must feel anything but well pleased, and the wrath of a whole country is not a thing easily restrained: these are circumstances about which you cannot but feel anxious.

For Further Reflection

■ The Chinese high commissioner appeared to base his arguments, and those of his emperor, largely on a moral rather than an economic frame of reference. Were his points effective, and did his reasoning bring forth any hypocritical discrepancies in European beliefs?

Source: Reasons for the proclamation ordering foreigners to deliver up opium smuggled into China. In *Readings in Modern European History.* By James Harvey Robinson and Charles A. Beard. Volume II. Boston: Ginn & Company, 1909. pp. 419–422.

MAP 31.3   East Asia in the nineteenth century.

Notice the division of China, which technically remained a sovereign nation, into spheres of influence by various European nations and Japan.

What impact would such spheres of influence have had on the Chinese government in Beijing?

The Opium War Outraged by the Chinese action against opium (despite their awareness that the trade was illegal), British commercial agents pressed their government into a military retaliation designed to reopen the opium trade. The ensuing conflict, known as the **Opium War** (1839-1842), exposed the military power differential between Europe and China. In the initial stages of the conflict, steam-powered British naval vessels easily demonstrated their superiority on the seas. Meanwhile, equipped with antiquated muskets, swords, and spears, the defenders of Chinese coastal towns were no match for the firepower of well-drilled British infantry armed with rifles. But neither the destruction of Chinese war fleets nor the capture of coastal forts and towns persuaded the Chinese to sue for peace.

British forces broke the military stalemate when they decided to strike at China's jugular vein—the Grand Canal, which linked the Yangzi and Yellow River valleys—with the aid of steam-powered gunboats. Armed, shallow-draft steamers could travel speedily up and down rivers, projecting the military advantage that European ships enjoyed on the high seas deep into interior regions. In May 1842 a British armada of seventy ships—led by the gunboat *Nemesis*—advanced up the Yangzi River. The British fleet encountered little resistance, and by the time it reached the intersection of the river and the Grand Canal, the Chinese government had sued for peace. China experienced similar military setbacks throughout the second half of the nineteenth century in conflicts with Britain and France (1856-1858), France (1884-1885), and Japan (1894-1895).

Unequal Treaties In the wake of those confrontations came a series of pacts collectively known in China as **unequal treaties,** which curtailed China's sovereignty. Beginning with the **Treaty of Nanjing,** which Britain forced China to accept at the conclusion of the Opium War in 1842, these agreements guided Chinese relations with foreign states until 1943. The Treaty of Nanjing (1842) ceded Hong Kong Island to Britain; opened five Chinese ports—including Guangzhou and Shanghai—to foreign commerce and residence; compelled the Qing government to extend most-favored-nation status to Britain; and granted extraterritoriality to British subjects, which meant they were not subject to Chinese laws. The Treaty of Nanjing governed relations only between Britain and China, but France, Germany, Denmark, the Netherlands, Spain, Belgium, Austria-Hungary, the United States, and Japan later concluded similar unequal treaties with China. Collectively these treaties broadened the concessions given to foreign powers; they legalized the opium trade, permitted the establishment of Christian missions throughout China, and opened additional treaty ports. To encourage sales of foreign goods, various treaties also prevented the Qing government from levying tariffs on imports to protect domestic industries. By 1900 ninety Chinese ports were under the effective control of foreign powers, foreign merchants controlled much of the Chinese economy, Christian missionaries sought converts throughout China, and foreign gunboats patrolled Chinese waters. Several treaties also released Korea, Vietnam, and Burma (now known as Myanmar) from Chinese authority and thereby dismantled the Chinese system of tributary states.

The Taiping Rebellion

The weakening of the Chinese Empire at the end of the nineteenth century was as much a result of internal turmoil as it was a consequence of foreign intervention. Large-scale rebellions in the later nineteenth century reflected the increasing poverty and discontent of the Chinese peasantry. Between 1800 and 1900 China's population rose by almost 50 percent, from 330 million to 475 million. But the amount of land under cultivation increased only slowly during the same period, making it difficult to feed so many

The final assault on the Taipings at Nanjing by Qing forces in 1864. Losses were devastating: about one hundred thousand Taiping soldiers were killed, and then Qing forces massacred most of the city's inhabitants after emerging victorious.
Photo12/UIG/Getty Images

more people. The concentration of land in the hands of wealthy elites aggravated peasant discontent, as did widespread corruption of government officials. After 1850, rebellions erupted throughout China: the Nian rebellion (1851–1868) in the northeast, the Muslim rebellion (1855–1873) in the southwest, and the Tungan rebellion (1862–1878) in the northwest. Most dangerous of all was the **Taiping rebellion** (1850–1864), which raged throughout most of China and brought the Qing dynasty to the brink of collapse.

The Taiping Program The village schoolteacher Hong Xiuquan, who we met in the introduction to this chapter, provided both inspiration and leadership for the Taiping rebellion. His call for the destruction of the Qing dynasty and his program for the radical transformation of Chinese society appealed to millions of men and women. The Qing dynasty had ruled China since 1644, and Qing elites had adapted to Chinese ways, but many native Chinese subjects despised the Manchu ruling class as foreigners. The Taiping reform program contained many radical features that appealed to discontented subjects, including the abolition of private property, the creation of communal wealth to be shared according to needs, the prohibition of foot binding and concubinage, free public edcation, simplification of the written language, and literacy for the masses. Some Taiping leaders also called for the establishment of democratic political institutions and the building of an industrial society. Although they divided their army into separate divisions of men and women soldiers, the Taipings decreed the equality of men and women. Taiping regulations prohibited sexual intercourse among their followers, including married couples, but Hong and other high leaders maintained large harems.

After sweeping through southeastern China, Hong and his followers in the Society of God Worshipers took Nanjing in 1853 and made it the capital of their Taiping ("Great Peace") kingdom. From Nanjing they campaigned throughout China, and as the rebels passed through the countryside whole towns and villages joined them—often voluntarily but sometimes under coercion. By 1855 a million Taipings were poised to attack Beijing. Qing forces repelled them, but five years later, firmly entrenched in the Yangzi River valley, the Taipings threatened Shanghai.

Taiping Defeat The radical nature of the Taiping program ensured that the Chinese gentry would side with the Qing government to support a regime dedicated to the preservation of the established order. After imperial forces consisting of Manchu soldiers failed to defeat the Taipings, the Qing government created regional armies staffed by Chinese instead of Manchu soldiers and commanded by members of the scholar-gentry class, a shift encouraged by the empress dowager Cixi (1835–1908), a former imperial concubine who established herself as effective ruler of China during the last fifty years of the Qing dynasty. With the aid of European advisers and weapons, these regional armies gradually overcame the Taipings. By 1862 Hong Xiuquan had largely withdrawn from public affairs, as he sought solace in

religious reflection and diversion in his harem. After a lingering illness, he committed suicide in June 1864. In the following months Nanjing fell, and government forces slaughtered some one hundred thousand Taipings. By the end of the year, the rebellion was over. But the Taiping rebellion had taken a costly toll. It claimed twenty million to thirty million lives, and it caused such drastic declines in agricultural production that people in war-torn regions frequently resorted to eating grass, leather, hemp, and even human flesh.

Reform Frustrated

The Taiping rebellion altered the course of Chinese history. Contending with aggressive foreign powers and lands ravaged by domestic rebellion, Qing rulers recognized that changes were necessary for the empire to survive. From 1860 to 1895, Qing authorities tried to fashion an efficient and benevolent Confucian government to solve social and economic problems while also adopting foreign technology to strengthen state power.

The Self-Strengthening Movement Most imaginative of the reform programs was the **Self-Strengthening Movement** (1860–1895), which flourished especially in the 1860s and 1870s. Empowered with imperial grants of authority that permitted them to raise troops, levy taxes, and run bureaucracies, several local leaders promoted military and economic reform. Adopting the slogan "Chinese learning at the base, Western learning for use," leaders of the Self-Strengthening Movement sought to blend Chinese cultural traditions with European industrial technology. While holding to Confucian values and seeking to reestablish a stable agrarian society, movement leaders built modern shipyards, constructed railroads, established weapons industries, opened steel foundries with blast furnaces, and founded academies to develop scientific expertise.

Although it laid a foundation for industrialization, the Self-Strengthening Movement brought only superficial change to Chinese economy and society. For one thing, it did not introduce enough industry to bring real military and economic strength to China. It also encountered obstacles in the imperial government: for example, the empress dowager Cixi diverted funds intended for the navy to build a magnificent marble boat to grace a lake in the imperial gardens. Furthermore, elites worried that industrialization would bring fundamental social change to an agrarian land and that education in European curricula would undermine the commitment to Confucian values.

Spheres of Influence The Self-Strengthening Movement also did not prevent continuing foreign interference into Chinese affairs. During the latter part of the nineteenth century, foreign powers began to dismantle the Chinese system of tributary states. In 1885 France incorporated Vietnam into its colonial empire, and in 1886 Great Britain detached Burma from Chinese control. In 1895 Japan forced China to recognize the independence of Korea and cede the island of Taiwan

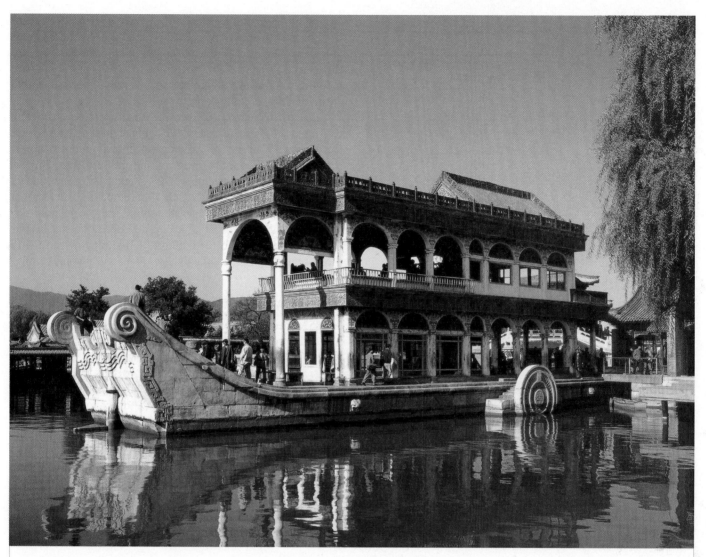

Empress Dowager Cixi diverted government funds intended for the construction of modern warships to the construction of a huge marble vessel to decorate a lake in the gardens of the Summer Palace near Beijing.

David Ball/Alamy Stock Photo

and the Liaodong peninsula in southern Manchuria. By 1898 foreign powers had carved China into spheres of economic influence. The Qing government was also forced to grant exclusive rights for railway and mineral development to Germany in Shandong Province, to France in the southern border provinces, to Great Britain in the Yangzi River valley, to Japan in the southeastern coastal provinces, and to Russia in Manchuria. Only distrust among the foreign powers prevented the total dismemberment of the Middle Kingdom.

The Hundred Days Reforms These setbacks sparked the ambitious but abortive **Hundred Days reforms** of 1898. The leading figures of the reform movement were the scholars Kang Youwei (1858–1927) and Liang Qichao (1873–1929), who published a series of treatises reinterpreting Confucian thought in a way that justified radical changes in the imperial

system. Kang and Liang did not seek to preserve an agrarian society and its cultural traditions so much as to remake China and turn it into a powerful, modern industrial society. Impressed by their ideas, the young Emperor Guangxu (r. 1875–1898) launched a sweeping program to transform China into a constitutional monarchy, guarantee civil liberties, root out corruption, remodel the educational system, encourage foreign influence in China, modernize military forces, and stimulate economic development. The broad range of reform edicts produced a violent reaction from members of the imperial household; their allies in the gentry; and the young emperor's aunt, the ruthless and powerful empress dowager Cixi. After a period of 103 days, Cixi nullified the reform

Kang Youwei (kahng yoo-way)
Liang Qichao (lee-yahng chee-chow)

Photograph of a Chinese Boxer in 1900, during the revolt.
Courtesy of Everett Collection/Shutterstock

decrees, imprisoned the emperor in the Forbidden City, and executed six leading reformers. Kang and Liang, the spiritual guides of the reform movement, escaped to Japan.

The Boxer Rebellion Believing that foreign powers were conspiring to effect her retirement, Cixi threw her support behind an antiforeign uprising known as the **Boxer rebellion,** a violent movement spearheaded by militia units calling themselves the Society of Righteous and Harmonious Fists. The foreign press referred to the rebels as Boxers. In 1899 the Boxers organized to rid China of "foreign devils" and their influences. With the empress dowager's encouragement, the Boxers went on a rampage in northern China, killing foreigners and Chinese Christians as well as Chinese who had ties to foreigners. Confident that foreign weapons could not harm them, some 140,000 Boxers besieged foreign embassies in

Beijing in the summer of 1900. A heavily armed force of British, French, Russian, U.S., German, and Japanese troops quickly crushed the Boxer movement in bloody retaliation for the assault. The Chinese government had to pay a punitive indemnity and allow foreign powers to station troops in Beijing at their embassies and along the route to the sea.

Because Cixi had instigated the Boxers' attacks on foreigners, many Chinese regarded the Qing dynasty as bankrupt. Revolutionary uprisings gained widespread public support throughout the country, even among conservative Chinese gentry. Cixi died in November 1908, one day after the sudden, unexpected, and mysterious death of the emperor. In her last act of state, the empress dowager appointed the two-year-old boy Puyi to the imperial throne. But Puyi never had a chance to rule: revolution broke out in the autumn of 1911, and by early 1912 the last emperor of the Qing dynasty had abdicated his throne.

THE TRANSFORMATION OF JAPAN

In 1853 a fleet of U.S. warships steamed into Tokyo Bay and demanded permission to establish trade and diplomatic relations with Japan. Representatives of European states soon joined U.S. agents in Japan. Heavily armed foreign powers intimidated the Tokugawa shogun and his government, the bakufu, into signing unequal treaties providing political and economic privileges similar to those obtained earlier from the Qing dynasty in China. Opposition forces in Japan used the intrusion of foreigners as an excuse to overthrow the discredited shogun and the **Tokugawa bakufu.** After restoring the emperor to power in 1868, Japan's new rulers worked for the transformation of Japanese society to achieve political and economic equality with foreign powers. The changes initiated during the Meiji period turned Japan into a political, military, and economic powerhouse.

From Tokugawa to Meiji

Crisis and Reform By the early nineteenth century, Japanese society was in turmoil. Declining agricultural productivity, periodic crop failures and famines, and harsh taxation contributed to economic hardship and sometimes even led to starvation among the rural population. A few cultivators prospered during this period, but many had to sell their land and become tenant farmers. Economic conditions in towns and cities, where many peasants migrated in search of a better life, were hardly better than those in the countryside. As the price of rice and other commodities rose, the urban poor experienced destitution and hunger. Even **samurai** and daimyo (discussed in chapter 26) faced hardship because they fell into debt to a growing merchant class. Under those conditions, Japan experienced increasing peasant protest and rebellion during the late eighteenth and early nineteenth centuries.

The Tokugawa bakufu responded with limited reforms. Between 1841 and 1843 the shogun's chief adviser, Mizuno Tadakuni, initiated measures to stem growing social and economic decline and to shore up the Tokugawa government.

Tokugawa (TOH-koo-GAH-wah)
Meiji (MAY-jee)

Painting of Commodore Matthew Perry (1794–1858) meeting the royal commissioner at Yokohama in 1853.
Bettmann/Getty Images

Mizuno canceled debts that samurai and daimyo owed to merchants, abolished several merchant guilds, and compelled peasants residing in cities to return to the land and cultivate rice. Most of his reforms were ineffective, and they provoked strong opposition that ultimately drove him from office.

Foreign Pressure Another problem facing the Tokugawa bakufu was the insistence on the establishment of diplomatic and commercial relations by foreign lands. Beginning in 1844, British, French, and U.S. ships visited Japan seeking to establish relations. The United States in particular sought ports where its Pacific merchant and whaling fleets could stop for fuel and provisions. Tokugawa officials refused all requests and stuck to the policy of excluding all European and American visitors to Japan except for a small number of Dutch merchants, who carried on a carefully controlled trade in Nagasaki. In the later 1840s the bakufu began to make military preparations to resist potential attacks.

The arrival of a U.S. naval squadron in Tokyo Bay in 1853 abruptly changed the situation. The American commander, **Commodore Matthew C. Perry,** trained his guns on the bakufu capital of Edo (modern Tokyo) and demanded that the shogun open Japan to diplomatic and commercial relations and sign a treaty of friendship. Under the pressure of force, the shogun quickly acquiesced to Perry's demands. Representatives of Britain, the Netherlands, and Russia soon won similar rights. Like Qing diplomats a few years earlier, Tokugawa officials agreed to a series of unequal treaties that opened Japanese ports to foreign commerce, deprived the government of control over tariffs, and granted foreigners extraterritorial rights.

The End of Tokugawa Rule The sudden intrusion of foreign powers precipitated a domestic crisis in Japan that resulted in the collapse of the Tokugawa bakufu and the restoration of imperial rule. When the shogun complied with the demands of U.S. and European representatives, he aroused

Japanese artist Miyagawa Shuntei offered a late-nineteenth-century contrast in fashion in his depiction of two women at the seaside. One wears European swimwear, and the other has donned a kimono.

John Stevenson/Corbis Historical/Getty Images

the opposition of conservative daimyo and the emperor, who resented the humiliating terms of the unequal treaties and questioned the shogun's right to rule Japan as "subduer of barbarians." Opposition to Tokugawa authority spread rapidly, and the southern domains of Choshu and Satsuma became centers of discontented samurai. By 1858 the imperial court in Kyoto—long excluded from playing an active role in politics—had become the focal point for opposition. Dissidents there rallied around the slogan "Revere the emperor, expel the barbarians."

The Meiji Restoration Tokugawa officials did not yield power quietly. Instead, they vigorously responded to their opponents by forcibly retiring dissident daimyo and executing

Mutsuhito (MOO-tsoo-HEE-taw)
Fukuzawa Yukichi (foo-koo-ZAH-wah yoo-KEE-chee)
Ito Hirobumi (EE-toh heer-oh-BOO-mee)

or imprisoning samurai critics. In a brief civil war, however, bakufu armies suffered repeated defeats by militia units trained by foreign experts and armed with imported weapons. With the Tokugawa cause doomed, the shogun resigned his office.

Meiji Reforms

On January 3, 1868 the boy emperor **Mutsuhito**—subsequently known by his regnal name, Meiji ("Enlightened Rule")—took the reins of power. Emperor Meiji (1852–1912) reigned during a most eventful period in Japan's history. The **Meiji restoration** returned authority to the Japanese emperor and brought an end to the series of military governments that had dominated Japan since 1185. It also marked the birth of a new Japan. Determined to gain equality with foreign powers, a conservative coalition of daimyo, imperial princes, court nobles, and samurai formed a new government dedicated to the twin goals of prosperity and strength: "rich country, strong army." The Meiji government looked to the industrial states of Europe and the United States to obtain the knowledge and expertise to strengthen Japan and reverse the unequal treaties. The Meiji government sent many students and officials abroad to study everything from technology to constitutions, and it also hired foreign experts to encourage economic development and the creation of indigenous expertise.

Foreign Influences Among the most prominent of the Meiji-era travelers were **Fukuzawa Yukichi** (1835–1901) and **Ito Hirobumi** (1841–1909). Fukuzawa began to study English soon after Perry's arrival in Japan, and in 1860 he was a member of the first Japanese mission to the United States. Later, he traveled in Europe, and he reported his observations of foreign lands in a series of popular publications. He applauded the constitutional government and modern educational systems that he found in the United States and western Europe, and he argued strongly for equality before the law in Japan. Ito ventured abroad on four occasions. His most important journey came in 1882 and 1883, when he traveled to Europe to study foreign constitutions and administrative systems, as Meiji leaders prepared to fashion a new government. He was especially impressed with recently united Germany, and he drew inspiration from the German constitution in drafting a governing document for Japan.

Abolition of the Social Order The first goal of the Meiji leaders was to centralize political power, a difficult task that required destruction of the old social order. After persuading daimyo to yield their lands to the throne in exchange for certificates of nobility, reformers replaced the old domains with prefectures and metropolitan districts controlled by the central government. Reformers then appointed new prefectural governors to prevent the revival of old loyalties. As a result, most daimyo found themselves effectively removed from power. The government also abolished the samurai class and the stipends that supported it. Gone as well were the rights of daimyo and samurai to carry swords and wear their hair in the distinctive topknot that signified their military status. When Meiji leaders raised a conscript army, they deprived the samurai of the military monopoly they had held for centuries. Many samurai felt betrayed by these actions, and Meiji officials sought to ease their discontent by awarding them government bonds. But as the bonds diminished in value because of inflation, former warriors had to seek employment or else suffer impoverishment. Frustrated by these new circumstances, some samurai rose in rebellion, but the recently created national army crushed all opposition. By 1878 the national government no longer feared internal military challenges to its rule.

Revamping the Tax System Japan's new leaders next put the regime on secure financial footing by revamping the tax system. Peasants traditionally paid taxes in grain, but because the value of grain fluctuated with the price of rice, so did government revenue. In 1873 the Meiji government converted the grain tax into a fixed-money tax, which provided the government with predictable revenues and left peasants to deal with market fluctuations in grain prices. The state also began to assess taxes on the potential productivity of arable land, no matter how much a cultivator actually produced. This measure virtually guaranteed that only those who maximized production could afford to hold on to their land. Others had to sell their land to more efficient producers.

Constitutional Government The reconstruction of Japanese society continued in the 1880s under mounting domestic pressure for a constitution and representative government. Those demands coincided with the rulers' belief that constitutions gave foreign powers their strength and unity. Accordingly, in 1889 the emperor issued the Meiji constitution as "a voluntary gift" to his people. Drafted under the guidance of Ito Hirobumi, this document established a constitutional monarchy with a legislature, known as the Diet, composed of a house of nobles and an elected lower house. The constitution limited the authority of the Diet and reserved considerable power to the executive branch of government. Thus, the "sacred and inviolable" emperor commanded the armed forces, named the prime minister, and appointed the cabinet. Both the prime minister and the cabinet were responsible to the emperor rather than the lower house, unlike European parliamentary systems. The emperor also had the right to dissolve the parliament, and whenever the Diet was not in session he had the prerogative of issuing ordinances. Effective power thus lay with the emperor, whom the parliament could advise but never control. The Meiji constitution recognized individual rights, but it provided that laws could limit those rights in the interests of the state, and it established property restrictions on the franchise, ensuring that delegates elected to the lower

How the Past Shapes the Future

The Birth of Nationalism

Nationalism came to Japan as a result of contact with the aggressive trade policies of the United States and other European nations. An elite group of reformers believed that, to avoid domination by western powers, they had to modernize and industrialize on the Western model—which included embracing the idea of a Japanese nation whose citizens would work together to promote the interests of the new state. In this case, then, the idea of creating a strong nation was initiated from the top down rather than from a groundswell of popular sentiment. This was accomplished in part through mandatory, state-funded education programs to teach both literacy and an appreciation of state-sanctioned national values. Consider the role mandatory public education has played in building nationalist feelings among populations around the world. Do such programs always serve the interests of states?

house represented the most prosperous social classes. In the elections of 1890 less than 5 percent of the adult male population was eligible to cast ballots. Despite its conservative features, the Meiji constitution provided greater opportunity for debate and dissent than ever before in Japanese society.

Remodeling the Economy Economic initiatives matched efforts at political reconstruction. Convinced that a powerful economy was the foundation of national strength, the Meiji government created a modern transportation, communications, and educational infrastructure. The establishment of telegraph, railroad, and steamship lines tied local and regional markets into a national economic network. The government also removed barriers to commerce and trade by abolishing guild restrictions and internal tariffs. Aiming to improve literacy rates—40 percent for males and 15 percent for females in the nineteenth century—the government introduced a system of universal primary and secondary education. Universities provided advanced instruction for the best students, especially in scientific and technical fields. This infrastructure supported rapid industrialization and economic growth. Although most economic enterprises were privately owned, the government controlled military industries and established pilot programs to stimulate industrial development. During the 1880s the government sold most of its enterprises to private investors who had close ties to government officials. The result was a concentration of enormous economic power in the hands of a small group of people, collectively known as *zaibatsu,* or financial cliques.

Costs of Economic Development Economic development came at a price, as the Japanese people bore the social and political costs of rapid industrialization. Japanese peasants, for example, supplied much of the domestic capital that

zaibatsu (zeye-BAHT-soo)

This Japanese illustration of Emperor Mutsuhito demonstrates the visual and martial transformations in Meiji Japan.
The Print Collector/Print Collector/Getty Images

supported the Meiji program of industrialization. The land tax of 1873, which cost peasants 40 to 50 percent of their crop yields, produced almost 90 percent of government revenue during the early years of Meiji development. Foreign exchange to purchase industrial equipment came chiefly from the export of textiles produced in a labor-intensive industry staffed by poorly paid workers.

The difficult lot of peasants came to the fore in 1883 and 1884 with a series of peasant uprisings aimed at moneylenders and government offices holding records of loans. The Meiji government responded by deploying military police and army units to put down these uprisings, and authorities imprisoned or executed many leaders of the rebellions. Thereafter, the government did virtually nothing to alleviate the suffering of the rural population. Hundreds of thousands of families lived in destitution—many malnourished to the point of starvation. Those who escaped rural society to take up work in the burgeoning industries learned that the state did not tolerate labor organizations that promoted the welfare of workers: Meiji law treated the formation of unions and the organization of strikes as criminal activities, and the government crushed a growing labor movement in 1901.

Nevertheless, in a single generation Meiji leaders transformed Japan into a powerful industrial society poised to play a major role in world affairs. Achieving political and economic equality with western European lands and the United States was the prime goal of Meiji leaders, who sought an end to humiliating treaty provisions. In this they were successful. In 1899 they were able to end extraterritoriality on Japanese soil for all foreign powers, and in 1902 they concluded a military alliance with Britain as an equal power. Their new status as a major military power was confirmed by stunning victories in wars first with the Chinese Empire (1894-1895) and then with the Russian Empire (1904-1905).

CONCLUSION

During the nineteenth century, Ottoman, Russian, Chinese, and Japanese societies faced severe external and internal challenges. Confrontations with western European and U.S. forces showed that the agrarian societies were militarily at a great disadvantage compared to industrial states. Ottoman, Russian, Chinese, and Japanese societies suffered also from domestic problems brought on by growing populations, the slowing of agricultural productivity, official corruption, and declining imperial revenues. To combat these problems, each of these societies embarked on ambitious reform programs that drew inspiration from western European and U.S. models to solve the crises caused by domestic discontent and foreign intrusions on their sovereignty. But reform programs had very different results in different lands. In the Ottoman, Russian, and Chinese empires, conservative ruling elites limited the scope of reform: although they generally supported industrialization and

military reform, they stifled political and social reforms that might threaten their positions in society. In Japan, however, dissent led to the collapse of the Tokugawa bakufu, and reformers had the opportunity to undertake a much more thorough program of reform than did their counterparts in Ottoman, Russian, and Chinese societies. By the early twentieth century, on the basis of reforms implemented by Meiji leaders, Japan was becoming a political, military, and economic powerhouse.

STUDY TERMS

Abdül Hamid II (675)
Boxer rebellion (688)
capitulations (674)
Cixi (671)

cohong (681)
Commodore Matthew C.
    Perry (689)
Crimean War (677)

Duma (681)

Emancipation Manifesto (677)

Fukuzawa Yukichi (690)

Hundred Days reforms (687)

Ito Hirobumi (690)

Janissaries (672)

Lin Zexu (682)

Mahmud II (674)

Meiji restoration (690)

Muhammad Ali (673)

Mutsuhito (690)

Nicholas II (680)

Opium War (685)

pogroms (680)

Qing (671)

samurai (688)

Self-Strengthening
  Movement (686)

Sergei Witte (678)

Sultan Selim III (674)

Taiping rebellion (686)

Tanzimat era (675)

Tokugawa bakufu (688)

Treaty of Nanjing (685)

Tsar Alexander II (677)

unequal treaties (685)

Xiuquan (670)

Young Turks (676)

zaibatsu (691)

zemstvos (678)

FOR FURTHER READING

Michael R. Auslin. *Negotiating with Imperialism: The Unequal Treaties and the Culture of Japanese Diplomacy.* Cambridge, Mass., 2004. Diplomatic history that examines Japan's interaction with Western imperialism and the country's emergence as a world power.

David Anthony Bello. *Opium and the Limits of Empire: Drug Prohibition in the Chinese Interior, 1729–1850.* Cambridge, Mass., 2005. Explores Qing China's efforts at controlling and prohibiting the domestic opium trade.

Carter Vaughn Findley. *Turkey, Islam, Nationalism, and Modernity.* New Haven, 2011. A leading scholar examines the historical dynamics driving two centuries of Ottoman and Turkish history.

Andrew Gordon. *A Modern History of Japan: From Tokugawa Times to the Present.* Oxford, 2013. A rich and detailed narrative of the transformation of Japan since the Tokugawa period.

Peter Kolchin. *Unfree Labor: American Slavery and Russian Serfdom.* Cambridge, Mass., 1990. A remarkable and stimulating comparative study of American slavery and Russian serfdom.

Sevket Pamuk. *The Ottoman Empire and European Capitalism, 1820–1913: Trade, Investment, and Production.* Cambridge, 2010. Closely examines complex economic entanglements.

Nicolas Spulber. *Russia's Economic Transitions: From Late Tsarism to the New Millennium.* Cambridge, 2006. This massive and challenging work examines the three major transitions in Russian economic history between the early 1860s and 2000.

John W. Steinberg, ed. *The Russo-Japanese War in Global Perspective: World War Zero.* Boston, 2005. Collection of essays that examines the Russo-Japanese War as a harbinger of World War I.

Francis William Wcislo. *Tales of Imperial Russia: The Life and Times of Sergei Witte.* Oxford, 2011. Explores the life of one of the chief engineers of modern, industrial Russia prior to the 1917 revolution.

Richard Wortman. *Scenarios of Power: Myth and Ceremony in the Russian Monarchy.* Princeton, abridged, 2006. An innovative study exploring the means by which Romanov rulers held on to their autocratic prerogatives despite fundamental changes in Russian society.

ZOOMING IN ON ENCOUNTERS

Emperor Menelik II of Ethiopia and His Warning to European Empire Builders

Emperor Menelik II of Ethiopia (r. 1889–1913) on the throne in coronation garb.
MARKA/Alamy Stock Photo

In 1889, Emperor Menelik II (1844–1913) came to the throne of the independent state of Ethiopia, in the horn of Africa. Long before taking the throne, Menelik had focused on obtaining the most up-to-date European firearms as a means of strengthening his power. In the wake of the Berlin West Africa Conference (1884–1885)—in which European powers divided up the continent of Africa among them—Menelik observed with increasing concern the violent conquest of huge portions of African territory. In 1891, Menelik decided to make his position about attempts to conquer Ethiopia clear by sending a letter to the European heads of state. He began the letter by informing his European readers about the current boundaries of Ethiopia, adding that he intended to expand these in the future. He continued by saying that "if powers at a distance come forward to partition Africa between them, I do not intend to be an indifferent spectator . . . As the Almighty has protected Ethiopia up to this day, I have confidence He will continue to protect her, and increase her borders in the future. I am certain He will not suffer her to be divided among other Powers."

Menelik did not simply rely on the power of persuasion to keep Europeans out of Ethiopia. Instead, he set about stockpiling more than eighty thousand European rifles and other weapons, including a canon. So when an Italian army—with the blessing of the British and French governments—invaded Ethiopia in 1896, the Ethiopians were ready. On March 1, they routed the Italians in the battle of Adwa, killing almost 40 percent of the force (about five thousand men), injuring another fifteen hundred, and taking a further three thousand prisoner. The battle was decisive: the Italians retreated and the European nations formally recognized Ethiopian sovereignty and independence.

But Menelik's success against European invaders was unique in the late nineteenth and early twentieth centuries. Resistance to conquest was nearly universal among African leaders and included diplomacy, seeking protection from other powers, treaties, and armed conflict. But no other state or group had been able to purchase and stockpile such a large quantity of the latest weaponry, nor had they been able to command a large, unified army to use it. As a result, Europeans maintained a technological advantage in most of the rest of Africa and used it to conquer more than 90 percent of the continent by 1910.

CHAPTER OVERVIEW

Throughout history strong societies have often sought to dominate their neighbors by subjecting them to imperial rule. They have built empires for various reasons: to gain control over natural resources, to subdue potential enemies, to seize wealth, to acquire territory for expansion, and to keep territories out of the hands of other powers. From the days of ancient Mesopotamia and Egypt to the present, imperialism has been a prominent theme of world history.

But in the second half of the nineteenth century, as the Ottoman and Qing empires weakened, a handful of western European states wrote a new chapter in the history of imperialism. Industrialization equipped them with the most effective tools and the most lethal weapons available anywhere in the world. Strong nationalist sentiments enabled them to mobilize their populations for purposes of overseas expansion. Three centuries of experience with maritime trade in Asia, Africa, the Americas, and Oceania provided them with extensive knowledge of the world and its peoples. With those advantages, western European peoples conquered foreign armies, overpowered local rulers, used their economic power, and imposed their hegemony throughout the world. Toward the end of the century, the United States and Japan joined European states as imperial powers with overseas territories.

The establishment of global empires in this period had far-reaching effects. In many ways, imperialism forcibly tightened links between the world's societies. Imperial powers demanded trade between dominant states and their overseas colonies, for example, and they organized mass migrations of laborers to work in agricultural and industrial ventures. Yet imperialism also fostered divisions between the world's peoples. Powerful tools, deadly weapons, and global hegemony led European peoples to consider themselves superior to their subjects throughout the world. In fact, modern racism is one of the legacies of imperialism. Another effect of imperialism was the development of anticolonial resistance in subject territories, including nationalism. Just as invasion and occupation by Napoleonic armies stimulated the development of nationalism in Europe, so the imposition of foreign rule provoked anticolonial and nationalist responses in colonized lands. Although the formal empires of this period were relatively short-lived and nearly all colonies had won their independence by 1970, the influence of global imperialism continues to shape the contemporary world.

CHRONOLOGY	
1772–1833	Life of Ram Mohan Roy
1838–1917	Life of Queen Lili'uokalani
1840	Treaty of Waitangi
1857	Sepoy rebellion
1859–1869	Construction of the Suez Canal
1860–1864	Land wars in New Zealand
1874–1904	Life of Raden Adjeng Kartini
1884–1885	Berlin West Africa Conference
1884–1896	Can Vuong Movement
1885	Founding of the Indian National Congress
1894–1895	Sino-Japanese War
1898–1899	Spanish-Cuban-American War
1899–1902	South African War (Boer War)
1904–1905	Russo-Japanese War
1904–1914	Construction of the Panama Canal
1906	Founding of All-India Muslim League

FOUNDATIONS OF EMPIRE

Campaigns to conquer foreign territories have always been dangerous and expensive ventures. They have arisen from a sense that foreign conquest is essential, and they have entailed the mobilization of political, military, and economic resources. In nineteenth-century Europe, advocates of empire advanced a variety of political, economic, and cultural arguments to justify the conquest and control of foreign lands. The imperialist ventures they promoted enjoyed such dramatic success largely because of the military, transportation, and communications technologies developed by European industry in the first half of the nineteenth century.

Motives of Imperialism

Modern Imperialism As we know, the building of empires was not a new phenomenon in world history. By the nineteenth century, however, even contemporary observers recognized that empires of their day were different from those of earlier times. By mid-century they began to speak of *imperialism,* and by the 1880s the recently coined term had made its way into popular speech and writing throughout western Europe. In contemporary usage, imperialism referred to the domination by European powers—and later by the United States and Japan as well—over subject territories overseas. Sometimes that domination was won by force of arms, but often it arose from trade, investment, and business activities that enabled imperial powers to profit from subject societies and influence their affairs without exercising direct political control.

Modern Colonialism Like the building of empires, the establishment of colonies in foreign territories is a practice dating from ancient times. Here, however, colonialism refers not just to the sending of colonists to settle new lands but also to the political, social, economic, and cultural structures that enabled imperial powers to dominate subject lands. In some places such as North America, Chile, Argentina, Algeria, Australia, New Zealand, and South Africa, European powers established settler colonies populated by large numbers of migrants from Europe. Yet contemporary scholars also speak of European colonies in India, southeast Asia, and sub-Saharan Africa, even though European migrants did not settle there in large numbers. European agents, officials, and businesspeople effectively turned those lands into colonies and profoundly influenced their historical development by controlling their domestic and foreign policies, integrating local economies into the network of global capitalism, introducing European business techniques, transforming educational systems according to European standards, and promoting European cultural preferences.

During the second half of the nineteenth century, many Europeans came to believe that imperial expansion and colonial domination were crucial for the survival of their states and societies—and sometimes for their personal fortunes as well. European merchants and entrepreneurs sometimes became extremely wealthy from business ventures in Asia or Africa, and they argued for their home states to pursue imperialist policies partly to secure and enhance their own enterprises. A notorious example was **Cecil John Rhodes** (1853–1902), who built a massive fortune by exploiting African laborers to mine for diamonds in southern Africa. Having made his fortune, Rhodes became a tireless advocate for the extension of British rule to the rest of the world.

Economic Motives of Imperialism A wide range of motives encouraged European peoples to launch imperialist campaigns of conquest and control. Some advocates argued that imperialism was in the economic interests of European societies as well as individuals. They pointed out that overseas colonies could serve as reliable sources of raw materials not available in Europe that came into demand because of industrialization: rubber, tin, and copper were vital products, for example, and by the late nineteenth century petroleum had also become a crucial resource for industrialized lands. Imperialists ruthlessly exploited wild rubber resources in the Congo River basin and established rubber plantations in Malaya. Abundant supplies of tin were available from colonies in southeast Asia and copper in central Africa. The United States and Russia supplied most of the world's petroleum in the nineteenth century, but by the early twentieth century the oil fields of southwest Asia attracted the attention of European industrialists and imperialists alike.

Proponents of imperialism also held that colonies would consume manufactured products and provide a haven for European migrants in an age

How the Past Shapes the Future ▷ ▷ ▷ ▷

The Birth of Nationalism

State governments sometimes used popular nationalist sentiment for their own purposes when it came to imperial expansion. One characteristic feature of nationalism is that nationalists often define their common bonds in opposition to other peoples and traditions: thus, national unity tends to be most strongly expressed when members feel threatened by outside forces. During the nineteenth century, some governments sought to capitalize on this characteristic of nationalism to gain popular support for imperial expansion and also to manipulate political opinion at home. The Abyssinian campaign of 1862 is but one example of this phenomenon: during an election year, the British Conservative party used an incident in which several British citizens had been taken hostage by the Ethiopian king as a way to whip up nationalist outrage against both the Ethiopians and the ruling British Liberal party. In part because of this nationalist fervor, the Liberals were defeated and the Conservatives were voted into power. What might be the short- and long-term consequences of manipulating nationalist feeling for political purposes?

Rubber tapping on a plantation in Sumatra in the Dutch East Indies (modern Indonesia) in the early twentieth century.
Sepia Times/Universal Images Group/Getty Images

of rapidly increasing population. In fact, manufactured goods did not flow to most colonies in large quantities, and European migrants went overwhelmingly to independent states in the Americas rather than to overseas colonies. Nevertheless, arguments arising from national economic interest generated considerable support for imperialism.

Geopolitical Motives of Imperialism

In the last half of the nineteenth century, geopolitical concerns became one of the most influential motivations for imperialism. Advocates argued that even if colonies were not always economically beneficial, they were crucial for political and military reasons. Territories that occupied strategic sites on the world's sea lanes or harbors ideal for supplying commercial and naval ships attracted particular attention. Proponents of imperialism sought to acquire these sites for their own states and especially to deny them to other states. The British occupation of Egypt in 1882 is a good example of this because the British government was extremely anxious to protect the Suez Canal—the main route to India from Britain—from falling into the hands of a rival. Sometimes political motivations for imperial expansion were rooted in the desire for global power and prestige. In the late nineteenth century, for example, French enthusiasm for imperial expansion increased after its humiliating defeat in the Franco-Prussian war of 1870–1871. In Germany as well, public opinion demanded colonies as a way of marking Germany's entry to great power status after the state's achievement of nationhood in 1871.

Imperialism also had its uses for domestic politics. In an age when socialists and communists directly confronted industrialists, European politicians and national leaders sought to defuse social tension and inspire patriotism by focusing public attention on imperialist ventures. Beginning in the mid-nineteenth century and continuing into the twentieth, European leaders frequently organized colonial exhibitions where they convinced or coerced colonized people to display their dress, music, and customs for tourists and the general public in imperial metropoles like London and Paris, all in an effort to win popular support for imperialist policies.

Cultural Justifications of Imperialism

Cultural motivations also helped justify imperial expansion in this period. European missionaries, for example, believed it was their duty to seek out converts to Christianity around the world, and imperial expansion allowed them the protection of European governments as they did so. European missionaries did not always see eye to eye with European entrepreneurs or colonial officials and were sometimes deeply critical of aspects of colonial rule. Nevertheless, they often facilitated communications between imperialists and subject peoples, and they sometimes provided European officials with information they needed to maintain control of overseas colonies. Missionary settlements also served as convenient meeting places for Europeans overseas and as distribution centers for European manufactured goods.

While missionaries specifically sought to introduce Christianity to subject peoples, other Europeans thought it was their duty to bring the values and practices associated with European "civilization" to people around the world. These included ideas ranging from the establishment of European-style legal systems, modes of dress, expected gender relations, and emphasis on market consumerism. French imperialists routinely invoked the ***mission civilisatrice*** ("civilizing mission") as

---

mission civilisatrice (mih-see-on sih-vih-lees-ah-TRIHS) justification for their expansion into Africa and Asia, and the English writer and poet Rudyard Kipling (1864–1936) defined the "white man's burden" as the duty of European and Euro-American peoples to bring their ideas of order and enlightenment to distant places.

Tools of Empire

Even the strongest motives would not have enabled imperialists to impose their rule throughout the world without the powerful technological advantages that industrialization conferred on them. Ever since the introduction of gunpowder in the thirteenth century, European states had competed vigorously to develop increasingly powerful military technologies. Industrialization enhanced those efforts by making it possible to produce huge quantities of advanced weapons and tools. During the nineteenth century, industrialists devised effective technologies of war, transportation, communication, and medicine that enabled European imperialists to exert enormous influence in the world during the nineteenth and first half of the twentieth centuries.

Military Technologies The most advanced firearms of the early nineteenth century were smoothbore, muzzle-loading muskets, meaning that ammunition was projected from a smooth inner casing and that the weapon had to be loaded from the end where the ammunition was shot. When large numbers of infantry fired their muskets at once, the resulting volley could cause havoc among opponents. Yet it took a skilled musketeer about one minute to reload a weapon, and on top of that, the smoothbore interior reduced the accuracy

of the musket. By mid-century European armies were using breech-loading firearms with rifled bores—in which weapons were loaded quickly from the top and ammunition was projected from a grooved interior—that were far more accurate and reliable than muskets. By the 1870s Europeans were experimenting with rifled machine guns, and in the 1880s they adopted the Maxim gun, a light and powerful weapon that fired eleven bullets per second.

Those firearms provided European armies with an arsenal vastly stronger than any other in the world. When European states sought to impose their will against others that didn't yet have the latest rifles or machine guns, as they often did in this period, they were able to inflict devastating defeats. In 1898, for example, a British army with twenty machine guns and six gunboats engaged a huge Sudanese force that sought to expel the British from the area at Omdurman, near Khartoum on the Nile River. During five hours of fighting, the British force lost a few hundred men while machine guns and explosive charges fired from gunboats killed close to twenty thousand Sudanese in a matter of hours. The battle of **Omdurman** became the first step in the establishment of British colonial rule in Sudan.

Communications Technologies Communications also benefited from industrialization, and in turn aided European imperial expansion. Oceangoing steamships reduced the time required to deliver messages from imperial capitals to colonial lands. In the 1830s it took as long as two years for a British correspondent to receive a reply to a letter sent to India by sailing ship. By the 1850s, however, after the introduction of steamships, correspondence could make the round-trip between

A British Maxim gun at Chilas Fort on India's Northwest Frontier in the late nineteenth century.
Hulton Archive/Getty Images

Thousands of spectators gathered on the banks of the Suez Canal in 1869 to watch a parade of ships that opened the canal by proceeding from the Mediterranean to the Red Sea. The Suez and Panama canals became the most strategic waterways in the world because they significantly shortened maritime routes both between Europe and the lands bordering the Indian and Pacific oceans and between one coast of North America and ports on the other side of South America. Chronicle/Alamy Stock Photo

London and Bombay in four months. After the opening of the Suez Canal in 1869, steamships traveled from Britain to India in less than two weeks.

The invention of the telegraph made it possible to exchange messages even faster. Telegraph wires carried communications over land beginning in the 1830s, but only in the 1850s did engineers devise reliable submarine cables for the transmission of messages across the oceans. By 1870, submarine cables carried messages between Britain and India in about five hours. By 1902, cables linked all parts of the British Empire throughout the world, and other European states maintained cables to support communications with their own colonies. Their monopoly on telegraphic communications provided imperial powers with distinct advantages over their colonial territories. Imperial officials could rapidly mobilize forces to deal with troubles, and merchants could respond quickly to developments of economic and commercial significance. Rapid communication was an integral structural element of empire.

Medical Technologies When Europeans traveled to the tropical and subtropical regions where they sought to impose their rule, they frequently became ill and died from malaria, a mosquito-borne disease. When they discovered an effective treatment for the disease in the form of quinine, it became a powerful weapon in the European quest to conquer and rule distant lands during the nineteenth century.

The remedy for malaria came to Europe from Peru, where indigenous peoples used the bark from the cinchona tree to treat various fevers. This "Jesuit bark," as it was known because of the missionaries' role in conveying this information to other Europeans, also worked well against malaria. When it became clear that cinchona bark could be used not only to treat malaria but also to prevent it, the bark quickly became the favored treatment for malaria. In 1820, two French chemists, Pierre Pelletier and Joseph Caventou, extracted the alkaloid of quinine from cinchona bark, and by the 1840s European colonizers kept quinine pills by their bed stands. The use of quinine proved to be a major force in the expansion of European empires and ultimately permitted small European populations to survive in tropical regions. By the time the British in India and the Dutch in Java began commercially planting cinchona trees in the 1880s to create a reliable supply of the bark, its active ingredient, quinine powder, had become crucial to the health of European colonizers wherever malaria existed.

Transportation Technologies The most important innovations in transportation as they related to imperial expansion involved steamships and railroads. Small steamboats plied the waters of the United States and western Europe from the early nineteenth century. During the 1830s British naval engineers adapted steam power to military uses and built large, ironclad ships equipped with powerful guns. These steamships traveled much faster than sailing vessels, and as an additional advantage they could ignore the winds and travel in any direction. Because they could travel much farther upriver than sailboats, which depended on convenient winds, steamships enabled imperialists to project power deep into the interior regions of foreign lands. For example, as we saw in chapter 31, in 1842 the British ironclad steamship *Nemesis* led an expedition up the Yangzi River that brought the Opium War to a conclusion. Steam-powered gunboats later helped to project European power to inland sites throughout Africa and Asia.

The construction of new canals enhanced the effectiveness of steamships. Both the **Suez Canal** (constructed 1859–1869) and the **Panama Canal** (constructed 1904–1914) facilitated the building and maintenance of empires by enabling naval vessels to travel more rapidly than ever before between the world's seas and oceans. They also lowered the costs of trade between imperial powers and subject lands.

Once imperialists had gained control of overseas lands, they often constructed railroads to help them maintain their hegemony and organize local economies to their own advantage. Rail transportation enabled colonial officials and armies to travel quickly through the colonies. It also facilitated the exploitation of raw materials and the distribution of European manufactured goods in the colonies.

EUROPEAN IMPERIALISM

Aided by powerful technologies, European states launched an unprecedented round of empire building in the second half of the nineteenth century. Imperial expansion began with the British conquest of India. Competition between imperial powers led to European intrusion into central Asia and the establishment of colonies in southeast Asia. Fearful that rivals might gain control over some region that remained free of imperial control, European states embarked on a campaign of frenzied expansion in the 1880s that brought almost all of Africa and Pacific Ocean territories into their empires. Competition between imperial powers led to European intrusion into central Asia, the establishment of colonies in southeast Asia, and interference in the Ottoman and Qing empires in southwest and east Asia (discussed in chapter 31). Throughout this period, Europeans were engaged simultaneously in projects of settler colonialism, formal imperialism without large numbers of settlers, and informal imperialism in which sovereignty was compromised by widespread economic interference. Whether European powers engaged in one kind or another of imperial project depended largely on rivalries with other European powers, the strategic or economic importance of a given area, and the level and type of resistance offered by indigenous peoples.

The British Empire in India

The British Empire in south Asia and southeast Asia grew out of the mercantile activities of the English **East India Company,** which enjoyed a monopoly on English trade with India. In 1600, the East India Company obtained permission from the Mughal emperors of India to build fortified posts on the coastlines. There, company agents traded for goods and stored commodities in warehouses until company ships arrived to transport them to Europe. In the seventeenth century, company merchants traded mostly for Indian pepper and cotton, Chinese silk and porcelain, and fine spices from southeast Asia. During the eighteenth century, tea and coffee became the most prominent trade items, and European consumers acquired a taste for both beverages that they have never lost.

Company Rule After the death of the emperor Aurangzeb in 1707, the Mughal state entered a period of decline, and many local authorities asserted their independence of Mughal rule. The East India Company took advantage of Mughal weakness

to strengthen and expand its trading posts. In the 1750s company officials embarked on the outright conquest of India. Through diplomacy or military campaigns, the company conquered autonomous Indian kingdoms and reduced Mughal rule to only a small area around Delhi. Part of the British policy of expansion was the "doctrine of lapse," greatly resented by Indians. If an Indian ruler failed to produce a biological male heir to the throne, his territories lapsed to the company upon his death. By the mid-nineteenth century, the English East India Company had annexed huge areas of India and had established control over present-day Pakistan, Bangladesh, Burma, and Sri Lanka. Company rule was enforced by a small British army and a large number of Indian soldiers known as sepoys.

Indian Rebellion The British imposition of rule in south Asia was often insulting to both Hindu and Muslim religious traditions and frequently cut off the political ambitions of influential leaders without any kind of political compensation. Discontent with the British reached even to the sepoys of the East India Company, and in 1857 large portions of the army rebelled.

The rebellion in the army quickly spread to a general anti-British revolution in central and north India. Sepoys were now joined by Indian princes and their followers, whose territories had been annexed by the British, and people whose ways of life and sources of income had been disrupted by British trade, missionary activities, and misguided social reforms. What had begun as a rebellion by Indian troops in the employ of the English East India Company turned into a full-fledged war of independence against British rule. To regain control, the British waged a bloody campaign of retribution in which many thousands of Indians—including civilians not directly involved in the rebellion—were killed in summary hangings and the destruction of whole villages. After several months of inconclusive battles, British forces finally gained the upper hand by late 1857, and peace was officially declared on 8 July 1858.

British Imperial Rule The widespread but unsuccessful rebellion against British rule in India had far-reaching consequences. The British government officially abolished the East India Company in favor of the direct rule of India by the British government. In 1858 Queen Victoria (reigned 1837-1901) assigned responsibility for Indian policy to the newly established office of secretary of state for India. A viceroy represented British royal authority in India and administered the colony through an elite Indian civil service staffed almost exclusively by the English. Indians served in low-level bureaucratic positions, but British officials formulated all domestic and foreign policy in India.

Under both the East India Company and direct colonial administration, British rule transformed India. As they extended their authority to all parts of India and Ceylon (modern Sri Lanka), British officials cleared forests, restructured landholdings, and encouraged the cultivation of crops, such as tea, coffee, and opium, that were especially valuable trade items.

Troops loyal to the British hang two participants of the sepoy rebellion on a makeshift gallows. During the rebellion, British forces frequently resorted to summary execution without trial for those they suspected of involvement.
Felice Beato/Universal History Archive/Universal Images Group/Getty Images

They built extensive railroad and telegraph networks that tightened links between India and the larger global economy. They also constructed new canals, harbors, and irrigation systems to support commerce and agriculture. Especially after 1857, British colonial authorities made little effort to promote Christianity, but they established English-style schools for the children of Indian elites, and they suppressed Indian customs that conflicted with European law or values. Most prominent of those customs were sati (the practice of widows burning themselves on their husbands' funeral pyres), infanticide, and slavery.

Imperialism in Central Asia and Southeast Asia

As the East India Company and British colonial agents tightened their grip on India, competition among European states kindled further empire-building efforts. Beginning in the early nineteenth century, French and Russian strategists sought ways to undermine British power and establish their own colonial presence in India. French efforts stalled after the fall of Napoleon in 1815, but Russian interest in India fueled a prolonged contest for power in central Asia.

MAP 32.1   Imperialism in Asia, ca. 1914. Date is year of conquest.

Note the claims made by various industrial powers.

Which territories remained unclaimed, and why? Which power claimed the most imperial territory in Asia?

Russians had been interested in central Asia as early as the sixteenth century, but only in the nineteenth century did they undertake a systematic effort to extend Russian authority south of the Caucasus. The weakening of the Ottoman and Qing empires in Central Asia gave them their opportunity. By the 1860s Russians had overcome Tashkent, Bokhara, and Samarkand, the great caravan cities of the Silk Roads, and approached the ill-defined northern frontier of British India. For the next half century, military officers and imperialist adventurers engaged in a risky pursuit of influence and intelligence that British agents referred to as the **"Great Game."**

The Great Game Russian and British explorers ventured into parts of central Asia never before visited by Europeans. They mapped terrain, scouted mountain passes, and sought alliances with local rulers from Afghanistan to the Aral Sea—all in an effort to prepare for the anticipated war for India. In fact, the outbreak of global war in 1914 and the collapse of the tsarist state in 1917 ensured that the contest for India never took place. Nevertheless, imperial expansion brought much of central Asia into the Russian empire and subjected the region to intense Russian influence that persisted until the disintegration of the Soviet Union in 1991.

Competition among European powers led also to further imperialism in southeast Asia. The Philippines had come under Spanish colonial rule in the sixteenth century, and many southeast Asian islands were conquered by the Dutch in the seventeenth century. As imperial rivalries escalated in the nineteenth century, Dutch officials tightened their control and extended their authority throughout the Dutch East Indies, the archipelago that makes up the modern state of Indonesia. Along with cash crops of sugar, tea, coffee, and tobacco, exports of rubber and tin made the Dutch East Indies a valuable colony for the Netherlands, even while Dutch colonial policy impoverished indigenous populations.

British Colonies in Southeast Asia In the interests of increasing trade between India, southeast Asia, and China, British imperialists moved in the nineteenth century to establish a presence in southeast Asia. As early as the 1820s, colonial officials in India came into conflict with the kings of Burma (modern Myanmar) while seeking to extend their influence to the Irrawaddy River delta. By the 1880s they had established colonial authority in Burma, which became a source of teak, ivory, rubies, and jade. In 1824 Thomas Stamford Raffles founded the port of Singapore after signing a treaty with the local rulers of

SOURCES FROM THE PAST

Raden Adjeng Kartini on Life as a Colonized Subject in the Dutch East Indies

Raden (an honorific title) Adjeng Kartini (1879–1904) was born to a noble family on the island of Java, part of the Dutch colony of the East Indies (now Indonesia). Her father worked for the Dutch government, which allowed Kartini to attend a Dutch school—a privilege reserved only for Indonesians of the highest social class and usually only for boys. In the course of her schooling, Kartini became a fierce critic of colonial racism and the oppression of women in both Dutch and Javanese culture. Yet she was forced to leave school as an adolescent because her family believed that it was inappropriate for a young, noble woman to participate in the public world. In hopes of escaping her social isolation, Kartini agreed to marry at the age of twenty-three. With the support of her husband and the Dutch government, in 1903 she opened the first primary school for Indonesian girls that did not discriminate on the basis of social class. Kartini had dreams of expanding her efforts on behalf of Indonesian women, but she died tragically from complications of childbirth only two years later, at the age of twenty-five. Below, she writes to the Dutch feminist Stella Zeehandelaar about Dutch prejudice and the coming emancipation of Indonesian men and women.

January 12, 1900

The Hollanders laugh and make fun of our stupidity, but if we strive for enlightenment, then they assume a defiant attitude toward us. What have I not suffered as a child at school through the ill will of the teachers and of many of my fellow pupils? Not all of the teachers and pupils hated us. Many loved us quite as much as the other children. But it was hard for the teachers to give a native the highest mark, never mind how well it may have been deserved . . .

With heavy hearts, many Europeans here see how the Javanese, whom they regard as their inferiors, are slowly awakening, and at every turn a brown man comes up, who shows that he has just as good brains in his head, and a just as good heart in his body, as the white man . . .

> Why does Kartini say that the Europeans view the "awakening" of Javanese people with "heavy hearts"?

But we are going forward, and they cannot hold back the current of time. I love the Hollanders very, very much, and I am grateful for everything that we have gained through them. Many of them are among our best friends, but there are also others who dislike us, for no other reason than we are bold enough to emulate them in education and culture.

In many subtle ways they make us feel their dislike. "I am a European, you are a Javanese," they seem to say, or "I am the master, you the governed." Not once, but many times, they speak to us in broken Malay; although they know very well that we understand the Dutch language . . .

Why do many Hollanders find it unpleasant to converse with us in their own language? Oh yes, now I understand; Dutch is too beautiful to be spoken by a brown mouth.

A few days ago we paid a visit to Totokkers [Europeans new to the East Indies]. Their domestics were old servants of ours, and we knew that they could speak and understand Dutch very well. I told the host this, and what answer did I receive from my gentleman? "No, they must not speak Dutch." "No, why?" I asked. "Because natives ought not to know Dutch." I looked at him in amazement, and a satirical smile quivered at the corners of my mouth. The gentleman grew fiery red, mumbled something into his beard, and discovered something interesting in his boots, at least he devoted all of his attention to them.

> Why did Kartini's smile embarrass the Dutch man?

In the last few days, articles written by natives have been published in the "Locomotief," the foremost paper of India [the Dutch East Indies]. In these articles they lay bare the opinions, which have secretly been held for years about, not all, but by far the greater number of Indian officials [Dutch officials in the East Indies]. Not only the highest in the land, but also the most humble are allowing their voices to be heard. The paper calls this a good sign of the times, and rejoices. . . . It is also urged that the Dutch language be used officially in business between European and native chiefs. Splendid! . . . In July, the question of the education of women will come up too. The Javanese are emancipating themselves.

Still this is only a beginning, and it is splendid that men of influence and ability are supporting our [women's] cause. The strife will be violent, the combatants will not have to fight against opposition alone, but also against the indifference of our own countrywomen, in whose behalf they would break their lances. While this agitation among the men is on the tapis, that will be the time for the women to rise up and let themselves be heard. Poor men—you will have your hands full.

For Further Reflection

■ Kartini was a noble woman and daughter of a high-ranking official who worked for the Dutch. In what ways does the passage above give away her social status? How might Kartini's focus have been different if she had been a woman of a much lower social status?

Source: Raden Adjeng Kartini, *Letters of a Javanese Princess.* This edition originally published in 1920. Project Gutenberg. http://www.gutenberg.org/files/34647/34647-h/34647-h.htm.

Warships provide covering fire as British troops prepare to storm the Burmese port of Rangoon in 1824. By the 1880s the British had established colonial authority in Burma and were using it as a source of such valuable commodities as teak, ivory, rubies, and jade. The British Library/Robana/Getty Images

the island, which soon became the busiest center of trade in the Strait of Melaka. Administered by the colonial regime in India until 1867 and then as a crown colony ruled directly from Britain, Singapore served as the base for the British conquest of Malaya (modern Malaysia) in the 1870s and 1880s. Besides offering outstanding ports that enabled the British navy to control sea lanes linking the Indian Ocean with the South China Sea, Malaya provided abundant supplies of tin and rubber.

French Indochina Although they were unable to oust the British and establish themselves in India, French imperialists built the large southeast Asian colony of French Indochina, consisting of the modern states of Vietnam, Cambodia, and Laos, between 1859 and 1893. Like their British counterparts in India, French colonial officials introduced European-style schools and sought to establish close connections with native elites. Unlike their rivals, French officials also encouraged conversion to Christianity, and as a result the Roman Catholic church became prominent throughout French Indochina, especially in Vietnam.

By century's end, all of southeast Asia had come under European imperial rule except for the kingdom of Siam (modern Thailand), which preserved its independence largely because colonial officials regarded it as a convenient buffer state between British-dominated Burma and French Indochina.

The Scramble for Africa

The most striking expansion of European imperialism in this period took place in Africa. As late as 1875, Europeans had only a limited presence in Africa. They held several small coastal colonies and fortified trading posts, but their only sizable possessions were the Portuguese colonies of Angola and Mozambique, the French settler colony in northern Algeria, and a cluster of settler colonies populated by British and Dutch migrants in southern Africa. After the end of the slave trade in 1807, a lively commerce developed around the exchange of African gold, ivory, and palm oil for European textiles, guns, and manufactured goods.

Between 1875 and 1900, however, the relationship between Africa and Europe dramatically changed. Within a quarter century, European imperial powers partitioned and colonized almost the entire African continent. Prospects of exploiting African resources and geopolitical rivalries between European powers help to explain this frenzied quest for empire, often referred to as the **"scramble for Africa."**

Precursors to the Scramble for Africa
Europeans did not know much about the huge and diverse interior of the African continent before the mid-nineteenth century. But a series of explorers who went on to write and speak about their journeys to Africa stimulated intense interest among Europeans. The best known of these explorers was Dr. David Livingstone, a Scottish minister, who made three extremely well publicized trips to Africa to explore territories unknown to Europeans and to convert Africans to Christian-

This 1912 photograph documents the missing hands of two young people in the Belgian Congo. Amputations were a frequent punishment for failing to meet rubber quotas.

Cultural Heritage Images/Universal Images Group/Newscom

violence to induce inhabitants to collect rubber from wild vines. When inhabitants could not meet rubber quotas set by the state, colonial officials resorted to burning villages, amputations, whippings, and murder. Between four to eight million Congolese died as a result of these practices. Although all European colonial administrations used violence to enforce their will, when missionaries and journalists eventually exposed the brutality of the Congo Free State, global opinion turned sharply against Leopold. In an effort to mitigate some of the worst abuses of the regime, in 1908 the Belgian government took control of the colony away from Leopold and thereafter administered it as the Belgian Congo. While Leopold's Congo had been conceived in a climate of European fascination for Africa, it foreshadowed the many abuses that would result as Europeans sought to divide the continent between them for their own gain.

ity. Livingstone's books attracted many thousands of readers, and when he seemed to disappear for four years during his third journey in the African interior, the editor for the *New York Herald* ordered the American journalist Henry Morton Stanley to lead an expedition to find him. After a highly publicized journey of eight months, in 1871 Stanley found Livingstone in the town of Ujiji, Tanganyika. By that time, Europeans and Americans from many backgrounds—including merchants, missionaries, and government officials—were determined to mine Africa's potential for their own purposes.

One of these people was the King of Belgium, **Leopold II** (r. 1865–1909). By the 1870s, Leopold had become convinced that the only way for a tiny state like Belgium to play a major role in world affairs was to acquire colonies as Britain and France did. He had avidly followed Stanley's journey to find Livingstone and became convinced that Belgium could carve out a colony in the Congo River basin, whose forests were rich with natural rubber so desired by industrialized nations. Under the pretense of encouraging free trade in the area, Leopold hired Stanley to help develop commercial ventures and establish a colony called the Congo Free State (modern-day Democratic Republic of the Congo). Leopold's greed for wealth from rubber led him to establish a regime in the Congo Free State that openly used forced labor and extreme

South Africa Long before the scramble for Africa, a European presence had grown at the southern tip of the African continent, where the Dutch East India Company had established Cape Town (1652) as a supply station for ships en route to Asia. Soon after, former company employees plus newly arrived settlers from Europe moved into territories beyond company control to take up farming and ranching. Many of these settlers, known first as Boers (the Dutch word for "farmer") and then as Afrikaners (the Dutch word for "African"), believed that God had predestined them to claim the people and resources of the Cape. The area under white settler control expanded during the eighteenth century as a steady stream of European migrants—chiefly Dutch, Germans, and French Huguenots (Protestants) fleeing religious persecution—continued to swell the colony's population. As European settlers spread beyond the reaches of the original colony, they began encroaching on lands occupied by **Khoikhoi** and **Xhosa** peoples. Competition for land soon led to hostility, and by the early eighteenth century, warfare, enslavement, and smallpox epidemics had led to the virtual

Khoikhoi (KOY-koy)
Xhosa (KOH-suh)

extinction of the Khoikhoi. After a century of intermittent warfare, the Xhosa too had been decimated, losing lives, land, and resources to European settlers.

When the British took over the Cape from the Dutch during the Napoleonic Wars (1799–1815), Afrikaners pushed further into the interior of southern Africa. The establishment of British rule in 1806 deeply disrupted Afrikaner society, for in its wake came the imposition of English law and language. The institution of slavery—a defining feature of rural Afrikaner society—developed into the most contentious issue between British administrators and Afrikaner settlers because Afrikaners believed that enslaved labor was vital to their livelihoods. Chafing under British rule, and in particular the British abolition of slavery in 1833, Afrikaners started to leave their farms in Cape Colony and gradually migrated east in what they called the Great Trek. That colonial expansion sometimes led to violent conflict with indigenous peoples, but the superior firepower of Afrikaner *voortrekkers* (Afrikaans for "pioneers") overcame first Ndebele and then Zulu resistance. The colonizers interpreted their successful expansion as evidence that God approved of their dominance in South Africa. By the mid-nineteenth century, *voortrekkers* had created several independent republics: the Republic of Natal, annexed by the British in 1843; the Orange Free State in 1854; and the South African Republic (Transvaal territories) in 1860.

The British in South Africa were not particularly concerned about the establishment of these states until the discovery of large mineral deposits in Afrikaner-populated territories—diamonds in 1867 and gold in 1886. When the existence of these minerals became clear, thousands of British miners and prospectors flocked to the Afrikaner states, leading to tensions between British authorities and Afrikaners. By 1899, these tensions erupted in the **South African War** (1899–1902; sometimes called the Boer War), in which Britons and Afrikaners fought over the right to control the land and resources of the Orange Free State and the Transvaal. The war was both expensive and brutal—both sides possessed modern weapons, Afrikaners engaged in guerilla warfare, and the Afrikaner lifestyle included training in marksmanship. Although the British eventually prevailed, they were forced to assemble a force of five hundred thousand men (at a cost of about two hundred million pounds) to defeat the eighty-eight thousand Afrikaners ranged against them. Moreover, to break the will of Afrikaners, the

French cartoon depicting the Berlin Conference of 1884–1885. Germany's Otto von Bismarck carves a large cake called "Africa" while other European delegates look on.

Historia/Shutterstock

British resorted to a policy of imprisoning Afrikaner women and children in concentration camps, where at least twenty-eight thousand died. And although the war was between Britons and Afrikaners, nearly twenty thousand black Africans also died in the conflict. When Afrikaners conceded defeat in 1902, the British determined to unite their territories in the Cape and Natal with the Orange Free State and the Transvaal, creating the Union of South Africa in 1910. British attempts at improving relations between English speakers and Afrikaners after the war centered on shoring up the privileges of white colonial society over black Africans.

The Berlin Conference In 1882, a British army occupied Egypt in order to protect British financial and strategic interests in the Suez Canal (and its quickest sea route to India). The British government justified its actions by claiming the need to stabilize the country from military rebellion, which itself had occurred in response to high taxes imposed to pay off a crushing Egyptian debt to European lenders. In addition to provoking hostility among Egyptians, the British occupation also angered other European colonial powers who believed British control of the Suez would tip the global balance of power even further in its favor. These tensions, and the threat of war they raised, led to the **Berlin West Africa Conference** (1884–1885), during which the delegates of twelve European states as well as the United States and the Ottoman Empire devised the ground rules for the division of African territories by outsiders. Not a single African was present. Half the nations represented, including the United States, had no colonial ambitions on the continent, but they had been invited to give the proceedings a veneer of unbiased international approval. The Berlin Conference produced agreement for future claims on African lands with the goal of avoiding war between the great powers: each colonial power had to notify the others of its claims, and each claim had to be followed up by "effective occupation" of the claimed territory. Occupation was commonly accomplished either by getting a signed agreement from a local African ruler or by military conquest. Conference participants also spelled out so-called noble-minded objectives for colonized lands: an end to the slave trade, the extension of civilization and Christianity, and increased commerce and trade. Although the conference did not parcel out African lands among the participant nations, it nevertheless

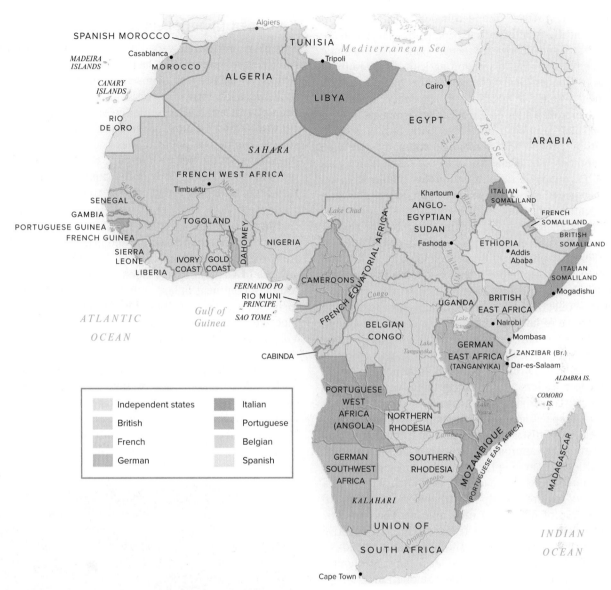

MAP 32.2   Imperialism in Africa, ca. 1914.

By 1914, only Ethiopia and Liberia remained free of European control.

How was it possible for Europeans to gain such domination?

served public notice that European powers were poised to carve the continent into colonies.

During the next twenty-five years, European imperialists sent armies to consolidate their claims and impose colonial rule. Armed with the latest weapons technology, including the newly developed machine gun and artillery with explosive shells, they rarely failed to defeat African forces. All too often, battles were one-sided. As we have already seen, in 1898, at Omdurman (a city in central Sudan near the junction of the White and Blue Nile rivers) British forces killed close to 20,000 Sudanese in a matter of hours while suffering only minor losses themselves. As we saw in the introduction to this chapter, the only indigenous African state to resist colonization successfully was Ethiopia. Besides Ethiopia, the only African state to remain independent was Liberia, a small republic in west Africa populated by formerly enslaved people that was effectively a dependency of the United States.

Systems of Colonial Rule
In the wake of rapid conquest came problems of colonial occupation. Imperial powers commonly assumed that, following an initial modest investment, colonial administration would become financially self-sufficient. For decades, Europeans struggled to identify the ideal system of rule, only to learn that colonial rule in Africa could be maintained only through exceedingly high expenditures.

The earliest approach to colonial rule involved "concessionary companies" such as the German Colonial Society for

German Southwest Africa (founded in 1885). European governments typically granted private companies large concessions of territory and empowered them to undertake economic activities such as mining, plantation agriculture, or railroad construction. Concessionary companies also had permission to implement systems of taxation and labor recruitment. Although that approach allowed European governments to colonize and exploit immense territories with only a modest investment in capital and personnel, company rule also brought liabilities. The brutal use of forced labor, which provoked a public outcry in Europe, and profits smaller than anticipated persuaded most European governments by the early twentieth century to curtail the powers of private companies and to establish their own rule. Usually, government rule took the form of either **direct rule,** typical of French colonies, or **indirect rule,** characteristic of British colonies.

Under direct rule, colonies featured administrative districts headed by European personnel who assumed responsibility for tax collection, labor and military recruitment, and the maintenance of law and order. Administrative boundaries intentionally cut across existing African political and ethnic boundaries to divide and weaken potentially powerful indigenous groups. Direct rule aimed at removing strong kings and other leaders and replacing them with more malleable persons. Underlying the principle of direct rule was the desire to keep African populations in check and to permit European administrators to engage in a "civilizing mission." However, that approach to colonial rule presented its own difficulties. Key among them was the constant shortage of European personnel. For example, in French West Africa some thirty-six hundred Europeans tried to rule over an African population of more than nine million. The combination of long distances and slow transport limited effective communication between regional authorities and officials in remote areas. An inability to speak local languages and a limited understanding of local customs among European officials further undermined their effective administration.

The British colonial administrator Frederick D. Lugard (1858-1945) was the driving force behind the doctrine of indirect rule, which the British employed in many of their African colonies. Lugard stressed the moral and financial advantages of exercising control over subject populations through indigenous institutions. He was particularly keen on using existing "tribal" authorities and "customary laws" as the foundation for colonial rule. Forms of indirect rule worked in regions where Africans had already established strong and highly organized states, but elsewhere erroneous assumptions concerning the "tribal" nature of African societies weakened the effectiveness of indirect rule. Bewildered by the complexities of African societies, colonial officials frequently imposed their own ideas of what constituted "tribal boundaries" or "tribal authorities." The invention of rigid tribal categories and the establishment of artificial tribal boundaries became one of the greatest obstacles to nation building and regional stability in much of Africa during the second half of the twentieth century.

European Imperialism in the Pacific

European imperial powers did not overlook opportunities to establish their presence in the Pacific Ocean basin even as they divided Africa between themselves. Imperialism in the Pacific took two main forms. In Australia and New Zealand, European powers established settler colonies and dominant political institutions. In most of the Pacific islands, however, they sought commercial opportunities and reliable bases for their operations but did not wish to go to the trouble or expense of outright colonization. Only in the late nineteenth century did they begin to impose direct colonial rule on the islands.

Settler Colonies in the Pacific European mariners explored the Australian coastline and made occasional landfalls from the early sixteenth century, but only after the Pacific voyages of Captain James Cook did Europeans travel to the southern continent in large numbers. In 1770 Cook anchored his fleet for a week at Botany Bay, near modern Sydney, and reported that the region would be suitable for settlement. In 1788 a British fleet with about one thousand settlers, most of them convicted criminals, arrived at Sydney harbor and established the colony of New South Wales. The migrants supported themselves mostly by herding sheep. Lured by the opportunity to acquire land, voluntary migrants outnumbered convicts by the 1830s, and the discovery of gold in 1851 brought a surge in migration to Australia. European settlers established communities also in New Zealand. Europeans

An anonymous contemporary painting depicts the signing of the Treaty of Waitangi on 6 February 1840. British military and colonial officials look on as about fifty Maori chiefs put their names to the document.
Chronicle/Alamy Stock Photo

MAP 32.3 Imperialism in Oceania, ca. 1914.

Observe the many small, distant islands of the Pacific.

Why would imperial powers have thought it so important to claim these islands in the late nineteenth and early twentieth centuries?

first visited New Zealand while hunting whales and seals, but the islands' fertile soils and abundant stands of timber soon attracted their attention and drew large numbers of migrants.

European migration devastated the indigenous societies of Australia and New Zealand, partially as a result of the introduction of European diseases such as smallpox and measles. The aboriginal population of Australia fell from about 650,000 in 1800 to 90,000 in 1900, whereas the European population rose from a few thousand to 3.75 million during the same period. Similarly, the population of indigenous **Maori** in New Zealand fell from about 200,000 in 1800 to 45,000 a century later, while European numbers climbed to 750,000.

Increasing migration also fueled conflict between European settlers and native populations. Large settler societies pushed indigenous peoples from their lands, often following violent confrontations. Because the nomadic foraging peoples of Australia did not occupy lands permanently, British settlers considered the continent *terra nullius*—"land belonging to no one"—that they could seize and put to their own uses. They undertook brutal military campaigns to evict aboriginal

peoples from lands suitable for agriculture or herding. Despite strong resistance, by 1900 the British had succeeded in displacing most indigenous Australians from their traditional lands and dispersing them throughout the continent.

A similarly disruptive process transpired in New Zealand. Representatives of the British government encouraged Maori leaders in 1840 to sign the **Treaty of Waitangi,** which was designed to place New Zealand under British protection. Because the British underplayed the effect of the treaty on Maori sovereignty, many Maori chiefs agreed to sign it. However, the treaty actually signaled the coming of official British colonial control in New Zealand (1841) and thereafter inspired effective and long-lasting Maori opposition to British attempts to usurp their land and sovereignty. Conflicts over land confiscations and disputed land sales, for example, helped to spark the New Zealand Wars, a series of military confrontations between autonomous Maori groups and British troops and settlers that extended from the mid- to the late nineteenth century.

Maori (MAY-oh-ree)

Various Maori also cooperated in the Maori King Movement (or *Kingitanga*), beginning in 1856, as a means of forwarding Maori unity and sovereignty. While political and military battles continued, the British managed by the end of the century to force many Maori into poor rural communities separated from European settlements.

Pacific Islands European diseases also ravaged indigenous populations in the Pacific islands, although most did not attract large populations of European settlers. During the nineteenth century the principal European visitors to Pacific islands were whalers, merchants, and missionaries, and for most of the century the imperialist powers had little desire to establish direct colonial rule over Pacific islands. But that situation changed in the late nineteenth century. Just as European rivalries drove the scramble for Africa, so they encouraged the imperialist powers to stake their claims in the Pacific. In an era of global imperialism, European states sought reliable coaling stations for their steamships and ports for their navies. To that end, France established protectorates in Tahiti, the Society Islands, and the Marquesas as early as 1841 and imposed direct colonial rule in 1880. France also annexed New Caledonia in 1853. Britain made Fiji a crown colony in 1874, and Germany annexed several of the Marshall Islands in 1876 and 1878. Then at the Berlin Conference in 1884–1885, diplomats agreed on a partition of Oceania as well as Africa, and Britain, France, Germany, and the United States proceeded to claim almost all of the Pacific islands. By 1900 only the kingdom of Tonga remained independent, and even Tonga accepted British protection against the possibility of encroachments by other imperial powers.

In addition to their value as ports and coaling stations, the Pacific islands offered economic benefits to imperial powers. For example, Hawai'i and Fiji were the sites of productive sugarcane plantations. Samoa, French Polynesia, and many Melanesian and Micronesian islands were sources of copra—dried coconut, which produced high-quality vegetable oil for the manufacture of soap, candles, and lubricants. New Caledonia had rich veins of nickel, and many small Pacific islands had abundant deposits of guano—bird droppings that made the world's best fertilizer.

Queen Lili'uokalani, last monarch of Hawai'i, before her deposition in 1893. Wearing a European dress (she had received a western education by missionaries and had traveled widely in Europe and America), the queen sits on a throne covered with a traditional royal cape made of bird feathers.
Everett Collection Inc/Alamy Stock Photo

THE EMERGENCE OF NEW IMPERIAL POWERS

Nineteenth-century imperialism was mostly a European affair. Toward the end of the century, however, two new imperial powers joined Europeans in their efforts to divide the world into colonies: the United States and Japan. Both states experienced rapid industrialization in the late nineteenth century, and both built powerful armed forces. As European imperial powers forcibly claimed territories throughout the world, leaders of the United States and Japan decided that they too needed to establish an imperial presence overseas.

U.S. Imperialism in Latin America and the Pacific

The very existence of the United States was due to European imperialism. After the new republic had won its independence, U.S. leaders brought almost all the temperate regions of North America under their authority. Although they purchased some of this territory from other European powers (i.e., the Louisiana Purchase in 1803) or acquired it by treaty after war (i.e., the Mexican Cession in 1848), all westward movement in the United States involved the forcible and violent removal of indigenous populations from their hereditary lands. In that sense, the settlement of the United States was no different than the settler colonialism of Australia or New Zealand, even though Americans obscured these similarities by claiming they had a "manifest destiny" to settle North America from coast to coast.

The Monroe Doctrine But westward expansion on the North American continent was only part of the story of U.S. imperial expansion. Early in its history as an independent republic, the fledgling United States also sought to wield power outside North America. In 1823 President James Monroe (in office 1817–1825) issued a proclamation that warned European states against imperialist designs in the Western Hemisphere. In essence Monroe claimed all of the Americas as a U.S. protectorate, and his proclamation, known as the **Monroe Doctrine,** served as a justification for later U.S. intervention in hemispheric affairs. Until the late nineteenth century, however, the United States mostly sought to ensure that other European powers did not establish new colonies in the Americas and that U.S. entrepreneurs could profit from bringing the natural resources and agricultural products of the Americas to the world market.

SOURCES FROM THE PAST

Queen Lili'uokalani's Protest against the Annexation of Hawai'i

Queen Lili'uokalani (1838–1917) was the last monarch of the Kalakalua dynasty, which had ruled the Hawaiian Islands since 1810. Before taking the throne in 1891, Lili'uokalani had traveled extensively in the United States and Europe, and had served in the royal court. In 1887, American businessmen forced King Kalakaua, her older brother, to sign a constitution (called the "Bayonet Constitution") that limited the powers of the monarchy. Lili'uokalani adamantly opposed this constitution, and when she acceded to the throne she tried to implement a new constitution that would return her power. But in 1893, a group of European and American businessmen—with the help of U.S. Marines—staged a coup and deposed Lili'uokalani. Even after she was deposed, the queen continued to protest to the U.S. government against the loss of her power and against the rise of American power in Hawai'i. Her efforts were in vain, however, as the government of president William McKinley annexed Hawai'i in July, 1898. Below is her letter of protest to the U.S. House of Representatives from December of that year.

I, Liliuokalani of Hawaii, named heir apparent on the 10th day of April, 1877, and proclaimed Queen of the Hawaiian Islands on the 29th day of January, 1891, do hereby earnestly and respectfully protest against the assertion of ownership by the United States of America of the so-called Hawaiian Crown Lands amounting to about one million acres and which are my property, and I especially protest against such assertion of ownership as a taking of property without due process of law and without just or other compensation.

Therefore, supplementing my protest of June 17, 1897, I call upon the President and the National Legislature and the People of the United States to do justice in this matter and to restore to me this property, the enjoyment of which is being withheld from me by your Government under what must be a mis-apprehension of my right and title.

Done at Washington, District of Columbia, United States of America, this nineteenth day of December, in the year one thousand eight hundred and ninety-eight. ——————

> What is the significance of the fact that Lili'uokalani went to Washington, D.C., to make this protest?

For Further Reflection

■ What, according to Lili'uokalani, is the nature of the injustices she has had to endure? Why does she say that the government must not understand her right and title?

Source: https://www.archives.gov/historical-docs/todays-doc/?dod-date=707. Records of the U.S. House of Representatives, HR 55A-H28.3, Record Group 233, National Archives.

As the United States consolidated its continental holdings, U.S. leaders became interested in acquiring territories beyond the temperate regions of North America. In 1867 the United States purchased Alaska from Russia and in 1875 it claimed a protectorate over the islands of Hawai'i, where U.S. entrepreneurs had established highly productive sugarcane plantations. The Hawaiian kingdom survived until 1893, when a group of American and European planters and businesspeople overthrew the last monarch, Queen **Lili'uokalani** (reigned 1891–1893), and invited the United States to annex the islands. U.S. president Grover Cleveland (in office 1885–1889 and 1893–1897) opposed annexation, but his successor, William McKinley (in office 1897–1901), was more open to American expansion and agreed to acquire the islands as U.S. possessions in 1898.

The Spanish-Cuban-American War The United States emerged as an important imperial and colonial power after the brief **Spanish-Cuban-American War** (1898–1899). By the end of the nineteenth century U.S. business interests had made large investments in the Spanish colonies of Cuba and Puerto Rico. When the U.S. battleship *Maine* exploded and sank while an-

chored in the Cuban port of Havana in 1898, U.S. leaders claimed sabotage and declared war on Spain. The United States quickly defeated Spain and took possession of Cuba and Puerto Rico. U.S. leaders then turned their attention to Spain's Pacific colonies: Guam and the Philippines. After the U.S. navy destroyed the Spanish fleet at Manila in a single day, the United States took possession of both colonies to prevent them from falling under German or Japanese control.

The United States quickly established colonial governments in its new possessions. It also intervened directly in the affairs of Caribbean and Central American territories that were not U.S. possessions whenever it felt its business interests were threatened. U.S. military forces occupied Cuba, the Dominican Republic, Nicaragua, Honduras, and Haiti in the early twentieth century.

The consolidation of U.S. authority in the Philippines was especially brutal. The Spanish-Cuban-American War coincided with a Filipino revolt against Spanish rule, and U.S.

Lili'uokalani (lee-lee-oo-oh-kah-LAH-nee)

leaders promised to support independence of the Philippines if Filipino rebels allied with the United States against Spain. After the victory over Spain, however, President William McKinley decided to bring the Philippines under American control instead. The United States paid Spain twenty million dollars for rights to the colony, which was important to American businesspeople and military leaders because of its strategic position in the South China Sea. Outraged at their betrayal by the United States, Filipino rebels led by **Emilio Aguinaldo**—known to his followers as the George Washington of his country—turned their arms against the new intruders. The result was a bitter war that raged until 1902 and flared sporadically until 1906. The conflict claimed the lives of fifteen thousand rebel troops and forty-two hundred American soldiers, as well as about two hundred thousand Filipino civilians.

The Panama Canal To facilitate communication and transportation between the Atlantic and the Pacific oceans, the United States sought to build a canal across a narrow stretch of land in Central America. Engineers identified the isthmus of Panama in northern Colombia as the best site for a canal, but Colombia was unwilling to cede land for the project. Under President Theodore Roosevelt (in office 1901–1909), an enthusiastic champion of imperial expansion, the United States supported a rebellion against Colombia in 1903 and helped rebels establish the breakaway state of Panama. In exchange for this support, the United States won the right to build a canal across Panama and to control the adjacent territory, known as the Panama Canal Zone. Given this expansion of U.S. interests in Latin America, Roosevelt added a corollary to the Monroe Doctrine in 1904. The **Roosevelt Corollary** exerted the U.S. right to intervene in the domestic affairs of nations within the hemisphere if they demonstrated an inability to maintain the security deemed necessary to protect U.S. investments. The Roosevelt Corollary, along with the Panama Canal when it opened in 1914, strengthened U.S. military and economic claims in the region.

Imperial Japan

Strengthened by rapid industrialization during the Meiji era, Japan also joined the ranks of imperial powers in the late nineteenth century. Japanese leaders deeply resented the unequal treaties that the United States and European powers forced them to accept in the 1860s (discussed in chapter 31). They resolved to eliminate the diplomatic handicaps imposed by the treaties and to raise Japan's profile in the world. While founding representative political institutions to demonstrate to European and American diplomats their commitment to western values, Japanese leaders also made a bid to stand alongside the world's great powers by launching a campaign of imperial expansion.

Early Japanese Expansion The Japanese drive to empire began in the east Asian islands. During the 1870s Japanese leaders consolidated their hold on Hokkaido and the Kurile Islands to the north, and they encouraged Japanese migrants to populate the islands to prevent Russian expansion there. By 1879 they had also established their hegemony over Okinawa and the Ryukyu Islands to the south.

In 1876 Japan purchased modern warships from Britain, and the newly strengthened Japanese navy immediately began to pursue military intervention in Korea. After a confrontation between the Korean navy and a Japanese surveying vessel, Meiji officials dispatched a gunboat expedition and forced Korean leaders to submit to the same kind of unequal treaty that the United States and European states had imposed on Japan. As European and U.S. imperialists divided up the world in the 1880s and 1890s, Meiji political and military leaders made plans to project Japanese power abroad. They developed contingency plans for a conflict with China, staged maneuvers in anticipation of a continental war, and built a navy with the capacity to fight on the high seas.

The Sino-Japanese War In 1894, conflict erupted between Japan and China over the status of Korea. Taking advantage of the unequal treaty of 1876, Japanese businesses had developed substantial interests in Korea. When an antiforeign rebellion broke out in Korea in 1893, Meiji leaders feared that the land might fall into anarchy and become an inviting target of European or U.S. imperialism. Qing rulers sent an army to restore order and reassert Chinese authority in Korea, but Meiji leaders were unwilling to recognize Chinese control over a place so important to Japanese business interests. Thus in August 1894 they declared war on China. The Japanese navy quickly gained control of the Yellow Sea and demolished the Chinese fleet in a battle lasting a mere five hours. The Japanese army then pushed Qing forces out of the Korean peninsula. Within a few months the conflict was over. When the combatants made peace in April 1895, Qing authorities recognized the independence of Korea, thus making it essentially a dependency of Japan. They also ceded Taiwan, the Pescadores Islands, and the Liaodong peninsula, which strengthened Japanese control over east Asian waters. Alongside territorial acquisitions, Japan gained unequal treaty rights in China like those enjoyed by European and American powers.

The unexpected Japanese victory startled European imperial powers, especially Russia. Tensions between Japan and Russia soon mounted, as both imperial powers had territorial ambitions in the Liaodong peninsula (in northeastern China), Korea, and Manchuria. During the late 1890s Japanese military leaders vastly strengthened both their navy and their army with an eye toward a future conflict with Russia.

The Russo-Japanese War War broke out in 1904, and Japanese forces overran Russian outposts before reinforcements could arrive from Europe. The enhanced Japanese navy destroyed the Russian Baltic fleet, which had sailed halfway around the world to support the war effort. By 1905 the war was over, and Japan won international recognition of its

---

Emilio Aguinaldo (eh-MEE-lyoh AH-gee-NAHL-doh)

Japanese painting of a Japanese naval victory over a Chinese vessel. China's defeat in the Sino-Japanese War showed how the Qing dynasty had been weakened militarily, especially by the Opium War, and demonstrated how successful modernization had been for Japan since the Meiji restoration.

The Artchives/Alamy Stock Photo

colonial authority over Korea and the Liaodong peninsula. Furthermore, Russia ceded the southern half of Sakhalin island to Japan, along with a railroad and economic interests in southern Manchuria. Victory in the **Russo-Japanese War** transformed Japan into a major imperial power.

LEGACIES OF IMPERIALISM

Imperialism and colonialism profoundly influenced the development of world history. In some ways, they tightened links between the world's peoples: trade and migration increased dramatically as imperial powers exploited the resources of subject territories and recruited laborers to work in colonies throughout the world. Yet imperialism and colonialism also brought peoples into conflict and heightened senses of difference between peoples. European, Euro-American, and Japanese imperialists all came to think of themselves as superior to the peoples they conquered. Meanwhile, foreign intrusion stimulated the development of anticolonial and nationalist identities in colonized territories, and over time these identities served as a foundation for anticolonial independence movements.

Empire and Economy

One of the principal motives of imperialism was the desire to gain access to natural resources and agricultural products. As imperial powers consolidated their hold on foreign territories, colonial administrators reorganized colonized societies so they would become efficient suppliers of timber, rubber, petroleum, gold, silver, diamonds, cotton, tea, coffee, cacao, and other products. As a result, global trade in those commodities surged during the nineteenth and early twentieth centuries. However, profits from that trade went mostly to the colonial powers, who exported raw materials for processing in the industrialized societies of Europe, North America, and Japan.

Economic and Social Changes Sometimes colonial rule transformed the production of crops and commodities that had long been prominent in subject societies. In India, for example, the cultivation of cotton began probably before 5000 B.C.E. For most of history, cultivators spun thread and wove their own cotton textiles or else supplied local artisans with raw materials. Beginning in the late eighteenth century, however, colonial administrators reoriented the cultivation of cotton to serve the needs of the emerging British textile industry. They encouraged cultivators to produce cotton for export rather than for local consumption, and they built railroads deep into the subcontinent to transport raw cotton to the coast quickly. They shipped raw cotton to England, where mechanized factories rapidly turned out large volumes of high-quality textiles. They also allowed the import of inexpensive British textiles to India, which undermined Indian cotton cloth production. The value of raw cotton exported from India went from 10 million

What's Left Out?

Textbooks often overlook the fact that colonial policies seemingly unrelated to gender nevertheless frequently altered gender relations between colonized men and women. For example, the imposition of new systems of taxation often went hand in hand with European assumptions that men should be heads of households and thus the responsible parties for paying taxes to the state. In places where both women and men had held property and produced crops, such as colonial Tanganyika (modern Tanzania), these assumptions led to tax collection policies that put economic responsibility in the hands of men. This resulted in the marginalization of colonized women in public life and a rise in the political and economic power of colonized men, thus changing the gender dynamics between the sexes. The imposition of colonial law also similarly led to changes in gender relations. In Northern Ghana, for example, the implementation of the British judicial system brought about a deterioration in the legal status of indigenous women. Even though marriage practices in the region had given women an extraordinary amount of autonomy in both choosing and changing partners, British notions about the authority of husbands increasingly led to legal decisions that enforced the idea that wives were the property of their husbands. Over time, the colonial justice system allowed men to claim increasing legal control over their wives. While most textbooks do not have space to explore the many and varied ways colonialism shaped gender relations within the colonies, it is important to remember that the imposition of economic and legal policies could have an impact on seemingly unrelated—and quite intimate—issues such as gender relations.

Source: Jean Allman, Susan Geiger, and Nakanyike Musisi. *Women in African Colonial Histories* (Bloomington: Indiana University Press, 2002).

rupees in 1849 to 60 million rupees in 1860 and 410 million rupees in 1913, whereas the value of finished cotton products imported into India rose from 50,000 rupees in 1814 to 5.2 million rupees in 1829 and 30 million rupees in 1890. Thus colonial policies transformed India from the world's principal center of cotton manufacture to a supplier of raw cotton and a consumer of textiles produced in the British isles.

In some cases, colonial rule led to the introduction of new crops that transformed both the landscape and the social order of subject lands. In the early nineteenth century, for example, British colonial officials introduced tea bushes from China to Ceylon (modern Sri Lanka) and India. The effect on Ceylon was profound. British planters felled trees in much of the island, converted rain forests into tea plantations, and recruited Ceylonese women by the thousands to carry out the labor-intensive work of harvesting mature tea leaves. Consumption of tea in India and Ceylon was almost negligible, so increased supplies met the growing demand for tea in Europe, where the beverage became accessible to individuals of all social classes. The value of south Asian tea exports rose from about 309,000 pounds sterling in 1866 to 4.4 million pounds sterling in 1888 and 6.1 million pounds sterling in 1900. Malaya and Sumatra underwent a

similar social transformation after British colonial agents planted rubber trees there in the 1870s and established plantations to meet the growing global demand for rubber products.

Labor Migrations

Efforts to exploit the natural resources and agricultural products of subject lands led imperial and colonial powers to encourage mass migrations of workers during the nineteenth and early twentieth centuries. Two patterns of labor migration were especially prominent during this period. European migrants went mostly to temperate lands, where they worked as free cultivators or industrial laborers. In contrast, migrants from Asia, Africa, and the Pacific islands moved largely to tropical and subtropical territories, where they worked as indentured laborers on plantations or manual laborers for mining enterprises or large-scale construction projects. Between them, these two streams of labor migration profoundly influenced the development of societies, especially in the Americas and the Pacific basin.

European Migration Between 1800 and 1914 some fifty million European migrants left their homes and sought

An engraving depicts the East India Railway about 1863. Though originally built to transport goods, railroads quickly became a popular means of passenger travel in India. Chronicle/Alamy Stock Photo

opportunities overseas. Most of those migrants left the relatively poor agricultural societies of southern and eastern Europe, especially Italy, Russia, and Poland, although sizable numbers came also from Britain, Ireland, Germany, and Scandinavia. A majority of the migrants—about thirty-two million—went to the United States. Many of the early arrivals went west in search of cheap land to cultivate. Later migrants settled heavily in the northeast, where they provided the labor that drove U.S. industrialization after the 1860s. Settler colonies in Canada, Argentina, Australia, New Zealand, and South Africa also drew large numbers of European migrants, who mostly became free cultivators or herders but sometimes found employment as skilled laborers in mines or fledgling industries. Most European migrants traveled as free agents, but some went as indentured laborers. They were

MAP 32.4   Imperialism and migration during the nineteenth and early twentieth centuries.

An unprecedented intercontinental migration of people characterized the age of imperialism.

What factors encouraged and facilitated migration on this extraordinary scale?

able to find opportunities in temperate regions of the world because of European and Euro-American imperialism in the Americas, South Africa, and Oceania.

Indentured Labor Migration In contrast to their European counterparts, migrants from Asia, Africa, and the Pacific islands generally traveled as indentured laborers. As the institution of slavery went into decline, planters sought large numbers of laborers to replace enslaved people who left the plantations. The planters relied primarily on indentured laborers recruited from relatively poor and densely populated places. Between 1820 and 1914 about 2.5 million indentured laborers left their homes to work in distant parts of the world. Labor recruiters generally offered workers free passage to their destinations and provided them with food, shelter, clothing, and modest compensation for their services in exchange for a commitment to work for five to seven years. Sometimes recruiters also offered free return passage to workers who completed a second term of service.

The majority of the indentured laborers came from India, but sizable numbers also came from China, Japan, Java, parts of Africa, and the Pacific islands. Indentured laborers went mostly to tropical and subtropical lands in the Americas, the Caribbean, Africa, and Oceania. The **indentured labor** trade began in the 1820s when French and British colonial officials sent Indian migrants to work on sugar plantations in the Indian Ocean islands of Réunion and Mauritius. Shortly thereafter, large numbers of Indian laborers went to work on rubber plantations in Malaya and sugar plantations in South Africa; the Pacific island of Fiji; the Guianas; and the Caribbean islands of Trinidad, Tobago, and Jamaica. After the Opium War ended in 1842, recruiters also, began to seek workers in China. Large numbers of Chinese laborers went to sugar plantations in Cuba and Hawai'i; guano mines in Peru; tin mines in Malaya; gold mines in South Africa and Australia; and railroad construction sites in the United States, Canada, and Peru. After the Meiji restoration in Japan, a large contingent of Japanese laborers migrated to Hawai'i to work on sugar plantations, and a smaller group went to work in guano mines in Peru. Indentured laborers from various parts of Africa went mostly to sugar plantations in Réunion, the Guianas, and Caribbean islands. Those from Pacific islands went mostly to plantations in other Pacific islands and Australia.

Empire and Migration All of the large-scale migrations of the nineteenth century reflected the global influence of imperial powers. European migrations were possible only because European and Euro-American peoples had established settler societies in temperate regions around the world. Movements of indentured laborers were possible because colonial officials were able to recruit workers and dispatch them to distant lands where their compatriots had already established plantations or opened mines. In combination the nineteenth-century migrations profoundly influenced

societies around the world by establishing large communities of people with distinctive ethnic identities in places far from their original homes.

Empire and Society

Colonial Conflict The policies adopted by imperial powers and colonial officials forced peoples of different societies to deal with one another on a regular and systematic basis. Their interactions often led to violent conflicts between colonizers and subject peoples. The sepoy rebellion was the most prominent effort to resist British colonial authority in India, but it was only one among thousands of insurrections organized by discontented Indian subjects between the mid-nineteenth and the mid-twentieth centuries. Colonized people in southeast Asia and Africa also strongly resisted foreign rule, the tyrannical behavior of colonial officials, the introduction of European schools and curricula, high taxation, and requirements that subject peoples cultivate certain crops or provide compulsory labor for colonists' enterprises.

Many rebellions drew strength from traditional religious beliefs, and priests or prophets often led resistance to colonial rule. Some rebellions sought to expel colonial intruders and return territories to their precolonial rulers. The Can Vuong (Loyalty to the King) movement in what is now Vietnam was one such movement. In 1884, the twelve-year-old Ham Nghi came to the throne of the Nguyen dynasty in the province of Annam (modern Vietnam). Ham Nghi's advisers watched with horror as the French began to take control of the provinces around Annam and issued regular and vehement anti-French statements. In response, a French force raided Ham Nghi's royal palace in the city of Hue, forcing the young king and his advisers to flee. From the dense forests of Annam, Ham Nghi became the centerpiece of a resistance movement whose goal was to put the king back on the throne and to drive the French out of Indochina altogether. Ham Nghi was captured and exiled in 1888, but some of his supporters continued to resist French influence until 1895 by killing French soldiers and murdering Vietnamese converts to Christianity. While the Can Vuong movement did not succeed in driving out the French, the movement did provide training for some of the most important Vietnamese revolutionaries of the twentieth century. Just as important, the Can Vuong movement was only one of hundreds around the colonized world that sought to overthrow colonial rule by force. Even when subject peoples dared not revolt because they could not match European weaponry, they resisted colonial rule by boycotting European goods, organizing political parties and pressure groups, publishing anticolonial newspapers and magazines, and pursuing anticolonial policies through churches and religious groups.

Colonial policies also led to conflicts among peoples brought together artificially into multicultural societies. When indentured laborers from different societies congregated on plantations, for example, tensions sometimes developed between workers and their supervisors and among different groups of workers themselves. In Hawai'i, which had one of the most diverse multicultural societies created by the labor migrations of the nineteenth century, workers on sugar plantations came primarily from China, Japan, and Portugal, but there were also sizable contingents from the Philippines, Korea, and other Pacific islands. Workers and their families normally lived in villages dominated by their own ethnic groups, but there were plentiful opportunities for individuals and groups to mix with one another at work or in the larger society. Although the various ethnic communities readily adopted their neighbors' foods and sometimes took spouses from other groups, linguistic, religious, and cultural differences provided a foundation for strong ethnic identities throughout the plantation era and beyond.

Scientific Racism Social and cultural differences were the foundation of an academic pursuit known as **scientific racism,** which became prominent especially after the 1840s. Theorists such as the French nobleman Count Joseph Arthur de Gobineau (1816–1882) took race as the most important index of human potential. In fact, there is no basis for separating humans into different races because differences such as skin color are purely physical and do not signal differences in biological makeup. Nevertheless, nineteenth-century theorists assumed that the human species consisted of several distinct racial groups. Gobineau himself divided humanity into four main racial groups, each of which had its own peculiar traits. Throughout the later nineteenth and early twentieth centuries, racial theorists sought to identify racial groups on the basis of skin color, bone structure, nose shape, cranial capacity, and other physical characteristics. Although they did not always agree on the details about racial differences, one thing they did agree on was the superiority of Europeans to all others—a belief that seemed to be justified by the dominance of European imperial powers in the larger world.

After the 1860s, scientific racists drew heavily from the writings of Charles Darwin (1809–1882), an English biologist whose book ***The Origin***

Fig. 339. — Apollo Belvidere.

Fig. 341. — Negro.

Fig. 340.

Greek.

Fig. 342.

Creole Negro.

Fig. 343. — Young Chimpanzee.

Fig. 344.

Young Chimpanzee.

(458)

Scientific racists often argued that Europeans had reached a higher stage of evolution than other peoples. An illustration from a popular book by Josiah Clark Nott and G. R. Gliddon, *Indigenous Races of the Earth,* deliberately distorted facial and skull features to suggest a close relationship between African peoples and chimpanzees.
Science Source

of Species (1859) argued that all living species had evolved over thousands of years in a ferocious contest for survival. Species that adapted well to their environment survived, reproduced, and flourished, according to Darwin, whereas others declined and went into extinction. The slogan **"survival of the fittest"** soon became a byword for Darwin's theory of evolution. Theorists known as social Darwinists seized on those ideas, which Darwin had applied exclusively to biological matters, and adapted them to explain the development of human societies. For example, the English philosopher Herbert Spencer (1820–1903) relied on theories of evolution to explain differences between the strong and the weak: successful individuals and races had competed better in the natural world and consequently evolved to higher states than did other, less fit peoples. On the basis of that reasoning, Spencer and others justified the domination of European imperialists over subject peoples as the inevitable result of natural scientific principles.

Popular Racism On a more popular level, there was no need for elaborate scientific theories to justify racist prejudices. Representatives of imperial and colonial powers routinely adopted racist views on the basis of personal experience, which seemed to confirm their superiority to subject peoples. For many, the simple fact of European conquest seemed to demonstrate European superiority over those they colonized since an inability to resist conquest seemed to demonstrate fundamental weakness.

Racist views were by no means a monopoly of European imperialists: U.S. and Japanese empire builders also developed a sense of superiority over the peoples they conquered and ruled. During the war to defeat Emiliano Auginaldo's independence fighters, U.S. forces in the Philippines disparaged the rebels they fought with racial slurs, and they did not hesitate to torture enemies in a conflict that was publicly justified as an effort to "civilize and Christianize" the Filipinos. In the 1890s Japanese newspapers portrayed Chinese and Korean peoples as dirty, backward, stupid, and cowardly. Some Japanese scholars concocted speculative theories that the Japanese

Connecting the Sources

Thinking about colonized peoples' responses to colonization

The problem   For many years, the history of imperialism and colonialism was written from the point of view of the various colonizing powers. Colonial officials produced copious amounts of official and unofficial documents about colonial policies, their own experiences, and their opinions of colonized people. Not surprisingly, the histories written about colonialism using such sources tended to be biased in favor of the colonizers and frequently marginalized the experiences of colonized peoples themselves. In the last four decades, however, a plethora of histories have appeared that explore the colonial past from the point of view of colonized peoples, relying on previously underutilized sources such as court records, letters, memoirs, oral interviews, and fiction. Such sources have altered the way historians understand the massive imperial expansion that occurred in Asia and Africa in the nineteenth and first half of the twentieth centuries.

Let us consider two sources generated by people responding to British policies—one from China, the other from southern Africa—in order to think about what sources generated by the people who experienced colonialism can and cannot tell us.

The British Ironclad steamship HMS *Nemesis* destroying Chinese ships during the Opium War in 1841.

Dea picture library/De Agostini/Getty Images

The documents   Read the documents below, and consider carefully the questions that follow.

Document 1:

The following resolution was produced in 1842—just after the defeat of the Chinese Empire by the British in the Opium War—by Chinese citizens at a large public meeting in the city of Canton (Guangzhou).

> *Behold that vile English nation! Its ruler is at one time a woman, then a man, and then perhaps a woman again; its people are at one time like vultures, and then they are like wild beasts, with dispositions more fierce and furious than the tiger or wolf, and natures more greedy than anacondas or swine. These people having long steadily devoured all the western barbarians, and like demons of the night, they now suddenly exalt themselves here.*
>
> *During the reigns of the emperors Kien-lung [Qianlong] and Kia-king [Jiaqing] these English barbarians humbly besought an entrance and permission to deliver tribute and presents; they afterwards presumptuously asked to have Chu-san [the city of Zhoushan]; but our sovereigns, clearly perceiving their traitorous designs, gave them a determined refusal. From that time, linking themselves with traitorous Chinese traders, they have carried on a large trade and poisoned our brave people with opium.* ——————
>
> *Verily, the English barbarians murder all of us that they can. They are dogs, whose desires can never be satisfied. Therefore we need not inquire whether the peace they have now made be real or pretended. Let us all rise, arm, unite, and go against them.*
>
> *We do here bind ourselves to vengeance, and express these our sincere intentions in order to exhibit our high principles and patriotism. The gods from on high now look down upon us; let us not lose our just and firm resolution.*

> Which actions of the British caused the authors to find them so untrustworthy?

Document 2:

The following letter was written in 1858 by Moshweshewe I, founder of Basutoland and chief of the Basuto people in South Africa. It was directed to Sir George Grey, then governor of the Cape

Colony and high commissioner of South Africa, regarding Moshweshewe's treatment at the hands of white South African Afrikaners (called Boers by Moshweshewe).

. . . About twenty-five years ago my knowledge of the White men and their laws was very limited. I knew merely that mighty nations existed, and among them was the English. These, the blacks who were acquainted with them, praised for their justice. Unfortunately it was not with the English Government that my first intercourse with the whites commenced. People who had come from the Colony first presented themselves to us, they called themselves Boers. I thought all white men were honest. Some of these Boers asked permission to live upon our borders. I was led to believe they would live with me as my own people lived, that is, looking to me as to a father and a friend.

About sixteen years since, one of the [British] Governors of the [Cape] Colony, Sir George Napier, marked down my limits on a treaty he made with me. I was to be ruler within those limits. A short time after, another Governor came, it was Sir P. Maitland. The Boers then began to talk of their right to places I had then lent to them. Sir P. Maitland told me those people were subjects of the Queen, and should be kept under proper control; he did not tell me that he recognized any right they had to land within my country, but as it was difficult to take them away, it was proposed that all desiring to be under the British rule should live in that part near the meeting of the Orange and Caledon rivers.

Then came Sir Harry Smith, and he told me not to deprive any chief of their lands or their rights, he would see justice done to all, but in order to do so, he would make the Queen's Laws extend over every white man. He said the Whites and Blacks were to live together in peace. I could not understand what he would do. I thought it would be something very just, and that he was to keep the Boers in my land under proper control, and that I should hear no more of their claiming the places they lived on as their exclusive property. But instead of this, I now heard that the Boers consider all those farms as their own, and were buying and selling them one to the other, and driving out by one means or another my own people.

In vain I remonstrated. Sir Harry Smith had sent Warden to govern in the Sovereignty. He listened to the Boers, and he proposed that all the land in which those Boers' farms were should be taken from me. . . . One day he sent me a map and said, sign that, and I will tell those people . . . to leave off fighting: if you do not sign the map, I cannot help you in any way. I thought the Major was doing very improperly and unjustly. I was told to appeal to the Queen to put an end to this injustice. I did not wish to grieve Her Majesty by causing a war with her people. I was told if I did not sign the map, it would be the beginning of a great war. I signed, but soon after I sent my cry to the Queen. I begged Her to investigate my case and remove "the line," as it was called, by which my land was ruined. I thought justice would soon be done, and Warden put to rights. [Hostilities then broke out between the Boers and Moshweshewe's people, and Moshweshewe was thus requesting arbitration by Grey, the high commissioner]

Moshweshewe I, 1786–1870.
A Short History of Lesotho by Stephen Gill

What was the main issue between Moshweshewe and the Boers (Afrikaners)?

Questions

1. What can these documents definitively tell you about their respective writers' situations? What facts can be gleaned from these brief sources?
2. In Document 1, how do the Chinese who produced the resolution feel about the recent British victory? What have the British done to deserve such condemnation, in the group's view? How does the group propose to remedy the problem of the British in China?
3. In Document 2, why does Moshweshewe carefully recount his interactions with the various British officials who oversee the area in which Basutoland is situated? What kind of tone does Moshweshewe take in this letter, and why? Do you think Moshweshewe believes he has been treated fairly by the Boers and the British? What do you think happened when he signed the map?
4. What can these two documents tell us about the experience of colonialism in general? Do you imagine that the responses to domination suggested by these documents were common reactions to colonial expansion, or do you think responses would differ depending on the interests of the colonized group?
5. Sources such as these make up the building blocks on which historians base their interpretations of the past. How many sources do you think it would take in order to make accurate interpretations?

Sources: **Document 1:** "China, Japan, and the Islands of the Pacific, Vol. I." in *The World's Story: A History of the World in Story, Song, and Art,* edited by Eva March Tappan, 197. Boston: Houghton Mifflin, 1914. **Document 2:** Letter from the Chief Moshesh to the High Commissioner in 1858." in *Basutoland Records: Copies of Official Documents of Various Kinds, Accounts of Travellers, &, Volume 2,* edited by George McCall Theal, 384. Bosman Street: Government of Capetown, 1883.

people were more akin to the "Aryans," who supposedly had conquered much of the Eurasian landmass in ancient times, than to the "Mongolians" who populated China and Korea. After the Japanese victory in the Russo-Japanese War, political and military leaders came to believe that Japan had an obligation to oversee the affairs of their backward neighbors and help civilize their "little Asian brothers."

Anticolonial and Nationalist Movements

While imperialists convinced themselves of their racial superiority, colonial rule provoked subject peoples to develop a sense of their own identities. Just as Napoleon's invasions aroused national feelings and led to the emergence of nationalist movements in Europe, so imperial expansion and colonial domination prompted the organization of anticolonial movements and the formation of national identities. In the late nineteenth and early twentieth centuries, the potential of imperialism and colonialism to push subject peoples toward nationalism was most evident in India.

Ram Mohan Roy   During the nineteenth century, educated Indian elites helped forge a sense of Indian identity. Among the most influential of them was **Ram Mohan Roy** (1772–1833), a prominent Bengali intellectual sometimes called the "father of modern India." Roy argued for the construction of a society based on both modern European values and the Indian tradition of devotional Hinduism. He supported some British

colonial policies, and he worked with Christian social reformers to improve the status of Indian women by providing them with education and property rights. Yet Roy saw himself as a Hindu reformer who drew inspiration from the Vedas and Upanishads and who sought to bring Hindu spirituality to bear on the problems and conditions of his own time. During the last two decades of his life, Roy tirelessly published newspapers and founded societies to mobilize educated Hindus and advance the cause of social reform in colonial India.

Reform societies flourished in nineteenth-century India. Many of them appealed to upper-caste Hindus, but some were Muslim organizations, and a few represented the interests of peasants, landlords, or lower castes. After mid-century, reformers increasingly called for self-government or at least greater Indian participation in government. Their leaders often had received an advanced education at British universities, and they drew inspiration from European Enlightenment values such as equality, freedom, and popular sovereignty. But they invoked those values to criticize the British colonial regime in India and to call for political and social reform.

The Indian National Congress   The most important of the reform groups was the **Indian National Congress,** founded in 1885 as a forum for educated Indians to communicate their views on public affairs to colonial officials. Representatives from all parts of the subcontinent aired grievances about Indian poverty, the transfer of wealth from India to Britain, trade and tariff policies that harmed Indian businesses, the inability of

Much of western India experienced severe famine in 1896–1897, and epidemics of bubonic plague broke out among weakened populations. British relief efforts were often heavy-handed and insensitive, and they did little to alleviate the problems.
Historic Images/Alamy Stock Photo

colonial officials to provide effective relief for regions stricken by drought or famine, and British racism toward Indians. By the end of the nineteenth century, the congress openly sought Indian self-rule within a larger imperial framework. In 1916 the congress joined forces with the All-India Muslim League, the most prominent organization working to advance the political and social interests of Muslims, who made up about 25 percent of the Indian population.

Faced with increasing demands for Indian participation in government, in 1909 colonial authorities granted a limited franchise that allowed wealthy Indians to elect representatives to local legislative councils. By that time, however, the drive for political reform had become a mass movement. Indian nationalists called for independence, mounted demonstrations to build support for their cause, and organized boycotts of British goods. Other anticolonial activists turned to violence and sought to undermine British rule by bombing government buildings and assassinating colonial officials.

Although local experiences varied considerably, Indian anticolonial and nationalist movements served as models for anticolonial campaigns in other lands. In many cases, the leaders of those movements were European-educated elites who absorbed Enlightenment values and then turned those values into an attack on European colonial rule in foreign lands.

CONCLUSION

The construction of global empires in the nineteenth century noticeably increased the tempo of world integration. Armed with powerful transportation, communication, and military technologies, European peoples imposed their rule on much of Asia and almost all of Africa. Toward the end of the nineteenth century, the United States and Japan joined European states as global imperialists. All the imperial powers profoundly influenced the development of the societies they ruled. They shaped the economies and societies of their colonies by pushing them to supply natural resources and agricultural commodities in exchange for manufactured products, and they facilitated the movement of workers to lands where there was high demand for labor on plantations or in mines. They also developed racist ideologies that sought to justify conquest and brutal violence. In response, colonized people developed increasingly strong anticolonial and nationalist movements whose goal was to remove the imperial powers altogether. From the early twentieth century forward, much of global history has revolved around issues stemming from the world order established by imperialism and colonialism.

STUDY TERMS

Berlin West Africa Conference (706)
Cecil John Rhodes (696)
direct rule (708)
East India Company (700)
Emilio Aguinaldo (712)
Great Game (702)
indentured labor (716)
Indian National Congress (720)
indirect rule (708)
Khoikhoi (705)
Leopold II (705)
Lili'uokalani (711)
Maori (709)
mission civilisatrice (697)
Monroe Doctrine (710)
Omdurman (698)
The Origin of Species (717)
Panama Canal (699)
Ram Mohan Roy (720)
Roosevelt Corollary (712)
Russo-Japanese War (713)
scientific racism (717)
scramble for Africa (705)
South African War (706)
Spanish-Cuban-American War (711)
Suez Canal (699)
survival of the fittest (717)
terra nullius (709)
Treaty of Waitangi (709)
Xhosa (705)

FOR FURTHER READING

Clare Anderson. *Subaltern Lives: Biographies of Colonialism in the Indian Ocean World, 1790-1920*. Cambridge, 2012. Explores the experience of colonialism through the perspective of convicts, sailors, enslaved people, and indentured laborers.

Tony Ballantyne and Antoinette Burton. *Bodies in Contact: Rethinking Colonial Encounters in World History*. Durham, 2005. Collection of essays that explore the body as a critical site of cultural encounter in the context of colonialism.

Sugata Bose. *A Hundred Horizons: The Indian Ocean in the Age of Global Empires*. Cambridge, Mass., 2006. A bold interregional history that argues that the peoples of the Indian Ocean littoral shared a common historical destiny.

Jane Burbank and Frederick Cooper. *Empires in World History: Power and the Politics of Difference*. Princeton, 2010. A major study that considers modern empires in historical context.

Ken S. Coates. *A Global History of Indigenous Peoples: Struggle and Survival*. Houndmills, U.K., 2004. Stressing the active role of indigenous peoples, this work examines the dynamics of colonial encounters.

John Darwin. *Unfinished Empire: The Global Expansion of Britain*. London and New York, 2013. The author has fashioned a sweeping and sober account of one of the longest-lived and most influential empires in world history.

Daniel R. Headrick. *Power over Peoples: Technology, Environments, and Western Imperialism, 1400 to the Present*. Princeton, 2009. Explores the central role of technological innovation in the rise and fall of imperialism.

Eric T. L. Love. *Race over Empire: Racism and U.S. Imperialism, 1865-1900*. Chapel Hill, N.C., 2004. In this critical reinterpretation, the author challenges the prevailing notion that racism abetted imperialism, notwithstanding the fact that many imperialists were racists.

Heather Streets-Salter and Trevor Getz. *Empires and Colonies in the Modern World*. Oxford, 2015. Explores the structures and ideologies of imperialism and colonialism since 1400 from a global perspective.

H. L. Wesseling. *The European Colonial Empires: 1815-1919*. New York, 2004. Puts the process of colonization into a comparative and long-term perspective.

ZOOMING IN ON ENCOUNTERS

An Assassination That Led to Global War

Archduke Franz Ferdinand (1863–1914) of Austria-Hungary was aware that his first official visit to Sarajevo was fraught with danger. That ancient city was the capital of Bosnia-Herzegovina, twin provinces that had been under Ottoman rule since the fifteenth century before being occupied in 1878 and finally annexed by Austria-Hungary in 1908. The provinces were home to large numbers of ethnic Serbians who sought incorporation into the neighboring kingdom of Serbia rather than into the Austro-Hungarian Empire, and as a result they became the hotbed of pan-Serbian nationalism. Even though Ferdinand himself favored diplomacy rather than hard-line tactics when it came to Serbian nationalism, most Serbian nationalists nevertheless hated the dynasty and the empire represented by the heir to the throne of Austria-Hungary.

Ferdinand and his wife Sophie arrived in Sarajevo on the warm Sunday morning of June 28, 1914. As their motorcade moved from the train station through the narrow streets of Sarajevo, seven Serbian nationalists armed with bombs and revolvers were waiting on the designated route to assassinate Ferdinand. The first would-be assassin did not take a shot, but the next man in line threw a hand grenade into the open car. Bouncing off Ferdinand's arm, the grenade exploded near another vehicle and injured dozens of spectators.

This contemporary painting by C. R. W. Nevinson, called "The Paths of Glory," testifies to the appalling scale of death and destruction during the battles of World War I.
Photo12/Universal Images Group/Getty Images

Undeterred, Ferdinand and Sophie went on to a reception at city hall; after the reception Ferdinand instructed his driver to take them to the hospital where those wounded in the earlier attack were being treated. On the way, a young Bosnian Serb named Gavrilo Princip (1894–1918) lunged at the archduke's car and fired a revolver. The first bullet blew a hole in the side of Ferdinand's neck. A second bullet intended for the governor of Bosnia went wild and entered the stomach of the expectant

Sophie. Turning to his wife, the archduke pleaded: "Sophie dear! Don't die! Stay alive for our children!" By the time medical aid arrived, however, the archduke and the duchess were dead.

In the meantime, Princip swallowed poison in an attempt to kill himself after the successful attack. But the poison was old and only made him sick. When he tried to turn the gun on himself, a crowd prevented him from doing so and held him for the police. When the police arrived, they took out their fury on Princip: they kicked him, beat him, and scraped the skin from his neck with the edges of their swords. Three months later a court found Princip guilty of treason and murder, but because he committed his crime before his twentieth birthday, he was not subject to the death penalty. Sentenced to twenty years in prison, Princip died in April 1918 from tuberculosis.

The assassination on 28 June 1914 allowed hard-liners in Austria to take control of the government, and they demanded extensive reparations from the Serbian government, which they blamed for the assassination. When the Serbian government refused the terms demanded by the Austrian government, Austria declared war on Serbia on July 28. But the stakes of the conflict quickly expanded beyond Austria and Serbia. Indeed, nationalist aspirations, international rivalries, and an inflexible alliance system transformed the conflict into a general European war and ultimately into a global struggle involving thirty-two nations and nearly all of the colonies of the various empires. Twenty-eight of those nations, collectively known as the Allies and the Associated Powers, fought the coalition known as the Central Powers, which consisted of Germany, Austria-Hungary, the Ottoman Empire, and Bulgaria. The generation that survived the carnage called this clash of arms the Great War because its scope and its casualties exceeded all previous wars. Sadly, though, a subsequent generation of survivors renamed the conflict World War I because it was only the first of two devastating wars that engulfed the world in the first half of the twentieth century.

CHAPTER OVERVIEW

The Great War lasted from August 1914 to November 1918 and ushered in history's most violent century. In geographic extent the conflict surpassed all previous wars, compelling men, women, and children on five continents to participate directly or indirectly. The Great War also had the distinction of being the first total war in human history, as governments mobilized every available human and material resource for the conduct of war, including those in colonial territories. The industrial nature of the conflict meant that it was the bloodiest in the annals of organized violence. It took the lives of millions of combatants and civilians, physically maimed untold multitudes, and emotionally scarred an entire generation. The military casualties passed a threshold beyond previous experience: approximately fifteen million soldiers died, and an additional twenty million combatants suffered injuries.

The war of 1914–1918 did more than destroy individual lives. It seriously damaged national economies. The most visible signs of that damage were huge public debts and soaring rates of inflation. The international economy witnessed a shift in power away from western Europe. By the end of the conflict, the United States emerged as an economic world power that, despite its self-imposed isolation during the 1920s and 1930s, played a key role in global affairs in the coming decades. Politically, the war led to the redrawing of European boundaries and caused the demise of four dynasties and their empires—the Ottoman Empire, the Russian Empire, the Austro-Hungarian Empire, and the German Empire. The Great War also gave birth to nine new nations: Yugoslavia, Austria, Hungary, Czechoslovakia, Poland, Lithuania, Latvia, Estonia, and Finland. The war helped unleash the Bolshevik Revolution of 1917, which had profound consequences for the whole world. Finally, the Great War was responsible for an international realignment of power. It undermined the preeminence and prestige of western European society, signaling an end to Europe's global primacy.

CHRONOLOGY	
1914	Assassination of Archduke Franz Ferdinand
1915	German submarine sinks the *Lusitania*; Japan makes Twenty-one Demands on China; Gallipoli campaign
1916	Battles at Verdun and the Somme
1917	German resumption of unrestricted submarine warfare; United States declaration of war on Germany; Bolshevik Revolution
1918	Treaty of Brest-Litovsk; Armistice suspends hostilities
1919	Paris Peace Conference
1920	First meeting of the League of Nations
1923	Atatürk proclaims Republic of Turkey

THE DRIFT TOWARD WAR

As we have seen, the catalyst for war was the assassination of Archduke **Franz Ferdinand,** heir to the throne of the Austro-Hungarian Empire, by a Serbian nationalist. Yet without deeper underlying developments, Gavrilo Princip's bullets would have had limited effect. The underlying causes for the war of 1914–1918 were many, including intense nationalism, frustrated national ambitions and ethnic resentments, the pursuit of exclusive economic interests, abrasive colonial rivalries, and a general struggle over the balance of power in Europe and in the world at large. Between 1871 and 1914, European governments adopted foreign policies that steadily increased the likelihood of a general war between them. To avoid finding themselves alone in a hostile world, national leaders sought alignments with other powers. The establishment and maintenance in Europe of two hostile alliances—the Allies and the Central Powers—helped spread the war from the Balkans to most of the rest of the world.

Nationalist Aspirations

The French revolution and subsequent Napoleonic conquests spread nationalism throughout most of Europe by the end of the nineteenth century (see chapter 28). Inherent in nationalism was the idea that peoples with the same ethnic origins, language, and political ideals had the right to form sovereign states; this concept is called **self-determination.** The dynastic and often reactionary powers that dominated European affairs during the early nineteenth century either ignored or opposed the principle of self-determination, thereby denying national autonomy to Germans, Italians, and Belgians, among others. Before long, however, a combination of powerful nationalistic movements, revolutions, and wars allowed Belgians to gain independence from the Netherlands in 1830, promoted the unification of Italy in 1861, and secured the unification of Germany in 1871. Yet at the end of the nineteenth century, the issue of nationalism remained unresolved in other areas of Europe, most notably in eastern Europe and the Balkans. There the nationalist aspirations of subject minorities threatened to tear apart the multinational empires of the Ottoman, Hapsburg, and Russian dynasties and with them the regional balance of power. In those instances, opposition to foreign rule played a large role in the construction of national identities and demands for self-determination.

The Ottoman Empire had controlled the Balkan peninsula since the fifteenth century, but after 1829 the Turkish empire lost huge portions of its territories. European powers, especially Austria and Russia, were partly responsible for these losses in Europe, but in other areas the slicing away of Turkish territory resulted mostly from nationalist revolts by the sultan's subjects. Greece was the first to gain independence (in 1830), and within a few decades Serbia, Romania, and Bulgaria followed suit.

As the Ottoman territories succumbed to the forces of nationalism, Austria-Hungary confronted the nationalist aspirations of Slavic peoples—Poles, Czechs, Slovaks, Serbs, Croats, and Slovenes. Most militant were the Serbs, who pressed for unification with the now-independent kingdom of Serbia. Russia added fuel to this volatile situation by promoting Pan-Slavism, a nineteenth-century movement that stressed the ethnic and cultural kinship of the various Slav peoples of eastern and east central Europe and that sought to unite those peoples politically. Pan-Slavism, as advocated by Russian leaders, supported Slav nationalism in lands occupied by Austria-Hungary. The purpose behind that policy was to promote secession by Slav areas, thereby weakening Austrian rule and perhaps preparing territories for future Russian annexation. Russia's support of Serbia, which supported Slav nationalism, and Germany's backing of Austria-Hungary, which tried desperately to counter the threat of national independence, helped set the stage for international conflict.

National Rivalries

Aggressive nationalism was also manifest in economic competition and colonial conflicts, fueling dangerous rivalries among the major European powers. The industrialized nations of Europe competed for foreign markets and engaged in tariff wars, but the most unsettling economic rivalry involved Great Britain and Germany. By the twentieth century, Germany's rapid industrialization threatened British economic predominance. In 1870 Britain, the first industrial nation, produced almost 32 percent of the world's total industrial output, compared with Germany's share of 13 percent, but by 1914 Britain's share had dropped to 14 percent, roughly equivalent to that of Germany. British reluctance to accept the relative decline of British industry vis-à-vis German industry strained relations between the two economic powers.

The Naval Race An expensive naval race worsened tensions between the two nations. Germans and Britons convinced themselves that naval power was vital for securing and protecting merchant shipping. Military leaders and politicians also saw powerful navies as a means of controlling the seas in times of war, a control they viewed as decisive in determining the outcome of any war. Thus, when Germany's political and military leaders announced their program to build a fleet with many large battleships, they seemed to undermine British naval supremacy. The British government moved to meet the German threat through the construction of battleships known as **dreadnoughts.** Dreadnoughts represented an entirely new generation of warships, characterized in part by the high speed supplied by steam turbines. Rather than discouraging the Germans from their naval buildup, the British determination to retain naval superiority stimulated the Germans to build their own flotilla of dreadnoughts. This expensive naval race contributed further to international tensions and hostilities between nations.

Colonial Disputes Economic rivalries also encouraged colonial competition. During the late nineteenth and early twentieth centuries, European nations searched aggressively for new colonies or dependencies to bolster economic performance. In their haste to conquer and colonize, the imperial powers sometimes stumbled over each other, repeatedly clashing in one corner of the globe or another: Britain and Russia competed for influence in Persia (modern-day Iran) and Afghanistan; Britain and France both sought a controlling influence in Siam (modern-day Thailand) and the Nile valley; Britain and Germany competed for territory in east and southwest Africa; and Germany and France almost came to blows over attempts to influence affairs in Morocco and west Africa.

Virtually all the major powers engaged in the scramble for empire, but the competition between Britain and Germany and between France and Germany were the most intense. Germany, a unified nation only since 1871, embarked on the colonial race belatedly but aggressively, insisting that it too must have its "place in the sun." German imperial efforts were frustrated, however, by the simple fact that British and French

imperialists had already carved up much of the world. German-French antagonisms and German-British rivalries were important in shaping the international alliances that contributed to the spread of war after 1914.

Between 1905 and 1914, a series of international crises and two local wars raised tensions and almost precipitated a general European war. The first crisis resulted from a French-German confrontation over Morocco in 1905. French influence had been growing in the area, and to counter this the German government announced its support of Moroccan independence. The French responded to German interference by threatening war. An international conference in Algeciras, Spain, in the following year prevented a clash of arms, but similar crises threatened the peace in subsequent years. Contributing to the growing tensions in European affairs were the Balkan wars. Between 1912 and 1913, the states of the Balkan peninsula—including Bulgaria, Greece, Montenegro, Serbia, and Romania—fought two consecutive wars for possession of the remaining European territories held by the Ottoman Empire. The Balkan wars strained European diplomatic

Dissident German cartoonist Walter Trier's satirical map of Europe in 1914. Trier's work stands in stark contrast to the press of the time, which fueled the chauvinist desires of competing national publics. What message was Trier trying to convey with this map?
akg-images/Alamy Stock Photo

relations and helped shape the tense circumstances that led to the outbreak of the Great War.

Public Opinion Public pressure also contributed to national rivalries. Many European societies were characterized by a high degree of political participation and chauvinism (excessive patriotism) on the part of citizens who identified strongly with the state. These citizens wanted their nation to outshine others, particularly in the international arena. New means of communication nourished the public's desire to see their country "come in first," whether in the competition for colonies or in the race to the South Pole. The content of inexpensive, mass-produced newspapers, pamphlets, and books fueled feelings of national arrogance and aggressive patriotism. However, public pressure calling for national greatness placed policymakers and diplomats in an awkward situation. Compelled to achieve headline-grabbing foreign policy successes, these leaders ran the risk of paying for short-lived triumphs with long-lasting hostility from other countries.

Understandings and Alliances

Escalating national rivalries and nationalist aspirations of subject minorities led to a system of entangling alliances. Fundamental to all of these alliances was that they outlined the circumstances under which countries would go to war to support one another. Although they were meant to preserve the peace, in fact rival alliance systems created a framework whereby even a small international crisis could set off a chain reaction leading to a much larger war. In 1914, the Great War erupted in large part because Europe's major powers had aligned themselves into two hostile camps—the Triple Alliance and the Triple Entente.

The Central Powers The Triple Alliance, also known as the **Central Powers,** grew out of the close relationship that developed between the leaders of Germany and Austria-Hungary during the last three decades of the nineteenth century. In 1879 the governments of the two empires entered into the Dual Alliance, a defensive pact that ensured reciprocal protection from a Russian attack and neutrality in case of an attack from any other power. Fear of a hostile France motivated Germans to enter into this pact, whereas Austrians viewed it as giving them a free hand in pursuing their Balkan politics without fear of Russian intervention. Italy, fearful of France, joined the Dual Alliance in 1882, thereby transforming it into the Triple Alliance. From the outset, however, the Italian policy of expansion at the expense of the Ottoman Empire and Italy's rivalry with Austria-Hungary in the Balkans threatened to wreck the alliance. Thus the Italian declaration of war on the Ottoman Empire in 1911 and the subsequent drive to annex

the Tripoli region of northern Africa strained the Triple Alliance because the German government was interested in cultivating friendly relations with the Ottomans.

The Allies The Central Powers sought to protect the political status quo in Europe, but the leaders of other nations viewed this new constellation of power with suspicion. This response was especially true of French leaders, who neither forgot nor forgave France's humiliating defeat during the Franco-Prussian War of 1870–1871. The French government was determined to curb the growing might of Germany.

The tsarist regime of Russia was equally disturbed by the new alignment of powers, especially by Germany's support of Austria, and British leaders were traditionally suspicious of any nation that seemed to threaten the balance of power on the Continent. The result was the **Triple Entente,** a combination of nations that had once been rivals, commonly referred to as the Allies. The Triple Entente originated in a series of agreements between Britain and France (1904) and between Britain and Russia (1907) that aimed to resolve colonial disputes. Between 1907 and 1914 cooperation between the leaders of Britain, France, and Russia led to the signing of a military pact in the summer of 1914. Reciprocal treaty obligations, which the governments felt compelled to honor lest they face the risk of being alone in a hostile world, made it difficult for diplomats to contain what otherwise might have been relatively small international crises.

War Plans The preservation of peace was also difficult because the military staffs of each nation had devised inflexible military plans and timetables to be carried out in the event of war. For example, French military strategy revolved around Plan XVII, which revolved around offensive maneuvers. The French master plan could be summed up in one word, *attack,* to be undertaken always and everywhere. This strategy viewed the enemy's intentions as inconsequential and gave no thought to the huge number of casualties that would invariably result from repeated attacks. Yet it was German war plans in particular that played a crucial role in the events leading to the Great War. Germany's fear of encirclement encouraged its military planners to devise a strategy that would avoid a war on two fronts. It was based on a strategy developed in 1905 by General Count Alfred von Schlieffen (1833–1913).

The **Schlieffen plan** called for a swift attack on France, followed by defensive action against Russia. German planners based their strategy on the knowledge that the Russians could not mobilize their soldiers and military supplies as quickly as the French, thus giving German forces a few precious weeks during which they could concentrate their full power on France. But the Schlieffen plan raised serious logistical problems, not the least of which was moving 180,000 soldiers and their supplies into France and Belgium on five hundred trains, with fifty wagons each. More important, Germany's military strategy was a serious obstacle to those seeking to preserve the

---

Triple Entente (ahn-TAHNT)
Schlieffen (SHLEE-fn)

peace. In the event of Russian mobilization, Germany's leaders would feel compelled to stick to their war plans of attacking France first, thereby setting in motion a military conflict of major proportions.

GLOBAL WAR

War came to Europe during harvest time, and most ordinary people heard the news as they worked in the fields. Most reacted not with enthusiasm but with shock and fear. Other people, especially intellectuals and young city dwellers, met the news with euphoria. Many of them had long expected war and saw it as a liberating release of pressure that would resolve the various political, social, and economic crises that had been building for years. The philosopher Bertrand Russell observed that the average Englishman positively wanted war, and the French writer Alain-Fournier noted that "this war is fine and just and great." In the capitals of Europe, people danced in the streets when their governments announced formal declarations of war. When the first contingents of soldiers left for the front, jubilant crowds threw flowers at the feet of departing men, who expected to return victorious after a short time.

Reality crushed any expectations of a short and triumphant war. On most fronts the conflict quickly bogged down and became a war of attrition in which the firepower of modern weapons slaughtered soldiers by the millions. For the first time in history, belligerent nations (meaning those nations that entered the war) engaged in total war. Even in democratic societies, governments assumed dictatorial control to marshal the human and material resources required for continuous war. One result was increased participation of women in the labor force. Total war had repercussions that went beyond the borders of Europe. Imperial ties drew millions of Asians, Africans, and residents of the British dominions into the war to serve as soldiers and laborers. Struggles in and over colonies further underlined the global dimension of this war. Last, the war gained a global flavor through the entry of Japan, the United States, and the Ottoman Empire, nations whose leaders professed little direct interest in European affairs.

The Guns of August

The shots fired from Gavrilo Princip's revolver on that fateful day of 28 June 1914 were heard around the world, for they triggered the greatest war in human history up to that point. By July, Austrian investigators had linked the assassins to a terrorist group known as the **Black Hand.** Centered in neighboring Serbia, this organization was dedicated to the unification of all south Slavs, or Yugoslavs, to form a greater Serbia. As far as Serbian nationalists were concerned, the principal obstacle to Slavic unity was the Austro-Hungarian Empire, which explains why the heir to the Hapsburg throne was a symbolic victim. This viewpoint also explains Austria's unyielding and violent response to the murder.

Declarations of War The assassination set in motion a flurry of diplomatic activity that quickly escalated into war. Austrian leaders in Vienna were determined to teach the unruly Serbs a lesson, and on 23 July the Austrians issued a nearly unacceptable ultimatum to the government of Serbia. The Serbian government accepted all the terms of the ultimatum except one, which infringed on its sovereignty. The ultimatum demanded that Austrian officials take part in any Serbian investigation of persons found on Serbian territory connected to the assassination of Franz Ferdinand. On 28 July, after declaring the Serbian reply to be unsatisfactory, Austria-Hungary declared war on Serbia. The war had begun, and politicians and generals discovered that it could not be easily limited to a local conflict. The subsequent sequence of events was largely determined by two factors: complex mobilization plans and the logic of the alliance system.

On 29 July the Russian government under Tsar Nicholas II began mobilizing its troops to defend its Serbian ally and itself from Austria. Russia then ordered mobilization against Germany. Nicholas II (1868–1918) took that decisive step

This French propaganda poster, "The Heroes of Belgium, 1914," was intended to rouse French patriotism by depicting German soldiers as inhuman monsters.
National Archives

reluctantly and only after his military experts convinced him that a partial mobilization against the Austrians would upset complex military plans and timetables based on the existing alliance system. Delayed mobilization might invite defeat, they advised, should the Germans enter the war to defend their Austrian allies. That action precipitated a German ultimatum to Russia on 31 July, demanding that the Russian army cease its mobilization immediately. Another ultimatum addressed to France demanded to know what France's intentions were in case Germany and Russia went to war. The Russians replied with a blunt "impossible," and the French never answered. Thus on 1 August the German government declared war on Russia, and France started to mobilize.

After waiting two more days, the Germans declared war on France, on 3 August. On the same day, German troops invaded Belgium in accordance with the Schlieffen plan. Key to this plan was an attack on the weak left flank of the French army by a massive German force through Belgium. The Belgian government, which had refused to permit the passage of German troops, called on the signatories of the treaty of 1839, which guaranteed Belgium's neutrality. On 4 August the British government, one of the signatories, sent an ultimatum to Germany demanding that Belgian neutrality be respected. When Germany's wartime leaders refused, the British immediately declared war. A local conflict had become a general European war a mere five weeks after the assassination of Archduke Franz Ferdinand.

Mutual Butchery

Everyone expected the war to be brief. In the first weeks of August 1914, twenty million young men donned uniforms, took up rifles, and left for the front. Many of them looked forward to heroic charges, rapid promotions, and a quick homecoming. Some dreamed of glory and honor, and they believed that God was on their side. The inscription on the belt buckle of German recruits read *Gott mit uns* ("God is with us"), a sentiment echoed by Russian troops, who fought for "God and Tsar," and British soldiers, who went into battle "For God, King, and Country." Several years later Americans believed they were entering the war to "make the world safe for democracy." Similar attitudes prevailed among the political and military leaders of the belligerent nations. Unfortunately, the war strategies devised by the finest military thinkers of the time

Crowds of young men happily pose outside a recruiting office in Toronto, Canada, while waiting to enlist.
Shawshots/Alamy Stock Photo

paid little attention to matters of defense. Instead, they were preoccupied with visions of sweeping assaults; envelopments; and, above all, swift triumphs.

The Western Front

The German march toward Paris in August 1914 was stopped by the French army (with British support) along the river Marne. Both sides then repeatedly tried to outflank the other, which led to a series of movements that took both armies to the North Sea (later, this movement was called the "race to the sea"). By October 1914, the German and Franco-British armies faced each other along a battlefront—called the **western front**—that stretched from the border of Switzerland to the North Sea. For the next three years, the battle lines remained virtually stationary, as both sides dug vast networks of defensive trenches and slugged it out in a war of attrition that lasted until the spring of 1918. Each belligerent tried to break through the other's defensive lines and to inflict continuous damage and casualties, only to have their own forces suffer heavy losses in return. Farther south, Italy left the Triple Alliance and then entered the war on the side of the Allies in 1915. By the terms of the Treaty of London, the Allies promised, once victory was secured, to cede to Italy Austro-Hungarian-controlled territories, specifically south Tyrol and most of the Dalmatian coast. Allied hopes that the Italians would pierce Austrian defenses quickly faded. After a disastrous defeat at Caporetto in 1917, Italian forces maintained a defensive line only with the help of the French and the British.

Stalemate and New Weapons

The stalemate on the western and southern fronts reflected technological developments that favored defensive tactics. Barbed wire, which had confined cattle on America's Great Plains, proved highly effective in frustrating the advance of soldiers across **no-man's-land,** the deadly territory between opposing trenches. The rapid and continuous fire of machine guns further contributed to the battlefield stalemate, turning infantry charges across no-man's-land into suicide missions. First deployed by Confederate troops during the U.S. Civil War, the machine gun had been a key weapon for overcoming resistance to nineteenth-century colonial expansion before Europeans trained the weapon on one another during the Great War. The machine gun represented one of the most important advances in military technology and compelled military leaders on all sides to rethink their battlefield tactics.

Poison gas was lethal for humans and animals. Millions of horses were used for military purposes by both sides during the war. When poison gas attacks were anticipated, horses near the battle lines wore gas masks too.
Photo12/UIG/Getty Images

The immobility of trench warfare and the desire to reintroduce movement to warfare prompted the development of weapons that supplied the power necessary to break the deadly stalemate. Both sides subsequently developed many new and potent weapons. The most unconventional weapon was poisonous gas, first used by German troops in January 1915. Especially hated and much feared by troops in the trenches was **mustard gas,** a liquid agent that, when exposed to air, turned into a noxious yellow gas, hence its name. The effects of mustard gas did not appear for some twelve hours following exposure, but then it rotted the body from both within and without. After blistering the skin and damaging the eyes, the gas attacked the bronchial tubes, stripping off the mucous membrane. Death usually occurred in four to five weeks. In the meantime, victims endured excruciating pain. Like the machine gun, gas proved a potent weapon, and both sides lost a total of about 1.2 million soldiers as a result of its use. But even though chemical agents were effective in producing heavy casualties, gas attacks failed to deliver strategic breakthroughs, and the anticipated return to more fluid battle lines never materialized.

Other weapons developed to break the stalemate on the western front included tanks and airplanes. The British first introduced tanks in September 1916, and the Allies deployed them to break down German defensive trenches. Despite its effectiveness during the final offenses of the war, the tank did not produce the longed-for strategic advantage. In most cases, German counterattacks quickly regained the ground won by tanks. Military leaders also hoped that airplanes, just recently invented in 1914, would help restore mobility to the western front. However, because airplanes could not carry enough weapons to do serious damage to troops or installations on the ground, their real asset during the Great War was aerial reconnaissance. In fact, the much publicized and glamorized aerial combat of the Great War featuring "ace fighters" and "dogfights" were not large-scale battles in themselves but, rather, were attempts to prevent the enemy from conducting such reconnaissance. The plane and the tank figured more prominently as important strategic weapons during the Second World War. Other weapons systems, such as the submarine, had made earlier appearances in warfare but did not play a significant role until the Great War. It was not until the Great War, when the German navy deployed its diesel-powered submarine fleet against Allied commercial shipping, that the

MAP 33.1   The Great War in Europe and southwest Asia, 1914–1918.

Note the locations of both the eastern and the western fronts in Europe during the war.

Why didn't the same kind of trench warfare immobilize opposing armies on the eastern front the way it did on the western front?

submarine proved its military effectiveness. Although the German navy relied more heavily on submarines, the allied navies of Great Britain and the United States also deployed their own fleets of diesel-powered submarines.

No-Man's-Land   The most courageous infantry charges, even when preceded by pulverizing artillery barrages and clouds of poisonous gas, were no match for determined de-

fenders. Shielded by the dirt of their trenches and by barbed wire and gas masks, they unleashed a torrent of lethal metal with their machine guns and repeating rifles. In every sector of the front, those who fought rarely found glory. Instead, they encountered death. No-man's-land was strewn with shell craters, cadavers, and body parts. The grim realities of trench warfare—the wet, cold, waist-deep mud, lice, and corpse-fed rats—contrasted sharply with the encouraging

A dogfight (close combat between military aircraft) between German and British planes during the Great War. Dogfights as a new type of combat resulted from the attempt of each contestant to prevent the enemy from conducting aerial reconnaissance.

Historica Graphica Collection/Heritage Images/Getty Images

and optimistic phrases of politicians and generals justifying the unrelenting slaughter.

The Eastern Front In eastern Europe and the Balkans, the battle lines were more fluid. After a staunch defense, a combination of Austrian and German forces overran Serbia, Albania, and Romania. Farther north, Russia took the offensive early by invading Prussia in 1914. The Central Powers recovered quickly, however, and by the summer of 1915 combined German and Austrian forces drove the Russian armies out of East Prussia and then out of Poland, establishing a defensive line extending from the Baltic to the Ukraine. Russian counterattacks in 1916 and 1917 collapsed amid massive casualties. The huge scale of Russian defeats in turn undermined the popularity of the tsar and his government and played a significant role in fostering revolutionary ferment within Russian society.

Bloodletting Many battles took place, but some were so horrific, so devastating, and so futile that their names are synonymous with human slaughter. The casualty figures attested to this bloodletting. In 1916 the Germans tried to break the deadlock with a huge assault on the fortress of **Verdun.** The French rallying cry was "They shall not pass," and they did not—but at a tremendous cost: while the defeated Germans suffered a loss of 280,000, the victorious French counted 315,000 dead. Survivors recovered fewer than 160,000 identifiable bodies. The rest were unrecognizable or had been blown to bits by high explosives and sucked into the mud. To relieve the pressure on Verdun, British forces counterattacked at the Somme, and by November they had gained a few thousand yards at the cost of 420,000 casualties. The Germans suffered similar losses, although in the end neither side gained any strategic advantage.

New Rules of Engagement Dying and suffering were not limited solely to combatants. Because they were crucial to the war effort, millions of civilians became targets of enemy military operations. On 30 August 1914, Parisians looked up at the sky and saw a new weapon of war, a huge, silent German zeppelin (a hydrogen-filled airship) whose underbelly rained bombs. Although the attack killed just one person, it heralded a new kind of warfare—air war against civilians. A less novel but more effective means of targeting civilian populations was the naval blockade. Military leaders on both sides used blockades to deny food to whole populations, hoping that starving civilians would force their governments to capitulate. The British blockade of Germany during the war contributed to the deaths of an estimated half-million Germans.

Total War: The Home Front

Helmuth Karl von Moltke (1800–1891), former chief of the Prussian General Staff, showed an uncanny insight long before 1914 when he predicted that future wars would not end with a single battle because the defeat of a nation would not be acknowledged until the whole strength of its people was broken. He was right. As the Great War ground on, it became a conflict of attrition (gradually wearing down the enemy) in which the organization of material and human resources was of paramount importance. War became total, fought between entire societies, not just between armies; and total victory was the only acceptable outcome that might justify the terrible sacrifices made by all sides. The nature of total war created a military front and a home front. The term **home front** expressed the important reality that the outcome of the war hinged on how effectively each nation mobilized its economy and activated its noncombatant citizens to support the war effort.

The Home Front As the war continued beyond 1914 and as war weariness and a decline in economic capability set in, the response of all belligerents was to limit individual freedoms and give control of society increasingly over to military leaders.

How the Past Shapes the Future ▷ ▷ ▷ ▷ ▷ ▷ ▷ ▷ ▷

The Destructive Potential of Industrial Technologies

By the last half of the nineteenth century, a variety of European and American intellectuals believed that industrialization—which resulted in mass-produced goods, new and more rapid forms of communication, and all manner of mechanized devices—had led to a marked improvement in the human condition. Moreover, these same intellectuals were optimistic that industrialization would continue to contribute to the overall progress of humanity into the distant future. In many ways their expectations were realized: during the twentieth century industrial machinery made it possible to feed billions of people, build vast networks of roads, and create hundreds of millions of cars and airplanes. Mass-produced medicines made it possible to virtually eliminate smallpox, the plague, and a variety of other health scourges from much of the world, while mass-produced consumer goods allowed people to purchase, at relatively low cost, a bewildering variety of items designed to make them more comfortable. At an aggregate level, humans in the twentieth century lived longer, were less poor, were more connected to one another, and had access to more everyday comforts than their predecessors in previous centuries.

The Machinery of War

Yet the twentieth century also revealed the enormous costs of industrialization—costs that reverberate right up to the present. Indeed, although industrialization allowed the manufacture of goods and materials that brought people together or made life more convenient, it also allowed for the manufacture of items designed for destruction on a hitherto unimaginable scale. In this chapter we have already seen how the belligerent European nations involved in World War I marshaled their industrial power to manufacture deadly weapons, ammunition, chemical gases, tanks, and submarines. Few humans alive even in 1900 could have imagined the devastation—in both life and property—made possible when industrial powers put their energies toward destruction. In fact, disillusion with the destructive capacities of industrial technologies played an important role in the widespread atmosphere of anxiety that permeated intellectual and popular circles in Europe after the war—a process discussed in chapter 34. Such anxieties did not prevent industrialized nations from continuing to develop more and better ways to destroy their enemies, however. During World War II, opposing sides used industrial technology to kill ever more efficiently and quickly. In the case of Germany, Adolf Hitler took industrialized killing to a chilling new level when

Women at work in an English munitions factory. The Great War drew huge numbers of men out of the workforce at a time of great industrial need. Women replaced them, for the first time assuming traditionally "male" jobs.
Universal History Archive/Universal Images Group/Getty Images

he authorized the use of advanced industrial techniques to kill millions of Jews, Gypsies, Slavs, dissidents, and homosexuals (chapter 36). After the war, the creation of the atom bomb used with such devastating effect in Hiroshima and Nagasaki made it clear that scientists had designed industrial weaponry capable of destroying entire populations in one blow. From that point until the dissolution of the Soviet Union in 1991, people all over the world were subjected to the threat of nuclear annihilation if the "cold" war between the United States and the Soviet Union ever erupted into a "hot" war (chapter 36). During the twentieth century, indeed, the threat of mass destruction via industrial technologies was a reality that significant segments of the world's population learned to live with, however uncomfortably.

Environmental Impact

Industrial technologies also proved to be destructive during the twentieth century in terms of their environmental impact. Since the nineteenth century, industrial economies relied on fossil fuels to function. In addition, industrial manufacturing required the widespread exploitation of raw materials such as cotton and timber. During the nineteenth and much of the twentieth centuries, industrializing states operated as though fossil fuels and raw materials would be endlessly available. Over time, however, it became clear that large-scale industrialization resulted in air and water pollution as well as in deforestation, erosion, and the loss of biodiversity. During the post–World War II period, these problems intensified as a variety of new states sought to establish industrialized economies of their own—a process discussed in chapter 37. By the end of the twentieth century, moreover, the majority of the world's scientists concluded that the pollution generated by more than a century of industrialization had caused changes in climate on a planetary scale (chapter 38). The ultimate impact of these changes remains unclear, although some scientists fear that it may be too late to undo the damage that has been set in motion from industrialization.

These are only a small sampling of the destructive potential of industrial technologies, both through time and across space. When reading subsequent chapters, try to identify additional developments whose origins can be traced to the consequences of industrialization, whether of a positive or destructive nature.

Because patriotism and courage alone could not guarantee victory, the governments of belligerent nations assumed control of the home front. Initially, ministers and generals were reluctant to resort to compulsive measures, even conscription of recruits, but they quickly changed their minds. Each belligerent government eventually militarized civilian war production by subordinating private enterprises to governmental control and imposing severe discipline on the labor process.

Economic measures were foremost in the minds of government leaders because the war created unprecedented demands for raw materials and manufactured goods. Those material requirements compelled governments to institute tight controls over economic life. Planning boards reorganized entire industries, set production quotas and priorities, and determined what would be produced and consumed. Government authorities also established wage and price controls, extended work hours, and in some instances restricted the movement of workers. Because bloody battlefields caused an insatiable appetite for soldiers, nations responded by extending the age range for compulsory military service. In Germany, for example, men between the ages of sixteen and sixty were eligible to serve at the front. By constantly tapping into the available male population, the war created an increasing demand for workers at home. Unemployment—a persistent feature of all prewar economies—vanished virtually overnight.

Women at War As men went off to war, women replaced them at work. Conscription took men out of the labor force, and wartime leaders exhorted women to fill the gaps in the workforce. A combination of patriotism and high wages drew women into formerly "male" jobs. The lives of women changed as they left home or domestic service for the workplace. Some women took over the management of farms and businesses left by their husbands, who went off to fight. Others found jobs as postal workers and police officers. Behind the battle lines, women were most visible as nurses, physicians, and communications clerks.

Perhaps the most crucial work performed by women during the war was the making of shells. Several million women, and sometimes children, put in long, hard hours in munitions factories. This work exposed them to severe dangers. The first came from explosions because keeping sparks away from highly volatile materials was impossible. Many women died in these incidents, although government censorship during the war made it difficult to know how many. The other, more insidious danger came from working with TNT explosives. Although authorities claimed that this work was not dangerous, exposure to TNT caused severe poisoning, depending on the length of exposure. Before serious illnesses manifested themselves, TNT poisoning marked its victims by turning their skin yellow and their hair orange. Long-term health

Perhaps the most crucial work performed by women during the war was the making of shells. This photograph shows a female assembly-line worker in a munitions factory in England in 1917.

Hulton Deutsch/Corbis Historical/Getty Images

SOURCES FROM THE PAST

Dulce et Decorum Est

The Great War produced a wealth of poetry. The poetic response to war covered a range of moods, from early romanticism and patriotism to cynicism, resignation, and the angry depiction of horror. One of the best-known war poets was Wilfred Owen (1893–1918), whose poems are among the most poignant of the war. Owen, who enlisted for service on the western front in 1915 at the age of twenty-two, was injured in March 1917 and sent home. Declared fit for duty in August 1918, he returned to the front. German machine-gun fire killed him on 7 November, four days before the armistice that ended the war, when he tried to cross the Sambre Canal. This poem was published in 1920, two years after his death.

Bent double, like old beggars under sacks,
Knock-kneed, coughing like hags, we cursed through sludge,
Till on the haunting flares we turned our backs
And towards our distant rest began to trudge.
Men marched asleep. Many had lost their boots
But limped on, blood-shod. All went lame; all blind;
Drunk with fatigue; deaf even to the hoots
Of gas-shells dropping softly behind.

> What is Owen trying to convey about the physical demands of service during the war?

Gas! GAS! Quick, boys!—An ecstasy of fumbling,
Fitting the clumsy helmets just in time;
But someone still was yelling out and stumbling
And floundering like a man in fire or lime.—
Dim, through the misty panes and thick green light
As under a green sea, I saw him drowning.

In all my dreams, before my helpless sight,
He plunges at me, guttering, choking, drowning.
If in some smothering dreams you too could pace
Behind the wagon that we flung him in,
And watch the white eyes writhing in his face,
His hanging face, like a devil's sick of sin;
If you could hear, at every jolt, the blood
Come gargling from the froth-corrupted lungs,
Obscene as cancer, bitter as the cud
Of vile, incurable sores on innocent tongues,—
My friend, you would not tell with such high zest
To children ardent for some desperate glory,
The old Lie: Dulce et decorum est
Pro patria mori.*

> How does Owen describe the effects of a gas attack? Is his literary depiction more or less effective than detached descriptions of war's effects?

*Author's note: "Sweet and fitting is it to die for one's country" comes from a line by the Roman poet Horace (65–8 B.C.E.).

For Further Reflection

■ What is Owen's overall message in this poem? Do you think he intended to take a political stand on war or that he was simply describing his experience?

Source: Owen, Wilfred. Dulce et Decorum, 1918.

effects included damage to the eyes and skin, liver damage, reproductive problems, and severe anemia. The accepted though ineffectual remedy for TNT poisoning was rest, good food, and plenty of fresh milk.

Middle- and upper-class women often reported that the war was a liberating experience, freeing them from older attitudes that had limited their work and their personal lives. These women, who had not typically worked outside the home, frequently remarked on a sense of mission and the knowledge that they were important to the war effort. Working-class women, in contrast, had long been accustomed to earning wages, and for them war work proved far less liberating. Most of the belligerent governments promised equal pay for equal work, but in most instances that promise remained unfulfilled. Although women's industrial wages rose during the war, measurable gaps always remained between the incomes of men and women. In the end, female employment on such a large scale was a temporary phenomenon that ended when the war was over. At the end of the war, women were encouraged (and often required) to leave their wartime jobs in order to accommodate the men returning from service. Nevertheless, the extension of voting rights to women shortly after the war, in Britain (1918, for women thirty years and older), Germany (1919), and Austria (1919), was in part an acknowledgment of the important roles women assumed during the Great War.

Propaganda To maintain the spirit of the home front and to counter threats to national unity, governments resorted to the restriction of civil liberties, censorship of bad news, and vilification of the enemy through propaganda campaigns. While government officials busily censored war news, including letters from soldiers at the front, people who had the temerity to criticize their nation's war effort were prosecuted as traitors. In France, for example, former prime minister Joseph Caillaux spent two years in prison awaiting trial because he had publicly suggested that the best interest of France would be to reach a compromise peace with Germany.

The propaganda offices of the belligerent nations tried to convince the public that military defeat would mean the destruction of everything worth living for, and to that end they did their utmost to discredit and dehumanize the enemy. Posters, pamphlets, and "scientific" studies depicted the enemy as subhuman savages who engaged in vile atrocities. While German propaganda depicted Russians as "semi-Asiatic barbarians", French authorities chronicled the atrocities committed by the German "Hun" in Belgium. In 1917 the *Times* of London published a story claiming that Germans converted human corpses into fertilizer and food. With much less fanfare a later news story admitted that this information resulted from a sloppy translation: the German word for *horse* had been mistakenly translated as "human." German propaganda stooped equally low. One widely distributed poster invoked racist tropes by showing caricatures of black Allied soldiers raping German women, including pregnant women, to suggest the horrors that would follow if the nation's war effort failed. Most atrocity stories originated in the fertile imagination of propaganda officers, and their falsehood eventually engendered public skepticism and cynicism. Ironically, public disbelief of wartime propaganda led to skepticism about actual abominations perpetrated during subsequent wars.

Conflict in East Asia and the Pacific

For many people outside Europe, the Great War was a murderous European civil war that quickly turned into a global conflict. There were three reasons for the war's expansion. First, European governments carried their animosities into their colonies, embroiling them—especially African societies—in their war. Second, because of massive casualties among European recruits, the British and the French augmented their ranks by recruiting men from their colonies. Millions of Africans and Asians were drawn into the war. Behind their trenches the French employed soldiers and laborers from Algeria, West Africa, and French Indochina, while the British recruited more than a million Indian soldiers as well as African troops for combat. The British also relied on troops furnished by the dominion lands, including Australia, New Zealand, Canada, Newfoundland, and South Africa. Third, the Great War assumed global significance because the desires and objectives of some principal actors that entered the conflict—Japan, the United States, and the Ottoman Empire—had little to do with the murder in Sarajevo or the other issues that drove the Europeans to battle.

Japan's Entry into the War On 15 August 1914 the Japanese government, claiming that it desired "to secure firm and enduring peace in Eastern Asia," sent an ultimatum to Germany demanding the handover of the German-leased territory of Jiaozhou (northeastern China) to Japanese authorities without compensation. The same note also demanded that the German navy unconditionally withdraw its warships from Japanese and Chinese waters. When the Germans refused to comply, the Japanese entered the war on the side of the Allies on 23 August 1914. With the blessing of their British allies (including the assistance of two British battalions), Japanese forces took the fortress of Qingdao, a German-held port in China's Shandong Province, in November 1914. Then, between August and November of that year, Japanese forces also took possession of the German-held Marshall Islands, the Mariana Islands, Palau, and the Carolines. Forces from New Zealand and Australia joined in the Japanese quest for German-held islands in the Pacific, capturing German-held portions of Samoa in August 1914 and German-occupied possessions in the Bismarck Archipelago and New Guinea.

The Twenty-one Demands After seizing German bases on the Shandong peninsula and on Pacific islands, Japan shrewdly exploited Allied support and European preoccupation to advance its own imperial interests in China. On 18 January 1915 the Japanese presented the Chinese government with twenty-one secret demands. The terms of that ultimatum, if accepted, would have reduced China to a protectorate of Japan. The most important demands were that the Chinese confirm the Japanese seizure of Shandong from Germany, grant Japanese industrial monopolies in central China, place Japanese overseers in key government positions, give Japan joint control of Chinese police forces, restrict their arms purchases to Japanese manufacturers, and make those purchases only with the approval of the Tokyo government. China submitted to most of the demands but rejected others. Chinese diplomats leaked the note to the British authorities, who spoke up for China, thus preventing total capitulation. The **Twenty-one Demands** reflected Japan's determination to dominate east Asia and served as the basis for future Japanese pressure on China.

Africa and Africans in the War

The geographic extent of the conflict also broadened beyond Europe when the Allies targeted German colonies in Africa. When the war of 1914–1918 erupted in Europe, all of sub-Saharan Africa (except Ethiopia and Liberia) consisted of European colonies, with the Germans controlling four: Togoland, the Cameroons, German Southwest Africa, and German East Africa. Thus, one immediate consequence of war for Africans in 1914 was that the Allies invaded those German colonies. Specific strategic interests among the Allies varied. British officers and soldiers, trying to maintain naval supremacy, attempted to put German port facilities and communications systems out of action. The British also anticipated that victory in the German colonies would mean the acquisition of German territory in Africa after the war. France's objective was to recover territory in Cameroon that it had ceded to Germany in 1911. The Germans, in contrast, simply tried to hold on to what they had.

An Indian gun crew in the Somme area, 1916. During the Great War, colonial powers relied on millions of Asian and African men to fight or labor for their respective sides.

National Archives (165-BO-1602)

Battles in Africa Although their position in Africa was far less powerful than that of either the British or the French, by resorting to guerrilla tactics some fifteen thousand German troops tied sixty thousand Allied forces down for the duration of the war. While Togoland fell to an Anglo-French force after three weeks of fighting, it took extended campaigns ranging over vast distances to subdue the remaining German footholds in Africa. The Allied force included British, Portuguese, French, and Belgian troops and large contingents of Indian, Arab, and African soldiers. Fighting took place on land and sea; on lakes and rivers; in deserts, jungles, and swamps; and in the air. Germs were frequently more deadly than battles; tens of thousands of Allied soldiers and workers succumbed to deadly tropical diseases. The German flag did not disappear from Africa until after the armistice took effect on 11 November 1918.

Africans in the War More than one million African soldiers participated directly in military campaigns, in which they witnessed firsthand the spectacle of

What's Left Out?

For decades after the Great War, historians focused on the European causes of the Great War and its major European battlefronts. While understandable given the scale of destruction in Europe, such a focus obscured the profound ways World War I affected even neutral territories thousands of miles away. One of the reasons is because the German government established the principle of instigating revolutions in Allied colonies as an explicit war aim. Germany was especially interested in starting a revolution in India because it was Britain's most important colony and provided over a million soldiers for the war effort. For this reason, the German Foreign Office created the Committee for Indian Independence and staffed it with Indian revolutionaries who planned the immediate overthrow of British rule. Indian revolutionaries were already active before the war, but now they found common cause with a powerful state willing to provide them with money, weapons, and logistical support. During the war, the German government funded initiatives aimed at fomenting revolution in India, including establishing a secret military training base for Indians in Siam (Thailand), smuggling weapons to India from the United States via China and the Dutch East Indies, and distributing propaganda intended to whip up popular Indian support for rebellion. These efforts all required revolutionaries to move around the world and to coordinate their efforts with German consuls in neutral territories as diverse as the Dutch East Indies, the United States, Siam, and China (the latter three were neutral until 1917). These contacts, in turn, brought the politics of the war right into neutral territories because officials in those places feared they would be dragged into the war if the Central Powers were caught plotting against the Allies on their soil. As a result, each had to devote significant energy and money toward stopping German coordination with colonial revolutionaries. This example helps us to see that the enmities between the Allied and the Central Powers were not simply fought out on European battlefronts and in European colonies, but even in neutral territories halfway around the world.

Source: Heather Streets-Salter, *World War One in Southeast Asia* (Cambridge: Cambridge University Press, 2017).

A company of Askari riflemen fighting for the Germans march in German East Africa.
Pictorial Press Ltd/Alamy Stock Photo

white people fighting one another. They fought on African soil, in the lands of southwest Asia, and on the western front in Europe. Even more men, as well as women and children, served as carriers to support armies in areas where supplies could not be hauled by conventional methods such as road, rail, or pack animal. The colonial powers raised recruits for fighting and carrier services in three ways: on a purely voluntary basis, in levies supplied by African chiefs that consisted of volunteer and impressed (coerced) personnel, and through formal conscription. In French colonies, military service became compulsory for all males between the ages of twenty and twenty-eight, and by the end of the war more than four hundred eighty thousand colonial troops had served in the French army. The British also raised recruits in their African colonies. In 1915 a compulsory service order made all men aged eighteen to twenty-five liable for military service. In the Congo, the Belgians impressed more than half a million porters. Ultimately, more than one hundred fifty thousand African soldiers and carriers lost their lives, and many more suffered injury or became disabled.

Battles in Southwest Asia

The most extensive military operations outside Europe took place in the southwest Asian territories of the Ottoman Empire. When war broke out between the Allied and Central powers in 1914, the Ottoman government feared that the victors would carve up what was left of its empire if it did not ally with one side or the other. After being rebuffed by the British, the Ottoman government turned to the Germans and entered into a formal alliance on October 28, 1914. Once a member of the Central Powers, the Germans convinced the Ottomans—as the seat of the caliph, or the nominal leader of Sunni Muslims around the world—to declare a *jihad*

(religious war) against the Allies. This, they hoped, would undermine support for the Allies by the millions of Muslim colonial subjects ruled by Britain, France, and Russia. Although the jihadist strategy was not as effective as the Germans had hoped, the Allies viewed it with alarm and made a concerted effort to undermine the Ottoman Empire in a variety of its territories.

Gallipoli Ottoman entry into the war also seemed to offer a way for the Allies to break the stalemate on the western front. To accomplish this, Winston Churchill (1874–1965), first lord of the Admiralty (British navy), suggested an Allied strike against the Ottomans via the Ottoman-controlled Dardanelles Strait (see Map 33.1). Early in 1915 British and French naval forces conducted an expedition to seize the approach to the Strait in an attempt to open a warm-water supply line to Russia. After bombing the forts that defended the strait, Allied ships were damaged by floating mines and withdrew without accomplishing their mission. After withdrawing the battleships, the British high command decided to land a combined force of soldiers from Britain, Canada, Austrialia, and New Zealand on the beaches of the Gallipoli peninsula. The campaign was a disaster. Turkish defenders, ensconced in the cliffs above, quickly pinned down the Allied troops on the beaches. Trapped between the sea and the hills, Allied soldiers dug in and engaged in their own version of trench warfare. The resulting stalemate produced a total of 250,000 casualties on each side. Despite the losses, Allied leaders took nine months to admit that their campaign had failed.

Gallipoli was a debacle with long-term consequences. Although the British directed the ill-fated campaign, it was mostly Canadians, Australians, and New Zealanders who suffered terrible casualties. That recognition led to a weakening of imperial ties and paved the way for emerging national identities. In Australia the date of the fateful landing, 25 April 1915, became enshrined as Anzac (an acronym for Australian and New Zealand Army Corps) Day and remains the country's most significant day of public homage. On the Ottoman side, the battle for the strait helped launch the political career of the commander of the Turkish division that defended Gallipoli. Mustafa Kemal (1881–1938) went on to play a crucial role in the formation of the modern Turkish state.

Armenian Massacres The war provided the pretext for the Ottoman government to begin a campaign of extermination against the two million Armenians living under its rule. Armenians were the last remaining major non-Muslim ethnic group living under Ottoman rule, and like other Christians who had once been subject to Ottoman rule, they sought autonomy and eventual independence. Friction between Armenians and Ottoman authorities went back to the nineteenth century, when distinct nationalist feelings stirred many of the peoples who lived under Ottoman rule.

Initially, Armenians had relied on government reforms to prevent discrimination against non-Muslim subjects by corrupt officials and extortionist tax collectors. When abuses persisted, Armenians resorted to confrontation. Armenian demonstrations against Ottoman authorities in 1890 and 1895 led to reprisals by a government that had become increasingly convinced that the Armenians were seeking independence, as other Christian minorities of the Balkans had done in previous decades.

After 1913 the Ottoman state adopted a new policy of Turkish nationalism intended to strengthen morale within the shrinking empire. The new nationalism stressed Turkish culture and traditions, which aggravated tensions between Turkish rulers and non-Turkish subjects of the empire. In particular, the state viewed Christian minorities as an obstacle to Turkish nationalism. During the Great War, the Ottoman government branded Armenians as a traitorous internal enemy, who threatened the security of the state, and then unleashed a murderous campaign against them. Forced mass evacuations, accompanied by starvation, dehydration, and exposure, led to the death of tens of thousands of Armenians. The Ottoman government also organized massacres of Armenians through mass drowning, incineration, or assaults with blunt instruments.

The wartime Ottoman campaign against its Armenian subjects has become known as the **Armenian Genocide.** Scholars estimate that close to a million Armenians perished during the genocide. Yet the Turkish government rejects the label of genocide and claims that Armenian deaths resulted not from a state-sponsored plan of mass extermination but from disease, famine, and religious fighting between ordinary Christians and Muslims.

The Ottoman Empire After successfully fending off Allied forces on the beaches of Gallipoli in 1915 and in Mesopotamia in 1916, Ottoman armies retreated slowly on all fronts. The British in particular were instrumental in coordinating multiple attacks against the Ottomans, using armies that drew heavily on recruits from Egypt, India, Australia, and New Zealand to invade Ottoman territory. As the armies smashed the Ottoman state—one entering Mesopotamia and the other advancing from the Suez Canal toward Palestine—they received significant support from an Arab revolt against the Turks. In 1916, aided by the British, the nomadic bedouin of Arabia under the leadership of Hussein bin Ali, sharif of Mecca and king of the Hejaz (1856-1931), and others rose up against Turkish rule. The motivation for the Arab revolt centered on securing independence from the Ottoman Empire—a goal the British government promised to help Arabs reach—and subsequently creating a unified Arab nation spanning lands from Syria to Yemen.

The British government did not keep its promise of Arab independence after the war. Instead, the British and French governments, with the assent of Russia, forged a secret agreement, the **Sykes-Picot Treaty** of 1916, and divided Ottoman territory in southwest Asia between them in the aftermath of their victory in the war. Further complicating the issue and creating a future source of conflict was the 1917 **Balfour Declaration,** by which the British government publicly declared its support for "the establishment in Palestine of a national home for the Jewish people."

THE END OF THE WAR

The war produced strains within all the belligerent nations, but most of them managed, often ruthlessly, to cope with food riots, strikes, and mutinies. In the Russian Empire, the war amplified existing stresses to such an extent that the Romanov dynasty was forced to abdicate in favor of a provisional government in the spring of 1917. Eight months later, **Bolshevik** revolutionaries took power from the provisional government. The Bolsheviks then promptly took Russia out of the war early in 1918. This blow to the Allies was offset by the entry of the United States into the conflict in 1917, which turned the tide of war in 1918. The resources of the United States finally compelled the exhausted Central Powers to sue for peace in November 1918.

In 1919 the victorious Allies gathered in Paris to hammer out a peace settlement. The settlements that resulted were compromises that pleased few of the parties involved. The most significant consequence of the war was Europe's diminished role in the world, though this was not immediately visible to contemporaries. The war of 1914-1918 undermined Europe's power and simultaneously promoted nationalist aspirations among colonized peoples who clamored for self-determination and national independence. For the time being, however, the major imperialist powers kept their grip on their overseas holdings.

Revolution in Russia

The February Revolution The Great War had seriously undermined the Russian state. In the spring of 1917, disintegrating armies, mutinies, and food shortages provoked a series of street demonstrations and strikes in Petrograd (St. Petersburg). The inability of police forces to suppress the uprisings, and the subsequent mutiny of troops garrisoned in the capital, persuaded Tsar Nicholas II (reigned 1894-1917) to abdicate the throne in March of that year. Thus Russia ceased to be a monarchy, and the **Romanov dynasty** disappeared after more than three hundred years of uninterrupted rule. Russians called this the **February Revolution** because Russians used the Julian calendar rather than the Gregorian calendar in use by western European states.

The Struggle for Power After its success in Petrograd, the revolution spread throughout the country, and political power in Russia shifted to two new agencies: the provisional government and the Petrograd soviet of Workers' and Soldiers' Deputies. Soviets, which were revolutionary councils organized by socialists, appeared for the first time during the

---

Sykes-Picot (sikes pee-coh)
Bolshevik (BOHL-sheh-vihk)

Vladimir Lenin (1870–1924) makes a speech in Red Square on the first anniversary (1918) of the Bolshevik revolution.
Hulton Deutsch/Corbis Historical/ Getty Images

thought and writing political pamphlets. In contrast to Marx, Lenin viewed the industrial working class as incapable of developing the proper revolutionary consciousness that would lead to effective political action. To Lenin the industrial proletariat required the leadership of a well-organized and highly disciplined party, a workers' vanguard that would serve as the catalyst for revolution and for the realization of a socialist society.

In a moment of high drama, the German High Command transported Lenin and other revolutionaries in 1917 to Russia in a sealed train, hoping that this committed antiwar activist would stir up trouble and bring about Russia's withdrawal from the war. Lenin headed the Bolsheviks, the radical wing of the Russian Social Democratic Party. In April he began calling for the transfer of legal authority to the soviets and advocated uncompromising opposition to the war. Initially, his party opposed his radicalism, but he soon succeeded in converting his fellow Bolsheviks to his proposals.

Russian revolution of 1905 (see chapter 31). In 1917, soviets of Workers' and Soldiers' Deputies surfaced all over Russia, wielding considerable power through their control of factories and segments of the military. The period between March and November witnessed a political struggle between the provisional government and the powerful Petrograd soviet. At first the new government enjoyed considerable public support as it disbanded the tsarist police; repealed all limitations on freedom of speech, press, and association; and abolished laws that discriminated against ethnic or religious groups. But it failed to satisfy popular demands for an end to war and for land reform. It claimed that, being provisional, it could not make fundamental changes such as confiscating land and distributing it among peasants. Any such change had to be postponed for decision by a future constituent assembly. The government also pledged itself to "unswervingly carry out the agreements made with the Allies" and promised to continue the war to a victorious conclusion. The Petrograd soviet, in contrast, called for an immediate peace. The soviets were the only ones in Russia determined to end the war and hence gained more support from the people of Russia.

Lenin Into this tense political situation stepped **Vladimir Ilyich Lenin** (1870–1924), a revolutionary Marxist who had been living in exile in Switzerland. Born into a warm and loving family, Lenin grew up in the confines of a moderately prosperous family living in the provincial Russian town of Simbirsk. In 1887, shortly after his father's death, the police arrested and hanged his older brother for plotting to assassinate the tsar, an event that seared Lenin's youth. Following a brief career as a lawyer, Lenin spent many years abroad, devoting himself to studying Marxist

The October Revolution The Bolsheviks, who were a small minority among revolutionary working-class parties, eventually gained control of the Petrograd soviet. Crucial to that development was the provisional government's insistence on continuing the war, its inability to feed the population, and its refusal to undertake land reform. Those policies led to a growing conviction among workers and peasants that their problems could only be solved by the soviets. The Bolsheviks capitalized on that mood with effective slogans such as "All Power to the Soviets" and, most famous, "Peace, Land, and Bread." In September, Lenin persuaded the Central Committee of the Bolshevik Party to organize an armed insurrection and seize power in the name of the All-Russian National Congress of Soviets, which was then convening in Petrograd. During the night of 6 November and the following day, armed workers, soldiers, and sailors stormed the Winter Palace, the home of the provisional government. By the afternoon of 7 November (although called the **October Revolution** in Russia because of the Julian calendar), the

Vladimir Ilyich Lenin (VLAD-uh-meer IL-yich LEHN-in)

virtually bloodless insurrection had run its course, and power passed from the provisional government into the hands of Lenin and the Bolshevik Party. The U.S. journalist John Reed (1887–1920), who witnessed the Bolshevik seizure of power, understood the significance of the events when he referred to them as "ten days that shook the world." Lenin and his followers were poised to destroy the traditional patterns and values of Russian society and challenge the institutions of capitalist society everywhere.

Treaty of Brest-Litovsk   The Bolshevik rulers ended Russia's involvement in the Great War by signing the **Treaty of Brest-Litovsk** with Germany on 3 March 1918. The treaty gave the Germans possession or control of much of Russia's territory (the Baltic states, the Caucasus, Finland, Poland, and the Ukraine) and one-quarter of its population. The terms of the treaty were harsh and humiliating, but taking Russia out of the war gave the new government an opportunity to deal with internal problems. Russia's departure from the war meant that Germany could concentrate all its resources on the western front.

U.S. Intervention and Collapse of the Central Powers

The year 1917 was crucial for another reason: it marked the entry of the United States into the war on the side of the Allies. In 1914 the American public firmly opposed intervention in a European war. Woodrow Wilson (1856–1924) was reelected president in 1916 because he campaigned on a nonintervention platform. That sentiment soon changed. After the outbreak of the war, the United States pursued a neutrality that favored the Allies, and as the war progressed, the United States became increasingly committed economically to an Allied victory.

Economic Considerations   During the first two years of the war, the U.S. economy coped with a severe business recession that saw thousands of businesses fail and unemployment reach 15 percent. Economic recovery became dependent on sales of war materials, especially on British orders for munitions. Because U.S. companies sold huge amounts of supplies to the Allies, insistence on neutrality seemed hypocritical at

In 1915, artist Willy Stower depicted a ship sinking as a result of a submarine attack. The Germans used submarines to great effect to disrupt the shipping of essential supplies to Great Britain.
Bettmann/Getty Images

best. With the war grinding on, the Allies took out large loans with American banks, which persuaded some Americans that an Allied victory made good financial sense. Moreover, by the spring of 1917, the Allies had depleted their means of paying for essential supplies from the United States and probably could not have maintained their war effort had the United States remained neutral. An Allied victory and, hence, the ability to pay off Allied war debts could be accomplished only by direct U.S. participation in the Great War.

Submarine Warfare The official factor in the United States' decision to enter the war was Germany's resumption of

This 1917–1918 U.S. army recruitment poster depicts an apish monster leaving war-torn Europe and emerging on the shores of America. Wielding a club labeled Kultur, and wearing a spiked helmet associated with Prussian and German militarism, this is a less than subtle caricature of the threat emanating from a warmongering Germany.
Library of Congress Prints & Photographs Division [LC-DIG-ds-03216]

unrestricted submarine warfare in February 1917. At the outset of the war, U.S. government officials asserted the traditional doctrine of neutral rights for American ships because they wanted to continue trading with belligerents, most notably the British and the French. With the German surface fleet bottled up in the Baltic, Germany's wartime leaders grew desperately dependent on their submarine fleet to strangle Britain economically and break the British blockade of the Central Powers. German military experts calculated that submarine attacks against the ships of Great Britain and all the ships headed to Great Britain would bring about the defeat of Great Britain in six months. German subs often sank neutral merchant ships without first giving a warning as required by international law. On 7 May 1915, a German submarine sank the British passenger liner *Lusitania* off the Irish coast, with a loss of 1,198 lives, including 128 U.S. citizens. Technically, the ship was a legitimate target because it carried 4,200 cases of ammunition and traveled through a declared war zone. Nevertheless, segments of the American public were outraged, and during the next two years the country's mood increasingly turned against Germany.

American public opinion became further enraged in 1917 when the content of a coded telegram came to light, dispatched by the foreign secretary of the German Empire, Arthur Zimmermann, to the German ambassador in Mexico. This so-called **Zimmermann telegram** was a diplomatic proposal for Mexico to join the Central Powers in the event of the United States entering World War I on the side of the Triple Entente. In return for a military alliance, Mexico was promised territories in Texas, New Mexico, and Arizona. The Mexican government was not tempted by this offer. It ignored the proposal and officially rejected it after the United States entered the war.

America Declares War Even though the British naval blockade directed at the Central Powers constantly interfered with American shipping, Woodrow Wilson nonetheless moved his nation to war against Germany. In January 1917, with his country still at peace, Wilson began to enumerate U.S. war aims, and on April 2 he urged the Congress of the United States to adopt a war resolution. In his ringing war message, Wilson equated German "warfare against commerce" with "warfare against mankind," intoning that "the world must be made safe for democracy." Republican senator George W. Norris, arguing for U.S. neutrality, countered by saying, "I feel that we are about to put the dollar sign upon the American flag." That protest was to no avail, and on April 6, 1917, the United States declared war against Germany. The U.S. entry proved decisive in breaking the stalemate.

Collapsing Fronts The corrosive effects of years of bloodletting showed. For the first two years of the conflict, most people supported their governments' war efforts, but the continuing ravages of war took their toll everywhere. In April 1916 Irish nationalists mounted the Easter Rebellion, which attempted unsuccessfully to overthrow British rule in Ireland.

German prisoners of war in 1917. Over six million prisoners of war were captured by both sides during the conflict, creating strains on wartime economies. Imprisoned enlisted men were put to work to supplement labor shortages by both the Allies and the Central Powers.
GL Archive/Alamy Stock Photo

The Central Powers suffered from food shortages as a result of the British blockade, and increasing numbers of people took to the streets to demonstrate against declining food rations. Food riots were complemented by strikes as prewar social conflicts reemerged. Governments reacted harshly to those challenges by suppressing demonstrators and jailing dissidents. Equally dangerous was the breakdown of military discipline. At the German naval base in Kiel, sailors revolted in the summer of 1917 and again, much more seriously, in the fall of 1918. In the wake of another failed offensive during the spring of 1917, which resulted in ghastly casualties, French soldiers also lost confidence in their leadership. When ordered to attack once again, they refused. The extent of the mutiny was enormous: 50,000 soldiers were involved, resulting in 23,385 courts-martial and 432 death sentences. So tight was French censorship that the Germans, who could have taken advantage of this situation, did not learn about the mutiny until the war was over.

Against the background of civilian disillusionment and deteriorating economic conditions, Germany took the risk of throwing its remaining might at the western front in the spring of 1918. The gamble failed, and as the offensive petered out, the Allies—reinforced with fresh troops from the United States—broke through the front and started pushing the Germans back. By that time Germany had effectively exhausted its human and material means to wage war. Meanwhile, Bulgaria capitulated to the invading Allies on 30 September, the Ottomans

concluded an armistice on 30 October, and Austria-Hungary surrendered on 4 November. Finally, the Germans accepted an armistice, which took effect on 11 November 1918. At last the guns went silent.

After the War

The immediate effects of the Great War were all too obvious. Aside from the physical destruction, which was most visible in northern France and Belgium, the war had killed, disabled, orphaned, or rendered homeless millions of people. Conservative estimates suggest that the war killed fifteen million people and wounded twenty million others. In the immediate postwar years, millions more succumbed to the effects of starvation, malnutrition, and epidemic diseases.

The Influenza Pandemic of 1918 The end of the Great War coincided with the arrival of one of the worst pandemics ever recorded in human history. No one knows its origins or why it vanished in mid-1919, but by the time this virulent influenza disappeared, it had left more than twenty million dead. The disease killed more people than did the Great War, and it hit young adults—a group usually not severely affected by influenza—with particular ferocity.

The Great War did not cause the **influenza pandemic** of 1918–1919, but wartime traffic on land and sea probably contributed to the spread of the infection. It killed swiftly wherever it went. From the remotest villages in Arctic climates and crowded cities in India and the United States to the battle-fields of Europe, men and women were struck down by high fever. Within a few days they were dead. One estimate puts deaths in India alone at seven million. In Calcutta, the postal service and the legal system ground to a halt. In the United States, the flu killed more Americans than all the wars fought in the twentieth century put together. In cutting a swath across west Africa, it left in its deadly path more than one million victims. The Pacific islands suffered worst of all as the flu wiped out up to 25 percent of their entire population.

There was no cure for the flu of 1918 and the influenza plague never discriminated. It struck the rich as fiercely as the poor. It decimated men and women equally. It did not distinguish between the hungry and the well nourished, and it took the healthy as well as the sick.

The Paris Settlement Before the costs of the war were assessed fully, world attention shifted to Paris. There, in 1919, the victorious powers convened to arrange a postwar settlement and set terms for the defeated nations. At the outset, people on both sides of the war had high hopes for the settlement, but in the end it left a bitter legacy. Because the twenty-seven nations represented at Paris had different and often conflicting aims, many sessions of the conference deteriorated into pandemonium. Ultimately, **Georges Clemenceau** (1841–1929), **Lloyd George** (1863–1945), and **Woodrow Wilson**—the representative leaders of France, Great Britain, and the United States—dominated the deliberations. The Allies did not permit representatives of the Central Powers to participate. In addition, the Allies threatened to renew the war if the terms they laid down were not accepted. Significantly, the Soviet Union was not invited to the conference. Throughout this time the British blockade of Germany remained in effect, adding a sense of urgency to the proceedings. That situation later gave rise to the charge of a dictated peace.

Wilson's Fourteen Points One year before the opening of the **Paris Peace Conference** in January 1918, U.S. president Woodrow Wilson forwarded a proposal for a just and enduring postwar peace settlement. Wilson's postwar vision had subsequently prompted the defeated Central Powers to announce their acceptance of his so-called Fourteen Points as the basis for the armistice. They also expected the Allies to use them as the foundation for later peace treaties. Key among Wilson's **Fourteen Points** were the following recommendations: open covenants (agreements) of peace, openly arrived at; absolute freedom of navigation on the seas in peace and war; the removal of all economic barriers and the establishment of an equality of trade conditions among all nations; adequate guarantees for a reduction in national armaments; adjustments of colonial disputes to give equal weight to the interests of the controlling government and the colonial population; and a call for "a general association of nations." The idealism expressed in the Fourteen Points gave

The Great War exacted an awful toll on human life, in terms of both the dead and the disfigured survivors. This brutally scarred French soldier in 1918 vividly represented the human cost of the war. Exact figures will always remain in dispute, but the best estimates suggest that the Great War claimed the lives of some 8.5 million soldiers. A far greater number, some 21 million soldiers, suffered injuries, many of them so serious they scarred people permanently, as in the case of this soldier.

adoc-photos/Corbis Historical/Getty Images

Wilson a position of moral leadership among the Allies. Those same allies also opposed various points of Wilson's peace formula because those points compromised the secret wartime agreements by which they had agreed to distribute among themselves territories and possessions of the defeated nations. The defeated powers, in turn, later felt betrayed when they faced the harsh peace treaties that so clearly violated the spirit of the Fourteen Points.

Georges Clemenceau (jawrj klem-uhn-SOH)

The Peace Treaties The final form of the treaties represented a series of compromises among the victors. The hardest terms originated with the French, who desired the destruction or the permanent weakening of German power. Thus, in addition to requiring Germany to accept sole responsibility and guilt for causing the war, the victors demanded a reduction in the military potential of the former Central Powers. For example, the **Treaty of Versailles** (1919) denied the Germans a navy and an air force and limited the size of the German army to 100,000 troops. In addition, the Allies prohibited Germany and Austria from entering into any sort of political union. The French and the British agreed that the defeated Central Powers must pay for the cost of the war and required the payment of reparations either in money or in kind. Although the German government and the public decried the Treaty of Versailles as being excessively harsh, it was no more severe in its terms than the Treaty of Brest-Litovsk that the Germans imposed on Russia in 1918.

The Paris Peace Conference resulted in several additional treaties. Bulgaria accepted the Treaty of Neuilly (1919), ceding

Colonel Mustafa Kemal ("Ataturk") with Ottoman officers at the Battle of Gallipoli in 1915.
Scherl/Süddeutsche Zeitung Photo/Alamy Stock Photo

only small portions of territory, because the Allies feared that major territorial changes in the Balkans would destabilize the region. That view did not apply to the dual monarchy of Austria-Hungary, whose imperial unity disintegrated under the impact of the war. The peacemakers recognized the territorial breakup of the former empire in two separate treaties: the Treaty of St. Germain (1919), between the Allies and the Republic of Austria, and the Treaty of Trianon (1920), between the Allies and the kingdom of Hungary. Both Austria and Hungary suffered severe territorial losses, which the Allies claimed were necessary in order to find territorial boundaries that accorded closely with the principle of self-determination. For example, the peace settlement reduced Hungarian territory to one-third of its prewar size and decreased the nation's population from twenty-eight million to eight million people.

Arrangements between the defeated Ottoman Empire and the Allies proved to be a more complicated and protracted affair. The Treaty of Sèvres (1920) effectively dissolved the empire, calling for the surrender of Ottoman Balkan and Arab provinces and the occupation of eastern and southern Anatolia by foreign powers. The treaty was acceptable to the government of sultan Mohammed VI but not to Turkish nationalists, who rallied around their wartime hero Mustafa Kemal. As head of the Turkish nationalist movement, Mustafa Kemal set out to defy the Allied terms. He organized a national army that drove out Greek, British, French, and Italian occupation forces and abolished the sultanate and replaced it with the Republic of Turkey, with Ankara as its capital. In a great diplomatic victory for Turkish nationalists, the Allied powers officially recognized the Republic of Turkey in a final peace agreement, the Treaty of Lausanne (1923).

Atatürk As president of the republic, Mustafa Kemal, now known as **Atatürk** ("Father of the Turks"), instituted an ambitious program of modernization that emphasized economic development and secularism. Government support of critical industries and businesses, and other forms of state intervention in the economy designed to ensure rapid economic development, resulted in substantial long-term economic growth. The government's policy of secularism dictated the complete separation between the existing Muslim religious establishment and the state. The policy resulted in the replacement of religious with secular institutions of education and justice; the emancipation of women, including their right to vote; and the adoption of European-derived law, Hindu-Arabic numerals, the Roman alphabet, and Western clothing. Theoretically heading a constitutional democracy, Atatürk ruled Turkey as a virtual dictator until his death in 1938.

Turkey's postwar transformations and its success in refashioning the terms of peace proved to be something of an exception. In the final analysis, the peace settlements were strategically weak because too few participants had a stake in maintaining them and too many had an interest in revising them. German expansionist aims in Europe, which probably played a role in the nation's decision to enter the Great War, remained unresolved, as did Italian territorial designs in the

Balkans and Japanese influence in China. Those issues virtually ensured that the two decades following the peace settlement became merely a twenty-year truce, characterized by power rivalries and intermittent violence that led to yet another global war.

The League of Nations In an effort to avoid future destructive conflicts, the diplomats in Paris created the **League of Nations.** The League was the first permanent international security organization whose principal mission was to maintain world peace. At the urging of U.S. president Woodrow Wilson, the Covenant of the League of Nations was made an integral part of the peace treaties, and every signatory to a peace treaty had to accept this new world organization. Initially, the League seemed to be the sign of a new era: twenty-six of its forty-two original members were countries outside Europe, suggesting that it transcended European interests.

The League had two major flaws that ultimately rendered it ineffective. First, though designed to solve international disputes through arbitration, it had no power to enforce its decisions. Second, it relied on *collective security* as a tool for the preservation of global peace. The basic premise underlying collective security arrangements was the concept that aggression against any one state was considered aggression against all the other states, which had pledged to aid one another. Collective security could assume different forms, such as diplomatic pressure, economic sanctions, and ultimately force. However, the basic precondition for collective security—participation by all the great powers—never materialized because at any given time one or more of the major powers did not belong to the League. The United States never joined the organization because the U.S. Senate rejected the idea. Germany, which viewed the League as a club of Allied victors, and Japan, which saw it as an instrument of imperialism, left the League of Nations in 1933, as did some smaller powers. Italy, chastised by the League for invading Ethiopia in 1935, withdrew from it in 1937. The Soviet Union, which regarded the League as a tool of global capitalism, joined the organization in 1934, only to face expulsion in 1940. Although its failure to stop aggression in the 1930s led to its demise in 1940, the League established the pattern for a permanent international organization and served as a model for its successor, the United Nations.

Self-Determination One of the principal themes of the peacemaking process was the concept of self-determination, which was promoted most intensely by Woodrow Wilson. Wilson believed that self-determination was the key to international peace and cooperation. Yet Wilson's idea of self-determination was mostly directed at European populations. While Poland, Czechoslovakia, and Yugoslavia (kingdom of Serbs, Croats, and Slovenes until 1929) already existed as sovereign states by 1918, by the end of the conference the principle of self-determination had triumphed in many areas that were previously under the control of the Austro-Hungarian and Russian empires. Sometimes, however, peacemakers

pushed the principle of self-determination aside for strategic and security reasons, such as in Austria and Germany, whose peoples were denied the right to form one nation. At other times, diplomats violated the notion of self-determination because they found it impossible to redraw national boundaries in accordance with nationalist aspirations without creating large minorities on one side or the other of a boundary line. Poland was a case in point, as one-third of the population did not speak Polish. A more complicated situation existed in Czechoslovakia. The peoples who gave the republic its name—the Czechs and the Slovaks—totaled only 67 percent of the population, with the remaining population consisting of Germans (22 percent), Ruthenes (6 percent), and Hungarians (5 percent). On the surface, the creation of Yugoslavia ("Land of the South Slavs") represented a triumph of self-determination because it politically united related peoples who for centuries had chafed under foreign rule. Beneath that unity, however, there lingered the separate national identities embraced by Serbs, Croats, and Slovenes. Even in Europe, the results of the application of the principle of self-determination were far from perfect.

The Mandate System In other parts of the world, however, peacemakers did not even try to apply the principle of self-determination. This unwillingness became most obvious when the victors confronted the issue of what to do with Germany's former colonies and the Arab territories of the Ottoman Empire. Because the United States rejected the establishment of new colonies, the European powers came up with the idea of trusteeship. Article 22 of the Covenant of the League of Nations referred to the colonies and territories of the former Central Powers as areas "inhabited by peoples not yet able to stand by themselves under the strenuous conditions of the modern world." As a result, "The tutelage of such peoples should be entrusted to the advanced nations who . . . can best undertake this responsibility." The League divided the mandates into three classes based on the presumed development of their populations in the direction of fitness for self-government. The administration of the mandates fell to the victorious powers of the Great War.

The Germans rightly interpreted the **mandate system** as a division of colonial booty by the victors, who had conveniently forgotten to apply the tutelage provision to their own colonies. German cynicism was more than matched by Arab outrage. The establishment of mandates in the former territories of the Ottoman Empire violated promises by French and British leaders during the war. They had promised Arab nationalists independence from the Ottoman Empire and had promised Jewish nationalists in Europe a homeland in Palestine. Where the Arabs hoped to form independent states, the French (in Lebanon and Syria) and the British (in Iraq and Palestine) established mandates. The Allies viewed the mandate system as a reasonable compromise between the reality of imperialism and the ideal of self-determination. To the peoples who were directly affected, the mandate system was simply continued imperial rule draped in a cloak of respectability.

MAP 33.2   Territorial changes in Europe after the Great War.

Observe the territories ceded by the Central Powers and the Soviet Union.

Which power lost the most territory, and why?

Challenges to European Preeminence

The Great War changed Europe forever, but most people could not see this at the war's end. With the imperial powers still ruling over their old colonies and new mandates, it appeared that European global hegemony was even more secure than it had been in 1914. In hindsight, however, it is clear that the Great War did irreparable damage to European power and prestige and set the stage for a process of decolonization that gathered momentum during and after the Second World War.

SOURCES FROM THE PAST

Memorandum of the General Syrian Congress

Article 22 of the League of Nations Covenant established a system of mandates to rule the colonies and territories of the defeated powers, including parts of the former Ottoman Empire (comprising present-day Syria, Lebanon, Jordan, and Israel). The mandate system essentially substituted European mandates for Ottoman rule. The news of this arrangement came as a shock to the peoples of the defeated Ottoman Empire who had fought alongside the English and the French during the Great War and expected their independence, which they had indeed been promised. They quickly denounced the mandate system. The following selection is a memorandum addressed to the King Crane Commission, which was responsible for overseeing the transfer of Ottoman territory.

We the undersigned members of the General Syrian Congress, meeting in Damascus on Wednesday, July 2nd 1919, . . . provided with the credentials and authorizations by the inhabitants of our various districts, Moslems, Christians, and Jews, have agreed upon the following statement of the desires of the people of the country who have elected us. . . .

1. We ask absolutely complete political independence for Syria. . . .

2. We ask that the Government of this Syrian country should be a democratic civil constitutional Monarchy based on broad decentralization principles, safeguarding the rights of minorities, and that the King be the Emir Feisal, who carried on a glorious struggle in the cause of liberation and merited our full confidence and entire reliance.

3. Considering that the Arabs inhabiting the Syrian area are not naturally less gifted than other more advanced races and that they are by no means less developed than the Bulgarians, Serbians, Greeks, and Romanians at the beginning of their independence, we protest against Article 22 of the Covenant of the League of Nations, placing us among the nations in their middle stage of development which stand in need of a mandatory power. . . .

> Why did the Congress compare its constituents to European groups here?

6. We do not acknowledge any right claimed by the French Government in any part whatever of our Syrian country and refuse that she should assist us or have a hand in our country under any circumstances and in any place. . . .

7. We oppose the pretensions of the Zionists to create a Jewish commonwealth in the southern part of Syria, known as Israel, and oppose Zionist migration to any part of our country; for we do not acknowledge their title but consider them a grave peril to our people, from the national, economical, and political points of view. Our Jewish compatriots shall enjoy our common rights and assume the common responsibilities.

> Given the tone of this memorandum, how likely does it seem that people in Syria would accept mandate rule?

For Further Reflection

■ For what specifically was the Syrian Congress asking? Do you think the European powers expected this response to the League of Nations Covenant?

Source: "United States Department of State Papers Relating to the Foreign Relations of the United States." The Paris Peace Conference, 1919, Vol. XII. Washington, DC: U.S. Government Printing Office, 1919.

The war of 1914–1918 accelerated the growth of nationalism in the European-controlled parts of the world, fueling desires for independence and self-determination.

Weakened Europe The decline in European power was closely related to diminished economic capacity, a result of the commitment to total war. In time, Europe overcame many war-induced economic problems, such as high rates of inflation and huge public debts, but other economic dislocations were permanent and damaging. Most significant was the loss of overseas investments and foreign markets, which had brought huge financial returns. Nothing is more indicative of Europe's reduced economic might than the reversal of the economic relationship between Europe and the United States. Whereas the United States was a debtor nation before 1914, owing billions of dollars to European investors, by 1919 it was a major creditor.

A loss of prestige overseas and a weakening grip on colonies also reflected the undermining of Europe's global hegemony. Colonial subjects in Africa, Asia, and the Pacific often viewed the Great War as a civil war among the European nations, a bloody spectacle in which the haughty bearers of an alleged superior society vilified and slaughtered one another. Because Europe seemed weak, divided, and vulnerable, the white colonizers appeared far less powerful than before.

MAP 33.3   Territorial changes in southwest Asia after the Great War.

The Great War completed the process of disintegration of the Ottoman Empire and left much of the region to be ruled as virtual colonies by the major imperial powers.

What was the reaction in the region when European statesmen assigned former Ottoman territories to French or British control under the League of Nations mandates?

Colonial subjects who returned home from the war in Europe and southwest Asia reinforced those general impressions with their own firsthand observations. In particular, they were less inclined to be obedient imperial subjects.

Revolutionary Ideas The war also helped spread revolutionary ideas to the colonies. The U.S. war aims spelled out in the Fourteen Points raised the hopes of peoples under imperial rule and promoted nationalist aspirations. The peacemakers repeatedly invoked the concept of self-determination, and Wilson publicly proposed that in all colonial questions "the

interests of the native populations be given equal weight with the desires of European governments." Wilson seemed to call for nothing less than national independence and self-rule. Nationalists struggling to organize anti-imperialist resistance also sought inspiration from the Soviet Union, whose leaders denounced all forms of imperialism and pledged their support to independence movements. Taken together, these messages were subversive to imperial control and had a great appeal for colonial peoples. The postwar disappointments and temporary setbacks experienced by nationalist movements did not diminish their desire for self-rule and self-determination.

CONCLUSION

The assassination of the Austrian archduke Franz Ferdinand had a galvanizing effect on a Europe torn by national rivalries, colonial disputes, and demands for self-determination. In the summer of 1914, inflexible war plans and a tangled alliance system transformed a local war between Austria-Hungary and Serbia into a European-wide clash of arms that also immediately entangled the colonized world. With the entry of the Ottoman Empire, Japan, and the United States, the war of 1914–1918 became a truly global conflict. Although many belligerents organized their societies for total war and drew on the resources of their overseas empires, the war in Europe remained at a bloody stalemate until the United States entered the conflict in 1917. The tide turned, and the combatants signed an armistice in November 1918. The Great War, a brutal encounter between societies and peoples, inflicted ghastly human casualties, severely damaged national economies, and discredited long-established political and cultural traditions. The war also altered the political landscape of many places as it destroyed four dynasties and their empires, fostered the creation of several new European nations, and created new protectorates called mandates. In Russia the war served as a backdrop for the world's first successful socialist revolution. In the end the Great War sapped the strength of European colonial powers while promoting nationalist aspirations among colonized peoples.

STUDY TERMS

Armenian genocide (738)
Atatürk (744)
Balfour Declaration (738)
Black Hand (727)
Bolshevik (738)
Central Powers (726)
dreadnoughts (724)
February Revolution (738)
Fourteen Points (743)
Franz Ferdinand (724)
Gallipoli (737)
Georges Clemenceau (743)
home front (731)
influenza pandemic (742)
League of Nations (745)
Lloyd George (743)
mandate system (745)
mustard gas (729)
no-man's-land (729)
October Revolution (739)
Paris Peace Conference (743)
Romanov dynasty (738)
Schlieffen plan (726)
self-determination (724)
Sykes-Picot Treaty (738)
Treaty of Brest-Litovsk (740)
Treaty of Versailles (744)
Triple Entente (726)
Twenty-one Demands (735)
unrestricted submarine warfare (741)
Verdun (731)
Vladimir Ilyich Lenin (739)
western front (729)
Woodrow Wilson (743)
Zimmermann telegram (741)

FOR FURTHER READING

Mustafa Aksakal. *The Ottoman Road to War in 1914: The Ottoman Empire and the First World War.* Cambridge, 2008. Uses previously untapped sources to explore how and why the Ottomans entered the Great War on the side of the Central Powers.

Christopher Clark. *The Sleepwalkers: How Europe Went to War in 1914.* New York, 2013. This is the best researched, most readable one-volume account of a most contentious subject.

Peter Gatrell. *Russia's First World War: A Social and Economic History.* London, 2005. Traces the impact of World War I on Russian society before the revolution.

Robert Gerwarth and Erez Manela. *Empires at War, 1911–1923.* Oxford, 2014. An edited collection of top-notch essays that explore the Great War as a fundamentally imperial and global conflict.

Susan R. Grayzel. *Women and the First World War.* New York, 2002. This is an excellent introduction to the experiences and contributions of women during the war.

Margaret MacMillan. *Paris 1919: Six Months That Changed the World.* New York, 2002. This is the most engaging and lucid analysis written on the subject of the peace settlement.

John H. Morrow. *The Great War. An Imperial History.* New York, 2003. A global history of the Great War that places the conflict squarely in the context of imperialism.

Michael S. Neiberg. *Fighting the Great War.* Cambridge, Mass., 2005. A good blend of narrative and analysis, this work highlights the global reach of the conflict.

Susan Pedersen. *The Guardians: The League of Nations and the Crisis of Empire.* Oxford, 2015. Comprehensive study of the history of the League of Nations and its creation and management of the mandate system.

Hew Strachan. *The First World War.* New York, 2004. One of the leading historians of World War I offers a one-volume version of his projected three-volume work, treating the war in a global rather than European context.

ZOOMING IN ON TRADITIONS

The Evolution of a Dictator

Born on a lovely spring day in 1889, in a quaint Austrian village, he was the apple of his mother's eye. He basked in Klara's warmth and indulgence as a youth, enjoying the fine life of a middle-class child. As he grew older, he sensed a vague anxiety that stemmed from the competing expectations of his parents. Contented with being spoiled by Klara, he bristled at the demands of his father, Alois. Alois expected him to follow in his footsteps to a career in the Austrian civil service. He had no desire to become a bureaucrat. In fact, he envisioned a completely different life for himself as an artist. His school grades slipped, and that seemed an appropriate way to express his discontent and sabotage his father's plans for his future.

Alois's unexpected death in 1903 freed him from a future as a bureaucrat. He now had the freedom to daydream and indulge his imagination. He left school in 1905 with a ninth-grade education and moved to Vienna with plans to study to become an artist. But the Vienna Academy of Fine Arts rejected him in 1907. His beloved Klara died the following year, and he meandered the city streets of Vienna, living off a pension and the money he inherited from his mother. He immersed himself in Vienna, admiring the architecture of the city and attending the opera when his funds permitted. He especially enjoyed the music of Richard Wagner, who embraced heroic German myths in his compositions.

This is one of the few known photographs of a young Adolf Hitler, taken in 1923.

Bettmann/Getty Images

When he finally ran through all of his money, he began staying at a homeless shelter. There, he was exposed to a variety of political ideologies held by the shelter's other inhabitants. They discussed issues such as race, and he was particularly attracted to the viewpoints of those who hailed the supremacy of the Aryan race and the inferiority of the Jews. He immersed himself in reading, particularly the newspapers and pamphlets that gave him more information about those disturbing political issues. He came to hate Jews and Marxists, whom he thought had formed an evil union with the goal of destroying the world. He also despised liberalism and democracy, and in cheap cafés he began directing political tirades at anyone who would listen. Soon, he also began to engage in public debates about these issues.

He left Vienna in 1913 for Munich, where he volunteered for service in the German army. He discovered in himself a real talent for military service, and he remained in the army for the duration of the war, 1914–1918. Twice wounded and decorated for bravery, he nonetheless found himself in despair at war's end. He learned of Germany's defeat in the war while being treated in a hospital for exposure to mustard gas. Enraged, he believed with all his being that the Jews were responsible for this humiliation, and he also knew what he had to do: he had to enter the political arena in his chosen fatherland and save the nation. **Adolf Hitler** had finally found his mission in life: a mission that would have a devastating and deadly effect for millions of people.

CHAPTER OVERVIEW

Badly shaken by the effects of years of war, Europeans experienced a shock to their system of values, beliefs, and traditions. Profound scientific, intellectual, and cultural transformations that came to the fore in the postwar decades also contributed to a sense of loss and anxiety. As peoples in Europe and around the world struggled to come to terms with the aftermath of war, an unprecedented economic contraction gripped the international community.

Against the background of the Great Depression, dictators in Russia, Italy, and Germany tried to translate blueprints for utopias into reality. While Joseph Stalin and his fellow communists recast the former tsarist empire into a dictatorship of the proletariat, Benito Mussolini and his fascists along with Adolf Hitler and his Nazi Party forged a new kind of national community. These political innovations unsettled many Europeans and much of the world, contributing significantly to the anxiety of the age.

CHRONOLOGY	
1905	Einstein publishes special theory of relativity
1918–1920	Civil war in Russia
1919	Mussolini launches fascist movement in Italy
1921–1928	Lenin's New Economic Policy
1927	Heisenberg establishes the uncertainty principle
1928–1932	First Soviet Five-Year Plan
1929	U.S. stock market crash; Beginning of Great Depression; Ernest Hemingway and Erich Remarque publish antiwar novels
1933–1945	Hitler rules Germany
1935–1938	Stalin's Great Purge in the Soviet Union
1939	John Steinbeck publishes *The Grapes of Wrath*

NEW INTELLECTUAL FRONTIERS

The Great War discredited established social and political institutions and long-held beliefs about the superiority of European society. Writers, poets, theologians, and other European intellectuals lamented the decline and imminent death of their society. While some wrote obituaries, however, others embarked on bold new cultural paths that established the main tendencies of contemporary thought and taste. Most of these cultural innovators began their work before the war, but

it was in the two decades following the war that a revolution in science, psychology, art, and architecture attained its fullest development and potency.

The discoveries of physicists undermined the Newtonian universe, in which a set of inexorable natural laws governed events, with a new and disturbing cosmos. Uncertainty governed this strange universe, which lacked objective reality. Equally discomforting were the insights of psychoanalysis, which suggested that human behavior was fundamentally irrational. Disquieting trends in the arts paralleled the developments in science and psychology. Especially in painting, an aversion to realism and a pronounced preference for abstraction heralded the arrival of new aesthetic standards.

Postwar Pessimism

"You are all a lost generation," noted Gertrude Stein (1874–1946) to her fellow American writer Ernest Hemingway (1899-1961). Stein had given a label to the group of American intellectuals and literati who congregated in Paris in the postwar years. This **"lost generation"** expressed in poetry and fiction the malaise and disillusion that characterized U.S. and European thought after the Great War. The vast majority of European intellectuals had rallied enthusiastically to the war in 1914, viewing it as a splendid adventure. The brutal realities of industrialized warfare left no room for heroes, however, and most of these young artists and intellectuals quickly became disillusioned. During the 1920s they spat out their revulsion in a host of war novels such as Ernest Hemingway's *A Farewell to Arms* (1929) and Erich Maria Remarque's *All Quiet on the Western Front* (1929), works overflowing with images of meaningless death and suffering.

Postwar writers lamented the decline of Western society. A retired German schoolteacher named Oswald Spengler (1880-1936) made headlines when he published *The Decline of the West* (1918-1922). In this work, which was seen as an obituary of civilization, Spengler proposed that all societies pass through a life cycle of growth and decay comparable to the biological cycle of living organisms. His analysis of the history of western Europe led him to conclude that European society had entered the final stage of its existence. All that remained was irreversible decline, marked by imperialism and warfare. Spengler's gloomy predictions provided a kind of comfort to those who sought to rationalize their postwar despair, as did his conviction that all the nations of the world were equally doomed. In England the shock of war caused the historian Arnold J. Toynbee (1889-1975) to begin his twelve-volume classic, *A Study of History* (1934-1961), in which he analyzed the genesis, growth, and disintegration of twenty-six societies.

Religious Uncertainty Theologians joined the chorus of despair. In 1919 Karl Barth (1886–1968), widely recognized as one of the most notable Christian theologians, published a religious bombshell titled *Epistle to the Romans*. In his work Barth sharply attacked the liberal Christian theology that embraced the idea of progress, or the tendency of European thinkers to believe in limitless improvement as the realization of God's purpose. The Augustinian, Lutheran, and Calvinist message of original sin—the idea that humans are doomed to lives of sin as a result of Adam and Eve's disobedience—fell on receptive ears as many

Christians refused to accept the idea that contemporary human society was in any way a realization of God's purpose. The Russian orthodox thinker Niokolai Berdiaev (1874-1948) summed up these sentiments: "Man's historical experience has been one of steady failure, and there are no grounds for supposing it will be ever anything else."

Attacks on Progress The Great War destroyed long-cherished beliefs such as belief in the universality of human progress. Many idols of nineteenth-century progress came under attack, especially those in science and technology. The scientists' dream of leading humanity to a beneficial conquest of nature seemed to have gone awry because scientists had spent the war making poisonous gas and high explosives. Democracy was another fallen idol. The idea that people should have a voice in selecting the leaders of their government had enjoyed widespread support in European societies. By the early twentieth century, the removal of property and educational restrictions on the right to vote resulted in universal male suffrage in most societies. In the years following the Great War, most European governments extended the franchise to women. These developments led to an unprecedented degree of political participation as millions of people voted in elections and referendums. However, many intellectuals came to abhor what they viewed as a weak political system that championed the tyranny of the average person. Instead, they viewed democracy as a product of decay and as lacking in positive values, and they idealized elite rule. In Germany a whole school of conservatives lamented the "rule of inferiors." Common people, too, often viewed democracy as a decaying political system because they associated it with corrupt and ineffective party politics. However, antidemocratic strains were not confined to Germany. The widely read essay "Revolt of the Masses" (1930) by the Spanish

How the Past Shapes the Future

The Destructive Potential of Industrial Technologies

World War I is an instructive example of the long-term consequences of historical events on both intellectual and popular culture. Prior to the war, many Europeans believed that the technologies associated with industrialization—while not without their problems—would ultimately lead to greater human comfort, prosperity, and happiness. Yet the role of mass-produced war matériel in the huge scale of slaughter during the war caused Europeans to wonder with horror if, with industrial technologies, humans had created a monster that would ultimately bring about more death and destruction than happiness. In effect, the realities of the war made it impossible for Europeans to return to the optimism of the nineteenth century with regard to the benefits of modern technologies. Consider how this ambivalence, in turn, became an important feature of intellectual and popular culture not only in interwar Europe but also in many parts of the world right up to the present.

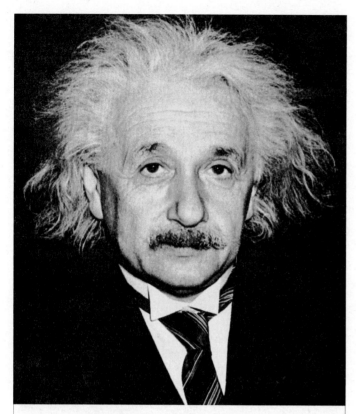

One of the best-known faces of the twentieth century, Albert Einstein (1879–1955) was the symbol of the revolution in physics.

Bettmann/Getty Images

Heisenberg (1901-1976), who in 1927 published a paper, "About the Quantum-Theoretical Reinterpretation of Kinetic and Mechanical Relationships," which established the **uncertainty principle.** According to Heisenberg, it is impossible to specify simultaneously the position and the velocity of a subatomic particle. The more accurately one determines the position of an electron, the less precisely one can determine its velocity, and vice versa. In essence, he argued that scientists cannot observe the behavior of electrons objectively because the act of observation interferes with them.

It quickly became evident that the uncertainty principle had important implications beyond physics. It also carried broader philosophical ramifications. Heisenberg's theory called into question established notions of truth and violated the fundamental law of cause and effect. Likewise, objectivity was no longer a valid concept because the observer was always

Sigmund Freud (1856–1939) formulated psychoanalysis, a theory and clinical practice to explore the mind and, by extension, its creations, such as literature, religion, art, and history.

Imagno/Getty Images

philosopher José Ortega y Gasset (1883-1955) warned readers about the masses who were destined to destroy the highest achievements of Western society.

New Visions in Physics, Psychology, and Art

The postwar decade witnessed a revolution in physics that transformed the character of science. **Albert Einstein** (1879-1955) struck the first blow with his theory of special relativity (1905), showing that there is no single spatial and chronological framework in the universe. According to the theory, it no longer made sense to speak of space and time as absolutes because the measurement of those two categories always varies with the motion of the observer. That is, space and time are relative to the person measuring them. To the layperson such notions—usually expressed in incomprehensible mathematical formulas—suggested that science had reached the limits of what could be known with certainty. A commonsense universe had vanished, to be replaced by a radically new one in which reality or truth was merely a set of mental constructs.

The Uncertainty Principle More disquieting even than Einstein's discoveries was the theory formulated by Werner part of the process under observation. Accordingly, any observer—an anthropologist studying another society, for instance—had to be alert to the fact that his or her very presence became an integral part of the study.

Freud's Psychoanalytic Theory Equally unsettling as the advances in physics were developments in psychology that challenged established concepts of morality and values. In an indeterminate universe governed by relativity, the one remaining fixed point was the human psyche, but the insights of **Sigmund Freud** (1856–1939) brought this into question as well. Beginning in 1896, the medical doctor from Vienna embarked on research that focused on psychological rather than physiological explanations of mental disorders. Through his clinical observations of patients, Freud identified a conflict between conscious and subconscious mental processes that lay at the root of neurotic (mentally unbalanced) behavior. That conflict, moreover, suggested to him the existence of a repressive mechanism that keeps painful memories or threatening events away from the conscious mind. Freud believed that dreams held the key to the deepest recesses of the human psyche. Using the free associations of patients to guide him in the interpretation of dreams, he identified sexual drives and fantasies as the most important source of repression. For example, Freud claimed to have discovered a so-called Oedipus complex in which male children develop an erotic attachment to their mother and hostility toward their father.

From dreams Freud analyzed literature, religion, politics, and virtually every other type of human endeavor, seeking always to identify the manifestations of the repressed conscious. He was convinced that his theory, known as **psychoanalysis,** provided the keys to understanding all human behavior. In the end, Freudian ideas shaped the psychiatric profession and established a powerful presence in literature and the arts. During the 1920s, novelists, poets, and painters acknowledged Freud's influence as they focused on the inner world—the hidden depths of memory and emotion—of their characters. The creators of imaginative literature used Freud's bold emphasis on sexuality as a tool for the interpretation and understanding of human behavior.

Experimentation in Art The sense of uncertainty and anxiety induced by advances in physics and psychology also found reflection in the arts, which in turn contributed to the unsettling atmosphere of the first half of the twentieth century. The point of departure for these developments was the brutality of the Great War, which gave birth to Dada or **Dadaism.** Although the origin of the name Dada is unclear, it is believed to be a deliberately nonsensical word. Between 1916 and 1920, the disillusioned artists of the Dada movement in Zurich, Paris, and New York used any available public forum to critique nationalism, materialism, and rationalism, which they felt had

This is one of German-Jewish artist Erwin Blumenfeld's Dadaist collages, which combined his photographs with magazine cutouts and reflected the critical changes in art and politics after the Great War.
Erwin Blumenfeld

contributed to a senseless war. They consistently rejected prevailing standards of art and declared an all-out assault on the unquestioning conformity of culture and thought. They imagined themselves to be nonartists who created nonart.

Also deeply affected by the horrors of war was a German art movement of the 1920s. Known as the *Neue Sachlichkeit* (New Objectivity), this genre was characterized by a realistic style of painting that reflected a cynical and highly critical attitude toward war. Many proponents of the Neue Sachlichkeit aggressively attacked and satirized the evils of postwar society, especially as symbolized by those in political power, all the while illustrating the devastating effects of the Great War. Wilhelm Heinrich Otto Dix (1891–1969) was a German painter and printmaker, notorious for his merciless and bitterly realistic depictions of society in the aftermath of war. Dix had enthusiastically volunteered for the German Army in 1914, took part in the Battle of the Somme, and then became quickly and profoundly affected and disillusioned by the sights of war. Along with George Grosz (1893–1959) he is

Sigmund Freud (SIG-muhnd froid)

Neue Sachlichkeit (no-yuh ZACH-kleekh-kite)

widely considered one of the most important artists of the Neue Sachlichkeit.

Not all artistic movements drew on the experiences of the Great War, but by the beginning of the twentieth century, the possibilities inherent in a new aesthetic led to the emergence of a bewildering variety of pictorial schools, all of which promised an entirely new and unsettling art. Regardless of whether they called themselves dadaists, surrealists, cubists, or abstractionists, artists generally agreed on a program "to abolish the sovereignty of appearance." Paintings no longer depicted recognizable objects from the everyday world, and beauty was expressed in pure color or shape. Some painters sought to express feelings and emotions through violent distortion of forms and the use of explosive colors; others, influenced by Freudian psychology, tried to tap the subconscious mind to communicate an inner vision or a dream. By the third decade of the twentieth century, it was nearly impossible to generalize about contemporary painting. All artists were acknowledged to have a right to their own reality, and generally accepted standards that distinguished between "good" and "bad" art disappeared.

GLOBAL DEPRESSION

After the horrors and debilitating upheavals of the Great War, much of the world yearned for a return to normality and prosperity. By the early 1920s the efforts of governments and businesses to rebuild damaged economies seemed to bear fruit. Prosperity, however, was short-lived. In 1929 the world plunged into economic depression that was so long-lasting, so severe, and so global that it has become known as the **Great Depression.** The old capitalist system of trade and finance collapsed, and until a new system took its place after 1945, a return to worldwide prosperity could not occur.

The Great Depression

By the middle of the 1920s, some semblance of economic normality had returned, and most countries seemed on the way to economic recovery. Industrial productivity had returned to prewar levels as businesses repaired the damages the war had inflicted on industrial plants, equipment, and transportation facilities. But that prosperity was fragile, perhaps even false, and many serious problems and dislocations remained in the international economy.

Economic Problems The economic recovery and well-being of Europe, for example, were tied to a tangled financial system that involved war debts among the Allies, reparations paid by Germany and Austria, and the flow of U.S. funds to Europe. In essence, the governments of Austria and Germany relied on U.S. loans and investment capital to finance reparation payments to France and England. The French and British governments, in turn, depended on those reparation payments

Soup kitchens and breadlines became commonplace in the United States during the earliest, darkest years of the Great Depression. They fed millions of starving and unemployed people.
Bettmann/Getty Images

to pay off loans taken out in the United States during the Great War. By the summer of 1928, U.S. lenders and investors started to withdraw capital from Europe, placing an intolerable strain on the financial system.

There were other problems as well. Improvements in industrial processes reduced worldwide demand for certain raw materials, causing an increase in supplies and a drop in prices. Technological advances in the production of automobile tires, for instance, permitted the use of reclaimed rubber. The resulting glut of natural rubber had devastating consequences for the economies of the Dutch East Indies, Ceylon, and Malaysia, which relied on the export of rubber. Similarly, the increased use of oil undermined the coal industry, the emergence of synthetics hurt the cotton industry, and the growing adoption of artificial nitrogen virtually ruined the nitrate industry of Chile.

One of the nagging weaknesses of the global economy in the 1920s was the depressed state of agriculture, the result of overproduction and falling prices. During the Great War, when Europe's agricultural output declined significantly, farmers in the United States, Canada, Argentina, and Australia expanded their production. At the end of the war, European farmers resumed their agricultural activity, thereby contributing to worldwide surpluses. Above-average global harvests between 1925 and 1929 aggravated the situation. As production increased, demand declined, and prices collapsed throughout the world. By 1929 the price of a bushel of wheat was at its lowest level in 400 years, and farmers everywhere became impoverished. The reduced income of farm families contributed to high inventories of manufactured goods, which in turn caused businesses to cut back production and to dismiss workers.

The Crash of 1929 The United States enjoyed a boom after the Great War: industrial wages were high, and production and consumption increased. Many people in the United States invested their earnings and savings in speculative ventures, particularly the buying of stock on margin—putting up as little as 3 percent of a stock's price in cash and borrowing the remainder from brokers and banks or by mortgaging their homes. By October 1929, hints of a worldwide economic slowdown and warnings from experts that stock prices were overvalued prompted investors to pull out of the market. On **Black Thursday** (October 24), a wave of panic selling on the New York Stock Exchange caused stock prices to plummet. Investors who had overextended themselves in a frenzy of speculative stock purchases watched in agony. Thousands of people, from poor widows to industrial tycoons, lost their life savings, and by the end of the day eleven financiers had committed suicide. The crisis deepened when lenders called in loans, thereby forcing more investors to sell their securities at any price.

Economic Contraction Spreads In the wake of this financial chaos came a drastic decrease in business activity, wages, and employment. Consumer demand no longer kept up with all the goods that businesses produced, and when businesses realized that they could not sell their inventories, they responded with cutbacks in production and layoffs. With so many people unemployed or underemployed, demand plummeted further, causing more business failures and soaring unemployment. In 1930 the slump deepened, and by 1932 industrial production had fallen to half of its 1929 level. National income had dropped by approximately half. Forty-four percent of U.S. banks were out of business, and the deposits of millions of people had disappeared. Because much of the world's prosperity depended on the export of U.S. capital and the strength of U.S. import markets, the contraction of the U.S. economy created a ripple effect that circled the globe.

Most societies experienced economic difficulties throughout the 1930s. Although the severity of the economic contraction varied in intensity, virtually every industrialized society saw its economy shrivel. Nations that relied on exports of manufactured goods to pay for imported fuel and food—Germany and Japan in particular—suffered the most. The depression also spread unevenly to primary producing economies in Latin America, Africa, and Asia. Hardest hit were countries that depended on the export of a few primary products—agricultural goods, such as coffee, sugar, and cotton, and raw materials, such as minerals, ores, and rubber.

Industrial Economies U.S. investors, shaken by the collapse of stock prices, tried to raise money by calling in loans and liquidating investments, and Wall Street banks refused to extend short-term loans as they became due. Banking houses in Austria and Germany became vulnerable to collapse because they had been major recipients of U.S. loans. Devastated by the loss of U.S. capital, the German economy experienced a precipitous economic slide that by 1932 resulted in 35 percent unemployment and a 50 percent decrease in industrial production. As the German economy ground to a virtual halt, the rest of Europe—which was closely integrated with the German economy—sputtered and stalled. The situation in Europe deteriorated further when businesses, desperate to raise capital by exporting goods to the United States, found that U.S. markets had virtually disappeared behind tariff walls. Foreign trade fell sharply between 1929 and 1932, causing further losses in manufacturing, employment, and per capita income. Because of its great dependence on the U.S. market, the Japanese economy felt the depression's effects almost immediately. Unemployment in export-oriented sectors of the economy skyrocketed as companies cut back on production.

Economic Nationalism The Great Depression destroyed the international financial and commercial network of the capitalist economies. As international cooperation broke down, governments turned to their own resources and practiced **economic nationalism.** By imposing tariff barriers, import quotas, and import prohibitions, politicians hoped to achieve a high degree of economic self-sufficiency. In an age of global interdependence, however, such goals remained unobtainable, and economic nationalism invariably backfired. Each new measure

In January 1932, ten thousand hunger strikers marched on Washington, D.C., seeking government relief for their misery.
Bettmann/Getty Images

Human faces of the Great Depression. This 1936 photograph of a mother with her two children in Oklahoma, taken by photographer Dorothea Lange, documented the extreme poverty of the Great Depression.
Pictorial Press Ltd/Alamy Stock Photo

designed to restrict imports provoked retaliation by other nations whose interests were affected. After the U.S. Congress passed the **Smoot-Hawley Tariff Act** in 1930, which raised duties on most manufactured products to prohibitive levels, the governments of dozens of other nations immediately retaliated by raising tariffs on imports of U.S. products. The result was a sharp drop in international trade. Instead of higher levels of production and income, economic nationalism yielded the opposite. Between 1929 and 1932, world production declined by 38 percent and trade dropped by more than 66 percent.

Despair and Government Action

By 1933 unemployment in industrial societies reached thirty million, more than five times higher than in 1929. Men lost their jobs because of economic contraction, and a combination of economic trends and deliberate government policy caused women to lose theirs also. Unemployment initially affected women less directly than men because employers paid women two-thirds to three-quarters the wages of men doing the same work. But before long, governments enacted policies to reduce female employment, especially for married women. The notion that a woman's place was in the home was already widespread and gained even further currency during the Depression. In 1931 a British royal commission on unemployment insurance declared that "in the case of married women as a class, industrial employment cannot be regarded as the normal condition." More candid was the French Nobel Prize–winning physician Charles Richet (1850–1935), who insisted that removing women from the workforce would solve the problem of male unemployment and increase the nation's dangerously low birthrate.

Personal Suffering The Great Depression caused enormous personal suffering. The stark, gloomy statistics documenting the failure of economies do not convey the anguish and despair of those who lost their jobs, savings, and homes, and often their dignity and hope. For millions of people the struggle for food, clothing, and shelter grew desperate. Shantytowns appeared overnight in urban areas, and breadlines stretched for blocks. Marriage, childbearing, and divorce rates declined, while suicide rates rose. The acute physical and social problems of those at the bottom of the economic ladder often magnified social divisions and class hatreds. Workers and farmers especially came to despise the wealthy, who, despite their reduced incomes, were shielded from the worst impact of the economic downturn and continued to enjoy a comfortable lifestyle. Adolescents completing their schooling faced an almost nonexistent job market.

That the Great Depression deflated economies as well as hope was especially noticeable in the literature of the period. Writers castigated the social and political order, calling repeatedly for a more just society. The U.S. writer John Steinbeck

SOURCES FROM THE PAST

Franklin Delano Roosevelt: Nothing to Fear

Franklin Delano Roosevelt (1882–1945) assumed the presidency of the United States on March 4, 1933, during the depths of the Great Depression. In his inaugural address to the nation, he conveyed both the anxiousness of the times and the seemingly unquenchable optimism that carried him—and his nation—through hard times. A vastly wealthy man serving as president during a time of devastating penury, Roosevelt nonetheless gained the admiration and respect of the people because of his warm eloquence and compassion. Although he hid his condition quite successfully during his time in public, FDR had contracted polio in the 1920s and had lost the use of his legs. This "crippled" president became a metaphor for the United States' economic collapse, but also for its ability to overcome fear itself. The excerpt below was part of Roosevelt's inaugural speech in 1933.

I am certain that my fellow Americans expect that on my induction into the Presidency I will address them with a candor and a decision which the present situation of our Nation impels. This is preeminently the time to speak the truth, the whole truth, frankly and boldly. Nor need we shrink from honestly facing conditions in our country today. This great Nation will endure as it has endured, will revive and will prosper. So, first of all, let me assert my firm belief that the only thing we have to fear is fear itself—nameless, unreasoning, unjustified terror which paralyzes needed efforts to convert retreat into advance. In every dark hour of our national life a leadership of frankness and vigor has met with that understanding and support of the people themselves which is essential to victory. I am convinced that you will again give that support to leadership in these critical days.

> What kind of spirit characterizes Americans during difficult times, according to Roosevelt?

In such a spirit on my part and on yours we face our common difficulties. They concern, thank God, only material things. Values have shrunken to fantastic levels; taxes have risen; our ability to pay has fallen; government of all kinds is faced by serious curtailment of income; the means of exchange are frozen in the currents of trade; the withered leaves of industrial enterprise lie on every side; farmers find no markets for their produce; the savings of many years in thousands of families are gone.

More important, a host of unemployed citizens face the grim problem of existence, and an equally great number toil with little return. Only a foolish optimist can deny the dark realities of the moment. . . .

> What was Roosevelt trying to accomplish by being so frank about the difficulties facing the United States?

Happiness lies not in the mere possession of money; it lies in the joy of achievement, in the thrill of creative effort. The joy and moral stimulation of work no longer must be forgotten in the mad chase of evanescent profits. These dark days will be worth all they cost us if they teach us that our true destiny is not to be ministered unto but to minister to ourselves and to our fellow men.

For Further Reflection

■ How does Roosevelt believe U.S. citizens can profit from the dark days of the Great Depression, and why is it that all they have to fear is fear itself?

Source: Franklin D. Roosevelt, First Inaugural Address, 4 March 1933, available at The Avalon Project at http://www.yale.edu/lawweb/avalon/president/inaug/froos1.htm.

(1902–1968) chillingly captured the official heartlessness and the rising political anger inspired by the depression. In *The Grapes of Wrath* (1939), the Joad family, prototypical "Okies," migrated from Oklahoma to California to escape the "dust bowl," a period of severe and damaging dust storms. In describing their journey Steinbeck commented on the U.S. government's policy of "planned scarcity," in which surplus crops were destroyed to raise prices while citizens starved. In one of the novel's most famous passages, Steinbeck portrayed the nation's rising political anguish:

The people come with nets to fish for potatoes in the river and the guards hold them back; they come in rattling cars to get the dumped oranges, but the kerosene is sprayed. And they stand still and watch potatoes float by, listen to the screaming pigs being killed in a ditch and covered with quicklime, watch the mountains of oranges slop down to a putrefying ooze; and in the eyes of the people there is the failure; and in the eyes of the hungry there is a growing wrath. In the souls of the people the grapes of wrath are filling and growing heavy, growing heavy for the vintage.

Economic Experimentation

Classical economic thought held that capitalism was a self-correcting system that operated best when left to its own devices. Governments responded to the economic crisis in one of two ways. Initially, most governments did nothing, hoping that the crisis would resolve itself. When the misery spawned by the depression sparked calls for action, some governments assumed more active roles, pursuing deflationary measures by balancing national budgets and curtailing public spending. In either case, rather than lifting national economies out of the doldrums, the classical prescriptions for economic ills worsened the depression's impact and intensified the plight of millions of people. Far from self-correcting, capitalism seemed to be dying. Many people called for a fundamental revision of economic thought.

Keynes **John Maynard Keynes** (1883-1946), the most influential economist of the twentieth century, offered a novel solution. His seminal work, *The General Theory of Employment, Interest, and Money* (1936), was his answer to the central problem of the depression—that millions of people who were willing to work could not find employment. To Keynes the fundamental cause of the depression was not excessive supply, but inadequate demand. Accordingly, he urged governments to play an active role and stimulate the economy by increasing the money supply, thereby lowering interest rates and encouraging investment. He also advised governments to undertake public works projects to provide jobs and redistribute incomes through tax policy, an intervention which would result in reduced unemployment and increased consumer demand, which in turn would lead to economic revival. Such measures, Keynes argued, were necessary even if they caused governments to run deficits and maintain unbalanced budgets.

The New Deal Although Keynes's theories did not become influential with policymakers until after World War II, the administration of U.S. President **Franklin Delano Roosevelt** (1882-1945) applied similar ideas. Roosevelt took aggressive steps to reinflate the economy and ease the worst of the suffering caused by the depression. His proposals for dealing with the national calamity included legislation designed to prevent the collapse of the banking system, to provide jobs and farm subsidies, to give workers the right to organize and bargain collectively, to guarantee minimum wages, and to provide social security in old age. This program of sweeping economic and social reforms was called the **New Deal.** Its fundamental premise, that the federal government was justified in intervening to protect the social and economic welfare of the people, represented a major shift in U.S. government policy and started a trend toward social reform legislation that continued long after the depression years. Nevertheless, it was the enormous military spending during World War II that did more to end the Great Depression in the United States than the specific programs of the New Deal.

CHALLENGES TO THE LIBERAL ORDER

Amid the gloom and despair of the Great Depression, it seemed to many that the capitalism and liberalism that had come to characterize much of western Europe and the United States no longer worked. At the same time, some voices promised to guide the way to more effective alternatives. Marxists, for example, believed that capitalist society was on its deathbed, and they sought to demonstrate that a new and better system based on rule by the proletariat (the working class) was being born out of the ashes of the Russian Empire. The new rulers of Russia, Vladimir Ilyich Lenin and then Joseph Stalin, transformed the former tsarist empire into the world's first communist society, the Union of Soviet Socialist Republics (1922). Once the Soviet Union was established, they also sought to export communism to the rest of the world.

Other people argued that only strong leadership from above, without the bureaucracy of democratic institutions, could build powerful societies. Fascist movements across Europe promoted their alternatives to socialism and offered revolutionary answers to the economic, social, and political problems that seemed to defy solution by traditional liberal democratic means. Among those fascist movements, the Italian and German ones figured most prominently.

Communism in Russia

In 1917 Lenin and his fellow Bolsheviks had taken power in the name of the Russian working class, but socialist victory did not bring peace and stability to the lands of the former Russian Empire. After seizing power, Lenin and his supporters had to defend the world's first dictatorship of the proletariat against numerous enemies, including dissident socialists, anti-Bolshevik officers and troops, peasant bands, and foreign military forces.

Civil War Opposition to the Bolshevik takeover—by now calling itself the Russian Communist Party—erupted into a civil war that lasted from 1918 to 1920. In order to maintain power, Lenin's government in Moscow began a policy of crushing all opposition. The communists began the Red Terror campaign in which suspected anticommunists known as Whites were arrested, tried, and executed. During this period, the newly developed secret police killed some 200,000 opponents of the regime. In July 1918 the Bolsheviks executed Tsar Nicholas II, Empress Alexandra, their five children, and their remaining servants because they feared that the Romanov family would fall into the hands of the Whites, thereby strengthening counterrevolutionary forces. The peasantry, meanwhile, largely supported the Bolsheviks, fearing that a victory by the Whites would result in the return of the brutally oppressive tsarist system. And indeed, White terror was often as brutal as Red terror. But the fight between the Whites and the Reds inside Russia was only part of the conflict. Russia's former allies—Britain, France, Japan, and the United States—were deeply opposed to the assumption of Bolshevik power, partially because it threatened their economic interests in Russia and partly because Russia's exit from the war had betrayed the alliance against the Germans. Thus in 1918, just as the Great War was ending, the Allies assembled an international coalition and sent troops to support the Whites. But the coalition was poorly organized, the troops were tired from four years of war, and their numbers were small. In addition, the presence of foreign troops on the side of the Whites had the effect of uniting Russians against the Whites. After three years of brutal civil war, the Whites were decisively defeated by the Red Army in 1920. One of the lasting legacies of the civil war was that the methods of terror the Reds resorted to in order to defeat the Whites—including the creation of a powerful secret police—now became a permanent part of communist rule in Russia.

War Communism   The need for access to funds to fight the civil war led the new Soviet government to embark on a hasty and unplanned course of nationalization, a policy known as **war communism.** After officially annulling private property, the Bolshevik government assumed ownership of banks, industry, and other privately held commercial properties. Landed estates and the holdings of monasteries and churches became national property, although the Bolsheviks explicitly exempted the holdings of poor peasants from confiscation. The government also abolished private trade, and seized crops from peasants to feed people in the cities. The policies that made up war communism were deeply unpopular with many segments of Russian society. In addition, they were disastrous for the Russian economy. By 1920 industrial production had fallen to about one-tenth of its prewar level and agricultural output to about one-half its prewar level.

In 1921, Lenin faced the daunting prospect of rebuilding a society that had been torn apart by war and civil war for the last seven years. The workers, in whose name he had taken power, were on strike. Other problems included depopulated cities, destroyed factories, and an army that demobilized soldiers faster than the workforce could absorb them. Lenin and the party tried to take strict control of the country by crushing workers' strikes, peasant rebellions, and a sailors' revolt. Yet Lenin recognized the need to make peace with those whose skills would rekindle industrial production. Faced with economic paralysis, in the spring of 1921 he decided on a radical reversal of war communism.

The New Economic Policy   Demonstrating his pragmatism and willingness to compromise, Lenin implemented the **New Economic Policy** (NEP), which temporarily restored the market economy and some private enterprise in Russia. Large industries, banks, and transportation and communications facilities remained under state control, but the government returned small-scale industries (those with fewer than twenty workers) to private ownership. The government also allowed peasants to sell their surpluses at free market prices. Other features of the NEP included a vigorous program of

electrification and the establishment of technical schools to train technicians and engineers. Lenin did not live to see the success of the NEP. After suffering three paralytic strokes, he died in 1924. His death was followed by a bitter struggle for power among the Bolshevik leaders.

Joseph Stalin   Many old Bolsheviks continued to argue for a permanent or continuous revolution, asserting that socialism in Russia would fail if socialism did not move from a national to an international stage. Others in the Politburo, the central governing body of the Communist Party, favored establishing socialism in one country alone, thus repudiating the role of the Union of Soviet Socialist Republics as torchbearer of worldwide socialist revolution. **Joseph Stalin** (1879–1953), who served in the unglamorous but powerful bureaucratic position of general secretary of the communist party, promoted the idea of socialism in one country. A Georgian by birth, an Orthodox seminarian by training, and a Russian nationalist by conviction, Stalin spoke Russian with a heavy accent, and was an intellectual misfit among the Bolshevik elite. However, by 1928, Stalin had

Joseph Stalin (1879–1953) at a Soviet congress in 1936. By 1928 Stalin had prevailed over his opponents to become the dictator of the Soviet Union, a position he held until his death in 1953.
Bettmann/Getty Images

completely triumphed over his rivals in the party by using his influence as general secretary and had cleared the way for an unchallenged dictatorship of the Soviet Union.

First Five-Year Plan

Stalin decided to replace Lenin's NEP with an ambitious plan for rapid economic development known as the **First Five-Year Plan.** The basic aim of this and subsequent five-year plans (the first was implemented in 1929) were to transform the Soviet Union from a predominantly agricultural country to a leading industrial power. The First Five-Year Plan set targets for increased productivity in all spheres of the economy but emphasized heavy industry—especially steel and machinery—at the expense of consumer goods. Through Gosplan, the central state planning agency, Stalin and the party attempted to coordinate resources and the labor force on an unprecedented scale. As the rest of the world teetered on the edge of economic collapse, this blueprint for maximum centralization of the entire national economy offered a bold alternative to market capitalism. Stalin repeatedly stressed the urgency of this monumental endeavor, telling his people, "We are 50 to 100 years behind the advanced countries. Either we do it, or we shall go under."

Collectivization of Agriculture

Integral to the drive for industrialization was the **collectivization of agriculture.** The Soviet state expropriated privately owned land to create collective or cooperative farm units whose profits were supposed to be shared by all farmers. The logic of communist ideology demanded the abolition of private property and market choices, but more practical considerations also played a role. Stalin and his regime viewed collectivization as a means of increasing the efficiency of agricultural production and ensuring that industrial workers would be fed. Collectivization was extremely unpopular among peasants, but it was not a choice. Stalin's government forced peasants onto the collectivized farms and ruthlessly punished those who resisted. The government specifically attacked a group called *kulaks* (relatively wealthy peasants who had risen to prosperity under Lenin's New Economic Policy), who strongly opposed collectivization.

In some places, outraged peasants reacted to collectivization by slaughtering their livestock and burning their crops. The government's response was outright murder or else removal to prison camps. Millions of farmers chose to leave the land altogether to avoid collectivization and instead migrated to cities in search of work. Once in the cities, these peasants further taxed the limited supplies of housing, food, and utilities in urban areas. Collectivized farms often set unrealistic production quotas, which peasants were unable to meet. Nevertheless, the farms continued to send what they did produce to feed urban workers, leaving peasants to starve to death on the land they once owned. Stalin called a halt to collectivization in 1931, when about half of the farms in the Soviet Union had been collectivized. Although he claimed the policy had made his government "dizzy with success," in reality at least three million peasants died as a direct result of collectivization.

The Soviet Union industrialized under Stalin even though the emphasis on building heavy industry first and consumer industries later meant that citizens postponed the gratifications of industrialization. Before refrigerators, radios, or automobiles became available, the government constructed steelworks and hydroelectric plants. The scarcity or nonexistence of consumer goods was to some degree balanced by full employment, low-cost utilities, and—when available—cheap housing and food in urban areas. Set against the collapse of the U.S. stock market and the depression-ridden

Men and women drive tractors out of one of the Soviet Union's Machine Tractor Stations to work fields on the new collectivized farms.
Sovfoto/Universal Images Group/Getty Images

SOURCES FROM THE PAST

Goals and Achievements of the First Five-Year Plan

In the aftermath of war, revolution, and civil strife, Vladimir Lenin in 1921 adopted the New Economic Policy (NEP) to prevent the collapse of the Russian economy. The NEP was relatively successful, but it rankled Marxist purists because it permitted the return of a limited form of capitalism. Lenin's successor, Joseph Stalin, was determined to build "socialism in one country" by replacing the NEP with a planned economy, whereby a centralized bureaucracy guided and regulated production. To that end, Stalin launched a series of Five-Year Plans designed to transform the Soviet Union into a modern, powerful state. In the following report, delivered to the Central Committee of the Communist Party of the Soviet Union in January 1933, Stalin outlined the goals and the achievements of the First Five-Year Plan.

The fundamental task of the five-year plan was to convert the U.S.S.R. from an agrarian and weak country, dependent upon the caprices of the capitalist countries, into an industrial and powerful country, fully self-reliant and independent of the caprices of world capitalism.

The fundamental task of the five-year plan was, in converting the U.S.S.R. into an industrial country, to completely oust the capitalist elements, to widen the front of socialist forms of economy, and to create the economic basis for the abolition of classes in the U.S.S.R., for the building of a socialist society.

The fundamental task of the five-year plan was to transfer small and scattered agriculture on to the lines of large-scale collective farming, so as to ensure the economic basis of socialism in the countryside and thus to eliminate the possibility of the restoration of capitalism in the U.S.S.R.

Finally, the task of the five-year plan was to create all the necessary technical and economic prerequisites for increasing to the utmost the defensive capacity of the country, enabling it to organize determined resistance to any attempt at military intervention from abroad, to any attempt at military attack from abroad.

What are the results of the five-year plan in four years in the sphere of industry?

We did not have an iron and steel industry, the basis for the industrialization of the country. Now we have one.

We did not have a tractor industry. Now we have one.

We did not have an automobile industry. Now we have one.

We did not have a machine-tool industry. Now we have one.

We did not have a big and modern chemical industry. Now we have one.

We did not have a real and big industry for the production of modern agricultural machinery. Now we have one.

> What areas of industry did the Soviet Union focus on during the First Five Year Plan, and what areas were neglected?

We did not have an aircraft industry. Now we have one.

In output of electric power we were last on the list. Now we rank among the first.

In output of oil products and coal we were last on the list. Now we rank among the first.

And as a result of all this the capitalist elements have been completely and irrevocably ousted from industry, and socialist industry has become the sole form of industry in the U.S.S.R.

Let us pass to the question of the results of the five-year plan in four years in the sphere of agriculture. The Party has succeeded in the course of some three years in organizing more than 200,000 collective farms and about 5,000 state farms devoted to grain growing and livestock raising, and at the same time it has succeeded during four years in expanding the crop area by 21 million hectares. The Party has succeeded in getting more than 60 per cent of the peasant farms to unite into collective farms, embracing more than 70 per cent of all the land cultivated by peasants; this means that we have fulfilled the five-year plan three times over. The Party has succeeded in converting the U.S.S.R. from a country of small-peasant farming into a country of the largest-scale agriculture in the world. Do not all these facts testify to the superiority of the Soviet system of agriculture over the capitalist system?

> Given that Stalin does not address here the three million lives lost during collectivization, is it possible that he similarly downplayed the human costs of the industrial achievements he lists above?

Finally, as a result of all this the Soviet Union has been converted from a weak country, unprepared for defense, into a country mighty in defense, a country prepared for every contingency, a country capable of producing on a mass scale all modern means of defense and of equipping its army with them in the event of an attack from abroad.

For Further Reflection

■ What were the fundamental aims and achievements of the First Five-Year Plan? What benefits, if any, did the peoples of the Soviet Union derive from this economic experiment in a planned economy?

Source: Stalin, J. V. "The Results of the First Five-Year Plan. Report Delivered at the Joint Plenum of the Central Committee and the Central Control Commission of the C.P.S.U.(B.), January 7, 1933." From J. V. Stalin *Marxists Internet Archive,* 1947, 578–630.

capitalist world, the ability of a centrally planned economy to create more jobs than workers could fill made it appear an attractive alternative.

The Great Purge Nevertheless, the results of Stalin's First Five-Year Plan generated controversy as the Communist Party prepared for its seventeenth congress in 1934, the self-proclaimed "Congress of Victors." Although Stalin proclaimed that it had been a great success, the disaster of collectivization and the ruthlessness with which it was carried out had raised doubts about his administration. Although themes of unity and reconciliation prevailed, Stalin learned of a plan to bring more pluralism back into leadership. The Congress of Victors became the "Congress of Victims" as Stalin incited a civil war within the party that was climaxed by highly publicized trials of former Bolshevik elites for treason and by a purge of two-thirds of the delegates. Between 1935 and 1938, in a campaign of political repression known as the **Great Purge,** Stalin removed from posts of authority all persons suspected of opposition, including two-thirds of the members of the 1934 Central Committee and more than one-half of the army's high-ranking officers. The victims faced execution or long-term suffering in labor camps. According to the declassified Soviet archives, during 1937 and 1938, Soviet security forces detained 1,548,366 persons, of whom 681,692 were shot.

The outside world watched the events unfolding within the Soviet Union with a mixture of contempt, fear, and admiration. Most observers recognized that the political and social upheavals that transformed the former Russian Empire were of worldwide importance. The establishment of the world's first dictatorship of the proletariat challenged the values and institutions of liberal society everywhere and seemed to demonstrate the viability of communism as a social and political system.

The Fascist Alternative

While socialism was transforming the former Russian Empire, another political force swept across Europe after the Great War. **Fascism,** a far-right, ultranationalist political movement and ideology that sought to create a new type of society, developed as a reaction against liberal democracy and the spread of socialism and communism. The term *fascism* derives from the word *fasces,* an ancient Roman symbol of authority consisting of a bundle of wooden rods strapped together around an axe. In 1919 Benito Mussolini adopted this symbol for the Italian Fascist movement that governed Italy from 1922 to 1943. Movements comparable to Italian fascism subsequently developed and sometimes dominated political life in many European societies, most notably in Germany in the guise of National Socialism (Nazism). Although fascism enjoyed widespread popularity in many European countries, it rarely threatened the political order and, with the exception of Italy and Germany, never overthrew a parliamentary system. Political and economic frustrations made fertile ground for fascist appeals

outside Europe, and potential fascist movements sprang up during the 1930s in Japan, China, and South Africa; in Latin American societies such as Brazil and Argentina; and in several Arab territories. Nevertheless, fascism was most influential in Europe in the era between the two world wars.

Defining Fascism During the 1920s and 1930s, fascist movements in Europe attracted millions of followers and proved especially attractive to middle classes and rural populations. These groups became radicalized by economic and social crises and were especially fearful of class conflict and the perceived threat from the political left, especially from communism. Fascism also proved attractive to nationalists of all classes, who denounced their governments for failing to realize the glorious objectives for which they had fought during the Great War. Asserting that society faced a profound crisis, fascists sought to create a new national community, which they defined either as a nation-state or as a unique ethnic or racial group. As part of their quest, fascist movements commonly dedicated themselves to the revival of allegedly lost national traditions and, hence, differed widely. Nevertheless, most fascist movements shared certain common features, such as the veneration of the state; a devotion to a strong leader; and an emphasis on ultranationalism, ethnocentrism, and militarism.

Fascist ideology consistently invoked the central role of the state, which stood at the center of the nation's life and history and which demanded the subordination of the individual to the service of the state. Strong and often charismatic leaders, such as Benito Mussolini in Italy or Adolf Hitler in Germany, embodied the state and claimed indisputable authority. Consequently, fascists were hostile to liberal democracy; its devotion to individualism; and its institutions, which they viewed as weak. Fascism was also extremely hostile to class-based visions of the future promoted by socialism and communism. Fascist movements emphasized **chauvinism** (an aggressive form of nationalism) and **xenophobia** (a fear of foreign people). Some fascist leaders, accordingly, viewed national boundaries as artificial restraints limiting their union with ethnic or racial comrades living in other states. The typical fascist state embraced *militarism,* a belief in the rigors and virtues of military life as an individual and national ideal. In practice, militarism meant that fascist regimes maintained large and expensive military establishments; tried to organize much of public life along military lines; and generally showed a fondness for uniforms, parades, and monumental architecture.

Italian Fascism

The first fascist movement developed in Italy after the Great War. Italians in 1918 were deeply disilluisioned with their uninspired political leadership and ineffective government, extensive economic turmoil and social discontent, and what

---

chauvinism (SHOH-vuh-niz-uhm)
xenophobia (zen-uh-FOH-bee-uh)

Benito Mussolini and Adolf Hitler watch a Nazi parade staged for the Italian dictator's visit to Germany in the fall of 1937. Hitler ordered a major display of military power for Mussolini and, by the end of the visit, Mussolini was convinced that an alliance with Germany would lead to Italy becoming more powerful in Europe.

Bettmann/Getty Images

seemed like a threatening rise of socialist movements. In addition Italians were extremely disappointed with Italy's territorial spoils from the peace settlement after the Great War, as many believed Italy should have received significant chunks of Austrian territory.

Benito Mussolini   The guiding force behind Italian fascism was **Benito Mussolini,** a former socialist and, from 1912 to 1914, editor of Italy's leading socialist daily *Avanti!* ("Forward!"). In 1914 he founded his own newspaper, *Il Popolo d'Italia* ("The People of Italy"), which encouraged Italian entry into the Great War. Mussolini was convinced that the war represented a turning point for the nation. The soldiers returning from the front, he argued, would spearhead the thorough transformation of Italian society and create a new type of state. But after the Great War, the one-time socialist advanced a political program that emphasized virulent nationalism, demanded repression of socialists, and called for a strong political leader. In 1919 he established the *Fasci Italiani di Combattimento* (Italian Combat Veteran League).

Mussolini's movement gained widespread support after 1920, and by 1921 his league managed to elect thirty-five fascists to the Italian parliament. Much of the newly found public support resulted from the effective use of violence against socialists by fascist armed squads known as Blackshirts. The Italian socialist party had organized militant strikes throughout Italy's northern industrial cities, causing considerable chaos. By early 1921 Italy hovered on the brink of civil war. In 1922, Mussolini and his followers decided the time was ripe for a fascist seizure of power, and on 28 October, they staged a march on Rome. While Mussolini stayed safely in Milan awaiting the outcome of events, thousands of his blackshirted troops converged on Rome. Rather than calling on the military to oppose the fascist threat, King Victor Emmanuel III hastily asked Mussolini on 29 October to become prime minister and form a new government. Mussolini inaugurated a fascist regime in 1922.

The Fascist State   Between 1925 and 1931, Italy's fascists consolidated their power through a series of laws that provided the legal basis for the nation's transformation into a one-party dictatorship. In 1926 Mussolini seized total power as dictator and subsequently ruled Italy as *Il Duce* ("the leader"). The regime moved quickly to eliminate all other political parties, curb freedom of the press, and outlaw free speech and association. A Special Tribunal for the Defense of the State, supervised by military officers, silenced political dissent. Thousands of Italians were marked as antifascist subversives and found themselves imprisoned or exiled on remote islands. Others faced capital punishment. Allying himself and his movement with business and landlord interests, *Il Duce* also crushed labor unions and prohibited strikes. In an effort to harmonize the interests of workers, employers, and the state, the regime tried to establish a corporatist order. This order was based on the vague fascist concept of corporatism, which viewed society as an organic entity through which the different interests in society came under the control of the state. Thus, in theory, a National Council of Corporations settled labor disputes and supervised wage settlements, but, in reality, this scheme was little more than a propaganda effort. In 1932, on the tenth anniversary of the fascist seizure of power, Mussolini felt confident enough to announce "that the twentieth century will be a century of fascism, the century of Italian power."

Racism and antisemitism were never prominent components of Italian fascism, but in 1938 the government suddenly issued antisemitic laws that labeled Jews unpatriotic, excluded them from government employment, and prohibited all marriages between Jews and so-called Aryans. This development was likely occasioned by Mussolini's newfound friendship with fellow dictator Adolf Hitler. In 1936 Mussolini told his followers that from now on, world history would revolve around a Rome-Berlin Axis. In May 1939 the leaders of fascist Italy and Nazi Germany formalized their political, military,

Il Duce (eehl DOO-cheh)

and ideological alliance by signing a ten-year Pact of Steel. This Pact of Steel illustrated the strong links between the Italian and German variants of fascism.

German National Socialism

Hitler and the Nazi Party After his postwar political awakening, Adolf Hitler came into contact with an obscure political party sympathetic to his ideas. In 1921 he became chairman of the party now known as the National Socialist German Workers' Party. National Socialism (the Nazi movement) made its first major appearance in 1923 when party members and Hitler attempted to overthrow the democratic Weimar Republic that had replaced the German Empire in 1919. The revolt quickly fizzled under the gunfire of police units; Hitler was jailed, and the Nazi movement and its leader descended into obscurity. When Hitler emerged from prison in 1924, he resolved to use new tactics. Recognizing the futility of armed insurrection, he reorganized his movement and launched it on a "path of legality." Hitler and his followers were determined to gain power legally through the ballot box and, once successful, to discard democracy altogether.

The Struggle for Power National Socialism made rapid gains after 1929 because it had broad appeal. Hitler attracted disillusioned people who felt alienated from society and frightened by the growing strength of the communist party in Germany. A growing number of people blamed the young German democracy for Germany's misfortunes: a humiliating peace treaty—the Treaty of Versailles—that identified Germany as responsible for the Great War and assigned reparation payments to the Allies, the hyperinflation of the early 1920s that wiped out the savings of the middle class, the suffering brought on by the Great Depression, and the seemingly unending and bitter infighting among the nation's major political parties. Adolf Hitler promised an end to all those misfortunes by creating a new order that would lead to greatness for Germany. By stressing racial doctrines, particularly antisemitism, the Nazis added a unique and frightening twist to their ideology. Although the Nazis avoided class divisions by recruiting followers from all strata of society, National Socialism in the main appealed to the members of the lower-middle classes: ruined shopkeepers and artisans, impoverished farmers, discharged white-collar workers, and disenchanted students.

The impact of the Great Depression and political infighting led to bloody street battles, shaking the foundations of Germany's fragile young democracy. The leaders of the nation's democratic and liberal parties groped for solutions to mounting unemployment but were hindered by lack of consensus and the public's loss of faith in the democratic system. The electorate became radicalized. Fewer and fewer Germans were willing to defend a parliamentary system they considered ineffective and corrupt. Between 1930 and 1932 the Nazi Party

"Against Starvation and Desperation—Vote for Hitler" is the translated slogan written on this election poster for the July 1932 federal election in Germany. The election resulted in great gains by the Nazi Party, which garnered 37 percent of the national vote and became the single largest party in the *Reichstag* (parliament).
picture alliance/Getty Images

became the largest party in parliament, and the reactionary and feeble president, Paul von Hindenburg (1847–1934), decided to offer Hitler the chancellorship. Promising to gain a majority in the next elections, Hitler lost little time in transforming the dying republic into a single-party dictatorship. He promised a German *Reich,* or empire, that would endure for a thousand years.

Consolidation of Power Under the guise of a state of national emergency, the Nazis used all available means to impose their rule. They began by eliminating all working-class and liberal opposition. The Nazis suppressed the German communist and socialist parties and abrogated virtually all constitutional and civil rights. Subsequently, Hitler and his government outlawed all other political parties, made it a crime to create a new party, and made the National Socialist Party the only legal party. Between 1933 and 1935 the regime replaced Germany's federal structure with a highly centralized state that eliminated the autonomy previously exercised by state and municipal governments. The National Socialist state then guided the destruction of trade unions and the elimination of collective bargaining, including the prohibition of strikes and lockouts. The Nazis also purged the judiciary and the civil service, took control of all police forces, and removed enemies of the regime—both real and imagined—through imprisonment or murder.

The Racial State Once securely in power, the Nazi regime translated its deeply racist ideology, especially notions about racial superiority and racial purity, into practice. The leaders of the Third Reich pursued the creation of a race-based national community by introducing measures designed to improve both the quantity and the quality of the German "race." Implicit in this racial remodeling was the conviction that there was no room for the "racially inferior" or for "biological outsiders." The racial program of the Nazis, implemented as early as 1933, was based on a diffuse mixture of racial anthropological, pseudo-scientific, and antisemetic theories that harkened back to the nineteenth century.

Hitler's perception of Jews originated within a broader racist view of the world based on concepts of the "inequality" of "races" and the alleged "superiority" of the "white race" over other "races." The notion of racial superiority, in turn, was frequently buttressed by a perversion of evolutionary theory known as "social Darwinism," a theory that emerged in England and the United States in the 1870s. Proponents of "social Darwinism" applied the biological concepts of natural selection and survival of the fittest to the alleged social and political realities of human society. Thus, some "social Darwinists" argued that different races are biologically driven to struggle against one another for living space. Paralleling these racial theories was an international scientific, political, and moral ideology known as **eugenics,** which reached its peak of popularity in the first decades of the twentieth century. The term and field of modern eugenics was first formulated by Sir Francis Galton in his 1883 book *Hereditary Genius.* Reflecting a growing faith in science, especially heredity science, eugenics aimed at improving the genetic quality of the human gene pool. As a practical matter, eugenics policies were divided into positive eugenics, the increased reproduction of those assumed to possess beneficial hereditary traits, and negative eugenics, the discouraging of reproduction among those with hereditary traits regarded as deficient. Eugenics was supported by prominent people, including Winston Churchill, Woodrow Wilson, Margaret Sanger, and Émile Zola, to mention just a few. Eugenic measures, such as the sterilization of certain mental patients, were implemented in the United States, Brazil, and Sweden, among other nations. The most infamous proponent of eugenics, however, was Adolf Hitler.

Women and Race Alarmed by declining birthrates in Germany, the Nazis launched a campaign to increase births of "racially valuable" children. This initiative was complementary

What's Left Out? ■ ■ ■ ■ ■ ■

Although Nazi Germany is most closely associated with the application of eugenics policies, in the 1920s and 1930s the United States also enacted a series of applied eugenics laws. Like Nazi Germany, eugenics in the United States—as promoted by the American Eugenics Society (founded in 1922)—focused mostly on negative eugenics, or eliminating negative traits from the population. Also like Nazi Germany, proponents of eugenics in the United States located most of these negative traits in minority populations. In the United States, poor and nonwhite populations were targeted as "undesirables," as were the mentally ill. In an effort to ensure that the most "undesirable" people within these groups did not reproduce, the eugenics movement in the United States focused on turning programs of forced sterilization into law. Indiana was the first state to enact a forced sterilization law in 1907, but by 1935 thirty-one other states had followed suit. In total, more than sixty thousand American citizens were sterilized against their will as a result of such laws. In one landmark 1927 case that made it all the way to the Supreme Court, chief justice Oliver Wendell Holmes justified the practice by writing, "It is better for all the world, if instead of waiting to execute degenerate offspring for crime, or to let them starve for their imbecility, society can prevent those who are manifestly unfit from continuing their kind. . . . Three generations of imbeciles are enough." In fact, Hitler himself boasted of studying American eugenics laws when developing his own programs of forced sterilization and euthanasia in the 1930s. When thinking about the crimes against humanity committed by Nazi Germany, it is worth remembering that these were justified by racist thinking masquerading under the guise of "scientific" ideas such as eugenics and that such racist thinking was widely believed—and put into practice—in the United States as well during the interwar period.

Source: Adam Cohen, *Imbeciles: The Supreme Court, American Eugenics, and the Sterilization of Carrie Buck* (New York: Penguin Press, 2016).

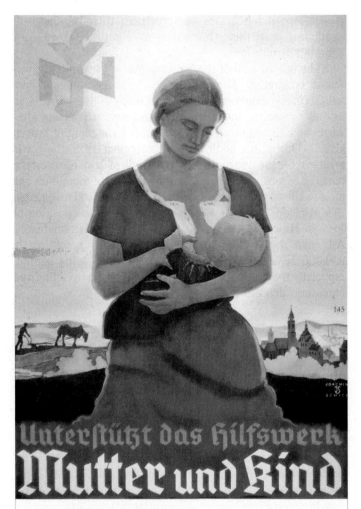

"Mother and Child" was the slogan on this poster created in the mid-1930s, idealizing and encouraging motherhood. The background conveys the Nazi predilection for the wholesome country life, a dream that clashed with the urban reality of German society.

akg-images/Newscom

Mother in three classes: bronze for those with more than four children, silver for those with more than six, and gold for those with more than eight. By August 1939 three million women carried this prestigious award, which many Germans cynically called the "rabbit decoration." In the long term, however, these pronatalist measures failed, and the birthrate remained below replacement level.

Nazi Eugenics The quantity of offspring was not the only concern of the new rulers. They were also obsessed with quality. Starting in 1933, the regime initiated a compulsory sterilization program for men and women the regime had identified as having "hereditarily determined" sicknesses, including schizophrenia, feeblemindedness, manic depression, hereditary blindness, hereditary deafness, chronic alcoholism, and serious physical deformities. Between 1934 and 1939 more than thirty thousand men and women underwent compulsory sterilization. Beginning in 1935 the government also sanctioned abortions—otherwise illegal in Germany—of the "hereditary ill" and "racial aliens." The mania for racial health culminated in a state-sponsored euthanasia program that was responsible for the murder of approximately two hundred thousand women, men, and children. Between 1939 and 1945 the Nazis systematically killed—by gassing, lethal injections, or starvation—those people judged useless to society, especially the physically and mentally handicapped. Nazi eugenics measures served as a precursor to the wholesale extermination of peoples classified as racial inferiors, such as Roma (also called Gypsies) and Jews.

A Nazi "racial expert" uses a caliper to measure the racial purity of a German, in this case as expressed in his facial features.

Henry Guttmann Collection/Hulton Archive/Getty Images

to Nazi ideology, which relegated women primarily to the roles of wife and mother. Through tax credits, special child allowances, and marriage loans, the government tried to encourage marriage and, they hoped, procreation among young people. Legal experts rewrote divorce laws so that a husband could get a divorce decree solely on the ground that he considered his wife sterile. At the same time, the regime outlawed abortions, closed birth control centers, restricted birth control devices, and made it difficult to obtain information about family planning. The Nazis also became enamored with pronatalist (in favor of pregnancy and childbirth) propaganda, and set in motion a veritable cult of motherhood. Annually on 12 August—the birth date of Hitler's mother—women who bore many children received the Honor Cross of the German

Antisemitism **Antisemitism,** or prejudice against Jews, was a key element in Nazi efforts to achieve a new racial order and became the hallmark of National Socialist rule. Immediately after coming to power in 1933, the Nazis initiated systematic measures to suppress Germany's Jewish population. Although Nazi antisemitism was based on biological racial theories, government authorities used religious descent to determine who was a Jew. A flood of discriminatory laws and directives designed to humiliate, impoverish, and segregate Jews from the rest of society followed. In 1935 the notorious **Nuremberg Laws** deprived German Jews of their citizenship and prohibited marriage and sexual intercourse between Jews and other Germans. The Nazi Party, in cooperation with government agencies, banks, and businesses, took steps to eliminate Jews from economic life and expropriate their wealth. Jewish civil servants lost their jobs, and Jewish lawyers and doctors lost their non-Jewish clients. Party authorities also supervised the liquidation of Jewish-owned businesses or argued for their purchase—at much less than their true value—by companies owned or operated by non-Jews.

The official goal of the Nazi regime, at least initially, was Jewish emigration. Throughout the 1930s thousands of Jews left Germany, depriving the nation of many of its leading intellectuals, scientists, and artists. The exodus gained urgency after what came to be known as **Kristallnacht** ("the night of broken glass"). During the night of 9–10 November 1938, the Nazis arranged for the destruction of thousands of Jewish stores, the burning of most synagogues, and the murder of more than one hundred Jews throughout Germany and Austria. This *pogrom* (Yiddish for "devastation") was a signal that the position of Jews in Hitler's Reich was about to deteriorate dramatically. Although they had difficulty finding refuge, approximately 250,000 Jews left Germany by 1938. Those staying behind, especially the poor and the elderly, would face a troubling and potentially deadly future.

CONCLUSION

In the decades after the Great War, European intellectuals questioned and challenged established traditions. While scientists and social thinkers conceived new theories that reshaped the ways humans encountered knowledge and perceptions, artists forged a contemporary aesthetic. In an age of global interdependence, the U.S. stock market crash of 1929 ushered in a period of prolonged economic contraction and social misery that engulfed much of the world and further added to a sense of crisis in Europe and the United States. As most of the industrialized world reeled under the impact of the Great Depression, the leadership of the Soviet Union embarked on a state-sponsored program of rapid industrialization. Though causing widespread human suffering, a series of five-year plans transformed the Soviet Union into a major industrial and military power and offered an alternative to liberal democracy.

European fascist regimes also offered alternatives to liberal democracy. Italians under the leadership of Mussolini rebuilt their state through fascist policies and imperial expansion. In Germany the effects of the Great Depression paved the way for the establishment of the Nazi state, which was based on the principle of racial inequality. Although many peoples suffered under the racist regime, Jews were the principal victims. Ultimately, Adolf Hitler's vision of a powerful and racially pure German state—crafted in an age of anxiety and uncertainty—helped lead to another world war less than two decades after the end of World War I.

STUDY TERMS

Adolf Hitler (751)
Albert Einstein (753)
antisemitism (768)
Benito Mussolini (764)

Black Thursday (756)
chauvinism (763)
collectivization of agriculture (761)
Dadaism (754)
economic nationalism (756)
eugenics (766)
fascism (763)
First Five-Year Plan (761)
Franklin Delano Roosevelt (759)
Great Depression (755)
Great Purge (763)
John Maynard Keynes (759)
Joseph Stalin (760)

Kristallnacht (768)
kulaks (761)
lost generation (752)
National Socialism (765)
Neue Sachlichkeit (754)
New Deal (759)
New Economic Policy (NEP) (760)
Nuremberg Laws (768)
pogrom (768)
psychoanalysis (754)
Sigmund Freud (754)
Smoot-Hawley Tariff Act (757)
uncertainty principle (753)
war communism (760)
xenophobia (763)

FOR FURTHER READING

H. H. Arnason and Elizabeth C. Mansfield. *History of Modern Art.* 7th ed. 2012. This is a comprehensive source for students studying the art of the late nineteenth to the twenty-first centuries.

R. J. B. Bosworth. *Mussolini's Italy: Life under the Fascist Dictatorship, 1915–1945.* New edition. New York, 2011. One of the world's leading authorities on modern Italian history successfully explores the complexities of *Il Duce* and his times.

Peter J. Bowler and Iwan Rhys Morus. *Making Modern Science: A Historical Survey.* Chicago, 2005. This work examines the relationship between science and modern thought more thoroughly than a typical survey.

Richard Evans. *The Third Reich in Power, 1933–1939.* New York, 2005. The second work in a three-volume series, this book starts with the Nazis' assumption of power and ends at the beginning of World War II in Europe.

Ian Kershaw. *Hitler: A Biography*. Reprint edition. New York, 2010. One of the foremost historians of the Nazi era pens the definitive biography of Adolf Hitler.

George Makari. *Revolution in Mind: The Creation of Psychoanalysis*. New York, 2008. A comprehensive history of the development of psychoanalysis and how it gained influence during the first half of the twentieth century.

John Moser. *Global Great Depression and the Coming of World War II*. London, 2015. Explores the ways various states responded to the crisis of the Great Depression and how these responses helped lead to World War II.

Norman Naimark. *Stalin's Genocides*. Princeton, N.J., 2010. This is a lucid analysis of Stalin's terror and brutal mass killings.

Robert Paxton. *The Anatomy of Fascism*. New York, 2004. This groundbreaking work focuses on what fascists did rather than on what they said.

Robert Service. *Stalin: A Biography*. Cambridge, Mass., 2005. The author of an acclaimed biography of Lenin provides the most complete portrait available of the Soviet ruler.

ZOOMING IN ON ENCOUNTERS

Shanfei Becomes a New and Revolutionary Young Woman in China

Shanfei lived in a time of great political turmoil. The daughter of a wealthy landowning man of the Chinese gentry, she grew up with luxuries and opportunities unknown to most girls. Her father reluctantly allowed her to attend school, and her mother clothed her in beautiful silk dresses. Shanfei, however, matured into a woman who rejected the rich trappings of her youth. Her formative years were marked by the unsettling cultural and political changes that engulfed the globe in the wake of the Great War. The rise of nationalism and communism in China after the revolution of 1911 and the Russian revolution in 1917 guided the transformation of Shanfei—from a girl ruled by tradition and privilege to an active revolutionary dedicated to freeing her country as a member of the Chinese Communist Party.

With the exception of Shanfei's father, the members of her family in Hunan province took in the new spirit of the first decades of the twentieth century. Her brothers returned from school with strange and compelling ideas, including some that challenged the subordinate position of women in China. Shanfei's mother, to all appearances a woman who accepted her subservience to her husband, proved instrumental to Shanfei's departure from the common destiny of Chinese girls. She listened quietly to her sons as they discussed new views, and then she applied

In this cigarette advertisement from 1935, Chinese women are shown wearing modern styles and smoking cigarettes. They would have been recognized around the world as "modern girls," who increasingly challenged traditional gender expectations in their choices of clothing, behavior, and occupation.
swim ink 2 llc/Corbis Historical/Getty Images

them to her daughter. She used every means at her disposal to persuade her husband to educate their daughter. He eventually agreed but still insisted that Shanfei receive an old-fashioned education and submit to foot binding and childhood betrothal.

When Shanfei was eleven years old, her father suddenly died, and his death emboldened her mother. She ripped the bandages off Shanfei's feet and sent her to a modern school far from home. In the lively atmosphere of her school, Shanfei became an activist. At sixteen she incited a student strike against the school administration, then transferred to a more modern school, and became famous as a leader in the student movement. She attended classes with men and broke tradition in her personal and political life. In 1926 Shanfei abandoned her studies to join the Communist Youth, and she gave up the fiancé that had been arranged for her for a free marriage to the man she loved: a peasant leader in the communist movement.

CHAPTER OVERVIEW

The twists of fate that altered the destiny of Shanfei had parallels throughout the colonial and neocolonial world after 1914. Two major events, the Great War and the Great Depression, defined much of the turmoil of those years. Disillusion and radical upheaval affected colonized and neocolonial areas all over the world, including those in Asia, Africa, and Latin America. As peoples around the world struggled to come to terms with the aftermath of war, an unprecedented economic contraction gripped the international community. The Great Depression complicated peoples' struggles for national sovereignty and financial solvency, especially in Asia, where Japan's militarist leaders sought to build national strength through imperial expansion. Latin American states worked to resist the economic domination of the United States, while people in sub-Saharan Africa suffered devastating economic consequences when European powers were no longer able to buy and use the raw materials produced in their colonies.

European empires still appeared to dominate global relations in the 1920s and 1930s, but the Great War had opened fissures within the European and U.S. spheres of influence. Nationalist and communist movements were already active in most colonial and neocolonial territories, and now they gathered strength. Indeed, in the postwar years resistance to foreign rule and a desire for national unity were stronger than ever. Movements to throw off foreign domination were especially strong in India and China, where various visions of national identity competed, but they also took on new momentum in sub-Saharan Africa and Latin America. While peoples in sub-Saharan Africa worked to become independent of outright imperial control, those in Latin America had to fight off the more indirect economic effects of postindependence colonialism, usually termed *neocolonialism*. And while we know that resistance to colonialism was as old as colonialism itself, the trauma of the Great War and the Depression that followed helped convince more people than ever before to join movements in order to secure the self-determination they desired.

CHRONOLOGY	
1909–1955	Life of Carmen Miranda
1912	Taft establishes dollar diplomacy as U.S. foreign policy
1919	May Fourth Movement in China
1920	Non-Cooperation Movement in India
1921	Rivera returns to Mexico to paint
1928	Socialist Party of Peru is founded
1929	Beginning of Great Depression
1930	Civil Disobedience Movement in India
1930s–1940s	Vargas's *estado novo* in Brazil
1931	Japanese invasion of Manchuria
1933	Roosevelt begins practice of the Good Neighbor Policy
1934	Long March by Chinese Communists
1934	Sandino is murdered in Nicaragua
1935	Government of India Act
1938	Cárdenas nationalizes oil industry in Mexico

PATHS TO AUTONOMY IN SOUTH AND EAST ASIA

In the decades following the Great War, nationalism and revolutionary anticolonialism developed into powerful political forces in Asia, especially in India and China. Achieving the twin ideals of independence from foreign powers and national unity became a goal of intellectuals, new political leaders, and ordinary people alike. Indian, Chinese, and Japanese societies underwent a prolonged period of disorder and struggle until a new order emerged. In India the quest for national identity focused on gaining independence from British rule, a pursuit that was complicated by sectarian (religious) differences between Hindus and Muslims. The Chinese path to national identity was fraught with foreign and civil war as two principal groups—the Nationalist and Communist Parties—contended for power. Deeply divided by ideologies, both parties opposed foreign domination, rejected the old order, and sought a unified Chinese state. Japanese militarists made China's quest for national unity more difficult because Japan struggled to overcome its domestic problems and enhance its national identity through conquests that focused on China.

India's Quest for Home Rule

By the beginning of the twentieth century, Indian nationalism already threatened the British Empire's hold on India. The construction of a vast railway network across India to facilitate the export of raw materials contributed to the idea of national unity by bringing the people of the subcontinent within easy reach of one another. Moreover, because it was impossible for a small group of foreigners to control and administer such a vast country, the British had trained an elite class of English-speaking, educated Indian administrators to help in this task. A European system of education familiarized the local middle-class intelligentsia with the political and social values of European society. Those values, however—democracy, individual freedom, and equality—were the antithesis of empire, and Indians educated within this system quickly saw their fundamental contradiction with the injustices of imperial rule in India.

Indian National Congress
Of all the associations dedicated to the struggle against British rule, the most influential was the **Indian National Congress,** founded in 1885. This organization, which enlisted the support of many prominent Hindus and Muslims, at first sought collaboration with the British to bring self-rule to India, but after the Great War the congress pursued that goal in opposition to the British. The formation of the Muslim League, established in 1906 with the encouragement of the British government, added a new current into the movement for national liberation. Both organizations were dedicated to achieving independence for India, but members of the Muslim League increasingly worried that Hindu oppression and continued subjugation of India's substantial Muslim minority might replace British rule.

During the Great War, more than one million Indians—Hindus and Muslims—served in the armies of the British at the western front and in Mesopotamia. During the war, the Indian National Congress supported the British and suspended its campaigns for self-rule. Many Indians hoped their active support in the war effort would result in British willingness to allow greater Indian autonomy. But shortages of goods and food during the war tried the patience of Indian subjects, and once the war was

over the British made it clear that their ideas of sharing power fell far short of Indian expectations. In April 1919, British-led troops opened fire on a group of unarmed Indian demonstrators in the city of Amritsar, killing 379 and wounding 1200 more. This massacre shocked millions of Indians and prompted Indian political leaders—including Mohandas Gandhi—to call not just for home rule but for total independence.

Mohandas K. Gandhi Into this turmoil stepped **Mohandas Karamchand Gandhi** (1869–1948), a remarkable and charismatic leader. Gandhi grew up in a prosperous and pious Hindu household, married at thirteen, and left his hometown in 1888 to study law in London. In 1893 he went to South Africa, part of the British Empire, to accept a position with an Indian firm,

Leader of the Indian civil disobedience revolt, Mohandas Gandhi marched to the shore at Dandi, a coastal village located on the Arabian Sea, to collect salt without paying taxes. This Salt March, also known as the Salt Satyagraha, sparked large-scale acts of civil protest against the British Raj (rule) and changed both global and British attitudes about Indian independence. On his left is Sarojini Naidu (1879–1949), a feminist activist who in 1925 was elected the first female president of the Indian National Congress.
Bettmann/Getty Images

Mohandas Karamchand Gandhi
(moh-huhn-DAHS kuhr-uhm-CHUND GAHN-dee)

SOURCES FROM THE PAST

M. N. Roy: The Awakening of the East

Narendra Nath Battacharya, who later adopted the name M. N. Roy, was born near Calcutta, India, in 1887. He began his political life as a radical Indian nationalist but became a Marxist while he lived in the United States during World War I. After helping to found the Mexican Communist Party in 1917, he was invited to Moscow to attend the Second World Congress of the Communist International (Comintern) in 1920. In Moscow, Roy became an influential leader in the Communist International. His ideas about the importance of the colonial world in the future communist revolution helped to shape Comintern policy toward the colonial world.

The world revolution, in order to accomplish its great mission, must cross the borders of the so-called Western Countries where capitalism has reached its climax. Until very recently this truth was almost entirely unknown among the revolutionaries of Europe and America, who hardly gave a moment's thought to the social and economic conditions of the Asiatic generally. It was generally maintained that, owing to their industrial backwardness, the hundreds of millions of the masses in the East would not count for anything in the great struggle between the exploiter and the exploited. Consequently the "World" of the world revolution was limited to Europe and America.

> Why does Roy think European revolutionaries never thought very much about the potential of revolutionaries in the colonized world?

But revolution is the result of objective conditions; it breaks out in the least suspected place if the dynamic forces are there. The inevitable result of oppression is that sooner or later the oppressed rebel. This is happening to-day in the Eastern countries, where the myriads of toilers have been groaning under the same exploitation against which their more fortunate and less downtrodden comrades of the Occident have been carrying on an heroic fight. The East is awakening: and who knows if the formidable tide, that will sweep away the capitalist structure of Western Europe, may not come from there . . .

During almost a century World Capitalism kept on invigorating itself by sucking the blood of the colonial toilers. But along with the bloody sword of organised exploitation, it carried in its womb the incipient forces that were destined to rise against it and build the new society upon its ruins. To-day these forces are manifesting themselves in the growing revolutionary fermentation among the Eastern peoples, who were considered till the other day negligible factors in the World Revolution. This awakening of the East must open a new vision before the revolutionary leaders of Europe. It ought to show them the way through which the retreat of the cunning enemy can be cut. A formidable upheaval of the colonial and "protected" peoples will take away from under the feet of Imperialist Capitalism, the rock of super-profit which has helped so far offset the effects of overproduction . . . The disruption of Empire is the only thing that will complete the bankruptcy of European capitalism; and the revolutionary upheavals in the Asiatic countries are destined to bring about the crumbling of the proud imperial structure of capitalism. . .

> Why does Roy believe that the awakening of the East is essential to undermining the capitalist world order?

For Further Reflection

■ Roy makes it clear that the fight against colonialism required a global strategy. How does this change our understanding of anticolonial movements in individual colonies?

Source: The Call, July 15, 1920, p. 5. Marxists Internet Archive (2007). https://www.marxists.org/archive/roy/1920/07/15.htm

and there he quickly became involved in organizing the local Indian community against a system of racial segregation that made Indians second-class citizens. During the twenty-five years he spent in South Africa, Gandhi embraced a moral philosophy of **ahimsa** (tolerance and nonviolence) and developed the technique of passive resistance that he called **satyagraha** ("truth and firmness"). His belief in the virtue of simple living led him to renounce material possessions, dress in the garb of a simple Indian peasant, and become a vegetarian. He renounced sex and extolled the virtues of a daily salt-

water enema. He also spent an hour each morning in careful study of the *Bhagavad Gita* (Sanskrit for "The Lord's Song"), one of the most sacred writings of Hinduism, which he regarded as a spiritual dictionary.

Gandhi returned to India in 1915, where he became active in Indian politics. He succeeded in transforming the Indian National Congress from an elitist body of anglicized gentlemen into a mass organization. Although the reform program

satyagraha (suh-TYA-gruh-hah)

of the congress appeared remote from the needs of common people, Gandhi translated their demands in a way that was meaningful for ordinary Indians. His unique mixture of spiritual intensity and political activism appealed to a broad section of the Indian population, and in the eyes of many he quickly achieved the stature of a political and spiritual leader, their Mahatma, or "great soul."

Under Gandhi's leadership the congress launched two mass movements: the Non-Cooperation Movement of 1920–1922 and the Civil Disobedience Movement of 1930. Convinced that economic self-sufficiency was a prerequisite for self-government, Gandhi called on the Indian people to boycott British goods and return to wearing rough homespun cotton clothing. He disagreed with those who wanted India to industrialize, advocating instead manual labor and the revival of rural cottage industries. Gandhi furthermore admonished Indians to boycott institutions operated by the British in India, such as schools, offices, and courts. Despite Gandhi's cautions against the use of force, violence often accompanied the protest movement, both by Indians who were protesting and by the British who sought to stop them.

The India Act For nearly two decades after the end of the Great War, the political situation in India was in constant turmoil. The Indian National Congress, led by Gandhi in the 1920s and 1930s, was only one of the movements seeking independence from Britain. Various revolutionary groups and the Indian Communist Party (founded in 1925) also agitated in favor of independence, sometimes using violence. Over time, it became clear to the British that repressive measures were simply not enough to quell such strong and sustained calls for an end to British rule. In an attempt to maintain some control over India, then, the British offered a political compromise. After years of commissions, reports, and tense conversations with Indian political leaders (including Gandhi), in 1935 the British parliament enacted the **Government of India Act**. The act established in India the institutions of a self-governing state, including the establishment of autonomous legislative bodies in the provinces of British India and the creation of a bicameral (two-chambered) national legislature. Acts of the legislature, however, were still subject to approval by the executive arm of government and remained under British control. Additionally, the British still controlled foreign policy. Although the India Act was not the independence called for by the Indian National Congress, Gandhi urged Indians to support it. A majority of Indians ended up approving the measure, which went into effect in 1937.

The India Act proved unworkable, however, because India's six hundred nominally sovereign princes refused to cooperate and because Muslims feared that Hindus would dominate the national legislature. These latter fears were

exacerbated by the Great Depression because Muslims constituted the majority of indebted tenant farmers in India, and they found themselves increasingly unable to pay rents and debts during the economic crisis. And since their landlords were mainly Hindus, Muslims increasingly perceived their experiences during the Depression as stemming from economic exploitation by Hindus. They were encouraged in these perceptions by **Muhammad Ali Jinnah** (1876–1948), an eloquent and brilliant lawyer who headed the Muslim League. Jinnah and Muslim League leaders increasingly warned that a unified India represented nothing less than a threat to the Muslim faith and its Indian community. By 1940, Jinnah proposed that British India be divided into two independent states: India, for India's Hindus, and Pakistan, for India's Muslims. Thus in spite of hundreds of years of Hindus and Muslims living peacefully together in the same communities, these increasing sectarian tensions in the interwar period would come to dominate the independence process on the Indian subcontinent.

China's Campaigns to End Foreign Domination

As Shanfei's life story suggested in the introduction to this chapter, during the first half of the twentieth century China was in a state of almost continual revolutionary upheaval. The conflict's origins dated from the nineteenth century, when the Chinese Empire came under relentless pressure from imperialist powers that rushed in to fill the vacuum created by China's internal political disintegration (see chapter 31). As revolutionary and nationalist uprisings gained widespread support, a revolution in 1911 forced the **Xuantong** emperor (also known as Puyi), to abdicate at the age of five. The Qing empire fell with relative ease. Dr. **Sun Yatsen** (1866–1925), a leading opponent of the old regime, proclaimed a Chinese republic in Nanjing in 1912 and briefly assumed the office of president. The dynasty was dead, but there remained the problems of what to put in its place.

The Republic The revolution of 1911 did not establish a stable government. Sun Yatsen controlled only a portion of China around Nanjing, while many others in different parts of the country had their own claim to leadership. As a result, the republic soon plunged into a state of political anarchy and economic disintegration marked by the rule of disaffected generals from the old imperial Chinese army and their troops who established themselves as provincial or regional rulers. Because the generals were responsible for the neglect of irrigation projects crucial to the survival of farmers; for the revival of the opium trade, which they protected; and for the decline of crucial economic investments, Chinese society went into economic decline in this period. Yet the rule of the generals was just one symbol of the disintegration of the political order. The fragmented relationship between Chinese authority and foreign powers was another. Since the nineteenth century, a collection of treaties, known in China as the unequal treaties, had guided Chinese relations with foreign countries. Those treaties had established

Muhammad Ali Jinnah (moo-HAHM-ahd ah-lee JIN-uh)
Xuantong (shoo-ahn-tohng)

a network of foreign control over the Chinese economy that effectively hindered Chinese economic development even as it greatly benefited the foreign powers. The continued sway of unequal treaties and other concessions permitted foreigners to intervene in Chinese society and protect their own interests. While foreigners did not control every aspect of the state, through their privileges they greatly impaired its sovereignty.

Chinese Nationalism After the Great War, nationalist sentiment developed rapidly in China. Youths and intellectuals, who in the previous decade had looked to Europe and the United States for models and ideals for the reform of China, eagerly anticipated the results of the 1919 Peace Conference in Paris. They expected the U.S. government to support the termination of the treaty system and the restoration of full Chinese sovereignty. Those hopes were shattered, however, when the peacemakers did none of these things and instead approved increasing Japanese interference in China. That decision gave rise to the **May Fourth Movement.** Spearheaded by students and intellectuals in China's urban areas, the movement galvanized the country, and all classes of Chinese protested against foreign, especially Japanese, interference. In speeches, newspapers, and novels, the movement's leaders pledged themselves to rid China of imperialism and reestablish national unity. Student leaders such as Shanfei rallied their comrades to the cause.

Disillusioned by the cynical self-interest of the United States and the European powers, some Chinese became interested in Marxism (see chapter 33) and the social and economic experiments under way in the Soviet Union. The anti-imperialist rhetoric of the Soviet leadership struck a responsive chord, and in 1921 a group of Chinese activists organized the **Chinese Communist Party (CCP)** in Shanghai. Among its early members was **Mao Zedong** (1893–1976), a former teacher and librarian who viewed a Marxist-inspired social revolution as the cure for China's problems. Mao's political radicalism extended to the issue of women's equality, which he and other

communists championed. As Shanfei's personal experience suggested, Chinese communists believed in divorce, opposed arranged marriages, and campaigned against the practice of foot binding.

Sun Yatsen Even prior to the founding of the Chinese Communist Party, Sun Yatsen—who had helped bring down the Qing government—sought to organize Chinese people into a party based on nationalism and modernization. In 1912 he founded the *Guomindang* (Nationalist People's Party), which became a powerful political force in the first half of the twentieth century. The Guomindang's platform was based on Sun's ideology, summarized in his *Three Principles of the People,* which called for elimination of special privileges for foreigners, national reunification, economic development, and a democratic republican government based on universal suffrage. While Sun was not a communist, he recognized the utility of forming an alliance with the powerful Soviet Union and the Chinese Communist Party in order to achieve his nationalist goals. In 1923, the Soviet Union brokered a deal in which the Guomindang and the Chinese Communist Party agreed to enter into a partnership (now known as the First United Front), in which both would work toward the common goal of uniting China and driving out foreign imperialists. To improve its chances of success, the Soviet Union agreed to provide military training, funding, and arms. This partnership was deeply alarming to the foreign powers active in China—including, especially, Britain, France, and Japan—because none of them wanted a strong Chinese state to limit their profits or privileges.

Civil War When Sun Yatsen died in 1925, the leadership of the Guomindang fell to **Jiang Jieshi** (Chiang Kai-shek, 1887–1975), a young general who had been trained in Japan and the Soviet

Guomindang (GWOH-mihn-dahng)

Jiang Jieshi (jyahng jeh-she)

Adversaries in the struggle for power in China: at left, Jiang Jieshi (Chiang Kai-shek) (1887–1975); at right, Mao Zedong (1893–1976).
Bettmann/Getty Images

MAP 35.1   The struggle for control in China, 1927–1936.

Compare the continental territories controlled by Japan and the Guomindang in 1934.

How would the size of Japan's territories in Manchuria and Korea influence Chinese abilities to challenge Japanese expansion?

Union. Unlike Sun, Jiang distrusted the Chinese communists he was supposed to be working with and was suspicious that communists were gaining too much power in the Guomindang. In 1926, Jiang maintained the partnership of the United Front in order to wage a political and military offensive, known as the Northern Expedition, to unify the nation and bring China un-

der Guomindang rule. But once the offensive had proven successful and Jiang's forces had taken the cities of Shanghai and Nanjing in early 1927, Jiang's forces brutally and unexpectedly turned against his former communist allies, bringing the alliance of convenience between the Guomindang and the CCP to a bloody end. On April 12, 1927, Jiang unleashed armed men on communists in the city of Shanghai, murdering thousands and arresting many more over the two weeks that followed. In the following year, nationalist forces occupied Beijing, set up a central government in Nanjing, and declared the Guomindang the official government of a unified and sovereign Chinese state. Meanwhile, the badly mauled communists retreated to a remote area of southeastern China, where they tried to reconstitute and reorganize their forces.

The nationalist government had to deal with many concerns, but Chinese leaders evaded one major global crisis—the Great Depression. China's large agrarian economy and small industrial sector were connected only marginally to the world economy. Foreign trade in such items as tea and silk, which did decline, made up only a small part of China's economy, which was otherwise dominated by its large domestic markets. Although the new government in China generally avoided having to contend with global economic devastation, it did have to confront three major problems during the 1930s. First, the nationalists actually controlled only part of China, leaving the remainder of the country in the hands of various generals. Second, by the early 1930s communist activity in China became a major threat since now communists sought to eliminate their nationalist enemies. Third, the Guomindang faced increasing Japanese aggression. In dealing with those problems, Jiang Jieshi gave priority to eliminating the CCP and its Red Army. No longer able to ward off the relentless attacks of nationalist forces, the communists took flight in October 1934 to avoid annihilation. Bursting through a military blockade around their bases in Jiangxi province in southeastern China, some eighty-five thousand troops and auxiliary personnel of the Red Army began the legendary **Long March,** an epic journey of 10,000 kilometers (6,215 miles). After traveling across difficult terrain and fighting for survival against hunger, disease, and Guomindang forces, the marchers arrived in a remote area of Shaanxi province in northwestern China in October 1935 and established headquarters at Yan'an. Although thousands died in this forced retreat, the Long March inspired many Chinese to join the Communist Party. During the Long March, Mao Zedong emerged as the leader and the principal theoretician of the Chinese communist movement. He came up with a Chinese form of Marxist-Leninism, or Maoism, an ideology grounded in the conviction that peasants rather than urban proletarians were the foundation for a successful revolution. Village power, Mao believed, was critical in a country where most people were peasants.

Imperial and Imperialist Japan

After the Great War, Japan achieved great power status and appeared to accept the international status quo that the major powers fashioned in the aftermath of war. After joining the League of Nations as one of the "big five" powers, the Japanese government entered into a series of international agreements that sought to improve relations among countries with conflicting interests in Asia and the Pacific. As a signatory to several Washington Conference treaties in 1922, Japan agreed to limit naval development, pledged to evacuate Shandong province in China, and guaranteed China's territorial integrity. In 1928 the Japanese government signed the Kellogg-Briand Pact, which renounced war as an instrument of national policy. Concerns about earlier Japanese territorial ambitions, highlighted by the Twenty-one Demands on China in 1915, receded from the minds of the international community.

Japan's limited involvement in the Great War gave a dual boost to its economy. Japanese businesses profited from selling munitions and other goods to the Allies throughout the war, and they gained a bigger foothold in Asia as the war led Europe's trading nations to neglect Asian markets. Economic prosperity was short-lived, however, as the postwar economy of Japan faced serious challenges. Rapid inflation and labor unrest set in by 1918, followed by a series of recessions that culminated in a giant economic slump caused by the Great Depression. Like the economies of other industrial nations tied into the global economy, Japan's economy experienced plummeting industrial production, huge job layoffs, declining trade, and financial chaos. Economic contraction set the stage for social unrest and radical politics.

Public demands for sweeping political and social reforms, including a broadening of the franchise, protection for labor unions, and welfare legislation, figured prominently in Japanese domestic politics throughout the 1920s. Yet conservatives blocked any major advances beyond the suffrage law of 1925, which established universal male suffrage. By the early 1930s an increasingly frustrated public blamed its government for the nation's continuing economic problems and became more disenchanted with leading politicians tainted by bribery scandals and corrupt connections to business conglomerates. Right-wing political groups called for an end to party rule, and xenophobic nationalists dedicated themselves to the preservation of a unique Japanese culture and the eradication of Western influences. A campaign of assassinations, targeting political and business leaders, culminated in the murder of Prime Minister **Inukai Tsuyoshi** (1855–1932).

Politicians who supported Japan's role in the international industrial-capitalist system faced increasing opposition from those who were inclined toward a militarist vision of a self-sufficient Japan that would dominate east Asia. The hardships of the depression undermined support for the internationalist position, and the militarists were able to benefit from Japanese martial traditions and their own unwillingness to be constrained by international cooperation. Meanwhile, China's unification threatened Japan's economic interests in Manchuria. At the same time, China's political instability, the result of nationalists and communists vying for power, made China an inviting target. Manchuria had historically been Chinese

Inukai Tsuyoshi (ee-NO-kigh ts-yo-she)

territory, but by the twentieth century it was a sphere of influence where Japan maintained the Manchurian Railroad (built in 1906), retained transit rights, and stationed troops. In 1931 Japan's military forces in Manchuria acted to assert control over the region.

The Mukden Incident   On the night of September 18, 1931, Japanese troops used explosives to blow up a few feet of rail on the Japanese-built South Manchuria Railway north of Mukden. They accused the Chinese of attacking their railroad. This **"Mukden incident"** became the pretext for war between Japanese and Chinese troops. Although the civilian government in Japanese tried to halt this military incursion, by 1932 Japanese troops controlled all of Manchuria, thereby ensuring Japan preeminence and protecting its long-term economic and industrial development of the region. The Japanese established a puppet state called Manchukuo, but in reality Japan had absorbed Manchuria into its empire, challenged the international peace system, and begun a war. In response to the Manchurian invasion, the Guomindang (Nationalist Party) leader Jiang Jieshi appealed to the League of Nations to halt Japanese aggression. After a lengthy investigation, the league called for the withdrawal of Japanese forces and for the restoration of Chinese sovereignty. The Japanese responded by leaving the league, and, although China gained the moral high ground in international eyes, nothing was done to stop the aggression. This reaction set the pattern for future responses to the actions of expansionist nations such as Japan. Embarking

on conquests in east Asia, Japanese militarists found a sure means to promoting a new militant Japanese national identity. They also helped provoke a new global war.

The Great War and the Great Depression made signal contributions to the ongoing political upheavals taking place throughout Asia. Revolutionary and nationalist ideologies intersected with old conflicts to complicate the processes of independence and national unification in India and China. And while the global economic crisis led to some lessening of European imperial influence, it prompted an industrialized Japan to exert its imperial will on the Asian sphere.

SUB-SAHARAN AFRICA UNDER COLONIAL DOMINATION

The Great War and the Great Depression similarly complicated quests for national independence and unity in sub-Saharan Africa. The colonial ties that bound African colonies to European powers had ensured that Africans became participants in the Great War, willing or not (see chapter 33). As in India, Africans expected that their participation in the Great War on behalf of the various colonial powers would lead to greater control over their governments and economies. But instead, colonial governments ignored African pleas for social and political reform.

Indeed, rather than retreating, colonialism consolidated its hold on the African continent including sub-Saharan Africa. In the decades following the Paris Peace Conference that ended

The Victoria Falls Bridge, completed in 1905 but under construction in this photograph, is an example of the railroad infrastructure undertaken by colonial powers in sub-Saharan Africa. The bridge was constructed in Britain by British engineers and assembled mostly by African workers over the Zambezi River in what was then Rhodesia (now Zambia and Zimbabwe). The purpose of the railroad was to link coalfields with copper mining enterprises in Rhodesia.
History and Art Collection/ Alamy Stock Photo

the Great War in 1919, the European powers focused on the economic exploitation of their colonies. The imposition of a rapacious form of capitalism destroyed the self-sufficiency of many African economies and turned the resulting colonial economies into extensions of those of the colonizing powers. As a result, African economic life became enmeshed in the global economy. The persistence of colonialism led to the development of African anticolonial movements and the establishment of nationalist parties. During the decades following the Great War, African intellectuals searched for new national identities and looked forward to independence from colonial rule.

The Colonial Economy

The decades following the Great War witnessed a thorough transformation of economic life in sub-Saharan Africa. Colonial powers pursued two key economic objectives in sub-Saharan Africa: they wanted to make sure that colonized people paid for the institutions—bureaucracies, judiciary, police, and military forces—that kept them in subjugation; and they developed export-oriented economies characterized by the exchange of unprocessed raw materials or minimally processed cash crops for manufactured goods from abroad. In pursuit of those goals, colonial authorities imposed economic structures that altered, subordinated, or destroyed preexisting economies in sub-Saharan Africa. In their place came colonial economies, tightly integrated into and dependent on a

European-dominated global economy. The Great Depression of the 1930s exposed the vulnerability of dependent colonial economies. As international markets for primary products shrank under the impact of the depression, European companies that controlled the export of African products suffered accordingly. Trade volume often fell by half, and commodity prices dropped even more sharply.

Infrastructure The economic integration of sub-Saharan Africa required investment in infrastructure. Thus, during the early twentieth century, the new colonial economy first became visible in the form of port facilities, roads, railways, and telegraph wires. Transportation and communication networks not only facilitated conquest and rule but also linked the agricultural or mineral wealth of a colony to the outside world. Although Europeans later claimed that they had "given" sub-Saharan Africa its first modern infrastructure, Europeans and their businesses were its main beneficiaries. Indeed, although Africans paid for the infrastructure with their labor and taxes, Europeans did not consider the needs of local African economies.

Farming and Mining Colonial taxation was an important tool designed to drive Africans into the labor market. To earn the money to pay the taxes colonial powers levied on land, houses, livestock, and people themselves, African farmers had to become cash crop farmers or seek wage labor on

Two workers in a diamond mine in Northern Rhodesia. Although this photograph was taken in the 1950s, it nevertheless depicts the difficult conditions involved in the mining industries of sub-Saharan Africa in the interwar period. INTERFOTO/Alamy Stock Photo

plantations and in mines. Cash crop farming embraced the largest proportion of sub-Saharan Africans. In most colonies, farmers who had their own land specialized in one or two crops, generally destined for export to the country governing them. Farmers in sub-Saharan Africa grew a variety of cash crops for the international marketplace, among them peanuts from Senegal and northern Nigeria, cotton from Uganda, cocoa from the Gold Coast, rubber from the Congo, and palm oil from the Ivory Coast and the Niger delta. In areas with extensive European settlement, such as in Kenya, Rhodesia, and South Africa, settler agriculture was most prominent. Production of agricultural commodities intended for overseas markets remained in the hands of white settlers, whose governments saw to it that they received large and productive areas of land. In British-controlled Kenya, for example, four thousand white farmers seized the Kikuyu highlands, which comprised seven million acres of the colony's richest land. In South Africa, the government reserved 88 percent of all land for whites, who made up just 20 percent of the total population.

Colonial mining enterprises relying on African labor loomed large in parts of central and southern Africa. These enterprises usually involved the extraction of mineral wealth such as copper, gold, and diamonds, and they required vast numbers of laborers. Colonial mining companies found this labor by recruiting men from rural areas, who they paid only minimal wages. These recruitment practices set in motion a vast pattern of labor migration that persisted throughout the twentieth century. The absence of male labor and the payment of minimal wages had the effect of impoverishing the rural areas.

Labor Practices Colonial authorities and settlers frequently could not recruit the number of laborers they needed, in spite of the high taxes they imposed. In these cases, colonial officials resorted to outright forced labor. Indeed, forms of forced labor and barely disguised variants of slavery were prominent features of the colonial economy. A white settler in Kenya candidly expressed the view held by many colonial administrators: "We have stolen his land. Now we must steal his limbs. Compulsory labor is the corollary to our occupation of the country." Infrastructure-building projects such as the construction of railways and roads also commonly depended on forced labor regimes. When the French undertook the construction of the Congo-Ocean railway from Brazzaville to the port at Point-Noir, for example, they rounded up some ten thousand workers annually. Labor practices were so brutal that within a few years between fifteen and twenty thousand African laborers had perished from starvation, disease, and maltreatment.

African Nationalism

In the decades following the Great War, European powers consolidated their political control over sub-Saharan Africa and imposed economies designed to exploit its natural and labor resources. Many Africans were disappointed that their contributions to the war went unrewarded. Instead, in place of anticipated social reforms or some degree of greater political participation came an extension and consolidation of the colonial system. This reality, coupled with an awareness of the demands of anticolonial movements in other parts of the

What's Left Out? ▮▮ ▬ ▬ ▬ ▬ ▬

As we have seen in this chapter, the interwar period was characterized by numerous anticolonial movements all over the world. It is impossible to capture all of these anticolonial movements in one chapter, but it is even more difficult to capture the ways in which the people involved in these movements were not only aware of each other but often knew each other personally. One of the primary reasons for this was that many anticolonial activists in this period spent time living in European cities like Paris, Berlin, and London, often while attending university. People from all over the colonized world lived in these cities, as did people from places like Latin America and China. As a result, people from diverse areas came into contact with one another through their participation in student groups, social activities, and political movements. When they interacted, they learned about colonial and neocolonial conditions in other places, thus helping them see imperialism as a global problem rather than as a problem specific to a particular imperial power. One organization designed for just this purpose was the League Against Imperialism, which held its first major conference in Brussels, Belgium, in 1927. In February of that year, 174 delegates from the colonial and neocolonial world (including India's Jawaharlal Nehru, Indonesia's Mohammad Hatta, Senegal's Lamine Senghor, and Algeria's Messali Hadj, to name just a few) gathered together with leftist Europeans to learn about global colonial oppression and to make resolutions calling for an end to imperialism. Through connections like these, anticolonial activists were inspired by each other, gained information about events happening elsewhere, and learned new techniques to fight against colonialism. When they returned home, they brought this knowledge with them and used it in their own anticolonial struggles. It was thus no accident that so many anticolonial movements flourished at roughly the same time in the interwar period.

Source: Michael Goebel, *Anti-Imperial Metropolis: Interwar Paris and the Seeds of Third World Nationalism* (Cambridge, 2015).

SOURCES FROM THE PAST

Africa for Africans

Marcus Garvey (1887–1940) is best remembered as a pivotal figure in the pan-African movement. He inspired many African leaders. A powerful orator, Garvey preached the greatness of the African heritage and called on European colonial powers to leave Africa. Convinced that blacks in the diaspora could never secure their rights as minorities, Garvey rejected the idea of integration and instead championed a "Back to Africa" movement. According to Garvey, a Jamaican who also lived for a time in the United States, only in Africa would it be possible to establish an autonomous black state that featured its own unique culture. In the excerpt below, Garvey addressed the Second International Convention of Negroes in New York City in 1921.

George Washington was not God Almighty. He was a man like any Negro in this building, and if he and his associates were able to make a free America, we too can make a free Africa. Hampden, Gladstone, Pitt and Disraeli were not the representatives of God in the person of Jesus Christ. They were but men, but in their time they worked for the expansion of the British Empire, and today they boast of a British Empire upon which "the sun never sets." As Pitt and Gladstone were able to work for the expansion of the British Empire, so you and I can work for the expansion of a great African Empire. Voltaire and Mirabeau were not Jesus Christs, they were but men like ourselves. They worked and overturned the French Monarchy. They worked for the Democracy which France now enjoys, and if they were able to do that, we are able to work for a democracy in Africa. Lenin and Trotsky were not Jesus Christs, but they were able to overthrow the despotism of Russia, and today they have given to the world a Social Republic, the first of its kind. If Lenin and Trotsky were able to do that for Russia, you and I can do that for Africa. Therefore, let no man, let no power on earth, turn you from this sacred cause of liberty. I prefer to die at this moment rather than not to work for the freedom of Africa. If liberty is good for certain sets of humanity it is good for all. Black men, Colored men, Negroes have as much right to be free as any other race that God Almighty ever created, and we desire freedom that is unfettered, freedom that is unlimited, freedom that will give us a chance and opportunity to rise to the fullest of our ambition and that we cannot get in countries where other men rule and dominate.

> Why is it important to Garvey to point out that the various leaders listed here were not gods?

We have reached the time when every minute, every second must count for something done, something achieved in the cause of Africa. . . . It falls to our lot to tear off the shackles that bind Mother Africa. Can you do it? You did it in the Revolutionary War. You did it in the Civil War; You did it at the Battles of the Marne and Verdun; You did it in Mesopotamia. You can do it marching up the battle heights of Africa. Let the world know that 400,000,000 Negroes are prepared to die or live as free men. Despise us as much as you care. Ignore us as much as you care. We are coming 400,000,000 strong. We are coming with our woes behind us, with the memory of suffering behind us—woes and suffering of three hundred years—they shall be our inspiration. My bulwark of strength in the conflict of freedom in Africa, will be the three hundred years of persecution and hardship left behind in this Western Hemisphere.

> What is the three hundred years of suffering to which Garvey refers here?

For Further Reflection

■ In his speech, how does Marcus Garvey convey the significance of Africa for both Africans and those involved in the black diaspora?

Source: Garvey, Marcus. *The Philosphy and Opinions of Macus Garvey*, edited by Amy Jacques Garvey, 95–96. New Preface by Tony Martin. Dover, MA: The Majority Press Inc.

world, led Africans in sub-Saharan colonies to develop their own anticolonial movements. An emerging class of urban intellectuals, frequently educated in Europe, became especially involved in the formation of ideologies that sought freedom from colonialism and promoted new national identities.

Sub-Saharan Africa's New Elite Colonialism prompted the emergence of a new African social class, sometimes called the "new elite." This elite derived its status and place in society from employment and education. The upper echelons of sub-Saharan Africa's elite class contained high-ranking civil servants, physicians, lawyers, and writers, most of whom had studied abroad either in western Europe or sometimes in the United States. For example, **Jomo Kenyatta** (1895–1978), spent almost fifteen years in Europe, during which time he attended various schools and universities, including the London School of Economics. Like many other colonized subjects who lived in Europe, Kenyatta made contact with colonized subjects from other regions in sub-Saharan Africa, India, and the Caribbean. Through discussions and meetings and friendships, colonized subjects like Kenyatta were able to view imperialism as a global problem that needed to be eliminated everywhere. Later, Kenyatta led Kenya to independence from the British. Other members of the new elite included teachers, clerks, and interpreters who had obtained a European-derived primary or secondary education. Although some individuals were self-employed, such as lawyers and doctors, most held jobs with colonial governments, foreign companies, or Christian missions. In short, these were the Africans who spoke European languages and outwardly adopted European cultural norms such as wearing European-style clothes or adopting European names. It was within the ranks of this new elite that anticolonial mass movements emerged.

African nationalists frequently embraced the European concept of the nation as a means of forging unity among disparate African groups. This was partly a practical response to the artificial borders Europeans had drawn to create sub-Saharan African colonies in the first place. Even when such borders did not make sense in terms of ethnic and cultural ties, it was nevertheless true that the borders placed all the people within them under a single colonizer and a common legal and political regime. As such the idea of the nation—as defined by these borders—seemed to offer the best chance to mount effective resistance to colonialism.

Alternatives to the Nation Some anticolonial sub-Saharan Africans were not convinced that independent nations—especially as constituted within borders drawn by European colonizers—were what anticolonial movements should be striving for. Instead, some looked to the precolonial past for inspiration. There they found identities based on ethnicity, religion, and languages, and they believed that any future state must reconstitute institutions crucial to those identities, such as distinctively African forms of spiritual and political authority. Race had provided colonial powers with one rationale for conquest and exploitation; hence it was not surprising that some anticolonial activists used the

Portrait of the Jamaican Pan-Africanist Marcus Garvey (1887–1940), taken in 1924.
Library of Congress, Prints and Photographs Division [LC-USZ61-1854]

concept of an African race as a foundation for identity, solidarity, and state building. Race figured as an important concept in another important strain of African anticolonialism, which originated in the Western Hemisphere among the descendants of slaves. Pan-Africanists thought of Africans and African-descended peoples from around the world as members of a single race and promoted the unification of all people of African descent into a single African state. Many pan-Africanists came from North America and the Caribbean, though the idea also attracted followers in Africa. Some of the most well-known representatives of this **pan-Africanism** were the black U.S. activist and intellectual **W. E. B. DuBois** (1868–1963) and the Jamaican nationalist leader **Marcus Garvey** (1887–1940), who preached black pride and called on blacks living in the African diaspora to go "Back to Africa." Collectively these ideas influenced the development of anticolonial movements in sub-Saharan Africa during the 1930s and 1940s, but the need to oppose colonial powers from within existing colonial borders made it difficult to enact proposed alternatives that moved across them.

LATIN AMERICAN STRUGGLES WITH NEOCOLONIALISM

Having gained their independence in the nineteenth century, most sovereign nations in Latin America thereafter struggled to achieve political and economic stability in the midst of interference from foreign powers. The era of the Great War and the Great Depression proved crucial to solidifying and exposing the neocolonial structures that dominated affairs in Latin America. Generally seen as an indirect and more subtle form of imperial control, neocolonialism usually took shape as foreign economic domination but did not exclude more typically imperial actions such as military intervention and political interference. In Central and South America, as well as in Mexico and the Caribbean, this imperial influence came not from former colonial rulers in Spain and Portugal but, rather, from wealthy, industrial-capitalist powerhouses such as Great Britain and, especially, the United States. Neocolonialism impinged on the independent political and economic development of Latin American states, but it did not prevent nationalist leaders from devising strategies to combat it.

The Impact of the Great War and the Great Depression

Reorientation of Political and Nationalist Ideals The Great War and the Russian revolution, along with the ongoing Mexican revolution (see chapter 27), spread radical ideas and the promise of new political possibilities throughout Latin America. The disparate ideals emerging from this time of political ferment found receptive audiences in Latin America before but especially during the global economic crisis of the Great Depression. Marxism, Vladimir Lenin's theories on capitalism and imperialism, and a growing concern for the impoverished indigenous population as well as exploited peasants and workers in Latin American societies informed the outlooks of many intellectuals and artists who sought a path to greater social and political equality. Although those revolutionary doctrines did not achieve full-scale adoption by Latin American states during the interwar era, their increasing popularity and perceived viability as political options suggested the alternatives open to nations in the future.

University Protests and Communist Parties The Great War had propelled the United States into a position of world economic leadership. The peoples of Latin America came to experience this increased U.S. economic power most intensely, and it was no coincidence that the capitalism embraced by the United States came under attack. One of the first institutions in many Latin American states to witness this rebelliousness were the universities. Taking their inspiration from the Mexican and Russian revolutions—both deeply anti-capitalist—students in the 1920s began to demand reforms in their own countries. Their political activism resulted in the long-term politicization of the student bodies at Latin American universities. Universities thereafter became training grounds for future political leaders, including the Cuban **Fidel Castro** (1926–2016), and the ideas explored within an academic setting—from Marxism to anti-imperialism—exerted great influence on those budding politicians.

The currency of radicalism also expressed itself in the formation of political parties that either openly espoused communism or otherwise adopted anti-capitalist and anti-imperialist agendas for change. Peruvians, for example, created a number of radical new political parties, many of which had connections to a self-educated young Marxist intellectual, **José Carlos Mariátegui** (1895–1930). Mariátegui felt particular concern for the poor and for indigenous Indians, who constituted approximately 50 percent of Peru's population. He castigated Peru's leaders in journals and newspapers for not helping the downtrodden, and he suffered exile to Europe as a

Diego Rivera (1886–1957) finishing a mural in the lobby of the Cordiac Institute, Mexico City, Mexico, circa 1930.
FPG/Getty Images

result. He came back from Europe a dedicated Marxist and in 1928 established the Socialist Party of Peru. Mariátegui continued to write and rally in support of laborers, and he was in the midst of helping to create the Peruvian Communist Party when he died from cancer in 1930.

The same agitation that filled José Carlos Mariátegui affected others in Peru and led in the 1920s and 1930s to violence and strikes. The *Alianza Popular Revolucionaria Americana* (Popular American Revolutionary Alliance, or APRA) gave another voice to those critical of Peru's ruling system. This party's followers, known as *Apristas*, advocated indigenous rights and anti-imperialism among other causes. *Aprismo* offered a radical but noncommunist alternative to Peruvians, and it stemmed from the ideas of **Victor Raúl Haya de la Torre** (1895-1979). Haya de la Torre began his political activism as a student protester and as a supporter of a workers' movement. Exiled like Mariátegui, Haya de la Torre nonetheless imparted his eclectic views to APRA, including both staunch anti-imperialism and a plan for capitalist development that had peasants and workers cooperating with the middle class. The more traditional power of the military and landed elites in Peru managed to contain these rebellious movements, but the cultural and political popularity of radicalism and its intellectual proponents persisted.

Diego Rivera and Radical Artistic Visions The ideological transformations apparent in Latin America became stunningly and publicly visible in the murals painted by famed

José Carlos Mariátegui (ho-SAY car-lohs ma-ree-AH-teh-gee)

Mexican artist **Diego Rivera** (1886–1957). After studying art in Mexico in his youth, Rivera went to study in Europe in 1907 and did not return to Mexico until 1921. Influenced by the art of both Renaissance artists and cubists, Rivera also experienced the turmoil and shifting political sensibilities taking place in Europe during the Great War and its aftermath. He blended his artistic and political visions in vast murals that he intended for viewing and appreciation by the masses. He believed that art should be on display for working people. Along with other Mexican muralists, such as David Alfaro Siqueiros (1896–1974) and José Clemente Orozco (1883–1949), Rivera shaped the politicized art of Mexico for decades.

Diego Rivera celebrated indigenous Mexican art and pre-Columbian folk traditions, and he incorporated radical political ideas in his style and approach to mural painting. The government commissioned him in the late 1920s and 1930s to create large frescoes for public buildings, and Rivera artistically transcribed the history of Mexico, replete with its social ills, on the walls of such structures as the National Palace and the Ministry of Education in Mexico City. An activist in the Mexican Communist Party (founded in 1917), he taught briefly in Moscow in the late 1920s. In the early 1930s the Detroit Institute of Arts commissioned him to paint murals for a U.S. audience, although this migration of his art to the United States soon caused a controversy.

In 1933 Rivera received a request to paint murals for the RCA building in Rockefeller Center in New York City. He included in one panel a portrait of Vladimir Lenin, which outraged those who had commissioned the work. John D. Rockefeller himself ordered the mural to be plastered over and replaced. Rivera in turn undertook a series of twenty-one paintings on United States history titled *Portrait of America*. He labeled one of the most pointed and critical paintings *Imperialism,* which visualized and advertised the economic interference and political repressiveness engendered by U.S. neocolonialism in Latin America. Rivera depicted massive guns and tanks extending over the New York Stock Exchange. In the foreground and at the edges of the Stock Exchange are a variety of Latin American victims of this monied-military oppression, including Central Americans laboring for the United Fruit Company and others toiling for the Standard Oil Company. Overlooking all of this in the upper-right corner is **Augusto César Sandino** (1893–1934), the martyred nationalist hero who opposed U.S. intervention in Nicaragua. Rivera made visible the impact of U.S. imperialism on Latin American societies, and by doing so he helped spread political activism in the Americas.

The Evolution of Economic Imperialism

United States Economic Domination Latin American states were no strangers to foreign economic domination in the nineteenth and early twentieth centuries. Their export-oriented economies had long been tied to global finances and had long been subject to controls imposed by foreign investors,

largely those from Great Britain, the United States, France, and Germany. The major evolution in economic neo-colonialism during this period concerned the growing predominance of the United States in the economic affairs of Latin American nations. The Great War sealed this transition to U.S. supremacy, and U.S. investments in Latin America soared in the 1920s. Between 1924 and 1929, U.S. banks and businesses more than doubled their financial interests in Latin America as investments grew from $1.5 billion to $3.5 billion. Much of that money went toward the takeover of businesses extracting vital minerals, such as copper-mining firms in Chile and oil-drilling concerns in Venezuela.

Dollar Diplomacy That U.S. neocolonialism was meant to be largely economic became evident in the policies of President William Howard Taft (1857–1931). In his final address to Congress in 1912, Taft argued that the United States should substitute "dollars for bullets" in its foreign policy. He wanted businesses to develop foreign markets through peaceful commerce and believed that expensive military intervention should be avoided as much as possible. Likewise, by replacing European investments with U.S. investments, the United States would face fewer tests of the Monroe Doctrine or its 1904 Roosevelt corollary, which justified direct intervention in Latin American nations deemed unstable by the United States. This new vision of U.S. expansion abroad, dubbed **"dollar diplomacy"** by critics, encapsulated the gist of what those in Latin America perceived as "Yankee imperialism."

Economic Depression and Experimentation The economic crisis of the Great Depression demonstrated the extent to which Latin America had become integrated in the world economy. With some exceptions, exports had continued in the interwar period to help nations achieve basic solvency and even enough economic expansion to institute social reforms. The Great Depression, however, halted fifty years of economic growth in Latin America and illustrated the region's susceptibility to global economic crises. The increasing U.S. capital investments for budding industries and other financial concerns during the 1920s could not be maintained during this catastrophic economic downturn. Most Latin American states, because they exported agricultural products or raw materials, were further vulnerable to the effects of the depression. The prices of sugar from the Caribbean, coffee from Brazil and Colombia, wheat and beef from Argentina, tin from Bolivia, nitrates from Chile, and many other products fell sharply after 1929. Attempts by producers to raise prices by holding supplies off the market—Brazilians, for example, set fire to coffee beans or used them in the construction of highways—failed, and throughout Latin America unemployment rates increased rapidly. The drastic decline in the price of the region's exports and the drying up of foreign capital prompted Latin American governments to raise tariffs on foreign products and impose various other restrictions on foreign trade. Those same conditions also encouraged domestic

VOL. XLIX. No. 1257.   PUCK BUILDING, New York, April 6th, 1901.   PRICE TEN CENTS.

COLUMBIA'S EASTER BONNET.

The cover of American humor and satire magazine *Puck,* from 6 April 1901, featured Columbia wearing a warship bearing the words "World Power" as her Easter bonnet. Columbia is the female personification of the United States of America.
Library of Congress, Prints and Photographs Division [LC-DIG-ppmsca-25515]

manufacturing, which made important gains in many Latin American nations in this period.

Indeed, although the weaknesses of export-oriented economies and industrial development financed by foreigners became evident during the Great Depression, the international crisis also allowed Latin American nations to take alternative paths to economic development. Economic policy stressing internal economic development was most visible in Brazil, where dictator-president (1930–1945, 1950–1954) **Getúlio Dornelles Vargas** (1883–1954) turned his nation into an *estado novo* (new state). Ruling with the backing of the military but without the support of the landowning elite, Vargas and his government during the 1930s and 1940s embarked on a program of industrialization that created new enterprises. Key

among them was the iron and steel industry. The Vargas regime also implemented protectionist policies that shielded domestic production from foreign competition, which pleased both industrialists and urban workers. Social welfare initiatives accompanied industrial development, protecting workers with health and safety regulations, minimum wages, limits on working hours, unemployment compensation, and retirement benefits. The Great Depression contributed in many ways to the evolution of both economic neocolonialism and economic experimentation within Latin American states.

Conflicts with a "Good Neighbor"

The "Good Neighbor Policy" The pressures of the Great Depression and the instability of global politics led to a reassessment of U.S. foreign policy in Latin America during the late 1920s and 1930s. U.S. leaders realized the costliness and the ineffectiveness of their previous direct interventions in Latin America, especially when committing U.S. Marines as peacekeeping forces. To extricate U.S. military forces and rely more fully on dollar diplomacy, policymakers instituted certain innovations that nonetheless called into question any true change of heart among U.S. neocolonialists. They approved "sweetheart treaties" that guaranteed U.S. financial control in the Caribbean economies of Haiti and the Dominican Republic, for example, and the U.S. Marines provided training for indigenous police forces to keep the peace and maintain law and order. These national guards tended to be less expensive than maintaining forces of U.S. Marines, and the guards' leaders usually worked to keep cordial relations with the United States. This revamped U.S. approach to relations with Latin America became known as the **Good Neighbor Policy,** and it was most closely associated with the administration of Franklin D. Roosevelt (1882–1945). Although Roosevelt appeared more well-intentioned in his exercise of the policy, events in Nicaragua before and during the beginning of his administration highlighted the limits of U.S. neighborliness.

Nicaragua and the *Guarda Nacional* U.S. financial interests had long influenced the economy of Nicaragua, and those substantial investments—whether in the transportation industry or in bananas—served to justify U.S. intervention when revolts or civil wars broke out. The mid- and late 1920s again witnessed the outbreak of civil war in Nicaragua and the repeated insertion of U.S. Marines to restore order. Leading the opposition to Nicaraguan conservatives and the occupation of Nicaragua by U.S. Marines was Augusto César Sandino, a nationalist and liberal general who refused to accept any peace settlement that left Marines on Nicaraguan soil.

As part of a plan to remove U.S. forces, the United States established and trained the ***Guarda Nacional,*** or National Guard, in Nicaragua. The U.S.-supervised elections of 1932

Getúlio Dornelles Vargas (zhi-TOO-lyoo door-NEH-lis VAHR-guhs)

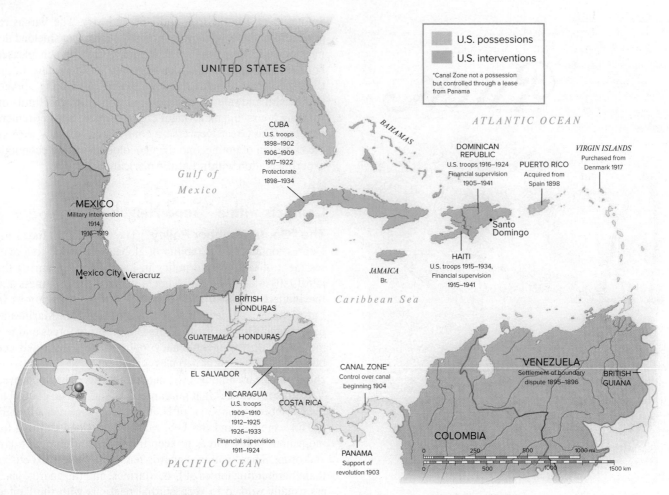

MAP 35.2   The United States in Latin America, 1895–1941.

Note the number of Latin American states where U.S. troops intervened in local politics.

On what basis did U.S. policymakers justify those interventions?

How the Past Shapes the Future ▷▷▷▷▷▷▷▷

The Destructive Potential of Industrial Technologies

One of the features of mid-twentieth-century nationalist movements in both Brazil and China was an emphasis on economic development through industrialization. It is easy to understand the rationale behind such plans: one of the things nationalists in Asia, Africa, and Latin America agreed upon was their objection to economic exploitation by the industrial powers of Europe, Japan, or the United States. To counter such exploitation, nationalists in this period began to seek control over their economies by producing their own industrial goods and by exploiting their own natural resources. Yet the model of industrialization established by the powers that had industrialized first was one that paid little attention to the environmental consequences of resource extraction or industrial pollution. As a result, those states seeking to industrialize in the mid-twentieth century tended to perpetuate patterns of resource depletion; monocrop cultivation; soil erosion; and air, soil, and water pollution begun by the original industrial powers. Consider the aggregate environmental effects of this pattern of industrialization at the planetary level, especially as increasing numbers of states sought to escape economic domination through internal industrialization over the course of the twentieth century.

brought Juan Batista Sacasa (president, 1932-1936) into power, and U.S. troops departed, having positioned the brutal but trusted **Anastacio Somoza Garcia** (1896-1956) as commander of the Guard. Even though conflicts between Sandino's forces and Somoza's Guard persisted, Sandino explored options with Sacasa and Somoza for ending the rebellion given the departure of U.S. Marines. But officers from the National Guard murdered Sandino in 1934, and Somoza soon after fulfilled his ambitions and became president of his country. Somoza endeavored successfully to maintain the loyalty of the National Guard and to prove himself a good neighbor to the United States. He visited Washington, D.C., in 1939 and renamed the Nicaraguan capital city's main thoroughfare after Roosevelt. He also began to collect what became the largest fortune in Nicaragua's history and to establish a political dynasty that ruled the nation for decades to come. In the meantime, Sandino gained heroic status as a martyr who died in part because he fought the good neighbor to the north, while ordinary Nicaraguans suffered under a brutal dictatorship supported by those same neighbors.

Mexico Under Cardenas's Rule However flawed, the Good Neighbor Policy evolved under Roosevelt into a more conciliatory U.S. approach to Latin American relations. The interventionist corollary to the Monroe Doctrine enunciated previously by President Theodore Roosevelt (1859-1919) was formally renounced in December 1933, when Secretary of State Cordell Hull attended the Seventh International Conference of American States in Montevideo, Uruguay. Hull signed the Convention on the Rights and Duties of States, which held that "no state has the right to intervene in the internal or external affairs of another." That proposition faced a severe challenge in March 1938 when Mexican president **Lázaro Cárdenas** (1895-1970) nationalized the oil industry, much of which was controlled by foreign investors from the United States and Great Britain.

Given the history of tempestuous relations between the United States and Mexico, including multiple U.S. military incursions into Mexico during the revolution, there was little chance for a peaceful resolution to this move on the part of Cárdenas. Cárdenas took this step after Mexican oil workers went on strike in protest of their difficult working conditions and low pay. The Mexican government intervened and drew up a new labor agreement between Mexican workers and the foreign oil companies, but the foreign oil companies refused to abide by it. Cárdenas took this as a direct challenge to Mexican sovereignty and thus resolved to nationalize the oil industry. Despite calls for a strong U.S. and British response including those who advocated an all-out war, Roosevelt and his administration officials resisted the demands of big businesses and instead called for a cool, calm response and negotiations to end the conflict. This plan prevailed, and the foreign oil companies ultimately had to accept only $24 million in compensation rather than the $260 million that they initially demanded because Cárdenas cleverly based the compensation

A 1920s photograph of Nicaraguan patriot leader Augusto César Sandino. Sandino opposed the presence of the United States in Nicaragua and fought to expel U.S. Marines in his country. He was murdered by officers from the U.S.-friendly National Guard in 1934.
Bettmann/Getty Images

price on the tax value claimed by the oil companies. The nationalization of Mexican oil proved popular with Mexican people, not least because it had demonstrated Mexico's ability to stand up to the exploitative capitalist economies of the United States and western Europe.

Lázaro Cárdenas (LAH-sah-roh CAR-deh-nahs)

Neighborly Cultural Exchanges?

Although the nationalization crisis in Mexico ended in a fashion that suggested the strength of the Good Neighbor Policy, a good deal of the impetus for that policy came from economic and political concerns associated with the Great Depression and the deterioration of international relations in the 1930s. The United States wanted to cultivate Latin American markets for its exports, and it wanted to distance itself from the militarist behavior of Asian and European imperial powers. The U.S. government knew it needed to improve relations with states in Latin America, if only to secure those nations' support in the increasingly likely event of another global war.

Hollywood added to this process by promoting more positive images of Latin America through its adoption of singer and dancer **Carmen Miranda** (1909–1955). Born in Portugal but raised from childhood in Brazil, Miranda found fame on a Rio de Janeiro radio station and recorded hundreds of hit songs. A Broadway producer recruited her to the United States, where she then became a popular sensation in World War II–era films such as *Down Argentine Way* (1940). Carmen Miranda appeared as an exotic Latin American woman, usually clothed in sexy, colorful costumes that featured headdresses adorned with the fruits grown in Latin America—such as bananas. She softened representations of Latin Americans for audiences in the United States, providing a less threatening counterpoint to la-boring migrants or women guerrilla fighters in Mexico's revolution. She also became a source of pride for Brazilians, who reveled in her Hollywood success. At the same time, Miranda's deliberately sexualized image and her use of Latin American fruits and symbols in her costumes did not provide audiences in the United States with a realistic vision of Latin American people. Instead, Miranda's performances simply encouraged them to trade one set of stereotypes for a more palatable alternative.

Chiquita Banana, an advertising icon used to promote a good image of the United Fruit Company, was a replica in fruit of the singing and acting sensation Carmen Miranda. Fort Worth Star-Telegram/Tribune News Service/Getty Images

And indeed, U.S. companies like the United Fruit Company—whose profits were based on the brutal exploitation of Central Americans on banana plantations—co-opted Carmen Miranda's image for their own purposes. The **United Fruit Company** owned 160,000 acres of land in the Caribbean by 1913, and already by 1918 U.S. consumers bought fully 90 percent of Nicaragua's bananas. Not content with such market control, the United Fruit Company's advertising executives in 1944 crafted "Chiquita Banana," a female banana look-alike of Carmen Miranda. In singing radio commercials, Chiquita Banana taught U.S. consumers about the storage and various uses of bananas ("I'm Chiquita Banana / And I've come to say / Bananas have to ripen / In a certain way"). This singing banana promoted the sales of United Fruit Company bananas, and for consumers in the United States, it gave the prototypical neocolonial company in Latin America a softer, less threatening image—one that challenged, for example, the more ideologically raw representation in Diego Rivera's *Imperialism*.

While Hollywood and U.S. companies were softening images of Latin American people and products for their own reasons, treatment of Mexican migrants to the United States in the same period revealed the persistence of negative attitudes toward Latin American people. During the Great War, hundreds of thousands of Mexican men, women, and children migrated to the United States to fill the labor void created when Europeans could not travel overseas to find work. In spite of the fact that their work was desperately needed, many Mexican migrants were treated poorly by U.S. citizens, who considered them "cheap Mexican labor." These attitudes hardened further during the Great Depression, when federal and local officials managed to deport thousands of Mexicans who had come to the United States at the urging of agricultural and industrial companies.

CONCLUSION

In the decades after the Great War, and in the midst of the Great Depression, intellectuals and political activists in Asia, sub-Saharan Africa, and Latin America challenged the ideological and economic underpinnings of empire and neocolonialism. Often embracing the ideas and theories that activists encountered in their travels and around the globe as a result of the war—including self-determination, socialism, communism, and anti-imperialism—radicals and nationalists crafted new visions of a future in which political and economic independence was possible.

Meanwhile, the Japanese government embarked on a policy of militarism in East Asia, while the United States increased its efforts to intervene in Latin American economies. European colonial rulers also continued to limit, often brutally, the freedom of peoples in Asia and Africa. Yet like Shanfei, young intellectuals and older political leaders alike fought against these trends during the interwar period. Although their efforts to achieve economic and political autonomy did not come to fruition until after World War II, this period was critical to formulating their social, political, and economic responses to all forms of imperial control.

STUDY TERMS

ahimsa (773)
Anastacio Somoza Garcia (787)
Augusto César Sandino (784)
Carmen Miranda (788)
Chinese Communist
   Party (CCP) (775)
Diego Rivera (784)
dollar diplomacy (784)
estado novo (785)
Fidel Castro (783)
Getúlio Dornelles Vargas (785)
Good Neighbor Policy (785)
Guarda Nacional (785)
Guomindang (775)
India Act (774)
Indian National
   Congress (772)
Inukai Tsuyoshi (777)
Jiang Jieshi (775)

Jomo Kenyatta (781)
José Carlos Mariátegui (783)
Lázaro Cárdenas (787)
Long March (777)
Mao Zedong (775)
Marcus Garvey (782)
May Fourth Movement (775)
Mohandas Karamchand
   Gandhi (772)
Muhammad Ali Jinnah (774)
Mukden incident (778)
pan-Africanism (782)
satyagraha (773)
Sun Yatsen (774)
United Fruit Company (788)
Victor Raúl Haya de la
   Torre (783)
W. E. B. DuBois (782)
Xuantong (774)

FOR FURTHER READING

Victor Bulmer-Thomas. *The Economic History of Latin America Since Independence* (Cambridge Latin American Studies). 3rd ed. New York, 2014. This well-known classic remains the best economic history of Latin America.

Ian Buruma. *Inventing Japan, 1853–1964.* New York, 2003. A respected journalist compresses a century of complex history into a short and elegant book.

Toyin Falola. *Nationalism and African Intellectuals.* Rochester, 2002. Explores the ways African intellectuals shaped anticolonial nationalist movements in the colonial period and then state-building movements after independence.

William Gould. *Hindu Nationalism and the Language of Politics in Late Colonial India.* New York, 2004. Political history of India on the eve of independence.

Robert E. Hannigan. *The New World Power: American Foreign Policy, 1898–1917.* Philadelphia, 2002. A detailed account of U.S. foreign relations that links class, race, and gender influences to policymakers.

Michele Louro. *Comrades against Imperialism: Nehru, India, and Interwar Nationalism.* Cambridge, 2018. Argues that Jawaharlal Nehru, the first president of independent India, was deeply shaped by the internationalism of the interwar period—particularly by the League Against Imperialism.

Roland Oliver and Anthony Atmore. *Africa Since 1800.* 5th ed. Cambridge, 2005. An updated version of a well-regarded survey.

S.C.M. Paine. *The Wars for Asia, 1911–1949.* Cambridge, 2012. Explores the competing visions of Chinese, Japanese, and Russians for the future of China in the period encapsulated by the two World Wars.

Steve Striffler and Mark Moberg, eds. *Banana Wars: Power, Production, and History in the Americas.* Durham, N.C., 2003. Interdisciplinary analysis of the transformative impact of the banana industry on global trade and the consequences for Latin American societies and economies.

Odd Arne Westad. *Decisive Encounters: The Chinese Civil War, 1946–1950.* Stanford, 2003. An engaging work that introduces the reader to the salient political and military events that led to the eventual defeat of the Guomindang.

ZOOMING IN ON ENCOUNTERS

Victor Tolley finds Tea and Sympathy in Nagasaki

On 6 August 1945, as he listened to the armed services radio on Saipan (a U.S.-controlled island in the north Pacific), U.S. marine Victor Tolley heard the news: the president of the United States announced that a "terrible new weapon" had been deployed against the city of Hiroshima, Japan. Tolley and the other marines rejoiced, realizing that the terrible new weapon—the atomic bomb—might end the war and relieve them of the burden of invading Japan. A few days later Tolley heard that the city of Nagasaki had also been hit with an atomic bomb. He remembered the ominous remarks that accompanied the news of this atomic destruction: radio announcers suggested it might be decades before the cities would be inhabitable.

Imagine Tolley's astonishment when a few weeks later, after the Japanese surrender, he and his fellow marines were assigned to the U.S. occupation forces in Nagasaki. Assured by a superior officer that Nagasaki was "very safe," Tolley lived there for three months, during which he became very familiar with the devastation wrought by the atomic bomb. As he noted, "It was just like walking into a tomb. There was total silence. You could smell this death all around ya. There was a terrible odor."

Tolley also became acquainted with some of the Japanese survivors in Nagasaki, which proved to be an eye-opening

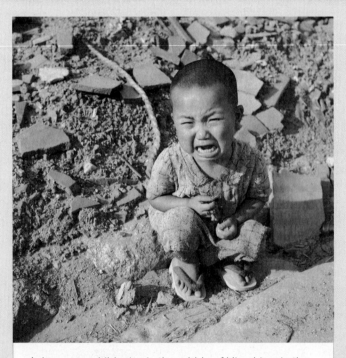

A Japanese child cries in the rubble of Hiroshima in the aftermath of the atomic bombing, expressing the profound sadness of war and its devastating weapons.
Bettmann/Getty Images

experience. After seeing "young children with sores and burns all over," Tolley, having become separated from his unit, encountered another young child. He and the boy communicated despite the language barrier between them. Tolley showed the child pictures of his wife and two daughters. The Japanese boy excitedly took Tolley home to meet his surviving family, his father and his pregnant sister. Tolley recalled,

> This little kid ran upstairs and brought his father down. A very nice Japanese gentleman. He could speak English. He bowed and said, "We would be honored if you would come upstairs and have some tea with us." I went upstairs in this strange Japanese house. I noticed on the mantel a picture of a young Japanese soldier. I asked him, "Is this your son?" He said, "That is my daughter's husband. We don't know if he's alive. We haven't heard." The minute he said that, it dawned on me that they suffered the same as we did. They lost sons and daughters and relatives, and they hurt too.

Before his chance meeting with this Japanese family, Tolley had felt nothing except contempt for the Japanese. He pointed out, "We were trained to kill them. They're our enemy. Look what they did in Pearl Harbor. They asked for it and now we're gonna give it to 'em. That's how I felt until I met this young boy and his family." But after coming face-to-face with his enemies, Tolley saw only their common humanity, their suffering, and their hurt. The lesson he learned was that "these people didn't want to fight us."

CHAPTER OVERVIEW

The civility that reemerged at the end of the war was barely evident during the war itself. The war began in 1931 when Japan invaded Manchuria, thereby ending the post–Great War peace, and it ended after the United States dropped atomic bombs on Hiroshima and Nagasaki. Between 1931 and 1945 the conflict expanded well beyond east Asia. By 1941 World War II was a truly global war. Hostilities spread from east Asia and the Pacific to Europe, north Africa, and the Atlantic, and people from large and small nations in North America, Asia, Europe, Africa, and Australia came into sustained contact for the duration of the war. Beyond its immense geographic scope, World War II exceeded even the Great War (1914–1918) in demonstrating the enormous sacrifices in lives and other resources required for achieving complete victory. At least sixty million people perished in the war, with civilian deaths outnumbering military casualties. In this total war, contacts with enemies, occupiers, and liberators affected populations around the world on a greater scale than any other conflict before or since. World War II also redefined gender roles and changed the shape of the colonial world, as women contributed to their nations' war efforts and as colonial peoples exploited the war's weakening of imperial nations.

Postwar recovery was complicated by the atomic and age and cold war that followed. Over time, the cold war illustrated how deep the rift between the United States of America and the Union of Soviet Socialist Republics (USSR) had grown and signaled a major realignment in international relations and the global balance of power. The cold war was a strategic struggle that, after World War II, involved the United States and its allies on the one hand and the USSR and its allied communist countries on the other. It was this clash between the forces of capitalism and communism, each armed with increasingly powerful nuclear weapons, that gave rise to a new set of global relationships, shaping the foreign policies, economic systems, and political institutions of nations throughout the world. The hostility between these new adversaries resulted in a divided world. First Europe, and Germany in particular, split into separate blocs and states. Then the cold war became global as the superpowers came into conflict in Korea and Cuba. Over the course of four decades, the cold war evolved from mutual hostility to peaceful coexistence and détente, finally coming to a close near the end of the twentieth century.

CHRONOLOGY	
1937	Invasion of China by Japan; The "Rape of Nanjing"
1939	Nazi-Soviet pact; Invasion of Poland by Germany
1940	Fall of France, Battle of Britain
1941	German invasion of the Soviet Union; Attack on Pearl Harbor by Japan
1942	U.S. victory at Midway
1943	Soviet victory at Stalingrad
1944	D-Day, Allied invasion at Normandy
1945	Capture of Berlin by Soviet forces; Atomic bombing of Hiroshima and Nagasaki; Establishment of United Nations
1947	Truman Doctrine
1948	Marshall Plan
1949	Division of Berlin and Germany; Establishment of the People's Republic of China
1950–1953	Korean War
1961	Construction of Berlin Wall
1962	Cuban missile crisis

ORIGINS OF WORLD WAR II

In 1941 two major alliances squared off against each other. Japan, Germany, and Italy, along with their conquered territories, formed the **Axis powers.** The **Allied powers** included France and its empire, Great Britain and its empire and Commonwealth allies (such as Canada, Australia, and New Zealand), the Soviet Union, China, and the United States and its allies in Latin America. The construction of these global alliances took place over the course of the 1930s and early 1940s.

Driven in part by a desire to revise the peace settlements that followed the Great War and affected by the economic distress of the worldwide depression, Japan, Italy, and Germany engaged in a campaign of territorial expansion that ultimately broke apart the structure of international cooperation that had kept the world from violence in the 1920s. These **revisionist powers,** so called because they revised, or overthrew, the terms of the post–Great War peace, confronted nations that were committed to the international system and to the avoidance of another world war. To expand their global influence, the revisionist nations remilitarized and conquered territories they believed were central to their territorial and resource needs. The Allies did not take action against the revisionist powers' early aggressive actions, but after they had been attacked, in the late 1930s and early 1940s, the Allies engaged the Axis powers in a total war.

Japan's War in China

The global conflict opened with Japan's attacks on China in the 1930s: the conquest of Manchuria between 1931 and 1932 was the first step in Japan's goal of expansion to meet critical strategic and resource needs. Within Japan a battle continued between supporters and opponents of the aggressive policies adopted in Manchuria, but during the course of the 1930s the militarist position dominated, and for the most part civilians lost control of the government and the military. In 1933, after the League of Nations condemned its actions in Manchuria, Japan withdrew from the league and followed an ultranationalist and promilitary policy.

Seeing territorial control as essential to its survival, Japan launched a full-scale invasion of China in 1937. A battle between Chinese and Japanese troops at the Marco Polo Bridge in Beijing in July 1937 was the opening move in Japan's undeclared war against China. Japanese troops took Beijing and then moved south toward Shanghai and Nanjing, the capital of China. Japanese naval and air forces bombed Shanghai, killing thousands of civilians, and secured it as a landing area for armies bound for Nanjing. By December 1937 Shanghai and Nanjing had fallen, and during the following six months Japanese forces won repeated victories.

The Rape of Nanjing China became the first nation to experience the horrors of World War II in the form of brutal warfare against civilians and repressive occupation. During

Japanese soldiers execute Chinese prisoners in 1937. In the Japanese invasion of China that year, four hundred thousand Chinese people were brutally murdered.
Hulton-Deutsch Collection/Corbis Historical/Getty Images

the invasion of China, Japanese forces used methods of warfare that led to mass death and suffering on a new, almost unimaginable level. Chinese civilians were among the first to feel the effects of aerial bombing of urban centers; the people of Shanghai died by the tens of thousands when Japanese bombers attacked the city to soften Chinese resistance. What became known as the **Rape of Nanjing** demonstrated the horror of the war as the residents of Nanjing became victims of Japanese troops inflamed by a sense of racial superiority. Over the course of two months, Japanese soldiers raped seven thousand women, murdered hundreds of thousands of unarmed soldiers and civilians, and burned one-third of the homes in Nanjing. Four hundred thousand Chinese lost their lives as Japanese soldiers used them for bayonet practice and machine-gunned them into open pits.

Chinese Resistance Despite Japanese military successes and the subsequent Japanese occupation of Chinese territory, Chinese resistance persisted throughout the war. Japanese aggression aroused feelings of nationalism among the Chinese that continued to grow as the war wore on. By September 1937 nationalists and communists, who had spent the past decade fighting one another, put aside their differences to fight the

Japanese soldiers in 1938 engaged in strenuous physical education in order to keep fit for the challenges of war.
Bettmann/Getty Images

Japanese together. This alliance was known as the second "united front" (the first lasted from 1923 to 1927; see chapter 35), and it resulted in a combined army of 1.7 million soldiers. Although Chinese forces were not able to defeat the Japanese, who retained naval and air superiority, by 1941 the Japanese had to engage half of their land army, 750,000 soldiers, in order to maintain control in China. This was crucial because it meant these troops could not be deployed elsewhere when the Japanese army needed them.

Throughout the war, the second united front between nationalists and communists was fragile. Although neither side was willing to risk open civil war, the two groups engaged in numerous military clashes as their forces competed for both control of enemy territory and political control within China. Those clashes rendered Chinese resistance less effective, for while both sides continued the war against Japan, each understood that the alliance was temporary and thus ultimately fought for its own advantage. The nationalists suffered major casualties in their battles with Japanese forces, but they kept the Guomindang government alive by moving far inland to Chongqing. Meanwhile, the communists carried on guerrilla operations against the Japanese invaders. Lacking air force and artillery, communist guerrillas staged hit-and-run operations from their mountain bases, sabotaged bridges and railroads, and harassed Japanese troops. While the guerrillas did not defeat the Japanese, they captured the loyalty of many Chinese peasants through their resistance to the Japanese and their moderate policies of land reform in territories they controlled.

The Japanese invasion of China met with intense international opposition, but other world powers—distracted by depression and military aggression in Europe—could offer little in the way of an effective response to Japanese actions. The government of Japan aligned itself with the other revisionist nations, Germany and Italy, by signing the Tripartite Pact, a ten-year military and economic pact, in September 1940. Japan also cleared the way for further empire building in Asia and the Pacific basin by concluding a neutrality pact with the Soviet Union in April 1941, thereby precluding hostilities on any other front, especially in Manchuria. Japan did not face determined opposition to its expansion until December 1941, when conflict with the United States created a much broader field of action for Japan and its growing empire.

Italian and German Aggression

Italy's expansionism helped destabilize the post-Great War peace and spread World War II to the European continent. Italians suffered tremendously in World War I. Six hundred thousand Italian soldiers died, and the national economy never recovered sufficiently for Italy to function as an equal to other European military and economic powers. Many Italians expected far greater recompense and respect than they received at the conclusion of the Great War. Rather than being treated as a real partner in victory by Britain and France, Italy found itself shut out of the divisions of the territorial spoils of war.

Italy **Benito Mussolini** (1883-1945) promised to bring glory to Italy through the acquisition of territories that it had been denied after the Great War. Italy's conquest of Ethiopia in 1935 and 1936, when added to the previously annexed Libya, created an overseas empire. Italy also intervened in the **Spanish Civil War** (1936-1939) on the side of General Francisco Franco (1892-1975), whose militarists overthrew the republican government. Mussolini also annexed Albania in 1939 in preparation for further expansion into the Balkans. The invasion and conquest of Ethiopia in particular infuriated other nations, but, as with Japan's invasion of Manchuria, the League of Nations was not able to offer effective opposition.

Outsiders—from state leaders to ordinary people—were horrified by Italy's conquest of Ethiopia both because they feared another war and because of Italy's excessive use of force during the invasion. Mussolini sent an army of 250,000 soldiers armed with tanks, poison gas, artillery, and aircraft to conquer the Ethiopians, who were entirely unprepared for the assault. The mechanized troops mowed them down. Italy lost 2,000 soldiers while Ethiopia lost 275,000. Although the Italian government did not commit to an alliance when it invaded Ethiopia in 1935, by 1938 the Italians had made it clear that they were firmly on the side of the Axis.

Emperor Haile Selassie (1892–1975) of Ethiopia speaking at the League of Nations in 1936. Selassie strongly protested against the Italian invasion of his nation in 1935, and expressed his deep disappointment in the League for its inaction in bringing Italy to account.
Scherl/Süeddeutsche Zeitung Photo/Alamy Stock Photo

Germany Japan and Italy were the first nations to challenge the post–World War I settlements through territorial conquest, but it was Germany that systematically undid the Treaty of Versailles and the fragile peace of the interwar years. Most Germans and their political leaders were unwilling to accept defeat and deeply resented the harsh terms imposed on their nation in 1919. In addition, even the governments of other European nations came to recognize the extreme nature of the Versailles treaty's terms, which in turn caused them to be more tolerant of the revisionist actions of **Adolf Hitler** (1889–1945) and his government. Hitler came to power in 1933, riding a wave of public discontent with Germany's postwar position of powerlessness and the suffering caused by the Great Depression. Hitler referred to the signing of the 1918 armistice as the "November crime" and blamed it on those he viewed as Germany's internal enemies: Jews, communists, and liberals of all sorts. Neighboring European states—Poland, France, Czechoslovakia, Yugoslavia, Hungary, and Austria—also shared in the blame. Hitler's scheme for ridding Germany of its enemies and reasserting its power was remilitarization—which was legally denied to Germany under the Versailles treaty. Germany's dictator abandoned the peaceful efforts of his predecessors to ease the provisions of the treaty and proceeded unilaterally to destroy it step by step. Hitler's aggressive foreign

policy helped relieve the German public's feeling of war shame and depression trauma. After withdrawing Germany from the League of Nations in 1933, his government carried out an ambitious plan to strengthen the German armed forces. Hitler reinstated universal military service in 1935, and in the following year his troops entered the previously demilitarized Rhineland that bordered France. Germany joined with Italy in the Spanish Civil War, during which Hitler's troops, especially the air force, honed their skills. In 1938 Hitler began the campaign of expansion that ultimately led to the outbreak of World War II in Europe.

Hitler began with the forced annexation of Austria (known as the *Anschluss*) in March 1938. He justified this annexation as an attempt to unite all Germans into a single homeland. Europe's major powers, France and Britain, did not respond by taking action against Germany, thus enhancing Hitler's reputation in the German military. Soon thereafter, using the same rationale of uniting Germans, the Nazis attempted to gain control of the **Sudetenland,** the western portion of Czechoslovakia. This region was inhabited largely by ethnic Germans, whom Hitler conveniently regarded as persecuted minorities. Although the Czech government was willing to make concessions to the Sudeten Germans, Hitler in September 1938 demanded the immediate cession of the Sudetenland to the German Reich. Against the desires of the Czechoslovak government, the leaders of France and Britain accommodated Hitler and allowed Germany to annex the Sudetenland.

Anschluss (AHN-shloos)
Sudetenland (soo-DEYT-n-land)

Neither the French nor the British were willing to risk a military confrontation with Germany—and thus another general European war—to defend Czechoslovakian territory.

Peace for Our Time In September 1938, European politicians anxious to avoid war held a conference in Munich where they consolidated the policy that came to be known throughout the 1930s as **appeasement.** The **Munich Conference** was attended by representatives of Italy, France, Great Britain, and Germany and revealed how most nations outside the revisionist sphere had decided to deal with territorial expansion by aggressive nations, especially Germany. In conceding demands to Hitler, or "appeasing" him, the British and French governments extracted a promise that Hitler would not expand German territorial aims beyond the Sudetenland. Their goal was to keep peace in Europe, even if it meant making major concessions. Britain's prime minister, Neville Chamberlain (1869-1940), arrived home from Munich to announce that the meeting had achieved "peace for our time." Unprepared for war and distressed by the depression, nations sympathetic to Britain and France also embraced peace as an admirable goal in the face of aggression by the revisionist nations.

Hitler, however, quickly broke the promises he made in the Munich agreement, and in March 1939 German troops occupied and annexed most of Czechoslovakia. But when Hitler appeared ready to invade Poland just a short time later, the European nations that had supported appeasement realized that the policy had failed. Britain and France therefore guaranteed the security of Poland, which meant that they would declare war against Germany if it decided to invade. Meanwhile, in August 1939 Hitler and the Soviet Union's **Joseph Stalin (1879-1953)** concluded the **German-Soviet Non-Aggression Pact,** an agreement that shocked and outraged the world. By the terms of the pact, the two nations agreed not to attack each other, and they promised neutrality in the event that either of them went to war with a third party. Additionally, a secret protocol divided eastern Europe into German and Soviet spheres of influence. The protocol provided for German control over western Poland while granting the Soviet Union a free hand in eastern Poland, eastern Romania, Finland, Estonia, Latvia, and Lithuania. Hitler was now ready to conquer Europe.

TOTAL WAR: THE WORLD UNDER FIRE

Two months after the United States became embroiled in World War II, President Franklin Roosevelt (1882-1945) delivered one of his famous radio broadcasts, known as fireside chats. In it he explained the nature of the war: "This war is a new kind of war," he said. "It is warfare in terms of every continent, every island, every sea, every air lane." There was little exaggeration in FDR's analysis. Before World War II was over, almost every nation and colonial territory in the world had participated in it. Battles raged across the vast Pacific and Atlantic oceans, across Europe and northern Africa, and throughout much of Asia. Virtually every weapon known to humanity was thrown into

the war. Even more than the Great War, this was a conflict in which entire societies engaged in warfare and mobilized every available material and human resource.

Japan and China had already been at war for over eight years when, between 1939 and 1941, nations and territories inside and outside Europe were drawn into the conflict. They included the French and British colonies in Africa and India as well as the British Dominion allies of Canada, Australia, and New Zealand. Germany's stunning military successes in 1939 and 1940 focused attention on Europe, but after the Soviet Union and the United States entered the war in 1941, the conflict took on global proportions.

Blitzkrieg: Germany Conquers Europe

During World War II it became common for aggressor nations to avoid overt declarations of war. Instead, the new armed forces relied on surprise, stealth, and swiftness for their conquests. Germany demonstrated the advantages of that strategy in Poland. German forces, banking on their air force's ability to soften resistance on the ground and on their *Panzer* ("armored") columns' unmatched mobility and speed, moved into Poland unannounced on 1 September 1939. Within a month they subdued its western expanses while the Soviets

German dive-bombers like this one dominated the early air war in World War II and played a significant role in the German technique known as Blitzkrieg.
Bettmann/Getty Images

took the eastern sections in accordance with the Nazi-Soviet pact. The Germans stunned the world, especially Britain and France, with their *Blitzkrieg* ("lightning war") and sudden victory. The term *Blitzkrieg* was coined by journalists and is still used today, although it was never an official doctrine or concept of the German armed forces.

Honoring their commitment to guarantee the security of Poland, Britain and France declared war on Germany on September 3. While they gathered their forces to defend Europe, however, the war in the Atlantic began immediately. The battle of the Atlantic was the longest-running battle of the war, lasting from September 1939 through April 1945. During that time, German submarines (*Unterseeboote*) attempted to cut off imports of food and war material to Britain, while the British navy formed convoys of ships to protect against submarine attack. In 1942 British intelligence cracked the secret German code used by submarines, which greatly aided the Allies. Despite having the codes, however, only 10 percent of the intercepted messages were decrypted in time to prevent attacks on British ships. The battle of the Atlantic thus remained an important and dangerous theater for the duration of the war.

The Fall of France In April 1940 the Germans occupied Denmark and Norway, then launched a full-scale attack on western Europe. By seizing control of Norway, the Germans gained control of the eastern North Sea and prevented Britain's navy from implementing a blockade. The German offensive against Belgium, France, and the Netherlands began in May, and again the Allies were overwhelmed by Blitzkrieg tactics. Belgium and the Netherlands fell in May, while the French signed an armistice in June. The fall of France convinced Italy's Benito Mussolini that the Germans were winning the war, and it was time to enter the conflict and reap any potential benefits his partnership with the Germans might offer.

Before the battle of France, Hitler had boasted to his staff, "Gentlemen, you are about to witness the most famous victory in history!" Given France's rapid fall, Hitler was not far wrong. Field Marshal Erwin Rommel put it more colorfully: "The war has become practically a lightning Tour de France!" In a moment of exquisite triumph, Hitler had the French sign their armistice in the very railroad car in which the Germans had signed the armistice in 1918. Trying to rescue some Allied troops before the fall of France, the British engineered a retreat at the coastal town of Dunkirk, but it could not hide the bleak failure of the Allied troops in their mission to defend Europe from Germany. Britain now stood alone against the German forces.

The Battle of Britain The Germans next turned their attention to defeating Britain. In July 1940 they launched the **Battle of Britain,** led by the German air force, the *Luftwaffe.* The goal was to defeat Britain almost solely through air attacks. "The Blitz," as the British called this air war, rained

---

Luftwaffe (LOOFT-vaff-uh)

Lebensraum (LAY-behnz-rahwm)

Adolf Hitler proudly walks through conquered Paris in 1940, with the Eiffel Tower as a backdrop.
Harwood/Keystone/Hulton Archive/Getty Images

bombs on heavily populated metropolitan areas, especially London, and killed more than forty thousand British civilians. The Royal Air Force staved off defeat, however, and by the end of October 1940 Hitler abandoned plans to invade Britain. But Hitler's successes continued elsewhere. By the summer of 1941, his conquests included the Balkans, and the battlefront extended to north Africa, where the British fought both the Italians and the Germans. The swastika-bedecked Nazi flag now waved from the streets of Paris to the Acropolis in Athens, and Hitler had succeeded beyond his dreams in his quest to reverse the outcome of World War I.

The German Invasion of the Soviet Union

Flush with victory in the spring of 1941, Hitler next turned his attention to the Soviet Union. Notwithstanding his nonaggression pact with the Soviet Union, Hitler had long coveted Soviet territory, where Jews, Slavs, and Bolsheviks could be expelled or exterminated to create more *Lebensraum* ("living space") for resettled Germans. Believing firmly in the bankruptcy of the Soviet system, Hitler said of **Operation Barbarossa,** the code name for the June invasion of the Soviet Union, "You only have to kick in the door, and the whole rotten structure will come crashing down."

Operation Barbarossa

On June 22, 1941, Adolf Hitler ordered his armed forces to invade the Soviet Union. To do so, the German military assembled the largest and most powerful invasion force in history, attacking with 3.6 million soldiers, thirty-seven hundred tanks, and twenty-five hundred planes. Military contingents from Italy, Romania, Hungary, Slovakia, Croatia, and Finland—totaling some thirty divisions—augmented the German invasion force. The invasion, along a front of 3,000 kilometers (1,900 miles), took Stalin by surprise and caught the Red Army off guard. By December 1941 the Germans had captured the Russian heartland, Leningrad had come under siege, and German troops had reached the gates of Moscow. Germany seemed assured of victory.

But the German Blitzkrieg tactics that had earlier proved so effective in Poland and western Europe failed the Germans in the vast expanses of Russia. Hitler and his military leaders underestimated Soviet personnel reserves and industrial capacity. Within a matter of weeks, the 150 German divisions faced 360 divisions of the Red Army. Also, in the early stages of the invasion Stalin ordered Soviet industry to relocate to areas away from the front. About 80 percent of firms manufacturing war matériel moved to the Ural Mountains between August and October 1941. As a result, the capacity of Soviet industry outstripped that of German industry. The Soviets also received crucial equipment from their allies, notably trucks from the United States. By the time the German forces reached the outskirts of Moscow, fierce Soviet resistance had produced eight hundred thousand German casualties.

The arrival of winter—the most severe in decades—helped Soviet military efforts and prevented the Germans from capturing Moscow. The Germans had been so sure of a quick victory that they did not bother to supply their troops with winter clothing and boots. One hundred thousand German soldiers suffered frostbite, and two thousand of them underwent amputation. The Red Army, in contrast, prepared for winter and found further comfort as the United States manufactured thirteen million pairs of felt-lined winter boots. By early December, Soviet counterattacks along the entire front had halted German advances.

German forces regrouped and inflicted heavy losses on the Red Army during the spring of 1942. The Germans briefly regained the military initiative, and by June German armies raced toward the oil fields of the Caucasus and the city of **Stalingrad.** As the Germans came on Stalingrad in September, Soviet fortunes of war reached their nadir. At this point the Soviets dug in. "Not a step back," Stalin ordered, and he called on his troops to fight a "patriotic" war for Mother Russia. Behind those exhortations lay a desperate attempt to stall the Germans with a bloody street-by-street defense of Stalingrad until the Red Army could regroup for a counterattack.

Russian prisoners captured by the Germans after the battle of Kiev in September 1941. The German military engaged in murderous policies toward Soviet prisoners of war, killing 3.3 million men (out of a total of 5.7 million) through summary execution, exposure, and starvation.
Heinrich Hoffmann/ Mondadori/Getty Images

Battles in Asia and the Pacific

The United States, though officially neutral, inched toward greater involvement in the war between 1939 and 1941. In 1939 it instituted a cash-and-carry policy of supplying the British, in which the British paid cash and carried the materials across the Atlantic on their ships. More significant was the lend-lease program initiated in 1941, in which the United States "lent" destroyers and other war goods to the British in return for the lease of naval bases. The program later extended such aid to the Soviets, the Chinese, and many others.

Pearl Harbor German victories over the Dutch and the French in 1940 and Great Britain's precarious military position in Europe and in Asia encouraged the Japanese to project their influence into southeast Asia. Particularly attractive were the Dutch East Indies (now Indonesia) and British-controlled Malaya, regions rich in raw materials such as tin, rubber, and petroleum. In September 1940, moving with the blessings of the German-backed Vichy government in France, Japanese forces began to occupy French Indochina (now Vietnam, Laos, and Cambodia). The government of the United States responded to that situation by freezing Japanese assets in the United States and by imposing a complete embargo on oil. Great Britain, the British Commonwealth of Nations, and the colonial government of the Dutch East Indies supported the U.S. oil embargo.

Economic pressure, however, did not persuade the Japanese to comply with U.S. demands, which included the renunciation of the Tripartite Pact with Germany and Italy and the withdrawal of Japanese forces from China and southeast Asia. To Japanese militarists, given the equally unappetizing alternatives of giving in to U.S. demands or engaging the United States in war, war seemed the lesser of two evils. In October 1941, defense minister general Tojo Hideki (1884–1948) assumed the office of prime minister, and he and his cabinet set in motion plans for war against Great Britain and the United States.

The Japanese hoped to quickly destroy American naval capacity in the Pacific with an attack at **Pearl Harbor.** The attack would then clear the way for the conquest of southeast Asia and the creation of a defensive Japanese perimeter that would prevent the Allies' from striking at Japan's homeland. On December 7, 1941, Japanese pilots took off from six aircraft carriers to attack Hawai`i. More than 350 Japanese bombers, fighters, and torpedo planes struck in two waves, sinking or disabling eighteen ships and destroying more than two hundred aircraft. Except for the U.S. aircraft carriers, which were out of the harbor at the time, American naval power in the Pacific was devastated. The next day, on December 8, the United States and Great Britain declared war on Japan.

On December 11, 1941, though not compelled to do so by treaty, Hitler and Mussolini declared war on the United States. That move provided the United States with the only reason

Flames consumed U.S. battleships in Pearl Harbor after the Japanese attack on 7 December 1941.
Bettmann/Getty Images

it needed to declare war on Germany and Italy. The United States, Great Britain, and the Soviet Union came together in a coalition that linked two vast and interconnected theaters of war, the European and Asian-Pacific theaters, and ensured the defeat of Germany and Japan. Adolf Hitler's gleeful reaction to the outbreak of war between Japan and the United States proved mistaken: "Now it is impossible for us to lose the war: We now have an ally who has never been vanquished in three thousand years." More accurate was **Winston Churchill** (1874–1965), prime minister of Britain, who expressed a vast sense of relief and a more accurate assessment of the situation when he said, "So we had won after all!"

Japanese Victories After Pearl Harbor the Japanese swept on to one victory after another. The Japanese coordinated their strike against Pearl Harbor with simultaneous attacks against the Philippines, Guam, Wake Island, Midway Island, Hong Kong, Thailand, and British Malaya. For the next year the Japanese military maintained the initiative in southeast Asia and the Pacific, capturing Borneo, Burma, the Dutch East Indies, and several Aleutian Islands off Alaska. Australia and New Zealand were now in striking distance. The Japanese navy emerged almost unscathed from these campaigns. The humiliating surrender of British-held Singapore in February 1942 dealt a blow to British prestige and shattered any myths of European military invincibility.

Singapore was a symbol of European power in Asia. The slogan under which Japan pursued expansion in Asia was "Asia for Asians," implying that the Japanese would lead Asian peoples to independence from the despised European imperialists and the international order they dominated. In this struggle for Asian independence, Japan required the region's resources and therefore sought to build what they called a **Greater East Asia Co-Prosperity Sphere.** The appeal to Asian independence at first struck a responsive chord among some anticolonial activists such as Sukarno in the Dutch East Indies, but conquest and brutal occupation made it soon obvious to most Asians that the real agenda was "Asia for the Japanese." Proponents of the Greater East Asia Co-Prosperity Sphere advocated Japan's expansion in Asia and the Pacific while cloaking their territorial and economic designs with the idealism of Asian nationalism.

Defeat of the Axis Powers

The entry of the Soviet Union and the United States into the war in 1941 was decisive because personnel reserves and industrial capacity were the keys to the Allied victories in the European and Asia-Pacific theaters. Despite the brutal exploitation of conquered territories, neither German nor Japanese war production matched that of the Allies, who outproduced their enemies. The U.S. automotive industry alone,

After the Pearl Harbor attack, Americans expressed great hostility toward the Japanese nationals and Japanese Americans living in the United States, primarily on the west coast. In 1942 President Franklin Roosevelt authorized the forcible removal of approximately 120,000 Japanese and Japanese Americans to relocation or internment camps. This photograph shows interned Japanese people behind barbed wire at Santa Anita camp in California.
Everett Collection Historical/ Alamy Stock Photo

for instance, produced more than four million armored, combat, and supply vehicles of all kinds during the war. In the Atlantic, although German submarines sank a total of 2,452 Allied merchant ships and 175 Allied warships over the course of six years, after 1942 U.S. naval shipyards simply built more "Liberty Ships" than the Germans could sink. By the end of 1943, sonar, aircraft patrols, and escort aircraft from carriers eliminated the U-boat as a strategic threat.

Allied Victory in Europe By 1943, German forces in Russia lost momentum and faced bleak prospects as the Soviets retook territory. Moscow never fell, and the battle for Stalingrad, which ended in February 1943, marked the first large-scale

victory for Soviet forces. Desperate German counteroffensives failed repeatedly, and the Red Army, drawing on enormous personnel and material reserves, pushed the German invaders out of Russian territory. By 1944 the Soviets had advanced into Romania, Hungary, and Poland, reaching the suburbs of Berlin in April 1945. At that point, the Soviets had inflicted more than six million casualties on the German enemy—twice the number of the original German invasion force. The Red Army had broken the back of the German war machine.

With the eastern front disintegrating under the Soviet onslaught, British and U.S. forces attacked the Germans from north Africa and then through Italy. In August 1944 the Allies forced Italy to withdraw from the Axis and to join them. In the

MAP 36.1   High tide of Axis expansion in Europe and north Africa, 1942–1943.

Observe the number of nations occupied by or allied with the Axis powers.

Given Axis dominance in Europe, what factors finally allowed the Allies to turn the tide of war in their favor?

meantime, the Germans also prepared for an Allied offensive in the west, where the British and U.S. forces opened a front in France. On **D-Day,** June 6, 1944, British and U.S. troops landed on the French coast of Normandy. Although the fighting was deadly for all sides, the Germans were overwhelmed. With the two fronts collapsing around them and round-the-clock strategic bombing by the United States and Britain leveling German cities, German resistance faded. Since early 1943, Britain's Royal Air Force had committed itself to area bombing in which city centers became the targets of nighttime raids. U.S. planes attacked industrial targets in daytime. The British firebombing raid on Dresden in February 1945 was particularly devastating, as one hundred thirty-five thousand German men, women, and children died in the firestorm. A brutal

street-by-street battle in Berlin between Germans and Russians, along with a sweep through western Germany by British and U.S. troops, forced Germany's unconditional surrender on May 8, 1945. A week earlier, on April 30, as fighting flared right outside his Berlin bunker, Hitler committed suicide along with his mistress Eva Braun, as did many of his Nazi compatriots. He therefore did not live to see the Soviet red flag flying over the Berlin *Reichstag,* Germany's parliament building.

Turning the Tide in the Pacific The turning point in the Pacific war came in a naval engagement near the Midway Islands on June 4, 1942. The United States prevailed there partly because U.S. aircraft carriers had survived the attack on Pearl Harbor. Although the United States had few carriers,

MAP 36.2 World War II in Asia and the Pacific.

Compare the geographic conditions of the Asian-Pacific theater with those of the European theater.

What kinds of resources were necessary to win in the Asian-Pacific theater as opposed to the European theater?

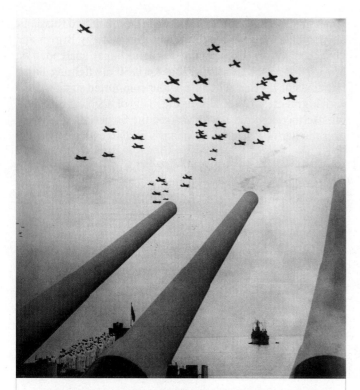

A photograph titled *Planes over Tokyo Bay,* taken from the U.S.S. *Missouri,* visually captured a sense of U.S. power and victory on V-J Day (Victory over Japan Day), 1945.

Hulton Deutsch/Corbis Historical/Getty Images

it did have a secret weapon: a code-breaking operation known as *Magic,* which enabled a cryptographer monitoring Japanese radio frequencies to discover the plan to attack Midway. On the morning of 4 June, thirty-six carrier-launched dive-bombers attacked the Japanese fleet, sinking three Japanese carriers in one five-minute strike and a fourth one later in the day. This victory changed the character of the war in the Pacific. Although there was no immediate shift in Japanese fortunes, the Allies took the offensive. They adopted an island-hopping strategy, capturing islands from which they could make direct air assaults on Japan. Deadly fighting characterized these battles in which the United States and its allies gradually retook islands in the Marianas and the Philippines and then, early in 1945, moved toward areas more threatening to Japan: the islands of Iwo Jima and Okinawa.

Iwo Jima and Okinawa The fighting on **Iwo Jima** and **Okinawa** was savage. Innovative U.S. amphibious tactics were matched by the sacrifice of Japanese soldiers and pilots. On Okinawa the Japanese introduced the *kamikaze*—pilots who "volunteered" to fly planes with just enough fuel to reach an Allied ship and dive-bomb into it. In the two-month battle, the Japanese flew nineteen hundred kamikaze missions, sinking dozens of ships and killing more than five thousand U.S.

soldiers. The kamikaze, and the defense mounted by Japanese forces and the 110,000 Okinawan civilians who died refusing to surrender, convinced many people in the United States that the Japanese would never willingly surrender.

Japanese Surrender The fall of Saipan in July 1944 and the subsequent conquest of Iwo Jima and Okinawa brought the Japanese homeland within easy reach of U.S. strategic bombers. Because high-altitude strikes in daylight failed to do much damage to industrial sites, military planners changed tactics. The release of napalm firebombs during low-altitude missions at night met with devastating success. The firebombing of Tokyo in March 1945 destroyed 25 percent of the city's buildings, killed approximately one hundred thousand people, and made more than a million people homeless. The final blows came on August 6 and 9, 1945, when the United States used a revolutionary new weapon, the atomic bomb, against the cities of **Hiroshima** and **Nagasaki.** The atomic bombs either instantaneously vaporized or slowly killed by radiation poisoning upward of two hundred thousand people.

The Soviet Union declared war on Japan on 8 August 1945, and this new threat, combined with the devastation caused by the bombs, persuaded Emperor Hirohito (1901–1989) to surrender unconditionally. The Japanese surrendered on 15 August, and the war was officially over on 2 September 1945. When Victor Tolley—who we met in the introduction to this chapter—sipped his conciliatory cup of tea with a Nagasaki family, the images of ashen Hiroshima and firebombed Tokyo lingered as reminders of how World War II brought the war directly home to millions of civilians.

LIFE DURING WARTIME

The widespread bombing of civilian populations during World War II, from its beginning in China to its end in Hiroshima and Nagasaki, meant that there was no safe home front during the war. The arrival of often brutal occupation forces in the wake of Japanese and German conquests in Asia and Europe reinforced this reality. Strategic bombing slaughtered men, women, and children around the world, and occupation troops forced civilians to labor and die in work and extermination camps. In this total war, civilian death tolls far exceeded military casualties. Yet alongside such terrible brutality remains the record of human endurance, personified in the contributions of resistance groups battling occupying forces, in the determination of mobilized civilians, and in the survivors of bombings or concentration camps.

Occupation, Collaboration, and Resistance

Axis bombardments and invasion were followed by occupation, but the administration imposed on conquered territories by Japanese and German forces varied in character. In territories such as **Manchukuo,** Japanese-controlled China, Burma, and the Philippines, Japanese authorities installed puppet governments that served as agents of Japanese rule. Thailand

kamikaze (KAH-mih-kah-zee)

The writing on the board displayed by German security forces in Minsk, Belarus, reads, "We are partisans who shot at German soldiers." The Germans murdered some 700,000 civilians, mostly Belarusians and Poles, in so-called antipartisan reprisals. Women and children were included in the "reprisal" because they were considered an encumbrance. Sueddeutsche Zeitung Photo/Alamy Stock Photo

remained an independent state after it aligned itself with Japan, for which it was rewarded with grants of territory from bordering Laos and Burma. Other conquered territories either were considered too unstable or unreliable for self-rule or were deemed strategically too important to be left alone. Thus territories such as Indochina (Laos, Cambodia, and Vietnam), Malaya, the Dutch East Indies, Hong Kong, Singapore, Borneo, and New Guinea came under direct military control.

In Europe, Hitler's racist ideology played a large role in determining how occupied territories were administered. As a rule, Hitler intended that most areas of western and northern Europe—populated by people he believed to be "racially valuable"—would become part of a Greater Germanic Empire. Accordingly, Denmark retained its elected government and monarchy under German supervision. In Norway and Holland, whose governments had gone into exile, the Germans left the civilian administration intact. Though northern France and the Atlantic coast came under military rule, the **Vichy** government remained the civilian authority in the unoccupied southeastern part of the country. Named for its locale in central France, the Vichy government provided a prominent place for those French willing to collaborate with German rule. The Germans had varying levels of involvement in eastern European and Balkan countries, but most conquered territories came under direct military rule as a prelude to brutal harsh occupation, economic exploitation, and German settlement.

Exploitation Japanese and German authorities administered their respective empires for economic gain and proceeded to exploit the resources of the lands under their control for their own benefit, regardless of the consequences for conquered peoples. The occupiers pillaged all forms of economic wealth that could fuel the German and Japanese war machines. The most notorious form of economic exploitation involved the use of slave labor. As the demands of total war stimulated an insatiable appetite for workers, Japanese and German occupation authorities used prisoners of war (POWs) and local populations to help meet labor shortages. By August 1944, more than seven million foreign workers labored inside Germany's Third Reich. And in China alone, the Japanese military mobilized more than ten million civilians and prisoners of war for forced labor. These enslaved laborers worked under horrific conditions and received little in the way of sustenance. Reaction to Japanese and German occupation varied from willing collaboration and acquiescence to open resistance.

Atrocities The treatment of POWs by German and Japanese authorities spoke to the horrors of the war as well. The death rate among soldiers in Japanese captivity averaged almost 30 percent, although it was even higher among Chinese POWs. The racial ideologies of Hitler's regime were reflected in the treatment meted out to Soviet prisoners of war in particular. By February 1942, 2 million out of the 3.3 million Soviet soldiers in German custody had died from starvation, exposure, disease, or outright murder.

Vichy (vee-shee)

Beyond the callous mistreatment of POWs, both German and Japanese authorities engaged in painful and often deadly medical experiments on thousands of unwilling subjects. In China, special Japanese military units, including the most infamous Unit 731, conducted cruel experiments on civilians and POWs. Victims, for example, became the subject of vivisection (defined as experimental surgery conducted on a living organism) or amputation without anesthesia. Tens of thousands of Chinese became victims of germ warfare experiments after they were deliberately infected with bubonic plague, cholera, anthrax, and other diseases. German physicians carried out similarly unethical medical experiments in concentration camps. Experimentation ranged from bone-grafting surgeries without anesthesia to exposing victims to phosgene and mustard gas in order to test possible antidotes. German doctors also directed painful experiments to determine how different "races" withstood various contagious diseases.

Collaboration The majority of people resented occupation forces but tried to go on with life as much as possible. That response was especially true in many parts of Japanese-occupied lands in Asia, where local populations found little to resent in the change from one colonial administration to another. In Asia and Europe, moreover, local notables often joined the governments sponsored by the conquerors because collaboration offered them the means to gain power. Businesspeople and companies often collaborated because they prospered financially from foreign rule. Still other people became collaborators and assisted occupation authorities by turning in friends and neighbors to get revenge for past grievances. In western Europe, anticommunism motivated Belgians, French, Danish, Dutch, and Norwegians to join units of Hitler's elite military formations, the Waffen SS, creating in the process a multinational army tens of thousands strong. In violation of its own racial policies, the SS also accepted volunteers from the Balkans, eastern Europe, and the Caucasus. In China several Guomindang generals went over to the Japanese, and local landowners and merchants in some regions of China set up substantial trade networks between the occupiers and the occupied.

Resistance Occupation and exploitation created an environment for resistance that took various forms. The most dramatic forms of resistance were campaigns of sabotage, armed assaults on occupation forces, and assassinations. Resistance fighters as diverse as Filipino guerrillas and Soviet partisans harassed and disrupted the military and economic activities of the occupiers by blowing up ammunition dumps, destroying communication and transportation facilities, and sabotaging industrial plants. Less conspicuously, other resisters gathered intelligence, hid and protected refugees, or passed on clandestine newspapers. Resistance also comprised simple acts of defiance such as scribbling anti-German graffiti or walking out of bars and restaurants when Japanese soldiers entered. In the Netherlands, people associated the royal House of Orange

with national independence and defiantly saluted traffic lights when they turned orange.

German and Japanese citizens faced different decisions about resistance than conquered peoples did. For them, any form of noncompliance constituted an act of treason that might assist the enemy and lead to defeat. Moreover, many institutions that might have formed the core of resistance in Japan and Germany, such as political parties, labor unions, or churches, were weak or had been destroyed. As a result, there was little or no overt opposition to the state and its policies in Japan, and in Germany resistance remained generally sparse and ineffective. The most spectacular act of resistance against the Nazi regime came from a group of officers and civilians who tried to kill Adolf Hitler on July 20, 1944. The plot failed when their bomb explosion killed several bystanders but inflicted only minor injuries on Hitler.

Attempts to eradicate resistance movements often fanned the flames of rebellion because of the indiscriminate reprisals against civilians. Despite the deadly retaliation meted out to people who resisted occupation, widespread resistance movements grew throughout the war. Life in resistance movements was tenuous at best and entailed great hardship—changing identities, hiding out, and risking capture and death. Nevertheless, the resisters kept alive their nations' hopes for liberation.

The Holocaust

By the end of World War II, the Nazi regime and its accomplices had murdered millions of Jews, Slavs, Roma (or Gypsies),

This photograph, taken in 2003, shows a portion of the perimeter fence at Auschwitz concentration camp. The sign in the foreground reads: "Caution. High Voltage. Danger to Life." The Auschwitz complex established in German-occupied Poland was essentially two camps in one, a labor camp and an extermination camp that took the lives of some one million Jews.
Courtesy of Herbert F. Ziegler

How the Past Shapes the Future

The Destructive Potential of Industrial Technologies

World War I had demonstrated that states were willing to harness industrial technologies on a massive scale for the purpose of destroying their enemies. Many observers were horrified by this, as we know, and as a result large numbers of people around the world advocated peace as a global priority during the interwar years. But during World War II, states nevertheless unleashed even more destructive industrial technologies on their enemies than they had in World War I—and now, they specifically targeted civilian populations in addition to enemy combatants. One particularly chilling example of this was Hitler's "final solution," which sought to exterminate all the Jewish people using industrial technologies and methods. Using railways, poison gas, and a factory-like system that maximized the numbers of people who could be moved, murdered, and disposed of, the German system industrialized genocide. Consider the extent to which the use of industrial technologies during World War I might have impressed the young Adolf Hitler, who himself had fought in the war.

and others targeted as undesirables. Jews were the primary target of Hitler's racially motivated genocidal policies. These policies resulted in what has come to be known as the **Holocaust,** or the near elimination of European Jews by Germany, which was a human disaster on an unprecedented scale.

The murder of European Jews was preceded by a long history of vilification and persecution. For centuries Jewish communities had been singled out by Christian society as a "problem," and by the time the Nazi regime assumed power in 1933, anti-Semitism had contributed significantly to widespread tolerance for anti-Jewish measures. Marked as outsiders, Jews found few defenders in their societies. Nazi determination to destroy the Jewish population in Europe and Europeans' passive acceptance of anti-Semitism laid the groundwork for genocide.

MAP 36.3   The Holocaust in Europe, 1933–1945.

Observe the geographic locations of the concentration and extermination camps.

Why were there more concentration camps in Germany and more extermination camps in Poland?

SOURCES FROM THE PAST

"We Will Never Speak about It in Public"

On 4 October 1943, Heinrich Himmler, leader of the SS and chief of the German police, gave a three-hour speech to an assembly of SS generals in the city of Posen (Poznan), in what is now Poland. In the following excerpt, Himmler justified Nazi anti-Jewish policies that culminated in mass murder. The speech, recorded on tape and in handwritten notes, was entered into evidence at the Nuremberg war crimes trials in 1945.

I also want to speak to you here, in complete frankness, of a really grave chapter. Amongst ourselves, for once, it shall be said quite openly, but all the same we will never speak about it in public. . . .

I am referring here to the evacuation of the Jews, the extermination of the Jewish people. This is one of the things that is easily said: "The Jewish people are going to be exterminated," that's what every Party member says, "sure, it's in our program, elimination of the Jews, extermination—it'll be done." And then they all come along, the 80 million worthy Germans, and each one has his one decent Jew. Of course, the others are swine, but this one, he is a first-rate Jew. Of all those who talk like that, not one has seen it happen, not one has had to go through with it. Most of you men know what it is like to see 100 corpses side by side, or 500 or 1,000. To have stood fast through this and except for cases of human weakness to have stayed decent, that has made us hard. This is an unwritten and never-to-be-written page of glory in our history. . . .

> What was Himmler's point here about "decent" Jews?

The wealth they possessed we took from them. I gave a strict order, which has been carried out by SS *Obergruppenfuehrer* Pohl, that this wealth will of course be turned over to the Reich in its entirety. We have taken none of it for ourselves. Individuals who have erred will be punished in accordance with the order given by me at the start, threatening that anyone who takes as much as a single Mark of this money is a dead man. A number of SS men, they are not very many, committed this offense, and they shall die. There will be no mercy. We had the moral right, we had the duty towards our people, to destroy this people that wanted to destroy us. But we do not have the right to enrich ourselves by so much as a fur, as a watch, by one Mark or a cigarette or anything else. We do not want, in the end, because we destroyed a bacillus, to be infected by this bacillus and to die. I will never stand by and watch while even a small rotten spot develops or takes hold. Wherever it may form we will together burn it away. All in all, however, we can say that we have carried out this most difficult of tasks in a spirit of love for our people. And we have suffered no harm to our inner being, our soul, our character. . . .

> Why was it so important to Himmler that individual Germans not take the wealth of murdered Jews?

For Further Reflection

■ Himmler argued that SS officers and soldiers "stayed decent" while overseeing the extermination of the Jews; how, according to him, was this possible?

Source: Heinrich Himmler, " We Will Never Speak about It in Public" (*The Complete Text of the Poznan Speech*), October 4, 1943, Translation used with permission of the Holocaust History Project (www.holocaust-history.org).

During the 1930s through the early years of the war, the German government encouraged Jewish emigration. Although tens of thousands of Jews availed themselves of the opportunity to escape from Germany and Austria, many more were unable to do so. Most nations outside the Nazi orbit limited the migration of Jewish refugees, especially if the refugees were impoverished (as many were because Nazi authorities had previously appropriated their wealth). This situation worsened as German armies overran Europe, bringing an ever-larger number of Jews under Nazi control. At that point

Nazi "racial experts" toyed with the idea of deporting Jews to Nisko, a proposed reservation in eastern Poland, or to the island of Madagascar, near Africa. Those ideas, however, proved to be impractical.

The Final Solution The German occupation of Poland in 1939 and invasion of the Soviet Union in the summer of 1941 gave Hitler an opportunity to solve what he considered the problem of Jews in Germany and in Europe. When German armies invaded the Soviet Union in June 1941, the Nazis dispatched three thousand troops in mobile detachments known as SS *Einsatzgruppen* ("action squads") to kill entire populations of Jews, Roma (or Gypsies), and many non-Jewish Slavs in the newly occupied territories. The action squads undertook mass shootings in ditches and ravines that became mass graves. By the spring of 1943, the special units had killed over one million Jews, and tens of thousands of Soviet citizens and Roma.

Sometime during 1941 the Nazi leadership committed to what they called the **"final solution"** of the Jewish question, a plan to murder every Jew living in Europe. At the **Wannsee Conference** on January 20, 1942, fifteen leading Nazi bureaucrats gathered to discuss and coordinate the implementation of the final solution. They agreed to evacuate all Jews from Europe to camps in eastern Poland, where they would be worked to death or exterminated. Soon after, German forces—aided by collaborating authorities in foreign countries—rounded up Jews and deported them to specially constructed concentration camps in occupied Poland. The victims, whether they were from nearby Polish ghettos or distant assembly points all across Europe, traveled to their destinations by train. On the way the sick and the elderly often perished in overcrowded freight cars. The Jewish victims packed into these suffocating railway cars never knew their destinations, but rumors of mass deportations and mass deaths nonetheless spread among Jews remaining at large and among the Allied government leaders, who were frequently apathetic to the fate of Jews.

In camps such as Kulmhof (Chelmno), Belzec, Majdanek, Sobibor, Treblinka, and Auschwitz, the final solution took on an organized and technologically sophisticated character. Here, the killers introduced gassing as the most efficient means for mass extermination, though other means of destruction were always retained, such as electrocution, phenol injections, flamethrowers, hand grenades, and machine guns. The largest of the camps was Auschwitz, where at least one million Jews perished. Nazi camp personnel subjected victims from all corners of Europe to industrial work, starvation, medical experiments, and outright extermination. The German commandant of **Auschwitz** explained proudly how his camp became the most efficient at killing Jews: by using the fast-acting crystallized prussic acid Zyklon B as the gassing agent, by enlarging the size of the gas chambers, and by lulling victims into thinking they were going through a delousing process. At Auschwitz and elsewhere, the Germans also constructed large crematories to incinerate the bodies of gassed Jews and hide the evidence of their crimes. This systematic murder of Jews constituted what war crime tribunals later termed a "crime against humanity."

Jewish Resistance The murder of European Jewry was carried out with the help of the latest technology and with the utmost efficiency. For most of the victims, the will to resist was sapped by prolonged starvation, disease, and mistreatment. Nevertheless, there was fierce Jewish resistance

throughout the war. Thousands of Jews joined anti-Nazi partisan groups and resistance movements while others led rebellions in concentration camps or participated in ghetto uprisings from Minsk to Krakow. The best-known uprising took place in the Warsaw ghetto in the spring of 1943. Lacking adequate weapons, sixty thousand Jews who remained in the ghetto that had once held four hundred thousand rose against their tormentors. It took German security forces using tanks and flamethrowers three weeks to crush the uprising. In total, approximately 5.7 million Jews perished in the Holocaust.

Women and the War

Observing the extent to which British women mobilized for war, the U.S. ambassador to London noted, "This war, more than any other war in history, is a woman's war." A poster encouraging U.S. women to join the **WAVES** (Women Appointed for Volunteer Emergency Service in the navy) mirrored the thought: "It's A Woman's War Too!" While hundreds of thousands of women in Great Britain, the United States, and the Soviet Union joined the armed forces or entered war industries, women around the world were affected by the war in a variety of ways. Some nations, including Great Britain and the United States, barred women from engaging in combat or carrying weapons, but Soviet and Chinese women took up arms, as did women in resistance groups. In fact, women often excelled at resistance work because they were less suspect in the eyes of occupying security forces and less subject to searches. Nazi forces did not discriminate, though, when rounding up Jews for transport and extermination: Jewish women and girls died alongside Jewish men and boys.

Women's Roles Women who joined military services or took jobs on factory assembly lines gained an independence and confidence previously denied them, but so too did women who were forced to act as heads of household in the absence of husbands killed or away at war, captured as prisoners of war, or languishing in labor camps. Women's roles changed during the war, often in dramatic ways, but those new roles turned out to be temporary. After the war, especially in western Europe and the United States, women warriors and workers were expected to resume their traditional roles as wives and mothers. In the meantime, though, women made the most of their opportunities. In Britain, women served as noncombatant pilots, drove ambulances and transport vehicles, and labored in the fields to produce foodstuffs. More than 500,000 women joined British military services, and approximately 350,000 women did the same in the United States. In the Soviet Union, women recruits exceeded

Einsatzgruppen (INE-zahts-GROO-pen)

Connecting the Sources

Exploring perspective and neutrality in the historical interpretation of World War II

The problem   More than sixty million people died in World War II. Millions more suffered intensely but ultimately survived the ordeal. Because World War II occurred within living memory, millions of individuals around the world still feel intimately connected with it—if not through their own experiences, then through the stories of their family members of an older generation. As a result, it is still understandably difficult for historians and nonhistorians alike to consider the war from a neutral perspective. Moreover, although all the countries that actively participated in the war engaged in brutalities, both the German and the Japanese states sanctioned extreme brutalities against civilian populations—which included massive campaigns of genocide, forced prostitution, forced labor, and medical experiments. These appalling events have resulted in a marked reluctance to discuss the suffering of ordinary Germans not targeted by the Holocaust or of ordinary Japanese because doing so has been associated with cheapening the experience of the millions who suffered and died as a result of German and Japanese national policies. The implication, though not usually stated explicitly, is that not all human suffering in World War II should be explored equally. Let us consider two sources as a way of considering the ways that our own proximity to traumatic historical events might affect the ways we interpret the past.

Indonesians who had been recruited by the Japanese to work as *romushas* (forced laborers).
Image bank WW2 – NIOD

The documents   Read the documents below, and consider carefully the questions that follow.

Document 1:

Dulrahman, a Javanese farmer born in 1920, was one of approximately 250,000 laborers forced by the Japanese to work on various war-related projects in southeast Asia during World War II. These work battalions were called romushas. *Although* romushas *were told they would receive pay when they were recruited, instead they found themselves working without pay in extremely difficult conditions and with little food. As a result, over half did not survive the war.*

In June 1942, a Japanese soldier by the name of Kawakubu came to our village and asked my father if there were any people who could work, for wages, of course. My father then gave him my name. They first assigned me to help build a tunnel at Parangtritis, south of Yogya, on the coast. We didn't get paid at all, however, and they told my father they'd kill him if he'd come to fetch me. Sure, the Japanese told us repeatedly: "We've come to free you from colonial oppression." But meanwhile they forced us to work for them!

We left from Gunung Kidul for Parangtritis with about 500 people. My estimate is that about 300 survived. It's hard to be precise, for people were not buried but simply tossed into the sea. Some eight months later they shipped us out by the hundreds, including about 100 people belonging to the Gunung Kidul group. It turned out that they had taken us to Digul (in Irian Jaya, a former Dutch penal colony in what was then New Guinea) to cut trees for building a road and a prison. Compared to this place, Parangtritis had been pleasant. There at least we got a piece of cassava the size of my fist, and we could fetch water from a small mountain lake. In Digul, however, we were left to our own devices and so we had to forage for ourselves. For food, you had to look in the jungle. We ate leaves, and any snake you'd find was good for roasting.

Finally, they told us we could go home. Everybody was elated. . . . But about halfway, in the middle of the ocean, we began to ask ourselves: "Where on earth are they taking us this time?" There was no land to be seen anywhere. The voyage took a month. We finally arrived and got off the ship and that's when we panicked: Where on earth were we? This wasn't Indonesia, but then what country was it? After one week, I found out that we were in Burma.

> Why did Dulrahman's father agree to let his son work for the Japanese in 1942?

Devastation in the aftermath of the bombing of Hiroshima.
Bettmann/Getty Images

In Burma, life for a romusha was terrible. But compared to Digul it was better. . . . if we did anything wrong, [the Japanese would] beat us up vigorously with their rubber truncheons. That was no joke. If you got beaten with that truncheon it would remove your skin when bouncing back, and that caused a lot of pain.

We spent exactly one year in Burma. . . . One day, our foreman let it slip that we'd be going home in two weeks. . . . When I arrived [back home], everybody cried. They thought I'd been dead long since. I certainly looked quite different. . . . During the first month, my family treated me a bit like a retiree, as it were. I was not allowed to work and they fed me very well. . . .

I still dream a lot about those days, especially about the work we did: dragging stones, that sort of thing. And about that voyage across the sea. Those high waves. That results in a nightmare once in a while, and then I find myself screaming out loud. . . . My gosh, to think that after 50 years I'm still dreaming about that!

Document 2

Kosaku Okabe was a young Japanese soldier who had seen combat many times over the course of the war. The day after the Hiroshima bombing, on August 7, he and some fellow soldiers took the train to Hiroshima, knowing only that a bomb had been dropped on the city. The passengers were told to get out on the outskirts of the city, as the train was going no further. Once Kosaku got out, he realized it was because the train tracks had been completely destroyed. What follows is what Kosaku saw as he moved closer to the epicenter.

In front of me, smoke still overhung the city, and there was increasing confusion as the people leaving the city met those trying to enter it. I began to come across people with tattered clothing and injuries of a kind I had never seen before. By now the area around me was a burned-out wasteland, with no houses standing. It was when I crossed what I think was the Ota River, though, that I really seemed to step into hell . . . Dead bodies lay where they had fallen. The great cherry trees that had lined the embankment were stripped of their branches, which were now hanging down in shreds from their trunks. Looking downstream to the river mouth, I saw strange black shapes almost obliterating the sparkling sandbars . . . . as I drew nearer I realized that in reality they were dead bodies, possibly deposited there by the river . . . Farther on, in the water, floated countless bodies of men, women, and children. The misery was indescribable.

> What difference does it make to read about civilian deaths versus those of military combatants? Is it more difficult or the same for both groups? Why?

Questions

1. What can these documents definitively tell you about their respective situations? What facts can be gleaned from these brief sources?
2. In Document 1, what was it like for Dulrahman to serve as a romusha? According to this source, how did the experience affect him after the war? Does Dulrahman's story elicit your sympathy, even though he was working in a Japanese-led work battalion? If yes, are you able to determine what factors of the story make you sympathetic? If no, are you able to determine the reasons why not?
3. In Document 2, does Kosaku's story elicit your sympathy, even though he was a Japanese soldier who had actively supported the Japanese war effort? If yes, what parts of his story make you feel sympathetic? If no, are you able to determine the reasons why not?
4. Taking both documents together, do you believe that either Dulrahman or Kosaku deserve more sympathy than the other? Do you find that your answer to this question is affected by the nationality of either person? Do you think it would be difficult for individuals who had experienced the war to be impartial about the suffering of individuals in enemy nations? Why or why not?
5. Sources such as these make up the building blocks on which historians base their interpretations of the past. When interpreting the relatively recent past, it is especially important that historians remain aware of the ways in which their own personal and national backgrounds affect both the sources they use as well as their interpretations of them.

Source Citations: **Document 1:** http://www.opendemocracy.net/arts-photography/war_2764.jsp, from Open Democracy, Jan Banning exhibition, 2005: Traces of War: Dutch and Indonesian Survivors. **Document 2:** Gaynor Sekinori and Naomi Shohno, *Hibakusha: Survivors of Hiroshima and Nagasaki* (Kosei Publishing, 1989), pp. 33–34.

Natalya Kravtsova (left) and Irina Sebrova (right) were pilots in the Soviet Airforce's 588th Night Bomber Regiment, and are pictured here in front of a PO 2 aircraft. Sebrova flew 825 bombing missions during World War II, and in 1945 was awarded the title "Hero of the Soviet Union" for her service.
TASS/Getty Images

even these high numbers. There, about 800,000 women enlisted in the armed forces during the war. While many served as medics and nurses, thousands also served in active combat as pilots, snipers, and machine gunners.

Comfort Women Women's experiences in war were not always empowering. The Japanese army forcibly recruited, conscripted, and coerced as many as two hundred thousand women aged fourteen to twenty to serve in military brothels, called "comfort houses" or "consolation centers." The army presented the women to the troops as a gift from the emperor. The majority of women came from China and the Japanese colony of Korea, though others came from Japanese colonies and occupied territories in Taiwan, Manchuria, the Philippines, and elsewhere in Southeast Asia.

Once forced into this imperial prostitution service, the **"comfort women"** catered to between twenty and thirty men each day. Stationed in war zones, the women often confronted the same risks as soldiers, and many became casualties of war. Others were killed by Japanese soldiers, especially if they tried to escape or contracted venereal diseases. At the end of the war, soldiers massacred large numbers of comfort women to cover up the operation. The impetus behind the establishment of comfort houses for Japanese soldiers came from the horrors of Nanjing, where the mass rape of Chinese women had taken place. In trying to avoid such atrocities, the Japanese army created another horror of war. Comfort women who survived the war experienced deep shame and hid their past or faced being shunned by their families. They found little comfort or peace after the war.

Four Korean "comfort women," who were forced into prostitution by the Japanese during World War II, sit beside a rocky cliff in China at the end of the war in 1945.
CPA Media Pte Ltd/Alamy Stock Photo

THE COLD WAR

The end of World War II produced moving images of peace, such as Soviet and U.S. soldiers clasping hands in camaraderie at the Elbe River, celebrating their victory over the Germans. But by the time Germany surrendered in the spring of 1945, the wartime alliance between the Soviet Union, the United States, and Great Britain was disintegrating. Within two years the alliance forged by mutual danger gave way to a cold war between two principal rivals and their allies. It was a contest in which neither side gave way; yet, in the end, a direct clash of arms was always avoided, hence the term *cold war.*

The **cold war** became a confrontation for global influence principally between the United States and the Soviet Union. The geopolitical and ideological rivalry between the Soviet Union and the United States and their respective allies lasted almost five decades and affected every part of the world. The cold war was responsible for the formation of military and political alliances, the creation of client states, and an arms race of unprecedented scope. It engendered diplomatic crises, spawned military conflicts, and at times brought the world to the brink of nuclear annihilation. Among the first manifestations of the cold war was the division of the European continent into competing political, military, and economic blocs—one dependent on the United States and the other subservient to the USSR—separated by what Winston Churchill in 1946 famously called an "iron curtain."

Origins of the Cold War

The United Nations Despite their many differences, the Allies were among the nations that agreed to the creation of the **United Nations (UN)** in October 1945, a supranational organization dedicated to keeping world peace and security. The commitment to establish a new international organization derived from Allied cooperation during the war. Unlike its predecessor, the League of Nations (1920), which failed in its basic mission to prevent another world war, the United Nations created a powerful Security Council responsible for maintaining international peace. Recognizing that peace could be maintained only if the great powers were in agreement, the UN founders made certain that the Security Council consists of five permanent members and six rotating elected members. The United States, the Soviet Union, Great Britain, France, and China—the members of the full Allied alliance in World War II—are the five permanent powers, and their unanimous vote is required on all substantive matters. The decisions of the Security Council are binding on all members.

Despite this initial cooperation, the wartime unity of the former Allies began to crack. In addition to a long history of philosophical differences between the Soviet Union and the western European powers, at the end of the war the Allies were already expressing differences over the future of Poland and eastern European nations liberated and subsequently occupied by the Soviet Red Army. On the surface, all sides agreed at the wartime conference at Yalta (February 4-11,

What's Left Out? ■■ ■■■ ■■ ■■ ■■

Historians used to assume that antagonism between capitalist and communist systems was natural and that, therefore, the intense rivalry that emerged between the United States and the Soviet Union during the cold war needed no historical explanation. But cold war antagonisms had a history that predated the end of World War II by almost three decades. The leading capitalist powers—including Great Britain and the United States—had actively tried to put an end to the Russian revolution in 1918 when they sent troops to help overthrow the Bolsheviks as World War I was ending. In 1919 they grew even more alarmed about the Soviet state when it established the Communist International (Comintern), whose express purpose was to provide funds and strategies for colonized and marginalized people to overthrow capitalism through violent revolution. In fact, it is no exaggeration to say that metropolitan and colonial authorities—especially from Great Britain and France—were convinced that international communism posed a fundamental danger to the stability of the Euro-American global system in the interwar period. During the 1920s and 1930s, both Britain and France expended enormous energy and capital trying to root out and persecute communists around the world (especially in their colonies), and in efforts to gain allies in their anticommunist campaign. British authorities in particular were influential in shaping the anticommunist attitudes of U.S. authorities at this time, encouraging them to fear the influence of communism both in their own overseas empire and among U.S. workers. So even though the capitalist powers were able to put aside their animosity toward the Soviet Union in order to fight the Axis powers, it is hardly surprising that this decades-long rivalry flared up again at the end of the war. The difference now was that the United States, rather than Great Britain or France, was leading the campaign. What is important to remember is that the United States took over the campaign but did not invent it and that the struggle between communism and anticommunism was critical to international politics long before the United States became the primary adversary of the Soviet Union.

Source: Anne Foster. "Secret Police Cooperation and the Roots of Anti-Communism in Interwar Southeast Asia." *Journal of American-East Asian Relations* 4:4 (1995).

MAP 36.4   Occupied Germany, 1945–1949.

Locate the city of Berlin in Soviet-controlled territory.

How was it possible for the British, American, and French to maintain their zones of control in Berlin, given the geographic distance from West Germany?

1945) to "the earliest possible establishment through free elections of governments responsive to the will of the people." But the Soviet Union had just suffered a devastating invasion by the German army through this territory, and Joseph Stalin was determined that postwar governments in the region would be controlled by the Soviet Union in order to safeguard against any future threat from Germany. From the American and British perspectives, Stalin's intentions signaled the permanent Soviet domination of eastern Europe and the threat of Soviet-influenced communist parties coming to power in the democracies of western Europe. Their fears were realized in 1946 and 1947, when the Soviets helped bring communist

governments to power in Romania, Bulgaria, Hungary, and Poland. Communists had previously gained control in Albania and Yugoslavia in 1944 and 1945.

Truman Doctrine   The enunciation of the **Truman Doctrine** on 12 March 1947 crystallized the U.S. perception of a world divided between "free" and "enslaved" peoples. Articulated partly in response to crises in Greece and Turkey, where communist movements seemed to threaten democracy and U.S. strategic interests, the Truman Doctrine starkly drew the battle lines of the cold war. As President Harry Truman (1884–1972) explained to the U.S. Congress: "At the present moment in world history nearly every nation must choose between alternative ways of life. I believe that it must be the policy of the United States to support free peoples who are resisting attempted subjugation by armed minorities or by outside pressures." The United States then committed itself to an interventionist foreign policy, dedicated to the "containment" of communism, which meant preventing any further expansion of Soviet influence.

Marshall Plan Just after the announcement of the Truman Doctrine, the U.S. government developed a plan to help shore up the destroyed infrastructures of western Europe. The European Recovery Program, commonly called the **Marshall Plan** after U.S. Secretary of State George C. Marshall (1880–1959), proposed to rebuild European economies through cooperation and capitalism, forestalling communist or Soviet influence in the devastated nations of Europe. Proposed in 1947 and funded in 1948, the Marshall Plan provided more than $13 billion to reconstruct western Europe. Although initially included in the nations invited to participate in the Marshall Plan, the Soviet Union became infuriated over what it correctly saw as a U.S. attempt to make communism seem less attractive to Europeans devastated by the war. In response, the Soviet government came up with its own aid program for the satellite nations around it, establishing an economic Council for Mutual Economic Assistance (**COMECON**) in 1949. COMECON offered increased trade within the Soviet Union and eastern Europe as an alternative to the Marshall Plan, which Soviet officials denounced as capitalist imperialism.

Military Alliances The creation of the U.S.-sponsored North Atlantic Treaty Organization (**NATO**) and the Soviet-controlled **Warsaw Pact** signaled the militarization of the cold war. In 1949 the United States established NATO as a regional military alliance against Soviet aggression. The original members included Belgium, Canada, Denmark, France, Great Britain, Iceland, Italy, Luxembourg, the Netherlands, Norway, Portugal, and the United States. The intent of the alliance was to maintain peace in postwar Europe through collective security, which implied that a Soviet attack on any NATO member was an attack against all of them. NATO assumed a more military focus with the Soviet Union's detonation of its first atomic bomb in 1949 and with the outbreak of the Korean War in 1950. When NATO admitted West Germany and allowed it to rearm in 1955, the Soviets formed the Warsaw Pact as a countermeasure. A military alliance of seven communist European nations, the Warsaw Pact matched the collective defense policies of NATO.

A Divided Germany The fault lines of early cold war Europe were most visible in Germany. An international crisis arose there in 1948–1949 when the Soviet Union pressured the western powers to give up their jurisdiction over Berlin. After the collapse of Hitler's Third Reich, the forces of the

United States, the Soviet Union, Britain, and France occupied Germany and its capital, Berlin, both of which they divided for administrative purposes into four zones. When the western powers decided to merge their occupation zones in Germany—including their sectors in Berlin—the Soviets retaliated by blockading all road, rail, and water links between Berlin and western Germany. The last thing the Soviet government wanted was a strong Germany. If it could not prevent its former allies from merging their sectors to ease German recovery, it hoped at least to force them to surrender their control over the city of Berlin, which sat deep within the Soviet sector.

Blockade and Airlift In the first serious test of the cold war, the Americans and the British responded with an airlift designed to keep West Berlin's inhabitants alive, fed, and warm. For eleven months, in a massive display of airpower, American and British aircrews flew around-the-clock missions to supply West Berlin with the necessities of life. Tensions remained high during the airlift, but the cold war did not turn hot. Stymied by British and U.S. resolve, the Soviet leadership called off the blockade in May 1949. In the aftermath of the blockade, the U.S., British, and French zones of occupation coalesced to form the Federal Republic of Germany (West Germany) in May 1949. In October the German Democratic Republic (East Germany) emerged out of the Soviet zone of occupation. A similar process repeated itself in Berlin. The Soviet sector formed East Berlin and became the capital of the new East Germany. The remaining three sectors united to form West Berlin, and the West German capital moved to the small town of Bonn.

Barbed wire and a concrete wall in front of the Brandenburg Gate in Berlin symbolized the cold war division of Europe.
Keystone-France/Gamma-Keystone/Getty Images

The Berlin Wall By 1961 the communist East German state was hemorrhaging from a steady drain of refugees who preferred life in capitalist West Germany. Between 1949 and 1961 nearly 3.5 million East Germans—many of them young and highly skilled—left their homeland, much to the embarrassment of East Germany's communist leaders. In August 1961 the communists reinforced the border between East and West Germany, and also constructed a fortified wall that divided the city of Berlin. The wall, which began as a layer of barbed wire, quickly turned into a barrier several layers deep, with watchtowers, searchlights, antipersonnel mines, and border guards who had orders to shoot to kill. The **Berlin Wall** accomplished its purpose of stemming the flow of refugees, though at the cost of shaming a regime that seemed to be unpopular even among its own people.

Cold War Culture and Censorship Somewhat ironically, despite their intense competition, during the cold war societies in the Soviet Union and the United States came to resemble one another in some ways, especially in their internal censorship policies. In the United States, cold war concerns about the spread of communism reached deeply into the domestic sphere. Politicians, agents of the Federal Bureau of Investigation (FBI), educators, and social commentators warned of communist spies trying to undermine the institutions of U.S. life. Senator **Joseph McCarthy** (1909–1957) became infamous in the early 1950s for his largely unsuccessful but nonetheless intimidating quest to expose communists in the U.S. government. Thousands of citizens who supported any radical or liberal cause—especially those who were or once had been members of the Communist Party—lost their jobs and reputations after being held up as risks to their nation's security. The culture industry, and Hollywood in particular, came under great scrutiny for its suspected ties to left-wing politics, which had the effect of limiting overt criticism of the United States and its foreign policies.

In the Soviet Union and Eastern Europe, cold war ideologies also profoundly influenced domestic culture and politics. After the war, Stalin imposed Soviet economic planning on governments in Eastern Europe and expected the peoples of the Soviet Union and Eastern Europe to conform to anticapitalist ideological requirements. Rebellious artists and novelists found themselves silenced or denounced in a mirrored form of the McCarthyism evident in the United States. This policy of repression relaxed somewhat after Stalin's death in 1953, but there remained limits on Soviet liberalization. Soviet troops cracked down on Hungarian rebels in 1956, and Soviet novelist **Boris Pasternak** (1890–1960), author of *Doctor Zhivago,* was not allowed to receive his Nobel Prize in Literature in 1958. There is little doubt that societies and cultures in the Soviet Union and the United States underwent dramatic transformations as a result of the international competition between communism and capitalism, and such changes continued to engulf these societies as the cold war globalized.

The Globalization of the Cold War

The People's Republic of China
The establishment of a communist China in 1949 simultaneously ended a long period of imperialist intrusion in China and further transformed the cold war, as it seemed to enhance the power of the Soviet Union and its communist allies. Although China had not been formally ruled by an imperial power, many countries had impinged on its sovereignty in the nineteenth and early twentieth centuries. During the 1920s, two groups had arisen to reassert Chinese control over internal affairs: the nationalists and the communists (see chapter 35). When World War II broke out, these two groups had been engaged in a civil war, but they came together to fight against the Japanese invasion. Once World War II was over, however, the civil war resumed. In 1948 and 1949, the communists inflicted heavy military defeats on the nationalists. With the communist People's Liberation Army controlling most of mainland China, the national government under Jiang Jieshi (Chiang Kai-shek) sought refuge on the island of Taiwan, taking along most of the nation's gold reserves. Although Jiang Jieshi continued to proclaim that the government in Taiwan was the legitimate government of all China, Mao Zedong, chairman of the Chinese Communist Party, proclaimed the establishment of the People's Republic of China on 1 October 1949. That declaration brought to an end the long period of imperialist intrusion in China and spawned a close relationship between the world's largest and most powerful socialist states.

Fraternal Cooperation
China and the Soviet Union drew closer during the early years of the cold war. This relationship was hardly surprising because the leaders of both communist states felt threatened by a common enemy, the United States, which sought to establish anticommunist bastions throughout Asia. Most disconcerting to Soviet and Chinese leaders was the American-sponsored rehabilitation of their former enemy, Japan, and the forming of client states in South Korea and Taiwan. The Chinese-Soviet partnership matured during the early 1950s and took on a distinct form when China recognized the Soviet Union's undisputed authority in world communism in exchange for Russian military equipment and economic aid.

Confrontations in Korea
In conjunction with the communist victory in China, the outbreak of hostilities on the Korean peninsula in the summer of 1950 shifted the focus of the cold war from Europe to east Asia. At the end of World War II, the leaders of the Soviet Union and the United States had partitioned Korea along the thirty-eighth parallel (the thirty-eighth line of latitude) into a northern Soviet zone and a southern U.S. zone. Because the superpowers were unable to agree on a framework for the reunification of the country, in 1948 they consented to the establishment of two separate Korean states: in the south, the Republic of Korea, with Seoul as its capital, and in the north, the People's Democratic Republic of Korea,

with Pyongyang as its capital. After arming their respective clients, each of which claimed sovereignty over the entire country, U.S. and Soviet troops withdrew.

On the early morning of June 25, 1950, the unstable political situation in Korea came to a head. Determined to unify Korea by force, the Pyongyang regime in North Korea ordered more than one hundred thousand troops across the thirty-eighth parallel in a surprise attack, quickly pushing back South Korean defenders and capturing Seoul on June 27. Convinced that the USSR had given its blessing for the invasion, the United States persuaded the United Nations to adopt a resolution to drive the North Koreans out. Armed with a UN mandate and supported by small armed forces from twenty countries, the U.S. military went into action, and within months had pushed the North Koreans back to the thirty-eighth parallel. However, sensing an opportunity to unify Korea under a pro-U.S. government, they pushed on into North Korea and within a few weeks had occupied Pyongyang. But subsequent U.S. advances toward the Yalu River on the Chinese border brought the Chinese into the war. A combined force of Chinese and North Koreans pushed U.S. forces and their allies back into the south, and the war settled into a stalemate near the original border at the thirty-eighth parallel. After two more years of fighting that raised the number of deaths to three million—mostly Korean civilians—both sides finally agreed to a cease-fire in July 1953. The failure to conclude a peace treaty ensured that the Korean peninsula would remain in a state of suspended strife that constantly threatened to engulf the region in a new round of hostilities.

Beyond the human casualties and physical damage it wrought, the Korean conflict also encouraged the globalization of the U.S. strategy of containment. Viewing the North Korean offensive as part of a larger communist conspiracy to conquer the world, the U.S. government extended military protection and economic aid to noncommunist governments in the rest of Asia. It also entered into security agreements that culminated in the creation of the Southeast Asian Treaty Organization (SEATO), an Asian counterpart of NATO. By 1954 U.S. President Dwight D. Eisenhower (1890–1969), who had contemplated using nuclear weapons in Korea, asserted the famous **domino theory**. This strategic theory rationalized worldwide U.S. intervention on the assumption that if one country became communist, neighboring ones would collapse to communism the way a row of dominoes falls sequentially until none remains standing. Subsequent U.S. administrations extended the policy of containment to areas beyond the nation's vital interests and applied it to local or imagined communist threats in Central and South America, Africa, and Asia.

Cracks in the Soviet-Chinese Alliance Despite the assumptions of U.S. leaders, there was no one monolithic communist force in global politics, as was demonstrated by the divisions that developed between Chinese and Soviet communists. The Chinese had embarked on a crash program of industrialization, and the Soviet Union rendered valuable assistance in the form of economic aid and technical advisers. By the mid-1950s the Soviet Union was China's principal trading partner, annually purchasing roughly half of all Chinese exports. But the Chinese grew offended that the Soviets would not share the technology for nuclear weapons with them and were furious when the Soviet Union did not support them in their war with India in 1962. By the end of 1964, the rift between the Soviet Union and the People's Republic of China became embarrassingly public, with both sides engaging in name-calling. In addition, both nations openly competed for influence in Africa and Asia, especially in the nations that had recently gained independence. The fact that China conducted successful nuclear tests in 1964, without the help of the Soviet Union, enhanced its prestige. An unanticipated outcome of the Chinese-Soviet split was that many countries gained an opportunity to pursue a more independent course by playing capitalists against communists and by playing Soviet communists against Chinese communists. It also opened the door for an eventual truce between China and the United States because both countries now saw the Soviet Union as their principal enemy.

The Nuclear Arms Race A central feature of the cold war world was a costly arms race and the terrifying proliferation of nuclear weapons. The Soviet Union had broken the U.S. monopoly on atomic weaponry by testing its own atomic bomb in 1949, but because the United States was determined to retain military superiority and because the Soviet Union was equally determined to reach parity with the United States, both sides amassed enormous arsenals of nuclear weapons and developed a multitude of systems for deploying those weapons. In the 1960s and beyond, the superpowers acquired so many nuclear weapons that they reached the capacity for mutually assured destruction, or MAD. This balance of terror, while often frightening, tended to restrain the contestants and stabilize their relationship, with one important exception.

Cuba: Nuclear Flashpoint Ironically, the cold war confrontation that came closest to unleashing nuclear war took place not at the expected flashpoints in Europe or Asia but on the island of Cuba. In 1959 a revolutionary movement headed by Fidel Castro Ruz (1926–2016) overthrew the autocratic Fulgencio Batista y Zaldivar (1901–1973), whose regime had gone to great lengths to maintain the country's subservient relationship with the United States, especially with the U.S. sugar companies that controlled Cuba's economy. Fidel Castro's new regime gladly accepted a Soviet offer of massive economic aid—including an agreement to purchase half of Cuba's sugar production—and arms shipments. In return for Soviet aid, Castro declared his support for the USSR's foreign policy. In December 1961 he confirmed the U.S. government's worst suspicions when he publicly announced: "I have been a Marxist-Leninist all along, and will remain one until I die."

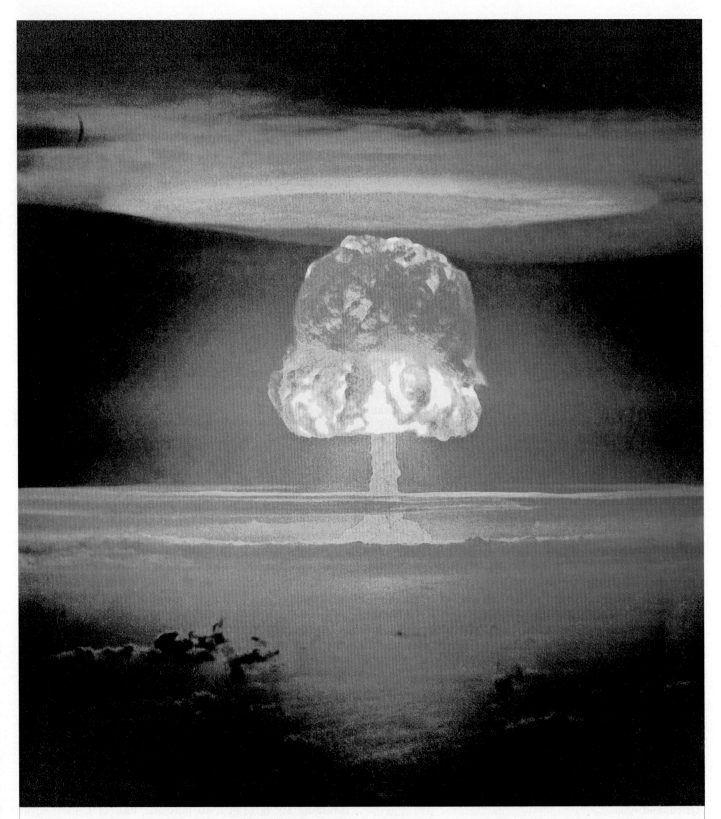

A nuclear test in the Marshall Islands in 1954. Between World War II and the end of the twentieth century, nations with the capacity to produce nuclear weapons conducted more than two thousand tests. Though most tests were conducted in remote regions, they inflicted severe damage on animal populations and on the environment.
Galerie Bilderwelt/Getty Images

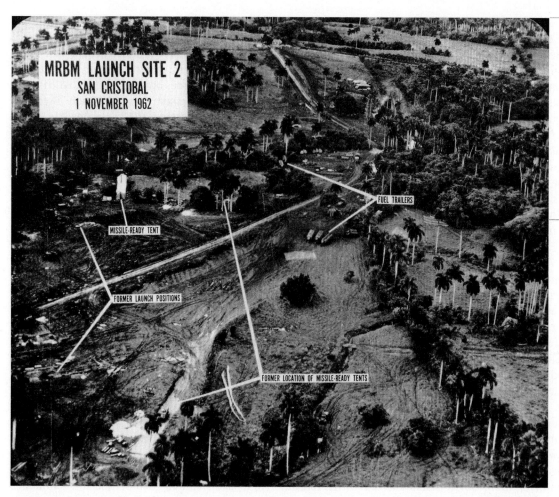

MRBM LAUNCH SITE 2
SAN CRISTOBAL
1 NOVEMBER 1962

FUEL TRAILERS

MISSILE-READY TENT

FORMER LAUNCH POSITIONS

FORMER LOCATION OF MISSILE-READY TENTS

U.S. aerial reconnaissance photograph taken on 1 November 1962, showing clearly the existence of a medium-range ballistic missile launch site at San Cristobal, Cuba. National Archives and Records Administration

Bay of Pigs Invasion Cuba's alignment with the Soviet Union spurred the U.S. government to action. Newly elected president John F. Kennedy (1917–1963) authorized a clandestine invasion of Cuba to overthrow Castro and his supporters. In April 1961 a force of fifteen hundred anti-Castro Cubans trained, armed, and transported by the Central Intelligence Agency (CIA) landed on Cuba at a place called the **Bay of Pigs.** The arrival of the invasion force failed to incite a hoped-for internal uprising, and when the promised American air support failed to appear, the invasion quickly fizzled. Within three days, Castro's military had either captured or killed the entire invasion force. The Bay of Pigs fiasco diminished U.S. prestige, especially in Latin America. It also strengthened Castro's position in Cuba and encouraged him to accept the deployment of Soviet nuclear missiles in Cuba as a deterrent to any future invasion.

Cuban Missile Crisis On October 26, 1962, the United States learned that Soviet technicians were assembling launch sites for medium-range nuclear missiles on Cuba. The deployment of nuclear missiles that could reach targets in the United States within minutes represented an unacceptable threat to U.S. national security. Thus President John F. Kennedy

issued an ultimatum, calling on the Soviet leadership to withdraw all missiles from Cuba and stop the arrival of additional nuclear armaments. To back up his demand, Kennedy imposed an air and naval quarantine on the island nation. The superpowers seemed poised for nuclear confrontation, and for two weeks the world's peoples held their collective breath. After two weeks, finally realizing the imminent possibility of nuclear war, the Soviet government yielded to the U.S. demands. In return, Soviet Premier Nikita Khrushchev (1894–1971) extracted an open pledge from Kennedy to refrain from attempting to overthrow Castro's regime and a secret deal to remove U.S. missiles from Turkey. The world trembled during this **Cuban missile crisis,** awaiting the apocalypse that potentially lurked behind any superpower encounter.

Dissent, Intervention, and Rapprochement

De-Stalinization Even before the Cuban missile crisis, developments within the Soviet Union caused serious changes in eastern Europe. Within three years of Joseph Stalin's death in 1953, several communist leaders startled the world when they openly attacked Stalin and questioned his methods of rule. The most vigorous denunciations came from Stalin's successor,

Soviet Premier Nikita Khrushchev, who embarked on a policy of **de-Stalinization,** that is, the end of the rule of terror and the partial liberalization of Soviet society. Government officials removed portraits of Stalin from public places, renamed institutions and localities bearing his name, and commissioned historians to rewrite textbooks to deflate Stalin's reputation. The de-Stalinization period, which lasted from 1956 to 1964, also brought a "thaw" in government control and resulted in the release of millions of political prisoners. With respect to foreign policy, Khrushchev emphasized the possibility of "peaceful coexistence" between different social systems and the achievement of communism by peaceful means. This change in Soviet doctrine reflected the recognition that a nuclear war was more likely to lead to mutual annihilation than to victory.

Soviet Intervention The new political climate in the Soviet Union tempted communist leaders elsewhere to experiment with domestic reforms and seek a degree of independence from Soviet domination. Eastern European states also tried to become their own masters, or at least to gain a measure of autonomy from the Soviet Union. The nations of the Soviet bloc did not fare well in those endeavors. East Germans staged an uprising crushed in 1953, but the most serious challenge to Soviet control came in 1956 from nationalist-minded communists in Hungary. When the communist regime in Hungary embraced the process of de-Stalinization, large numbers of Hungarian citizens demanded democracy and the breaking of ties to Moscow and the Warsaw Pact. Soviet leaders viewed those moves as a serious threat to their national security. In the late autumn of 1956, Soviet tanks entered Budapest and crushed the Hungarian uprising.

Twelve years after the Hungarian tragedy, Soviets again intervened in eastern Europe, this time in Czechoslovakia. In 1968 the Communist Party leader, Alexander Dubček (1921-1992), launched a "democratic socialist revolution." He supported a liberal movement known as the **Prague Spring**

and promised his fellow citizens "socialism with a human face." The Czechs' move toward liberal communism aroused fear in the Soviet Union because such ideas could lead to the unraveling of Soviet control in eastern Europe. Intervention by Soviet and Warsaw Pact forces brought an end to the Prague Spring. Khrushchev's successor, Leonid Ilyich Brezhnev (1906-1982), justified the invasion of Czechoslovakia by the Doctrine of Limited Sovereignty. This policy, more commonly called the **Brezhnev doctrine**, reserved the right to invade any socialist country that was deemed to be threatened by internal or external elements "hostile to socialism." The destruction of the dramatic reform movement in Czechoslovakia served to reassert Soviet control over its satellite nations in eastern Europe and led to tightened controls within the Soviet Union.

Détente Realizing the extreme danger posed by mutually assured destruction, by the late 1960s the leaders of the Soviet Union and the United States agreed on a policy of *détente,* or a reduction in hostility, in which they tried to slow the costly arms race and decrease their competition in developing countries. Although détente did not resolve the deep-seated antagonism between the superpowers, it did signal a relaxation of cold war tensions and prompted a new spirit of cooperation. The spirit of détente was most visible in negotiations designed to reduce the threat posed by strategic nuclear weapons. The two cold war antagonists cooperated despite the tensions caused by the U.S. incursion into Vietnam, Soviet involvement in Angola and other African states, and continued Soviet repression of dissidents in eastern Europe. Likewise symbolic of the relaxation of tensions between democratic and communist nations were the state visits in 1972 to China and the Soviet Union made by U.S. President Richard Nixon (1913-1994). Nixon had entered politics in 1946 on the basis of his service in World War II and his staunch belief in anticommunism, and his trips to the two global centers of communism suggested a possible beginning to the end of cold war divisions.

CONCLUSION

World War II was a total global war that forced violent encounters between peoples and radically altered the political shape of the world. Beginning in Japan and China in 1931, this global conflagration eventually engulfed Europe and its empires, the Pacific Ocean, and the rest of Asia. Men, women, and children throughout the world were subjected to the horrors of war as victims of civilian bombing campaigns, as soldiers and war workers, and as slave laborers and comfort women. When the Allies defeated the Axis powers in 1945, destroying the German and Japanese empires, the world had to rebuild just as another conflict began. The end of the war saw the breakup of the alliance that had defeated Germany and Japan, and within a short time the United States and the Soviet Union and their respective allies squared off against each other in a cold war, a

rivalry waged on political, economic, and propaganda fronts. as well as via proxy wars with client states. When former colonial territories began to win their independence in the postwar period, they emerged as new nations into this bipolar world: a reality that limited their choices and shaped their futures.

STUDY TERMS

Adolf Hitler (794)

Allied powers (792)

Anschluss (794)

appeasement (795)

Auschwitz (807)

Axis powers (792)

Battle of Britain (796)

Bay of Pigs (817)

Benito Mussolini (793)

Berlin Wall (814)

Blitzkrieg (796)

Boris Pasternak (814)

Brezhnev doctrine (818)

cold war (811)

COMECON (813)

comfort women (810)

Cuban missile crisis (817)

D-Day (801)

de-Stalinization (818)

détente (818)

domino theory (815)

Einsatzgruppen (807)

experimental surgery (804)

final solution (807)

German-Soviet
    Non-Aggression Pact (795)

Greater East Asia
    Co-Prosperity Sphere (799)

Hiroshima (802)

Holocaust (805)

Iwo Jima (802)

Joseph McCarthy (814)

Joseph Stalin (795)

kamikaze (802)

Lebensraum (796)

Luftwaffe (796)

Manchukuo (802)

Marshall Plan (813)

Munich Conference (795)

Nagasaki (802)

NATO (813)

Okinawa (802)

Operation Barbarossa (797)

Pearl Harbor (798)

Prague Spring (818)

Rape of Nanjing (792)

revisionist powers (792)

Spanish Civil War (793)

Stalingrad (797)

Sudetenland (794)

Truman Doctrine (812)

United Nations (UN) (811)

Unterseeboote (796)

Vichy (803)

Wannsee Conference (807)

Warsaw Pact (813)

WAVES (807)

Winston Churchill (799)

FOR FURTHER READING

Svetlana Alexievich. *The Unwomanly Face of War: An Oral History of Women in World War II*. New York, 2017. A meticulously researched history of Soviet women's contributions to the war effort.

Christopher Bayly and Tim Harper. *Forgotten Armies: The Fall of British Asia, 1941–1945*. Cambridge, 2005. Broad study of the impact of World War II on Britain's Asian empire.

John Lewis Gaddis. *The Cold War: A New History*. New York, 2005. A fresh and concise history of the cold war by the dean of cold war historians.

Brian Masaru Hayashi. *Democratizing the Enemy: The Japanese American Internment*. Princeton, N.J., 2004. Important account of the experience of Japanese Americans in World War II.

Waldo Heinrichs and Marc Gallicchio. *Implacable Foes: War in the Pacific, 1944–1945*. Oxford, 2017. Explores both the battles and the bitter debates over strategy in the last eighteen months of the Pacific war.

Keith Lowe. *Savage Continent: Europe in the Aftermath of World War II*. New York, 2012. The author presents an absorbing and chilling picture of a continent brutalized by war.

Rana Mitter. *Forgotten Ally: China's World War II, 1937–1945*. Boston, 2013. This is an important account of how a brutal conflict shaped modern China.

Richard Overy. *The Bombers and the Bombed: Allied Air War over Europe 1940–1945*. New York, 2014. In this impressive work the author explores the military, technological, and ethical issues of strategic bombing, and challenges the notion that the Allies fought a "moral" war.

Timothy Snyder. *Bloodlands: Europe between Hitler and Stalin*. New York, 2010. This is a nuanced and pathbreaking study of Europe's killing fields, where the murderous regimes of Hitler and Stalin claimed the lives of fourteen million noncombatants.

Odd Arne Westad. *Global Cold War: Third World Interventions and the Making of Our Times*. New York, 2007. In a reexamination of the global conflict between the United States and the Soviet Union, the author argues that cold war interventionism helped shape present-day international affairs.

37 The End of Empire in an Era of Cold War

ZOOMING IN ON ENCOUNTERS
Mohandas Gandhi's Last Words

"Hé Ram" were the last words that escaped Gandhi's lips after three bullets ripped through his frail body. Roughly translated, he uttered, "O! God," and then died. It had begun as a day much like any other in the life of **Mohandas K. Gandhi** (1869–1948), or "Bapuji" (dear father) as he was fondly called. On January 30, 1948, a few months after India gained its independence from Great Britain, he awakened at Birla House in Delhi at an early hour, 3:00 A.M., to continue his work hammering out solutions to the problems that plagued the country. That morning, he labored on a draft of a new constitution for the **Indian National Congress,** stressing as usual his major concerns for the newly independent and strife-ridden nation: that villages be empowered, that discrimination based on the caste system be abolished, that religious intolerance and violence between Hindus and Muslims cease. Still distraught over the partitioning of his land into a Hindu India and Muslim Pakistan, he had weakened himself after independence through fasts and hunger strikes in protest against the killings of Hindus and Muslims and the mistreatment of Pakistan. He weighed a mere 107 pounds that day.

Alternating between working, talking with visitors, and napping, Gandhi finally took a meal at 4:30 P.M. He nibbled on raw and cooked vegetables and oranges, and drank goat's milk and a special brew made with aloe juice, lemons, ginger, and strained butter. A little over half an hour later, he made his way to the evening prayer meeting he was to lead. A bit late, the skies already darkening, he took a shortcut across the green, finely trimmed lawns of Birla House to reach the dais where he would speak. As he approached the dais, he

An American air strike against anti-American Viet Cong positions during the Vietnam war results in the destruction of a Vietnamese village.
Larry Burrows/Time & Life Pictures/Getty Images

stopped to press his palms together, offering the traditional Hindu greeting to the crowd waiting at the meeting. At that moment, Nathuram Godse—a Hindu extremist—stepped out of the crowd, pulled a pistol from his pants pocket, and fired the three shots that ended the life of the man many saw as the very soul and conscience of India. The force of the shots crumpled Gandhi's thin body. As he slumped to the ground, his glasses fell from his face, his sandals slipped from his feet, and large crimson bloodstains spread starkly over his white homespun shawl. After he whispered "Hé Ram," his breathing stilled. Godse's actions made it clear that not all Hindus agreed with Gandhi's lifelong rejection of violence and his insistence that Hindus and Muslims should tolerate one another's religious beliefs. Indeed, before he was executed by hanging in 1949, Godse declared Gandhi a "curse for India, a force for evil."

CHAPTER OVERVIEW

Gandhi's murder suggested the troubles and traumas faced by nations and peoples adjusting to independence from colonial rule, a process that occurred in almost every colonized territory in the three decades after World War II. Although most colonies won their independence in this period, they did not do so without a fight. Few colonial powers transferred power willingly, though the type of struggle ranged from intense negotiations to all-out war. During this period of **decolonization,** those fighting for independence not only had to actually win, but they also had to determine who would be included and excluded in the new states, whether or not established colonial borders would be adequate, how ethnic and religious minorities would be treated, and what kind of governments would be established in place of colonial rule.

European imperialism was an important theme in world history beginning in the sixteenth century. As we saw in chapter 32, by the turn of the twentieth century much of the world was dominated not only by European empires but also by empires claimed by the United States and Japan. And although we know that colonized people resisted colonial rule from its very beginnings, a series of developments in the first half of the twentieth century fundamentally undermined colonial rule around the world. One catalyst for change was the Great War (World War I), which sapped the strength and the prestige of the major colonial powers such as Great Britain and France. The Great Depression further undermined the strength of the imperialist nations, as did World War II. While the imperial powers were losing strength, anticolonial independence movements were growing stronger. The increasing ease of travel and communication that characterized the twentieth century meant that many activists seeking independence were not only aware of events outside their own colonies but that their leaders had made contact with one another in their travels to Europe and the United States. Activists fighting for independence also made use of the press, steam travel, and modern communications to spread their ideas to a very wide public. By 1994, anticolonial movements had swept away colonial rule and given birth to over ninety new nations.

This process of decolonization was aided by several factors. It became increasingly apparent that there was a significant growth of democratic and anti-imperialist sentiments within imperial countries themselves, and political leaders could no longer count on a war-weary public to make serious sacrifices to maintain overseas colonies. The short-lived Japanese Empire contributed to colonial revolutions throughout Asia, where European military prestige had been severely and permanently damaged after the Japanese defeated the British in Burma and Malaya, the French in Indochina, the Dutch in Indonesia, and the United States in the Philippines. With the emergence of the two postwar superpowers, the United States and the Soviet Union, both of which opposed European colonialism, the stage was set for a drastic overturning of colonial rule. The end of empire was one of the most important outcomes of World War II.

CHRONOLOGY

1940s–1970	El Milagro Mexicano
1947	Partition of India
1948	Creation of Israel
1948–1989	Apartheid in South Africa
1954	French defeat at Dien Bien Phu
1954–1962	Algerian war of liberation
1955	Bandung Conference
1956	Suez crisis
1957	Ghana gains independence
1958–1961	Great Leap Forward in China
1963	Founding of Organization of African Unity
1973	Arab-Israeli War
1976	Reunification of Vietnam
1979	Revolution in Iran
1980–1988	Iran-Iraq War
1997	Transfer of British Hong Kong to People's Republic of China

But decolonization frequently did not lead to the kind of freedom and stability most formerly colonized people had fought for. In some places, this was because the withdrawal of colonial rule brought religious, ethnic, or cultural divisions into high relief as once-colonized people struggled over who would take power. In other places, newly independent people realized that colonial rule had left them impoverished and without adequate infrastructure to compete on an equal footing in an increasingly globalized world. In still others, independence threw new states right into the midst of Cold War competition between the United States and the Soviet Union. This competition frequently entailed intervention and influence by one or the other Cold War powers, which limited the ability of new states to determine their own futures. Thus while freedom did not remain elusive for colonized people, peace and prosperity often did.

INDEPENDENCE IN ASIA

In the wake of World War II, the power of Asian anticolonial movements was irrepressible. In the decades that followed, new states emerged in south, southwest, and Southeast Asia. While colonized people faced different kinds of struggles in each territory, ranging from civil disobedience to guerrilla warfare, the end result across the whole region was independence from colonial rule.

India's Partitioned Independence

In the 1930s Indians had fought for, and won, numerous reforms from the British colonial government. The most significant of these reforms was the India Act of 1935, which laid out a structure for Indian home rule (control over internal affairs). But the India Act faced challenges in the form of increasing calls for independent yet separate Hindu and Muslim states, while the eruption of World War II suspended home rule altogether.

The Coming of Self-Rule Under the leadership of **Winston Churchill,** who despised Gandhi and vowed never "to preside over the liquidation of the British empire," the British ordered India to support the war effort and temporarily halted the implementation of home rule. British resistance to Indian independence evaporated after the war, however. The British people voted Churchill out of office. His conservative government was replaced with a Labour government more inclined to work with Indian nationalists, whose demands for independence had continued during the war. Faced with the necessity of waging a costly war to maintain British rule against such strong Indian resistance, the war-weary and economically weakened British government now decided to work toward independence.

The issue of Muslim separatism grew in importance as Indian independence became more certain. In particular, Muslims expressed concerns about their minority status in a free India dominated by Hindus. **Muhammad Ali Jinnah** (1876–1948), leader of the **Muslim League,** argued that these concerns could only be met through the establishment of a separate

Jawaharlal Nehru (left) and Mohammad Ali Jinnah (right) sit down with the British Viceroy of India Lord Mountbatten (center) to discuss the Partition of India in 1946.
World History Archive/ Alamy Stock Photo

Muslim state, even as Congress Party leaders such as **Jawaharlal Nehru** (1889–1964) and Gandhi urged all Indians to act and feel as one nation, undivided by what came to be known as communalism (emphasizing religious over national identity). In August 1946, in the midst of negotiations with the British to reach terms regarding independence, the Muslim League called for a Day of Direct Action, even though the league's leaders recognized that Muslim demonstrations might lead to rioting and fighting between Muslims and Hindus. Some six thousand people died in the Great Calcutta Killing that resulted, further fueling communal feeling and adding weight to Jinnah's claim: "The only solution to India's problem is Pakistan."

Partition and Violence Gandhi and Nehru only reluctantly came to accept the notion of a divided and independent India. Gandhi condemned what has come to be known as the **partition of India** as a "vivisection," a term that refers to the cutting up of a living body. He avoided the celebrations on August 15, 1947, that accompanied independence for India and Pakistan, glumly prophesying that "rivers of blood" would flow in the wake of partition. Indeed, communal violence between Hindus and Muslims had already become a major problem in parts of India in the months leading up to partition and independence. Both Hindus and Muslims were involved in propaganda campaigns intended to stir up animosities between the two religious traditions, while rumors about the dire consequences of remaining in the "wrong" state inspired fear and uncertainty among ordinary people. To make matters worse, the British government did not make it clear exactly where the boundaries of the new states would be, leaving that task to the new Indian government two days after independence. Hindus and Muslims who lived in the areas that would likely be affected were terrified that they would suddenly be in hostile territory once independence was declared, and thus millions began to move to what they hoped would be "safe" Muslim or Hindu territory during the summer of 1947. Muslims and Hindus who had once been neighbors and friends now began to see one another as the enemy, and in the highly charged atmosphere, individuals began to resort to violence. Acts of violence perpetrated by Hindus toward Muslims, and vice versa, spawned further violence in order to exact revenge, and quickly the cycle of violence spun out of control. By mid-1948 an estimated ten million refugees had made the torturous journey to one state or the other, and between half a million and one million people died in the violence that accompanied those massive human migrations. The hostility between migrating Hindus and Muslims spilled over into the enmity between the two states, complicating efforts to build their independent nations.

In spite of the tragic violence of partition, Indian independence became a reality with momentous consequences for the process of decolonization. India was the most important British colony, and its breakaway marked a significant turning point. Just as Gandhi's nonviolent resistance to British rule inspired anticolonial activists around the globe before and after World War II, independence in India and Pakistan further encouraged anti-imperial movements throughout Asia and Africa. Another way in which Indian independence inspired nations and set a pattern for grappling with decolonization in the midst of the Cold War was through Nehru's promotion of a nonalignment strategy. In his role as the first president of independent India, Nehru proved instrumental in fashioning a compelling position for newly independent nations caught in the Cold War and in the superpower tug-of-war contests for the loyalties of new nations. He became one of the impassioned defenders of nonalignment, especially at the Bandung Conference, where he was one of the most visible participants.

Nonalignment Leaders of new African and Asian countries first discussed nonalignment at the Bandung Conference. In April 1955, leaders from twenty-three Asian and six African nations met in Bandung, Indonesia, partly to find a "third path," an alternative to choosing either the United States or the Soviet Union. Bandung was the precursor of the broader **Nonaligned Movement,** which held occasional meetings so that its members could discuss matters of common interest, particularly their relations with the United States and the Soviet Union. The movement's primary goal was to maintain formal neutrality. However, the Nonaligned Movement suffered from a chronic lack of unity among its members and ultimately failed to present a genuinely united front. Although theoretically nonaligned with either Cold War superpower, many member states did in fact maintain close ties to one or the other.

Nationalist Struggles in Vietnam

In contrast to India, the Vietnamese struggle for independence became deeply enmeshed in the politics of the Cold War. As a result, Vietnam's independence occurred only after decades of fighting bloody wars to defeat first the French and then the Americans.

Fighting the French Vietnamese anticolonial activists had been fighting against French rule in Indochina since the late nineteenth century. By the 1930s, the Indochinese Communist Party was among the groups fighting to drive out the French. **Ho Chi Minh** (1890–1969), the man who would become the first president of North Vietnam, had helped found the Indochinese Communist Party but spent the 1930s in exile as a wanted man in his home country. When the Japanese invaded Indochina in 1940 with the agreement of the French Vichy regime (which was collaborating with the Nazis), Ho was infuriated that after so many years of fighting French colonizers, the Vietnamese now faced another. In that year he returned to Indochina to coordinate a resistance movement against the Japanese and worked with U.S. operatives from the Office of Strategic Services to undermine their common enemy. By 1945, when it was clear that Japan was going to lose the war and before the French could return to reclaim Indochina, Ho and his party issued the Vietnamese Declaration of Independence and proclaimed Vietnam an independent republic. However, the French, humiliated by their country's easy defeat and occupation by the Germans, sought to reclaim their world-power status through their imperial possessions. By October 1945, the French had retaken Saigon and much of southern Vietnam, and by 1946, war had broken out between the French and the Vietnamese communist forces of the north, known as the Viet Minh. The French were brutal in the battles that ensued as they moved north. For example, they indiscriminately bombed the cities of Hanoi and Haiphong, killing at least ten thousand civilians. By 1947 the French appeared to have secured their power, especially in the cities, but that security proved to be temporary. Much like the Chinese communists in their battles against the Japanese and then against the nationalists in the postwar years, the Vietnamese resistance forces, led by Ho Chi Minh and former history teacher General **Vo Nguyen Giap** (1912–2013), took to the countryside and mounted a campaign of guerrilla warfare. This campaign grew even more effective after 1949, when communist China sent aid and arms to the Viet Minh. In 1954, the Viet Minh

Vo Nguyen Giap (voh winn zahp)

defeated French forces at their fortress at **Dien Bien Phu,** leading the French to sue for peace.

The Geneva Conference and Partial Independence

The peace conference, held in Geneva in 1954, was dominated by Cold War concerns. Even though U.S. forces had aided Ho Chi Minh's resistance against the Japanese during World War II, by 1954 the United States was unwilling to accept that French defeat would leave Ho's communist party in control of Vietnam. As a compromise, the conference participants agreed that Vietnam should be temporarily divided at the seventeenth parallel; North Vietnam would be controlled by Ho Chi Minh and the communist forces, whereas South Vietnam would remain in the hands of noncommunists. In the context of growing tensions with the Soviet Union and China, U.S. president Dwight Eisenhower invoked the "domino theory," arguing that a communist Vietnam would lead to the spread of communism throughout Southeast Asia. The terms of the **Geneva Conference** required elections within two years in both North and South Vietnam that would reunite the country, and

MAP 37.1
Decolonization in Asia. Date is year of independence.

Note the dates of independence for the colonies of Great Britain, the Netherlands, the United States, and France.

Why did independence occur in such a short time span for most of these colonies?

it seemed clear to all that Ho would easily win. Instead of allowing Ho's communist government to be fairly elected, the United States supported a South Vietnamese anti-communist leader, and together both ignored calls for new elections. But Ngo Dinh Diem (1901–1963), the first president of the Republic of (South) Vietnam, was dictatorial, corrupt, and deeply unpopular with the people, and growing discontent sparked the spread of guerrilla war in the south.

In 1960, Vietnamese nationalists in the south formed the National Liberation Front (NLF) to fight for freedom from South Vietnamese rule (the military arm of the NLF became known as the **Viet Cong**). Although Vietnamese from the south made up the majority in this organization, it received direction, aid, weapons, and ultimately troops from the north. In turn, the government in the north received economic and military assistance from the Soviet Union and China, and a Cold War stalemate ensued.

Ho Chi Minh, leader of North Vietnam from 1945 to 1969 and one of southeast Asia's most influential communist leaders.
Bettmann/Getty Images

the conflict. Nixon extended the war into Cambodia through bombing and invasion in 1969 and 1970, and he resumed the heavy bombing of North Vietnam. He also opened diplomatic channels to the Soviet Union and China, hoping to get them to pressure North Vietnam into a negotiated end to the war. U.S. troops gradually withdrew from the conflict, and in January 1973 the "American War," as the Vietnamese termed it, ended with the negotiated Paris Peace Accords. With the Americans out of the way, forces from North Vietnam, in partnership with the Viet Cong, began to move south. In April 1975, North Vietnamese tanks rolled into Saigon. The next year, Vietnam was officially reunited as one nation, twenty-two years after the partition of the country by Cold War powers. War itself did not end, as forces from North Vietnam and the NLF continued their struggle to conquer South Vietnam and unite the nation. They achieved their goals with the military defeat of South Vietnam in 1975 and with national reunification in 1976.

Vietnam's "American War" Given the lack of popular support for the U.S.-backed Diem regime, the Viet Cong's attacks against the South Vietnamese government met with continued success. Believing in the dire consequences of a communist victory for the stability of Southeast Asia, in 1965 President **Lyndon Johnson** (1908–1973) embarked on a course of action that exponentially increased U.S. involvement in Vietnam. He ordered a bombing campaign against North Vietnam and sent U.S. ground troops to augment the South Vietnamese army. Yet, even with the overwhelming firepower and military personnel, the best the United States and South Vietnam could achieve against the Viet Cong was a draw. The United States had completely underestimated the ability and the resolve of both the Viet Minh and the Viet Cong—not to mention their civilian supporters—to fight effectively for Vietnamese self-determination. But the sacrifices were terrible: between 1965 and 1975, scholars estimate that nearly 900,000 Vietnamese soldiers and civilians were killed as a result of the war.

Vietnamese Victory Faced with such strong and effective resistance against U.S. intervention, incensed by the loss of over 58,000 American soldiers, and shocked by daily depictions of the war's brutality on American television, public opinion in the United States began to turn against the war. In 1968, the war had become so divisive that president Lyndon Johnson pledged not to run for re-election, while Richard Nixon successfully campaigned on a pledge to end the war. After Nixon's election, he implemented his strategy of turning the war over to the South Vietnamese—termed **Vietnamization**—by escalating

Arab National States and the Problem of Palestine

With the exception of Palestine, and in stark contrast to Vietnam, the Arab states of Southwest Asia had little difficulty freeing themselves from the colonial powers of France and Britain by the end of World War II. Before World War II, anticolonial activists in Arab states had already won concessions for self-rule under the mandate system established after the Great War. For example, Egyptians had won almost complete autonomy from British rule, although this autonomy continued to be limited by British military control of the strategic Suez Canal and the oil-rich Persian Gulf.

Arab Independence By 1946, Syria, Iraq, Lebanon, and Jordan had gained complete independence. But as in Egypt, significant vestiges of imperial rule impeded Arab sovereignty. The battle to rid Southwest Asia of those remnants of imperialism was deeply complicated by the Cold War, as both the United States and the Soviet Union sought influence in the region because of its vast reserves of oil, the lifeblood of the Cold War's military-industrial complexes. Throughout, one ambiguous legacy of imperialism—Palestine—absorbed much of the region's energies and emotions.

Palestine Great Britain served as the mandate power in Palestine after the Great War and, before and during its mandate, made conflicting promises to the Palestinian Arabs and to the Jews migrating to Palestine to establish a secure home-land where they could avoid persecution. With the Balfour Declaration of 1917, the British government committed itself to the support of a homeland for Jews in Palestine, a commitment engendered in part by the vibrant Zionist movement that had been growing in Europe since the 1890s. Zionists were dedicated to combating the violent anti-Semitism prevailing in central and eastern Europe by establishing a national Jewish state. The Zionist dream of returning to Palestine, the site of the original Jewish homeland, received a boost from the Balfour Declaration and from the Allies' support for it at the Paris Peace Conference in 1919. Thus the British were compelled to allow Jewish migration to Palestine under their mandate, but they also had to respond to the fears of those in possession of the land—the Palestinian Arabs. The British therefore limited the migration and settlement of Jews and promised to protect the Arabs' political and economic rights.

At the end of World War II, a battle brewed. The Holocaust, along with the British policy of limiting Jewish migration

to Palestine after the war, intensified the Jewish commitment to build a state capable of defending the world's remaining Jews. At the same time, as Arab states around Palestine gained their freedom from imperial rule, they developed a pan-Arab nationalism sparked by support for their fellow Arabs in Palestine and opposition to the possibility of a Jewish state there.

The Creation of Israel The British could not adjudicate the competing claims of the Arabs and the Jews in Palestine. While the Arabs insisted on complete independence under Arab rule, in 1945 the Jews embarked on a course of violent resistance to the British to compel recognition of Jewish demands for self-rule and open immigration. The British gave up in 1947, stating that they intended to withdraw from Palestine and turn over the region to the newly created United Nations. Delegates to the UN General Assembly debated the idea of dividing Palestine into two states, one Arab and the other Jewish. The United States and the Soviet Union lent their support to that notion, and in November 1947 the General Assembly announced a proposal for the division of Palestine into two distinct states. Arabs

MAP 37.2 The Arab-Israeli conflict, 1947–1982.

Compare the boundaries proposed by the UN partition of Palestine with the substantially larger territories claimed by Israel after 1948–1949.

What were the strategic advantages of the extra territories claimed by Israel in 1948–1949?

Proposed UN Two-State Plan
- Jewish state
- Arab state
- Jerusalem district

- Israel after UN partition of Palestine, 1947
- New Israeli territory after War of 1948–1949
- Occupied by Israel after Six-Day War, 1967
- Occupied by Israel after October War, 1973
- Returned to Egypt, 1978–1982

inside and outside Palestine found that solution unacceptable, and in late 1947 civil war broke out. Arab and Jewish troops battled each other as the British completed their withdrawal from Palestine, and in May 1948 the Jews in Palestine proclaimed the creation of the independent state of Israel.

Israel's proclamation of statehood provoked a series of military conflicts between Israeli and various Arab forces spanning decades, most notably in 1948-1949, 1956, 1967, 1973, and 1982. As a result of those wars, Israel substantially increased the size of its territory beyond the area granted to it by the original UN partition and forced hundreds of thousands of Palestinians to become refugees outside the state of Israel. Because Arabs and Israelis could not reach a comprehensive and permanent peace agreement, hostilities continued. Beginning in 1987 a popular mass movement known as the *intifada* initiated a series of demonstrations, strikes, and riots against Israeli rule in the Gaza Strip and other occupied territories. Violence continues well into the twenty-first century, and the future of the occupied territories remains undetermined.

Egypt and Arab Nationalism Egyptian military leaders, under the direction of **Gamal Abdel Nasser** (1918-1970), committed themselves to opposing Israel and taking command of the Arab world. When Israel had declared independence in 1948, Egypt—along with Jordan, Iraq, Syria, and Lebanon—declared war against the new state. But instead of defeating

Gamal Abdel Nasser was president of Egypt from 1954 until his death in 1970.

Bettmann/Getty Images

Israel, the Arab coalition was not only defeated but lost territory. Egyptians were deeply unhappy with their leadership and staged a number of riots. In July 1952 Nasser and other officers staged a bloodless coup that ended the monarchy of Egypt's King Farouk. Two years later, Nasser named himself prime minister and took control of the government. He then labored assiduously to develop Egypt economically and militarily and make it the fountainhead of pan-Arab nationalism.

In his efforts to strengthen Egypt, Nasser adopted an internationalist position based, like India's Nehru, on the idea of nonalignment (in fact, Nasser attended the Bandung Conference on nonalignment in 1955). Nasser argued that Cold War power politics were simply a new form of imperialism. Nasser condemned states that joined with either the United States or the Soviet Union in military alliances. In practice, however, Nasser played both sides off the other, and he used his political savvy to extract pledges of economic and military assistance from the United States and the Soviet Union. In so doing, Nasser demonstrated how newly independent nations could evade becoming trapped in either ideological camp and could force the superpowers to compete for influence.

Nasser also dedicated himself to ridding Egypt and the Arab world of imperial interference, which he believed included destroying the state of Israel. He also gave aid to the Algerians in their war against the French. Nasser did not neglect the remaining imperial presence in Egypt: he abolished British military rights to the Suez Canal in 1954. Through such actions and through his country's antipathy toward Israel, he laid claim to pan-Arab leadership throughout Southwest Asia and north Africa.

The Suez Crisis Nasser sealed his reputation during the **Suez crisis,** which left him in a dominant position in the Arab world. The crisis erupted in 1956, when Nasser decided to nationalize the Suez Canal and use the money collected from the canal to finance construction of a massive dam of the Nile River at Aswan. When he did not bow to international pressure to provide multinational control of the vital Suez Canal, British, French, and Israeli forces conspired to wrest control of the canal away from him. Their military campaign was successful, but they failed miserably on the diplomatic level and tore at the fabric of the Cold War world system. They had not consulted with the United States, which strongly condemned the attack and forced them to withdraw. The Soviet Union also objected forcefully, thereby gaining a reputation for being a staunch supporter of Arab nationalism. Nasser gained tremendous prestige, and Egypt solidified its position as leader of the charge against imperial holdovers in Southwest Asia and north Africa.

Despite Nasser's successes, he did not achieve his goal of defeating Israel, which instead continued to grow stronger and gain more territory. And although Nasser succeeded in playing the Cold War powers off one another and in sowing disunity between the United States and its European allies during the Suez Crisis, the superpowers nevertheless continued to intervene in the region because of its strategic value as an oil-producing region. These interventions, along with the continuation of the Arab-Israeli conflict, contributed to long-term instability in Southwest Asia long after the end of empire.

DECOLONIZATION IN AFRICA

Independence struggles in Africa took many forms—some peaceful and some violent—depending on the type of colony, the colonial power, and the nature of opposing anticolonial movements. In some colonies, like Angola, the colonial powers refused to relinquish their power without long and bloody wars. In others, like Ghana, decolonization was seen as an inevitability. In colonies where imperial rule had the support of European settlers, as in Algeria or Kenya, decolonization often became violent. Complicating the decolonization process were internal divisions in African societies, which undermined attempts to forge national or pan-African identities. Ethnic, religious, and linguistic divides within and between state boundaries, all of which colonial rulers had exploited, posed a challenge to African leaders. Whatever the path and in spite of many challenges, between 1957 and 1980 Africans from every region had won their independence.

Forcing the French out of North Africa

In 1956, Morocco and Tunisia peacefully won their independence from France. Four years later, thirteen French colonies in west and equatorial Africa also won their independence, leading some to dub 1960 as "the year of Africa." But in Algeria, the French resisted decolonization, sparking a brutal war that lasted eight years.

France and Algeria   The French government treated Algeria differently than its other African colonies for two reasons. First, Algeria was a settler colony, meaning that a substantial number of Europeans had made Algeria their permanent home in the nineteenth and twentieth centuries. By the mid-1940s, two million French and other Europeans had either settled in or had been born in Algeria. Second, unlike its other colonies in Africa, the French constitution of 1848 had incorporated Algeria as a region of France rather than as a separate colony. Thus, when Algerian nationalists began to advocate for independence from France and freedom from domination by white settlers just after World War II, the French government saw their actions as a threat to the integrity of France itself. The event that touched off the Algerian revolt came in May 1945.

War in Algeria   Algerian discontent with French rule soared in May 1945. French colonial police in the town of Sétif fired shots into an otherwise

Two female members of the National Liberation Army in combat gear during the war for Algerian independence. Thousands of women were active participants in the fight for independence from the French.
Keystone-France/Gamma-Keystone/Getty Images

How the Past Shapes the Future ▷ ▷ ▷ ▷

The Destructive Potential of Industrial Technologies

In both Algeria and Vietnam, France and the United States employed vast quantities of sophisticated weaponry—including fighter planes, helicopters, bombs, chemical agents, rifles, and grenades—to defeat the forces that opposed them. Yet even though Algerian and Vietnamese revolutionaries did not possess technological parity with French and American military might, they were not defeated. The reasons included military aid (indirect and direct) from the Soviet Union (and China, in the case of Vietnam), but also a willingness to resort to guerrilla warfare, suicide bombings, or sabotage to maximize the effectiveness of individual efforts in fighting against massive force. Consider the circumstances in which the deployment of sophisticated military technologies might not be enough to defeat a less well-armed opposition.

Legend:
- Great Britain
- France
- Italy
- Belgium
- Portugal
- Spain

MAP 37.3   Decolonization in Africa. Date is year of independence.

Compare this map with Map 32.2.

How do the borders of the newly independent African states compare with those drawn by European powers in the late nineteenth century?

peaceful demonstration in support of Algerian and Arab nationalism. Algerian rioting and French repression of the disturbances took place in the wake of the incident. In the resulting fighting more than eight thousand Algerian Muslims died, along with approximately one hundred French. Discontent simmered following the disaster, but it was only in 1954 that the Algerian war of liberation began in earnest under the command of the Front de Libération Nationale (**FLN,** or National Liberation Front). The FLN adopted tactics similar to those of nationalist liberation groups in Asia, relying on bases in outly-

ing mountainous areas and resorting to guerrilla warfare. The French did not realize the seriousness of the challenge they faced until 1955, when the FLN moved into more urbanized areas. At that point, France sent thousands of troops to Algeria to put down the revolution, and by 1958 it had committed half a million soldiers to the war. The war was brutal and ugly: Algerians serving with the French had to kill fellow Algerians or be killed by them; Algerian civilians became trapped in the crossfire of war, often accused of and killed for aiding FLN guerrillas; thousands of French soldiers died. By the war's end in 1962, when the Algerians gained independence from France, hundreds of thousands of Algerians had died.

Frantz Fanon One revolutionary from the Algerian war left a legacy for anticolonial activists everywhere. **Frantz Fanon** (1925–1961) gained fame as a supporter of Algerian independence and as an influential proponent of national liberation for colonial peoples through violent revolution. Born in Martinique in the West Indies, Fanon studied psychiatry and medicine in France, went to Algeria to head a hospital's psychiatric department, and then participated in Algeria's battle to free itself from French rule. Fanon furthered his fame and provided ideological support for African nationalism and revolution in his writings. In works such as *Black Skin, White Masks* (1952), he exposed the deep and damaging effects of colonial racism. Later, in *The Wretched of the Earth* (1961), he urged the use of violence against colonial oppressors as a means of overcoming the racist degradation experienced by peoples in developing or colonial nations. Fanon died shortly before Algeria achieved independence in 1962, but his ideas influenced the independence struggles that were still ongoing in Africa.

Black African Nationalism and Independence

Anticolonial movements were widespread in sub-Saharan Africa by the end of World War II. Some of these movements drew from the pan-African movements that emerged in the United States and the Caribbean in the early twentieth century (see chapter 34). For example, African intellectuals, especially in French-controlled west Africa, established a movement to promote *Négritude* ("Blackness"). Reviving Africa's great traditions, poets and writers expressed a widely shared pride in the rich and diverse cultures and histories of Africa.

Growth of African Nationalism This celebration of African culture was accompanied by grassroots protests against European imperialism in nearly every colony. A new urban African elite created organizations that held demonstrations and protests, and put pressure on colonial governments. Especially widespread, if sporadic, were workers' strikes against oppressive labor practices and low wages in areas such as the Gold Coast and Northern Rhodesia. Some independent Christian churches also provided avenues for anticolonial agitation, as prophets such as Simon Kimbangu in the Belgian Congo promised his churchgoers that God would deliver them from imperial control. And in the years after World War II, African poets associated with the *Négritude* movement continued to encourage Africans to turn away from European culture and colonial rule.

African Independence European colonizers frequently tried to stall independence in sub-Saharan Africa. Often assuming that black Africans were incapable of self-government, imperial powers planned for a slow transition to independence. The presence of white settlers in certain African colonies also complicated the process of decolonization. The politics of the Cold War allowed imperial powers to justify oppressive actions in the name of rooting out a subversive communist presence. Despite delays, however, sub-Saharan states slowly but surely won their independence as each newly

Roadside portraits of Queen Elizabeth II (1926–) and Kwame Nkrumah (1909–1972) in Accra. The British monarch made a postindependence visit to Ghana in November 1961.
Express Newspapers/ Hulton Royals Collection/ Getty Images

SOURCES FROM THE PAST

Kwame Nkrumah on the Future of Africa

As the leader of the first African nation to gain independence, Kwame Nkrumah (1909–1972) became a respected spokesperson for African unity as a strategy for dealing with decolonization during the cold war. In addition to his own speeches and writings, like-minded African nationalists also sought his stamp of approval by asking him to endorse their work. In this foreword to Africa Unbound: Reflections of an African Statesman, *Nkrumah did just that, while also reminding readers of his own vision for the future of Africa.*

The decade following the early 1950s may truly be regarded as Africa's decade. Breathtaking and significant changes have taken place on the African continent that were undreamed of twelve or fifteen years earlier. The independence of Ghana in March, 1957, proved to be the beginning of a great avalanche which was soon to sweep before it the "possessions" and "spheres of influence" of the colonial powers. A majority of these so called possessions have been transformed in our time into sovereign, independent states, and the process of decolonization goes on unabated.

Our next goal is to attain the political unification of the African continent so as to give form and substance to our independence through total disengagement from imperialist and colonialist entanglements . . .

Africans [are making efforts] to complete the liberation of their continent from all forms of imperialism, colonialism, racialism, and neocolonialism. In this way, we may secure the establishment of the personality of the African and the fulfillment of his destiny in an interdependent world.

> Why, according to Nkrumah, was the political unification of Africa so important for its future?

For Further Reflection

■ What role do you think Nkrumah sees for Ghana in this African future? Does Nkrumah seem optimistic or pessimistic? Why?

Source: Alex Quaison-Sackey, *Africa Unbound: Reflections of an African Statesman.* New York: Frederick Praeger, 1963, foreword.

---

independent nation inspired and often aided other territories to win their freedom.

Freedom and Conflict in Sub-Saharan Africa

Ghana Ghana, located in west Africa, was the first sub-Saharan country to achieve independence from colonial rule. Its people had been engaged in trade with Europe since the fifteenth century. Trading originally centered on gold but then shifted to the slave trade in the seventeenth century. By the time the British established Ghana as a Crown colony in 1874 (known at that time as the Gold Coast), its economy had developed into an important center for growing and exporting cacao.

Ghana's success in achieving its freedom from British rule in 1957 served as a hallmark in Africa's end of empire. Under the leadership of **Kwame Nkrumah** (1909–1972), political parties and strategies for mass action took shape. Although the British subjected Nkrumah and other nationalists to jail terms and repressive control, they eventually conceded to reforms and negotiated the transfer of power in their Gold Coast colony.

After it became independent in 1957, Ghana emboldened and inspired other African anticolonial movements. More than thirty other African countries followed Ghana's example and won their own independence within the next decade. Nkrumah, as a leader of the first sub-Saharan African nation to gain independence from colonial rule, became a persuasive spokesperson for pan-African unity. These efforts were aided by the optimism for the future in Ghana, whose immediate postcolonial economic prospects were bright. Indeed, in 1957 Ghana's gross domestic product was roughly equal to that of South Korea and was only slightly behind Portugal. Nkrumah's leadership of this prosperous new state symbolized the changing times in Africa.

Anticolonial Rebellion in Kenya The process of attaining independence was sometimes extremely violent. The battle for independence that took place in the British colony of Kenya in east Africa was one of these cases. The situation in

Kwame Nkrumah (KWAH-mee en-KROO-mah)

Kenya turned tense and violent in a clash between powerful white settlers and their elite, land-holding African allies on the one hand and landless Africans who had been impoverished by colonial rule on the other. Most of those involved were Kikuyu, one of Kenya's largest ethnic groups, because the British had disproportionately dispossessed the Kikuyu from their lands in the fertile Kenyan highlands. Beginning in 1947, Kikuyu seeking to drive out the British embarked on an intermittently violent campaign against both Europeans and against the Africans who had allied themselves with them. The settlers who controlled the colonial government in Nairobi refused to see the uprisings as a legitimate expression of discontent with colonial rule. Rather, they branded the Kikuyu rebels as radicals bent on a racial struggle for primacy. But it was the British settlers who displayed their own deep racism with comments such as, "Why the hell can't we fight these apes and worry about the survivors later?" Members of the militant anticolonial movements were labeled by the British government as **Mau Mau** subversives.

Kikuyu who became involved in the Mau Mau movement were deeply dissatisfied with British rule in Kenya. Their resentment originated in particular from their treatment in the 1930s and 1940s, when white settlers pushed them off the most fertile highland farm areas, often relegating them to overcrowded "tribal reserves." Resistance began in the early 1940s with labor strikes and violent direct action campaigns

These Kikuyu children were photographed in 1952 in a British government prison camp, where rebel nationalists and their families were detained.
Hulton Deutsch/Corbis Historical/Getty Images

designed to force or frighten the white settlers off the land. In the 1950s, attacks on white settlers—and on Africans the Kikuyu believed were collaborating with them—escalated, and in 1952 the British established a state of emergency to crush the anticolonial guerrilla movement through a violent counterinsurgency program that involved rounding up and imprisoning over a hundred thousand Kikuyu in detention camps. Conditions inside the camps were dismal, and many thousands died from abuse, disease, and execution. Unable or unwilling to distinguish violent activism from nonviolent agitation, the British moved to suppress all anticolonial groups and jailed Kenyan nationalist leaders, including Jomo Kenyatta (1895-1978) in 1953. Amid growing resistance to colonial rule, the British mounted major military offenses against rebel forces, supporting their army troops with artillery, bombers, and jet fighters. By 1956 the British had effectively crushed all military resistance in a conflict that claimed the lives of twelve thousand Africans and one hundred Europeans.

Despite military defeat, Kikuyu fighters broke British resolve in Kenya and gained increasing international recognition of African grievances. The British resisted the radical white supremacism and political domineering of the settlers in Kenya and instead responded to calls for Kenyan independence. In 1959 the British lifted the state of emergency, and as political parties formed, nationalist leaders like Kenyatta reemerged to lead those parties. By December 1963 Kenya had negotiated its independence.

Internal Colonialism in South Africa As elsewhere in Africa, the presence of large numbers of white settlers in South Africa long frustrated, complicated, and delayed the arrival of freedom for black South Africans. Even though black South Africans made up almost 70 percent of the population by 1946, white settlers had violently driven them off the best lands and deprived them of political rights. Anticolonial agitation thus was significantly different in South Africa than in the rest of sub-Saharan Africa: it was a struggle against internal colonialism, against an oppressive white regime that denied basic human and civil rights to tens of millions of South Africans.

Apartheid The ability of whites to resist majority rule was aided by the South African economy, the strongest on the continent. That strength had two sources: extraction of minerals and industrial development, which received a huge boost during World War II. The growth of the industrial sector opened many jobs to black South Africans, allowing some to build wealth, to organize into labor unions, and to demand serious political reform. These changes deeply alarmed white South Africans, who had built their rule on the political and economic oppression of black South Africans. In 1948 the Afrikaner National Party, which was dedicated to quashing any move toward black equality, came to power. Under the National Party the government instituted a harsh new set of laws designed to extend their control over the increasingly organized black population; these new laws constituted the system known as **apartheid,** or "separateness."

The system of apartheid institutionalized the racial segregation established in the years before 1948. The government designated approximately 87 percent of South Africa's territory for white residents. Remaining areas were designated as homelands for black and colored citizens. Nonwhites were classified according to a variety of ethnic identifications—colored or mixed-race peoples, Indians, and "Bantu," which in turn was subdivided into numerous distinct tribal affiliations (for example, Zulu, Xhosa, Sotho). As other imperial powers had done in Africa, white South Africans divided the black and colored population in the hope of preventing the rise of unified liberation movements. The apartheid system, complex and varied in its composition, evolved into a system designed to keep blacks in a position of political, social, and economic subordination.

Black South Africans resisted apartheid, just as they had resisted oppressive laws prior to 1948. The **African National Congress** (ANC), formed in 1912, gained new young leaders such as **Nelson Mandela** (1918–2013), who inspired direct action campaigns to protest apartheid. In 1955 the ANC (itself inspired by the Indian National Congress) published its Freedom Charter, which proclaimed the ideal of multiracial democratic rule for South Africa. Because its goals directly challenged white rule, the ANC and all black activists in South Africa faced severe repression. The government declared all its opponents communists and escalated its actions against black activists. Protests increased in 1960, the so-called year of Africa when multiple African nations won their independence from European colonial powers, and on 21 March 1960 white police gunned down unarmed black South African demonstrators in Sharpeville, near Johannesburg. Sixty-nine people, among them many young adults and ten children, were killed and almost two hundred more were wounded. Sharpeville, however, only increased radical activism by black South Africans.

At the same time, the egregious use of violence and repression by the white regime in South Africa also increased international opposition to white South African rule. Newly independent nations in Asia and Africa called for UN sanctions against South Africa while anticolonial and antiracist activists sought to publicize the government's repeated human rights violations. In 1961 South Africa declared itself a republic and withdrew from the British Commonwealth. Two years later, government forces captured the leaders of the ANC's military unit, including Nelson Mandela, and sentenced them to life in prison. Thereafter, Mandela and others became symbols of oppressive white rule. Protests against the system persisted in the 1970s and 1980s, spurred especially by student activism and awareness of successful independence struggles in neighboring states. The combined effects of widespread resistance and agitation with a powerful international anti-apartheid boycott eventually led to a growing recognition that, if it was to survive, South Africa had to change.

The End of Apartheid When **F. W. de Klerk** (1936–) became president of South Africa in 1989, he and the National Party began to dismantle the apartheid system. De Klerk

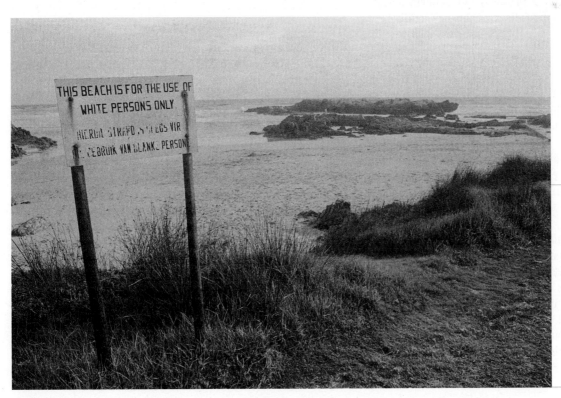

A sign in English and Afrikaans instructing visitors that the beach is for white persons only. From the Cape Province in South Africa in 1974, during the period of apartheid. Jonathan C. Katzenellenbogen/Getty Images

released Mandela from jail in 1990, legalized the ANC, and worked with Mandela and the ANC to negotiate the end of white minority rule. Collaborating and cooperating, the National Party, the ANC, and other African political groups created a new constitution and in April 1994 held elections that were open to people of all races. The ANC won overwhelmingly, and Mandela became the first black president of South Africa. In 1963, at the trial that ended in his jail sentence, Mandela proclaimed, "I have cherished the ideal of a democratic and free society in which all persons live together in harmony and with equal opportunities. It is an ideal which I hope to live for and to achieve. But if needs be, it is an ideal for which I am prepared to die." Mandela lived to see his ideal fulfilled. In 1994, echoing the words of Martin Luther King Jr., President Mandela proclaimed his nation "free at last."

AFTER INDEPENDENCE: LONG-TERM STRUGGLES IN THE POSTCOLONIAL ERA

Political and economic stability proved elusive after independence, particularly in those nations struggling to build political and economic systems free from the domination of more powerful nations. The legacies of imperialism, either direct or indirect, hindered the creation of democratic institutions in many parts of the world—from recently decolonized nations, such as those of Africa, to nations that won their independence a century earlier, such as those in Latin America. Continued interference by the former colonial powers or the Cold War superpowers impeded stability and prosperity all over the world. Indeed, few developing or newly independent nations escaped the legacies of imperialism or the new realities of Cold War rivalries as they sought to find their place in the postcolonial world.

Communism and Democracy in Asia

Except for Japan and India, the developing nations in south, southeast, and east Asia adopted some form of authoritarian or militarist political system, and several followed a communist or socialist path of political development. Under Mao Zedong (1893-1976), China served as a guide and inspiration for those countries seeking a means of political development distinct from the ways of the former colonial powers.

Mao's China Mao reunified China for the first time since the collapse of the Qing dynasty, transforming European communist ideology into a distinctly Chinese communism. After 1949 he embarked on programs designed to accelerate development in China. The economic and social transformation of Chinese society centered on rapid industrialization and the collectivization of agriculture (making landownership collective, not individual). Emulating earlier Soviet experiments, the Chinese introduced their first Five-Year Plan in 1955. Designed to speed up economic development, the Five-Year Plan emphasized im-

A 1966 poster shows Mao Zedong (1893–1976) inspiring young people to launch the Great Proletarian Cultural Revolution (1966–1976).
Hulton Archive/Getty Images

provements in infrastructure and the expansion of heavy industry at the expense of consumer goods. A series of agrarian laws promoted an unprecedented transfer of wealth among the population, virtually eliminating economic inequality at the village level. The government achieved this by confiscating the landholdings of rich peasants and landlords and redistributing the land so that virtually every peasant had at least a small plot of land. Between 1954 and 1960, however, the government oversaw the gradual collectivization of individual landholdings into agricultural communes in which land ownership existed only at the level of the commune. In the same period, the government took over the grain market and prohibited farmers from marketing their own crops. Collectives also became responsible for the provision of health care and primary education, which permitted the extension of social services to larger segments of the population. In the wake of economic reforms came social reforms, many of which challenged and often eliminated Chinese family traditions. Supporting equal rights for women, Chinese authorities introduced marriage laws that eliminated practices such as child or forced marriages, gave women equal access to divorce, and legalized abortion. Foot binding, a symbol of women's subjugation, was outlawed.

SOURCES FROM THE PAST

China's Marriage Law, 1949

When the Chinese Communist Party came into power under Mao Zedong in 1949, the new government quickly instituted the "Marriage Law," which made Chinese men and women legal equals in marriage. This was truly revolutionary because women traditionally held very low status in China's highly patriarchal social structure. Although actual equality was more elusive than legal equality, the Marriage Law marked a significant step toward granting women more rights in Chinese society.

Chapter I. General Principles

Article 1. The arbitrary and compulsory feudal marriage system, which is based on the superiority of man over woman and which ignores the children's interests, shall be abolished. The new democratic marriage system, which is based on free choice of partners, on monogamy, on equal rights for both sexes, and on protection of the lawful interests of women and children, shall be put into effect.

> Why might this article have seemed revolutionary in 1949?

Article 2. Bigamy, concubinage, child betrothal, interference with the remarriage of widows, and the exaction of money or gifts in connection with marriage shall be prohibited. . . .

Chapter III. Rights and Duties of Husband and Wife

Article 7. Husband and wife are companions living together and shall enjoy equal status in the home.

Article 8. Husband and wife are in duty bound to love, respect, assist, and look after each other, to live in harmony, to engage in production, to care for the children, and to strive jointly for the welfare of the family and for the building up of a new society.

Article 9. Both husband and wife shall have the right to free choice of occupation and free participation in work or in social activities.

> Why might it have seemed important to the authors of this law to include this article?

Article 10. Both husband and wife shall have equal right in the possession and management of family property.

Article 11. Both husband and wife shall have the right to use his or her own family name.

Article 12. Both husband and wife shall have the right to inherit each other's property.

For Further Reflection

■ In what ways were these marriage laws similar to or different from the demands for gender equality made by feminists in the United States and western Europe during the 1960s and 1970s?

Source: Dennis Sherman et al., *World Civilizations: Sources, Images, and Interpretations*, 3rd ed., Volume 2. Boston and New York: McGraw-Hill, 2002.

Mao's drive for development and revolutionary change was epitomized by the **Great Leap Forward** (1958-1961) and the **Great Proletarian Cultural Revolution** (1966-1976). These were far-reaching movements intended to bring rapid progress to China. In practice, however, they undermined the very political and economic development that Mao sought.

Mao envisioned his Great Leap Forward as a way to quickly overtake the industrial production of more developed nations. To achieve this, Mao extended the program of agricultural collectivization with the goal of collectivizing all land and managing all business and industrial enterprises collectively. Private ownership was abolished, and both farming and industry became communal. But the Great Leap Forward—or "Giant Step Backward" as some have dubbed it—failed. Most disastrous was its impact on agricultural production in China: the peasants did not meet production quotas set by the government, and a series of bad harvests contributed to one of the deadliest famines in history. Rather than face reality, Mao blamed the sparrows for the bad harvests, accusing these "counterrevolutionaries" of eating too much grain. He ordered tens of millions of peasants to kill the feathered menaces, leaving insects free to consume what was left of the crops. Between 1959 and 1962 as many as twenty million Chinese may have died of starvation and malnutrition in this crisis.

Chinese students stage a pro-democracy sit-in at Tiananmen Square in Beijing, in June 1989, with the historic Forbidden City in the background. Such protests were repressed violently by the Chinese government.

Chris Niedenthal//Time Life Pictures/Getty Images

The Cultural Revolution In 1966 Mao tried again to mobilize the Chinese and reignite the revolutionary spirit with the inauguration of the Great Proletarian Cultural Revolution. Designed to root out the revisionism (anti-revolutionary sentiment) Mao perceived in Chinese life, especially among Communist Party leaders and others in positions of authority, the Cultural Revolution subjected millions of people to humiliation, persecution, and death. The elite—intellectuals, teachers, professionals, managers, and anyone associated with foreign or bourgeois values—constituted the major targets of the Red Guards, teenagers Mao had empowered to cleanse Chinese society of opponents to his rule. Victims were beaten and killed, jailed, or sent to corrective labor camps or to toil in the countryside. The Cultural Revolution, which cost China years of stable development and gutted its educational system, did not end until after Mao's death in 1976. It fell to one of Mao's political heirs, Deng Xiaoping, to begin to heal the nation.

Deng's Revolution Although he was a colleague of Mao, **Deng Xiaoping** (1904–1997) suffered the same fate as millions of other Chinese during the Cultural Revolution: he had to recant criticisms of Mao, identify himself as a petit-bourgeois intellectual, and labor in a tractor-repair factory. When a radical faction failed to maintain the Cultural Revolution after Mao's death, China began its recovery from the turmoil. Deng came to power in 1981, and the 1980s are often referred to as the years of "Deng's Revolution." Deng moderated Mao's commitment to Chinese self-sufficiency and isolation and engineered China's entry into the international financial and

trading system, a move that was facilitated by the normalization of relations between China and the United States in the 1970s.

Tiananmen Square To facilitate China's economic development, Deng opened the nation to the influences that had been suspect under Mao as foreign, capitalist values. His actions included sending tens of thousands of Chinese students to foreign universities to rebuild the professional, intellectual, and managerial elite needed for modern development. But Deng's openness to foreign values only extended so far. When some of the students who had studied abroad staged prodemocracy demonstrations in Beijing's **Tiananmen Square** in 1989, Deng, whose experiences in the Cultural Revolution made him wary of revolutionary movements, approved a bloody crackdown. Not surprisingly, Deng faced hostile world opinion after crushing the student movement. The issue facing China as it entered the global economy was how (or whether) to reap economic benefits without compromising its identity and its authoritarian political system. This issue gained added urgency as Hong Kong, under British administration since the 1840s and in the throes of its own democracy movement, reverted to Chinese control in 1997. Chinese leaders in the twenty-first century have managed to maintain both centralized political control over China and impressive economic growth and development, though political control has depended on swift repression of dissenting voices.

Indian Democracy Whereas other nations turned to dictators, military rule, or authoritarian systems, India was able to maintain its political stability and its democratic system after gaining independence in 1947. Even when faced with ethnic and religious conflict, wars, poverty, and overpopulation, India remained committed to free elections and a critical press. Its first postindependence prime minister, Jawaharlal Nehru, guided this commitment to democratic rule for seventeen years, until his death in 1964.

In 1966 **Indira Gandhi** (1917–1984), Nehru's daughter (and no relation to Mohandas K. Gandhi), became leader of the Congress Party. She served as prime minister of India from 1966 to 1977 and from 1980 to 1984, and under her leadership India embarked on the "green revolution" that increased agricultural yields for India's eight hundred million people. Although the new agricultural policies aided wealthier farmers, the masses of peasant farmers were unable to buy the high-yield seeds, chemical fertilizers, insecticides, and farm equipment central to the green revolution, and thus they fell even deeper into poverty than before. In addition to continued poverty, India during Gandhi's administration was beset by problems relating to overpopulation and sectarian conflicts.

Those problems prompted Indira Gandhi to take decidedly undemocratic action to maintain control. To quell growing opposition to her government, she declared a national emergency that suspended democratic processes from 1975 until 1977. She used her powers under the emergency to move forward with one of India's most needed social reforms, birth control. But rather than persuading or tempting Indians to control the size of their families (offering gifts of money for those who got vasectomies, for example), the government engaged in repressive birth control policies, including forced sterilization. A record eight million sterilization operations were performed in 1976 and 1977, prompting huge riots.

When Indira Gandhi allowed elections to be held in 1977, Indians voted against her because of her violation of democratic principles and her harsh birth control policies. But she was voted back into power in 1980, this time in the midst of fierce religious, ethnic, and secessionist movements. One such movement was an uprising by Sikhs who wanted greater autonomy in the Punjab region. The Sikhs, representing perhaps 2 percent of India's population, practiced a monotheistic religion, maintained a distinctive physical appearance, and had a history of serving in the Indian army. When partition occurred, the traditional Sikh homeland had been split between India and Pakistan, leaving Sikhs to desire its reunification under Sikh rule. When Sikh separatists occupied the sacred Golden Temple in Amritsar and began stockpiling weapons, Indira Gandhi ordered the Indian army to attack, killing hundreds of separatists. In retaliation, two of her Sikh bodyguards—hired for their martial skills—assassinated her a few months later in 1984.

Indira Gandhi's son **Rajiv Gandhi** (1944–1991) took over the leadership of India in 1985 and offered reconciliation to the Sikhs. However, he was assassinated by a terrorist in 1991 while attempting to win back the office he lost in 1989. Despite assassinations, violations of democratic rule, and continued problems with poverty and sectarian division, India has maintained its democratic institutions into the twenty-first century.

Pan-Arab and Islamic Resurgence in Southwest Asia and North Africa

The geographic convergence of the Arab and Muslim worlds in Southwest Asia and north Africa encouraged the development of Arab nationalism in states of those regions that gained independence after World War II. Whether in Libya, Algeria,

A photographer captured this image of Indira Gandhi (1917–1984) in 1976. Gandhi led India into the "green revolution," which sought to increase agricultural production to help feed the country's eight hundred million people. The campaign's mixed results, among other reasons, led to her temporarily losing power in 1977 before regaining it in 1980.
Henri Bureau/Sygma/Corbis/VCG/Getty Images

or Egypt in north Africa or in Syria, Saudi Arabia, or Iraq in Southwest Asia, members of Arab nations were attracted by the idea of pan-Arab unity as a way of fending off European, U.S., and Soviet influence in the region. In north Africa, Egypt's Gamal Abdel Nasser provided the leadership for this pan-Arab nationalism, and Arab opposition to the state of Israel held the dream together.

The hopes attached to pan-Arab unity did not materialize. Although Arab lands shared a common language and religion, divisions were frequent and alliances shifted over time. The Cold War split the Arab world; some states allied themselves with the United States, while others allied with the Soviet Union. Some countries also shifted between the two, as Egypt did when it left the Soviet orbit for the U.S. sphere in 1976. Governments in these nations included military dictatorships, monarchies, and revolutionary Islamist regimes.

Islamism In the 1970s, **Islamism**—or the revival of Islamic values in the political and social sphere—emerged as an alternative to pan-Arab unity. Some Islamic thinkers called for the rigorous enforcement of the *sharia* (Islamic law), emphasized pan-Islamic unity, and urged the elimination of non-Muslim economic, political, or cultural influences in the Muslim world. In the view of many proponents, the Muslim world had been slipping into a state of decline, brought about by the abandonment of Islamic traditions. Many Muslims had become skeptical about European and American models of economic development and political and cultural norms, which they blamed for economic and political failure as well as for secularization and its attendant breakdown of traditional social and religious values. Disillusionment and anger with European and American societies, and especially with the United States, became widespread. The solution to the problems faced by Muslim societies lay, according to Islamists, in the revival of Islamic identity, values, and power. A small minority of Islamists argued that these goals could only be realized through violence.

The Iranian Revolution The **Iranian Revolution** that took place in 1979 demonstrated the power of Islam as a means of staving off secular foreign influences. Islamist influences emerged in Iran during the lengthy regime of Shah Mohammed Reza Pahlavi (1919–1980), whom the United States helped bring to power in 1953 in a CIA-engineered coup. The shah used the money from Iran's vast supply of oil to industrialize the country, and the United States provided the military equipment that enabled Iran to become a bastion of anticommunism in the region. But devout Muslim leaders despised the shah's secular regime, Iranian small businesses detested the influence of U.S. corporations on the economy, and leftist politicians rejected the shah's repressive policies. When the shah left Iran to get medical treatment in 1979, Ayatollah Ruhollah Khomeini (1900–1989) coordinated an Islamist revolution that deposed the shah.

The revolution took on a strongly anti-U.S. cast, mostly because of the long-term U.S. role in bringing the shah to power and maintaining his oppressive rule. During the revolution, Iranians captured sixty-nine hostages at the U.S. embassy in Tehran, fifty-five of whom remained captives until 1981. In the meantime, Iranian leaders shut U.S. military bases and confiscated U.S.-owned economic ventures. This Islamic power play against a developed nation such as the United States inspired other Muslims to stand up for themselves as well. Yet the resurgent Islamism of Iran did not lead to a new era of solidarity. Iranian Islam was the minority sect of Shia Islam, and one of Iran's neighbors, Iraq, attempted to take advantage of the revolution to invade Iran.

By the late 1970s Iraq had built a formidable military machine, largely owing to oil revenues and the efforts of **Saddam Hussein** (1937–2006), who became president of Iraq in 1979. Hussein launched his attack on Iran in 1980, believing that victory would be swift and perhaps hoping to become the new leader of a revived pan-Arab nationalism. (Iran is Muslim in religion but is not ethnically Arab.) Although they were initially successful, Iraqi troops faced a determined counterattack by Iranian forces, and the conflict became a war of attrition that did not end until 1988.

The Iran-Iraq and Gulf Wars The **Iran-Iraq War** killed as many as one million soldiers. In Iran the human devastation is still visible, if not openly acknowledged, in a nation that permits little dissent from Islamist orthodoxy. Young people are showing signs of a growing discontent caused by the war and by the rigors of a revolution that also killed thousands. Signs of recovery and a relaxation of Islamist strictness appeared in Iran in the late 1990s, but the destruction from war also remained visible. Islamism has reemerged in twenty-first-century Iran and has aroused some international concern, particularly for the United States. A conservative supreme leader, the Ayatollah Khamenei (1939–), and a conservative president, **Mahmoud Ahmadinejad** (1956–), represented this trend. Ahmadinejad took office in 2005 and touted Iran's nuclear program and his antipathy to the state of Israel, which had the effect of increasing his status in the Islamic world while intensifying tensions with the United States.

Iraqis continued on a militant course. Two years after the end of the Iran-Iraq War, Hussein's troops invaded Kuwait (1990) and incited the Gulf War (1991). The result was a decisive military defeat for Iraq, at the hands of an international coalition led by the United States, and further hardships for the Iraqi people.

Mahmoud Ahmadinejad (mah-MOOD ah-mah-DIH-nee-zhahd)

Iranian women and men protesting in favor of the revolution to remove the shah from power, Tehran 1979. Thousands of women took an active part in the Iranian revolution. Several people hold posters depicting Ayatollah Khomeini.
Michael Norcia/Sygma/ Getty Images

Colonial Legacies in Sub-Saharan Africa

The optimism that accompanied decolonization in sub-Saharan Africa faded as the prospects for political stability gave way in some areas to civil wars and territorial disputes. This condition largely reflected the impact of colonialism. As European powers departed their decolonized lands, they left behind territories whose borders were artificial conveniences that did not correspond to any indigenous economic or ethnic divisions. Historically distinct communities found themselves jammed into a single "national" state. In other instances, populations found themselves in newly independent states whose borders were unacceptable to neighboring states. As a result, decolonization was sometimes accompanied or followed by civil wars and border disputes that resisted resolution.

The **Organization of African Unity** (OAU), created in 1963 by thirty-two member states, recognized some of those problems and attempted to prevent conflicts that could lead to intervention by former colonial powers. The artificial boundaries of African states, though acknowledged as problematic, were nonetheless held inviolable by the OAU to prevent disputes over boundaries. International law also treated postcolonial borders as inviolable. The OAU also promoted pan-African unity, at least in the faction headed by Kwame Nkrumah, as a vehicle for African states to resist interference and domination by foreign powers. In its early years, the OAU successfully mediated border disputes between Morocco and Algeria (1964–1965) and between Somalia and its neighbors (1965–1967). But the drive for African political unity by leaders like Kwame Nkrumah of Ghana was not always appreciated. It was so unpopular in Ghana that it contributed to Nkrumah's overthrow in a military coup in 1966. In addition, the OAU could not prevent extensive interference by the Cold War superpowers in places like the Democratic Republic of the Congo, Angola, and Mozambique. Nevertheless, in spite of continuing instability and poverty, African leaders in the early postcolonial period sought to integrate their new nations into the global economy by making the most of their rich mineral deposits, raw materials, and agricultural products.

Politics and Economics in Latin America

The uneasy aftermath of independence visible throughout Asia and Africa also affected states on the other side of the world—states that gained their freedom from colonial rule more than a century before postwar decolonization. Nations in Central and South America along with Mexico grappled with the conservative legacies of Spanish and Portuguese colonialism, particularly the political and economic power of the landowning elite of European descent. Latin America moreover had to deal with neocolonialism because the United States not only intervened militarily when its interests were threatened but also influenced economies through investment and full or part ownership of enterprises such as the oil industry. In the nineteenth century Latin American states may have looked to the United States as a model of liberal democracy,

What's Left Out?

While textbooks often discuss how the process of decolonization became entangled with the Cold War, few offer extended treatment of the Portuguese colony of Angola. Yet Angola endured more than thirty years of war when a local communist anticolonial movement became enmeshed in a complex web of international aid and interference during the Cold War. Anticolonial activists in Angola began a widespread rebellion against Portuguese rule in 1961, just as Britain and France were in the process of decolonizing nearby territories in sub-Saharan Africa. War broke out when it became clear that Portugal would not even consider a path to Angolan independence. But Angolans were not united in their vision of independence and broke into three factions, one of which was communist in orientation. The factions turned to outside allies for help, with the result that the communist faction drew aid from communist Cuba and Yugoslavia, while the noncommunist factions drew aid from the United States and South Africa. Outside aid ensured the war would be long and bloody. But after fourteen years of fighting, new leadership in Portugal led the government to abruptly agree to Angolan independence. Before independence could even be declared, however, the three Angolan factions erupted in civil war as each sought sole control of the new country. Seeing an opportunity to determine the ideological allegiance of independent Angola, the United States and the South African government sent weapons, advisers, and (South African) troops to support the noncommunist factions. In response, Cuba sent its own weapons and troops to support the communist faction. With Cuban help, by 1976 the communist faction had won control of now-independent Angola, but even then the South African government continued to provide weapons to noncommunists. This, in turn, led both Cuba and the Soviet Union to continue providing material and financial aid to the victorious communist factions until the Cold War ended in 1991. By then, the Angolan civil war had resulted in massive destruction to the land and infrastructure, and a half million were dead. Thanks to the politics of the Cold War, then, the struggle for Angolan independence and power in the postcolonial era ended in the virtual destruction of the country.

Source: Jonathan Reynolds, *Sovereignty and Struggle: Africa and Africans in the Era of the Cold War,* 1945–1994 (New York and Oxford: Oxford University Press, 2015).

but by the twentieth century U.S. interference provoked negative reactions. That condition was true after World War I, and it remained true during and after World War II.

Mexico Only President Lázaro Cárdenas (in office 1934–1940) had substantially invoked and applied the reforms guaranteed to Mexicans by the Constitution of 1917. The constitution's provisions regarding the state's right to redistribute land after confiscation and compensation, as well as its claim to government ownership of the subsoil and its products, found a champion in Cárdenas. He brought land reform and redistribution to a peak in Mexico, returning forty-five million acres to peasants, and he wrested away control of the oil industry from foreign investors. Cárdenas's nationalization of Mexico's oil industry allowed for the creation of the *Petróleos Mexicanos* (PEMEX), a national oil company in control of Mexico's petroleum products. The revenues generated by PEMEX contributed to what has been called **"El Milagro Mexicano,"** or the Mexican economic miracle, a period of prosperity that lasted until the 1970s. Conservative governments thereafter, controlled by the one-party rule of the Institutional Revolutionary Party (PRI), often acted harshly and experimented with various economic strategies that decreased or increased Mexico's reliance on foreign markets and capital. The PRI came under attack in the 1990s as Mexican peasants in the Chiapas district protested their political oppression. Cuauhtémoc Cárdenas, the son of Lázaro Cárdenas, took on the leadership of an opposition party, the Democratic Revolutionary Party (PRD), and this shift to democratic political competition and multiparty elections has continued into the twenty-first century.

Argentina Mexico served as one model for political development in Latin America, and Argentina seemed to be another candidate for leadership in South America. It had a reasonably expansive economy based on cattle raising and agriculture, a booming urban life, the beginnings of an industrial base, and a growing middle class in a population composed mostly of migrants from Europe. Given its geographic position far to the south, Argentina remained relatively independent of U.S. control and became a leader in the Latin American struggle against U.S. and European economic and political intervention in the region. A gradual shift to free elections and a sharing of political power beyond that exercised by the landowning elite also emerged. Given the military's central role in its politics, however, Argentina became a model of a less positive form of political organization: the often brutal and deadly sway of military rulers.

Juan Perón During World War II, nationalistic military leaders gained power in Argentina and established a government controlled by the army. In 1946 **Juan Perón** (1895–1974), a former colonel in the army, was elected president. Although he was a nationalistic militarist, his regime garnered immense popularity among large segments of the Argentine population, partly because he appealed to ordinary Argentines. He promoted a nationalistic populism, calling for industrialization, support of the working class, and protection of the economy from foreign control.

Evita However opportunistic Perón may have been, his popularity with the masses was real. His wife, Eva Perón (1919–1952), helped to foster that popularity, as Argentines warmly embraced their **"Evita"** (little Eva). She rose from the ranks of the desperately poor. An illegitimate child who migrated to Buenos Aires at the age of fifteen, she found work as a radio soap-opera actress. She met Perón in 1944, and they were married shortly

In this 1950 photo taken in Buenos Aires, Eva Perón (1919–1952) waves to adoring *descamisados,* or "shirtless ones," to whose poverty she ceaselessly ministered. Although many thought of Eva Perón as a "saint," others viewed her own extravagant lifestyle as a sign of her opportunism.
Keystone/Hulton Archive/ Getty Images

thereafter. Reigning in the Casa Rosada (the Pink House) as Argentina's first lady from 1946 to 1952, Eva Perón transformed herself into a talented and fashionable political leader. While pushing for her husband's political reforms, she also tirelessly ministered to the needs of the poor, often the same *descamisados,* or "shirtless ones," who formed the core of her husband's supporters. Endless lines of people came to see her in her offices at the labor ministry—asking for dentures, wedding clothes, medical care, and the like. Eva Perón accommodated those demands and more: she bathed lice-ridden children in her own home, kissed lepers, and created the Eva Perón Foundation to institutionalize and extend such charitable endeavors. When she died of uterine cancer at the age of thirty-three, the nation mourned the tragic passing of a woman who came to be elevated to the status of "Santa Evita."

Some saw Eva Perón not as a saint but as a grasping social climber and a fascist sympathizer and saw her husband as a political opportunist, but after Juan Perón's ouster from office in 1955, support for the Perónist party remained strong. However, with the exception of a brief return to power by Perón in the mid-1970s, brutal military dictators held sway in Argentina for the next three decades. Military rule took a sinister turn in the late 1970s and early 1980s when dictators approved the creation of death squads that fought a "dirty war" against suspected subversives. Between six thousand and twenty-three thousand people disappeared between 1976 and 1983. Calls for a return to democratic politics increased in the aftermath of the dirty war, demands that were intensified by economic disasters and the growth of the poorest classes.

Liberation for Nations and Women

Revolutionary ideologies and political activism provided opportunities for Latin American women to agitate for both national and women's liberation. Nicaraguan women, for example, established the Association of Women Concerned about National Crisis in 1977 and fought as part of the Sandinista Front for National Liberation (FSLN). The **FSLN** was named in honor of the martyred Augusto Cesar Sandino (1893–1934), murdered for his opposition to U.S. intrusion in Nicaragua by the forces of Nicaraguan leader and U.S. ally Anastacio Somoza Garcia (1896–1956). Somoza's sons followed their father's brutal leadership practices, and Nicaraguan women dedicated themselves to ridding their nation of Somoza rule. In 1979 they renamed the organization the Luisa Amanda Espinoza Association of Nicaraguan Women (AMNLAE) to acknowledge the first woman who died in the battle against the Somoza regime. The group's slogan—"No revolution without women's emancipation: no emancipation without revolution"—suggested the dual goals of Nicaraguan women. By the mid-1980s, AMNLAE had over eighty thousand members. Despite facing problems typical of women's movements trying to navigate between national and personal needs, AMNLAE has been credited with forwarding women's participation in the public and political spheres, an impressive accomplishment in a region where women's suffrage had often been delayed. Although women in Ecuador attained

voting rights in 1929, women in Nicaragua could not vote until 1955; Paraguay's women waited for suffrage rights until 1961, when that nation became the last in Latin America to incorporate women into the political process.

The Search for Economic Equity

The late twentieth century witnessed a revival of democratic politics in Latin America, but economic problems continued to limit the possibility of widespread change or the achievement of economic and social equity. In many Latin American nations, the landowning elites who gained power during the colonial era were able to maintain their dominant position, which resulted in societies that remained divided between the few rich, usually backed by the United States, and the masses of the poor. It was difficult to structure such societies without either keeping the elite in power or promoting revolution on behalf of the poor, and the task of fashioning workable state and economic systems was made even more troublesome given the frequency of foreign interference by the United States. Indeed, in addition to long-standing economic interference, during the Cold War the U.S. government sanctioned either overt or covert military interference in multiple Latin American states, including Cuba, Guatemala, Brazil, the Dominican Republic, Chile, Nicaragua, and Grenada. In spite of such obstacles to stability, some Latin American states prospered in the mid-twentieth century. During World War II, many Latin American nations took advantage of world market needs and pursued greater industrial development. Profits flowed into these countries during and after the war, and nations in the region experienced sustained economic growth through expanded export trade and diversification of foreign markets. Exports included manufactured goods and traditional export commodities such as minerals and foodstuffs such as sugar, fruits, and coffee.

Dependency Theory

Latin American nations realized the need to reorient their economies away from exports and toward internal development. One influential Argentine economist, Raul Prebisch (1901–1985), who worked for the United Nations Commission for Latin America, explained Latin America's economic problems in global terms. Prebisch crafted the **"dependency"** theory of economic development, pointing out that developed industrial nations—such as those in North America and Europe—dominated the international economy and profited at the expense of less developed and industrialized nations burdened with the export-oriented, unbalanced economies that were a legacy of colonialism. To break the unequal relationship between what Prebisch termed the "center" and the "periphery," developing nations on the periphery of international trade needed to protect and diversify domestic trade and to use strategies of import-substituting industrialization to promote further industrial and economic growth.

Prebisch's theories about the economic ills of the developing world, though influential at the time, have since declined in currency. Latin American economies have shown resilience in the late twentieth and early twenty-first centuries, and Latin American nations have maintained links to global markets and money. Their economies appeared strong enough to limit the effects of their export-oriented systems and their use of foreign investment monies. Especially since the end of the Cold War and the resulting decline in military interference by the United States, further economic growth should aid in the search for social and economic stability in Latin America.

CONCLUSION

In the years immediately before and after World War II, a few nations claimed imperial territories that spanned much of the world. The imperial and colonial encounters between colonizers and colonized defined much of the recent history of the world before the mid-twentieth century. The decades following 1945 witnessed the stunningly rapid demise of the European, Japanese, and U.S. empires as colonized people everywhere fought for—and won—their independence. The process of decolonization was not easy and was frequently made more complicated by the presence of settlers, Cold War politics, and internal divisions. Nevertheless, by 1980 decolonization was nearly complete, and the world's peoples sought to reshape their identities and build relations with the rest of the world. This process was frequently hampered, however, by legacies of imperialism, such as lack of infrastructure, economic underdevelopment, poverty, and religious or ethnic conflict. Additionally, since decolonization occurred at precisely the same time as the Cold War, newly independent nations found their freedoms and stability compromised by the insistence of the two superpowers that they choose sides. Nevertheless, the global balance of power had been irrevocably altered by this attainment of worldwide independence and pointed to the emergence of a new kind of world order leading into the twenty-first century.

STUDY TERMS

African National
  Congress (ANC) (833)
apartheid (833)
decolonization (821)
Deng Xiaoping (836)
dependency theory (841)
Dien Bien Phu (824)
El Milagro Mexicano (840)
Evita (840)
FLN (829)
FSLN (841)
Frantz Fanon (830)
F. W. de Klerk (833)
Gamal Abdel Nasser (827)
Geneva Conference (824)
Great Leap Forward (835)

Great Proletarian Cultural
  Revolution (835)
Ho Chi Minh (823)
Indian National Congress (820)
Indira Gandhi (836)
intifada (827)
Iran-Iraq War (838)
Iranian Revolution (837)
Islamism (837)
Jawaharlal Nehru (823)
Juan Perón (840)
Kwame Nkrumah (831)
Lyndon Johnson (825)
Mahmoud Ahmadinejad (838)
Mau Mau (832)
Mohandas K. Gandhi (820)

Muhammad Ali Jinnah (822)
Muslim League (822)
Négritude (830)
Nelson Mandela (833)
Nonaligned Movement (823)
Organization of African
  Unity (OAU) (839)
partition of India (823)

Rajiv Gandhi (837)
Saddam Hussein (838)
Suez crisis (827)
Tiananmen Square (836)
Viet Cong (825)
Vietnamization (825)
Vo Nguyen Giap (824)
Winston Churchill (822)

FOR FURTHER READING

Abdel Monem Said Aly, Shai Feldman, and Khalil Shikaki. *Arabs and Israelis: Conflict and Peacemaking in the Middle East.* New York, 2013. An insightful book by three eyewitnesses who represent multiple perspectives on a controversial topic.

Nancy L. Clark and William H. Worger. *South Africa: The Rise and Fall of Apartheid.* New York, 2004. A survey of the history of the apartheid regime from 1948 to its collapse in the 1990s.

Prasenjit Duara, ed. *Decolonization (Rewriting Histories).* New York, 2004. The perspective of the colonized is privileged through a selection of writings by leaders of the colonizing countries.

Carlene J. Edie. *Politics in Africa: A New Beginning?* New York, 2002. Examines the domestic and external pressures that have transformed postcolonial African states and societies.

Caroline Elkins. *Imperial Reckoning: The Untold Story of Britain's Gulag in Kenya.* New York, 2005. Exposes the extreme violence and brutality of the British response to the Mau Mau rebellion in Kenya.

Rebecca Karl. *Mao Zedong and China in the Twentieth-Century World.* New Haven, 2010. Explores Mao and the Chinese revolution in a wide global context of imperialism, decolonization, and the Cold War.

Yasmin Khan. *The Great Partition: The Making of India and Pakistan.* New Haven: 2007. A thoughtful analysis of the context in which partition occurred, as well as its execution and legacy into the present.

Todd Shepherd. *Voices of Decolonization: A Brief History with Documents.* Boston, 2014. An excellent summary of decolonization with a variety of supporting documents authored by colonizers and anticolonial activists.

Martin Shipway. *Decolonization and its Impact: A Comparative Approach to the End of the Colonial Empires.* Hoboken, 2008. Explores the process of decolonization across all of the empires, with a special emphasis on under-studied areas.

Thomas E. Skidmore and Peter H. Smith. *Modern Latin America.* 8th ed. New York, 2013. A thorough and comprehensive overview of the region.

The End of the Cold War and the Emergence of a Unipolar World

The Global Economy

Cross-Cultural Exchanges and Global Communications

Urgent Global Issues in the Early Twenty-First Century

ZOOMING IN ON ENCOUNTERS

Kristina Matschat and a Falling Wall

On November 9, 1989, Kristina Matschat felt excitement and tension in the night air of Berlin. She had joined thousands of other East Germans at Checkpoint Charlie, one of the most famous crossing points in the Berlin Wall. Anticipating that some momentous event was soon to occur at the wall, that the wall might come down that night, she also shivered in fear at the proximity of the *Volkspolizei* ("people's police")— the same force who since 1961 gunned down East Germans

Neon McDonald's sign in Arabic, Amman, Jordan. Critics of globalization often point to the spread of McDonald's restaurants as both a sign of globalization and as a sign of the Americanization of global culture. Proponents of globalization point out that people in different cultures experience McDonald's differently, and that they make the restaurant chain their own by adding culturally specific foods and drinks to the menu. As of 2020, McDonald's had restaurants in 100 countries around the world, with over 38,000 individual locations.

A. Astes/Alamy Stock Photo

attempting to scale the wall and escape to freedom in West Berlin. She wore running shoes in case she needed to sprint away if shooting broke out.

Matschat remembered that "everybody was full of fear—but also full of hope." Her hope overcame her fears, though, as she chanted with her fellow compatriots, "Tear the wall down! Open the gates!" She could see that on the other side of the wall massive crowds of West Berliners had gathered to join their demonstration. Thrilled by this open protest against an iconic symbol of the Cold War, she was nonetheless unprepared for how quickly victory came. Just before midnight East German soldiers suddenly began not only opening gates in the Wall but also gently helping East Germans cross to the West, many for the first time in their lives. Her near disbelief at the swift downfall of Berlin's decades-old barricade registered in the word she heard shouted over and over again by those passing through the wall: *Wahnsinn* ("craziness").

Kristina Matschat remained at the wall until 3:00 or 4:00 A.M., celebrating with the hundreds of thousands of other Berliners who now mingled, drinking champagne and dancing on top of the wall. While celebrating the fall of the barbed wire and mortar structure, she became aware of the significance of what had just happened: "Suddenly we were seeing the West for the first time, the forbidden Berlin we had only seen on TV or heard about from friends. When we came home at dawn, I felt free for the first time in my life. I had never been happier." The fall of the Berlin Wall brought down one of the world's most notorious borders and symbolized the start of a new era in the contemporary world.

CHAPTER OVERVIEW

The fall of the Berlin Wall signaled the end of the Cold War, a phenomenon that had shaped the world in multiple ways for more than forty years. The post–Cold War era that followed the fall of the wall was characterized by an increased level of economic interaction between countries and a tighter economic integration of the world. The forces driving the world economy in this direction, often referred to as *globalization,* included advances in communication technology, an enormous expansion of international trade, and the emergence of new global enterprises as well as governments and international organizations that favored market-oriented economics.

Cultural integration also resulted from the never-ending stream of ideas, information, and values spreading from one society to another. Consumer goods, popular culture, television, computers, and the Internet spread outward from advanced capitalist and industrialized nations but also increasingly moved the other way as well.

But the post–Cold War era was also characterized by a host of urgent issues, including climate change, women's rights, terrorism, mass migration, and global disease. Each of these issues cross national boundaries and require global, interconnected responses. Almost a quarter of the way into the twenty-first century, none have yet been solved. While no one can predict the future, the ability of the world's peoples to deal with these issues will determine how historians in the future will describe the successes and failures of the post–Cold War era.

CHRONOLOGY	
1947	Establishment of GATT
1948	UN adopts Universal Declaration of Human Rights
1950	World population at 2.5 billion
1960	Introduction of birth control pill; Creation of OPEC
1967	Establishment of ASEAN; Birth of European Community
1981	Identification of AIDS
1989	Fall of Berlin Wall
1991	Collapse of the Soviet Union
1992	Beginning of socialist market economy in China
2000	World population at 6 billion
2001	Terrorist attacks against the United States and war against Afghanistan
2003–2011	U.S. war in Iraq
2011	U.S. killing of Osama bin Laden
2012	Aung San Suu Kyi elected to Burmese parliament
2014	President Obama withdraws American troops from Afghanistan
2020	World Population at 7.8 billion

THE END OF THE COLD WAR AND THE EMERGENCE OF A UNIPOLAR WORLD

Between 1989 and 1991, the Soviet system in Europe collapsed. In this period, through a series of mostly nonviolent revolutions, the peoples of eastern and central Europe regained their independence, instituted democratic forms of government, and adopted market-based economies.

The downfall of communist regimes in Europe was the direct consequence of interrelated economic and political developments. The United States, particularly under President **Ronald Reagan** (in office 1981-1989), kept relentless pressure on the Soviet Union to match its enormous military spending. At the same time, internal economic difficulties in the communist regimes of central Europe and the Soviet Union became so apparent as to require reforms. The policies espoused by a new Soviet leader, **Mikhail S. Gorbachev** (1931-), who came to power in 1985, represented an effort to address these massive economic challenges, but they also unleashed a tidal wave of revolution that brought down communist governments. As communism unraveled throughout eastern and central Europe, Gorbachev desperately tried to save the Soviet Union from disintegration by restructuring the economy and liberalizing society. Caught between the rising tide of radical reforms and the opposition of entrenched interests, however, there was little he could do except watch as events unfolded beyond his control. By the time the Soviet Union collapsed in 1991, the Cold War system of states and alliances had become irrelevant to international relations.

Revolutions in Eastern and Central Europe

The inability to connect communism with national identities left communist regimes vulnerable throughout eastern and

Leszek Kolakowski (LEH-shek ko-lah-KOW-skee)

central Europe. Those regimes were born in Moscow, transplanted by the Soviet army, and shored up by tanks and bayonets. To most eastern and central Europeans, the Soviet-imposed governments lacked legitimacy from the beginning, and despite the efforts of local communist leaders, the regimes never became firmly established. The Polish intellectual **Leszek Kolakowski** echoed the sentiments of many when he bitterly complained in 1971 that "the dead and by now also grotesque creature called Marxist-Leninism still hangs at the necks of the rulers like a hopeless tumor."

Despite economic stagnation, an accelerated arms race with the United States that further strained the Soviet economy, and obvious signs of discontent, the rulers of eastern and central Europe were reluctant to confront the challenge and restructure their ailing systems. It remained for Gorbachev to unleash the forces that resulted in the disappearance of the Soviet empire in Europe. By the time Gorbachev visited East Berlin in 1989 on the fortieth anniversary of the founding of the German Democratic Republic, he had committed himself to a restructuring of the Soviet Union and to unilateral withdrawal from the Cold War. In public interviews he surprised his grim-faced hosts with the announcement that the Brezhnev Doctrine (in which the Soviet Union reserved the right to intervene in any eastern European nation if it compromised Soviet domination) was no longer in force and that from then on each country would be responsible for its own destiny. The new Soviet orientation led in rapid succession to the collapse or overthrow of regimes in Poland, Bulgaria, Hungary, Czechoslovakia, Romania, and East Germany.

Poland, Bulgaria, and Hungary The end of communism came first in Poland, where Solidarity—a combined trade union and nationalist movement—put pressure on the crumbling rule of the Communist Party. The Polish government

United States President Ronald Reagan and Soviet General Secretary Mikhail Gorbachev sit together at a summit meeting in Geneva, Switzerland in 1985.
Universal History Archive/Universal Images Group/Getty Images

Men and women climb atop the Berlin wall on November 9, 1989.
dpa/picture alliance/Getty Images

legalized the previously banned Solidarity movement and agreed to multiparty elections in 1989 and 1990. The voters favored Solidarity candidates, and **Lech Walesa** (1943-), the movement's leader, became president of Poland. In Bulgaria popular unrest forced **Todor Zhivkov** (1911-1998), eastern Europe's longest-surviving communist dictator, to resign in November 1989. Two months later a national assembly began dismantling the communist state. Hungarians tore down the Soviet-style political system between 1988 and 1989. In 1990 they held free elections and launched their nation on the rocky path toward democracy and a market economy.

Velvet and Violent Revolutions The disintegration of communism continued elsewhere in eastern Europe. In Czechoslovakia a "velvet revolution" swept communists out of office and restored democracy by 1990. The term *velvet revolution* derived from the fact that aside from the initial suppression of mass demonstrations, little violence was associated with the transfer of power in societies formerly ruled by an iron fist. The communist leadership stood by and watched events take their course. In 1993, disagreements over the time frame for shifting to a market economy led to a "velvet divorce," breaking Czechoslovakia into two new nations, the Czech Republic and Slovakia. In Romania, by contrast, the regime of dictator **Nicolae Ceauşescu** (1918-1989) refused to acknowledge the necessity of reform. In 1989 *Securitate,* a brutal secret police force, savagely repressed demonstrations, setting off a national uprising that ended within four days and left Ceauş escu and his wife dead.

Fall of the Berlin Wall East Germany had long been a staunchly communist Soviet satellite. Its aging leader, Erich Honecker (1912-1994), openly objected to Gorbachev's ideas and clung to Stalinist policies. When he showed genuine bewilderment at the fact that East German citizens fled the country by the thousands through openings in the iron curtain in Hungary and Czechoslovakia, his party removed him from power. It was too late for anything other than radical changes, and when the East German regime decided to open the Berlin Wall to intra-German traffic on 9 November 1989, the end of the German Democratic Republic was in sight. The end to a divided Berlin was also in sight, literally, as thousands of east and west Berliners like Kristina Matschat tore down the Berlin Wall in the last weeks of 1989. In 1990 the two Germanies, once divided by the Cold War, formed again as a united nation.

The Collapse of the Soviet Union

The desire to concentrate attention and resources on urgent matters at home motivated Gorbachev's decision to disengage his nation from the Cold War and its military and diplomatic extensions. When he came to power in 1985, Gorbachev was keenly aware of the need for economic reform and the liberalization of Soviet society, although he never intended the collapse of the whole system. Yet it proved impossible to fix parts of the system without undermining the whole.

Gorbachev's Reforms Gorbachev's reform efforts first focused on the ailing economy. Antiquated industrial plants, obsolete technologies, and inefficient government control of production resulted in shoddy and outmoded products.

Lech Walesa (LEHK wah-LEHN-sah)

Todor Zhivkov (TO-dohr JHIF-kof)

Nicolae Ceauşescu (nih-kuh-LIE chow-SHESS-koo)

The diversion of crucial resources to the military in order to keep up with U.S. military spending made it impossible to produce enough consumer goods—regardless of their quality. The failure of state and collective farms to feed the population compelled the Soviet government to import grains from the United States, Canada, and elsewhere. By 1990 the government imposed rationing to cope with the scarcity of essential consumer goods and food. Economic stagnation in turn contributed to the decline of the Soviet standard of living. Ominous statistics documented the disintegration of the state-sponsored health care system: infant mortality increased while life expectancy decreased. Funding of the educational system dropped precipitously, and pollution threatened to engulf the entire country. Demoralization affected ever-larger numbers of Soviet citizens as divorce rates climbed, corruption intensified, and alcoholism became more widespread.

Perestroika and Glasnost

Under the slogan of *uskorenie,* or "acceleration," Gorbachev tried to shock the economy out of its coma. Yet the old methods of boosting production and productivity through bureaucratic exhortation and harassment paid few dividends; in fact, they called attention to the drawbacks of centralized economic control. Gorbachev then contemplated different kinds of reform, using the term *perestroika,* or "restructuring," to describe his efforts to decentralize the economy. To make perestroika work, the Soviet leader linked it to *glasnost,* a term that referred to the opening of Soviet society to public criticism and admission of past mistakes.

Perestroika proved more difficult to implement than Gorbachev imagined, and glasnost unleashed a torrent of criticism that shook the Soviet state to its foundations. When Gorbachev pushed economic decentralization, the profit motive and the cost-accounting methods he instituted engendered the hostility of those whose privileged positions depended on being protected by the old system. Many of Gorbachev's comrades and certain factions of the military objected to perestroika and worked to undermine or destroy it. Glasnost also turned out to be a two-edged sword because it opened the door to public criticism of party leaders and Soviet institutions in a way unimaginable a short time earlier. While discontent with Soviet life burst into the open, long-repressed ethnic and nationalist sentiments bubbled to the surface, posing a threat to the multiethnic Soviet state. Only half of the 285 million Soviet citizens were Russian. The other half included numerous ethnic minorities, most of whom never fully reconciled themselves to Soviet dominance.

The pressures on the Soviet system were exacerbated by an ill-considered and costly Soviet military intervention in 1979 to save a Marxist regime in Afghanistan. For nine years well-equipped Soviet forces fought a brutal, unsuccessful campaign against *Afghan* **mujahideen,** or Islamic warriors, who gradually gained control of most of the countryside. Weapons and money from the United States, Saudi Arabia, Iran, Pakistan, and China sustained the mujahideen in their struggle. The Central Intelligence Agency of the United States supplied the decisive weapons in the war: ground-to-air Stinger missiles, which could be used to shoot down heavily armored Soviet helicopters, and thousands of mules to haul supplies from Pakistan. In 1986 the Kremlin decided to pull its troops out of the costly, unpopular, and unwinnable war. A cease-fire negotiated by the United Nations in 1988 led to a full Soviet withdrawal in 1989.

Collapse

By the summer of 1990, Gorbachev's reforms had spent themselves. As industrial and agricultural production continued their downward slide against a backdrop of skyrocketing inflation, the Soviet economy disintegrated. Inspired by the end of the Soviet empire in eastern and central Europe, many minorities now contemplated secession from the Soviet Union. The Baltic peoples—Estonians, Latvians, and Lithuanians—were first into the fray, declaring their independence in August 1991. In the following months the remaining twelve republics of the Soviet Union followed suit. The largest and most prominent of the Soviet republics, the Russian Soviet Federated Socialist Republic, and its recently elected president, Boris N. Yeltsin (1931–2007), led the drive for independence. Soviet leaders vacillated between threats of repression and promises of better treatment, but neither option could stop the movement for independence.

Although the pace of reform was neither quick nor thorough enough for some, others convinced themselves that reforms had gone too far. While Gorbachev was vacationing in the Crimea in August 1991, a group of conspirators—including discontented party functionaries, disillusioned KGB (secret police) officials, and dissatisfied military officers—decided to seize power. Gorbachev's former friend and ally, the flamboyant Boris Yeltsin, crushed the coup with the help of loyal Red Army units. Gorbachev emerged unscathed from house arrest, but his political career had ended. He watched from the sidelines as Yeltsin dismantled the Communist Party and pushed the country toward market-oriented economic reforms. As the Soviet system disintegrated, several of its constituent regions moved toward independence. On 25 December 1991 the Soviet flag fluttered for the last time atop the Kremlin, and by the last day of that year the Union of Soviet Socialist Republics ceased to exist.

The Unipolar Moment

With the demise of the Soviet Union, the Cold War suddenly ended. For forty years, the bipolar rivalry between the United States and the Soviet Union had dominated global politics and resulted in countless deaths as a result of "hot" proxy wars. And while millions of people rejoiced that nuclear war no longer seemed likely and the arms race could end, this massive shift in the global balance of power left a vacuum. In the three decades following 1991, the United States sought to influence

---

perestroika (pehr-eh-STROY-kuh)

glasnost (GLAHS-nost)

mujahideen (moo-jah-hih-deen)

	Russia and components of former Soviet Union
	Former Communist-controlled states

MAP 38.1 The collapse of the Soviet Union and European communist regimes, 1991.

Note the number of states suddenly created by the breakup of the Soviet Union.

How would this affect the ability of each to survive, both economically and politically?

world politics as the sole remaining superpower, while Russia sought to return to stability and to regain its earlier prestige. These efforts caused relations between the United States and Russia to deteriorate dramatically in the opening decades of the twenty-first century. At the same time, the end of the Cold War seemed to open space for other powers, especially China, to play major roles in global politics.

Instability versus Overconfidence In spite of initial optimism in and outside Russia in 1991, by the mid-1990s it was clear that the shift to a market economy could not immediately fix the country's many economic problems. Both industrial and agricultural production had dropped significantly, and one-third of the Russian population had sunk below the

poverty line. Crime was pervasive. To make matters worse, Boris Yeltsin—who became the first popularly elected president in Russia in 1991—proved to be an erratic ruler and badly mismanaged a war with the breakaway Chechen Republic.

In the midst of these difficulties, the U.S. government saw an opportunity to become the only world superpower and to dictate global politics on its own terms. In 1992 Paul Wolfowitz, President George H. W. Bush's undersecretary for defense, wrote a post–Cold War policy statement that advocated unilateral action and the use of the military force to prevent the reemergence of another superpower. This aggressive stance receded somewhat during President Bill Clinton's administration (1993–2001), but in this period, the United States nevertheless alarmed Russian leaders by inviting the former Soviet satellite states of Hungary, Poland, and the Czech Republic to join NATO, which they did in 1999. Given that NATO's original purpose at its founding in 1949 was to form a defensive alliance against the Soviet Union, the Russian government saw the incorporation of its traditional buffer states as a clear threat to national security.

The Bush Doctrine Under the administration of President George W. Bush (2001–2009), the U.S. government returned to an overtly aggressive foreign policy. The president's policies, which became known collectively as the **Bush Doctrine,** affirmed the legitimacy of the United States acting alone to pursue its own interests, even to the point of engaging in pre-emptive strikes. At this time the U.S. government regarded Russia as a second-rate power, and its leaders continued the policy of inviting former Soviet satellites into NATO. In 2004, NATO admitted Bulgaria, Estonia, Latvia, Lithuania, Romania, Slovakia, and Slovenia, further alarming and angering the Russian government.

Deteriorating Relations in the Early Twenty-First Century Meanwhile, Vladimir Putin, Boris Yeltsin's former prime minister, was elected to the Russian presidency in 2000. After serving an eight-year term, in 2008 Putin ceded the post to his protégé Dmitry Medvedev and became prime minister (all the while retaining his personal power). In 2012 he returned to the presidency, and in 2018 he was reelected for another six-year term. For the first two decades of the twenty-first century, Putin focused on winning back the prestige Russia had lost after the collapse of the Soviet Union, demonstrating to the world that Russia would not tolerate unilateral action by the United States, and gaining ever tighter control over domestic politics.

Relations between the United States and Russia hit a new low in 2014, when the pro-Russian president of Ukraine fled to Russia in response to popular protests against his rule. Putin's government then massed its forces along the Ukrainian border and annexed the Ukrainian region of Crimea, which had been part of the independent nation of Ukraine since 1991. In response, both the United States and the European Union imposed sanctions on Russian individuals and financial institutions. Confrontational relations between Russia and the United States continued in 2016, when the FBI announced an investigation of Russian hacking into the Democratic National Committee's computer system, and the Democratic Party accused Russia of meddling in the 2016 presidential election.

Tense relations between the United States and Russia in the twenty-first century have led some contemporaries to wonder if the world is experiencing a new cold war. Yet circumstances are quite different from the post–World War II era. Most important is that the world is no longer dominated by two superpower blocs. Since 1989, the United States has acted alone as the only superpower, but there are signs that this "unipolar moment" will give way to a multipolar world in the future. China in particular seems poised to take on a superpower role, which will have major consequences for the global power dynamic.

THE GLOBAL ECONOMY

With the collapse of the Soviet Union, the potential for a truly globalized economy now expanded to the former communist world. Economists pointed to a new economic order characterized by the expansion of trade between countries, the growth of foreign investments, the unfettered movement of capital, the privatization of former state enterprises, a wave of deregulation that undermined the control that national governments once exercised over economic activity, and the emergence of a new type of corporation. Supporting the new global economy were technological developments in communications; semiconductors, fiber-optic cables, and satellites virtually eliminated geographic distances, causing an ever-faster integration of the market economy. The forces driving the world economy toward increased economic integration have been responsible for a process termed *globalization.*

Economic Globalization

Globalization is a widely used term that can be defined in a number of ways. There is general agreement, however, that in an economic context, globalization refers to the reduction and removal of barriers between national borders to facilitate the flow of goods, capital, services, and labor. Global economic interaction and integration is not a new phenomenon. Ancient Rome and China, for example, controlled and economically integrated vast regions of the ancient world. In more recent centuries, the nations of western Europe—through their global outreach and encounters with far-flung societies—created worldwide empires in which goods and people moved with relative ease. The more recent phenomenon of globalization since 1945, however, has been different and unprecedented in both scope and speed, and it has transformed the social and political as well as the economic contours of the world.

Free Trade International trade proved to be a key driving force behind economic globalization. Trade across long distances especially has figured prominently in the shaping of human history, and for at least the past five hundred years it has served as an integrating force. Of more recent origin is the phrase **free trade,** meaning freedom from state-imposed limits and constraints on trade across borders. The issue of free trade engendered a debate about the extent to which free trade enhances the prosperity of a society. In the aftermath of World War II, leaders from industrialized nations, especially from the United States, took a decisive stand on the issue.

GATT and WTO At the end of World War II, the victors sought to establish an international trading system that would facilitate economic recovery after the destruction of the war. Believing that the protective tariffs characteristic of national policies during the Great Depression had only worsened the

Nestlé global corporate headquarters in Vevey, Switzerland. Nestlé is the largest food company in the world and has corporate offices all over the globe. In 2018 Nestlé generated sales of $93.4 billion.
Gunter Fischer/Education Images/ Universal Images Group/Getty Images

global economic crisis, they pushed instead for the elimination of restrictive trading practices that stood in the way of free trade. The main vehicle for the promotion of unrestricted global trade was the **General Agreement on Tariffs and Trade** (GATT), which was signed by the representatives of 23 noncommunist nations in 1947. In 1994, the member nations of GATT signed an agreement to establish the **World Trade Organization** (WTO), which took over the activities of GATT in 1995. The WTO has developed into a forum for settling international trade disputes, with the power to enforce its decisions. The WTO has 164 member nations and 23 observer nations, which accounts for 99 percent of all world trade.

Global Corporations The emergence of a new type of corporation played another key role in the development of the new economic order. Global corporations have increasingly replaced the more traditional international or multinational forms of corporate enterprises. International companies were born out of the desire to extend business activities across borders in pursuit of specific activities such as importation, exportation, and the extraction of raw materials. International companies evolved into multinationals, which conducted their business in several countries but had to operate within the confines of specific laws and customs of a given society. During the past twenty-five years, the transformation of the corporate landscape has resulted in the birth of some fifty thousand global corporations. In contrast to the multinational, the typical global corporation relies on a small headquarters staff while dispersing all other corporate functions around the globe in search of the lowest possible operating costs. Global corporations treat the world as a single market and act as if the nation-state no longer exists. Many multinational corporations, such as General Motors, Siemens AG, and Nestlé, have transformed themselves into global enterprises, both benefiting from and contributing to the ongoing process of globalization.

Global corporations have become the symbols of the new economy. They also have begun to transform the political and social landscape of many societies. Since the end of World War II, major corporations throughout the developed world have been required to contribute to the welfare of their respective home communities through a combination of collective bargaining agreements, tax laws, and environmental regulations. Highly mobile global corporations that are no longer bound to any particular location have managed, however, to escape those obligations. Competing with companies around the world, global corporations have moved jobs from high-wage facilities to foreign locations where wages are low and environmental laws are weak or nonexistent.

Economic Growth in Asia

Globalization and the acceleration of worldwide economic integration also benefited from economic developments in east and southeast Asia, where the economies of Japan, China, and the so-called **little tigers** (Hong Kong, Singapore, South Korea, and Taiwan) underwent dramatic economic growth. This Asian "economic miracle" was largely a result of economic globalization.

Japan U.S. policies jump-started Japan's economic revival after its defeat in 1945, and by 1949 the Japanese economy had already attained its prewar level of productivity. Just as western European countries had benefited from the Marshall Plan, so Japan benefited from direct U.S. financial aid ($2 billion) and investment. In addition, the United States placed no restrictions on the entry of Japanese products into the U.S. market.

Finally, because a 1952 treaty stipulated that the United States would be the military protector of Japan and that Japan could never spend more than 1 percent of its gross national product on defense, the country's postwar leaders were able to channel the savings into economic development.

At first sight, Japan's economy was ill equipped for intensive economic growth. Japan had lost its overseas empire and was hampered by a large population and a lack of natural resources. Japan's economic planners sidestepped many of those disadvantages by promoting an economic policy that emphasized export-oriented growth supported by low wages. The large workforce, willing to endure working conditions and wages considered unacceptable by organized labor in western Europe and the United States, gave Japanese employers a competitive edge over international rivals. Although Japanese industries had to pay for the import of most raw materials, the low cost of Japanese labor ensured the production of goods that could be sold inexpensively on the global market.

Initially, the Japanese economy produced labor-intensive manufactured goods such as textiles, iron, and steel slated for export to markets with high labor costs, particularly the United States. During the 1960s Japanese companies used their profits to switch to more capital-intensive manufacturing and produced radios, television sets, motorcycles, and automobiles. In the 1970s Japanese corporations took advantage of a highly trained and educated workforce and shifted their economic resources toward technology-intensive products such as random access memory chips, liquid crystal displays, and CD-ROM drives. By that time the label "Made in Japan," once associated with cheap manufactured goods, signified state-of-the-art products of the highest quality. Japan's economic achievements gave its banks, corporations, and government an increasingly prominent voice in global affairs. By the 1980s Japan seemed poised to overtake the United States as the world's largest economy. In the 1990s, however, it became clear that postwar growth rates were not sustainable, and the Japanese economy entered into a deep recession. Indeed, the recovery from this recession continued into the second decade of the twenty-first century. Nevertheless, the postwar Japanese success story served as an inspiration for other Asian countries.

The Little Tigers

The earliest and most successful imitators of the Japanese model for economic development were Hong Kong, Singapore, South Korea, and Taiwan. Their remarkable and rapid growth rates earned them the somewhat condescending label of the "four little tigers," and by the 1980s these newly industrializing countries had become major economic powers. Like Japan, all four countries suffered from a shortage of capital, lacked natural resources, and had to cope with overpopulation. But like Japan a generation earlier, they transformed apparent disadvantages into advantages through a program of export-driven industrialization. By the 1990s the four little tigers were no longer simply imitators of Japan but had become serious competitors. As soon as new Japanese products had carved out market niches, corporations based in the four little tigers moved in and undercut the original item with cheaper versions. By the turn of the millennium, Indonesia, Thailand, and Malaysia joined the original tigers in their quest for economic development and prosperity.

Perils of the New Economy

For the supporters of the new global economy, the spectacular economic development of so many Asian societies was proof that globalization could deliver on the promise of unprecedented prosperity. By the late 1990s, however, it seemed clear that globalization could also lead to economic ruin.

At the center of this bust was a financial crisis that came to a head in 1997. In the preceding twenty years, the developing Asian economies had started to embrace the market, opening their borders to imports and courting foreign investments. After years of generous lending and growing national debts, the international investment community suddenly lost confidence in the booming economies and withdrew support. The crisis began in Thailand in mid-1997, when the government decided to discontinue its policy of pegging the Thai national currency (the baht) to the U.S. dollar. This led many investors to turn to other markets, which in turn caused the value of the baht to plummet. The Thai stock market quickly lost 75 percent of its value, and the country found itself in the grip of a depression. For no obvious reason, the financial panic—and with it economic contraction—then moved to Malaysia, Indonesia, the Philippines, and South Korea. In each instance, the rise and fall of the individual economies resulted from their integration in the new global economy, which rewarded and punished its new participants with equal ease.

BRICs

Contrary to all expectations, the nations hit so hard by the financial crisis recovered quickly. Their recovery was matched by other emerging economies, often identified as **BRICs** because they include the fast-growing and developing economies of Brazil, Russia, India, and China. In the aftermath of the Cold War, the governments composing the BRICs initiated political and economic reforms that embraced capitalism and allowed their countries to join the world economy. To make these nations more competitive, their leaders have simultaneously emphasized education, domestic entrepreneurship, foreign investment, and domestic consumption, with varying levels of success. China is already the leading global supplier of manufactured goods, while Brazil and Russia supply much of the world's raw materials.

The Rise of China

After the death of Mao Zedong (see chapter 37), China's leaders launched economic reforms that opened Chinese markets to the outside world, encouraged foreign investment, and imported foreign technology. These changes promoted rapid economic growth, and in 1992 the Chinese government labeled its new economic model a "socialist market economy." In such a model, the government retains its authoritarian control over political life while allowing a functioning market economy. In the economic realm, demand for goods and services determines production and pricing, and the role of the government is limited to providing a stable but competitive environment. Besides acting as a major exporter, China benefited from its large pool of cheap labor, while its enormous domestic markets have made the Chinese economy the destination of choice for foreign investment capital. In December 2001 China became a member of the World Trade Organization, and in 2010 it overtook Japan as the second largest economy in the world after the United States.

Trading Blocs

In the rapidly changing global economy, some groups of nations have sought to reduce risk, achieve advantages, and gain

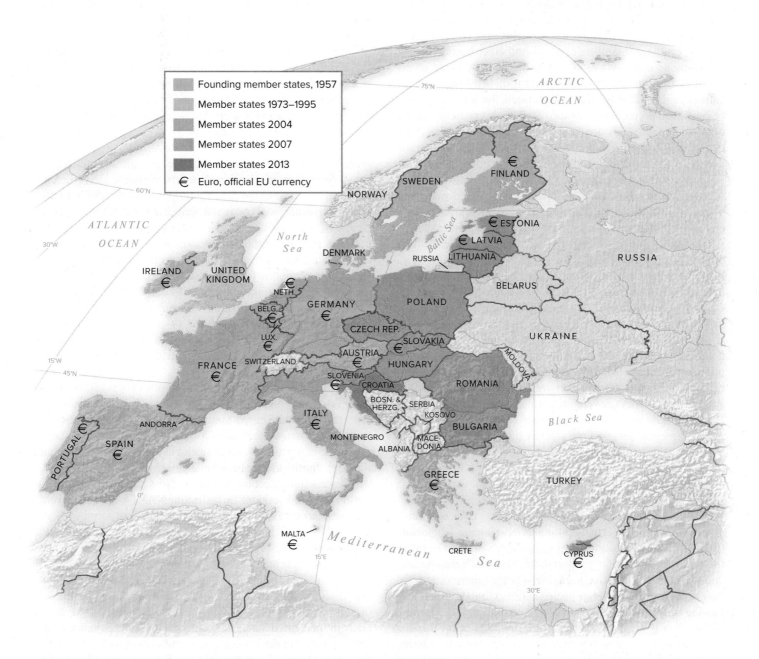

MAP 38.2   European Union membership, 2020.

In 2007 the European Union celebrated the fiftieth anniversary of its founding as a supranational and intergovernmental organization. The euro (sign: €) is the official currency of the eurozone, which consists of eighteen of the twenty-eight member states of the European Union. Note that Great Britain is no longer a member state, having left the European Union on January 31, 2020.

What major challenges face the European Union in the twenty-first century?

economic strength for their partners by entering into economic alliances known as trading blocs.

European Union The most strongly integrated regional bloc is the **European Union,** which is characterized by a common market and free trade. In March 1957, representatives of six nations—France, West Germany, Italy, the Netherlands, Belgium, and Luxembourg—took a significant step in this direction by signing the Treaty of Rome. This treaty established the European Economic Community—renamed the European Community in 1967. At the heart of this new community of nations lay the dismantling of tariffs and other barriers to free trade among member nations. Subsequent treaties created political institutions such as the Council of Ministers and the European Parliament, which facilitated the long-range goal of European political integration. The development of a supranational organization dedicated to increasing European economic and political integration culminated in the Maastricht Treaty of 1993, which established the European Union. By 2013, twenty-eight European nations submerged much of their national sovereignty in the European Union (twenty-seven as of 2020 with the exit of the United Kingdom), and since 1999 eighteen members have adopted a common currency.

Despite the European Union's many achievements, however, it has had its share of problems in the twenty-first century. Among the most serious have been concerns within member countries about the loss of control over social, political, and economic policies. Indeed, these concerns led to the first withdrawal from the EU by a member state when the United Kingdom voted to leave the union in 2016. "Brexit," as it has become known, was initiated by both economic and political concerns. Many Britons argued that the economic benefits of EU membership were no longer worth the price of a submerged British sovereignty. In addition, deep concerns over the movement of people across the European Union—particularly migrants seeking a better life from parts of Africa and the Middle East—triggered nationalist, xenophobic responses that called for reasserting control over Britain's borders. The British withdrawal became final on January 31, 2020.

OPEC One of the earliest and most successful economic alliances was the **Organization of Petroleum Exporting Countries** (OPEC), a producer cartel established in 1960 by the oil-producing states of Iran, Iraq, Kuwait, Saudi Arabia, and Venezuela, and later joined by Qatar, Libya, Indonesia, Abu Dhabi, Algeria, Nigeria, Ecuador, Congo, Equatorial Guinea, the United Arab Emirates, and Gabon. The purpose of OPEC is to control and negotiate the price of oil through cooperation with its mostly Arab or Muslim members. During the Arab-Israeli War of 1973, however, OPEC demonstrated that its economic control over oil prices could be used for political purposes. Because the United States supported Israel, the political enemy of many OPEC member nations, the cartel ordered an embargo on oil shipments to the United States and quadrupled the price of oil between 1973 and 1975.

The huge increase in the cost of petroleum triggered a global economic downturn, as did a curtailment of oil exports in the later 1970s. OPEC's policies therefore demonstrated how the alliance could exert control over the developed world and its financial system. OPEC's influence diminished in the 1980s and 1990s as a result of overproduction and dissension among its members over the Iran-Iraq War and the Gulf War. Additionally, in the twenty-first century, the increased use of hydraulic fracturing (often called "fracking") to extract oil from shale has dramatically increased production in the United States. In 2018 the United States was the world's largest oil-producing country, with 10 million barrels a day. Since this allows the United States to be less dependent on OPEC, it has also muted the political potential of OPEC actions. Nevertheless, OPEC members continue to control around 72 percent of the world's crude oil reserves and thus remain a critically important trading bloc.

ASEAN Another well-established economic partnership is the **Association of Southeast Asian Nations,** or **ASEAN.** Established in 1967 by the foreign ministers of Thailand, Malaysia, Singapore, Indonesia, and the Philippines, its principal objectives were to accelerate economic development and promote political stability in southeast Asia. Originally conceived as a bulwark against the spread of communism in the region, the economic focus of ASEAN became sharper after it signed cooperative agreements with Japan in 1977 and the European Community in 1980. In 1992 member states agreed to establish a free-trade zone and to cut tariffs on industrial goods over a fifteen-year period. By 2020, ASEAN member states had expanded to include Brunei, Cambodia, Lao, Vietnam, and Myanmar.

NAFTA Beginning in the 1980s, leaders of the North American nations of the United States, Canada, and Mexico also began to discuss the creation of a trading bloc to increase their economic competitiveness in the global marketplace. The result was the **North American Free Trade Agreement** (NAFTA), which went into effect on January 1, 1994, during the administration of U.S. President Bill Clinton. NAFTA worked toward the elimination of trade barriers among the three nations, allowing goods and services to move freely across borders, and set up mechanisms to resolve trade disputes. By 2018, NAFTA had quadrupled trade among the three nations, up from $290 billion in 1993 to $1.23 trillion. It had also dramatically increased foreign direct investment by the three countries in the economies of their neighbors. But NAFTA has also been criticized, especially in the United States, for causing a loss in U.S. jobs and for keeping wages in the United States artificially low. In 2018, U.S. President Donald Trump sought the renegotiation of NAFTA for the specific purposes of reducing the U.S. trade deficit with its partners and to safeguard U.S. jobs. The new agreement, called the United States Mexico Canada Agreement (USMCA), was signed in the United States in December 2019 and was ratified by all three countries by March 2020.

Globalization and Its Critics The global economy is still very much a work in progress, and it is not clear what the long-term effects will be on the economies and societies it touches. To its supporters, the global economy delivers markets that operate with efficiency, speedily directing goods and services wherever there is demand for them and always expecting the highest returns possible. Proponents of globalization also argue that the new economy is the only way to bring prosperity—the kind previously enjoyed only by industrialized nations—to the developing world. To its critics the global economy is a force that rewards the few and impoverishes the many. The specific charges leveled by antiglobalization groups and coalitions are many. They assert that globalization diminishes the sovereignty of local and national governments and transfers the power to shape economic and political destinies to transnational corporations and global institutions such as the WTO. Detractors of globalization also claim that the hallmark of globalization—rapid economic development—is responsible for the destruction of the environment; the widening gap between rich and poor societies; and the worldwide homogenization of local, diverse, and indigenous cultures. It is certain that globalization has been accompanied by major social and economic changes. But it is too soon to tell if these changes will be overwhelmingly destructive for the world's lands and peoples.

CROSS-CULTURAL EXCHANGES AND GLOBAL COMMUNICATIONS

Like trade and business organizations, cultural practices have also become globalized, thriving on a continuous flow of information, ideas, tastes, and values. At the turn of the twentieth century, local traditions—commonly derived from gender, social class, or religious affiliation—still determined the cultural identity of the vast majority of people. At the end of the twentieth century, thanks in part to advances in technology and communications, and the influence of international organizations, information and cultural practices were becoming truly global and more people than ever were aware of events and issues occurring far away. Their impact was summarized in a jingle popularized by the Walt Disney Company during the 1964–1965 World's Fair in New York City: "It's a small world after all."

Consumption and Cultural Interaction

New communications media have tied the world together and have promoted a global cultural integration whose hallmark is consumption. Beginning in the eighteenth century, industrialization and the subsequent rise in per capita income gave birth to a type of society in which the consumption of goods and services satisfied wants and desires rather than needs or necessities. Although the desire to consume is hardly novel, the modern consumer culture means more than simple

consumption. It implies that consumers want more than they need and that the items they consume take on symbolic value. Consumption, in other words, has become a means of self-expression as well as a source for personal identity and social differentiation. The peculiar shape of this consumer culture resulted from two seemingly contradictory trends: a tendency toward homogenization of cultural products and heightened awareness of local tastes and values. Critics sometimes refer to the homogenizing aspect of global culture as the "Americanization" or **"McDonaldization"** of the world.

Those terms suggest that the consumer culture that developed in the United States during the mid-twentieth century has been exported throughout the world, principally through advertising. Thus it is no accident that young people clad in blue jeans and T-shirts sing the same Usher or Eminem lyrics in San Francisco, Sarajevo, and Beijing. Still, nothing symbolizes the global marketing of U.S. mass culture more than the spread of its food and beverage products. While Pepsi and Coca-Cola fight battles over the few places on earth that their beverages have not yet dominated, fast-food restaurants such as Burger King, McDonald's, and Pizza Hut sell their standardized foods throughout the world. The closing of many bistros and cafés in France, for instance, is the result of more French people opting for fashionable fast food instead of taking the time for more traditional and lengthy lunches. So successful has the global spread of U.S. mass culture been that it seems to threaten local cultures everywhere.

The export of U.S. products and services is not the sole determinant of global cultural practices, however. Because the contemporary consumer culture stresses minute differences between products and encourages consumers to make purchase decisions based on brand names designed to evoke particular tastes, fashion, or lifestyle, it also fosters differentiation. Indeed, global marketing often emphasizes the local or indigenous value of a product. Genuinely Australian products, such as Drizabone wet-weather gear and Foster's Lager, have become international commodities precisely because they are Australian in origin. Likewise, young upwardly mobile consumers continue to prefer Rolex watches from Switzerland, Armani clothes from Italy, miniature electronics from Japan, and Perrier mineral water from France.

Multilateral Globalization Indeed, it would be a mistake to conceive of the globalization of culture as a one-way street emanating mainly from the United States. Rather, given the speed at which information and goods can travel, most any consumable item can gain worldwide popularity. For example, reggae music became a worldwide phenomenon after the Jamaican musician Bob Marley partnered with British-based Island Records in 1972 to produce the album *Catch a Fire*. Although reggae was a complex, hybrid musical style particular to Jamaica, its protest lyrics and beat found eager audiences in countercultures in almost every continent from North and South America to Europe and Africa, and it profoundly influenced musical traditions in the late twentieth century.

SOURCES FROM THE PAST

The Debate over Cultural Globalization

In 2003, Philippe Legrain tackled one of the thorniest issues related to culture and globalization: to what extent is the globalization of culture simply the Americanization of global culture? Drawing on his training as a journalist and economist, and drawing on his experiences with the World Trade Organization, Legrain rather forcefully challenged those observers and commentators who decried the omnipresence of American cultural imperialism (or what Legrain terms "Cocacolonization") in the age of globalization. In these excerpts from his article in The Chronicle of Higher Education, *titled "Cultural Globalization Is Not Americanization," Legrain made his position in the debate clear.*

Fears that globalization is imposing a deadening cultural uniformity are as ubiquitous as Coca-Cola, McDonald's, and Mickey Mouse. Europeans and Latin Americans, left-wingers and right, rich and poor—all of them dread that local cultures and national identities are dissolving into a crass all-American consumerism. That cultural imperialism is said to impose American values as well as products, promote the commercial at the expense of the authentic, and substitute shallow gratification for deeper satisfaction. . . .

It is a myth that globalization involves the imposition of Americanized uniformity, rather than an explosion of cultural exchange. For a start, many archetypal "American" products are not as all-American as they seem. Levi-Strauss, a German immigrant, invented jeans by combining denim cloth (or "serge de Nîmes," because it was traditionally woven in the French town) with Genes, a style of trousers worn by Genoese sailors. So Levi's jeans are in fact an American twist on a European hybrid. Even quintessentially American exports are often tailored to local tastes. MTV in Asia promotes Thai pop stars and plays rock music sung in Mandarin. CNN en Español offers a Latin American take on world news. McDonald's sells beer in France, lamb in India, and chili in Mexico.

In some ways, America is an outlier, not a global leader. Most of the world has adopted the metric system born from the French Revolution; America persists with antiquated measurements inherited from its British-colonial past. Most developed countries have become intensely secular, but many Americans burn with fundamentalist fervor—like Muslims in the Middle East. Where else in the developed world could there be a serious debate about teaching kids Bible-inspired "creationism" instead of Darwinist evolution?

> In what ways does Legrain argue that the United States is not necessarily a leader in globalization?

America's tastes in sports are often idiosyncratic, too. Baseball and American football have not traveled well, although basketball has fared rather better. Many of the world's most popular sports, notably soccer, came by way of Britain. Asian martial arts—judo, karate, kickboxing—and pastimes like yoga have also swept the world.

People are not only guzzling hamburgers and Coke. Despite Coke's ambition of displacing water as the world's drink of choice, it accounts for less than 2 of the 64 fluid ounces the typical person drinks a day. Britain's favorite takeaway is a curry, not a burger; Indian restaurants there outnumber McDonald's six to one. For all the concerns about American fast food trashing France's culinary traditions, France imported a mere $620 million in food from the United States in 2000, while exporting to America three times that. Nor is plonk [cheap alcohol] from America's Gallo displacing Europe's finest: Italy and France together account for three-fifths of global wine exports, the United States for only a twentieth. Worldwide, pizzas are more popular than burgers, Chinese restaurants seem to sprout up everywhere, and sushi is spreading fast. By far the biggest purveyor of alcoholic drinks is Britain's Diageo, which sells the world's best selling whiskey (Johnnie Walker), gin (Gordon's), vodka (Smirnoff), and liqueur (Bailey's). . . .

> In what ways is Legrain suggesting that globalization of culture can move in multiple directions?

In pop music, American crooners do not have the stage to themselves. The three artists who were featured most widely in national Top Ten album charts in 2000 were America's Britney Spears, closely followed by Mexico's Carlos Santana and the British Beatles. Even tiny Iceland has produced a global star: Björk. Popular opera's biggest singers are Italy's Luciano Pavarotti, Spain's José Carreras, and the Spanish-Mexican Placido Domingo. Latin American salsa, Brazilian lambada, and African music have all carved out global niches for themselves. In most countries, local artists still top the charts. . . .

The evidence is overwhelming. Fears about an Americanized uniformity are overblown: American cultural products are not uniquely dominant; local ones are alive and well.

For Further Reflection

■ Do you find Legrain's arguments and examples compelling? Could cultural exchanges such as those detailed in Legrain's article be more complicated or problematic than Legrain proposed? Consider how other cultural products—perhaps those from Africa or Asia—might either uphold or undermine Legrain's thesis on globalization.

Source: Philippe Legrain, "Cultural Globalization Is Not Americanization," *The Chronicle of Higher Education,* 49, no. 35 (May 9, 2003): B7. Used with permission.

Sushi consumption in the United States provides another example of the multidirectional nature of globalization. Although sushi was first introduced to the United States in the 1960s, in the 1990s sushi suddenly caught on outside major metropolitan areas as a healthy alternative to fatty, American-style food. In the last thirty years, sushi—which had been prepared in Japan since the eighth century—could be found in local Japanese restaurants across the United States, in airports, in the prepared foods section of grocery stores, and even in the refrigerated section of gas station convenience stores. Not only that, Americans have altered and modified sushi recipes to reflect ingredients more familiar in the United States or to give the varieties American-sounding names.

The phenomenon of modification is important to remember even with products or consumables that originate in the United States. Take the case of Music Television (MTV) Latino. When MTV Latino was launched in 1993 from Miami, many critics viewed it as just another case of foreign cultural intrusion, whereby Latin video deejays speak "Spanglish" or "Chequenos" ("check us out"), mixing Spanish and English. While Latin Americans once had called for protection against such alien influence, many soon relaxed their guard. Instead of cultural domination, they saw evidence of increased cultural sharing among Latin societies, noting that MTV and cable television have come to serve as a means of communication and unity by making the nations of Latin America more aware of one another. Thus, it is important to remember that cultural dominance is limited by the ability of many societies to blend and absorb a variety of foreign and indigenous practices.

The Networked World

Throughout history, technological advances provided the means to dissolve boundaries between localities and peoples and thus allowed cultural transmission to take place. Today virtually instantaneous electronic communications have dissolved time and space. Since the mid-1990s, the rise of the Internet and smartphones has swept away the social, economic, and political isolation of the past.

Communications technologies underwent a fundamental transformation during the 1990s with the rapid spread of the Internet. The Internet had arisen from Cold War imperatives: U.S. defense specialists wanted to establish a way to disseminate information after a nuclear attack and ultimately created a network (the Advanced Research Projects Agency Network, or ARPANET) in which computers at different locations could communicate with one another. In 1983, researchers began to use a communications protocol (called TCP/IP) by which different kinds of computers on different networks could communicate, and the Internet was officially born. However, it was not until 1991 that a platform for public use, called the World Wide Web, became available. When the institution that developed the World Wide Web (CERN) announced in 1993 that the platform was free for everyone to develop, its use exploded around the world. In 1998 Google

This CDC 7600 mainframe computer was built by the Control Data Corporation in the 1970s. Note its extremely large size in comparison to computers in the twenty-first century.
Science History Images/Alamy Stock Photo

went live, changing the way millions of people searched for information, and in 2004 Facebook launched its social media platform (though only for college students). By 2008, presidential candidates were taking full advantage of the Internet to conduct their campaigns, and by the second decade of the twenty-first century, the Internet had become fully integrated into the lives of most people living in developed nations.

Although the Internet fundamentally changed the way in which people communicated around the world, at first it was only available to people or companies who owned computers or who could pay to use them in "Internet cafés." But access to the Internet gradually became more democratized by the second decade of the twenty-first century through the use of smartphones—or mobile phones that could access wireless networks and thus the Internet. Mobile phones had been available publicly since the 1980s, but these were physically heavy and expensive to use. By the early 2000s, both the size and the cost of mobile phones had shrunk, and some phones began to be developed that could access wireless networks. The introduction of the first iPhone in 2007 revolutionized smartphone use: in little more than the span of a decade, a huge percentage of the human population had access to relatively inexpensive mobile phones that could function as telephones, computers, cameras, and video recorders, with ever-increasing coverage areas in nearly every part of the world. By 2019, the Pew Research Center estimated that five billion people had mobile phones and that half of these were smartphones. And while people in developed nations are more likely to own mobile phones, 45 percent of people in developing nations own them as well.

The use of the Internet, and especially of smartphones, has not only accelerated communications and proved convenient for everyday life activities, it has also changed the way people organize social movements. For example, during the social protests that swept the Arab world during the "Arab Spring" of 2011, activists used social media to advertise the locations of protests and to communicate what was happening with the outside world. Additionally, individuals have used social media as a platform to publicize human rights abuses they have filmed on their smartphones, often leading to public outcry and even policy changes. Yet even though the Internet, smartphones, and social media have transformed the way billions of people communicate in the twenty-first century, critics worry that over-reliance on such technologies might lead people to neglect face-to-face relations or that social media in particular might be detrimental to individual self-esteem. These debates have not been settled and will likely continue as Internet-driven technologies expand around the world.

International Organizations

As the world's peoples are becoming increasingly connected and interdependent as a result of new technologies, many have realized that they face issues that extend well beyond national borders. Since the end of World War II, this recognition has led to an increase in the number of organizations dedicated to solving global problems through international coordination and action. These institutions are important because they have the potential to tackle issues that do not respect territorial boundaries and thus cannot be effectively addressed by individual national governments.

Intergovernmental Organizations One type of international body is the intergovernmental organization, meaning that membership is made up of sovereign states rather than individuals or private groups. These organizations include the World Trade Organization, the North Atlantic Treaty Organization (NATO), the African Development Bank, and the European Union, to name a few. The main purposes behind intergovernmental organizations are to provide mechanisms for member states to work together to find solutions to maintain peace and security, or to enhance economic and social stability across national borders.

The best known intergovernmental organization is the United Nations (UN), which was established at the end of World War II to replace the League of Nations (1920-1946). The purpose of the UN is to find solutions to global problems and to deal with virtually any matter of concern to humanity. Unlike a national government, the UN does not legislate. Yet, in its meeting rooms and corridors, representatives of the vast majority of the world's countries (193 out of 195 total) have a voice and a vote in shaping the international community of nations. Under its charter, a principal purpose of the UN is "to maintain international peace and security." It has not been able to achieve this goal, partly because member states have often chosen to embark on wars or hostilities in spite of UN opposition. And unless all members of the UN Security Council (whose permanent members are made up of the five most powerful nations in the world) agree, the UN cannot send peacekeeping troops to help end a conflict.

But the UN has compiled an enviable record with respect to another role defined in its charter, namely, "to achieve international cooperation in solving international problems of an economic, social, cultural, or humanitarian character." Quietly and often without attracting attention from the international news media, the specialized agencies of the UN have achieved numerous successes. For example, in 1980 the World Health Organization (a division of the UN) proclaimed the worldwide eradication of smallpox as a result of its thirteen-year global program. On other fronts, UN efforts resulted in more than a 50 percent decrease in both infant and child mortality rates in developing countries between 1960 and 2002. Indeed, by 2015 the UN reported that its efforts had helped to save the lives of ninety million children worldwide since 1990. The organization's efforts also promoted an increase in female literacy, especially in Africa, where for the first time in history the majority of women—53.6 percent in 2010—were deemed to be literate. The UN also worked to provide access to safe water for over one billion people living in rural areas.

Nongovernmental Organizations Another type of international body is the nongovernmental organization (NGO), meaning that such an organization operates independently of any government. NGOs typically are nonprofit organizations and focus on a social, economic, environmental, or humanitarian issue that transcends national borders. Many NGOs have focused on the protection of human rights, or the notion that all persons are entitled to some basic rights, especially rights that protect an individual against state conduct prohibited by international law or custom. Universal recognition and acceptance of the concept of human rights came in the aftermath of World War II with the exposure of Nazi crimes. In 1948, the National Assembly of the UN adopted the **Universal Declaration of Human Rights,** which contributed to the codification of international human rights laws. The declaration singled out specific human rights violations such as extrajudicial or summary executions, arbitrary arrest and torture, and slavery or involuntary servitude as well as discrimination on racial, sexual, or religious grounds. Since then, concerned individuals and groups have formed human rights NGOs with the goal of ensuring these laws are upheld. For example, Amnesty International (founded 1961) seeks to expose human rights violations all over the world through massive media and lobbying campaigns, as well as to provide legal defense where possible. It is funded by individual members, which in 2020 had reached two million. Amnesty International has counted among its many victories campaigns on behalf of groups as well as individuals, from compelling Shell Oil to pay $55 million to the Nigerian government for oil spills to freeing a young woman in El Salvador who was imprisoned on suspicion of inducing an abortion.

In 2015, one organization estimated that there are ten million NGOs operating around the world. It is thus not surprising that they focus on many issues besides human rights. Many focus on global health, including organizations like Partners in Health (founded 1987), whose mission is to provide health care to the most marginalized populations in the world. Others focus on the environment and solutions to climate change. The Environmental Defense Fund (founded 1967), for example, seeks to find solutions to the most urgent environmental problems, whether in the air, in the oceans, or on land. Still others, such as Barefoot College (founded 1972), focus on education for the poor, in this case specifically by providing funding to educate and empower poor women from rural areas.

Given the intensity and acceleration of global interaction after World War II, the possibilities for solving global problems through international coordination is increasingly imaginable. And while both intergovernmental and nongovernmental international organizations are far from perfect, for the present they represent the closest thing humanity has to a global system of governance that can help the world's peoples meet the challenges of international problems.

URGENT GLOBAL ISSUES IN THE EARLY TWENTY-FIRST CENTURY

By the twenty-first century, it had become clear that the new millennium would bring with it a multitude of issues whose solution would require both a global perspective and global responses. Each of these issues—from climate change to women's empowerment to global pandemics—have the potential to affect all the world's people, and none have easy solutions.

Population Pressures and Climate Change

The post–World War II period has been accompanied by vast population increases. As the result of advances in agriculture, industry, science, and medicine global population has increased from 2.5 billion in 1950 to 7.8 billion in 2020. The widespread and successful use of vaccines, antibiotics, and insecticides, along with improvements in water supplies and increased agricultural yields, caused a dramatic decline in worldwide death rates in this period. The rapid decline in mortality among people who also maintained high levels of fertility led to explosive population growth in many areas of Asia and Africa. In some developing nations, population growth now exceeds 3.1 percent, a rate that ensures the doubling of the population within twenty-three years. Indeed, the population division of the United Nations has estimated that the earth's population will stabilize around 9.8 billion in 2050. In the meantime, 8.1 million people are joining the world's total population each year, and unless fertility declines to replacement levels—that is, two children per woman—the world's population will grow forever.

More optimistic voices, however, have pointed out that the odds of a population explosion and its dreaded consequences are exaggerated and are in fact receding. This is largely because fertility rates have been falling fast in the past two decades, both in rich and in poor societies. The same optimists also argue that despite rapid population growth, wages have risen and the cost of everything extracted or grown from the earth has declined. Equally significant is the fact that food production has more than kept pace with the growing population. Yet even if the earth can support its large and growing population in the short term, it seems clear that human actions have dramatically altered the physical environment in ways that may prove disastrous for the survival of the planet.

Climate Change The problem is not simply one of depleting nonrenewable resources or expanding populations. As increasing numbers of people are born, pollution levels increase, more habitats and animal and plant species disappear, and more natural resources are consumed. In recent decades one environmental issue has taken center stage: **climate change.** In the context of environmental debates and policymaking, climate change usually refers to a human-induced climate change known as **global warming.**

Global warming is the phenomenon of increasing average air temperature near the surface of the earth over the past two centuries. On the basis of detailed observations, scientists have concluded that the influence of human activities since the beginning of industrialization have altered the earth's climate. More specifically, the vast majority of scientists around the world are convinced that most of the observed temperature increases since the middle of the twentieth century are caused by increasing concentrations of greenhouse gases, which prevent solar heat from escaping from the earth's atmosphere. Like the glass panes in a greenhouse, hydrocarbon emissions from automobiles, and methane emitted from animal dung on commercial farms, trap heat within the atmosphere, leading to a rise in global temperatures. An average rise of global temperature by more than 2°C (3.6°F), would cause significant economic and ecological damage, particularly because this would cause a rise in sea levels as a result of melting in the polar ice caps.

A vigorous debate is in progress over the extent and seriousness of rising surface temperatures, their consequences for the environment, and the necessity to limit further warming. In the ancient Japanese capital of Kyoto, at a conference dedicated to climate change, the delegates from 187 nations agreed in 1997 to cut greenhouse emissions blamed for global warming. The Kyoto protocol went into force in 2005 and imposed targets for carbon emission reductions on developed countries until 2012. The protocol did not require developing countries—some of them major polluters, such as India and China—to reduce their emissions. The world's second-largest polluter after China, the United States, did not sign the protocol because it required nothing of developing countries. Since Kyoto, global carbon-dioxide emissions have risen by a third.

International efforts in dealing with climate change have been hampered by the fact that developing nations have been reluctant to commit themselves to cutting emissions. In part this is because their leaders believe that the only way to remain economically competitive in the globalized world is to continue industrializing. Additionally, some leaders resent being told they must cut back on emissions to solve environmental

Smokestacks in Siberia releasing carbon dioxide emissions into the atmosphere. Most scientists argue that emissions such as these, along with other hydrocarbon emissions and methane, contribute to global climate change.

Peter Turnley/Corbis/VCG/Getty Images

problems caused by developed nations over the span of more than a century. As a result, developing nations have insisted that developed nations bear the costs of reducing emissions. Efforts to find solutions have also been hampered by one of the most powerful developed nations and one of the world's greatest polluters: the United States. Politicians in the United States have worried about the economic effects of reducing emissions, and some have expressed skepticism about the existence of climate change at all. In spite of these obstacles, in December 2015 the United Nations Framework on Climate Change produced the Paris Agreement, which set global goals of capping greenhouse emissions. The Paris Agreement commits signatories to reducing emissions and to publicly tracking their progress in doing so. Unlike the Kyoto protocol, the Paris Agreement was signed by nearly every developing country (including China and India) as well as the United States. However, under the administration of President Donald Trump, who cited concern for American jobs and businesses, the United States withdrew from the Paris Agreement on June 1, 2017.

How the Past Shapes the Future

The Destructive Potential of Industrial Technologies

Nineteenth-century advocates of industrialization had envisioned a world in which mechanization and new technologies would lead to improvements in the human condition over the long term. Yet after only two centuries since industrialization began in Great Britain, it seems possible that the pollution associated with industrialization may have disastrous consequences for the whole planet if, as scientists predict, such pollution leads to global climate change. Think about how the issues associated with climate change are an excellent example of the ways historical events and processes can have consequences for the future in ways that contemporaries cannot even imagine.

Population Control For decades the issue of population control was highly politicized. Political leaders in developing countries, for example, charged representatives of industrialized countries with racism when they raised concerns regarding overpopulation. Industrialized nations were also accused of trying to safeguard their outrageous consumption patterns of the world's nonrenewable resources. Some leaders, such as Mexico's Luis Echeverría (president 1970–1976), went so far as to promote pronatalist measures (to increase births), urging his fellow citizens to have numerous children. The problems caused by rapid population growth eventually persuaded many governments to take action to control fertility. By that time, the old pervasive notion that a large population is a source of national power had given way to the idea that the best way to promote the health and well-being of a population is to control its growth.

As death rates declined persistently throughout the world during the latter part of the twentieth century, reducing birthrates became a central concern of many governments. The United Nations and two of its specialized agencies, the World Health Organization and the UN Fund for Population Activities, have aided many countries in organizing and promoting

A rare and endangered adult woolly spider monkey in the Atlantic Forest, Brazil. This species is one of about 30,000 endangered species, 85% of which are threatened as a result of habitat loss due to human expansion.
Paulo B. Chaves/Getty Images

family-planning programs. However, the availability and promotion of contraceptives does not guarantee effective control of fertility. Whereas China has, however stringently, significantly reduced its population growth rate and some Latin American societies also have experienced a decline in their birthrates, people in other societies have resisted efforts to reduce birthrates. In some instances, resistance stems from both religious and political motives. In India, for example, the Hindu emphasis on fertility has impeded birth control efforts. Thus global attempts to prevent excessive population growth have had mixed results.

Economic Inequities and Labor Servitude

The unequal distribution of resources and income, and the resulting poverty, have materialized as key concerns of the contemporary world. Several hundred million people, especially in the developing areas of eastern Europe, Africa, Latin America, and Asia, struggle daily for sufficient food, clean water, adequate shelter, and other basic necessities. Poverty is a lack of basic human necessities, and its effects are as wide-ranging as they are devastating. Malnutrition among the poor has led to starvation

This poster advertised China's one-child family rule, which was imposed in 1979. In 2013, Chinese authorities eased this restriction to allow a family to have two children if one of the parents was an only child. In 2016, the government began allowing all families to have two children.
Barry Lewis/Alamy Stock Photo

and death. As one of the most persistent effects of poverty, malnutrition is also responsible for stunted growth, poor mental development, and high rates of infection. Typically, vitamin and mineral deficiencies accompany malnutrition, causing mental disorders, organ damage, and vision failure among poor children and adults. Because of inadequate shelter, lack of safe running water, and the absence of sewage facilities, the poor have been exposed disproportionally to bacteria and viruses carried by other people, insects, and rodents. Poverty has correlated strongly with higher-than-average infant mortality rates and lower-than-average life expectancies.

The Causes of Poverty

The division between rich and poor has been a defining characteristic of all complex societies. Although relative poverty levels within a given society remain a major concern, it is the continuing division between rich and poor societies that has attracted the attention of the international community. A worldwide shortage of natural resources as well as the uneven distribution of resources have figured as major causes of poverty and have divided nations into the haves and have-nots. Excessively high population densities and environmental degradation have caused the depletion of available resources, leading to shortages of food, water, and shelter and ultimately to poverty. The other major cause of poverty, the unequal distribution of resources in the world economy, resulted from five hundred years of colonialism, defined by the appropriation of labor and natural resources. Pervasive poverty characterizes many former colonies and dependencies. All of these developing societies have tried to raise income levels and eliminate poverty through diversified economic development, but only a few, such as South Korea, Singapore, and Malaysia have accomplished their aims. In the meantime, economic globalization has generated unprecedented wealth for developed nations, creating an even deeper divide between rich and poor countries. A report issued by the antipoverty charity Oxfam noted that in 2018, 82 percent of the world's total wealth went to the richest 1 percent of the population, while the 3.7 billion people who make up the poorest half of the world saw no increase in their wealth.

Labor Servitude

Poor economic conditions have been closely associated with forms of servitude similar to slavery. Although legal slavery ceased to exist when Saudi Arabia and Angola abolished slavery officially in the 1960s, forced and bonded labor practices continue to affect millions of poor people in the developing world. Of particular concern is child-labor servitude. According to the International Labor Organization, a specialized agency of the United Nations, more than 250 million children between ages five and fourteen work around the world, many in conditions that are inherently harmful to their physical health and emotional well-being. Child-labor servitude is most pronounced in south and southeast Asia, affecting an estimated 50 million children in India alone. Most child labor occurs in agriculture, domestic service, family businesses, and the sex trade, making it difficult to enforce existing prohibitions and laws against those practices. Many children are born into a life of bonded labor because their parents have worked in debt bondage, a condition whereby impoverished persons work for very low wages, borrow money from their employer, and pledge their labor as security.

Trafficking

A growing and related global problem that touches societies on every continent is the trafficking of persons. In this insidious form of modern slavery, one to two million human beings annually are bought and sold across international and within national boundaries. Trafficking has appeared in many forms. In Russia and the Ukraine, for example, traffickers lure victims with the promise of well-paying jobs abroad. Once the victims arrive in the countries of their destination, they become captives of ruthless traffickers who force them into bonded labor, domestic servitude, or the commercial sex industry through threats and physical brutality—including rape, torture, starvation, incarceration, and death. Most of the victims of trafficking are girls and women, which is a reflection of the low social and economic status of women in many countries. In south Asia, for instance, it is common for poverty-stricken parents or other relatives to sell young women to traffickers for the sex trade or forced labor. The trafficking industry is one of the fastest growing and most lucrative criminal enterprises in the world, generating billions of dollars annually in profits.

The Continuing Inequality of Women

The status of women in many places around the world began changing after World War II. Women gained more economic, political, social, and sexual rights in highly industrialized states than in developing nations, but nowhere have they achieved full social, political, and economic equality with men. Although women have increasingly challenged cultural norms requiring their subordination to men and confinement in the family, attainment of even basic rights for many millions of women has been slow. Agitation for gender equality is often linked to women's access to employment, which is highest in industrialized nations. Women constitute 40 to 50 percent of the workforce in industrial societies, compared with only 20 percent in developing countries. Yet in all countries, the majority of women who do work for pay are engaged in low-paying jobs such as teaching, service, and clerical work. This does not include farming, as 40 percent of all farmers in the world are women. Rural African women, for example, do most of the continent's subsistence farming and produce more than 70 percent of Africa's food. Whether they are industrial, service, or agricultural workers,

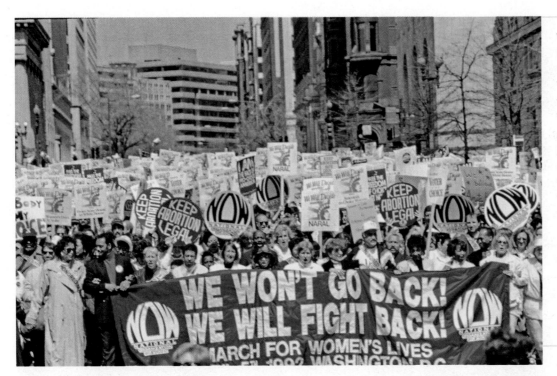

Women belonging to the U.S. feminist group the National Organization for Women (NOW) marching for equal rights in Washington, D.C., in 1992. Although American and European women have experienced many gains with respect to achieving full equality with men, they remain less powerful in many areas. Pressures against equality for women remain strong in many developing areas of the world.
Mark Reinstein/Corbis/Getty Images

women earn less than men earn for the same work and are generally kept out of the highest-paid professional careers.

In addition, a report issued by the UN and the World Bank in 2017 argued that more women live in extreme poverty in the world than men. At the same time, data collected by both the UN and many NGOs have demonstrated that programs to improve overall public health, improve access to education, and promote sustainable development in societies around the world meet with greater success when steps have been taken to improve the status of women.

The Struggle for Equality in Industrialized Nations

The discrimination that women faced in the workplace was a major stimulus for the **feminist movement** in industrialized nations. Women in most of those nations had gained the right to vote after the Great War (although women in France and Italy had to wait until 1944 and 1945), but they found that political rights did not guarantee economic or sexual equality. After World War II, when more and more women went to work, women started to protest job discrimination, pay differentials between women and men, and their lack of legal equality. In the 1960s those complaints expanded into a feminist movement that criticized all aspects of gender inequality. In the United States, the civil rights movement that demanded equality for African Americans influenced the women's movement and provided a training ground for many women activists.

Women in industrialized societies started to expose the ways in which a biologically determined understanding of gender led to their oppression. In addition to demanding equality in the workplace, women demanded full control over their bodies and their reproductive systems. Access to birth control and abortion became as essential to women's liberation as economic equality and independence. Only with birth control measures would women be able to determine whether or when to have children and thus avoid the notion that "biology is destiny." The introduction of the birth control pill in the 1960s gave millions of women the power to protect themselves from unwanted pregnancies. Shortly thereafter, beginning with the United Kingdom in 1967 and then extending to Canada (1967), the United States (1973), and many European countries, women won the fight to legalize abortion. But even though these developments provided women in industrialized nations with a measure of sexual freedom, women continued to lag behind men in terms of access to political power and equal wages for equal work. In addition, women often face sexual harassment in the workplace.

Gender Equality in China

Legally, the position of women most closely matches that of men in communist or formerly communist countries such as the Soviet Union, Cuba, and China. "Women hold up half the sky," Mao Zedong had declared, and that eloquent acknowledgment of women's role translated into a legal commitment to fairness. The communist dedication to women's rights led to improvement in the legal status of Chinese women once the communists gained power in China. In 1950, communist leaders passed a marriage law (see chapter 37) that mandated the protection of interests of both men and women within

Young girls study the Qu'ran at a madrassa (school) in Pakistan, 2005.
Robert Nickelsberg/Getty Images

marriage, legalized divorce, and abolished patriarchal practices such as child betrothal. It also upheld equal rights for men and women in the areas of work, property ownership, and inheritance.

Critics argue that despite such laws Chinese women have never gained true equality with men. For example, few women have gained high status in the Communist Party's leadership. And although most women in China have full-time jobs outside the home, they do not receive wages equal to those of men. They do most of the work at home as well. Nevertheless, they are able to enter most professions, although the majority of Chinese women engage in menial work. Long-standing cultural values continue to degrade the status of women, especially in rural areas. Traditionally, parents have overwhelmingly preferred boys over girls. One unintended consequence of China's population policies, which until 2016 limited couples to one child, was the mysterious statistical disappearance of a large number of baby girls. Demographers estimate that annually more than one-half million female births went unrecorded in government statistics. Although no one can with certainty account for the "missing" girls, some population experts speculate that a continued strong preference for male children caused parents to send baby girls away for adoption or to be raised secretly or, in some cases, to single them out for infanticide.

Domesticity and Abuse Although girls and women in industrial and communist nations are guaranteed basic if not fully equal legal rights and are educated in roughly the same numbers as boys and men, women in other areas of the world have long been denied access to education. Indeed, of the world's remaining 774 illiterate adults, two-thirds of these are women.

In India, for example, the literacy gap between men and women is stark, at 81.5 percent for men compared to 64.6 percent for women. Moreover, the participation of Indian women in the labor force is very low, at about 25 percent for rural women and 15 percent for urban women. At the same time, birthrates in India remain high in spite of greater access to birth control, at 2.33 births per woman as compared to 1.8 in the United States. These conditions have ensured a life of dependence for many Indian women. One indicator of the low social status of Indian women is the continued occurrence of dowry deaths. It is customary among many Indian communities to pay a dowry (gifts of money or goods) to the husband and his family upon a woman's marriage, although this requirement is difficult for many Indian families to meet. If the husband and his family perceive the dowry as inadequate, if the husband wants a new wife without returning his first wife's dowry, or in some cases if the wife has simply annoyed the husband or her in-laws, her new family douses her with kerosene and sets her on fire so that her death can be explained as a cooking accident. Although this practice is illegal and only occurs in a small minority of marriages, it is still widespread enough to make women's precarious position in society clear. In 2016 the government of India reported 7,621 dowry deaths, though unofficial estimates put the number closer to twenty-five thousand.

SOURCES FROM THE PAST

Malala Yousafzai on Why Girls Should Go to School

Malala Yousafzai (1997–) was eleven years old when the Taliban took control of her town in Pakistan. Malala wrote a diary protesting this, which was read by many people, and thereafter she became a target. When she dared to go to school in defiance of Taliban rules in 2012, a masked gunman boarded her school bus and shot her on the left side of the head, also wounding two of her friends. Malala survived the shooting, undergoing critical surgery in Pakistan before being flown to London for more surgeries. She and her family now live in London, where she is a vocal advocate for education, especially for girls. In 2014 she became the youngest recipient of the Nobel Peace Prize. Below are excerpts of the speech she gave at the United Nations on her sixteenth birthday.

I don't know where to begin my speech. I don't know what people would be expecting me to say. But first of all, thank you to God for whom we all are equal and thank you to every person who has prayed for my fast recovery and a new life. I cannot believe how much love people have shown me. . . .

Thousands of people have been killed by the terrorists and millions have been injured. I am just one of them.

So here I stand, one girl among many . . .

Dear sisters and brothers, I am not against anyone. Neither am I here to speak in terms of personal revenge against the Taliban or any other terrorist groups. I am here to speak up for the right of education of every child. I want education for the sons and the daughters of all the extremists especially the Taliban . . .

The wise saying, "The pen is mightier than sword" was true. The extremists are afraid of books and pens. The power of education frightens them. They are afraid of women. The power of the voice of women frightens them . . . That is why they are blasting schools every day. Because they were and they are afraid of change, afraid of the equality that we will bring into our society.

> Why, according to Malala, are the Taliban so against education, and for girls in particular?

I remember that there was a boy in our school who was asked by a journalist, "Why are the Taliban against education?" He answered very simply. By pointing to his book he said, "A Talib doesn't know what is written inside this book." They think that God is a tiny, little conservative being who would send girls to the hell just because of going to school. The terrorists are misusing the name of Islam and Pashtun society for their own personal benefits. Pakistan is peace-loving democratic country. Pashtuns want education for their daughters and sons. And Islam is a religion of peace, humanity and brotherhood. Islam says that it is not only each child's right to get education, rather it is their duty and responsibility.

> In what ways does Malala argue the Taliban misrepresents Islam?

Honourable Secretary General, peace is necessary for education. In many parts of the world especially Pakistan and Afghanistan, terrorism, wars and conflicts stop children to go to their schools. We are really tired of these wars. Women and children are suffering in many parts of the world in many ways. In India, innocent and poor children are victims of child labour. Many schools have been destroyed in Nigeria. People in Afghanistan have been affected by the hurdles of extremism for decades. Young girls have to do domestic child labour and are forced to get married at early age. Poverty, ignorance, injustice, racism and the deprivation of basic rights are the main problems faced by both men and women.

Dear fellows, today I am focusing on women's rights and girls' education because they are suffering the most. There was a time when women social activists asked men to stand up for their rights. But, this time, we will do it by ourselves . . .

Dear brothers and sisters, we want schools and education for every child's bright future. We will continue our journey to our destination of peace and education for everyone. No one can stop us. We will speak for our rights and we will bring change through our voice. We must believe in the power and the strength of our words. Our words can change the world.

So let us wage a global struggle against illiteracy, poverty and terrorism and let us pick up our books and pens. They are our most powerful weapons . . .

Education is the only solution. Education first.

For Further Reflection

■ Why is education so important to Malala? What does she believe education can do to help the poor and suffering?

Source: United Nations, Office of the Secretary General's Envoy on Youth. Malala Yousafzai addresses United Nations Youth Assembly. https://www.un.org/youthenvoy/video/malala-yousafzai-addresses-united-nations-youth-assembly/ Used with permission of the Malala Fund.

Women Leaders By 2015, women had gained the right to vote in almost every country in the world. In general, however, they do not exert political power commensurate with their numbers. Some women have nonetheless attained high political offices or impressive leadership positions. Somewhat ironically, the same south Asia that revealed so many continued barriers to women's rights on a day-to-day basis also elevated some women to positions of power. It was no accident, however, that all of these women came from powerful political families. **Indira Gandhi** (1917–1984) and **Benazir Bhuto** (1953–2007), both of whose fathers had been prime ministers, served as prime minister for India and Pakistan, respectively. Yet both women were controversial figures, and both were assassinated while in office. In 1994 **Chandrika Bandaranaike Kumaratunga** (1945–) became the first female president of Sri Lanka. Both her parents had previously served as prime ministers; her mother, Sirimavo Bandaranaike (1916–2000), became the first elected woman prime minister in 1960. As president, Kumaratunga appointed her mother to serve a third term as prime minister.

In Myanmar (formerly Burma), **Aung San Suu Kyi** (1945–) has emerged as a leader, also deriving her political authority from her father, Aung San, assassinated in 1947. Assuming the leadership of the democracy movement after her return from exile in 1988, Suu Kyi called for a nonviolent revolution against what she called Myanmar's "fascist government." The government placed her under house arrest from 1989 to 1995, during which time she created a new political institution, the "gateside meeting," speaking to her followers from behind the gates of her home. In the 1990 elections Suu Kyi and her party won a landslide victory, but they were not allowed to come to power. Awarded the Nobel Peace Prize for her efforts in 1991, she could not accept the award personally because she was still under house arrest. She remained in detention or under house arrest for much of the next two decades, released from her political imprisonment only in 2010. Aung San Suu Kyi was elected to the Burmese parliament in 2012, and in 2015 she led her party, the National League for Democracy, to a landslide victory in Myanmar's first openly contested elections. Although not allowed to serve as president because she has foreign-born children, she served as de facto leader of the country beginning in 2016. Since 2017, Suu Kyi has come under international criticism for her failure to stop attacks by Myanmar's army on Burma's indigenous Muslim minority, the Rohingya.

In spite of the fact that some women have served as leaders of their countries, the fact remains that by the end of the second decade of the twenty-first century, women still are vastly underrepresented as political leaders in nearly every

Pro-democracy leader Aung San Suu Kyi spoke at a press conference, appearing under the flag of her political party in Yangon, Burma.
EMMANUEL DUNAND/AFP/Getty Images

nation. There have only been nineteen female heads of state since 2000, and in 2020 only one in five members of lower or single houses of parliament are women worldwide. Women remain a small minority of corporate managers and senior officials everywhere in the world, and only 50 percent of working age women are in the labor force compared to 77 percent of men. We have seen that women are more likely to live in poverty than men, which has clear implications for their access to adequate health care, housing, and nutrition. Additionally, a UN report indicates that about one-third of women in the world have experienced sexual or physical violence by an intimate partner or have experienced sexual violence by a non-partner at some point in their lives. Thus, if it is true that programs for improving public health and sustainable development succeed best when women are empowered through access to education and work, much remains to be done.

Indira Gandhi (in-DEE-rah GAHN-dee)

Benazir Bhuto (BEN-ah-zeer BOO-toh)

Chandrika Bandaranaike Kumaratunga (CHAHN-dree-kah BAHN-dah-rah-nigh-kee koo-mah-rah-TOONG-ah)

Aung San Suu Kyi (ong sahn soo chee)

Global Terrorism

Terrorism has become a persistent feature of the globalized world since 1945. Although not a recent phenomenon, terrorism attained its greatest impact in a world distinguished by rapid technological advances in transportation, communications, and weapons development. Heightened media awareness, especially the ubiquity of worldwide television coverage, has exposed the grievances and demands of terrorists to millions of viewers, but it has also transformed the practice of terrorism. Acts of terror therefore punctuated the era following World War II, as individuals and groups the world over attempted to destabilize or overthrow political systems within or outside the borders of their countries. Terrorism figured prominently in anticolonial conflicts in Algeria and Vietnam; in struggles over a homeland between national groups such as Israelis and Palestinians; in clashes between religious denominations such as Protestants and Catholics in Northern Ireland; and between revolutionary forces and established regimes in states such as Indonesia, Iran, and Nicaragua.

Defining Terrorism No universally agreed-on definition of terrorism exists, but experts agree that a key feature of terrorism is the deliberate and systematic use of violence against civilians, with the aim of inspiring terror to advance political, religious, or ideological causes. Terrorists use violent means—from hijackings and hostage-taking to assassinations and mass murder—to magnify their influence and power. In contrast to the populations and institutions they fight, terrorists and their organizations are usually limited in size and resources. During the last decades of the twentieth century and the first decade of the twenty-first century, terrorism increasingly assumed a global character because instead of using terrorist techniques in local struggles, terrorist networks brought violence thousands of miles away to strike at the heart of their perceived enemies. To do this, they relied on the same sophisticated financial networks, modern modes of transportation, and communications technologies used by billions of other people in a globalized world. At the turn of the twenty-first century, this relatively novel kind of terrorism captured the attention of the world as a result of the September 11 attacks in the United States.

September 11 On the morning of September 11, 2001, New York City and Washington, D.C., became the targets of a coordinated terrorist attack that was unprecedented in scope, sophistication, and destructiveness. Hijackers seized four passenger jetliners and used them as guided missiles. Two of the planes crashed into the World Trade Center towers in New York City, causing the collapse of the two towers, the ancillary destruction of adjacent skyscrapers, and more than twenty-five hundred deaths. Before the morning was over, another plane crashed into the Pentagon, killing one hundred twenty-five people at the nerve center of the U.S. military in Washington, D.C., and the fourth jet crashed into

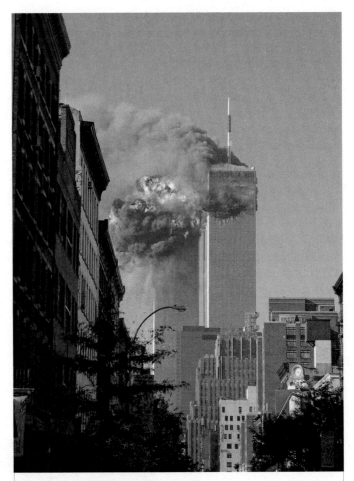

The north face of the south tower immediately after being struck by United Airlines flight 175 on September 11, 2001.
Laperruque/Alamy Stock Photo

a field outside Pittsburgh, Pennsylvania. Intended for another Washington, D.C., landmark, the fourth jet was thwarted in its mission when passengers stormed the hijackers and forced the plane to crash. As millions around the world watched events unfold on television, the U.S. government launched an intensive investigation and identified the Islamic militant **Osama bin Laden** (1957–2011) as the mastermind behind the attacks. Officials also accused bin Laden of directing previous attacks on U.S. interests in Africa and southwest Asia. Before the dust of the collapsed World Trade towers had settled, U.S. President George W. Bush (1946–) declared war on Osama bin Laden and global terrorism itself.

Osama bin Laden headed ***al-Qaeda*** ("the base"), the core of a global terrorist network. He became a popular figure in the U.S.-backed effort to aid mujahideen (Islamic warriors) who fought Soviet forces in Afghanistan. By the end of the Persian Gulf War (1990–1991), however, he began to consider the United States and its allies with unqualified hatred. The stationing of U.S. troops on what he regarded as the holy soil of Saudi Arabia, the bombing of Iraq, and supporting Israeli oppression of Palestinians, bin Laden claimed, were tantamount to a declaration of war against God. His radicalism led him first to be exiled and then, in 1994, to be stripped of his Saudi Arabian citizenship. He spent time in Sudan, where he took credit for the attack on two U.S. Black Hawk helicopters in 1993. He was expelled from Sudan in 1996, at which point he went to Afghanistan at the invitation of the radical and violent **Taliban** party. From his base there in 1998, bin Laden publicly called on every Muslim to kill Americans and their allies "wherever he finds them and whenever he can." Viewed by many as the personification of evil, yet admired by some for his convictions and aims, Osama bin Laden moved to the forefront of Islamist violence.

War in Afghanistan and Iraq The Taliban itself emerged out of the disorder and devastation of the Afghan-Soviet war (1979–1988) and the Afghan civil war that developed in its aftermath. Promoting itself as a new force for unity and determined to create an Islamic state according to its own austere interpretation of Islam, the Taliban proclaimed its followers the liberators who brought peace to Afghanistan. In their pursuit of what they claimed would be the purest Muslim state on earth, Taliban intolerance figured prominently, and Islamist strictures quickly alienated people both inside and outside Afghanistan. Dominated by Pashtuns—the majority ethnic

group of Afghanistan—the Taliban under its leading *mullah* (male religious leader), Mohammed Omar, fought a series of holy wars against other ethnic and Muslim groups, such as Afghanistan's Shia minority. At the same time, the Taliban provided sanctuary and training grounds for Islamist fighters in southwest and central Asia, most notably—as we have seen—for Osama bin Laden and al-Qaeda.

The Taliban enforced a strict interpretation of Islam that barred women from education and the workplace. As all forms of European and American dress became taboo, women had to be completely veiled in *burkas,* and men had to stop wearing neckties and grow full, untrimmed beards. The stringent form of Taliban-promoted Islam also called for a ban on television, movie theaters, photographs, and most styles of music. Some of those rules had nothing to do with Islam, but a religious police, the Ministry of the Promotion of Virtue and Prevention of Vice, nevertheless enforced them with an extremely harsh code of justice. The United Nations and most governments in the world withheld recognition of the Taliban as Afghanistan's legitimate government. Instead, they recognized a Taliban opposition force, the Northern Alliance, which was composed of the country's smaller religious and ethnic groups. The Northern Alliance became a crucial ally of the United States in its mission to find and punish those responsible for the September 11 attacks.

A photographer captured the ruin of Saddam Hussein in this image of a tiled mural pitted and pocked by the destruction in Baghdad as a result of Operation Iraqi Freedom.
Kevin Frayer/AP Photo

When the United States government announced its war against global terrorism, it also pointedly targeted "those harboring terrorists," that is, governments and states that supported and provided sanctuary for terrorists. The refusal of the Taliban government to surrender Osama bin Laden prompted the United States and its allies to begin military operations against Taliban military positions and terrorist training camps on October 7, 2001. The U.S. military and its international allies generally limited their operations to intelligence missions and massive air strikes, fighting the war on the ground through Afghan proxies, most notably the forces of the Northern Alliance. By November, U.S.-led bombardments permitted Northern Alliance troops to capture Kabul and other key Afghan cities. The United States' coalition hampered both the Taliban and al-Qaeda, but conflicts continued.

Another international action against terrorism separate from the war in Afghanistan came in March 2003, when President Bush coordinated what he termed **"Operation Iraqi Freedom."** A multinational coalition force some three hundred thousand strong, largely made up of U.S. and British troops but also including those from approximately two dozen other nations, carried out an invasion of Iraq designed to wage further war on terrorism by ousting the regime of **Saddam Hussein** and creating a democratic state. The coalition argued they had firm evidence that Hussein possessed a huge stockpile of chemical and biological weapons, otherwise termed "weapons of mass destruction," devastating implements of war that could presumably be employed by global terrorists to wreak destruction on a scale even greater than that of 11 September 2001. Hussein himself was another special target, although he eluded capture for months. Coalition forces managed to establish their military supremacy in Iraq, but they did not uncover any such cache of weapons nor did they immediately control Hussein. President Bush declared an end to major battle operations on 1 May 2003, and coalition forces since that time struggled in their efforts to occupy and stabilize Iraq. Hussein was finally caught in December 2003 and executed in 2006, but deadly resistance in Iraq persisted.

The costs of the Iraq War were enormous in terms of both casualties and expenditures. Tens of thousands of Iraqi military personnel and civilians died, as had more than 4,700 coalition soldiers by mid-2010. The United States spent approximately $4 billion per month to maintain troops in Iraq. While President Bush sustained the United States' willingness to pay such a price, some critics in the United States and around the globe balked at the president's aggressive approach to the war on terrorism. Seen as an expression of the "Bush Doctrine of Deterrence," his preemptive strike against Iraq—which had not overtly committed a terrorist act or been proven to harbor terrorists—set a troubling precedent in U.S. foreign policy. Moreover, the increased presence of foreign military personnel in Iraq appeared to intensify the sort of Islamist fervor already fanned by Osama bin Laden. U.S.

President **Barack Obama** (1961–), elected in 2008 and reelected in 2012, shifted the war on terror away from Iraq and back to Afghanistan and bin Laden. Obama announced in May 2011 that elite forces had fulfilled a major mission in the war on terror by carrying out the U.S.-sanctioned killing of Osama bin Laden in Pakistan. Further, the United States declared the war in Iraq over in December 2011, at least as far as U.S. troops were concerned, although Iraqis continued to face intense civil conflict. The Iraq War caused the deaths of almost forty-five hundred U.S. soldiers, led to the wounding of thirty thousand U.S. soldiers, cost the nation $1 trillion, and left an uncertain legacy for both the United States and Iraq.

Meanwhile, in Afghanistan President Obama announced first the draw-down (2011) and then the withdrawal of U.S. troops from Afghanistan in 2014, leaving only about ten thousand advisers. In December 2019, President Donald Trump withdrew about half of these and promised to withdraw the rest in 2020. Over nearly twenty years, the war resulted in one hundred fifty-seven thousand deaths, of which nearly forty-three thousand were civilians. The United States spent $975 billion on operations and still was unable to establish a stable government.

Migration

Migration, the movement of people from one place to another, is as old as humanity and has shaped the formation and identity of societies throughout the world. The massive influx of outsiders has transformed the ethnic, linguistic, and cultural composition of indigenous populations. With the advent of industrialization during the eighteenth century, population experts distinguished between two types of migration: internal migration and external or international migration. Internal migration describes the flow of people from rural to urban areas within one society, whereas external migration describes the movement of people across long distances and international borders. Both types of migration result from push factors, pull factors, or a combination of the two. Lack of resources such as land or adequate food supplies, population pressure, religious or political persecution, or discriminatory practices aimed at ethnic minorities push people to move. Conversely, opportunities for better employment, the availability of arable land, or better services such as health care and education pull people to move.

Internal Migration The largest human migrations in recent history are rural-urban flows. During the second half of the twentieth century, these internal migrations led to rapid urbanization in much of the world. Today the most highly urbanized societies are those of western and northern Europe, Australia, New Zealand, and temperate South America and North America. In these societies the proportion of people living in urban areas exceeds 75 percent; in some countries, such as Belgium, it exceeds 97 percent. The societies of tropical Latin America are in an intermediate

Seeking relief from rural poverty, large numbers of people throughout the developing world have migrated to urban areas ill equipped to meet their needs and have had to settle in slums such as this one in Rio de Janeiro.

Vittoriano Rastelli/Corbis Historical/Getty Images

stage of urbanization, with 50 to 65 percent of the population living in cities. In many countries in Africa and Asia, the process of urbanization is at a relatively early stage. But even though most people still reside in rural areas, the rate of urbanization is very high.

Urbanization In Latin America, Africa, and south Asia, large numbers of people have migrated to metropolitan areas in search of relief from rural poverty. Once in the cities, though, they often find themselves equally destitute. Life is bleak in the slums outside Mumbai; in the shantytowns around Kinshasa or Nairobi; and in the *barriadas, barrios,* and *villas miserias* of Lima, Mexico City, and Buenos Aires. More than ten million people cram the environs of cities such as Calcutta, Cairo, and Mexico City, straining those cities' resources. The few services originally available to those who moved to slum areas—potable water, electricity, and medical care—have diminished with the continuous influx of new

people. Among the unemployed or underemployed, disease runs rampant, and many suffer from malnutrition.

External Migration A combination of voluntary and forced international migrations has transformed the human landscape, especially during the past five hundred years. Between the sixteenth and the twentieth centuries, more than sixty million European migrants, for example, colonized the Americas, Australia, Oceania, and the northern half of Asia. Between 1820 and 1980, in the course of the Atlantic migration, thirty-seven million migrants of European descent made their home in the United States. Forced slave migrations supplemented those voluntary movements of people. Between the sixteenth and the nineteenth centuries, slave traders consigned about twelve million Africans to the Americas, though many died in the appalling conditions of the Atlantic voyages.

During World War II the Nazi regime initiated the largest mass expulsions of the twentieth century, deporting eight

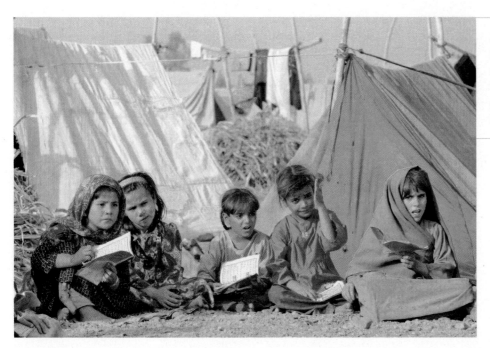

Afghan child refugees get a reading lesson at Jelozai Camp; they are just a few of the hundreds of thousands of forced displaced persons in the contemporary world.
Pascal Le Segretain/Sygma/Getty Images

million people to forced-labor sites and extermination camps. Following the war, the Soviet regime expelled ten million ethnic Germans from eastern and central Europe and transported them back to Germany. The largest migrations in the second half of the twentieth century have consisted of refugees fleeing war. For example, the 1947 partition of the Indian subcontinent into two independent states resulted in the exchange of six million Hindus from Pakistan and seven million Muslims from India. According to recent United Nations figures, more than forty-five million people worldwide had been forcibly displaced by 2013 as a result of conflict and persecution. More than fifteen million of the uprooted were refugees who fled their home countries, while another thirty million were people who remain displaced by conflict within their homelands. These numbers have been amplified in the second decade of the twenty-first century by a new wave of migrant refugees seeking safety and stability in the wake of civil war in Syria and instability in Afghanistan and Iraq. In 2015 alone, more than one million people sought refuge in Europe, both by land and by sea, and several hundred thousand followed in the ensuing four years. Many were desperate and allowed themselves to be illegally transported by human traffickers, and more than fifteen thousand died in the process. And while a variety of European countries initially agreed to take in migrants (especially Germany but also France, Sweden, Italy, and Austria), their presence has triggered a xenophobic backlash in many countries among Europeans who worry that such a large influx of foreigners will negatively affect their national cultures. Indeed, controversy over taking in migrants is believed to have contributed to the calls for British withdrawal from the European Union in 2016, and fear of migrants has led to an upsurge in right-wing parties across Europe whose rhetoric is openly racist.

Across the Atlantic, in 2012 many tens of thousands of refugees left their home countries in El Salvador, Guatemala, and Honduras for the United States. Although migration from Central America and Mexico was not a new phenomenon (over ten million Mexican migrants have settled in the United States since 1960), the rate of migration increased in that year from Central America because of extremely dangerous internal conditions. Homicide rates were among the highest in the world, and ordinary people grew desperate enough to sacrifice everything for a chance of finding stability elsewhere. As in Europe, though, this surge in migration stimulated controversy in the United States, as many Americans began to call for closing the border between Mexico and the United States to prevent migration from the south. In fact, President Donald Trump ran his presidential campaign in 2016 on a promise to build a wall between Mexico and the United States to keep migrants out. Once he took office, his administration stepped up efforts to prevent immigrants seeking asylum from entering the United States and even began to separate parents from their children in detainee camps to discourage refugees from attempting to enter the country.

In general, migrants leave their home countries because they seek a better life in countries with a higher standard of living and stable legal and political systems. They want better jobs and more readily available health care, educational opportunities, and a safe place to raise their children. Thus most contemporary mass migrations involve movement from developing countries to developed ones. Given the disparities and inequities between developed and developing countries, it seems likely that migration will continue to be a major issue in the short and long terms.

Migrants from Libya on an overcrowded boat trying to reach Europe in 2017. These passengers were rescued by a Spanish NGO, but many thousands died trying to cross the Mediterranean from North Africa to Europe. Samuel Nacar/SOPA Images/LightRocket/Getty Images

After their arrival on foreign shores, migrants often establish cultural and ethnic communities that maintain their social customs and native languages. The sounds of foreign languages as well as the presence of ethnic foods, arts, and music have transformed large cities into multicultural environments. Although the arrival of migrants has enriched societies in many ways, as we have seen it has also sparked resentment and conflict. People in host countries often believe that foreigners and their ways of life undermine national identity, especially if defined by language, religion, and other cultural characteristics. Beyond that, many citizens of host societies view migrants, who are often willing to work for low wages and not join labor unions, as competitors for jobs. When unemployment rates climb, there is a tendency to look for scapegoats, and all too frequently the blame falls on migrants. In many countries, governments have come under pressure to restrict immigration or even expel foreign residents. Thus, while migrants are reshaping the world outside their home countries, international mass migration poses challenges both to the migrants themselves and to the host society.

Global Diseases

For thousands of years, disease has played a significant role in the development of human communities. Its impact has been as dramatic as it has been destructive. For example, the most devastating impact of the Columbian exchange (see chapter 22) came in the wake of diseases that Europeans introduced into the Americas following the voyages of Christopher Columbus and others. The introduction of diseases to populations that lacked any form of immunity killed perhaps as many as 90 percent of Native Americans in the span of 150 years. More recently, an influenza pandemic that swept the globe in

1918 and 1919 killed between twenty and forty million people, far more than died as the result of the Great War that had just ended. Since then, medical experts, public health officials, and scientists scored major victories in their fight against diseases, eradicating smallpox and diphtheria, for example. Buoyed by those successes, the United Nations in 1978 called for the elimination of all infectious diseases by the year 2000. That goal was unrealistic and, in the meantime, ancient diseases once thought under control, such as malaria, tuberculosis, and even measles, are on the rise again. Moreover, the late twentieth century demonstrated the deadly potential of new diseases.

HIV/AIDS One of the most serious new diseases to emerge in this period was acquired immunodeficiency syndrome (AIDS). This fatal disorder of the immune system is caused by the human immunodeficiency virus (HIV), which slowly attacks and destroys the immune system, leaving the infected individual vulnerable to diseases that eventually cause death. AIDS is the last stage of HIV infection, during which time these diseases arise. The HIV infection is spread through sexual contact with an infected person; contact with contaminated blood; and transmission from mother to child during pregnancy and, after birth, through breast feeding.

Medical experts identified AIDS for the first time in 1981 among homosexual men and intravenous drug users in New York and San Francisco. Subsequently, evidence for an epidemic appeared among heterosexual men, women, and children in sub-Saharan Africa, and rather quickly AIDS developed into a worldwide epidemic that affected virtually every nation. At the end of 2019, the number of people living with **HIV/AIDS** was 37.9 million, and more than 32 million AIDS deaths had occurred since the beginning of the epidemic. More encouraging, both new HIV infections and the

In February 2020, medical staff in Wuhan, China work in an isolated intensive care unit for the treatment of patients with Covid-19.

Feature China/Barcroft Media/Getty Images

number of AIDS death have been declining during the past decade, thanks to the availability of new drug treatments. But the epidemic continues to disproportionately affect sub-Saharan Africa, home to 1.1 million new HIV infections in 2017. Equally worrisome, new infections have been on the rise in eastern Europe, central Asia, southwest Asia, and north Africa.

Although no vaccine has yet emerged to prevent or cure HIV infection, some advances have been made. When scientists first identified AIDS, there was no treatment for the disease. Existing antiviral drugs at best delayed the inevitable and at worst failed completely. By 1995, though, researchers succeeded in developing a new class of drugs known as protease inhibitors and, in combination with some of the older drugs, they produced what is now known as **highly active antiretroviral therapy,** or **HAART.** In most cases, HAART can prolong life indefinitely. Antiretroviral therapy not only prevents AIDS-related illness and death but also has the potential to significantly reduce the risk of HIV transmission and the spread of tuberculosis. The high cost of these sophisticated drugs initially prevented poor people from sharing in their benefits, but this too is changing. By 2018, 62 percent of the world's people living with HIV were receiving antiretroviral therapy.

Present and Future Concerns In spite of significant successes in the battle against HIV infection, global disease remains an urgent concern in the twenty-first century. Globalization has allowed ever more rapid circulations of people from one side of the globe to the other, meaning that new or mutated viruses—especially those spread through the air—can travel around the world in the space of a few hours. This was the case with the outbreak of the severe acute respiratory syndrome (SARS) virus in 2003 and the Middle East respiratory syndrome (MERS) virus in 2012. In these cases, people who had been exposed to the virus traveled in cars, trains, and planes before they knew they were sick and thus transmitted the diseases to distant locations rapidly. Viruses such as these have the potential to infect many thousands of people on every continent and require intensive international cooperation if a global pandemic is to be halted.

The incredible speed with which viruses can travel in an era of globalization was clearly demonstrated at the end of 2019, when authorities in China reported that a mysterious form of pneumonia had infected a cluster of people in the city of Wuhan. By January 7, 2020 the illness was identified as a novel coronavirus, which later became known as Covid-19. Case numbers rose quickly in China, and in an attempt to halt the spread of the epidemic, the government took drastic steps to place the city of Wuhan (with 11 million people) under strict quarantine. A week later, the United States and other nations halted travel to and from China. But these efforts were too late. The speed at which people travel ensured that individuals infected with the extremely contagious virus had already traveled to North America, Southeast Asia, Europe, and other countries in Asia. By March 11, the World Health Organization declared Covid-19 a pandemic, meaning that it was an uncontrolled disease that affected the whole world. By the beginning of June 2020, the number of people infected with the virus had reached 6.6 million, and the number of deaths exceeded 391,000.

Covid-19 revealed the weaknesses of international cooperation in halting pandemics. The World Health Organization, which was designed to coordinate international response to situations just like this, has been accused of moving too slowly to communicate the level of threat posed by the virus. Even more important, many countries—including the United States—failed to heed warnings about the virus until it had already spread widely, and thus failed to prepare by ensuring adequate levels of medical supplies or tests. Some countries sought to shift the blame for the virus to China, thus calling attention away from their own mismanagement. The pandemic also brought social inequalities into sharp relief, as it became clear that the poor and the marginalized died in far greater numbers than the rich and healthy. The worldwide lack of preparedness for dealing with a pandemic like Covid-19 meant that the only way to decrease the infection and death rates was to lock down societies by closing stores, halting gatherings and travel, and requiring people to stay at home. Indeed, by March 31 nearly one-third of humanity was living under some kind of lockdown. While lockdowns have largely been successful at reducing new infections, their negative impact on both local and global economies has been enormous.

Amidst the tragedies of so many lost lives and the mismanagement of the crisis by authorities around the world, the pandemic has also given us reason to be hopeful. In spite of political squabbles at the highest levels, tens of thousands of scientists, researchers, and healthcare workers have raced at record speed to develop effective treatments and vaccines to eliminate the threat of Covid-19. These people hail from every country, and have engaged in information-sharing and partnerships that defy national borders. Let us hope that we might learn from their example, in the likely event that a global pandemic will strike again in the future.

What's Left Out?

Historians are comfortable writing about events that happened long ago, even though they understand they can never fully comprehend the vast complexities of the past. But they are often far less comfortable writing about events that occurred in their own living memory—and grow increasingly uncomfortable as they move closer to the present. There are good reasons for this discomfort. The task of writing history is much easier when historians have perspective, which in this case means knowing what happened *after* the period under discussion. Perspective can also mean having distance from the events under discussion so that writers of history are not personally invested in the outcomes of their stories. When writing about the very recent past, it is difficult for historians to maintain either kind of perspective. This is because they might have been active participants in some of the events they write about, or because they personally knew active participants, or simply because they remember hearing about and reacting to events as they were happening. It is also because the events of the immediate past happened so recently that not enough time has elapsed to say with any certainty what their long-term effects will be. In both scenarios, it is extremely difficult for historians to maintain perspective—and especially for them to remain personally uninvolved in the way the story of the past is told. Of course, the personality and point of view of historians are always present in the histories they write. But it is worth thinking about how much more this is true when the subject matter is the very recent past. For example, although we cover the Covid-19 pandemic in this chapter, we do not yet know how the pandemic will end and what its larger effects will be in the future. And given that we lived through the pandemic, our vision of what it was like will be deeply informed by our personal experiences and where we are from. Both of these problems diminish our ability to maintain perspective.

Source: David Lowenthal, *The Past Is a Foreign Country Revisited*, 2nd ed. (Cambridge: Cambridge University Press, 2015), chapter 8.

CONCLUSION

In 1989, ordinary Germans like Kristina Matschat toppled the Berlin wall—an event that signaled the impending collapse of the Soviet Union and the end of the Cold War. The end of the Cold War changed the global balance of power in favor of the United States, although its unilateral actions in the following decades led to deteriorating relations with a variety of states, especially Russia. The decades after the end of the Cold War were also characterized by increasing globalization, which accelerated economic, political, and cultural connections between the world's peoples. While these connections and encounters in many cases aided economic growth and allowed for rich cultural exchanges, they also brought a host of urgent issues into high relief, including climate change, continuing inequalities, terrorism, migration, and global disease. Each of these issues continues to affect the whole world (although sometimes in different ways), and each appears unlikely to be solved in the short term. One thing is clear, however: if any solutions are to be found, they will require that nations work in cooperation with one another. Given the extremely violent and destructive twentieth century, in which nations killed tens of millions of people to achieve their goals, such cooperation would truly signal a new era in the history of the world.

STUDY TERMS

al-Qaeda (867)

Association of Southeast Asian
    Nations (ASEAN) (854)

Aung San Suu Kyi (866)

Barack Obama (869)

Benazir Bhuto (866)

BRICs (852)
Bush Doctrine (850)
Chandrika Bandaranaike
Kumaratunga (866)
climate change (859)
European Union (854)
feminist movement (863)
free trade (850)
General Agreement on Tariffs
and Trade (GATT) (851)
glasnost (848)
global warming (859)
globalization (850)
Highly Active Antiretroviral
Therapy (HAART) (873)
HIV/AIDS (872)
Indira Gandhi (866)
Lech Walesa (847)
Leszek Kolakowski (846)
little tigers (851)
McDonaldization (855)

Mikhail S. Gorbachev (846)
mujahideen (848)
North American Free Trade
Agreement (NAFTA) (854)
Nicolae Ceaușescu (847)
Organization of Petroleum
Exporting Countries
(OPEC) (854)
Operation Iraqi Freedom (869)
Osama bin Laden (867)
perestroika (848)
Ronald Reagan (846)
Saddam Hussein (869)
Taliban (868)
terrorism (867)
Todor Zhivkov (847)
Universal Declaration of
Human Rights (858)
velvet revolution (847)
World Trade Organization
(WTO) (851)

FOR FURTHER READING

Jagdish Bhagwati. *In Defense of Globalization.* New York, 2007. A convincing rebuttal to popular fallacies about global economic integration.

Gregory C. Chow. *China's Economic Transformation.* Oxford, 2007. This stands as the most accepted reference for understanding the world's most dynamic economy.

Jussi Hanhimäki and Bernhard Blumenau. *An International History of Terrorism: Western and Non-Western Experiences.* London, 2013. Analyzes the history and uses of terrorism for the last one hundred fifty years years from a variety of perspectives.

Mark Harrison. *Contagion: How Commerce Has Spread Disease.* New Haven, 2013. A scholarly examination of the connections between trade and infectious diseases, and the measures taken to limit the spread of disease.

Jason Hickel. *The Divide: Global Inequality from Conquest to Free Markets.* New York, 2018. An anthropologist explores the complex historical reasons behind the vast global inequalities between developed and developing countries.

Edward Luce. *In Spite of the Gods: The Rise of Modern India.* New York, 2008. A keen assessment of an up-and-coming economic and geopolitical giant.

David Marples. *The Collapse of the Soviet Union, 1985-1991.* London, 2015. Revisionist look at the collapse of the Soviet Union that emphasizes the role of Soviet national republics and Boris Yeltsin instead of the arms race with the United States.

J. R. McNeill. *Something New under the Sun: An Environmental History of the Twentieth-Century World.* New York, 2000. A brilliant but dark tale of the past century's interaction between humans and the environment.

Anne Sisson Runyan and V. Spike Peterson. *Global Gender Issues in the New Millennium.* London, 2019. Looks at the ways ideologies of gender have been used to perpetuate inequalities between men and women on a global stage and also feminist resistance and action to counteract these uses.

Joseph Stiglitz, *Globalization and Its Discontents Revisited: Anti-Globalization in the Era of Trump.* New York, 2017. Updated and revised edition of the classic 2007 book that argued for the destructive impact of the International Monetary Fund (IMF), World Bank, and trade agreements on developing nations.

Glossary & Pronunciation Guide

AH *a* sound, as in *car, father*
IH short *i* sound, as in *fit, his, mirror*
OO long *o* sound, as in *ooze, tool, crew*
UH short *u* sound, as in *up, cut, color*
A short *a* sound, as in *asp, fat, parrot*
EE long *e* sound, as in *even, meet, money*
OH long *o* sound, as in *open, go, tone*
EH short *e* sound, as in *ten, elf, berry*
AY long *a* sound, as in *ape, date, play*
EYE long *i* sound, as in *ice, high, bite*
OW diphthong *o* sound, as in *cow, how, bow*
AW diphthong *a* sound, as in *awful, paw, law*

Note on emphasis: Syllables in capital letters receive the accent. If there is no syllable in capitals, then all syllables get equal accent.

Abbasid dynasty (ah-BAH-sihd) Cosmopolitan Arabic dynasty (750–1258) that replaced the Umayyads; founded by Abu al-Abbas and reached its peak under Harun al-Rashid.

Abdül Hamid II Reigned 1876–1909 C.E. Sultan of the Ottoman Empire whose despotic style of rule led to the creation of many opposition groups and to his deposition by dissidents in 1909.

Abolitionism Antislavery movement.

Absolutism Political philosophy that stressed the divine right theory of kingship: the French king Louis XIV was the classic example.

Abu Bakr (ah-BOO BAHK-uhr) First caliph after the death of Muhammad.

Achaemenid empire (ah-KEE-muh-nid) First great Persian empire (558–330 B.C.E.), which began under Cyrus and reached its peak under Darius.

Adam Smith 1723–1790. Scottish philosopher and founder of modern political economy, and a key figure in the Scottish Enlightenment. Best known for *An Inquiry into the Nature and Causes of the Wealth of Nations,* published in 1776.

Adolf Hitler 1889–1945 C.E. German politician and leader of the Nazi Party, who came to power in 1933. He initiated the European theater of World War II by invading Poland in 1939 and oversaw the establishment of death camps that resulted in more than ten million deaths.

Adwa 1896 Battle in which the Ethiopians badly defeated would-be Italian conquerors.

Aegean Sea Sea located between the mainlands of modern Greece and Turkey.

Aeschylus (ES-kuh-luhs) Greek tragedian, author of the *Oresteia.*

Afonso d'Alboquerque 1453–1515 C.E. Commander of the Portuguese forces in the Indian Ocean in the early sixteenth century. He was responsible for seizing Hormuz, Goa, and Malacca, which allowed the Portuguese to control Indian Ocean trade.

African National Congress South African political party formed in 1912 that provided consistent opposition to the apartheid state, and eventually became the majority party at the end of the apartheid era in 1994.

Age grades Bantu institution in which individuals of roughly the same age carried out communal tasks appropriate for that age.

Ahimsa (uh-HIM-suh) Jain term for the principle of nonviolence to other living things or their souls.

Ahura Mazda (uh-HOORE-uh MAHZ-duh) Main god of Zoroastrianism who represented truth and goodness and was perceived to be in an eternal struggle with the malign spirit Angra Mainyu.

Akbar 1542–1605 C.E. The third Mughal emperor who ruled from 1556–1605 and was known for his religious tolerance.

Al-Andalus (al-ANN-duh-luhs) Islamic Spain.

Albert Einstein 1879–1955 C.E. German-born physicist who developed the theory of relativity and whose ideas had profound influence on the development of science in the twentieth century.

Alexander of Macedon Also known as Alexander the Great, Macedonian conqueror who defeated the Achaemenid Persian Empire and created an enormous empire in the mid-fourth century B.C.E.

Alexandria An important city of the ancient world, founded by Alexander on the Mediterranean coast of Egypt during the fourth century B.C.E.

Ali'i nui Hawaiian class of high chiefs.

Allah (AH-lah) God of the monotheistic religion of Islam.

al-Qaeda Militant Islamist organization founded by Osama bin Laden in 1988, which was responsible for the September 11, 2001, attacks in the United States.

Amon-Re (AH-muhn RAY) Egyptian god, combination of the sun god Re and the air god Amon.

Analects A collection of the sayings and teachings of the fifth century B.C.E. Chinese philosopher Confucius, collected by his students.

Anastacio Somoza Garcia 1896–1956. Brutal leader of the U.S.-trained Guarda Nacional in Nicaragua who became president and dictator in 1934.

Ancien Régime Meaning "old order," and refers to the period prior to the French Revolution in 1789.

Angkor (AHN-kohr) Southeast Asian Khmer kingdom (889–1432) that was centered on the temple cities of Angkor Thom and Angkor Wat.

Anti-Semitism Term coined in the late nineteenth century that was associated with a prejudice against Jews and the political, social, and economic actions taken against them.

Antigonid empire The smallest of the three states that split from Alexander the Great's massive empire in 275 B.C.E. The Antigonid empire occupied Greece and Macedon.

Antonianism African syncretic religion, founded by Dona Beatriz, that taught that Jesus Christ was a black African man and that heaven was for Africans.

Antonio López de Santa Anna 1794–1896 C.E. Mexican army officer and politician best known for his efforts to prevent Spain from recapturing Mexico. Served as president of Mexico several times.

Ao One of the six Shang dynasty (1766–1122 B.C.E.) capitals near the modern city of Zheng-zhou.

Apartheid (ah-PAHR-teyed) South African system of "separateness" that was implemented in 1948 and that maintained the black majority in a position of political, social, and economic subordination.

Appeasement British and French policy in the 1930s that tried to maintain peace in Europe in the face of German aggression by making concessions.

Arianism Early Christian heresy that centered on teaching of Arius (250–336 C.E.) and contained the belief that Jesus was a mortal human being and not coeternal with God; Arianism was the focus of the Council of Nicaea.

Armenian Genocide Campaign of extermination undertaken by the Ottomans against two million Armenians living in Ottoman territory during World War I.

Artha Hindu concept for the pursuit of economic well-being and honest prosperity.

Arthashastra (AR-thah-sha-strah) Ancient Indian political treatise from the time of Chandragupta Maurya; its authorship was traditionally ascribed to Kautalya, and it stressed that war was inevitable.

Aryans (AIR-ee-anns) Indo-European migrants who settled in India after 1500 B.C.E.; their union with indigenous Dravidians formed the basis of Hinduism.

Asceticism (uh-SET-uh-siz-uhm) The practice of severe self-discipline and avoidance of all forms of indulgence, typically for religious reasons.

Ashoka (ah-SHOW-kuh) Powerful ruler of the South Asian Mauryan Dynasty, who reigned from 268–232 B.C.E.

Association of Southeast Asian Nations (ASEAN) Regional organization established in 1967 by Thailand, Malaysia, Singapore, Indonesia, and the Philippines; the organization was designed to promote economic progress and political stability; it later became a free-trade zone.

Assyrians (uh-SEAR-ee-uhns) Southwest Asian people who built an empire that reached its height during the eighth and seventh centuries B.C.E.; it was known for a powerful army and a well-structured state.

Astrolabe Navigational instrument for determining latitude.

Ataturk 1881–1938 C.E. Meaning "Father of the Turks," his real name was Mustafa Kemal. He was a Turkish army officer, reformer, and the first president of the modern Republic of Turkey after the Ottoman defeat in World War I.

Aten Monotheistic god of Egyptian pharaoh Akhenaten (r. 1353–1335 B.C.E.) and a very early example of monotheism.

Athens Important city-state of ancient Greece, located in the Attica region.

Attica The region surrounding the ancient city of Athens.

Attila the Hun Warrior king of the Huns, who ruled the confederation from 434–453.

Audiencias Spanish courts in Latin America.

Augusto César Sandino 1893–1934. Nationalist and liberal general of Nicaragua who fundamentally opposed U.S. intervention. He was murdered in 1934 by Anastacio Somoza Garcia's forces.

Augustus Grandnephew and protégé of Julius Caesar, who served as de facto ruler of the Roman state from 27 B.C.E. until his death in 14 C.E.

Aung San Suu Kyi 1945–. Burmese politician and author who received the 1991 Nobel Peace Prize for her opposition to Burmese military rule. Leads the National League for Democracy party.

Aurangzeb 1618–1707 C.E. The sixth Mughal emperor, who ruled for forty-nine years over almost all of the Indian subcontinent.

Auschwitz Camp established by the Nazi regime in occupied Poland, which functioned both as a concentration camp and an extermination camp. Approximately one million Jews were killed there.

Australopithecus (ah-strah-loh-PITH-uhkuhs) "Southern ape," oldest known ancestor of humans; it lived from around four million down to around one million years ago, and it could walk on hind legs, freeing up hands for use of simple tools.

Austronesians People who as early as 2000 B.C.E. began to explore and settle islands of the Pacific Ocean basin.

Avesta Book that contains the holy writings of Zoroastrianism.

Axum African kingdom centered in Ethiopia that became an early and lasting center of Coptic Christianity.

Aztec empire Central American empire constructed by the Mexica and expanded greatly during the fifteenth century during the reigns of Itzcoatl and Motecuzoma I.

Babur (BAH-ber) 1483–1530 C.E. Central Asian descendant of Chinggis Khan and Tamerlane who founded the Mughal dynasty in northern India in 1526.

Bakufu The military government of Japan from 1192 to 1868 C.E., headed by a shogun.

Balfour Declaration British declaration from 1917 that supported the creation of a Jewish homeland in Palestine.

Ban Zhao 45–115 C.E. Renowned female historian and scholar of the Han dynasty, and author of the Book of Han.

Bantu (BAN-too) African peoples who originally lived in the area of present-day Nigeria; around 2000 B.C.E. they began a centuries-long migration that took them to most of sub-Saharan Africa; the Bantu were very influential, especially linguistically.

Barack Obama 1961–. Forty-fourth president of the United States, who served from 2009 to 2017. Obama was the first U.S. president of African heritage.

Baron de Montesquieu 1689–1755 C.E. French political philosopher who advocated the separation of legislative, executive, and judicial government powers.

Battle of Gaugamela October 1, 331 B.C.E. The final meeting between Alexander of Macedon and King Darius III of Persia, in which Alexander was victorious.

Battle of Marathon A battle fought in 490 B.C.E. between Greek and Persian forces, from which the Greeks emerged victorious.

Bedouins (BEHD-oh-ihnz) Nomadic Arabic tribespeople.

Benazir Bhutto 1953–2007 C.E. Pakistani politician who served twice as Pakistani prime minister: in 1988–1990 and then again in 1993–1996. She was assassinated in 2007.

Benefice Grant from a lord to a vassal, usually consisting of land, which supported the vassal and signified the relationship between the two.

Benito Juárez (beh-NEE-toh HWAHR-ez) 1806–1872 C.E. Mexican lawyer of indigenous origins who served as president of Mexico on five occasions.

Benito Mussolini 1883–1945 C.E. Italian politician and journalist who led the National Fascist Party and ruled as prime minister from 1922 to 1943.

Berlin Conference Meeting organized by German chancellor Otto von Bismarck in 1884–1885 that provided the justification for European colonization of Africa.

Bezant Byzantine gold coin that served as the standard currency of the Mediterranean basin from the sixth through the twelfth century.

Bhagavad Gita (BUH-guh-vahd GEE-tuh) "Song of the Lord," an Indian short poetic work drawn from the lengthy *Mahabharata* that was finished around 400 C.E. and that expressed basic Hindu concepts such as karma and dharma.

Bhakti movement (BAHK-tee) Indian movement that attempted to transcend the differences between Hinduism and Islam.

Black Hand Pre–World War I secret Serbian society; one of its members, Gavrilo Princip, assassinated Austrian archduke Francis Ferdinand and provided the spark for the outbreak of the Great War.

Blitzkrieg German style of rapid attack through the use of armor and air power that was used in Poland, Norway, Denmark, Belgium, the Netherlands, and France in 1939–1940.

Bloodletting rituals Ritual involving the shedding of human blood as a form of sacrifice to the gods, practiced by the Maya and Aztecs amongst many other societies.

Bodh Gaya Town southwest of Pataliputra in which Gautama (Buddha) received enlightenment while sitting under a bo tree.

Bodhisattvas (BOH-dih-SAT-vuhs) Buddhist concept regarding individuals who had reached enlightenment but who stayed in this world to help people.

Bogomils Bulgarian group active in the tenth and eleventh centuries that believed in rejecting the material world and extreme ascetisicm.

Bolshevik (BOHL-shih-vehk) Russian communist party headed by Lenin.

Book of Songs The oldest existing collection of Chinese poetry, dating from the eleventh to the seventh centuries B.C.E.

Bourgeoisie Middle class in modern industrial society.

Brahman Central concept of classical Vedic religion, the name of the "universal soul" at the heart of the cosmos.

Brahmins (BRAH-minz) Hindu caste of priests.

Brezhnev doctrine Policy developed by Leonid Brezhnev (1906–1982) that claimed for the Soviet Union the right to invade any socialist country faced with internal or external enemies; the doctrine was best expressed in the Soviet invasion of Czechoslovakia.

BRICs Acronym for the fast-growing and developing economies of Brazil, Russia, India, and China.

Buddha (BOO-duh) The "enlightened one," the term applied to Siddhartha Gautama after his discoveries that would form the foundation of Buddhism.

Buddhism (BOO-diz'm) Religion, based on Four Noble Truths, associated with Siddhartha Gautama (563–483 B.C.E.), or the Buddha; its adherents desired to eliminate all distracting passion and reach nirvana.

Bunraku (boon-RAH-koo) Japanese puppet theater.

Bush doctrine A set of policies during the administration of American president George W. Bush (2001–2009) that advocated preemptive strikes by the United States against potential enemies instead of containment or deterrence.

Byzantine empire (BIHZ-ann-teen) Long-lasting empire centered at Constantinople; it grew out of the end of the Roman empire, carried the legacy of Roman greatness, and was the only classical society to survive into the early modern age; it reached its early peak during the reign of Justinian (483–565).

Caesaropapism Concept relating to the mixing of political and religious authority, as with the Roman emperors, that was central to the church-versus-state controversy in medieval Europe.

Cahokia (kuh-HOH-kee-uh) Large structure in modern Illinois that was constructed by the mound-building peoples; it was the third largest structure in the Americas before the arrival of the Europeans.

Caliph (KAL-ihf) "Deputy," Islamic leader after the death of Muhammad.

Cambyses (kam-BIE-sees) Son of Cyrus and second ruler of the Achaemenid Persian Empire, reigned 530–522 B.C.E.

Camillo di Cavour 1810–1861 C.E. Prime Minister to King Vittorio Emmanuel II of Piedmont and Sardinia, and key figure in bringing about the unification of Italy.

Capetian (cah-PEE-shuhn) Early French dynasty that started with Hugh Capet.

Capitalism An economic system with origins in early modern Europe in which private parties make their goods and services available on a free market.

Capitulation Highly unfavorable trading agreements that the Ottoman Turks signed with the Europeans in the nineteenth century that symbolized the decline of the Ottomans.

Captain James Cook 1728–1779 C.E. British explorer, navigator, and cartographer who served in the British Royal Navy. Famous for his expeditions to the Pacific Ocean in the eighteenth century.

Carolingians Germanic dynasty that was named after its most famous member, Charlemagne.

Carthage Northern African kingdom, main rival to early Roman expansion, that was defeated by Rome in the Punic Wars.

Caste A system of social distinction that emerged in South Asia late in the second millennium B.C.E., which divides the population into a series of "classes" or varnas.

Çatal Hüyük Important Neolithic settlement in Anatolia (7250–6150 B.C.E.).

Cathars Medieval heretics, also known as the Albigensians, who considered the material world evil; their followers renounced wealth and marriage and promoted an ascetic existence.

Catherine the Great 1729–1796 C.E. Catherine II was the longest-serving female ruler of Russia (from 1762 to 1796). She came to power by overthrowing her husband, Peter III, in a coup.

Catholic Reformation Sixteenth-century Catholic attempt to cure internal ills and confront Protestantism; it was inspired by the reforms of the Council of Trent and the actions of the Jesuits.

Caudillos (KAW-dee-ohs) Latin American term for nineteenth-century local military leaders.

Cave paintings Paintings made on the walls and ceilings of caves by early human artists.

Central Powers World War I term for the alliance of Germany, Austria-Hungary, and the Ottoman empire.

Chaghatai One of Chinggis Khan's sons, whose descendants ruled central Asia through the Chaghatai khanate.

Chan Buddhism (CHAHN BOO-diz'm) Influential branch of Buddhism in China, with an emphasis on intuition and sudden flashes of insight instead of textual study.

Chanchan (chahn-chahn) Capital of the pre-Incan, South American Chimu society that supported a large population of fifty thousand.

Chandragupta Maurya (chuhn-dra-GOOP-tah MORE-yuh) Founding ruler of the South Asian Mauryan Dynasty, who reigned from 321 to 297 B.C.E.

Chang'an (chahng-ahn) Capital city for various early Chinese dynasties, including the Qin, Han, and Tang.

Charlemagne Ruler of the European Carolingian Empire from 748–814 C.E.

Charles V Reigned 1519–1556. Emperor who inherited the Hapsburg family's Austrian territories as well as the Kingdom of Spain. When he became emperor in 1519, his empire stretched from Austria to Peru.

Chavín culture Mysterious but very popular South American religion (1000–300 B.C.E.).

Chichén Itzá (chee-CHEN eet-SAH) Major Mayan city located in the northern Yucatan Peninsula of modern Mexico.

Chimu Pre-Incan South American society that fell to the Incas in the fifteenth century.

Chinampas Agricultural gardens used by Mexica (Aztecs) in which fertile muck from lake bottoms was dredged and built up into small plots.

Chinggis Khan (CHIHN-gihs Kahn) 1162–1227 C.E. Founder and first Kahn (emperor) of the Mongol Empire, which became the largest contiguous land empire in the history of the world up to that time.

Chivalry European medieval code of conduct for knights based on loyalty and honor.

Chola kingdom Southern Indian Hindu kingdom (850–1267), a tightly centralized state that dominated sea trade.

Christopher Columbus 1451–1506 C.E. Italian explorer and navigator who made four transatlantic voyages to the islands off North America, which in turn opened the way for European colonization of the Americas.

Chu Autonomous state in the central Yangzi region of China during the Zhou dynasty (1122–256 B.C.E.).

Chucuito Pre-Incan South American society that rose in the twelfth century and fell to the Incas in the fifteenth century.

City-state Urban areas that controlled surrounding agricultural regions and that were often loosely connected in a broader political structure with other city-states.

Civil Code Civil law code promulgated by Napoleon Bonaparte in 1804.

Civil service examinations A battery of grueling tests given at the district, provincial, and metropolitan levels that determined entry into the Chinese civil service during the Ming and Qing dynasties.

Cixi 1835–1908 C.E. Former imperial concubine who established herself as effective ruler of the Qing dynasty in the fifty years prior to the end of Qing rule in 1908. She was hated by millions for her lavish spending, corruption, and resistance to reform.

Cohong Specially licensed Chinese firms that were under strict government regulation.

Collectivization of agriculture Process beginning in the late 1920s by which Stalin forced the Russian peasants off their own land and onto huge collective farms run by the state; millions died in the process.

Colossal human heads Large carved heads made of basalt, produced by the Olmec during the late-second and early-first millennia B.C.E.

COMECON The Council for Mutual Economic Assistance, which offered increased trade within the Soviet Union and eastern Europe; it was the Soviet alternative to the United States' Marshall Plan.

Comfort women Mainly Korean, Taiwanese, and Manchurian women who were forced into service by the Japanese army to serve as prostitutes to the Japanese troops during World War II.

Communalism A term, usually associated with India, that placed an emphasis on religious rather than national identity.

Communism Philosophy and movement that began in middle of the nineteenth century with the work of Karl Marx; it has the same general goals as socialism, but it includes the belief that violent revolution is necessary to destroy the bourgeois world and institute a new world run by and for the proletariat.

Confucianism (kuhn-FYOO-shuhn-iz'm) Philosophy, based on the teachings of the Chinese philosopher Kong Fuzi (551–479 B.C.E.), or Confucius, that emphasizes order, the role of the gentleman, obligation to society, and reciprocity.

Congress of Vienna Gathering of European diplomats in Vienna, Austria, from October 1814 to June 1815. The representatives of the "great powers" that defeated Napoleon—

Britain, Austria, Prussia, and Russia—dominated the proceedings, which aimed to restore the prerevolutionary political and social order.

Conquistadores (kohn-KEE-stah-dohrayz) Spanish adventurers such as Cortés and Pizarro who conquered Central and South America in the sixteenth century.

Constantine Roman emperor who reigned from 306 to 337 C.E. and who moved the capital of the empire from Rome to Constantinople.

Constantinople The purpose-built capital of the late-Roman and Byzantine empires from the fourth to the fifteenth centuries. The name translates as "city of Constantine," the Roman emperor who founded the city.

Constitutionalism Movement in England in the seventeenth century that placed power in Parliament's hands as part of a constitutional monarchy and that increasingly limited the power of the monarch; the movement was highlighted by the English Civil War and the Glorious Revolution.

Containment Concept associated with the United States and specifically with the Truman Doctrine during the cold war that revolved around the notion that the United States would contain the spread of communism.

Corporation A concept that reached mature form in the 1860s in England and France; it involved private business owned by thousands of individual and institutional investors who financed the business through the purchase of stocks.

Corpus iuris civilis (KOR-puhs yoor-uhs sih-VEE-lihs) *Body of the Civil Law,* the Byzantine emperor Justinian's attempt to codify all Roman law.

Council at Nicaea (nahy-SEE-uh) An assembly of leading theologians that convened in the city of Nicaea in 325 to determine the orthodox position of the Church on a range of contentious theological matters.

Council of Trent 1545–1563. Assembly of high Roman Catholic church officials which met over a period of years to institute reforms in order to increase morality and improve the preparation of priests.

Crimean War 1853–1856 C.E. War fought on the Crimean peninsula between Russia on one side and Great Britain, France, the Ottoman Empire, and Sardinia on the other.

Criollos (kree-OH-lohs) Creoles, people born in the Americas of Spanish or Portuguese ancestry.

Cross staff Device that sailors used to determine latitude by measuring the angle of the sun or the pole star above the horizon.

Crystal Palace Glass and iron structure that housed an exhibition in London in 1851 to display industrial products.

Ctesiphon (TES-uh-phon) Capital city of the Sasanian Empire from the mid-third to mid-seventh centuries C.E.

Cult of Dionysis Devotees of the god of wine in ancient Greece. By the fifth century B.C.E. the cult had gone from wild, emotional displays to reserved, thoughtful tributes.

Cuneiform Written language of the Sumerians, probably the first written script in the world.

Cyrus Founder and first ruler of the Persian Achaemenid Empire, who reigned from 548 to 530 B.C.E.

Daimyo (DEYEM-yoh) Powerful territorial lords in early modern Japan.

Dao Key element in Chinese philosophy that means the "way of nature" or the "way of the cosmos."

Daodejing (DOW-DAY-JIHNG) Book that is the fundamental work of Daoism.

Daoism (DOW-i'zm) Chinese philosophy with origins in the Zhou dynasty; it is associated with legendary philosopher Laozi, and it called for a policy of noncompetition.

Dar al-Islam The "house of Islam," a term for the Islamic world.

Darius Third ruler of the Achaemenid Persian Empire, who reigned 521–486 B.C.E.

Dasas Ancient Aryan Indian term for enemies or subject peoples.

Declaration of Independence Drafted by Thomas Jefferson in 1776; the document expressed the ideas of John Locke and the Enlightenment, represented the idealism of the American rebels, and influenced other revolutions.

Declaration of the Rights of Man and the Citizen Document from the French Revolution (1789) that was influenced by the American Declaration of Independence and in turn influenced other revolutionary movements.

Decolonization Process by which former colonies achieved their independence, as with the newly emerging African nations in the 1950s and 1960s.

Deer Park of Sarnath Park near the city of Benares where the Buddha publicly announced his doctrine in the year 528 B.C.E.

Deism (DEE-iz'm) An Enlightenment view that accepted the existence of a god but denied the supernatural aspects of Christianity; in deism, the universe was an orderly realm maintained by rational and natural laws.

Deng Xiaoping (duhng show-ping) 1904–1997 C.E. Chinese politician who led the People's Republic of China from 1978 to his retirement in 1992.

Descamisados "Shirtless ones," Argentine poor who supported Juan and Eva Perón.

Détente A reduction in cold war tension between the United States and the Soviet Union from 1969 to 1975.

Devshirme Ottoman requirement that the Christians in the Balkans provide young boys to be slaves of the sultan.

Dharma (DAHR-muh) Hindu concept of obedience to religious and moral laws and order; also, the basic doctrine of Buddhism.

Dhimmi (dihm-mee) Islamic concept of a protected people that was symbolic of Islamic toleration during the Mughal and Ottoman empires.

Dhow Indian, Persian, and Arab ships, one hundred to four hundred tons, that sailed and traded throughout the Indian Ocean basin.

Diaspora People who have settled far from their original homeland but who still share some measure of ethnic identity.

Diocletian (dah-yuh-KLEE-shuhn) Roman emperor who reigned from 284 to 305 C.E.

Dionysus Greek god of wine, also known as Bacchus; Greek plays were performed in his honor.

Domingo Faustino Sarmiento 1811–1888 C.E. Argentine intellectual, writer, and activist who became the seventh president of Argentina.

Dominicans An order of mendicants founded by St. Dominic (1170–1221 C.E.) whose purpose was to live in poverty and serve the religious needs of their communities.

Dona Beatriz 1684–1706 C.E. Kongo prophet and religious leader who founded her own Christian movement, Antonianism, which taught that Jesus was from the Kongo.

Dravidians A family of languages spoken in southern India and Sri Lanka, or the peoples who speak them. Some scholars believe Dravidians were the original inhabitants of India prior to Aryan settlement, though this is controversial.

Dreadnoughts A class of British battleships whose heavy armaments made all other battleships obsolete overnight.

Duma Russian parliament, established after the Revolution of 1905.

Dunhuang Oasis in modern western China that became a site of Buddhist missionary activity by the fourth century C.E.

Durham Report Report issued in 1839 by the British Earl of Durham and recent governor-general of Canada, which advocated significant self-government for a united Canada.

Dutch learning European knowledge that reached Tokugawa Japan.

East India Company British joint-stock company that grew to be a state within a state in India; it possessed its own armed forces.

Economic nationalism Economic policies pursued by many governments affected by the Great Depression in which the nation tries to become economically self-sufficient by imposing high tariffs on foreign goods. The policy served to exacerbate the damaging effects of the Depression around the world.

Eight-legged essay Eight-part essays that an aspiring Chinese civil servant had to compose, mainly based on a knowledge of Confucius and the Zhou classics.

Eleanor of Aquitaine 1122–1204 C.E. Aristocratic woman from the city of Poitiers, modern France, who supported poets and entertainers known as troubadours.

Eleusinian mysteries Cult in ancient Greece that encouraged initiates to observe high moral standards.

Emancipation Manifesto Manifesto proclaimed by the Russian Tsar Alexander II in 1861 that abolished the institution of serfdom and freed 23 million serfs.

Emiliano Zapata (eh-mee-LYAH-no zuh-PAH-tuh) 1879–1919 C.E. Mexican revolutionary and leader of the peasant revolution during the Mexican Revolution whose followers were called Zapatistas.

Emilio Aguinaldo (eh-MEE-lyoh AH-gee-NAHL-doh) 1869–1964 C.E. Filipino revolutionary who declared independence from Spain and then fought against the United States during its war of occupation.

Emporia Commercial establishments that specialize in products and services on a large scale, vital to the conduct of transregional trade.

Encomienda (ehn-KOH-mee-ehn-dah) System that gave the Spanish settlers *(encomenderos)* the right to compel the indigenous peoples of the Americas to work in the mines or fields.

Engenho Brazilian sugar mill; the term also came to symbolize the entire complex world relating to the production of sugar.

English Civil War 1642–1649. A series of armed conflicts between the English crown and the English Parliament over political and religious differences.

Enlightenment Eighteenth-century philosophical movement that began in France; its emphasis was on the preeminence of reason rather than faith or tradition; it spread concepts from the Scientific Revolution.

Epicureans (ehp-ih-kyoo-REE-uhns) Hellenistic philosophers who taught that pleasure—as in quiet satisfaction—was the greatest good.

Equal-field system Chinese system during the Tang dynasty in which the goal was to ensure an equitable distribution of land.

Essenes Jewish sect that looked for the arrival of a savior; they were similar in some of their core beliefs to the early Christians.

Etruscans (ih-TRUHS-kuhns) Northern Italian society that initially dominated the Romans; the Etruscans helped convey Greek concepts to the expanding Romans.

Eugenics A late nineteenth- and early twentieth-century movement that sought to improve the gene pool of the human race by encouraging those deemed fit to have more children, and by discouraging those deemed unfit from reproducing. The movement was deeply tied to racism, and was eventually adopted by the German Nazi regime to justify the extermination of "undesirable" populations.

Eunuchs (YOO-nihks) Castrated males, originally in charge of the harem, who grew to play major roles in government; eunuchs were common in China and other societies.

European Community (EC) Organization of European states established in 1957; it was originally called the European Economic Community and was renamed the EC in 1967; it promoted economic growth and integration as the basis for a politically united Europe.

European Union Established by the Maastricht Treaty in 1993, a supranational organization for even greater European economic and political integration.

Fascism Political ideology and mass movement that was prominent in many parts of Europe between 1919 and 1945; it sought to regenerate the social, political, and cultural life of societies, especially in contrast to liberal democracy and socialism; fascism began with Mussolini in Italy, and it reached its peak with Hitler in Germany.

Ferdinand Magellan (FUR-dih-nand muh-JEHL-uhn) 1480–1521 C.E. Portuguese explorer famous for organizing the first circumnavigation of the globe, by ship, from 1519 to 1522.

Five Pillars of Islam The foundation of Islam: (1) profession of faith, (2) prayer, (3) fasting during Ramadan, (4) almsgiving, and (5) pilgrimage, or hajj.

Five-year plans First implemented by Stalin in the Soviet Union in 1928; five-year plans were a staple of communist regimes in which every aspect of production was determined in advance for a five-year period; five-year plans were the opposite of the free market concept.

Foot binding A practice that involved the tight wrapping of young girls' feet with strips of cloth that prevented natural growth of the bones and resulted in tiny, malformed curved feet.

Four Noble Truths The foundation of Buddhist thought: (1) life is pain, (2) pain is caused by desire, (3) elimination of desire will bring an end to pain, (4) living a life based on the Noble Eightfold Path will eliminate desire.

Franciscans An order of mendicants founded by St. Francis (1182–1226 C.E.) whose purpose was to live in poverty and serve the religious needs of their communities.

Franciso Pizarro 1478–1541 C.E. Spanish conquistador whose military expeditions led to the fall of the Inca Empire.

Franklin Delano Roosevelt 1882–1945 C.E. American politician who served as the thirty-second president of the United States from 1933 until his death.

Franks Germanic peoples who founded a successful dynasty in France, which went on to rule a substantial European empire in the eighth and ninth centuries.

Frederick Barbarossa 1152–1190 C.E. Medieval emperor with lands in modern southern Germany who tried and failed to conquer Lombardy in modern Italy.

Friedrich Engels 1820–1895 C.E. German socialist philosopher who, with Karl Marx, founded modern communism and co-authored *The Communist Manifesto* (1848).

Front de Libération Nationale (FLN) The Algerian organization that fought a bloody guerrilla war for freedom against France.

Fu Hao Favorite consort of King Wu Ding of the Shang dynasty (thirteenth century B.C.E.), whose richly appointed tomb remained intact until the modern era.

Fukuzawa Yukichi 1835–1901. Prominent Japanese who traveled around Europe and North America after the Meiji Restoration to evaluate foreign administrative systems and constitutions.

Fulani (foo-LAH-nee) Sub-Saharan African people who, beginning in the seventeenth century, waged a series of wars designed to impose their own strict interpretation of Islam.

Funan Southeast Asian state that ruled the lower reaches of the Mekong River (including parts of modern Cambodia and Vietnam) between the first and sixth centuries C.E.

Galileo Galilei 1564–1642 C.E. Italian astronomer, engineer, and physicist from the town of Pisa, whose observations had a huge impact on the development of modern science.

Gamal Abdel Nasser 1918–1970 C.E. Second president of Egypt who led the overthrow of the monarchy in 1952 and served from 1954 until his death.

Gandhara Kingdom in modern Pakistan and Afghanistan established by the Persian emperor Darius in about 520 B.C.E.

Gathas (GATH-uhs) Zoroastrian hymns believed to be compositions by Zarathustra.

Gauchos (GOW-chohz) Argentine cowboys, highly romanticized figures.

Gaul Name of the region of modern France during the ancient Greek and Roman period.

General Agreement on Tariffs and Trade (GATT) Free-trade agreement first signed in 1947; by 1994 it had grown to 123 members and formed the World Trade Organization (WTO).

Ghana (GAH-nuh) Kingdom in west Africa during the fifth through the thirteenth century whose rulers eventually converted to Islam; its power and wealth was based on dominating trans-Saharan trade.

Ghazi (GAH-zee) Islamic religious warrior.

Ghaznavids Turkish tribe under Mahmud of Ghazni who moved into northern India in the eleventh century and began a period of greater Islamic influence in India.

Gilgamesh Legendary king of the Mesopotamian city-state of Uruk (ca. 3000 B.C.E.), subject of the *Epic of Gilgamesh,* world's oldest complete epic literary masterpiece.

Glasnost (GLAHS-nohst) Russian term meaning "openness" introduced by Mikhail Gorbachev in 1985 to describe the process of opening Soviet society to dissidents and public criticism.

Global warming The emission of greenhouse gases, which prevents solar heat from escaping the earth's atmosphere and leads to the gradual heating of the earth's environment.

Globalization The breaking down of traditional boundaries in the face of increasingly global financial and cultural trends.

Glorious Revolution 1688–1689. The events that led to the replacement of the Catholic English King James II by his Protestant daughter Mary II and her Dutch husband William of Orange.

Golden Horde Mongol tribe that controlled Russia from the thirteenth to the fifteenth century.

Gracchi Brothers Tiberius and Gaius, brothers in the Roman Republic who worked to limit the amount of land individuals could hold in order to alleviate social conflict during the second century B.C.E.

Grand Canal A huge network of canals that linked the Yangzi and Huang He river systems, and that eventually extended 2000 kilometers (1200 miles).

Great Game Nineteenth-century competition between Great Britain and Russia for the control of central Asia.

Great Zimbabwe Large sub-Saharan African kingdom in the fifteenth century.

Greater East Asia Co-Prosperity Sphere Japanese plan for consolidating east and southeast Asia under their control during World War II.

Greek fire Devastating incendiary weapon used mainly at sea by Byzantine forces in the seventh and eighth centuries C.E.

Greenpeace An environmental organization founded in 1970 and dedicated to the preservation of earth's natural resources.

Griots Professional singers, historians, and story-tellers in sub-Saharan Africa.

Guomindang (GWOH-mihn-dahng) Chinese nationalist party founded by Sun Yatsen (1866–1925) and later led by Jiang Jieshi; it has been centered in Taiwan since the end of the Chinese civil war.

Gupta (GOOP-tah) Indian dynasty (320–550 C.E.) that briefly reunited India after the collapse of the earlier Mauryan dynasty.

Guru Kabir 1440–1518 C.E. A blind weaver who became the most important teacher in the bhakti movement, which sought to harmonize Hinduism and Islam.

Hacienda (HAH-see-ehn-dah) Large Latin American estates.

Hadith A collection of sayings of the Prophet Muhammad and accounts of his deeds.

Hagia Sophia (HAH-yah SOH-fee-uh) Massive Christian church constructed by the Byzantine emperor Justinian and later converted into a mosque.

Hajj (HAHJ) Pilgrimage to Mecca.

Hammurabi's Code (hahm-uh-RAH-beez) Sophisticated law code associated with the Babylonian king Hammurabi (r. 1792–1750 B.C.E.).

Han Feizi (hahn fay-zi) Third-century B.C.E. scholar credited as one of the founders of the ideology of Legalism.

Han Wudi One of the most important emperors of the Early Han Dynasty, who reigned from 141 to 87 B.C.E.

Hangzhou Capital of the Southern Song dynasty in the late thirteenth century.

Hannibal Barca Carthaginian general who devastated the Italian peninsula during the Second Punic War, 218–201 B.C.E.

Hanseatic League (han-see-AT-ik) A commercial confederation of merchant guilds and market towns in northwestern Europe that dominated Baltic trade from the thirteenth to the fifteenth centuries.

Harappan (hah-RAP-puhn) Early brilliant Indian society centered in Harappa and Mohenjo-daro.

Harijans "Children of God," Gandhi's term for the Untouchables.

Harsha Ruler of northern India from 606 to 648 C.E.

Harun al-Rashid Powerful ruler of the Abbasid Caliphate who reigned from 789 to 809 C.E.

Hebrews Semitic-speaking nomadic tribe influential for monotheistic belief in Yahweh.

Heian (HAY-ahn) Japanese period (794–1185), a brilliant cultural era notable for the world's first novel, Murasaki Shikibu's *The Tale of Genji.*

Hellenistic Era Phase in Greek history (328–146 B.C.E.), from the conquest of Greece by Philip of Macedon until Greece's fall to the Romans; this era was a more cosmopolitan age facilitated by the conquests of Alexander the Great.

Helots Servants to the Spartan state, who were neither chattel slaves nor free.

Hernán Cortés 1485–1587 C.E. Spanish conquistador whose military expeditions led to the fall of the Aztec Empire.

Hieratic Simplified writing script that was used for day-to-day administration in Egypt.

Hieroglyphics (heye-ruh-GLIPH-iks) Ancient Egyptian written language.

Hijra Muhammad's migration from Mecca to Medina in 622, which is the beginning point of the Islamic calendar and is considered to mark the beginning of the Islamic faith.

Hinayana (HEE-nah-yah-nuh) Branch of Buddhism known as the "lesser vehicle," also known as Theravada Buddhism; its beliefs include strict, individual path to enlightenment, and it is popular in south and southeast Asia.

Hinduism Main religion of India, a combination of Dravidian and Aryan concepts; Hinduism's goal is to reach spiritual purity and union with the great world spirit; its important concepts include dharma, karma, and samsara.

Hiroshima bombing Bombing of the Japanese city on August 6, 1945 by an American bomber, which—along with the bombing of Nagasaki on August 9—led the Japanese to surrender and end World War II.

Hittites Indo-European-speaking peoples who constructed a powerful empire in Anatolia and Mesopotamia in the mid-second millennium B.C.E.

Ho Chi Minh 1890–1969 C.E. North Vietnamese revolutionary and politician who first fought the French and then the Americans, and then became the first prime minister of North Vietnam in 1945.

Holocaust German attempt in World War II to exterminate the Jews of Europe.

Home front Term made popular in World War I and World War II for the civilian "front" that was symbolic of the greater demands of total war.

Homer Supposed author of the ancient Greek epic poems the *Iliad* and the *Odyssey.*

Hominid (HAWM-ih-nihd) A creature belonging to the family Hominidae, which includes human and humanlike species.

Homo erectus (HOH-MOH ee-REHK-tuhs) "Upright-walking human," which existed from two million to two hundred thousand years ago; *Homo erectus* used cleavers and hand axes and learned how to control fire.

Homo sapiens (HOH-MOH SAY-pee-uhns) "Consciously thinking human," which first appeared around two hundred fifty thousand years ago and used sophisticated tools.

Hongwu 1328–1398 C.E. Personal name Zhu Yuanzhang, was the founding emperor of the Ming dynasty in China. Reigned 1368–1398.

Huitzilopochtli (wee-tsee-loh-pockt-lee) Sun god and patron deity of the Aztecs.

Hundred Days of Reform Chinese reforms of 1898 led by Kang Youwei and Liang Qichao in their desire to turn China into a modern industrial power.

Hundred Years' War 1337–1453 C.E. Series of intermittent wars between France and England over the control of modern France.

Huns A militarized confederation of Central Asian nomads whose westward migration helped precipitate the collapse of the Western Roman Empire.

Hyksos (HICK-sohs) Invaders who seized the Nile delta and helped bring an end to the Egyptian Middle Kingdom.

Ibn Battuta (ih-bun BAH-too-tah) Born 1304 in Morocco. Was the greatest Muslim traveler of his time. He covered 75,000 miles and visited almost every Muslim country and China.

Ibn Rushd (IB-uhn RUSHED) Known as Averroes in the West, he was an important Islamic philosopher whose intellectual contributions were also appreciated by many European scholars. He lived from 1126 to 1198 C.E.

Iconoclasts (eye-KAHN-oh-klasts) Supporters of the movement, begun by the Byzantine Emperor Leo III (r. 717–741), to destroy religious icons because their veneration was considered sinful.

Ilkhanate (EEL-kahn-ate) Mongol state that ruled Persia after abolition of the Abbasid empire in the thirteenth century.

Imperialism Term associated with the expansion of European powers and their conquest and colonization of African and Asian societies, mainly from the sixteenth through the nineteenth century.

Inca empire Powerful South American empire that would reach its peak in the fifteenth century during the reigns of Pachacuti Inca and Topa Inca.

Indentured labor Labor source for plantations; wealthy planters would pay the laboring poor to sell a portion of their working lives, usually seven years, in exchange for passage.

India Act 1935 British Act that transferred to India the institutions of a self-governing state.

Indian Partition Period immediately following Indian and Pakistani independence in 1947, in which millions of Muslims sought to move to Pakistan from India, and millions of Hindus sought to move from Pakistan to India. It was marked by brutal sectarian violence, and the deaths of between one half million and a million people.

Indian Rebellion of 1857 Ultimately unsuccessful rebellion in North and Central India by a large portion of the Bengal Army and the civil population against British rule.

Indira Gandhi 1917–1984 C.E. Indian politician and daughter of Jawaharlal Nehru who became the first Indian female prime minister in 1966.

Indo-Aryans Indo-European-speaking peoples who migrated from Central Asia into the Indus Valley and India subcontinent during the second millennium B.C.E.

Indo-Europeans Tribal groups from southern Russia who, over a period of millennia, embarked on a series of migrations from India through western Europe; their greatest legacy was the broad distribution of Indo-European languages throughout Eurasia.

Indra Early Indian god associated with the Aryans; Indra was the king of the gods and was associated with warfare and thunderbolts.

Intifada Palestinian mass movement against Israeli rule in the Gaza Strip and other occupied territories.

Investiture (ihn-VEHST-tih-tyoor) One aspect of the medieval European church-versus-state controversy, the granting of church offices by a lay leader.

Iron metallurgy The adoption and use of iron for weapons and tools.

Iroquois (EAR-uh-kwoi) Eastern American Indian confederation made up of the Mohawk, Oneida, Onondaga, Cayuga, and Seneca tribes.

Isaac Newton 1643–1727 C.E. English mathematician, physicist, and astronomer who played a key role in the Scientific Revolution.

Isfahan Capital city of the Safavid Empire (modern Iran), founded by Shah Abbas in the early seventeenth century.

Islam Monotheistic religion announced by the prophet Muhammad (570–632); influenced by Judaism and Christianity, Muhammad was considered the final prophet because the earlier religions had not seen the entire picture; the Quran is the holy book of Islam.

Ismail. Reigned 1501–1524. Founder of the Safavid dynasty in modern Iran.

Israelites A branch of the Hebrews who settled in Palestine (modern-day Israel) after 1200 B.C.E.

Jainism (JEYEN-iz'm) Indian religion associated with the teacher Vardhamana Mahavira (ca. 540–468 B.C.E.) in which every physical object possessed a soul; Jains believe in complete nonviolence to all living beings.

Janissaries Highly respected, elite infantry units of the Ottoman Empire, who formed the first modern standing army in Europe.

Jati Indian word for a Hindu subcaste.

Java An island in modern Indonesia, and formerly home to the capital of the Dutch East Indies at the city of Batavia (modern Jakarta), founded 1619.

Jawaharlal Nehru 1889–1964 C.E. Indian activist and politician who fought for decades for Indian independence and became the first prime minister of India.

Jenne-jeno Settlement in the middle Niger River region in Africa that flourished from the fourth to the eighth centuries C.E. Known for iron production.

Jesus of Nazareth A charismatic Jewish teacher who lived from 4 B.C.E. to the early 30s C.E, recognized as the founder of the religion of Christianity.

Jews A member of the people and cultural community whose traditional religion is Judaism and who trace their origins through the ancient Hebrew people of Israel to Abraham.

Jiang Jieshi (jyahng jeh-she) 1887–1975 C.E. Also known as Chiang Kai-Shek. Chinese nationalist revolutionary, military leader, and politician who led the Republic of China from 1928 to 1975, first in mainland China and then in Taiwan after the communist party won the civil war between them in 1949.

Jihad An Arabic term that literally translates as "struggle," and which has various meanings to Muslims, each of which refer to the imperative to spread Islam throughout the world.

Jizya (JIHZ-yuh) Tax in Islamic empires that was imposed on non-Muslims.

John of Montecorvino 1247–1328 C.E. Franciscan missionary who traveled to China in 1291 in order to win converts to Christianity.

Joint-stock companies Early forerunner of the modern corporation; individuals who invested in a trading or exploring venture could make huge profits while limiting their risk.

Jomo Kenyatta 1891–1978 C.E. Kenyan independence leader and politician who governed Kenya from its independence in 1963 until his death.

Joseph Stalin 1878–1953 C.E. Soviet revolutionary who led the Soviet Union from the mid-1920s to his death, whose policies resulted in the deaths of twenty million people.

Julius Caesar Major late-Republican Roman ruler who served as consul and later as dictator of the Roman state, assassinated in 44 B.C.E.

Junks Ships used by merchants and others in the seas off China and Southeast Asia to carry commercial cargo.

Justinian Important early emperor of the Byzantine Empire, who reigned from 527 to 565 C.E.

Ka'ba (KAH-buh) Main shrine in Mecca, goal of Muslims embarking on the hajj.

Kabuki (kah-BOO-kee) Japanese theater in which actors were free to improvise and embellish the words.

Kama Hindu concept of the enjoyment of physical and sexual pleasure.

Kamikaze (KAH-mih-kah-zee) A Japanese term meaning "divine wind" that is related to the storms that destroyed Mongol invasion fleets; the term is symbolic of Japanese isolation and was later taken by suicide pilots in World War II.

Kangxi (kahng-shee) 1654–1722 C.E. Fourth emperor of China's Qing dynasty, whose sixty-one-year rule was the longest in Chinese history.

Kanun (KAH-noon) Laws issued by the Ottoman Süleyman the Magnificent, also known as Süleyman Kanuni, "the Lawgiver."

Kapu Hawaiian concept of something being taboo.

Karl Marx 1818–1883 C.E. German philosopher and socialist revolutionary who founded, with Friedrich Engels, the modern communist movement and co-authored *The Communist Manifesto* (1848).

Karma (KAHR-mah) Hindu concept that the sum of good and bad in a person's life will determine his or her status in the next life.

Khoikhoi South African people referred to pejoratively as the Hottentots by Europeans.

Khubilai Khan (KOO-bih-lie Kahn) 1215–1294 C.E. Grandson of Chinggis Khan and founder of the Yuan dynasty in China in 1271.

Khwarazm Shah Ruler of Afghanistan and Persia in 1218, when Chinggis Khan sought to trade with his realm. After Khwarazm shah murdered Chingiss Khan's envoys, Chinggiss' forces devastated Persia in 1219.

King Kashta Circa 750 B.C.E. Kushite king who Egyptianized Nubia and conquered Upper Egypt.

King Nzinga Mbemba (Afonso I) (N-zinga MEHM-bah) 1456–1543 C.E. Ruler of Kongo in the first half of the sixteenth century, who became the first vassal king to Portugal.

Knossos City on the island of Crete that flourished during the Minoan period during the third millennium B.C.E.

Kong Fuzi 551-479 C.E. Original name of Confucius, Chinese philosopher and teacher of ethics.

Kongo Central African state that began trading with the Portuguese around 1500; although their kings, such as King Affonso I (r. 1506-1543), converted to Christianity, they nevertheless suffered from the slave trade.

Koumbi-Saleh Important trading city along the trans-Saharan trade route from the eleventh to the thirteenth century.

Krishna One of the incarnations of the Hindu god Vishnu, who appears in the Bhagavad-Gita as the teacher of Arjuna.

Kshatriyas (KSHAHT-ree-uhs) Hindu caste of warriors and aristocrats.

Kulaks Land-owning Russian peasants who benefited under Lenin's New Economic Policy and suffered under Stalin's forced collectivization.

Kumiss An alcoholic drink of the nomadic groups of Central Asia made of fermented mare's milk.

Kush Nubian African kingdom that conquered and controlled Egypt from 750 to 664 B.C.E.

Kushan empire Major Eurasian empire that controlled much of Central Asia and modern Pakistan and India during the first three centuries of the Common Era.

Kwame Nkruhmah (KWAH-mee en-KROO-mah) 1909-1972 C.E. Ghanaian politician and revolutionary who led the Gold Coast to independence in 1957 and served as the new country of Ghana's first prime minister.

La Reforma Political reform movement of Mexican president Benito Juárez (1806-1872) that called for limiting the power of the military and the Catholic church in Mexican society.

Lamaist Buddhism (LAH-muh-ihst BOOdiz'm) Branch of Buddhism that was similar to shamanism in its acceptance of magic and supernatural powers.

Laozi Semi-legendary sixth-century B.C.E. Chinese philosopher traditionally recognized as the founder of the ideology of Daoism.

Lapita Earliest known Austronesian migrants to sail out into the Pacific Ocean and establish settlements on Pacific Islands.

Latifundia (LAT-ih-FOON-dee-uh) Huge state-run and slave-worked farms in ancient Rome.

Lawbook of Manu Circa 500 B.C.E. Book of verses in the Hindu canon that spells out the norms of religious, domestic, and social life in ancient India.

Lázaro Cárdenas 1895-1970. President of Mexico who nationalized the oil industry in 1938.

League of Nations Forerunner of the United Nations, the dream of American president Woodrow Wilson, although its potential was severely limited by the refusal of the United States to join.

Lebensraum (LAY-behnz-rowm) German term meaning "living space"; the term is associated with Hitler and his goal of carving out territory in the east for an expanding Germany.

Lech Walesa (LEHK WAH-lehn-sah) Leader of the Polish Solidarity movement.

Legalism Chinese philosophy from the Zhou dynasty that called for harsh suppression of the common people.

Leonardo da Vinci 1452-1519 C.E. Noted Italian painter, sculptor, architect, and engineer of the Renaissance period.

Levée en masse (leh-VAY on MASS) A term signifying universal conscription during the radical phase of the French revolution.

Lex talionis (lehks tah-lee-oh-nihs) "Law of retaliation," laws in which offenders suffered punishments similar to their crimes; the most famous example is Hammurabi's Laws.

Li (LEE) Confucian concept, a sense of propriety.

Li Bai 701-761 C.E. One of the most popular poets of the Tang era, famous for his commentary on Chinese social life.

Lili'uokalani 1838-1917 C.E. The first and only queen of Hawaii, and the last Hawaiian sovereign to rule the islands prior to Hawai'i's annexation by the United States in 1898.

Lin Zexu 1785-1850 C.E. Chinese scholar and official appointed by the Qing government to destroy the illegal opium trade conducted by the British and other European and American traders.

Linear A Minoan written script.

Linear B Early Mycenaean written script, adapted from the Minoan Linear A.

Little Ice Age Period beginning in about 1300 C.E. when global temperatures declined for about 500 years.

Louis Riel 1844-1885 C.E. Leader of metis and indigenous people who organized the unsuccessful Northwest Rebellion against Canadian settlement in 1885. Riel was executed by Canadian authorities.

Louis the Pious 814-840 C.E. Only surviving son of Charlemagne, who held his father's empire together until his sons split it up after his death in 843.

Louis XIV (LOO-ee) 1638-1715 C.E. Also known as the Sun King, his seventy-two-year reign was the longest of any monarch in European history.

Louis XVI 1754-1793 C.E. The last king of France before the end of the French monarchy during the French Revolution, who was executed by guillotine.

Luddites Early-nineteenth-century artisans who were opposed to new machinery and industrialization.

Machismo (mah-CHEEZ-moh) Latin American social ethic that honored male strength, courage, aggressiveness, assertiveness, and cunning.

Madrasas (MAH-drahs-uhs) Islamic institutions of higher education that originated in the tenth century.

Magi Member of a priestly caste in ancient Persia.

Magyars (MAH-jahrs) Hungarian invaders who raided towns in Germany, Italy, and France in the ninth and tenth centuries.

Mahabharata (mah-hah-BAH-rah-tah) Massive ancient Indian epic that was developed orally for centuries; it tells of an epic civil war between two family branches.

Mahayana (mah-huh-YAH-nah) The "greater vehicle," a more metaphysical and more popular northern branch of Buddhism.

Maize A plant whose domestication was crucial to the emergence of complex states in early Mesoamerica.

Majapahit (MAH-ja-PAHT) Southeast Asian kingdom (1293-1520) centered on the island of Java.

Mali (MAH-lee) West African kingdom founded in the thirteenth century by Sundiata; it reached its peak during the reign of Mansa Musa.

Malintzin 1500-1529 C.E. Nahua woman who acted as interpreter and advisor for Hernan Cortes.

Manchus Manchurians who conquered China, putting an end to the Ming dynasty and founding the Qing dynasty (1644-1911).

Mandarin A Chinese bureaucrat-scholar who worked for the government in Imperial China.

Mandate of heaven Chinese belief that the emperors ruled through the mandate, or approval, of heaven contingent on their ability to look after the welfare of the population.

Mandate system System that developed in the wake of World War I when the former colonies ended up mandates under European control, a thinly veiled attempt at continuing imperialism.

Manichaeism (man-ih-KEE-iz'm) Religion founded by the prophet Mani in the third century C.E., a syncretic version of Zoroastrian, Christian, and Buddhist elements.

Manila City in modern Phillipines, and formerly capital of the Spanish colony of the Philippines, founded in 1565.

Manor Large estates of the nobles during the European middle ages, home for the majority of the peasants.

Mansa Musa (MAHN-suh MOO-suh) Reigned 1312-1337 C.E. Ruler of the wealthy and powerful Mali Empire in West Africa.

Mao Zedong 1893-1976 C.E. Chinese communist revolutionary who ruled China as the chairman of the Communist Party from 1949, when the communists defeated the nationalist Guomindang Party and forced its leaders to flee to Taiwan, until his death.

Maori (mow-ree) Indigenous people of New Zealand.

Marae Polynesian temple structure.

Marathon Battlefield scene of the Athenian victory over the Persians in 490 B.C.E.

Marco Polo 1254–1324 C.E. Italian merchant whose account of his travels to China and other lands became legendary.

Maroons Runaway African slaves.

Marshall Plan U.S. plan, officially called the European Recovery Program, that offered financial and other economic aid to all European states that had suffered from World War II, including Soviet bloc states.

Martin Luther 1483–1546. German monk and Catholic priest who became a critical figure in what became known as the Protestant Reformation after challenging the corruption of the church in his *Ninety-Five Theses,* published 1517.

Mary Wollstonecraft 1759–1797. English writer, philosopher, and advocate of women's rights, who wrote *A Vindication of the Rights of Woman* in 1792.

Matteo Ricci (maht-TAY-oh REE-chee) 1552–1610 C.E. Italian Jesuit who was one of the founders of the Jesuit China missions.

Mauryan empire Indian dynasty (321–185 B.C.E.) founded by Chandragupta Maurya and reaching its peak under Ashoka.

May Fourth Movement Chinese movement that began 4 May 1919 with a desire to eliminate imperialist influences and promote national unity.

Maya ball game Game in which Maya peoples used a hard rubber ball to propel through a ring without using their hands. Often used for ritual and ceremonial purposes.

Maya (Mye-uh) Brilliant Central American society (300–1100) known for math, astronomy, and a sophisticated written language.

Mecca Important city in modern Saudi Arabia, in which the hajj is conducted annually.

Medes (meeds) Indo-European branch that settled in northern Persia and eventually fell to another branch, the Persians, in the sixth century B.C.E.

Medina A city 345 kilometers (214 miles) north of Mecca, to which the Prophet Muhammad and his followers migrated in 622 C.E. Medina means "the city," as in "the city of the prophet."

Meiji Restoration (MAY-jee) Restoration of imperial rule under Emperor Meiji in 1868 by a coalition led by Fukuzawa Yukichi and Ito Hirobumi; the restoration enacted western reforms to strengthen Japan.

Melaka (may-LAH-kah) Southeast Asian kingdom that was predominantly Islamic.

Mencius (MEN-shi-us) Late-fourth/early-third century BCE Chinese philosopher recognized as one the most important followers of Confucius.

Menes (mee-neez) Egyptian conqueror who, according to tradition, unified Upper and Lower Egypt c. 3100 B.C.E. (sometimes identified with Narmer).

Mesoamerica (mez-oh-uh-MER-i-kuh) Another term for Central America.

Mesopotamia Term meaning "between the rivers," in this case the Tigris and Euphrates; Sumer and Akkad are two of the earliest societies.

Mestizo (mehs-TEE-zoh) Latin American term for children of Spanish and native parentage.

Métis (may-TEE) Canadian term for individuals of mixed European and indigenous ancestry.

Mexica (MEHK-si-kah) Nahuatl-speaking people from the Valley of Mexico who were the rulers of the Aztec Empire.

Michaelangelo Buonarotti 1475–1564 C.E. An Italian painter, sculptor, and architect of the Renaissance whose worked shaped the development of western art.

Mikhail S. Gorbachev 1931–. Soviet politician who served as the last leader of the Soviet Union from 1985 until 1991, when the Soviet Union dissolved.

Millet An autonomous, self-governing community in the Ottoman empire.

Ming Chinese dynasty (1368–1644) founded by Hongwu and known for its cultural brilliance.

Minoan (mih-NOH-uhn) Society located on the island of Crete (ca. 2000–1100 B.C.E.) that influenced the early Mycenaeans.

Missi dominici (mihs-see doh-mee-neechee) "Envoys of the lord ruler," the noble and church emissaries sent out by Charlemagne.

Missionaries People who travel on religious missions to help spread their faith.

Mithradates I (mihth-rah-DAY-teez) Powerful ruler of the Parthian Empire, who reigned from 171 to 132 B.C.E.

Mithraism (MITH-rah-iz'm) Mystery religion based on worship of the sun god Mithras; it became popular among the Romans because of its promise of salvation.

Moche (moh-CHEE) Pre-Incan South American society (300–700) known for their brilliant ceramics.

Modu 210–174 B.C.E. Highly successful leader of the Xiongnu peoples of the Central Asian steppes.

Mohandas Karamchand Gandhi 1869–1948 C.E. Indian nationalist, politician, and lawyer who led the campaign against British rule by employing methods of nonviolent confrontation.

Mohenjo-daro Set of ancient cities in modern southeast Pakistan, near the Indus River, that flourished in the third millennium B.C.E.

Moksha Hindu concept of the salvation of the soul.

Monotheism (MAW-noh-thee-iz'm) Belief in only one god, a rare concept in the ancient world.

Monroe Doctrine American doctrine issued in 1823 during the presidency of James Monroe that warned Europeans to keep their hands off Latin America and that expressed growing American imperialistic views regarding Latin America.

Monsoon system Seasonal winds that blow across the Indian subcontinent and Indian Ocean Basin that facilitated maritime trade during the early Silk Roads eras.

Motecuzoma I (mo-tek-oo-ZO-mah) c. 1397–1468. Fifth Aztec ruler whose conquests significantly extended Aztec rule beyond the Valley of Mexico.

Motecuzoma II (mo-tek-oo-ZO-mah) 1466–1520 C.E. Aztec emperor at the time of Hernan Cortes' invasion.

Mughals (MOO-guhls) Islamic dynasty that ruled India from the sixteenth through the eighteenth century; the construction of the Taj Mahal is representative of their splendor; with the exception of the enlightened reign of Akbar, the increasing conflict between Hindus and Muslims was another of their legacies.

Muhammad Ali Jinnah (moo-HAHM-ahd ah-lee JIN-uh) 1876–1948 C.E. Politician and independence fighter who led the All-India Muslim League from 1913 until the founding of Pakistan in 1947 and then served as the first leader of independent Pakistan until his death.

Muhammad Ali Reigned 1805–1848. Egyptian general who built a powerful army on the European model and became the effective ruler of Egypt in spite of its official status as an Ottoman territory.

Muhammad (muh-HAH-mehd) Prophet of Islam (570–632).

Mujahideen Meaning "Islamic warriors," a group who fought against Soviet intervention in Afghanistan in 1979. They were supplied and trained by United States CIA operatives, which helped lead to a Soviet withdrawal in 1989.

Munich Conference 1938 meeting between Germany, Great Britain, Italy, and France in which attendees agreed to German expansion in Czechoslovakia. The conference is considered part of the policy of appeasement that led Adolf Hitler to believe he had a free hand in Europe.

Muslim A follower of Islam.

Mutsuhito (MOO-tsoo-HEE-taw) 1852–1912 C.E. The first Meiji emperor of Japan who reigned from 1867 until his death. During his reign Japan transformed from a feudal to an industrial economy.

Mycenaean (meye-seh-NEE-uhn) Early Greek society on the Peloponnese (1600–1100 B.C.E.) that was influenced by the Minoans; the Mycenaeans' conflict with Troy is immortalized in Homer's *Odyssey.*

Nam Viet Early Chinese name for the modern nation of Vietnam.

Napoleon Bonaparte (nuh-POH-lee-uhn BOH-nuh-pahrt) 1769–1821 C.E. French military leader during the French Revolution who later seized power and crowned himself emperor from 1804 to 1814, and again in 1815 until he was defeated and exiled.

Nara era Japanese period (710–794), centered on the city of Nara, that was the highest point of Chinese influence.

National Policy Nineteenth-century Canadian policy designed to attract migrants, protect industries through tariffs, and build national transportation systems.

NATO The North Atlantic Treaty Organization, which was established by the United States in 1949 as a regional military alliance against Soviet expansionism.

Ndongo (n'DAWN-goh) Angolan kingdom that reached its peak during the reign of Queen Nzinga (r. 1623–1663).

Neandertal (nee-ANN-duhr-tawl) Early humans (100,000 to 35,000 years ago) who were prevalent during the Paleolithic period.

Nebuchadnezzar (neb-uh-kud-NEZ-er) King of the Babylonian Empire who reigned between 600 and 550 B.C.E.

Negritude (NEH-grih-tood) "Blackness," a term coined by early African nationalists as a means of celebrating the heritage of black peoples around the world.

Nelson Mandela 1918–2013 C.E. South African revolutionary and politician who consistently fought against the apartheid state until its demise in 1994. He became the first black president of South Africa, and served from 1994 to 1999.

Neo-Confucianism (nee-oh-kuhn-FYOO-shuhn-iz'm) Philosophy that attempted to merge certain basic elements of Confucian and Buddhist thought; most important of the early Neo-Confucianists was the Chinese thinker Zhu Xi (1130–1200).

Neolithic New Stone Age (10,000–4000 B.C.E.), which was marked by the discovery and mastery of agriculture.

Nestorian (neh-STOHR-ee-uhn) Early branch of Christianity, named after the fifth-century Greek theologian Nestorius, that emphasized the human nature of Jesus Christ.

New Economic Policy (NEP) Plan implemented by Lenin that called for minor free-market reforms.

Nicholas II Reigned 1894–1917. Russian tsar who was first deposed and then executed, along with his family, in the Russian Revolution.

Nicolaus Copernicus 1473–1543 C.E. Polish astronomer who theorized that the Sun, rather than the Earth, lay at the center of the universe.

Nile River The world's longest river, it flows 6695 km (4160 mi) from Lake Victoria through Egypt to the Mediterranean Sea.

Nirvana (nuhr-VAH-nuh) Buddhist concept of a state of spiritual perfection and enlightenment in which distracting passions are eliminated.

Noble Eightfold Path Final truth of the Buddhist Four Noble Truths that called for leading a life of balance and constant contemplation.

Nonaligned Movement Movement in which leaders of former colonial states sought to assert their independence from either Soviet or U.S. domination. The initial meeting was held in 1955 in Bandung, Indonesia.

North American Free Trade Agreement (NAFTA) Regional accord established in 1993 between the United States, Canada, and Mexico; it formed the world's second largest free-trade zone.

Nubia (NOO-bee-uh) Area south of Egypt; the kingdom of Kush in Nubia invaded and dominated Egypt from 750 to 664 B.C.E.

Nubians a member of one of the group of peoples that formed a powerful empire between Egypt and Ethiopia from the sixth to the fourteenth centuries.

Oceania Term referring to the Pacific Ocean basin and its lands.

Odoacer Germanic general who deposed Romulus Augustus in 476 C.E., thus bringing about the end of the western Roman Empire.

Olaudah Equiano (oh-LAU-duh eh-kwee-AHN-oh) 1745–1797 C.E. Writer and abolitionist from the Kingdom of Benin who was sold into slavery but purchased his freedom in 1766.

Olmecs Early Mesoamerican society (1200–100 B.C.E.) that centered on sites at San Lorenzo, La Venta, and Tres Zapotes and that influenced later Maya.

Olympe de Gouges 1748–1793 C.E. French feminist who authored the Declaration of the Rights of Woman and the Female Citizen at the start of the French Revolution in 1789, which advocated for equal rights for women. De Gouges was later executed by the Jacobins during the Terror.

Olympic Games A Pan-Hellenic festival in which competitors from all over ancient Greece competed in athletic competitions, founded according to tradition in 776 B.C.E.

Oracle bones Chinese Shang dynasty (1766–1122 B.C.E.) means of foretelling the future.

Organization of African Unity (OAU) An organization started in 1963 by thirty-two newly independent African states and designed to prevent conflict that would lead to intervention by former colonial powers.

Organization of Petroleum Exporting Countries (OPEC) An organization begun in 1960 by oil-producing states originally for purely economic reasons but that later had more political influence.

Osama bin Laden 1957–2011 C.E. Saudi Arabian-born founder of the militant pan-Islamic organization al-Qaeda responsible for planning the September 11, 2001, attacks in the United States.

Osiris Ancient Egyptian god that represented the forces of nature.

Osman (os-MAHN) 1258–1326 C.E. Also known as Osman Gazi. Founder of the Ottoman dynasty and the Ottoman state.

Otto von Bismarck 1815–1898 C.E. Conservative German statesman who engineered the unification of Germany and then served as its first chancellor until 1890.

Ottoman empire Powerful Turkish empire that lasted from the conquest of Constantinople (Istanbul) in 1453 until 1918 and reached its peak during the reign of Süleyman the Magnificent (r. 1520–1566).

Paleolithic Old Stone Age, a long period of human development before the development of agriculture.

Palestinian Liberation Organization (PLO) Organization created in 1964 under the leadership of Yasser Arafat to champion Palestinian rights.

Papacy The office or authority of the pope.

Paris Peace Accords Agreement reached in 1973 that marked the end of the United States' role in the Vietnam War.

Parsis (pahr-SEES) Indian Zoroastrians.

Parthians Persian dynasty (247 B.C.E.–224 C.E.) that reached its peak under Mithradates I.

Pataliputra (pah-tal-ih-puh-tra) Purpose-built capital city of the South Asian Mauryan and Gupta Empires.

Paterfamilias (PAH-tur fuh-MEE-lee-ahs) Roman term for the "father of the family," a theoretical implication that gave the male head of the family almost unlimited authority.

Patriarch (PAY-tree-ahrk) Leader of the Greek Orthodox church, which in 1054 officially split with the pope and the Roman Catholic church.

Patricians Roman aristocrats and wealthy classes.

Paul of Tarsus Christian apostle who sought converts in the first-century Roman Empire and was executed for being a threat to peace and stability.

Pax romana (pahks roh-MAH-nah) "Roman Peace," a term that relates to the period of political stability, cultural brilliance, and economic prosperity beginning with unification under Augustus and lasting through the first two centuries C.E.

Peloponnesian War Bitter and destructive "civil war" fought between Sparta and her allies, and Athens and her allies, between 431 and 404 B.C.E.

Peninsulares (pehn-IHN-soo-LAH-rayz) Latin American officials from Spain or Portugal.

Perestroika (PAYR-eh-stroy-kuh) "Restructuring," a Russian term associated with Gorbachev's effort to reorganize the Soviet state.

Pericles Athenian statesmen who ruled his city from 461–429 B.C.E.

Period of the Warring States Last centuries of the Zhou dynasty (403–221 B.C.E.) when wars divided the region until the establishment of the Qin dynasty ended the disunity.

Persian Royal Road A long-distance road, partly paved with stone, built by the Persian Achaemenid Empire. It stretched for 2575 km (1600 mi) from the Mediterranean coast to the Persian heartland in modern Iran.

Peter the Great Reigned 1682–1725. Russian tsar of the Romanov family who sought to modernize Russia based on the model established by western European states.

Pharaohs (FARE-ohs) Egyptian kings considered to be gods on earth.

Philip of Macedon King of Macedon who reigned from 359 to 336 B.C.E. Responsible for bringing all of Greece under his control in 338 B.C.E.

Phoenicians Semitic-speaking peoples who settled on a narrow coastal strip between the Lebanon Mountains and Mediterranean Sea and established a series of successful commercial maritime states in the second and first millennia B.C.E.

Pico Pico della Mirandola, 1463–1494 C.E. Italian humanist who sought to harmonize the various religions and philosophies of the world.

Plato Athenian Greek philosopher, a pupil of Socrates, who lived from 430 to 347 B.C.E.

Plebians (plih-BEE-uhns) Roman common people.

Pogrom Yiddish word meaning "devastation," referring to an organized massacre of a particular ethnic group—especially Jews in Eastern Europe.

Polis (POH-lihs) Greek term for the city-state.

Pope Gregory I Important pope whose papacy lasted from 590 to 604, well known for his prolific writings.

Popol Vuh (paw-pawl vuh) Mayan creation epic.

Porcelain A very light, thin and adaptable type of pottery that, when fired with glazes, became a highly valuable export commodity during the Tang and Song dynasty.

Porfirio Díaz (pohr-FEER-eeo DEE-ahs) 1830–1915 C.E. Mexican general and politician who served seven terms as president, for a total of thirty-one years.

Potosí (paw-taw-SEE) City in the central highlands of modern-day Bolivia that became the world's largest silver-producing area after silver was discovered in 1545.

Prague Spring Period in 1968 in which the communist leader of Czechoslovakia, Alexander Dubcek, launched a reform movement aimed at softening Soviet-style rule. The movement was crushed when Russian forces invaded.

Prehistory The period before the invention of writing.

Proletariat Urban working class in a modern industrial society.

Protestant Reformation Sixteenth-century European movement during which Luther, Calvin, Zwingli, and others broke away from the Catholic church.

Protoindustrialization Also called the "putting-out system," in which entrepreneurs delivered raw materials to families in the countryside, who would then spin and weave the materials into garments. The entrepreneurs would then pick up the garments, pay the families, and sell them on the market.

Ptolemaic (TAWL-oh-may-ihk) Term used to signify both the Egyptian kingdom founded by Alexander the Great's general Ptolemy and the thought of the philosopher Ptolemy of Alexandria (second century C.E.), who used mathematical formulas in an attempt to prove Aristotle's geocentric theory of the universe.

Ptolemaic empire (TAWL-oh-may-ihk) Empire that ruled Egypt during the Hellenistic era.

Punic Wars A series of three wars fought between the Roman Republic and Carthage between 264 and 146 B.C.E.

Punt Land that traded with the ancient kingdoms of Egypt, whose exact whereabouts are unknown but may be in or near modern Eritrea.

Putting-out system Method of getting around guild control by delivering unfinished materials to rural households for completion.

Qadi Islamic judge.

Qanat (kah-NAHT) Persian underground canal.

Qi (chee) Chinese concept of the basic material that makes up the body and the universe.

Qianlong (chyahn-lawng) 1711–1799 C.E. Sixth emperor of China's Qing dynasty and grandson of Kangxi.

Qin Shihuangdi (chihn she-huang-dee) First emperor of the short-lived but highly influential Qin Dynasty, who reigned from 221 to 210 B.C.E.

Qin (chihn) Chinese dynasty (221–207 B.C.E.) that was founded by Qin Shihuangdi and was marked by the first unification of China and the early construction of defensive walls.

Qing (chihng) Chinese dynasty (1644–1911) that reached its peak during the reigns of Kangxi and Qianlong.

Qizilbash (gih-ZIHL-bahsh) Term meaning "red heads," Turkish tribes that were important allies of Shah Ismail in the formation of the Safavid empire.

Queen Hatshepsut Female pharaoh of ancient Egypt, who reigned from 1473 to 1458 B.C.E.

Queen Nzinga (N-zinga) 1583–1663 C.E. Seventeenth-century queen of the Ndongo and Matamba kingdoms in modern-day Angola.

Quetzalcoatl (keht-zahl-koh-AHT'l) Aztec god, the "feathered serpent," who was borrowed originally from the Toltecs; Quetzalcoatl was believed to have been defeated by another god and exiled, and he promised to return.

Quinto (KEEN-toh) The one-fifth of Mexican and Peruvian silver production that was reserved for the Spanish monarchy.

Quipu (KEE-poo) Incan mnemonic aid comprised of different-colored strings and knots that served to record events in the absence of a written text.

Quran (koo-RAHN) Islamic holy book that is believed to contain the divine revelations of Allah as presented to Muhammad.

Raja Sanskrit term for "king."

Ram Mohan Roy 1772–1833 C.E. Bengali intellectual who sought to harmonize aspects of European society with those of Indian society with the goal of reforming India along progressive lines.

Ramayana (rah-mah-yah-nah) Ancient Indian masterpiece about the hero Rama that symbolized the victory of *dharma* (order) over *adharma* (chaos).

Rape of Nanjing Japanese conquest and destruction of the Chinese city of Nanjing in the 1930s.

Re Sun god in ancient Egypt, and the chief deity among Egyptian gods.

Realpolitik (ray-AHL-poh-lih-teek) The Prussian Otto von Bismarck's "politics of reality," the belief that only the willingness to use force would actually bring about change.

Reconquista (ray-kohn-KEE-stah) Crusade, ending in 1492, to drive the Islamic forces out of Spain.

Reconstruction System implemented in the American South (1867–1877) that was designed to bring the Confederate states back into the union and also extend civil rights to freed slaves.

Relics Physical remains of saints or religious figures assembled by churches for veneration.

Rhapta Port that emerged as a principal commercial center in East Africa in the centuries around the turn of the millennium.

Roman Empire An empire that succeeded the Roman Republic during the reign of Augustus, which dates from 27 B.C.E. to 395 C.E.

Roman republic Period of Roman society from 509 B.C.E. to 27 B.C.E. characterized by republican form of government.

Romanov dynasty (ROH-mah-nahv) Russian dynasty (1610–1917) founded by Mikhail Romanov and ending with Nicholas II.

Ronald Reagan 1911–2004. Fortieth president of the United States, who served from 1981 to 1989. Reagan was noted for his anti-communism.

Rubaiyat (ROO-bee-aht) "Quatrains," famous poetry of Omar Khayyam that was later translated by Edward Fitzgerald.

Saddam Hussein 1937–2006 C.E. The fifth president of Iraq, who served from 1979 to 2003 until he was ousted by a coalition led by the United States.

Safavid empire (SAH-fah-vihd) Later Persian empire (1501–1722) that was founded by Shah Ismail and that became a center for Shiism; the empire reached its peak under Shah Abbas the Great and was centered on the capital of Isfahan.

Sakk Letters of credit that were common in the medieval Islamic banking world.

Saladin 1137–1193 C.E. Muslim leader and crusader who recaptured Jerusalem from the Christians in 1187.

Saljuqs (sahl-JYOOKS) Turkish tribe that gained control over the Abbasid empire and fought with the Byzantine empire.

Samsara (sahm-SAH-ruh) Hindu term for the concept of transmigration, that is, the soul passing into a new incarnation.

Samurai (SAM-uhr-eye) A Japanese warrior.

Sanskrit Original and "sacred" language of the Indo-Aryans.

Sappho Poetess who wrote around 600 B.C.E., known for writing about physical attraction between women.

Sargon of Akkad Ruler of the Mesopotamian city of Akkad who conquered most of the other city-states of the region to establish the first empire in world history.

Sasanians (suh-SAHN-iens) Powerful empire that ruled much of Central Asia and Mesopotamia from 224 to 651 C.E.

Sati (SUH-TEE) Also known as *suttee*, Indian practice of a widow throwing herself on the funeral pyre of her husband.

Satrapies System of provincial government in the Persian Empire, in which administration is divided into provinces, each of which was called a satrapy.

Satraps (SAY-traps) Persian administrators, usually members of the royal family, who governed a satrapy.

Satyagraha (SAH-tyah-GRAH-hah) "Truth and firmness," a term associated with Gandhi's policy of passive resistance.

Schism Mutual excommunication of the Roman pope and Byzantine patriarch in 1054 over ritual, doctrinal, and political differences between the two Christian churches.

Schlieffen plan (SHLEE-fn) The name of German war plans to deal with a war in which battles would have to be fought on two fronts. The plan was implemented at the start of World War I, when it was clear that Germany would go to war with Russia and France.

Scholasticism Medieval attempt of thinkers such as St. Thomas Aquinas to merge the beliefs of Christianity with the logical rigor of Greek philosophy.

Scientific racism Nineteenth-century attempt to justify racism by scientific means; an example would be Gobineau's *Essay on the Inequality of the Human Races.*

Scramble for Africa Period between about 1875 and 1900 in which European powers sought to colonize as much of the African continent as possible.

Seleucids (sih-LOO-sihds) Persian empire (323–83 B.C.E.) founded by Seleucus after the death of Alexander the Great.

Self-determination Belief popular in World War I and after that every people should have the right to determine their own political destiny; the belief was often cited but ignored by the Great Powers.

Self-Strengthening Movement Chinese attempt (1860–1895) to blend Chinese cultural traditions with European industrial technology.

Semitic (suh-miht-ihk) A term that relates to the Semites, ancient nomadic herders who spoke Semitic languages; examples of Semites were the Akkadians, Hebrews, Aramaics, and Phoenicians, who often interacted with the more settled societies of Mesopotamia and Egypt.

Sepoys Indian troops who served the British.

Serfs Peasants who, though not chattel slaves, were tied to the land and who owed obligation to the lords on whose land they worked.

Sergei Witte (SAYR-gay VIHT-tee) Late-nineteenth-century Russian minister of finance who pushed for industrialization.

Sericulture The cultivation of silkworms for the production of silk.

Shah Abbas the Great 1571–1629 C.E. Fifth Safavid Shah of Iran who is generally considered the strongest of the Safavid rulers.

Shah Jahan 1592–1666 C.E. Fifth Mughal emperor who commissioned the building of the Taj Mahal for his wife, Mumtaz.

Shamanism (SHAH-mah-niz'm) Belief in shamans or religious specialists who possessed supernatural powers and who communicated with the gods and the spirits of nature.

Shang dynasty Dynasty of ancient China that ruled, according to tradition, from 1766–1122 B.C.E.

Shang Yang 390–338 B.C.E. Minister to the Duke of Qin state in Western China, and important developer of the political philosophy of Legalism.

Sharia (shah-REE-ah) The Islamic holy law, drawn up by theologians from the Quran and accounts of Muhammad's life.

Shia (SHEE-ah) Islamic minority in opposition to the Sunni majority; their belief is that leadership should reside in the line descended from Ali.

Shintoism (SHIHN-toh-iz'm) Indigenous Japanese religion that emphasizes purity, clan loyalty, and the divinity of the emperor.

Shiva (SHEE-vuh) Hindu god associated with both fertility and destruction.

Shogun (SHOH-gun) Japanese military leader who ruled in place of the emperor.

Shudras (SHOO-druhs) Hindu caste of landless peasants and serfs.

Siberia Region to the east of Russia in northeastern Europe, which was conquered by the Russians between 1581 and 1639.

Siddhartha Gautama (sih-DHAR-tuh GOW-tau-mah) Indian *kshatriya* who achieved enlightenment and became known as the Buddha, the founder of Buddhism.

Sikhs (SIHKS) Adherents of an Indian syncretic faith that contains elements of Hinduism and Islam.

Silk Roads An extensive network of trade routes that linked much of Eurasia with North Africa during the Classical Period.

Silla dynasty Important early Korean dynasty that flourished during the seventh and eighth centuries.

Sima Qian Major ancient Chinese historian who lived during the second and early first centuries B.C.E. and wrote the first complete history of China to that point, the *Shiji.*

Simón Bolívar (see-MOHN boh-LEE-vahr) 1783–1830 C.E. Venezuelan military and political leader who led a number of Latin American states to independence from the Spanish.

Sinicization Process by which non–Han Chinese people come under the cultural or political domination of Han Chinese.

Sino-Japanese War War between China and Japan from 1897 to 1901, over the status of Korea. The Chinese were badly defeated.

Social Darwinism Nineteenth-century philosophy, championed by thinkers such as Herbert Spencer, that attempted to apply Darwinian "survival of the fittest" to the social and political realm; adherents saw the elimination of weaker nations as part of a natural process and used the philosophy to justify war.

Socialism Political and economic theory of social organization based on the collective ownership of the means of production; its origins were in the early nineteenth century, and it differs from communism by a desire for slow or moderate change compared with the communist call for revolution.

Socrates (SAHK-rah-teez) Athenian Greek philosopher who lived from 470 to 399 B.C.E.

Solidarity Polish trade union and nationalist movement in the 1980s that was headed by Lech Walesa.

Solon Aristocrat in Athens in the sixth century B.C.E. who forged a compromise between wealthy aristocrats and discontented common and landless classes who threatened rebellion.

Song Taizu (sawng tahy-zoo) First emperor of the Chinese Song dynasty who reigned from 960 to 976 C.E.

Song (SOHNG) Chinese dynasty (960–1279) that was marked by an increasingly urbanized and cosmopolitan society.

Soviets Russian elected councils that originated as strike committees during the 1905 St. Petersburg disorders; they represented a form of local self-government that went on to become the primary unit of government in the Union of Soviet Socialist Republics. The term was also used during the cold war to designate the Soviet Union.

Spanish Inquisition Institution organized in 1478 by Fernando and Isabel of Spain to detect heresy and the secret practice of Judaism or Islam.

Sparta Important city state of ancient Greece, located in the Peloponnesus region.

Srivijaya (sree-VIH-juh-yuh) Southeast Asian kingdom (670–1025), based on the island of Sumatra, that used a powerful navy to dominate trade.

St. Augustine 354–430 C.E. Bishop of the North African diocese of Hippo, and one of the leading intellectuals of the Late Roman Empire.

St. Basil 329-379 C.E. Byzantine Christian reformer who prepared regulations for monasteries emphasizing poverty, charity, and chastity.

St. Ignatius Loyola 1491-1556 C.E. A Basque nobleman and soldier who later devoted his life to religion and founded the missionary Society of Jesus (the Jesuits).

St. Thomas Aquinas (uh-KWIY-nuhs) 1225-1274 C.E. An Italian Dominican friar and Catholic priest whose religious writings became enormously influential in the school of Scholasticism.

Stateless societies Term relating to societies such as those of sub-Saharan Africa after the Bantu migrations that featured decentralized rule through family and kinship groups instead of strongly centralized hierarchies.

Stoics (STOH-ihks) Hellenistic philosophers who encouraged their followers to lead active, virtuous lives and to aid others.

Strabo (STRAH-boh) Greek geographer (first century C.E.).

Strategic Arms Limitation Talks (SALT) Agreement in 1972 between the United States and the Soviet Union.

Stupas (STOO-pahs) Buddhist shrines.

Sufis (SOO-fees) Islamic mystics who placed more emphasis on emotion and devotion than on strict adherence to rules.

Sui dynasty (SWAY) Chinese dynasty (589-618) that constructed the Grand Canal, reunified China, and allowed for the splendor of the Tang dynasty that followed.

Sui Yangdi (sway yahng-dee) Second emperor of the Chinese Sui Dynasty, responsible for the construction of the Chinese Grand Canal system, who reigned from 604-618 C.E.

Süleyman (SOO-lee-mahn) Ottoman Turkish ruler Süleyman the Magnificent (r. 1520-1566), who was the most powerful and wealthy ruler of the sixteenth century.

Sultan Selim III Reigned 1789-1807. Ottoman sultan whose efforts at reform threatened his elite fighting corps (the Jannissaries), who revolted and locked him up.

Sumerians (soo-MEHR-ee-uhns) Earliest Mesopotamian society.

Sun Yatsen 1866-1925 C.E. Chinese physician and politician who founded the Chinese nationalist Guomindang Party and then briefly served as the first president of the Republic of China.

Sundiata (soon-JAH-tuh) Founder of the Mali empire (r. 1230-1255), also the inspiration for the *Sundiata,* an African literary and mythological work.

Sunni (SOON-nee) "Traditionalists," the most popular branch of Islam; Sunnis believe in the legitimacy of the early caliphs, compared with the Shiite belief that only a descendant of Ali can lead.

Suu Kyi, Aung San (SOO KEY, AWNG SAHN) Opposition leader (1945-) in Myanmar; she was elected leader in 1990 but she was not allowed to come to power; she was a Nobel Peace Prize recipient in 1991. She was finally released from house arrest in November 2010.

Swahili (swah-HEE-lee) East African city-state society that dominated the coast from Mogadishu to Kilwa and was active in trade. Also a Bantu language of East Africa, or a member of a group who speaks this language.

Sykes-Picot Treaty Secret 1917 treaty between the British and French, with the agreement of Russia, to divide the modern Middle East between them after the end of World War I.

Taíno (TEYE-noh) A Caribbean tribe who were the first indigenous peoples from the Americas to come into contact with Christopher Columbus.

Taiping rebellion (TEYE-pihng) Rebellion (1850-1864) in Qing China led by Hong Xiuquan, during which twenty to thirty million were killed; the rebellion was symbolic of the decline of China during the nineteenth century.

Tale of Genji Japanese literary work written during the Heian Period (794-1185 C.E.) by the aristocratic woman Murasaki Shikibu.

Taliban Strict Islamic organization that ruled Afghanistan from 1996 to 2002.

Tamerlane (TAM-er-lane) 1336-1405 C.E. Also known as Timur. Founder of the Timurid Empire in modern-day Iran and Central Asia.

Tang dynasty Powerful and wealthy Chinese dynasty that ruled a vast East Asian empire from 618 to 907 C.E.

Tang Taizong (TAHNG TEYE-zohng) Chinese emperor (r. 627-649) of the Tang dynasty (618 to 907).

Tanzimat era "Reorganization" era (1839-1876), an attempt to reorganize the Ottoman empire on Enlightenment and constitutional forms.

Temüjin (TEM-oo-chin) Mongol conqueror (ca. 1167-1227) who later took the name Chinggis Khan, "universal ruler."

Tenochtitlan (the-NOCH-tee-tlahn) Capital of the Aztec empire, later Mexico City.

Teotihuacan (tay-uh-tee-wah-KAHN) Central American society (200 B.C.E.-750 C.E.); its Pyramid of the Sun was the largest structure in Mesoamerica.

Terra australis incognita Meaning "unknown southern land," it refers to land that European explorers had speculated must exist in the world's southern hemisphere from the second to the eighteenth centuries.

Terra Nullius Concept meaning "land belonging to no one" used frequently by colonial powers who sought to justify the conquest of nomadic lands.

Teutonic Knights Crusading European order that was active in the Baltic region.

Theodor Herzl 1860-1904 C.E. Jewish Austro-Hungarian writer and journalist who founded the modern Zionist movement.

Theodora Wife of the Emperor Justinian, who played a key role in the success of his reign.

Third Rome Concept that a new power would rise up to carry the legacy of Roman greatness after the decline of the Second Rome, Constantinople; Moscow was referred to as the Third Rome during the fifteenth century.

Three estates The three classes of European society, composed of the clergy (the first estate), the aristocrats (the second estate), and the common people (the third estate).

Three Principles of the People Philosophy of Chinese Guomindang leader Sun Yatsen (1866-1925) that emphasized nationalism, democracy, and people's livelihood.

Thucydides Athenian historian who wrote a history of the Peloponnesian war in the fifth century B.C.E.

Tian (TEE-ehn) Chinese term for heaven.

Tikal (tee-KAHL) Maya political center from the fourth through the ninth century.

Timbuktu (tim-buhk-TOO) City in the Mali Empire known for its large population, wealth, and places of learning.

Timur-i lang (tee-MOOR-yee LAHNG) "Timur the Lame," known in English as Tamerlane (ca. 1336-1405), who conquered an empire ranging from the Black Sea to Samarkand.

Tokugawa bakufu Feudal style of government that ruled Japan under the direction of shoguns from 1603 until the Meiji Restoration in 1868.

Tokugawa Ieyasu (TOH-koo-GAH-wah) 1543-1616 C.E. Founder and first shogun of the Tokugawa dynasty in Japan.

Tokugawa (TOH-koo-GAH-wah) Last shogunate in Japanese history (1600-1867); it was founded by Tokugawa Ieyasu who was notable for unifying Japan.

Toltecs Central American society (950-1150) that was centered on the city of Tula.

Toussaint Louverture (too-SAHNT loo-vehr-TOOR) 1743-1803 C.E. Haitian general and leader of the Haitian Revolution against the French until his death in a French prison.

Trail of Tears Forced relocation of the Cherokee from the eastern woodlands to Oklahoma (1837-1838); it was symbolic of U.S. expansion and destruction of indigenous Indian societies.

Treaty of Nanjing 1842 Treaty forced on China by Great Britain after Britain's victory in the first Opium War, which forcibly opened China to western trade and settlement.

Treaty of Versailles 1919 treaty between the victorious Entente powers and defeated Germany at the end of World War I, which laid the blame for the war on Germany and exacted harsh reparations.

Treaty of Waitangi Treaty between British government and indigenous Maori peoples of New Zealand in 1840 that was interpreted differently by both sides and thus created substantial Maori opposition to British settlement.

Triangular trade Trade between Europe, Africa, and the Americas that featured finished products from Europe, slaves from Africa, and American products bound for Europe.

Tribunes Officials elected by plebians (commoners) in the Roman Republic to represent their interests in the Roman government.

Triple Alliance Pre–World War I alliance of Germany, Austria-Hungary, and Italy.

Triple Entente (ahn-TAHNT) Pre–World War I alliance of England, France, and Russia.

Troubadors A class of traveling poets and entertainers enthusiastically patronized by Medieval aristocratic women in modern southern France and northern Italy.

Truman Doctrine U.S. policy instituted in 1947 by President Harry Truman in which the United States would follow an interventionist foreign policy to contain communism.

Tsar Alexander II 1818–1881 C.E. Emperor of Russia from 1855 until his assassination, best known for his emancipation of the serfs in 1861.

Tsar (ZAHR) Old Russian term for king that is derived from the term *caesar*.

Tula Original region of the Toltec people, located to the northwest of modern Mexico City.

Twelve Tables Rome's first set of laws, established in 449 B.C.E.

Twelver Shiism (SHEE'i'zm) Branch of Islam that stressed that there were twelve perfect religious leaders after Muhammad and that the twelfth went into hiding and would return someday; Shah Ismail spread this variety through the Safavid empire.

Uighurs (WEE-goors) Turkish tribe.

Ukiyo Japanese word for the "floating worlds," a Buddhist term for the insignificance of the world that came to represent the urban centers in Tokugawa Japan.

Ulaanbaatar (OO-lahn-bah-tahr) Mongolian city.

Ulama Islamic officials, scholars who shaped public policy in accordance with the Quran and the *sharia*.

Umayyad (oo-MEYE-ahd) Arabic dynasty (661–750), with its capital at Damascus, that was marked by a tremendous period of expansion to Spain in the west and India in the east.

Umma (UM-mah) Islamic term for the "community of the faithful."

United Nations (UN) Successor to the League of Nations, an association of sovereign nations that attempts to find solutions to global problems.

Untouchables Lowest caste (or varna) in the South Asian caste system.

Upanishads (oo-PAHN-ee-shahds) Indian reflections and dialogues (800–400 B.C.E.) that reflected basic Hindu concepts.

Urdu (OOR-doo) A language that is predominant in Pakistan.

Uruk (OO-rook) Ancient Mesopotamian city from the fourth millennium B.C.E. that was allegedly the home of the fabled Gilgamesh.

Utopian socialism Movement that emerged around 1830 to establish ideal communities that would provide the foundation for an equitable society.

Vaishyas (VEYES-yuhs) Hindu caste of cultivators, artisans, and merchants.

Vaqueros (vah-KEHR-ohs) Latin American cowboys, similar to the Argentine gaucho.

Varna (VAHR-nuh) Hindu word for caste.

Varuna (vuh-ROO-nuh) Early Aryan god who watched over the behavior of mortals and preserved the cosmic order.

Vedas (VAY-duhs) "Wisdom," early collections of prayers and hymns that provide information about the Indo-European Aryans who migrated into India around 1500 B.C.E.; *Rig Vedaf* is the most important collection.

Velvet revolution A term that describes the non-violent transfer of power in Czechoslovakia during the collapse of Soviet rule.

Venta, La (VEHN-tuh, lah) Early Olmec center (800–400 B.C.E.).

Venus figurines Small Paleolithic statues of women with exaggerated sexual features.

Vernacular (ver-NA-kyoo-lar) The language of the people; Martin Luther translated the Bible from the Latin of the Catholic church into the vernacular German.

Versailles (vehr-SEYE) Palace of French King Louis XIV.

Viet Minh North Vietnamese nationalist communists under Ho Chi Minh.

Vietnamization President Richard Nixon's strategy of turning the Vietnam War over to the South Vietnamese.

Vijayanagar kingdom (vee-juh-yah-NAH-gahr) Southern Indian kingdom (1336–1565) that later fell to the Mughals.

Vikings A group that raided the British Isles from their home at Vik in southern Norway.

Vishnu (VIHSH-noo) Hindu god, preserver of the world, who was often incarnated as Krishna.

Vladimir Ilyich Lenin (VLAD-uh-meer IL yich LEHN-in) 1870–1954 C.E. Russian revolutionary and politician who led the Bolshevik Revolution in November 1917 and became the first head of state of the Soviet Union until his death.

Vo Nguyen Giap 1912–2013. Vietnamese general who served as Ho Chi Minh's right-hand man and is credited with the strategy behind the Vietnamese victory at the battle of Dien Bien Phu.

Volksgeist (FOHLKS-geyest) "People's spirit," a term that was coined by the German philosopher Herder; a nation's volksgeist would not come to maturity unless people studied their own unique culture and traditions.

Volta do mar (VOHL-tah doh MAHR) "Return through the sea," a fifteenth-century Portuguese sea route that took advantage of the prevailing winds and currents.

Voltaire (vohl-TAIR) 1712–1778 C.E. French Enlightenment writer and philosopher famous for his wit and criticism of the Catholic church. His real name was Francois-Marie Arouet.

Voudou (voh-DOW) Syncretic religion practiced by African slaves in Haiti.

W. E. B. DuBois 1868–1963. African American activist and intellectual who championed the movement of American blacks back to Africa.

Waldensians Twelfth-century religious reformers who criticized the Roman Catholic church and who proposed that the laity had the right to preach and administer sacraments; they were declared heretics.

Wanli (wahn-LEE) Chinese Ming emperor (r. 1572–1620) whose refusal to meet with officials hurried the decline of the Ming dynasty.

War chariots An ancient horse-drawn two-wheeled vehicle used in war.

War Communism The Bolshevik policy of nationalizing industry and seizing private land during the civil war.

Warsaw Pact Warsaw Treaty Organization, a military alliance formed by Soviet bloc nations in 1955 in response to rearmament of West Germany and its inclusion in NATO.

White Huns A nomadic people from Central Asia who occupied Bactria (modern Afghanistan) in the fourth century C.E. and eventually crossed the Hindu Kush mountains into India.

William the Conqueror Reigned 1066–1087. William I, the first Norman king of England after the Norman invasion in 1066.

Wind wheels Prevailing wind patterns in the Atlantic and Pacific Oceans north and south of the equator; their discovery made sailing much safer and quicker.

Winston Churchill 1874–1965 C.E. British politician who was prime minister of the United Kingdom from 1940 to 1945, during which time he led the British to victory.

Witch hunts Period in the sixteenth and seventeenth centuries in which about 110,000 people (mainly women) were tried as witches in western Europe.

Woodrow Wilson 1856–1924. President of the United States during World War I and author of the "Fourteen Points," one of which envisioned the establishment of the League of Nations.

World Health Organization (WHO) United Nations organization designed to deal with global health issues.

World Trade Organization (WTO) An organization that was established in 1995 with more than 120 nations and whose goal is to loosen barriers to free trade.

Wu Zhao 626–706 C.E. Concubine of Emperor Tang Taizong, who seized imperial power for herself in 690 after Taizong became debilitated.

Wuwei (woo-WAY) Daoist concept of a disengagement from the affairs of the world.

Xia (shyah) Early Chinese dynasty (2200–1766 B.C.E.).

Xianyang (SHYAHN-YAHNG) Capital city of the Qin empire.

Xiao (SHAYOH) Confucian concept of respect for one's parents and ancestors.

Xinjiang (shin-jyahng) Western Chinese province.

Xuanzang (SHWEN-ZAHNG) Seventh-century Chinese monk who made a famous trip to India to collect Buddhist texts.

Xunzi (SHOON-dzuh) Third-century B.C.E. Chinese philosopher and administrator recognized as one the most important followers of Confucius.

Yahweh (YAH-way) God of the monotheistic religion of Judaism that influenced later Christianity and Islam.

Yang Jian (yahng jyahn) First emperor of the short-lived but effective Sui Dynasty which united China after centuries of division, reigned from 589 to 604 C.E.

Yangshao (YAHNG-show) Early Chinese society (2500–2200 B.C.E.).

Yangzi (YAHNG-zuh) River in central China.

Yellow Turban Uprising Major peasant revolt that broke out in the last decades of the Later Han Dynasty and was partly responsible for that dynasty's collapse.

Yin One of the six Shang dynasty (1766–1122 B.C.E.) capitals near the modern city of Anyang.

Yongle (YAWNG-leh) Chinese Ming emperor (r. 1403–1424) who pushed for foreign exploration and promoted cultural achievements such as the *Yongle Encyclopedia.*

Young Turks Nineteenth-century Turkish reformers who pushed for changes within the Ottoman empire, such as universal suffrage and freedom of religion.

Yu (yoo) Legendary founder of the Xia dynasty (ca. 2200 B.C.E.).

Yuan dynasty (yoo-AHN) Chinese dynasty (1279–1368) that was founded by the Mongol ruler Khubilai Khan.

Yucatan (yoo-kuh-TAN) Peninsula in Central America, home of the Maya.

Yurts (yuhrts) Tents used by nomadic Turkish and Mongol tribes.

Zaibatsu (zeye-BAHT-soo) Japanese term for "wealthy cliques," which are similar to American trusts and cartels but usually organized around one family.

Zambos (ZAHM-bohs) Latin American term for individuals born of indigenous and African parents.

Zamudio, Adela (ZAH-moo-dee-oh, ah-DEH-lah) Nineteenth-century Bolivian poet, author of "To Be Born a Man."

Zarathustra (zar-uh-THOO-struh) Persian prophet (ca. sixth century B.C.E.) who founded Zoroastrianism.

Zemstvos (ZEHMST-voh) District assemblies elected by Russians in the nineteenth century.

Zen Buddhism Japanese version of Chinese Chan Buddhism, with an emphasis on intuition and sudden flashes of insight instead of textual study.

Zhang Qian (jung-chen) Han Dynasty explorer and ambassador who was dispatched by Emperor Wudi during the late-second century B.C.E. to establish relations with states to the west of China.

Zheng He (jung ha) 1371–1433 C.E. Chinese mariner, explorer, and admiral during the early Ming Dynasty who traveled as far as Malindi in East Africa.

Zhou dynasty (JOH) Chinese dynasty (1122–256 B.C.E.) that was the foundation of Chinese thought formed during this period: Confucianism, Daoism, Zhou Classics.

Zhu Xi (ZHOO-SHEE) Neo-Confucian Chinese philosopher (1130–1200).

Ziggurats (ZIG-uh-rahts) Mesopotamian temples.

Zimbabwe (zihm-BAHB-way) Former colony of Southern Rhodesia that gained independence in 1980.

Zoroastrianism (zohr-oh-ASS-tree-ahn-iz'm) Persian religion based on the teaching of the sixth-century-B.C.E. prophet Zarathustra; its emphasis on the duality of good and evil and on the role of individuals in determining their own fate would influence later religions.

Index

Croatia, 797
Crompton, Samuel, 621, 624
Cromwell, Oliver, 483–484
crop rotation. *See* agriculture
cross staffs, 450, 450*i*
cross-cultural interactions. *See also*
    globalization
  animals, 462
  astronomy, 570
  biological interactions, 460–463
  calendars, 570
  China-Europe, 563
  colonial settlers and Native
    Americans, 509–510, 513, 517
  consumerism and, 855–857
  cuisine, 543, 656
  eastern-western hemispheres,
    501–502
  education, 563
  epidemic disease and, 462, 504–505
  ethics, 563
  food crops, 462–463, 489–490,
    533, 557
  Islamic empire's resistance to, 588
  Japan-Netherlands, 570
  maritime exploration and trade,
    448–449
  medicine, 570
  migration and, 463
  moral values, 563
  plantation society, 542–543
  technology and, 857–858
Cruelty to Animals Act, 636*i*
crusades, as motive for exploration, 452
Crystal Palace exhibition (1851), 621,
    631, 632*i*
Cuauhtemoc, Aztec emperor,
    502, 504
Cuba
  abolition of slavery in, 544, 609
  Bay of Pigs invasion, 817
  Columbus in, 456
  export crops, 661
  migration to, 667
  nuclear arms race and, 815, 817
  Santeria in, 543
  Spanish-Cuban-American War,
    711–712
  sugar plantations, 815
  U.S.S.R. economic aid to, 815
Cuban Missle Crisis, 817, 817*p*
cult of reason, 601
cults
  Antonian movement, 531–532
  syncretic, 531
cultural diversity, 661–664, 667
cultural interaction, 855
cultural nationalism, 612–613
Cultural Revolution (China),
    835–836
culture. *See* also *under specific countries*
  as justification of imperialism,
    697–698, 717, 720
  pan-American, 855–857
currency
  cowry shells as, 464
  silver as, 463, 681
currents, ocean, 451, 451*m*
Custer, George Armstrong, 648
Czechoslovakia, 794, 795, 817,
    818, 847

D
da Gama, Vasco, 448–449, 448*i*, 451,
    452, 453, 454, 456, 465, 528
Dada, 754
Dadaism, 754, 754*i*
Dahomey, kingdom of, 538, 539
daimyo, 563–564, 689
dar al-Islam. See Islam
Darwin, Charles, 717
Das Kapital (Marx), 640*i*
David, Jacques-Louis, 601*i*
D-Day, 801
de Klerk, F. W., South African
    president, 833–834
death
  afterlife beliefs, 648
  child mortality, 631–632
  industrial weapons of, 731–732
  infant mortality, 848
  of witches, statistics, 478–479
debt bondage, 862
debt peonage system, 514–515
Declaration of Independence (U.S.),
    596, 600, 646
Declaration of Independence
    (Vietnam), 823–824
*Declaration of the Rights of Man and
    the Citizen,* 599
*Declaration of the Rights of Woman and
    the Female Citizen* (Gouges), 611
The Decline of the West (Spengler), 752
decolonization. *See also* independence
    movements
  of Africa, 828–834, 829*m*
  chronology, 821
  importance of, 746
decolonization, in Asia, 824*m*
deforestation, industrialization and,
    623, 624
deism, 593
Delhi (India), 578
democracy
  Chinese pro-democracy
    demonstrations, 836*p*
  in Germany, 765
  in India, 836–837
  post-WWI thought, 752
Democratic Republic of the
    Congo, 705
Democratic Revolutionary Party
    (PRD), 840
demographic transition, 632–633
Deng Xiaoping, 836
Denmark, 544, 796, 803, 813
dependency theory of economic
    development, 841–842
Description of Africa, 531*i*
detente policy, 817, 818
Deus Destroyed (Fucan), 569
devshirme, 575
dhimmi, 584
diamonds, 696, 713
Dias, Bartolomeu, 454, 454*m*
diaspora, African, 539–546
Diaz, Porfirio, Mexican president,
    645, 655, 661
Diego, Juan, 502, 519
Dien Bien Phu (Vietnam), 824
diet
  African, 533
  African American, 543

cross-cultural interactions and,
    462–463, 489–490, 533
  disease immunity and, 490
  European, 462, 489–490
  industrialization and, 632
  population growth and, 533
  sailors, 456–457
  vegetarian, in India, 773
Diet (Japan), 691
diphtheria, 462
diplomacy, balance-of-power-, 489
diplomatic missions
  Fukuzawa Yukichi to U.S., 690
  Meiji Japan, 690
Directory (France), 601, 673
dirty war in Argentina, 841
disease. *See also* epidemics;
    specific diseases
  cross-cultural interactions, 462,
    504–505
  diet and immunity to, 490
  globalization and, 872–874
  industrialization and, 634
  migrations and, 463
  Native Americans and, 504–505
  Nazi experimentation victims, 804
  occupational disease, 634
  trade and spread of, 462
  vaccinations for, 631–632, 633*i*
  venereal, 522, 633
  from water pollution, 634
  WWI casualties from, 736
Diula people, 528
divine faith, 579, 584
divine-right theory, 485
division of labor
  the factory system, 625–626
  geographic, 642
  international, 642
divorce, 556, 601, 757, 767
Dix, Wilhelm Heinrich Otto, 754–755
Doctor Zhivago (Pasternak), 814
doctrine of lapse, 700
Doctrine of Limited Sovereignty
    (Brezhnev doctrine), 817, 818,
    846
dogs, 505, 530*i*, 636
doldrums, 759
domestic abuse, 864
domestic servants, 637
Dominican orders, 452, 563
Dominican Republic, 540, 602,
    711, 785
Dominion of Canada, 651*m*, 652, 666
domino theory, 815, 824
Down Argentine Way (film), 788
dowry deaths, 864
Drake, Sir Francis, 459
drama, kabuki theater, 567*i*, 568
dreadnoughts, 724
The Dream of the Red Chamber, 562
Dreyfus, Alfred, 613
droughts, 721
drumming, 543
Dual Alliance, 726
Dubĝek, Alexander, 818
Dubois, François, 474*i*
DuBois, W. E. B., 782
Duma (Russia), 681
Durham Report, 652
Dutch. *See* Netherlands

Dutch East India Company. *See* VOC
    (Vereenigde Oost-Indische
    Compagnie)
Dutch East Indies, 702, 703, 756, 798,
    799, 803
Dutch learning, 570
Dutch republic, 484–485. *See also*
    Netherlands
dysentery, 634

E
earth
  circumnavigation of the, 456–457
  gravitational influence of, 496
  planetary revolution around the, 495
east Africa. *See also specific countries*
  city-states, 528
  Islam in, 530–531
  states of, 526–528, 527*m*
East Asia, tradition and change, 549
East Berlin, 813, 846
East Germany, 813, 847. *See also*
    Germany
East India Company
  Dutch (VOC), 465–466, 468,
    490–491, 558, 583, 705
  English, 465–466, 490–491, 583,
    681–682, 700, 701
  French, 583
East India Railway, 714*i*
Eastern Orthodox church. *See*
    Christianity
Echeverria, Luis, 861
economic nationalism, 756–757
economic systems. *See also* capitalism;
    communism; imperialism;
    socialism
  fascism, 763–765
  supply and demand, 490, 592
  utopian socialism, 638–640
  war communism, 760
economy. *See also* global economy;
    Great Depression;
    industrialization; specific
    countries
  dependency theory of economic
    development, 841–842
  interwar era, 755–759
  Keynesian, 759
  WWI and the, 733*i*, 740–741, 742,
    755–756
  WWII and the, 760
Ecuador, 607
Edo (Japan), 564, 566, 567
education. *See also* literature;
    specific countries
  Canada, 663
  for children, 637, 639
  clan-supported, 556
  Confucian system of, 554, 561–562
  cross-cultural interactions, 563
  of girls, 668
  India, 584
  Islamic, 527, 531
  Jesuit, 478
  mandatory, 637
  Meiji Japan, 691
  missionary, 518
  of native Americans, 662*p*
  Ottoman empire reforms, 675
  religious, 584